BY THE SAME AUTHOR

Britain's Royal Families: The Complete Genealogy
The Six Wives of Henry VIII
The Princes in the Tower
The Wars of the Roses
The Children of Henry VIII
The Life of Elizabeth I
Eleanor of Aquitaine
Henry VIII: The King and His Court
Mary, Queen of Scots, and the Murder of Lord Darnley

QUEEN
ISABELLA

QUEEN ISABELLA

Treachery, Adultery,
and Murder in
Medieval England

ALISON WEIR

BALLANTINE BOOKS
New York

Published in the United States by Ballantine Books,
an imprint of The Random House Publishing Group,
a division of Random House, Inc., New York. Originally
published as *Isabella: She-Wolf of France, Queen of England*
in Great Britain by Jonathan Cape, a division of
Random House Ltd., London.

BALLANTINE and colophon are registered
trademarks of Random House, Inc.

Library of Congress Cataloging-in-Publication Data

Weir, Alison.
Queen Isabella : treachery, adultery, and murder in medieval
England / Alison Weir.
p. cm.
Includes bibliographical references and index.
ISBN 0-345-45319-0
1. Isabella, Queen, consort of Edward II, King of England,
1292–1358. 2. Great Britain—History—Edward II,
1307–1327—Biography. 3. Queens—Great Britain—
Biography. I. Title.
DA231.I83W45 2005
942.03'6'092—dc22
[B]
2005045383

Printed in the United States of America on acid-free paper

www.ballantinebooks.com

2 4 6 8 9 7 5 3 1

FIRST EDITION

Book design by Dana Leigh Blanchette

She-Wolf of France, with unrelenting fangs,
that tear'st at the bowels of thy mangled mate . . .
—Thomas Gray

It is not wise to set yourself in opposition to
the King. The outcome is apt to be unfortunate.
—*Vita Edwardi Secundi*

Acknowledgments

I should like to extend my grateful thanks to two fine authors and historians who have assisted me in my researches: Paul Doherty, who so kindly and generously sent me a copy of his authoritative 1977 thesis on Isabella of France, as well as the advance proofs of his fascinating book *Isabella and the Strange Death of Edward II;* and to Ian Mortimer, whose excellent biography of Roger Mortimer, *The Greatest Traitor,* I also had the privilege of reading at the advance proof stage, and whose comments I have found most valuable. Thank you both, most sincerely. Your works have been inspirational and of great assistance to me in this project. I should add that, although we have studied the same sources, my conclusions are rather different, which is entirely my responsibility!

As always, I owe a debt of gratitude to my agent, Julian Alexander, for his never-ending support; to my commissioning editors, Will Sulkin and Elisabeth Dyssegaard, for making this book possible, and for their great enthusiasm; and to my editorial director, Anthony Whittome, for his sensitive editing and creative vision.

I also owe a mention to all those other persons who have helped and inspired me over the past two years, and to those who have put up with not hearing from me for weeks on end while I finished this book. They are, in alphabetical order, Jacintha Alexander; Angela and John Bender; Neil and

Lesley Blyth; John and Joan Borman; Tracy Borman, Julian Humphreys, and the team at English Heritage; Terrence Cahill; Ewan and Lesley Carr at Carrbooks; Lucinda Cook and the team at L.A.W.; Jane Dunn; Sister Mary Fox; Kerry Gill-Pryde; Sarah Gristwood; Eileen Hannah; Jean and Nick Hubbard; Fraser Jansen and the team at Methvens; Roger Katz and all at Hatchards; Christian Lewis, Kate Worden, and Rosie Gailer at Random House; Jill and Wyndham Lloyd-Davies; Robin Loudon; Alison Montgomerie and Roger England at Hay-on-Wye and Chipping Sodbury; Hawk Norton at London History; Richard Pailthorpe at Syon House; Kim Poster; Deborah Queen; Graham and Mollie Turner; Christopher Warwick; Martha Whittome; and Ann Wroe.

Finally, to my much-loved family: to my husband, Rankin; children, John and Kate; parents, Doreen and Jim; uncle John; cousins Chris, Peter, David, and Catherine; and my in-laws, Kenneth and Elizabeth and Ronald and Alison: thank you all for your unstinting kindness and support during the difficult period when this book was in preparation.

Contents

PART THREE
Isabella

Author's Note

I have generally adopted the anglicized or Latin form of names. Thus, in the interests of using the name by which she is now commonly called (and which was in fact used by many chroniclers in her own time), I have chosen to refer to the subject of this book as Isabella rather than use the French form of her name, Isabelle, by which she would usually have been known in her lifetime, Norman-French being the language of the English court in the early fourteenth century.

Unless otherwise indicated, place names have been given in their modern form.

Unless they are contemporary quotes that appear in the text, the chapter titles have been taken from Christopher Marlowe's play *Edward the Second*.

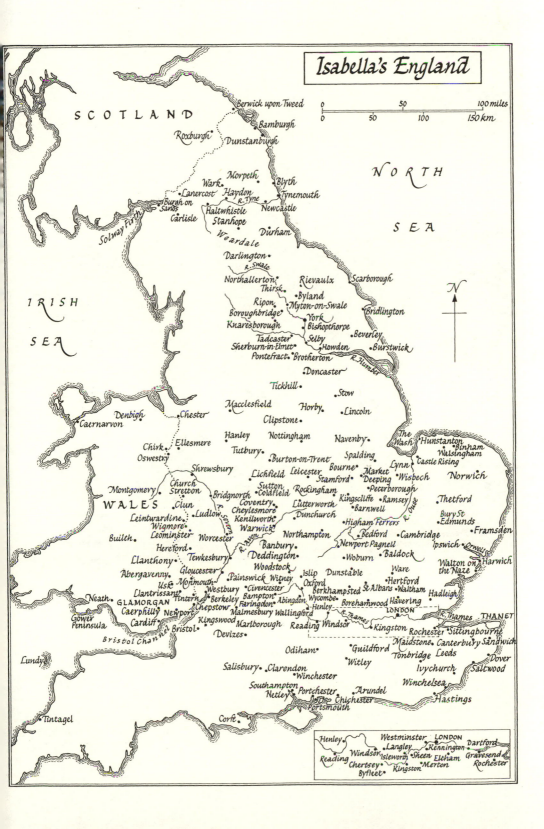

Isabella's England

SCOTLAND

NORTH SEA

IRISH SEA

WALES

GLAMORGAN

Bristol Channel

Berwick upon Tweed
Bamburgh
Roxburgh
Dunstanburgh
Morpeth
Wark
Blyth
Lanercost
Haydon
Tynemouth
Burgh on Sands
R. Tyne
Newcastle
Haltwhistle
Carlisle
Stanhope
Durham
Weardale
Darlington
R. Swale
Northallerton
Thirsk
Rievaulx
Scarborough
Ripon
Byland
Myton-on-Swale
Bridlington
Boroughbridge
York
Knaresborough
Bishopthorpe
Beverley
Tadcaster
Selby
Burstwick
Sherburn-in-Elmet
Howden
Pontefract
Brotherton
R. Humber
Doncaster
Tickhill
Stow
Macclesfield
Horby
Lincoln
Denbigh
Chester
Clipstone
Caernarvon
Hanley
Nottingham
Navenby
The Wash
Hunstanton
Chirk
Ellesmere
Tutbury
Spalding
Lynn
Binham
Walsingham
Oswestry
Burton-on-Trent
Castle Rising
Shrewsbury
Lichfield
Leicester
Bourne
Market Deeping
Wisbech
Norwich
Montgomery
Church Stretton
Sutton Coldfield
Stamford
Peterborough
Thetford
WALES
Clun
Bridgnorth
Rockingham
Kingscliffe
Ramsey
Leintwardine
Ludlow
Coventry
Lutterworth
Barnwell
Bury St Edmunds
Wigmore
Kenilworth
Dunchurch
Leominster
Worcester
Cheylesmore
Higham Ferrers
Framsden
Builth
Warwick
Northampton
Bedford
Cambridge
Hereford
Banbury
Newport Pagnell
Ipswich
Orwell
Llanthony
Tewkesbury
Deddington
Woburn
Baldock
Walton on the Naze
Harwich
Abergavenny
Gloucester
Woodstock
Ware
Usk
Painswick
Witney
Islip
Dunstable
Hertford
Westbury
Cirencester
Oxford
St Albans
Waltham
Hadleigh
Llantrissant
Tintern
Berkeley
Bampton
Berkhampsted
Havering
Neath
Chepstow
Faringdon
Abingdon
Boreham wood
Caerphilly
Malmesbury
Wallingford
Henley
LONDON
Gower Peninsula
Cardiff
Newport
Kingswood
Reading
Windsor
R. Thames
THANET
Lundy
Bristol
Marlborough
Kingston
Rochester
Sittingbourne
Devizes
Odiham
Guildford
Maidstone
Canterbury
Sandwich
Salisbury
Clarendon
Witley
Tonbridge
Leeds
Dover
Winchester
Ivychurch
Saltwood
Southampton
Portchester
Arundel
Winchelsea
Netley
Chichester
Hastings
Portsmouth
Tintagel
Corfe

N

0   50   100 miles
0   50   100   150 km

Henley
Westminster
LONDON
Windsor
Langley
Kennington
Dartford
Reading
Isleworth
Sheen
Eltham
Gravesend
Chertsey
Kingston
Merton
Rochester
Byfleet

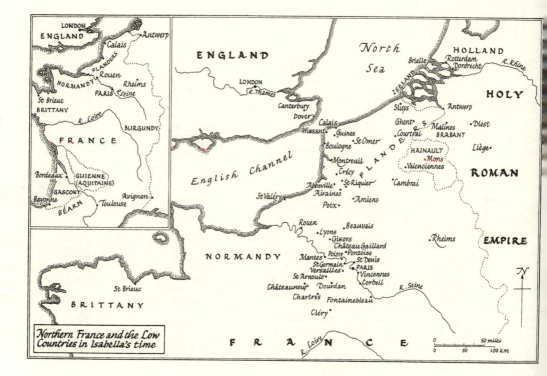

Inset map (upper left):

ENGLAND
LONDON
Antwerp
Calais
FLANDERS
NORMANDY Rouen
Rheims
PARIS R.Seine
St Brieuc
BRITTANY
R. Loire
BURGUNDY
FRANCE
Bordeaux
GUIENNE
(AQUITAINE)
GASCONY
Bayonne
Avignon
BÉARN Toulouse

Main map:

ENGLAND
North Sea
HOLLAND
Brielle
Rotterdam
Dordrecht
R. Rhine
LONDON
R. Thames
ZEELAND
HOLY
Canterbury
Dover
Sluys
Antwerp
Calais
Ghent
Malines
Diest
Wissant
Guines
Courtrai
BRABANT
St Omer
FLANDERS
Boulogne
HAINAULT
Liège
English Channel
Montreuil
Crécy
Mons
Valenciennes
ROMAN
Abbeville
St Riquier
Cambrai
Airaines
St Valéry
Amiens
Poix
Rouen
Beauvais
Lyons
Rheims
EMPIRE
Gisors
Château Gaillard
NORMANDY
Mantes
Poissy
Pontoise
St Germain St Denis
Versailles PARIS
St Arnoult
Vincennes
Châteauneuf Dourdan
Corbeil
Chartres
R. Seine
Cléry
Fontainebleau
BRITTANY
St Brieuc
F R A N C E
R. Loire

Northern France and the Low Countries in Isabella's time

50 miles
0   50
0   100 km

༈

The She-Wolf of France

I n Newgate Street, in the City of London, stand the meager ruins of
Christ Church, a stark reminder of the devastation caused by the Blitz
during the Second World War. This is the site of Christ's Hospital, the Blue
Coat School founded by Edward VI in the sixteenth century, destroyed during the Great Fire of 1666, and rebuilt by Sir Christopher Wren some years
later. Yet these ruins stand on the site of an even older foundation, the magnificent monastery of the Grey Friars, originally built in 1225 and later
endowed and reconstructed through the generosity of pious medieval
queens. In the fourteenth century, this was a royal mausoleum set to rival
Westminster Abbey as the resting place of crowned heads, yet tragically its
splendors are long gone, having disappeared after Henry VIII dissolved the
monastery in 1538, during the Reformation.

One of those who was buried in Greyfriars Church at Newgate, and
whose tomb was lost, was Isabella of France, Edward II's queen, one of the
most notorious femmes fatales in history. Nowadays, popular legend has it
that this sinister woman does not rest in peace but that her angry ghost can
sometimes be glimpsed amid the ruins, clutching the heart of her murdered husband to her breast.

It is also claimed, even in the reputable publications of English Heritage,
that this Queen's maniacal laughter and agonized screams can be heard on

stormy nights at Castle Rising in Norfolk, one of her favored residences. The belief still persists that, demented and insane, she was kept a prisoner here for twenty-eight years. And her unquiet ghost is also said to walk the secret passages below Nottingham Castle; she is believed to be searching in vain for her lost lover.

There is no doubt that the legends about Isabella of France paint a picture of a tragic, tormented, cruel, and essentially evil woman. And indeed, her historical reputation is not much more favorable. Since 1327, she has been more vilified than any other English queen. In her own lifetime, the chronicler Geoffrey le Baker called her "that harridan" or "that virago," referring to her as "Jezebel" and to her episcopal followers as "priests of Baal." Other chroniclers, although more discreet, were equally disapproving.

In 1592, in his play *The Tragedy of Edward the Second,* Christopher Marlowe wrote scathingly of "that unnatural Queen, false Isabel" and had Edward refer to her as "my unconstant Queen, who spots my nuptial bed with infamy." So, too, in his controversial 1991 filmed adaptation of the play, the director Derek Jarman showed little sympathy for Isabella, portraying her as a sexually repressed virago.

Shakespeare had invented the epithet "She-Wolf of France" for Margaret of Anjou, the scheming, vindictive wife of Henry VI, but in the eighteenth century, when England was at war with France, the poet Thomas Gray applied it to Isabella, and it has stuck ever since. In his "The Bard" (1757), he speaks, with horrific significance, of the

> . . . *She-Wolf of France, with unrelenting fangs,*
> *That tear'st the bowels of thy mangled mate.*

In the twentieth century, the German playwright and poet Bertolt Brecht revived the same theme in his *Life of Edward II of England.* In this, Isabella declares:

> *I shall become a she-wolf*
> *Ranging bare-toothed through the scrub,*
> *Not resting*
> *Until earth covers Edward . . .*
> *Drenched by the rain of exile,*
> *Hardened by foreign winds . . .*

And in 1960, in his novel *The She-Wolf of France,* the acclaimed French writer Maurice Druon describes Isabella as having small, sharp, pointed carnivore's teeth, like those of a she-wolf. Thus, the legend has become deeply entrenched in the popular consciousness.

Isabella has fared little better with the historians. In the mid-nineteenth century, Agnes Strickland wrote loftily that, since the days of "the fair and false Elfrida," who is believed to have arranged the murder of her stepson King Edward the Martyr in 979, "no Queen of England has left so dark a stain on the annals of female royalty as Isabella," who is "the only instance of a queen of England acting in open and shameless violation of the duties of her high vocation, allying herself with traitors and foreign agitators against her king and husband, and staining her name with the combined crimes of treason, adultery, murder and regicide." This proved almost too much for Miss Strickland, with her highly developed Victorian moral values, and her account was strictly bowdlerized, but even more modern historians have little that is good to say about Isabella, and most repeat the calumnies of the old chroniclers. In 1955, V. H. H. Green called her "a woman of no real importance or attraction," which is as inaccurate as it is dismissive, while in 1967, Kenneth Fowler denigrated her as "a woman of evil character, a notorious schemer" who was infamous "for her marital inconstancy," although he did concede that this was "in part excused by her husband's weaknesses." Elsewhere, Isabella is "one of the most beautiful but depraved women of her time," or simply "Isabella the Mad."

How, then, did Isabella acquire such a reputation? Married at twelve in 1308 to the homosexual Edward II, she grew up to be a legendary beauty yet was largely neglected by her weak husband and cruelly slighted by his vicious favorites. For many years, she endured this treatment, gaining renown as a model consort and a peacemaker. But in 1325, driven to desperation as a result of being deprived of her liberty, her children, and her income, she managed to escape to France, where she began a doubly adulterous affair with Roger, Lord Mortimer, an exiled English traitor. Together, they led the first successful invasion of England since the Norman Conquest, deposing Edward II and setting themselves up as regents for Isabella's eldest son, Edward III. Some months later, it was announced that Edward II had died in captivity, and soon afterward, rumor had it that he had been brutally murdered on the orders of Mortimer and Isabella. Before then, however, the unpopular policies of the regents had turned the people against them. When Edward III came of age in 1330, he overthrew their regime and had Mortimer executed. Isabella was spared any blame and spent the last twenty-eight years of her life in honorable retirement. Nevertheless, the taints of adultery, treason, and murder have blotted her name ever since.

Other queens have been accused of murder, treason, and adultery, but they have not attracted such enduring opprobrium, perhaps because the case against them has never been satisfactorily proved. Few now believe that Anne Boleyn betrayed Henry VIII with five men and also plotted his death. Katherine Howard always denied committing adultery. Monastic gossip accused Isabella of Angoulême of taking lovers: King John is said to have had them strung up above her bed, yet he never openly charged her with infidelity, and there is no question attached to the legitimacy of her children. Eleanor of Aquitaine was probably unfaithful to her first husband and led a rebellion against her second, Henry II, yet few writers now castigate her for it.

But Isabella is known to have lived in adultery for at least four years, in flagrant violation of the moral code of her time. Furthermore, with her lover, she plotted and mounted the successful invasion against her husband, which led to his deposition and his reputed murder. Such conduct on the part of a queen outraged conventional ideals of womanhood, which demanded that the King's wife be utterly loyal and sexually beyond reproach; and it also desecrated the sanctity of monarchy. Hence the charges of adultery and treason.

As for murder and regicide, the evidence is murkier. We are now not even certain that Edward II was murdered, still less that his estranged wife was a party to it, although many historians have assumed that she was.

It is her sexual misconduct that has above all made Isabella infamous. Her reputation rests largely on the prejudices of monkish chroniclers and Victorian historians. Yet as Norah Lofts has pointed out, if she had not taken a lover, her story would have been very different. An examination of contemporary records reveals that she had many fine qualities, and instead of incurring shame, dishonor, and revilement, she might have been seen as a liberator, the savior who unshackled England from a weak and vicious monarch and helped to put a strong king on its throne.

Changing social attitudes now permit a more tolerant and sympathetic view of Isabella's personal relationships. What comes across most strongly in her story is the sheer awfulness of the situation in which she eventually found herself and from which she managed to escape only by using her own initiative and cunning. She overcame male prejudice, won the sympathy of the people, and emerged as a heroine. It was her subsequent deeds that greatly shocked her contemporaries, who had hitherto perceived her to be a model queen. But this heroine was fatally flawed, and thereafter, she found herself on a downhill slide to tragedy and obloquy.

Remarkably, there has never been a full-length published biography of Isabella. An unpublished one exists in the form of Paul Doherty's 1977 thesis, primarily an academic study. Doherty's recent book on Isabella is not a biography, for it focuses mainly on the mystery surrounding Edward II's fate and Isabella's involvement in it. Isabella has been the subject of many learned articles in historical journals and, of course, of Agnes Strickland's greatly outdated life. A reappraisal is therefore long overdue.

Nowadays, after decades of change in the perception of the role of women, it is possible to view Isabella in a new light: to pity her, even to respect her. Women are no longer expected to be placid adornments of their husbands or the victims of circumstance; they are movers and shakers, able to shape their own destinies, make their own choices, and choose their own sexual partners. What once appeared so terrible seems so no longer.

Seduced by the drama of Isabella's life, I came to this project with many of the traditional misconceptions. I certainly didn't like her very much, and this rather concerned me, because I have always found, as a writer, that it helps to have a certain rapport with my subject. Eleanor of Aquitaine was undoubtedly a flawed woman, yet I had great admiration for her. Fortunately, and against all my expectations, while I was working on this book, my opinion of Isabella was gradually revised, as the sources revealed a rather different person from the one I had imagined. Isabella was every bit as vigorous and capable as Eleanor of Aquitaine, and in many ways, their experiences were similar. Both were spirited and cultivated Frenchwomen; both faced hardship and adversity; both were highly sexed and trapped in frustrating marriages; both had to cope with their spouses' infidelities, and both took lovers; more seriously, both led rebellions against their royal husbands, and both spent time under house arrest; both were adept at statecraft; and both were controversial in their own day. But unlike Eleanor, as we have seen, Isabella does not enjoy a brilliant posthumous reputation.

Now, having reevaluated all the evidence for Isabella's life, and having in the process stripped away the romantic legends and lurid myths, I have not only enormous sympathy for her but also considerable regard. Consequently, the aim of this book is to restore the reputation and rehabilitate the memory of a remarkable yet grossly maligned woman, who was the victim, not of her own wickedness, but of circumstances, unscrupulous men, and the sexual prejudices of those who chose to record her story. Like Eleanor, she was flawed, certainly, but her failings were very human ones, and there is much to like about her. What follows, therefore, is intended as the first realistic portrait of this most vilified of queens.

Alison Weir
Eddleston, Scottish Borders,
and Carshalton, Surrey
20 January to 5 August 2004

PART ONE

⚜

Isabella and Edward

I am your King,
though wanting majesty.

CHAPTER ONE

The Fair Maiden

On 20 May 1303, a solemn betrothal took place in Paris. The bride was seven years old, the groom, who was not present, nineteen. She was Isabella, the daughter of Philip IV, King of France; he, Edward of Caernarvon, Prince of Wales, the son and heir of Edward I, King of England.[1]

The Prince had sent the Earl of Lincoln and the Count of Savoy as his proxies, and during the ceremony, they formally asked the King and Queen of France for the hand of their daughter, the Lady Isabella, in marriage for the Prince of Wales. Consent was duly given, then Gilles, Archbishop of Narbonne, the presiding priest, required Isabella to plight her troth. Placing her hand in that of the Archbishop, she duly did so, giving her assent to the betrothal on condition that all the articles of the marriage treaty were fulfilled.[2]

This union had been arranged after tortuous negotiations to cement a lasting peace between those old warring enemies, England and France. Isabella's father, Philip IV, known as Philip the Fair, was the most powerful ruler in Christendom at that time and also the most controversial. Not only had he been engaged in territorial wars with both England and Flanders for the past seven years, he had also, despite boasting the title of "Most Christian King," become involved in a bitter conflict with the Papacy after imposing limitations on the Pope's authority in France. This was to lead to his excommunication only months after his daughter's betrothal.

Philip's war with Edward I was the result of a long-standing feud over England's possessions in France. In the twelfth century, through the marriage of Henry II to Eleanor of Aquitaine, the empire of the Plantagenets, the dynasty that Henry founded, had extended from Normandy to the Pyrenees, while the royal demesne of France had been limited to the regions around Paris. By 1204, Henry's son, King John, had lost most of the English territories, including Normandy, to the ambitious Philip II "Augustus" of France, and there were further French encroachments under John's son Henry III, as successive French monarchs sought to broaden their domain. By the time of Edward I, all that remained of England's lands in France was the prosperous wine-producing duchy of Gascony, the southern part of the former duchy of Aquitaine, along with the counties of Ponthieu and Montreuil, which had come to the English Crown through the marriage of Edward I to Eleanor of Castile in 1254.

Philip IV, who was vigorously carrying on his predecessors' expansionist policy, not surprisingly had his eye on Gascony, and in 1296, he invaded and took possession of it. There were two ways to settle a conflict: by military force or by diplomacy. Edward I wanted Gascony back, and Philip wanted to drive a wedge between Edward and the Flemings, who were uniting against him. By 1298, the two Kings were engaged in secret negotiations for a peace. Then Pope Boniface VIII intervened. In the spring of 1298, he suggested a double marriage alliance between France and England: his plan was that Edward I, a widower since the death of Eleanor of Castile in 1290, marry Philip's sister Marguerite, while Edward's son and heir, the Prince of Wales, be betrothed to Philip's daughter Isabella, then two years old. Once this peace had been sealed, Gascony could be returned to Edward I.[3]

Boniface's suggestion appealed to both parties; it conjured up for Philip the tantalizing prospect of French influence being extended into England and his grandson eventually occupying the throne of that realm; and for Edward I, it promised the return of Gascony and a brilliant match for his son. As the daughter of the King of France and the Queen of Navarre, Isabella was a great prize in the marriage market: no Queen of England before her had boasted such a pedigree.

The deal was agreed in principle, and two weeks later, on 15 May, King Edward appointed Henry de Lacy, Earl of Lincoln, to negotiate both marriages.[4] In March 1299, Parliament accepted the terms negotiated by Lincoln, and on 12 May following, plans were set in hand for the proxy betrothals. Three days later, the Earl of Lincoln, Amadeus, Count of Savoy, and the Earl of Warwick were appointed to act for Edward I and his son, and soon afterward, they departed for France. Edward I privately instructed the Count to find out as much as he could about the personal attributes of Marguerite of France, including the size of her foot and the width of her waist. The Count reported back that she was "a fair and marvellously virtuous lady," pious and charitable.

The Treaty of Montreuil, which provided for Isabella's future betrothal to Edward of Caernarvon, was drawn up on 19 June, ratified by Edward I and the Prince of Wales on 4 July, and amplified by the Treaty of Chartres on 3 August. Under its terms, Philip was to give Isabella a dowry of £18,000, and once she became Queen of England, she was to have in dower all the lands formerly held by Eleanor of Castile, which were in the interim to be settled by Edward I on Marguerite; these amounted to £4,500 per annum. Should Edward I default on the treaties, he would forfeit Gascony; if Philip defaulted, he would pay Edward a fine of £100,000.[5] On 29 August, at the instance of Edward I, the King and Queen of France gave solemn guarantees that the marriages would take place,[6] and in September, Marguerite of France, then aged twenty at most, arrived in England and was married to the sixty-year-old Edward I in Canterbury Cathedral. Against the odds, this proved to be a successful and happy union, and produced three children. In October 1299, Philip IV finally ratified the Treaty of Montreuil.[7] "When love buds between great princes, it drives away bitter sobs from their subjects," commented a contemporary.

In 1300, the French occupied Flanders, but two years later, they were humiliatingly defeated and massacred by the Flemings at Courtrai. Throughout this time, Edward I had continued to press for the immediate restoration of Gascony, but Philip would not agree to this until after the Prince of Wales had fulfilled his promise to marry Isabella,[8] who was still too young to wed.

By April 1303, Edward I was losing interest in the alliance and was beginning to look elsewhere for a bride for his son.[9] At this crucial point, fearing a war on two fronts, Philip IV played his trump card and agreed to restore the duchy of Gascony to Edward without further delay; his intention was, as he reminded Edward II in 1308, that it should in time become the inheritance of his grandchildren, the heirs of Edward and Isabella.[10] Edward I was now satisfied, and the Treaty of Paris, which officially restored the duchy, was signed on the same day that young Isabella and Edward of Caernarvon were betrothed. There would be further conflict between Edward I and Philip IV, but nothing serious enough to break this new alliance. Isabella was now destined to be Queen of England.

———

Isabella was probably born in 1295. There is conflicting evidence as to the year. Piers of Langtoft says she was "only seven years of age" in 1299, which places her birth in 1292, the date given in the *Annals of Wigmore*.[11] Yet she is described by both the French chronicler Guillaume de Nangis and Thomas Walsingham as being twelve years old at the time of her marriage in January 1308, which suggests she was born between January 1295 and January 1296. Given that twelve was the canonical age for marriage, and that in 1298, the Pope had stipulated that she should marry Prince Edward as soon as she reached that age,[12] these dates are viable. In the same document of June 1298, the Pope describes Isabella as being "under seven years," which places her birth at any time from 1291 onward. Furthermore, the Treaty of Montreuil (June 1299) provided for Isabella's betrothal and marriage to take place when she reached the respective canonical ages of seven and twelve.[13] So she must have reached seven before May 1303, and twelve before January 1308.

It has been suggested that Isabella had already reached the canonical age for marriage in 1305, when she and the Prince of Wales nominated representatives for a marriage by proxy.[14] This did not take place because of continued squabbles over Guienne,[15] but the fact that these nominations were made has been held as evidence that Isabella had then reached, or was soon to reach, the age of twelve, which would place her date of birth around 1293. Yet this theory is contradicted by a papal dispensation issued by Clement V in November 1305, giving the young couple permission to marry at once even though Isabella had not yet reached her twelfth year and was at present in her tenth year. This suggests a birth date between November 1294 and November 1295. The waters are muddied still further by a decree issued by Philip IV in 1310, in which Isabella is referred to as his "primogenita," or "firstborn," which suggests that she was born in 1288 at the latest, as her eldest brother Louis was born in October 1289. This date conflicts with all the other evidence and is probably the result of an error on the part of the official drawing up the document.

In conclusion, the evidence in the papal dispensations and documents and the Treaty of Montreuil is likely to be more reliable, and taken together, it supports a birth date between May and November 1295, which in turn is supported by the statements of Guillaume de Nangis and Thomas Walsingham. This would make Isabella seven years old at the time of her betrothal and twelve years old at the time of her marriage.

Isabella grew up in a period when society regarded women as inferior beings. "We should look on the female role as a deformity, though one which occurs in the ordinary course of nature," states a thirteenth-century edition of Aristotle's *Generation of Animals.* "Woman is the confusion of man, an insatiable beast, a continuous anxiety, an incessant warfare, a daily ruin, a house of tempest and a hindrance to devotion," fulminated the misogynistic Vincent de Beauvais in the thirteenth century. In 1140, the canon lawyer Gratian asserted that "women should be subject to their men. The natural order for mankind is that women should serve men and children their parents, for it is just that the lesser serve the greater."

The husband was his wife's lord and master: he was to her as Christ to the Church. Thus, if a woman murdered her husband, she was guilty of petty treason and could be burned at the stake. He, however, had the right to beat her if she displeased him; indeed, it was "the husband's office to be his wife's chastiser." He was not supposed to kill or maim her through such punishment, although, according to the legal code enshrined in the Customs of Beauvais, "in a number of cases men may be excused for the injuries they inflict on their wives, nor should the law intervene."

It was a woman's duty to love her husband and show him due obedience. In 1393, an anonymous Parisian writer instructed wives to obey their husbands' commandments, since "his pleasure should come before yours," and he advised them to "cherish your husband's person, give him plenty of attention, and the cheer of other delights, privy frolics, lovings and secret matters. Do not be quarrelsome, but sweet, gentle and amiable. And if you do all this he will keep his heart for you, and he will care nothing for other women." The onus was always on the wife to maintain the stability of a marriage.

In law, women were regarded as infants, so they had few legal rights. They were viewed as assets in the marriage market, chattels in property or land deals, or prizes in the game of courtly love, and their roles were very narrowly defined. When a group of noblewomen attempted to usurp male privilege and arrange a tournament in 1348, God "put their frivolity to rout by heavy thunderstorms and divers extraordinary tempests."[16] In the fifteenth century, one of Joan of Arc's chief crimes was the adoption of male attire, which was seen as tantamount to heresy.

Some highborn ladies were taught to read and write, but they were the fortunate few. In the thirteenth century, Philip of Navarre thought that generally women "should not learn to read or write unless they are going to be nuns, as much harm has come from such knowledge. For men will dare to send letters near them containing indecent requests in the form of songs or rhymes or tales, which they would never dare convey by message or word of mouth. And the Devil could soon lead her on to read the letters or"— even worse—"answer them."

Above all, in an age in which lineage and inheritance were paramount concerns, women were expected to be beyond moral reproach and to follow the virtuous example of the Virgin Mary. But because they were descended from Eve, who had committed the original sin, and were thus more likely to give in to temptation than men, they had to carefully guard their reputations. There was much comment on the frailty of women. "Wheresoever beauty shows upon the face, there lurks much filth beneath the skin." This anonymous Parisian writer also observed that "every good quality is obscured in the woman whose virginity or chastity falters. Women of sense avoid not only the sin itself, but also the appearance of it, so as to keep their good name. So you see in what peril a woman places her honour and that of her husband's lineage and of her children when she does not avoid the risks of such blame."

The Church taught that sex was primarily for procreation, not pleasure, and that intercourse was only permissible within marriage. Adultery was regarded as exceptionally sinful, especially on the part of a wife, for it jeopardized her husband's bloodline. In 1371, the author of the *Book of the Knight of La Tour Landry* insisted that "women who fall in love with married men are worse than whores in brothels, and a gentlewoman who has enough to live on yet takes a lover does it from nothing but the carnal heat of lust." A husband who caught his wife in adultery had the legal right to kill her.

There were, of course, many women who circumvented the conventions. Many ran farms or businesses, or administered estates. Some even practiced as physicians. A few wrote books. And queens, by virtue of their exalted marital status, could exercise political authority and the power of patronage. Isabella would have been brought up to know exactly what was required of her as a daughter and as a wife, and she had before her the example of her mother, who was a queen in her own right.

Isabella was born into the most illustrious royal house in Europe. It had gained its reputation largely through the careers of its thirteenth-century kings and the canonization in 1297 of her great-grandfather, Louis IX, one of the greatest of medieval monarchs. Her grandfather, Philip III, was a mild, mediocre man who briefly carried on the work of the sainted Louis, but it was left to his son, who became Philip IV in 1285 at the age of seventeen, to add to the prestige of the French monarchy. Philip IV extended the royal domain, effectively founded the Estates General, which evolved from his Paris *Parlement,* and centralized the royal administration.

In 1284, Philip had made a brilliant marriage with the eleven-year-old Jeanne, Queen of Navarre, who had succeeded to the throne of that kingdom in infancy. The acquisition of Navarre and Jeanne's counties of Champagne and Brie further strengthened Philip's power.

Philip IV was "the most handsome of men,"[17] and his stunning good looks earned him the nickname "Philip the Fair": in those days, an indication of good looks, not blond men. Exceptionally tall and strongly built, he also possessed a cold, calculating intelligence and a ruthless character. Yet there was, too, an ascetic side to his nature: beneath his costly velvets and furs was concealed a hair shirt, to mortify the flesh, and he regularly whipped himself with the monastic discipline on the orders of his confessor. Those who met him found his fixed stare, his long silences, and his mysterious manner disconcerting. "He is neither a man, nor a beast, but a statue," commented the Bishop of Pamiers.

As a ruler, Philip was authoritarian, despotic, efficient, and feared by his subjects. He was a resolute defender of the royal prerogative and obsessed with the acquisition of wealth. Being perennially short of money, he often resorted to drastic measures to get it. He dispossessed the Jews in his realm of vast sums, confiscated much of the property of the Lombard bankers, taxed the Church heavily, sold peerages to commoners, and notoriously, debased the coinage several times. His daughter Isabella would inherit his obsession with money and his avarice.

Isabella's mother, Jeanne of Navarre, was no beauty. Plump and plain, with a Moorish cast to her features, she was a dignified, pious, and intelligent woman, capable of managing her kingdom of Navarre and her other domains, although she tactfully adopted her husband's reforms in France as her administrative model. Twice, with great vigor, she successfully defended her territories, first against the Count of Bar and second against the combined might of Aragon and Castile. In 1298–99, the Queen, along with her mother, Blanche of Artois, and the Queen Dowager of France, Marie of Brabant, was actively involved in the diplomatic negotiations for her daughter Isabella's betrothal.

Generally, however, being frequently preoccupied with the business of childbearing, Jeanne chose not to dabble in French politics and confined her influence to the domestic and intellectual spheres. In Paris in 1304, she founded the College of Navarre, also known as the Hôtel de la Reine Jeanne, as a cultural center for the city's flourishing university. When Philip ventured forth on his frequent tours of the French provinces, Jeanne invariably went with him. Theirs had been a love match—on her part, at least—

for they had been brought up together at the château of Vincennes, after Jeanne's mother had seen fit to place her fatherless daughter under the protection of the King of France.

The career of her mother seems to have impressed itself upon Isabella's consciousness; she inherited many of her mother's abilities and may well have tried to emulate her example in later life. Certainly, she learned from Jeanne what a woman was capable of in a male-dominated society.

Philip's marriage to Jeanne produced seven children. Three sons survived childhood: the heir, Louis, born in 1289 in Paris; Philip, born around 1292–93 at Lyons; and Charles, probably born in 1294. All grew into "very handsome and great knights."[18] Isabella was the sixth child. Her two older sisters, Marguerite and Blanche, died young in or after 1294, and her younger brother, Robert, born in 1297, died at the age of eleven in 1308 at Saint-Germain-en-Laye. As the only surviving daughter, Isabella was much favored by her father and may well have been a little spoiled by him.

Through the marriages of his children, Philip was resolved to extend France's influence and borders. With any luck, his grandson, born of the union between Isabella and Edward, would sit on the English throne. In September 1305, Philip's eldest son, Louis,[19] was married to fifteen-year-old Marguerite of Burgundy, a granddaughter of Saint Louis on her mother's side, and the daughter of Robert II, Count of Burgundy. In 1307, Charles was married to Marguerite's cousin, eleven-year-old Blanche of Burgundy, and Philip was married to the latter's sister Jeanne; they were the daughters of Othon IV, Count of Burgundy. Through these unions, Franche-Comté and part of Burgundy became annexed to the French Crown.

In the early fourteenth century, France was the wealthiest and most heavily populated country in Europe: it had an estimated 21 million inhabitants, compared to 4.5 million in England; 80,000 people lived in Paris, twice the number who lived in London. French society was essentially feudal, and the royal domain now covered more than half of modern France; the rest was made up of vassal feudatories. The Capetian dynasty[20] had ruled since 987, since when the Crown had passed unfailingly from father to son.

France at that time was at the hub of European culture, and Paris was the intellectual center of Christendom. King Philip himself was a generous and discriminating patron of the arts, and Queen Jeanne, who descended from the brilliant and scholarly counts of Champagne, set a high cultural standard at court; in her retinue, she kept minstrels and trouvères, who provided sophisticated musical entertainment.

Isabella spent her childhood in the royal palaces around the Île de France and, of course, in Paris, at the Louvre, then a moated château, and the

Palace de la Cité, which was rebuilt by Philip IV. (The Palais de Justice now stands on the site.) Very little is known of her daily life during these early years. A few grants to her are recorded,[21] and, probably quite early on, a lady called Théophania de Saint-Pierre was appointed her nurse; Isabella became much attached to her, and Théophania would accompany her to England and remain with her for many years.

Isabella apparently received a good education for her time: she was lucky enough to be taught to read, and her love of books remained with her throughout her life. There is no evidence that she ever learned to write, although it is quite possible.[22] Above all, she must have grown up with a strong sense of her status and importance as the daughter of Europe's most powerful monarch and the future wife of the Prince of Wales, whose father was nearly as powerful. Promised when she was four, she could hardly have remembered a time when she was not aware that she would one day be Queen of England. Moreover, as the great-granddaughter of Saint Louis, she would certainly have been raised to believe in the sanctity of the royal House of Capet to which she belonged and its superiority over all other ruling dynasties. She may well also have cherished the naive expectation that all kings were like her father.

Although Isabella's childhood was privileged, it was overshadowed by war and by the quarrel her father waged with the Pope. She would have heard of Philip's envoys' physical assault on the violent and intransigent Boniface VIII in September 1303 and would have learned—doubtless to her distress—how the outraged Pontiff excommunicated her father the very next day. Even more shocking, later that month, Boniface died as a result of the assault. Fortunately for France, the election of a compliant elderly Frenchman, Clement V, in 1305 paved the way for a reconciliation, and in 1309, under pressure from Philip, Clement moved the seat of the Papacy from Rome to Avignon in southern France, where it was to remain for nearly seventy years, in thrall to the kings of France.

Meanwhile, in April 1305, when Isabella was not quite ten, her mother had died at Vincennes, aged only thirty-two. One French chronicler[23] accused her husband of poisoning her, but that is hardly credible, for Philip the Fair was grief-stricken at Queen Jeanne's passing, and his suffering was manifestly evident as he followed her funeral cortege to the Abbey of Saint-Denis, near Paris. There is no record of Isabella's being present. Jeanne was succeeded by her eldest son, Louis, who became King of Navarre. After her death, Philip remained faithful to her memory and never remarried, which was exceptional in an age in which royal marriages could secure valuable political advantages.

With Queen Jeanne's steadying influence removed, the French court lost much of its gravitas. The King's three young daughters-in-law now emerged as the leaders of fashionable society, and they were flighty, mischievous girls, intent only on pleasure. Soon, the court was plunged into a hectic round of fetes, dancing, and novel diversions, and moralists professed themselves shocked at the new fashions promoted by these princesses, who, along with other fripperies, set a trend for daringly slit skirts.

In the months after the Queen's death, Pope Clement began urging Edward I to press on with plans for his son's marriage to Isabella, and on 15 October, the Prince of Wales authorized the English envoys to conclude the contract.[24] There was talk of a proxy wedding at Lyons, to coincide with the new Pope's coronation there,[25] and on 11 November, Philip empowered Isabella to appoint her proxies.[26] The Pope issued the necessary dispensation for the marriage on 27 November,[27] and on 3 December, at the Louvre, Isabella named her proxies; they were her uncle, Louis of Evreux, Gilles de Saint Pol, and the Count of Dreux.[28] Yet there is no record of the proxy marriage ever taking place. The evidence suggests that it was prevented by further disputes over Gascony.

Still the tortuous preliminaries dragged on. In 1306, Clement sent Cardinal Peter the Spaniard to England to negotiate the final arrangements for the union between the Prince of Wales and "the fair maiden"[29] and expressed the hopeful opinion that peace between England and France was imminent.[30] Cardinal Peter was received by Edward I at Carlisle on 12 March 1307, and on the sixteenth, the King gave his formal consent to the union. When Parliament met at Easter at Carlisle,[31] the marriage was unanimously approved, and practical preparations for it were immediately put in hand. In late April, Prince Edward was supposed to go to France to marry Isabella at Poitiers; he even traveled to Dover and waited there nine days for his father's order to embark, but it never came.[32] Instead, the Prince was summoned to Scotland to assist his father in the Scottish campaign.[33] Apparently, the King was having doubts that this marriage would bring the lasting peace for which everyone was hoping.[34] He evidently had further thoughts, however, for two months later, shortly before he died on 7 July 1307, he belatedly commanded his son to marry Isabella. The next day, the Prince of Wales succeeded him as King Edward II.

The new King had shown no interest whatsoever in his coming marriage. There is no record of his sending any letter or gift to his future bride or even showing any curiosity about her. However, if he reneged on the marriage treaty, he stood to lose Gascony, and with Scotland in turmoil, he could not afford to fight a war on two fronts. Immediately after his acces-sion, therefore, he dispatched the Bishops of Durham and Norwich and the Earls of Lincoln and Pembroke to France to conclude the negotiations. They returned home with enthusiastic opinions of Isabella's beauty, and some chroniclers accuse Edward of being so eager to marry her that he abandoned his chances of conquering Scotland in his haste.[35] However, as will be seen, Edward had far more pressing personal concerns at this time.

Late in August, King Philip ordered his brother, Louis, Count of Evreux, to enter into negotiations with the English, and by 24 September, represen-tatives of Evreux had arrived in England; the Count was already in corre-spondence with King Edward.[36] In October, Parliament voted funds for the coming royal wedding and the coronation of the King and Queen that was to follow, and on 6 November, the King sent his envoys back to France to appoint a day for the nuptials and make the final arrangements.[37]

Four days later, Edward gave orders for preparations for his journey to France;[38] the wedding ceremony, which he wanted to take place at Boulogne;[39] and the reception of his bride in England. At the Palace of Westminster, he had the royal lodgings restored, the gardens freshly turfed with new trellises erected, the fish ponds cleaned and restocked, and the nearby "Queen's bridge," a pier on the Thames, repaired. A royal ship, *The Margaret of Westminster,* was commissioned to bring the new Queen home; Edward had it repainted and refitted, and he himself designed wardrobes and butteries inside it for his bride''s belongings.[40] He also ordered tapes-tries embroidered with the royal leopards and Gaveston's heraldic eagles for the coronation.[41]

Meanwhile, at the instance of the Pope, Philip agreed to the wedding's taking place at Boulogne in January.[42] He had a well-known devotion to Our Lady of Boulogne, and the location would be convenient for the English.[43] By now, Isabella was busy with her trousseau.[44]

These happy and auspicious plans were overshadowed in France by the mass arrest of about two thousand Knights Templar, on the King's orders, on 13 October. All over France, members of this monastic order, the Knights of the Temple of Solomon, founded in 1119 to protect pilgrims vis-iting the Holy Land, were taken into captivity on charges of heresy, fornica-tion, and worse, and their property was immediately sequestered by the Crown. It was not, of course, coincidental that the Templars had grown fabulously rich over the centuries and that King Philip was again desper-ately in need of funds. For the next seven years, the Templars in France would be accused of heresy, idolatry, sodomy, sacrilege, bestiality, and vari-ous other vile practices and interrogated, tortured, tried, and sometimes burned at the stake. Philip's treatment of the Templars paved the way for their condemnation by the Pope and the dissolution of the Order.

In England, in December 1307, Edward II gave offense to his future father-in-law by proclaiming that the charges against the Templars were unfounded, but just over a week later, he changed his mind and ordered the arrest of all members of the Order in his realm.[45] On 10 January 1308, the Order of the Temple was suppressed in England, too.

Shortly afterward, the English envoys returned from France, and on 22 January, King Edward set sail from Dover for Boulogne to marry Isabella.

Edward II was the youngest of the four sons of Edward I and Eleanor of Castile, and when he was born at Caernarvon Castle on 25 April 1284, just after his father's conquest of Wales, his one surviving elder brother, Alfonso, then aged ten, was heir to the English throne. It was only when Alfonso died of a fever the following August that the four-month-old Edward became his father's heir apparent. According to a famous legend, Edward I presented his newborn son on a shield to the Welsh as their prince, having promised them a native-born ruler; but this is a myth. Young Edward was not created Prince of Wales until February 1301, and the first account of his presentation was recorded as late as 1584 by John Stow, the Elizabethan antiquarian.

The Prince was born into a large family—Queen Eleanor presented her husband with sixteen children—but most of his siblings had either died young or been married off by the time he was born. Of those still in England, Joan of Acre (born 1272) was married in 1290 to Gilbert de Clare, Earl of Gloucester; Mary (born 1278) became a nun at Amesbury Abbey, Wiltshire, at the age of seven; and Elizabeth (born 1282) became in 1302 the wife of Humphrey de Bohun, Earl of Hereford and Essex. In 1286, Edward's parents went to Gascony for three years, leaving him in England; his younger sisters Beatrice and Blanche were both born there but died young.

Edward spent most of his early years at the royal manor of Langley near Saint Albans, which became his favorite residence. When his father and mother returned to England in 1289, they must have seemed like strangers to the young Prince. King Edward, now fifty years old, was a terrifying and remote authoritarian figure, and Queen Eleanor was already ailing: she died the following year. Edward of Caernarvon would therefore have been more or less emotionally isolated during his early childhood and was probably closer to his nurse, Alice Leygrave, than to anyone else; she was to remain in his service for twenty-nine years.[46] The forty-five-year gap between his father and himself cannot have made for closeness or understanding on either side.

Edward I was one of England's greatest medieval kings. "In build, he was handsome and of great stature, towering head and shoulders above the average." A drooping eyelid and a slight stammer or lisp did not detract from his aura of majesty, nor did he "lack a ready power of persuasion in argument."[47] He was autocratic, forceful, fierce-tempered, fearless, and full of boundless vigor. A born leader and a talented and dynamic ruler, he could still be unscrupulous, ruthless, cruel, and even violent. Even his second wife, Marguerite of France, who loved and respected him, conceded that he was "terrible to all the sons of pride."

Under Edward I, the prestige and authority of the English Crown reached its medieval zenith. In every respect, he personified contemporary ideals of kingship. A distinguished warrior, he inflicted a devastating conquest upon Wales, then spent the rest of his reign relentlessly trying to conquer Scotland. He streamlined the royal administration, enforced the royal prerogative, implemented far-reaching legal reforms, and promoted parliamentary government. He understood the need to curb the power of the great feudal lords, and by sheer force of character and judicious marriage alliances, he kept his barons firmly under control. It was only toward the end of the reign that aristocratic opposition to his policies grew vociferous, yet he would not brook any criticism or make concessions or changes.

Edward had married his first wife, Eleanor of Castile, in 1254, when he was fifteen and she only ten. They were devoted to each other, and when she died in November 1290, he was shattered by grief and retired for a time from public life. "My harp is turned to mourning," he wrote. "I loved her in life; I cannot cease to love her in death." In her memory, he built thirteen stone crosses to mark the route taken by her funeral procession from Harby in Nottinghamshire to Westminster Abbey, where a fine tomb with a bronze effigy still marks her resting place.

Edward I could show affection to his parents, his siblings, and his wives, but his children learned not to provoke his rages. On one occasion, he became so angry with one of his daughters that he pulled off her wedding circlet—she was about to be married—and threw it on the fire. Hundreds of his letters to his heir survive, and they are full of hectoring advice or stern reproofs. Yet his generosity was well known, and he did have a sense of humor. In his rare leisure time, he enjoyed hunting, hawking, and tournaments. He was also a pious and cultivated man, literate and well informed.

Since 1290, when he had been asked to arbitrate among thirteen claimants to its vacant throne, Edward I had cherished ambitions to annex

Scotland to the English Crown and to rule over a united kingdom. But his ambitions were continually frustrated by the resilience and tenacity of the Scots under the leadership of two great national heroes, William Wallace— whom Edward executed in 1305—and Robert Bruce, one of the most accomplished of military tacticians and an expert at guerrilla warfare. Yet Edward I was firm, even obsessive, in his resolve, and undeterred. When, in 1306, Bruce had himself crowned King of Scots, Edward declared him a traitor, dispatched an army, and drove him into hiding. Thereafter, the war dragged on bitterly and expensively until the end of the reign, by which time the English held every major fortress in Scotland. But Bruce was a doughty and intrepid fighter, and there was no end to the conflict in sight.

Edward of Caernarvon rarely enjoyed good relations with his father. Bound to emulate his magnificent sire and live up to his expectations, he was just not capable of doing so. At first, his lack of the requisite qualities was not apparent: he attended council meetings, fought ably on four campaigns in Scotland, and carried out ceremonial duties quite efficiently at home. But all too soon, he came under the influence of a young man whose name would soon become infamous.

Mindful that his son lacked companions of his own sex and age group, the King selected ten young men to be in constant attendance on the Prince. One was Piers Gaveston, the son of a leading Gascon baron who had fought for Edward I in France and Wales. Gaveston was born at Gabaston in Béarn; he first came to England in 1297 with his father, and in 1300, after serving in two campaigns in Scotland and impressing the King with his courtly demeanor, was placed in the Prince of Wales's household as one of his squires.[48] Before long, he had become "the most intimate and highly favoured member" of it.[49]

Piers was a handsome boy about the same age as the Prince;[50] he was graceful, active, intelligent, and skilled in arms.[51] Of his courage there is no doubt, nor of his boundless self-confidence. He was ambitious, indiscreet, greedy, extravagant, and arrogant: his pride, it was said, would have been intolerable even in a king's son. But that was later, after he had become notorious. The chroniclers were also fond of deriding Gaveston's "base and obscure" birth,[52] even though his family was an old and respected one; and in the sixteenth century, John Stow recorded an unfounded rumor that Piers's mother, Claramonde de Marsan, had been burned as a witch. Gaveston was also accused of leading the Prince's household into degeneracy— one claim that might have some truth in it.

Gaveston was a witty companion, but his tongue could be barbed, and he showed little respect for those of higher rank than he. Yet he could be charming when he wished, and he certainly charmed the Prince. "When the King's son saw him, he fell so much in love that he entered upon an enduring compact with him, and chose to knit an indissoluble bond of affection with him, before all other mortals."[53] Given that both were aged about sixteen at the time, this compact was probably that of two boys swearing blood brotherhood, an established medieval practice. From this time forward,[54] Edward was to refer constantly to Piers as "my brother" or "Brother Piers";[55] according to the *Annales Paulini,* he called him "brother" because of his excessive love for him. Yet the bond between Edward and Gaveston was indeed indissoluble: it lasted into adulthood and "surpassed the love of women";[56] even death could not sunder it. "I do not remember to have heard that one man so loved another," wrote the author of the *Vita Edwardi Secundi.* The conclusion is inescapable that Edward did fall in love with Piers—or "Perrot," as he sometimes called him—and that this love had homosexual connotations. Indeed, it is hard to interpret it in any other way.

It was common in the military society of the Middle Ages for men to form close friendships without there being any sexual overtones, yet that between Edward and Piers drew much comment, and even though most chroniclers refrained from overt accusation, especially in Edward's lifetime, it is clear what they are implying, for their tone is condemnatory. They say that Edward loved Gaveston "beyond measure"[57] and "uniquely,"[58] and that Gaveston loved him "inordinately."[59] The *Chronicle of Lanercost* accuses Edward of improper relations with Gaveston, Robert of Reading attacks the relationship as an "illicit and sinful union" that was "beyond the bounds of moderation" and charges Edward with desiring "wicked and forbidden sex," while the *Chronicle of Meaux* candidly states that Edward "particularly delighted in the vice of sodomy." The *Vita Edwardi Secundi* says that "the King's love for Gaveston was fiercer than that of David for Jonathan, whose love David valued above the love of all women, or Achilles for Patroclus.[60] But we do not read that they were immoderate." Thomas Walsingham calls Gaveston Edward's "beloved."

Ranulph Higden describes Edward as being "passionately devoted to one particular individual, whom he loved above all, showered with gifts and always put first; he could not bear separation from him, and honoured him more than anyone else. As a result, the beloved was loathed and the lover entangled himself in hatred and disaster."

In the fourteenth century, homosexuality was viewed as one of the vilest of crimes. Because it was regarded as a sin against nature and against the divinely appointed order of the universe, those found guilty of it faced, at the very least, excommunication by the Church, because it was seen as a form of heresy; some offenders were castrated or burned at the stake. It is hardly surprising, therefore, that the relationship between Edward and Piers was looked on with almost universal disapproval, even outrage, especially when the two men seemed to be flaunting their liaison.

It is true that both Edward and Gaveston married and fathered children, but that was what society expected of them, and it proves only that each man was capable of normal sexual relations. It is also true that Edward acknowledged a bastard son, Adam,[61] who was probably born before his accession. The Prince is further said to have been "given to the company of harlots"[62] in youth; when he was only fourteen, he paid 2s. (10p.) to a certain Maude Makejoy (whose name implies that she was a prostitute) for dancing before him. This all suggests either that he was uncertain of his sexuality in these early years or that he was truly bisexual.

Before long, however, it was Edward's passion for Piers that was fueling the relationship. It seems he had quickly come to terms with his sexual orientation, for thereafter, in his naive way, he appeared to see no wrong in it. And that was the root of the problem.

For a time, Edward I entertained no doubts about his son's friendship with Gaveston. Initially, he regarded it with approval and showed Gaveston great favor,[63] praising the example he set the Prince in his virtuous conduct and courtly manners. In 1303, the two young men earned further royal approbation when they served together in Scotland. However, in 1305, while on another northern campaign, Piers blotted his copybook by deserting the army, with several other young men, to take part in a tournament in France. Edward I was furious.[64]

By now, it was becoming clear to the old King that Gaveston was a bad influence on his son, especially after the pair of them, abetted by a gang of other youths, invaded the estates of Walter Langton, Bishop of Chester, the King's Treasurer, pulled down fences, and scattered the deer and other game. When the Bishop complained to the King, the Prince "uttered coarse and harsh words to him" and was sent in disgrace to Windsor Castle with only one servant in attendance, there to await his father's summons.[65] It did not come, and for the next six months, the boy remained in disgrace. Worst of all, from his point of view, he was banned from seeing Gaveston.

A reconciliation was finally effected in October 1305 through the good offices of Queen Marguerite. At Whitsun 1306, Edward and more than 260 other young men, including Gaveston, Hugh le Despenser, and Roger Mortimer (who were all to play fateful roles in Isabella's life story), were knighted in a great ceremony at Westminster, by which time Gaveston had his own household and had been granted land in ten counties. Soon afterward, the Prince and Gaveston joined Edward I in another campaign against the Scots. But early the next year, Edward of Caernarvon gave his father further offense when he asked him to give Piers, as a mark of royal favor, either the royal earldom of Cornwall or the counties of Ponthieu and Montreuil, which the Prince had inherited from his mother. Given the King's entrenched prejudices against the alienation of royal lands and the Prince's obvious and inappropriate infatuation with Piers, it is not surprising that Edward I erupted in rage. He grabbed his son by the hair and dragged him about the room, shouting, "You baseborn whoreson! Would you give away lands, you, who never gained any?"[66]

The King's fury masked a growing anxiety as to the precise nature of the relationship between Gaveston and his son. On 26 February 1307, "for certain reasons," which are unspecified in the written order,[67] he banished Gaveston to Gascony.[68] The *Chronicle of Lanercost* states that Piers was really exiled "on account of the undue intimacy which the younger Lord Edward had adopted towards him, publicly calling him his brother," while the *Annales Paulini* claim that the King was concerned about "the inordinate affection" that his son had for "a certain Gascon knight." Edward I further forbade the Prince to have his friend "near him or with him" and ordered him never to bestow on him any lands and titles. Even so, by providing so generously for Gaveston's maintenance, he made it clear that he thought Piers more sinned against than sinning.

The Prince and Gaveston were made to swear on the Blessed Sacrament and Edward I's "holiest relics" not to contravene the King's edict,[69] which in itself suggests how strong their friendship was perceived to be, then in May, a miserable Edward bade farewell to Gaveston at Dover, after lavishing gifts on him.[70] In the event, Piers went to Ponthieu rather than Gascony, and apparently with the King's blessing. The Prince announced his intention of visiting him there, but King Edward forbade it.[71]

At this time, Edward I was in the north, planning a new assault on Scotland. But he was a sick, bedridden man, possibly suffering from cancer of the rectum, and at Burgh-on-Sands, on 7 July 1307, he breathed his last, expiring as his servants were raising him to eat some food.[72] The Prince of Wales, now twenty-three, was King of England.

One of Edward I's legacies to his son was a kingdom nearly bankrupted by a war that looked to be unwinnable, with a great portion of his future revenues mortgaged to Italian bankers. Edward II also inherited a nobility that had chafed and grown resentful under the iron fist of the Crown and was determined to regain its lost influence and privileges. Nevertheless, the new King's accession was the occasion of "the greatest rejoicing,"[73] for he was young and debonair, had the common touch, and was seemingly deserving of the immense goodwill of his people. "God has bestowed every gift on him, and made him equal to, or indeed more excellent, than other kings," claimed Robert of Reading. "What high hopes he had raised as Prince of Wales!" commented Edward's biographer ominously,[74] while the Pope compared him to the biblical King Rehoboam, the son of Solomon, who lacked wisdom and relied on the advice of young, violent persons, through which his kingdom was grievously divided. In Scotland, Robert Bruce drily stated that he feared dead Edward's bones more than his living heir.

The people were soon to be bitterly disillusioned: "all hopes vanished when the Prince became King."[75] Edward II's first royal act was to recall Piers Gaveston.[76] "He had home his love," observed one chronicler. On 6 August, even before the favorite returned, his sovereign bestowed on him the earldom of Cornwall,[77] which until recently had been held only by members of the royal House and brought with it the vast income of £4,000 a year, almost as much as the Queen's dower. No commoner had ever been raised so high at a stroke, yet this creation was made "with the approval of some of the magnates," notably Henry de Lacy, Earl of Lincoln, one of the most loyal, honest, and able servants of Edward I[78] and a personal friend of that King. During his long career, Lincoln, now fifty-seven, had served the Crown faithfully as both a general and a diplomat; it was he who had helped to negotiate the new King's marriage to Isabella of France. Lincoln appears to have thought well of Gaveston at this period, and when some raised doubts as to whether the King could legally alienate the earldom of Cornwall, "which he held with the Crown, Earl Henry said that he could" because there were precedents. But the majority of the barons did not agree, "as much because Piers was an alien of Gascon birth, as through envy."[79]

Gaveston arrived in England around 13 August and was soon entrenched at court. The King "did him great reverence and worshipped him," almost as if he were a god. There is no doubt that, after the monarch, Gaveston was now the most important man in the realm. Unsurprisingly, "the magnates of the realm hated him because he alone found favour in the King's eyes, and lorded it over them like a second king, to whom all were subject and none equal. Almost all the land hated him too, and foretold ill of him, whence his name was reviled far and wide. Nor could the King's affection be alienated from Piers, for the more he was told, in attempts to damp his ardour, the greater grew his love and tenderness towards Piers."[80]

The King wasted no time in replacing some of his father's ministers and judges. Pricked on by Gaveston,[81] he began by dismissing his old adversary Bishop Langton and replacing him as Treasurer with Walter Reynolds, whom he made Bishop of Worcester. Reynolds, the son of a Windsor baker and former Keeper of the Prince's Wardrobe, was chosen apparently because he was Gaveston's friend and was skilled at mounting the theatrical entertainments that Edward so enjoyed.[82] Langton was imprisoned in the Tower of London and accused of the misappropriation of public funds; his public accounts were made the subject of an inquiry, and his treasure was given to Gaveston.[83] The King also urged the Pope to restore the archbishopric of Canterbury to his father's staunchest adversary, Robert Winchelsey, who was then in exile.[84]

Edward I's dying instructions to his son were to have the flesh boiled from his bones so that they could be carried at the head of a conquering army into Scotland.[85] Edward II ignored this request, just as he had quickly abandoned the war in Scotland, and on 27 October, his father's body was buried in Westminster Abbey, where the inscription "Malleus Scotorum" ("The Hammer of the Scots") was later inscribed on his tomb. Two days later, in order to "strengthen Piers and surround him with friends," the King had Gaveston betrothed to his niece, Margaret de Clare, daughter of Joan of Acre by the late Earl of Gloucester. The marriage took place on 1 November at Berkhamsted Castle, with the King as guest of honor.[86] This union not only brought Gaveston into the royal circle but did indeed "strengthen his position not a little, for it much increased the goodwill of his friends and restrained the hatred of the baronage."[87] This was partly because the bride's brother, Gilbert de Clare, the sixteen-year-old Earl of Gloucester, raised no objection to the marriage. He knew Gaveston well, having been brought up with him in the Prince's household.

Preparations for the King's marriage and coronation were already in hand, but Edward spent most of November in Gaveston's company at his favorite manor of Langley. On 2 December, with the aim of enhancing his "honour and glory," Gaveston held a great tournament at his castle of Wallingford, during which he unhorsed and "most vilely trod underfoot" the Earls of Arundel, Surrey, and Hereford, exulting triumphantly in his victory. The Earls never forgave him this insult. His pride, it was said, damaged him more than his prowess.[88]

According to the *Vita Edwardi Secundi,* "hatred for Gaveston mounted day by day, for he was very proud and haughty in bearing. All those whom the custom of the realm made equal to him he regarded as lowly and abject; nor could anyone, he thought, equal him in valour." The lords "looked down on him because, as a foreigner and formerly a mere man-at-arms, raised to such distinction and eminence, he was forgetful of his former rank. Thus he was an object of mockery to almost every one in the kingdom. But the King's unswerving affection for him prompted the issue of an edict from the court that no one should call him Piers Gaveston, but should style him Earl of Cornwall."[89]

Edward was due to depart for France after Christmas and had to leave his kingdom in the custody of a royal relative or some trustworthy noble. On 20 December, he appointed Piers Keeper of the Realm,[90] which provoked disgusted comments from the chroniclers[91] but surprisingly no overt criticism from the magnates, most of whom were better qualified than Gaveston for this high honor.

Edward and Piers spent Christmas together. Neither can have felt very happy at the prospect of the King's marriage. Gaveston had every reason to resent Isabella and what she stood for. He was a Gascon, and his family had been driven from the duchy during the French occupation. He therefore had good cause to hate and distrust Philip IV, and he would certainly have regarded Philip's daughter as an interloper and a threat to his ascendancy over the King. The evidence suggests that he did his best to stir up trouble between Edward and Philip in a last-ditch attempt to make Edward abandon his treaty with the French, urging that Philip would not rest until he had finally conquered Gascony. But there were others on Edward's council who greatly feared the consequences if their master reneged on his obligations to Philip, and for once, they prevailed over the favorite.

We have no means of knowing how much Isabella learned before her marriage, or understood, of her future husband's relationship with Piers Gaveston. It must have been common gossip at the French court, but the Princess may have been shielded from any adverse talk. It is inconceivable, however, that Philip IV was not aware of the furor and scandal that his future son-in-law's elevation of Gaveston was causing. Some historians have accused him of hypocrisy in giving his daughter to a reputed sodomite when he was charging the Templars with that very crime, but no doubt Philip would have taken a pragmatic view of such matters. This alliance would extend France's influence, so personal considerations must be set aside.

Isabella's preparations for her marriage were now complete. In her trousseau, she had numerous gowns, including some of baudekyn,[92] velvet, and shot taffeta. Six were of green cloth from Douai, six were beautifully marbled,[93] and six were of rose scarlet.[94] These gowns would have had tight-fitting bodices and sleeves, and circular skirts with trains.

Only unmarried girls, and queens on ceremonial occasions, wore their hair loose. It was fashionable for hair to be curled, and some of the representations of Isabella show her with curly hair. However, as a married woman, she would be obliged to wear a triangular-shaped linen or silk headdress comprising a chin-barbe, veil, and wimple, which was padded out at the sides with ramshorn and exposed the hair at the temples. Isabella had no fewer than seventy-two headdresses and coifs in her trousseau.

Ladies of rank wore heavy mantles, or cloaks, over their gowns, and furs in the cold weather, and Isabella brought many costly furs to England. She also had two gold crowns ornamented with gems, gold and silver drinking vessels, golden spoons, fifty silver porringers, twelve large silver gilt dishes, twelve small silver gilt dishes, and fifty silver plates. She was also provided with 419 yards of linen for her bath, body linen for chemises and hose (drawers were unknown before the sixteenth century), and tapestries blazoned with gold-embroidered lozenges framing the arms and heraldic emblems of England, France, and Navarre for her chamber.[95]

Early in the morning of Monday, 22 January 1308, Edward II sailed from Dover with a great retinue, arriving in Boulogne on the evening of the twenty-fourth, three days later than planned;[96] the delay was probably due to the vagaries of winter travel. Philip IV was waiting to greet him and present to him his bride.

Isabella was an enchanting child who would grow into "a most elegant lady and a very beautiful woman."[97] It was conventional for chroniclers routinely to describe queens and highborn ladies as being fair in visage, yet their praise for Isabella's looks is so fulsome and unanimous that she must indeed have been beautiful. Edward II himself gave her the nickname "Isabeau the Fair";[98] Walter of Guisborough, echoing Jean le Bel, calls her "one of the fairest ladies in the world"; Froissart, "the beautiful Isabella." She was "the fairest of the fair," "more beautiful than the rose," and "the beauty of beauties in the kingdom, if not all of Europe."[99]

Isabella, like her brother Charles, who was also nicknamed "the Fair," probably took after her father in looks. There is a French manuscript illustration of circa 1315 showing Philip IV with his sons and daughter,[100] but these are in no way portraits. Lacking any precise description, even a note of the color of her hair, we must look elsewhere for clues as to what Isabella really looked like. Contemporary ideals of beauty favored blonde, plump women, and we may therefore suppose that Isabella conformed to this type, but there is also some evidence that she had these attributes.

There are several extant representations of Isabella, some merely images of a queen, others possible attempts at an accurate portrayal. Most manuscript illustrations depicting Isabella date from the fifteenth century and owe much to the artist's imagination. There are a few pictures of her in more contemporary manuscripts, which will be discussed later, but which are, again, in no sense portraits. Isabella also appears on her seal, in the conventional image of a queen, whose figure stands between two shields.[101]

A corbel head of a woman in a crown and wimple in Beverley Minster, Yorkshire, is said to portray Isabella and bears a striking resemblance to the authenticated stone head of her that appears on the Oxenbridge tomb in Winchelsea Church, Sussex, which dates from circa 1320. Both depict a young woman with a plump face, arched brows, and curled hair and may be true likenesses.[102] Isabella traveled widely in England, and the men who sculpted these heads could well have seen her and attempted to produce her features with some veracity. On the other hand, a corbel head and a roof boss, both said to be Isabella, in Bristol Cathedral, and a boss in the choir of Exeter Cathedral, also purporting to be her, are probably purely representational. Three stone heads in Fyfield Church, Berkshire, are said to date from circa 1308 and to represent Isabella, Edward II, and the ship's master who had brought them from France, while a carved corbel head in the gatehouse of Caldicot Castle, Monmouthshire, is perhaps a crowned Isabella.

The heads at Beverley and Winchelsea also appear to bear a familial resemblance to the tomb effigies of Isabella's father and two eldest brothers at Saint-Denis, which are contemporary and sufficiently individualistic as to suggest attempts at likenesses. By this period, there was a definite trend toward realism in funerary effigies, although most were idealized images. Another representation of Isabella showing her crowned with curly hair escaping from her wimple is in the Psalter of Queen Isabella, which was probably commissioned by her. She is shown wearing a long gown belted under the bust and a cloak with an embroidered hem; in her hand is a shield bearing the royal fleurs-de-lis of France.[103]

As far as his appearance was concerned, Isabella's bridegroom was everything a young girl could dream of. Edward II was tall (about six feet) and muscular, "a fine figure of a handsome man"[104] and "one of the strongest men in his realm."[105] He had "better advantages of birth and nature than any other king," for "God had endowed him with every gift."[106] Even hostile chroniclers expressed admiration for his handsome looks, which he inherited from his father. He was well proportioned[107] and had curly, fair, shoulder-length hair, with a mustache and beard. He was also well spoken—his mother tongue was Norman-French—and articulate, and he dressed elegantly, even lavishly. He cannot have failed to make a good impression on his young bride.

Almost as soon as he arrived in France, Edward paid homage to Philip IV for his lands in France, and the French King in turn handed over Isabella's dowry of £18,000, which had been appropriated from the confiscated wealth of the Templars. On her marriage, Isabella was supposed to receive the lands customarily assigned to the queens of England, but as these were still in the possession of Edward I's widow, Marguerite of France, and Isabella would only get the reversion of them on Marguerite's death, King Edward undertook to dower her from his lands in France as well as giving her other lands in England.[108] To mark the marriage, Philip gave Edward and Isabella costly gifts of jewelry, rings, chains, and fine warhorses.[109]

On Thursday, 25 January, Edward and Isabella were married in the cathedral church of Our Lady of Boulogne.[110] Isabella was vibrantly dressed in a costly gown and overtunic of blue and gold, and a red mantle lined with yellow sindon,[111] which she was to preserve for the rest of her life.[112] On her head, she wore one of the crowns given her by her father, which glittered with precious stones. Her bridegroom was resplendent in a satin gardcorp (a sleeved cyclas) or surcoat and a cloak embroidered with jewels. Philip IV's robe was rose-colored.[113]

The importance of this union was underlined by the magnificence of the ceremony and the fact that no fewer than eight kings and queens were present: the King of England; the King of France and his son, the King of Navarre; the French Dowager Queen, Marie of Brabant; Albert of Habsburg, King of the Romans, and his Queen, Elizabeth of Tyrol; Charles II, King of Sicily; and Edward II's stepmother, Queen Marguerite,[114] who was also the bride's aunt and may have given her as a wedding gift a silver gilt casket bearing the arms of both Marguerite and Isabella in quatrefoils; it was presumably intended for use as a jewel casket or a receptacle for holy oils.[115] Leopold I, Archduke of Austria, and King Edward's brother-in-law, John II, Duke of Brabant, also attended the wedding, as well as a great throng of princes and nobles from all over Europe.[116]

After the ceremony, Edward and Isabella left for the lodgings that had been appointed for them near the cathedral; their retinues had to shiver in canvas tents, which had been set up in and around the town.[117] Medieval custom demanded that the bride and groom be ceremonially put to bed together on the first night, but there is no record of that happening in this case. Given the tender age of the bride (twelve was the minimum age permitted by the Church for a girl to have marital sex), the fact that she did not become pregnant for another four years, and the probable sexual inclinations of the groom, it is unlikely that the marriage of Edward and Isabella was consummated at this time.

Eight days of celebrations and tournaments followed the nuptials, with a great feast taking place on the twenty-eighth. Two days later, Edward entertained Philip's brothers, Louis of Evreux and Charles, Count of Valois, at a sumptuous dinner.[118] The merrymaking was marred, however, when Philip presented Edward with a list of grievances concerning Gascony and warned him not to think of having his marriage annulled, as certain persons in England had advised, because Gascony had been restored to him only because of his union with Isabella "and the children that would be born to them." Philip especially condemned those "who claim that the English King gains nothing by his marriage with the daughter of the King of France," which was probably an oblique but pointed reference to Gaveston. Edward retaliated by pettishly sending Philip's wedding gifts to Gaveston in England.[119] Furthermore, some of the English lords who had traveled to France with the King were already secretly scheming to get rid of Gaveston; at Boulogne, ten of them drew up a declaration of their intent to protect the honor of the King and the rights and privileges of the Crown.[120]

The festivities came to an end on 2 February,[121] which was none too soon, given the growing tensions, and the next day, accompanied by Isabella's uncles, the Counts of Evreux and Valois, the King of England and his new Queen bade their farewells and traveled along the coast to Wissant, whence they took ship and "returned joyfully" to England.[122]

CHAPTER TWO

The King Is Lovesick
for His Minion

In 1308, England was increasingly prosperous and had an expanding population. Society was still predominantly feudal and agrarian, yet the towns and cities were growing fast due to trade and mercantile enterprise. In the two and a half centuries since the Norman Conquest of 1066, Normans and English had learned to live together, although Norman-French was still the language of the court and the aristocracy, and Middle English the language of the commons. The kingdom was predominantly a land of great forests, green fields, quiet villages, and numerous churches, so numerous, in fact, that it was called "the ringing isle."

Isabella's first sight of the country of which she was now Queen was the white cliffs and Dover, where she and Edward landed on 7 February 1308.[1] Gaveston was waiting to greet them at the dockside, and with no thought for his bride or his dignity, Edward impulsively ran to him and greeted him with an embarrassing display of affection, falling into his arms, "giving him kisses and repeated embraces," and calling him "brother," while Isabella and her uncles looked on, visibly dismayed and displeased.[2] Even if the Queen knew nothing of the rumors about her husband and Gaveston, she was greatly offended by his publicly showing this man more affection than he had so far shown to her, his wife.

Gaveston had ordered the chief ladies of the Queen's newly established household to assemble at Dover, ready to greet her and attend her on her progress to Westminster.[3] Among them were Elizabeth, Countess of Hereford, the King's sister, now twenty-six; Alicia d'Avesne, the Flemish wife of Roger Bigod, Earl of Norfolk; Joan de Genville, the wife of Roger Mortimer, a leading baron; Joan Wake, who was French by birth;[4] and Isabella, the daughter of Louis de Brienne, Viscount de Beaumont. Isabella de Beaumont was married to John, Baron de Vesci, and she was to become as favored by the Queen as she already was by the King, who was related to her through his mother. Her two brothers, Henry and Louis, would also enjoy high favor with the royal couple. Henry was knighted in 1308; he received large grants of land from the King and was summoned to Parliament as Baron Beaumont. He was to serve Edward in a military capacity in Scotland and on diplomatic missions abroad and would be an enormously influential member of his household.

Edward and Isabella spent two nights at Dover, staying in the twelfth-century keep in the castle, where the royal apartments lay behind walls twenty feet thick. They probably held court in Arthur's Hall, built by Henry III in 1240, and may well have worshipped in the tiny Romanesque chapel dedicated to Saint Thomas à Becket, Edward's favorite saint. On 9 February, the King and Queen left Dover and traveled via Ospringe and Rochester to Eltham Palace, where they were to stay pending their state entry into London for their coronation.[5]

Eltham Palace, which lies some six miles southeast of London Bridge, and was originally a fortified manor built by the Clare family, had long been an important residence; both Henry III and Edward I had visited there, and in 1278, the latter granted it to the powerful baron John de Vesci. In 1295, his son William sold it to Anthony Bek, Bishop of Durham, who rebuilt it. Little is known about Bek's house, but it was turreted and had a tower and a moat surrounded by a stone wall; access was gained via a timber drawbridge. The great hall was tiled, and there was a wine cellar. The Bishop had also created a hunting park to the south of his palace. As will be seen, Eltham became one of Isabella's favorite places. Bishop Bek had already granted the reversion of the house to the King on his death, and Edward may have promised it to Isabella during their stay.

If he did, it was not enough to compensate for the discovery made by the dismayed young Queen that the income promised by her husband was showing no signs of materializing and that she had nothing to live on, since there was no money in the Treasury with which to dower her. Indignantly, she wrote to her father, complaining that she was expected to live in poverty.[6]

Philip responded by demanding that Edward state in writing exactly what financial provision he intended to make for Isabella and any children of the marriage. Edward replied that he had already drawn up such a statement for Isabella but that his advisers had counseled him not to put his seal to a copy for Philip in case it laid him open to further obligations in respect of their children if Isabella predeceased him.[7]

Then fuel was added to the fire when Isabella noticed Gaveston— "whose passion for finery was insatiable"—wearing not only the jewels and rings that Philip IV had given to the King but also some of the jewelry that she had brought from France as part of her dowry.[8] Again, she wrote to her father, expressing her fury at the avarice of Piers and the favor shown to him by her husband, who was neglecting his duty toward her. She was, she asserted, "the most wretched of wives."[9]

Isabella would have been comforted to know—and perhaps already did know—that the barons were determined to do something about Gaveston. The coronation was due to take place on 18 February, but they warned the King that, unless the favorite were banished, they would not take part in the ceremony, which was tantamount to refusing him their oaths of allegiance. At the same time, Isabella's uncles were angrily threatening to boycott the ceremony unless Gaveston were banished. By the time Edward had won them all round with fulsome promises "to undertake whatever they sought in the next Parliament," which was to meet in March, and agreed to a new clause in the coronation oath, the crowning had had to be postponed until 25 February.[10]

The King and Queen were magnificently received in the capital when they entered it in state on 19 February, the Lord Mayor and his aldermen and the members of the London guilds, all wearing new liveries, riding out to meet them and to ceremoniously surrender the keys to the City. Then the four-mile-long procession moved slowly through streets that were gaily decorated with banners and pennants, and thronged with thousands of people, who cheered their beautiful young Queen enthusiastically and took her to their hearts. Pageants were enacted in temporary castles of canvas or fairy bowers decked with artificial flowers, while free wine flowed in the City's conduits.

London at this period was a flourishing city, by far the largest and most powerful in England. Ships from all over Europe sailed up the Thames to its port, and the City was a great center for mercantile enterprise; it also played an important role in influencing public affairs. London occupied only a square mile at this period and was surrounded by stone walls; within them, its teeming narrow streets were crammed with jettied buildings, and space was at a premium. London also boasted more than a hundred churches, the largest of which was Saint Paul's Cathedral, built between 1251 and 1312 in the Gothic style. At 644 feet long, it was then the largest cathedral in England. The impressive stone bridge spanning the River Thames had been built in 1170, and its thoroughfare was lined with houses, shops, and a chapel. It linked the City to Southwark on the Surrey shore, where brothels plied their trade beyond the city boundaries. Two miles upriver lay West-minster, with its magnificent palace and abbey; this, the administrative and judicial hub of the kingdom, was beginning to be regarded as the central seat of government.

For the five nights following their arrival, Edward and Isabella lodged in the Tower of London,[11] on the north bank of the Thames. The central keep of this mighty fortress—known as the White Tower since 1240, when Henry III had had it whitewashed—had been built by William the Con-queror in the period 1076 to 1087 to stand sentinel over London. Various kings had added to it: Richard I encircled the bailey with a vast curtain wall bisected by towers, and Henry III built more towers and constructed a palace with a great aisled hall between the keep and the river; but the most recent and impressive improvements were those made by Edward I, who had created a moat and built massive concentric defenses, including a new watergate (now known as Traitor's Gate) and new royal apartments above it in Saint Thomas's Tower.

The Tower now housed the King's treasure, the Great Wardrobe—a repository for royal foodstuffs, furniture, jewels, and clothes—the state archives, the largest of the royal mints, and the greatest arsenal of weapons in the kingdom; consequently, it was one of the most important castles in England. It also contained a menagerie, created by Henry III in 1235 to house the animals that were sometimes given to monarchs as gifts. At vari-ous times, it held lions, bears, leopards, and even an elephant. In this period, the Tower had not gained its later notoriety as a state prison, although a few prominent persons had been held prisoner there over the centuries.

Edward and Isabella would have lodged in the sumptuous state apart-ments within Henry III's palace and its adjacent towers, which were located around what was now known as the Inmost Ward and could be accessed only by the Coldharbour Gate by the White Tower or from the river. These apartments were brilliantly decorated in bright colors and adorned with gold stars, heraldic emblems, and Purbeck marble fittings. There were hooded fireplaces, garderobes (lavatories) in the main chambers, and large pointed-arched Gothic windows. Edward II initially used the King's apartments in Saint Thomas's Tower, although he later came to prefer Henry III's suite, with its oratory and private watergate, in the nearby Hall Tower (now called the Wakefield Tower), so called because it gave access to the great hall.

Isabella's apartments were probably those created for Eleanor of Provence, Henry III's queen, and refurbished by Edward I for Marguerite of France; these lay at the west end of the great hall, beside the Hall Tower. The walls of the Queen's chamber were wainscoted, whitewashed, and painted with roses and trompe l'oeil pointing that looked like cut stonework. Her chapel windows were glazed.

Within the Tower precincts, there were gardens, a vineyard, and an orchard; in the northwest corner lay the chapel of Saint Peter ad Vincula, rebuilt by Edward I, and in the White Tower was the Norman Chapel of Saint John the Evangelist, with its Romanesque arches and brightly painted walls.[12]

On 24 February, Edward and Isabella left the Tower and rode in procession through the City of London to the Palace of Westminster, the chief residence of the English kings, where Isabella was to spend much of her life during the coming years. The original palace that stood on the site had been built by the Saxon King and saint Edward the Confessor, around 1050, but it had been rebuilt and extended over the centuries, and there was nothing left of it by Isabella's time. The palace site now occupied several acres along the north bank of the River Thames, and to the east lay Westminster Abbey, which had also been founded by Edward the Confessor but had been rebuilt by Henry III as a fittingly splendid setting for the Confessor's shrine and a mausoleum for himself and his descendants.

In 1097, William II built a huge great hall beside the Confessor's palace; measuring 240 feet by 67 feet, it was then probably the largest and grandest hall in Europe. Between 1154 and 1189, Henry II rebuilt the palace itself, extending the site to incorporate Old Palace Yard, a new "white" hall, a chapel dedicated to Saint Stephen, and a great chamber. He also instituted a sophisticated system of water supply, with fountains and conduits.

Around 1230, Henry III spent a fortune adding luxurious and brilliantly decorated royal apartments that would set a new and advanced standard for royal residences; he also rebuilt the great chamber as the famous Painted Chamber, so called because of its vast murals depicting events in the life of Saint Edward the Confessor and warlike scenes from the Bible. This room, with its great Gothic windows, glazed tiled floor, and private oratory, served as the King's bedchamber and was dominated by a large state bed with a gilded and painted carved wooden canopy and green curtains.

In 1237, Henry III built a new chamber for his Queen adjacent to the Painted Chamber, on the first floor overlooking the river; her Wardrobe was below it, and nearby was the "Maidens' Hall," which presumably was to house the Queen's damsels, or waiting women. The Queen's new chamber was wainscoted and had oriel windows with deep embrasures decorated with painted figures, and an allegorical figure of Winter painted on the wall over the fireplace hood; on the other walls were murals of the Four Evangelists. Beyond the Queen's chamber was her private chapel, which had pilasters with capitals and crowned heads flanking the arched doorways and the deeply molded lancet windows, the latter being "superbly gilt and coloured"; there was also a marble altar font and a green altar cloth. The walls in these rooms were painted in blue and red, while the sculptured reliefs and paneling were highlighted in gold, green, and yellow. The whole effect must have been startlingly vibrant.

Edward I erected a new main gateway northwest of Westminster Hall and began rebuilding Saint Stephen's Chapel, intending that it should rival the Sainte Chapelle in Paris, the private chapel of the kings of France. Edward II continued this project, but it was not finally completed until 1348.

There had, however, been disastrous fires at Westminster in 1263 and 1298. The latter destroyed the White Hall and rendered the Queen's apartments uninhabitable. When Marguerite of France came to England in 1299, Edward I arranged for her to stay in temporary accommodation in York Place, the Archbishop of York's palace that stood by the river between Westminster and Charing Cross.[13]

In 1307, Edward II had set about the restoration of the Palace of Westminster, so that it would be a fit place to receive his Queen. Throughout the autumn and winter, working by candlelight through the hours of darkness, masons had been cutting and dressing stone and marble, and craftsmen and workmen had shaped timbers, forged metalwork, painted walls, and glazed windows. The King himself had supervised the work, but it was still not finished by the time of Isabella's arrival and would not be until the following summer, by which time the cost of the repairs and refurbishments amounted to some £5,000.

The restored palace was just as impressive and comfortable as Henry III had intended, and its gardens were delightful, with returfed lawns, paved paths, pear and cherry trees, and vines. There was a "Queen's pool" and even an aviary, established by Eleanor of Castile. Inside the palace itself, the King had built two new "White Chambers": one attached to the Painted Chamber was to serve as his bedroom, and the other was added to the restored Queen's apartments; we may assume, therefore, that Isabella's accommodation was both spacious and stylish.

The Palace of Westminster was not only a royal residence but was now becoming established as the administrative center of the kingdom. It was near to London, which had long replaced Winchester as the capital of England, and it also housed the Treasury, the Exchequer, and the chief law courts, namely, the central Courts of Common Pleas and the King's Bench.[14]

The coronation of Edward II and Isabella of France took place on 25 February, the feast of Saint Matthias the Apostle.[15] The ceremony was performed by the Bishop of Winchester, assisted by the Bishops of Salisbury and Chichester, because the Archbishop of Canterbury had not yet returned to England.[16] Invitations to the ceremony had, for the first time, included the wives of peers in honor of the Queen.[17]

Gaveston had been given the responsibility of planning the coronation, and predictably, he accorded himself a central role in it, which many were to hold against him for a long time to come.

In the morning, the King and Queen went in stately procession from Westminster Hall to the Abbey, walking along a timber pathway laid with blue cloth strewn with herbs and flowers. Above their heads was an embroidered canopy borne by the Barons of the Cinque Ports. The crowds were so dense that the royal pair almost had to fight their way through, and to avoid this, they were obliged to enter the Abbey by a back door. In advance of the King had come the chief magnates, bearing the regalia: the Earl of Lancaster carried Curtana, Saint Edward the Confessor's blunted, edgeless Sword of Mercy; his brother Henry, the Rod with the Dove; the Earl of Hereford, the scepter with the Cross; the Earl of Lincoln, the royal staff; the Earl of Warwick, the three swords of state; and the Earl of Arundel, Thomas de Vere, Hugh le Despenser, and Roger Mortimer, the royal robes on a board covered with checkered cloth.[18]

But all heads turned when Gaveston appeared "so decked out that he more resembled the god Mars than an ordinary mortal."[19] It was not so much the magnificence of his clothes that caused mutterings at his effrontery but the fact that he was clothed in pearl-encrusted silk robes of imperial purple, a color that should have been reserved for the King himself, whose own finery was somewhat eclipsed by that of his favorite.[20] Gaveston also managed to upstage the other earls, who were wearing the traditional cloth of gold, the richest fabric normally permitted to those of their rank. All were bristling with jealousy.

What enraged the barons and shocked the people most, however, was that Gaveston, with his "soiled hands," was carrying that most sacred relic, the crown of Saint Edward the Confessor, into the Abbey,[21] a privilege that should have been bestowed on the highest noble in the land. Considering that Gaveston had only recently been elevated to the peerage, this was perceived to be a deliberate affront, and it would never be forgotten or forgiven. One earl was so furious with Gaveston that only consideration for the sensitivities of the Queen and the sanctity of the Abbey prevented him from coming to blows with him in the church itself.[22]

Edward II took his coronation oath in French rather than the traditional Latin.[23] In addition to the normal undertakings, he fulfilled his promise to the barons by promising to "uphold and defend the righteous laws and customs which the community of the realm shall determine."[24] After this, he was anointed with holy oil on the head, hands, and breast and then ascended to a high wooden platform on which was set the gilded and painted wooden coronation chair made by Edward I in 1297 to house the Stone of Scone, on which the kings of Scotland had long been crowned, and which had been seized by the English in 1296. Edward II seated himself in this chair—which has been used at every coronation since—and the crown was with due solemnity placed on his head.

After the peers had paid homage to the enthroned King, Isabella was anointed—on the hands only—and crowned Queen of England. The consort's crown was an open circlet surmounted by eight motifs interspersed with trefoils and set with many precious stones.[25]

Gaveston's ineptitude gave rise to several mishaps on coronation day. There were so many spectators crushed into the Abbey that a wall behind the altar collapsed, killing a knight.[26] Even at the moment of crowning, there was little space for the King and the officiating bishops, for the crowds were inadequately marshaled. After the rather disorganized ceremonies belatedly ended at 3:00 p.m., the King and Queen led the vast congregation back to Westminster Hall for the coronation banquet. All were seated in order of precedence, but the food was not ready; in fact, although there was an abundance of provisions of every kind—victuals had been commandeered from all the southern counties and a thousand pipes of wine had been sent from Gascony—no food was served until after dark, and when it did arrive, it was badly cooked, inedible, and ill served.[27] The King had chosen to sit next to Gaveston rather than the Queen. Again, the lords could barely contain their fury.[28]

Isabella's uncles, her brother Charles, and numerous French nobles and knights were guests at the coronation,[29] but they were appalled by the prominence accorded to Gaveston. When Evreux and Valois saw the tapestries bearing his arms alongside the King's,[30] they were incensed and demanded that the Queen's arms be arrayed next to Edward's. The excessive favor shown to Gaveston by the King seemed proof that the scandalous rumors about them were true.

As soon as the coronation celebrations were over, Evreux and Valois returned to France in disgust, declaring that their kinswoman was insulted because the King preferred the couch of Gaveston to that of his wife.[31] They may well have left a shocked Isabella in no doubt as to why he did so.

Queen Marguerite left court, too, and retired to Marlborough Castle in Wiltshire. Had she remained, she might have been able to advise Isabella on many aspects of her role as Queen of England, but without her aunt's wise counsel, the young and inexperienced Queen had no one but her French attendants to confide in and only her uninformed instincts to rely on. She had been taught that she must love, obey, and support her husband, but this was proving difficult, for already she apparently felt he was neglecting her for Gaveston, and her pique perhaps inclined her to side with Gaveston's critics. Without warning, she had been plunged into a predicament that would have taxed a mature adult, let alone a twelve-year-old girl who can have had little understanding of what she was dealing with.

Isabella was now discovering that her husband was quite unlike what she and most other people expected a king to be. For a start, he didn't even seem to want to be King; he wasn't interested in ruling England, and he cared nothing for his royal duties. On the contrary, he was quite content to share his power with Gaveston and use the advantages of his office to enrich his friend and enjoy himself. He didn't always conduct himself like a king, and he didn't personify contemporary ideals of kingship. He clearly was finding it impossible to impose his will on his barons and was consequently and rapidly forfeiting their respect. Yet it is clear also that he thought a king could do no wrong.

Edward had the oddest tastes for a monarch. Traditionally, medieval kings were war leaders and aristocrats, and their interests reflected this. They enjoyed hunting, tournaments, and planning military campaigns. Edward II certainly loved hunting and horse racing, and did not lack courage, but he hated tournaments and never went to war unless necessity drove him to it, which exasperated his martially minded barons beyond measure. It was said that "if he had habituated himself to arms, he would have exceeded the prowess of King Richard" the Lion-Hearted.[32] But Edward was content to throw away his advantages.

The barons were even more horrified by their sovereign's leisure activities, which included digging ditches on his estates, thatching roofs, trimming hedges, plastering walls, working in metal, shoeing horses, driving carts, rowing, swimming—even in February—"and other trivial occupations unworthy of a king's son."[33] The tragedy was that Edward had the potential to be a great king: "if only he had given to arms the labour that he expended on rustic pursuits, he would have raised England aloft, and his name would have resounded through the land."[34]

Worse still, his rustic pursuits inevitably led the King to fraternize in the most undignified way with the lower orders, whose company he actually preferred to that of his nobles.[35] His manner with the common people of his realm was affable and familiar—too familiar, in the opinion of his barons, who were horrified to see him consorting with grooms, carters, ditchers, mechanics, oarsmen, sailors, "villeins and vile persons." And they could only deplore his friendships with artists, buffoons, jesters, singers, choristers, actors, and jongleurs.[36]

To us, today, some of the company he kept suggests that Edward II was rather a cultivated man. Above all, he loved "theatricals" and was a great patron of writers and players. Sadly, not one of the plays—or "interludes"—that he enjoyed survives in its entirety; we only have a fragment from a comedy called *The Clerk and the Damsel*. But even this seemingly innocuous pleasure drew censure, for most of the aristocracy of the day despised amateur dramatics as being vulgar and disreputable.

The King was also literate, enjoyed poetry, and even wrote some himself.[37] Norman-French was his mother tongue, but he knew Latin, too,[38] and was a copious letter writer.[39] He collected exquisitely produced books of French romances and legends; he also borrowed, and did not return, manuscripts of the lives of Saint Anselm and Thomas à Becket from the monastic library at Christ Church, Canterbury. Edward had a passion for music and employed a group of Genoese musicians to entertain him: there were two trumpeters, a horn player, a harpist, and a drummer. The King himself owned a Welsh instrument known as a crwth, which was an early type of violin.[40]

Edward was undoubtedly a vain man; he was always elegant, and sometimes showy as a peacock in his dress, and he spent a great deal of money on clothes and jewelry. This did not attract overmuch criticism, because kings were expected to look the part, and with his good looks and strong physique, he certainly did. He loved luxuries and was "splendid in living"[41] but was also inclined to "vanities and frivolities." Given that he inherited huge debts from his father, his tastes were all too extravagant.[42]

The King loved animals; he was passionate about dogs and horses and was a skilled horseman. He bred and trained his own horses and hounds. At his behest, his huntsman, William Twici, wrote *L'Art de la Vénerie,* the earliest surviving hunting manual. As a young man, Edward owned a pet lion, which, tethered with a silver chain in its own cart, often traveled with him, attended by its keeper, and he also kept a camel in the stables at Langley.[43]

Edward had a boisterous sense of humor and enjoyed practical jokes and horseplay. He once paid a royal painter, Jack of Saint Albans, 50s. (£2.50) "for having danced on a table before the King and made him laugh beyond measure";[44] another man was rewarded for amusing his sovereign by falling off his horse in a comic manner.[45] Edward kept several fools in his employ and was not above indulging in mock fights with them; once, he had to pay compensation to a fool called Robert, whom he had accidentally injured during some boisterous games in the water.

Edward was an inveterate gambler; his Wardrobe accounts show that he lost large sums at vulgar games of chance such as dice, "chuck-farthing," "heads or tails," "cross and pile," or "pitch and toss."[46] He was also something of a gourmet, with a taste for good food and wines, but he frequently drank too much, and when he was inebriated would indiscriminately "let out his secret thoughts and quarrel with bystanders for feeble causes."[47] Even when sober, he was "quick and unpredictable in speech."[48]

Edward could also be wayward and difficult, petulant, vindictive, and viciously cruel when sufficiently provoked;[49] Higden says he was "savage" even with members of his household. Passion, anger, and resentment could smolder in him for years, and his outbursts of the famous Plantagenet temper left observers in no doubt as to whose son he was. He was weak; lacked judgment, intuition, and the ability to empathize with others; and in many ways was not very bright. He was lazy by nature, loving to lie abed late in the mornings,[50] and often maddeningly indecisive, failings that could be disastrous in a ruler in an age in which monarchs ruled as well as reigned.

However, once Edward's affection was given, he could be demonstrative, "prodigal in giving,"[51] and unswervingly loyal. In company, he was congenial and a good conversationalist, articulate and witty. He was also a good and loving father to his children.

The King was genuinely pious and had a special devotion to Saint Thomas à Becket, which Isabella would come to share. Both made frequent visits to that murdered saint's shrine at Canterbury, Edward going sixteen times in all. The King attended Mass often, spent a great deal of time with his chaplains, and was generous in his almsgiving. He had a particular affection for the Dominican Order of friars, whose house at Langley he founded and generously endowed.

Edward's good qualities, however, were insufficient to command the respect of his people; on the contrary, his faults—and in particular his indiscriminate promotion of unsuitable favorites, his determination to give matters concerning those favorites priority over matters of state, and his flaunting of his homosexuality—all looked set to damage the very institution of monarchy itself. Indeed, no king of England has ever attracted so much criticism from his contemporaries as Edward II did.

Edward II had begun his reign on a tide of public approval, but he was recklessly throwing that away through his irresponsible promotion of Gaveston, who was now "the person who is most talked about" at court. The King looked upon Gaveston as his equal and blood brother, almost as a second king and coruler,[52] was ruled by his advice while "despising the counsel of the other magnates,"[53] and gave him thousands of pounds from his already depleted Treasury.[54] It was Gaveston, and not the chief magnates, who controlled the network of royal patronage and Gaveston who took bribes for favors. This incensed the nobles, who resented having to pay for privileges that should have come direct to them from the King. It seemed to them that there were now two kings in England, "one in name and the other in reality."[55]

Gaveston's usurpation of patronage was one of the chief causes of the barons' "wrath and envy." Disgust at the nature of his relationship with the King may well have been another. But it was his arrogance that was beyond endurance. According to the *Vita Edwardi Secundi,* "Piers did not wish to remember that he had once been Piers the humble esquire. For Piers accounted no one his fellow, no one his peer, save the King alone. Indeed, his countenance exacted greater deference than that of the King. His arrogance was intolerable to the barons and a prime cause of hatred and rancour." This chronicler firmly believed that "if Piers had from the outset borne himself prudently and humbly towards the magnates, none of them would ever have opposed him."[56]

But Gaveston did nothing to placate the barons; tactless beyond measure, he seems to have gone out of his way to provoke their anger, without caring about the consequences. And the King, "who was incapable of moderate favour, and on account of Piers was said to forget himself,"[57] did nothing to curb his arrogance: "the more virulently people attacked Gaveston, the more keenly the King loved him."[58] Together, they were playing a very dangerous game.

It is abundantly clear that, from the first, Edward's marriage had made no difference to his relationship with Gaveston. In fact, it highlighted the strength of the King's "excessive and irrational"[59] love for the favorite, whom he "adored with a singular familiarity"[60] that fueled the jealousy not only of the magnates but of the neglected little Queen. Robert of Reading scathingly condemns the "mad folly of the King of England, who was so overcome with his own wickedness and desire for sinful, forbidden sex, that he banished his royal wife from his side and rejected her sweet embraces." Murimuth reports how it was common gossip that Edward "loved an evil male sorcerer more than he did his wife, a most handsome lady and a very beautiful woman."[61]

Isabella hated Gaveston, at least to begin with, and she was certainly resentful of his influence over the King and the fact that he took precedence over her. She told her father that he had caused "all her troubles, by alienating King Edward's affection from her, and leading him into improper company," and that her husband had become "an entire stranger to my bed."[62] But there was nothing she could do about it.

There was never any open rift between the Queen and Piers. Wisely, Isabella seems to have kept her feelings to herself and refrained from voicing any complaint that could prejudice her chances of establishing a good relationship with her husband; we know this because, in 1325, Edward declared that he had only ever rebuked her once in private, and that was for being too proud.[63] And even if she had remonstrated with him about the favorite, it would have done her no good. The King could hardly be blamed for preferring the company of a man of his own age above that of a mere child.

And it was as a child, no more, that Edward probably treated Isabella, indulging her now and then, or taking a fleeting interest in her. Of course, to a girl reared with a strong sense of her own importance and destiny, this was insulting and demeaning, and many of the barons were incensed on her behalf that she should be so slighted and resolved to take her part.

While Gaveston's star was in the ascendant, Isabella stood little chance of exercising any political influence as Queen. To begin with, of course, she was too young to do so. But it is clear, too, that she played a very insignificant part in the King's life during these early years and was therefore in no position to counteract the favorite's supremacy. She was effectively alone in a strange country and a court seething with tensions and hostility.

———

By now, Isabella would have become better acquainted with England's leading barons, most of whom were related in some way to either herself or her husband. Foremost among them were the Earl of Lincoln and his son-in-law, Thomas, Earl of Lancaster, the King's cousin. Lancaster was also Isabella's maternal uncle, being the son of her grandmother, Blanche of Artois, through her marriage to Edmund Crouchback, Earl of Lancaster, younger brother of Edward I. Jeanne of Navarre, Isabella's mother, had been the child of Blanche's first marriage, to Henry I, King of Navarre. Thomas thus boasted many royal connections.

He had been born around 1278–80 and had married Alice de Lacy before 1294. She was a great heiress, for, as her father's only surviving child, she stood to inherit great lands and earldoms on his demise. On his own father's death in 1296, Thomas inherited the earldoms of Lancaster, Leicester, and Derby, which made him the wealthiest landowner in England after the King. He maintained a huge private army and had as many knights in his service as the King did.

During Edward I's reign, Lancaster served the Crown in various small ways and was high in favor with Edward I. On 9 May 1308, Edward II confirmed his appointment as High Steward of England. But Lancaster had a low opinion of Edward. Well connected and blue-blooded as he was, he had every reason to expect to be the King's chief adviser; but Edward had chosen Gaveston instead and incurred Lancaster's undying jealousy.

Lancaster was tall, slim, and imposing and affected a flamboyant style of dress. In character, though, he was haughty, selfish, treacherous, and vicious. Like his cousin the King, he was lethargic and lacked vision or purpose. In fact, he had few redeeming features. A sulky, quarrelsome, and vindictive man,[64] he was quick to resort to violence. His speech was coarse, and he was promiscuous to excess; we are told that he "defouled a great multitude of women and gentle wenches." Unsurprisingly, his marriage was unhappy, and childless.

Humphrey de Bohun, Earl of Hereford and Essex and Constable of England, was thirty-two; in 1302, he had married Elizabeth, one of Edward I's daughters. He was a self-contained individual, prickly and quick-tempered, but also intelligent, with a sense of humor. As an official in the Prince of Wales's household, he had enjoyed good relations with Edward II before the latter's accession and had benefited from the Prince's generosity, but their friendship had been soured by Edward's excessive favoring of Gaveston, and the Earl, faced with a conflict of loyalties, was now reluctantly siding with the opposition.

Guy de Beauchamp, Earl of Warwick, was a fierce opponent of Gaveston. Now aged thirty-five or more, he was an exceptionally cultured and learned man who understood Latin, was well read, and owned an unusually large collection of books for a nobleman of this period. Warwick had served with great distinction in Scotland under Edward I, and he brought to his political career wisdom and good sense: "in prudence and counsel," he was "without parallel." Thus, his fellow magnates would often seek his advice before taking any action. Although he was also something of a thug, and could be ruthless and arrogant, the author of the *Vita Edwardi Secundi* lauded him as a hero.

John de Warenne, Earl of Surrey, was two years younger than the King and was married to Joan of Bar, a granddaughter of Edward I;[65] their marriage would, however, be annulled in 1315. Surrey was a nasty, brutal man with scarcely one redeeming quality; although they were his political allies, Lincoln and Lancaster loathed him, and he and Lancaster maintained a private feud for years. Surrey's sister, Alice de Warenne, was married to another young earl, Edmund FitzAlan, Earl of Arundel, now aged twenty-three; he, too, was an opponent of Gaveston.

Perhaps the most honorable and able of the magnates was the moderate Aymer de Valence, Earl of Pembroke, a tall, lean, and sallow man of forty who was the son of William de Valence, half brother of Henry III[66] and therefore cousin to the King. Pembroke had been one of Edward I's most trusted captains in his campaigns against the French and the Scots, and all his life he was a true servant of the Crown, a skilled diplomat who was known and respected both at home and abroad for his honesty and integrity. Pembroke, as a man of principle, deplored Edward II's reliance on his unworthy favorite because it threatened to undermine the prestige of the monarchy itself. Being no sycophant, he, too, was at times to find himself embroiled in a conflict of loyalties.

One baron who supported Edward II throughout the greater part of his reign was his Breton cousin John de Montfort, Earl of Richmond, a grandson of Henry III.[67] Aged forty-two in 1308, he had been granted his earldom by Edward I in 1306. Richmond became a favorite of Isabella and would play an important role in her life many years hence.

Immediately after the coronation, the magnates began to hold secret meetings. "It was only now that almost all the barons rose against Piers Gaveston, binding themselves by a mutual oath never to cease from what they had begun until Piers left England."[68] When Parliament met at Westminster on 3 March, they moved against "the King's idol," accused him of accroaching the powers of the Crown, and demanded his banishment. Their spokesman was Lincoln, who, appalled by Gaveston's arrogance, had now turned against him and become "his greatest enemy and persecutor,"[69] acting in what he sincerely believed were the interests of the Crown. The highly intransigent and uncompromising Archbishop Winchelsey, newly returned from exile, immediately supported the barons' stand, while Gloucester and Richmond remained neutral, and only Lancaster and Hugh le Despenser sided with the King. Not daring to criticize the mighty Lancaster, the other barons turned on Despenser and accused him of being a "hateful" man who, "more from a desire to please the King and a lust for gain than for any creditable reason, had become an adherent of Piers."[70]

In fact, Hugh le Despenser, who was now in his late forties and was married to Warwick's daughter, "was one of the most distinguished men of his day, both in judgement and in probity."[71] He had been one of Edward I's most faithful and able servants and was to prove as loyal to Edward II. He was an efficient administrator, a capable politician, and a trusted diplomat, courteous, easygoing, and genial. He had sent gifts to Prince Edward when the latter was in disfavor with his father, he was the only baron whom Edward could really trust, and—most important of all in Edward's eyes—he was friendly toward Gaveston, which earned him the King's undying affection and the implacable enmity of the other barons. It has to be said, however, that their accusations against him are borne out by contemporary records: he was indeed "brutal and greedy,"[72] with an insatiable desire for land and wealth, and he had over the years accumulated large estates through underhand means and sheer force. His success may be measured by the fact that in 1306, Edward I had agreed to the marriage of Despenser's son, Hugh the Younger, to his own granddaughter, Eleanor de Clare, whose sister Margaret married Piers Gaveston.

In response to the magnates' demands, Edward announced that he would defer discussion of such matters until after Easter. Meanwhile, he bestowed Berkhamsted Castle, which legitimately belonged to Queen Marguerite, on Piers, and at Easter, when Edward took Isabella to Windsor, journeying via Reading and Wallingford,[73] Gaveston joined them.

The situation between the King and his barons was now sufficiently grave for civil war to be a distinct possibility, and Edward spent most of April summoning men and fortifying castles. One person who offered his support to the King at this time was Roger Mortimer, who joined Edward at Windsor.

Roger Mortimer, who was to play such a fateful role in Isabella's life, was the most powerful member of a fiercely independent group of barons

known as Marcher lords, whose lands bestrode the Welsh border and whose
task it was to keep the peace in that region. Roger had been born probably
in 1287 and, in 1304, succeeded his father as eighth Baron of Wigmore,
where his family had been established since 1074, the first Roger Mortimer
having been a companion of the Conqueror. Edward I made this present
Roger, who had inherited considerable estates in Wales, the Marches, and
Ireland, a ward of Piers Gaveston, but Roger quickly purchased his independence.[74] In 1301, he married Joan de Genville, a well-connected[75] heiress
who brought him Ludlow in Shropshire and lands in Ireland and Gascony
and would bear him twelve children. Roger frequently took Joan with him
on his travels, which suggests that theirs was a close and companionable
relationship.[76]

Because of his Irish connections and his undoubted administrative talents and military reputation, and also because the King knew him to be
brave, loyal, and dependable, Roger Mortimer was to spend the best part of
the early years of Edward II's reign helping to govern Ireland. When he was
not in Ireland, he was serving in Scotland and Gascony, or ruling ruthlessly
and efficiently on the Marches and in Wales, in conjunction with his uncle,
the violent and lecherous Roger Mortimer of Chirk, almost like independent princes. Nevertheless, he came to court as often as he could and had
been present at the royal wedding in Boulogne. From the first, he appears
to have been on good terms with Queen Isabella, who corresponded with
him occasionally and, in 1311, helped him obtain the release of the Chamberlain of North Wales, who had been imprisoned on a false charge.[77]

Roger Mortimer was tall, swarthy of complexion, and strongly built. He
was one of the most outstanding military leaders of the period, tough,
energetic, decisive, and versatile in his talents. Like most barons, he was
arrogant, grasping, and ambitious, but he was also an excellent political
strategist and a faithful servant of the Crown who was well respected by his
peers. Clever, cultured, and literate,[78] he took a keen interest in his family's
history and its alleged descent from Brutus, the mythical British King, and
in the legends of King Arthur. He had refined tastes, loved fine clothes, lived
in some luxury, and undertook major architectural works to transform his
castles at Wigmore and Ludlow into veritable palaces. Typical of his caste,
he also loved tournaments, paid lip service to the knightly code of chivalry,
and amassed a considerable collection of weaponry.[79]

Edward sent Mortimer to Ireland in the autumn of 1308. In so doing, he
deprived himself of a valuable ally, because Roger's frequent absences would
mean that, for many years, he had little opportunity to become involved in
Edward's struggle with the barons.

When Parliament met at Westminster on 28 April, the magnates came armed "for self-defence," fearing treachery,[80] and demanded Gaveston's banishment on the grounds that he had seized royal funds for his own pleasure and had turned the King against his rightful advisers, themselves. Edward prevaricated, desperately playing for time, but although he still enjoyed the support of Lancaster and Hugh le Despenser, Despenser's son, Hugh the Younger, was on the side of the barons, and it was he who, with Lincoln, drafted a document in which the lords cunningly and defiantly declared that "a higher duty is owed to the Crown than to the person of the King. It is the magnates' professed duty to maintain the estate of the Crown, even if this should mean disobedience to the King."[81] Parliament also raised the issue of the Queen's dower, or lack of it, and on 3 May, the Great Council of barons tried to force Edward to agree in advance to any measures they might propose.

By April, Philip IV was becoming increasingly concerned about events in England and how they might affect his daughter and the alliance. After the coronation, apparently incensed at the reports brought back by Evreux and Valois, he had sent a clerk, Ralph de Rosseleti (the future Bishop of Saint Malo), to carry Isabella's Privy Seal and control her outgoing and incoming correspondence.[82] Possibly Philip feared that Gaveston might try to interfere in concerns that were legitimately hers; more likely, he wanted to establish a channel of communication between himself and his daughter; whatever the motive, there can be little doubt that Rosseleti acted as a spy and that Philip received far more information about his daughter's situation than is available to us today.

It seems that Isabella's complaints about Gaveston had also hit home, because on 12 May, it was reported in an anonymous newsletter that Philip had sent envoys to England, and two days later, another newsletter stated that these envoys were to "let it be known that, unless Piers Gaveston leaves the kingdom, their master will pursue as his mortal enemies all who support the said Piers."[83]

There is also evidence that, at the behest of her father and brothers, Isabella covertly offered her support to Gaveston's enemies. It has been claimed[84] that the Queen was at this time one of the leaders of the baronial opposition, but her very youth makes this improbable. It is more likely that the barons were only too happy to exploit her plight for their own purposes.[85] It is likely, too, that Rosseleti acted as a channel between Philip and Isabella in these secret negotiations and that Isabella played a more proactive part against Gaveston than will ever be fully known.

As early as the spring of 1308, the Queen's antagonism toward Gaveston and her alliance with his enemies were well known. Faced with the election of Gaveston's candidate as Abbot of Westminster, a monk called Roger de Aldenham urged his brethren to appeal to Queen Isabella, because it was recognized that, because of her hatred for Gaveston, she would do her utmost to hinder the election by enlisting the support of the King of France and the Pope; for whatever concerned Gaveston, "the Queen, the Earls, the Pope and the King of France would wish to impede it."[86]

Philip was angry with his son-in-law not only because of Gaveston but also on account of Isabella's parlous financial state. Aside from Edward's outrageous failure to provide her with a dower, she had not even received small sums for her daily expenses from the Exchequer or the Royal Wardrobe. Instead, she had been entirely dependent on the King, in whose household she had apparently been obliged to live. To add insult to injury, her husband had made her no gifts nor shown any mark of favor to her apart from granting three pardons to criminals at her instance.[87]

On his part, Philip had had to raise £200,000 through taxation for Isabella's wedding endowment, a measure that had met with many complaints and angry refusals on the part of his subjects.[88] Yet she had evidently received not a penny from her husband, even though he had not ceased to shower Gaveston with lands, gifts, and grants. Small wonder that Philip was indignant and ready to unite Gaveston's opponents in a cohesive party.[89]

Edward II had troubles enough without wishing further to antagonize his father-in-law, and on 14 May, in order that "his dearest consort Isabella, Queen of England, shall be honourably and decently provided with all things necessary for her chamber, and all expenses for jewels, gifts and every other requisite," he assigned the counties of Ponthieu and Montreuil to Isabella for her dower and directed Richard de Rokesley, "her seneschal of that province, to give the deputies of the Queen peaceful possession of the demesnes."[90]

This came not a moment too soon, for on the same day, an anonymous correspondent reported that King Philip and his sister, Queen Marguerite, had sent £40,000 to Lincoln and Pembroke to finance their campaign to oust Gaveston.[91] Marguerite herself had suffered as a result of the favorite's greed, and from Wiltshire, it appears, the Dowager Queen had kept abreast of events at court, and what she had heard had no doubt prompted her to write on her own behalf to Philip of her concerns about the favorite's influence and its effects on her niece. However, as Edward had intended, Philip was partly mollified by the settlement made on his daughter.

The French King's intervention had another effect, for on 18 May,

Edward, realizing that the opposition party was now too powerful to be
ignored, capitulated to Parliament's demands and agreed to strip Gaveston
of his title and banish him from his realm by midsummer day, 24 June.[92] Just
to make sure that Edward kept his word, Archbishop Winchelsey warned
that Gaveston would be excommunicated if he stayed in England one hour
too long.[93]

On 4 June, Edward, Isabella, and Gaveston were at Langley together, but
it seems likely that Isabella was largely ignored as her husband made the
most of his remaining time with Piers.

Langley, which had once belonged to Eleanor of Castile, was the King's
favorite residence; it was a pleasant manor house situated on a gentle rise on
the banks of the River Gade, six miles from Saint Albans, and it was surrounded by eight acres of parkland and 120 acres of farmland. In 1308,
Edward had founded a Dominican priory in the park. Fruit trees and vines
grew in the gardens, and the house, which was built round three courtyards,
boasted the very latest in interior decoration and had extensive suites of private apartments, with fireplaces in the royal bedchambers. The great hall
was embellished with fifty-four painted shields and a mural highlighted in
brilliant gold and vermilion, depicting knights riding to a tournament. There
was also a built-in organ. Isabella's rooms, probably the ones that had been
used by Queen Eleanor, overlooked the Great Court; she had a great chamber, a middle chamber, and a cloister, all paved; her Wardrobe was next to
her great chamber, her larder downstairs, and she even had a bathroom,
which had been installed for Queen Eleanor in 1279.[94]

On 7 June, while still at Langley, the King granted castles and manors to
Gaveston, as well as lands in Gascony, a strong indication that he did not
intend that his exile should last long.[95] Then, on 16 June, much to the barons'
chagrin, he appointed the favorite Lieutenant of Ireland with viceregal powers.[96] On the same day, with devastating naïveté, he wrote to his "dearest
lord and father," King Philip, begging him to intercede with his magnates to
bring about a concord over Gaveston, and to the Pope, asking him to annul
Winchelsey's threat to excommunicate Piers.[97]

Isabella remained at Langley when Edward traveled to Bristol with Piers
to see him off on a ship bound for Dublin.[98] On the day he sailed, 25 June,
the King took his earldom of Cornwall into his own hands until such time
as his beloved should return.[99] During his time in office in Ireland, Gaveston
proved an efficient and successful deputy. He suppressed two revolts, executed rebel chieftains, restored royal fortifications, and won the support of
the Irish nobles through lavish gifts.[100] Edward had given him blank royal
charters to use as he saw fit,[101] so he in effect wielded sovereign authority.

Once Gaveston had gone, the barons forced Edward to dismiss several officials from his household and Hugh le Despenser from his council, claiming that Despenser exercised an undesirable influence on the King.[102]

Bereft of Gaveston, Edward was plunged into misery, but over the next fourteen months, he used every persuasion to get his barons to agree to his return, bending "one after another to his will with gifts, promises and blandishments."[103] To begin with, he bought the loyalty of his nephew, Gloucester, with a large grant of land; then he set to work on the others, eventually reaching terms with Hereford and Lincoln. After that, most of the rest were willing to make terms.[104]

Isabella, meanwhile, had gone to Windsor, and Edward joined her there by 8 July. On the fourteenth, she left to go alone on a short pilgrimage to the shrine of Becket at Canterbury.[105]

Isabella was probably at Northampton when Parliament met there on 4 August. By now, Edward was enjoying better relations with his barons,[106] and later that month, Isabella, doubtless dutifully acting on her husband's orders, entertained some of them at a great feast at Westminster.[107]

In response to Edward's letter of 16 June, King Philip sent his brother Evreux and Bishop Guy of Soissons to England in September; their brief was to help bring about a concord between Edward and his lords and thus improve Isabella's situation.[108] The King dined with Evreux on the twenty-first,[109] and it is likely that they discussed Gaveston's possible return and its consequences. Soon afterward, emissaries of the Pope arrived in England, also bent on securing a peace. By now, Edward was reconciled with most of his leading nobles, but he was still granting rich wardships to the absent Gaveston and at the end of October sent Roger Mortimer to assist him in Ireland.

By November, however, a rift was growing between the King and Thomas of Lancaster. The Earl ceased to witness royal charters, and the King's patronage suddenly dried up.[110] This suggests that a quarrel of some sort had taken place, possibly because Lancaster had divined that Edward was scheming for Gaveston's return. Although it would be some months before Lancaster finally joined the barons in opposition, the loss of such a powerful supporter was to prove catastrophic to Edward. Much has been made by historians of Lancaster's supposed sympathy for his niece Isabella, but there is in fact very little evidence to show that he was especially supportive of her.

Fortunately, Isabella was in better case than before, for with Gaveston out of the way, Edward began treating her with greater respect and allowed her to assume at last her rightful place as Queen of England. She now appeared constantly at her husband's side and traveled everywhere with him. She also began to exercise the patronage that was her queenly prerogative; on 3 December, at Westminster, she granted one John de Peckbridge of Spalding, Lincolnshire, and all the men of Spalding, exemption from paying tolls.[111] At this time, the King made lavish grants of money to her and gave her manors in England and Wales, along with the right to appoint priests and clerks to benefices.[112]

The King and Queen spent Christmas at Windsor "with great solemnity." Isabella was now making a point of dutifully supporting her husband, which suggests that, with Gaveston gone, relations between them were kinder. In her innocence, Isabella may have believed that the favorite was gone for good. At the beginning of March, she made a point of dining with Richmond, Gloucester, and other royalist earls at Westminster,[113] possibly with a view to binding them closer in loyalty to the King.

In March and April, to show his gratitude, and doubtless sweeten his wife and her father in preparation for Gaveston's recall, Edward bestowed further grants and privileges on Isabella; among them were the manors of Macclesfield, Rhosfeir, Dolpennagen, and Peneham, and the Welsh commote[114] of Menai. These grants were backdated to the previous September.[115] On 4 March, the King ordered the immediate payment of all the Queen's gold—a percentage on payments made to the King—due to Isabella since her marriage.[116] In April, Isabella was also given the reversion of the manor of Ellesmere.[117]

Later in March, Edward wrote to the Pope, informing him, with false optimism, that the barons were now ready to agree to Gaveston's return,[118] he himself having promised to agree to certain administrative reforms. Edward was also going out of his way to win King Philip's support, dealing harshly with the Templars in his realm and showing himself most accommodating in disputes concerning Gascony.[119]

Philip, that shrewd man, was not to be moved. On 13 April, he was still opposing Gaveston's return,[120] but even so, Edward, increasingly desperate and as thick-skinned as ever, still had the nerve to ask his father-in-law outright to intercede with the lords on Gaveston's behalf.[121] Philip was understandably unwilling, but the Pope proved more accommodating. On 25 April, he issued a bull of absolution, quashing Archbishop Winchelsey's threat of excommunication and paving the way for Gaveston's sentence of banishment to be lifted.

But Edward had been mistaken in thinking that his barons were ready to agree to the favorite's return. When Parliament met at Westminster on

27 April, it refused his request outright. Isabella, who was in residence at Westminster at the time, must have been relieved to hear this.[122] But the King was biding his time, and as he and Isabella removed to Kennington Palace, south of the Thames, for further talks with his barons,[123] he was only waiting for the Pope's response to his plea. It arrived in June, and then he had the satisfaction of reading it aloud before a disconcerted and tight-lipped Winchelsey, who was painfully aware that he had been bested.

On 19 June, Edward, still naively hoping that Philip IV would act as mediator in his quarrel with the barons, requested a meeting with the French King.[124] By then, however, he had already summoned Gaveston home. Piers left Ireland around 23 June, and Edward, "rejoicing at his return," welcomed him at Chester on the twenty-seventh, "very thankfully receiving him with honour as his brother."[125] Isabella was conspicuous by her absence.

The King was "overjoyed at Piers's presence and, as one who receives a friend returning from a long pilgrimage, passed pleasant days with him."[126] The Queen's reaction is not recorded but may be guessed at.

A month later, King and favorite faced Parliament at Stamford, where, thanks to the intervention of the Pope and the conciliatory efforts of Glouces-ter, whose sister was married to Piers, the barons grudgingly gave their for-mal assent to Gaveston's return; only Warwick and Archbishop Winchelsey objected. "None of the barons now dared to raise a finger against Piers, or to lay any complaint about his return. Their ranks wavered and their party, divided against itself, broke up. So he who had twice been condemned to exile returned, exulting and in state."[127]

On 5 August, the earldom of Cornwall was restored to Gaveston, and on 4 September, a grateful Edward wrote to thank the Pope for his assis-tance.[128] Now that he no longer needed King Philip's support, he had aban-doned all plans for a meeting; and since Edward was continuing to treat Isabella with respect and generosity and to uphold her royal privileges,[129] Philip did not immediately choose to intervene, even though neither he nor his daughter welcomed the favorite's return.

Edward's tenacious efforts to win over and outwit his barons had borne fruit, but Gaveston's own behavior meant that this uneasy truce did not last.[130] Rashly, the King allowed him once more to control the flow of patronage; but this time, Piers did not bother to hide his contempt for those who had opposed him or his triumph at the victory he had scored over his opponents. "Now that he had regained his former status, his behaviour was worse than before."[131] Despite having promised Parliament that he would conduct himself circumspectly and live at peace, he "remained a man of big ideas, haughty and puffed up. Scornfully, rolling his upraised eyes in pride and abuse, he looked down upon all with pompous and supercilious countenance, which would have been unbearable enough in a king's son."[132]

He particularly provoked the barons by openly calling them by offensive and "degrading names."[133] The portly Lincoln was "Burstbelly"; Lancaster was the "Churl," the "Old Hog," "the Player," or "the Fiddler"; Warwick was the "Black Dog of Arden"—"Does he call me a dog?" retorted Warwick. "Let him take care lest I bite!"[134] The sallow-skinned Pembroke was "Joseph the Jew," and even Gloucester, who had been a friend to Gaveston, was called "Cuckold's Bird" and "Whoreson," both insulting allusions to his mother, the late Joan of Acre, who had defied Edward I and taken a second husband for love, despite his lowly birth. Even Queen Isabella herself was not exempted from Gaveston's sarcasm,[135] although we do not know what form it took. Such disrespect enraged the barons, even the moderate Pembroke.[136] And when Gaveston high-handedly made the King dismiss one of Lancaster's retainers in favor of one of his own, he finally drove the furious Earl wholeheartedly into the arms of the opposition, vowing that he would destroy the favorite.[137]

The barons now accused Gaveston of filling the court with his foreign relatives and greedily appropriating the revenues of the kingdom to such an extent that the King could not meet the charges of his court. As a result, it was claimed, the Queen was subjected to unworthy reductions in her income and was provoked once more into complaining to her father.[138]

By October, baronial hostility to Gaveston was once again simmering dangerously, and for safety, the King took him and Isabella to York. When visiting the city, Edward I had stayed in York Castle, first raised by William the Conqueror and rebuilt in 1244–45 by Henry III with an unusual quatrefoil-shaped keep known as Clifford's Tower. However, whenever Edward II and Isabella visited York, they usually lodged in the Franciscan Priory of the Friars Minor, founded in 1232 and relocated in 1243 to a site between Castlegate and the River Ouse. Here there were spacious apartments for visitors and gardens that stretched as far as the outworks that encircled the nearby Clifford's Tower.[139]

While in York, Edward summoned Parliament to meet there on 18 October, but Lancaster, Arundel, Hereford, Oxford, and Warwick categorically refused to attend because of Gaveston's presence at the King's side.[140] Edward postponed the session and issued new summonses to Westminster for 8 February.

In November, concerned at the prospect of civil war in England, and also no doubt provoked by his daughter's complaints, King Philip sent

Evreux once more to England, to act as mediator between Edward and his barons.

The King, Isabella, and Gaveston left York on 17 November and journeyed southward.[141] In December, in order to forestall his opponents, Edward ordered that scandalmongers be arrested and forbade any armed gatherings of the barons.[142] He spent Christmas at Langley with the Queen and Gaveston. Isabella's stay at Langley cannot have been a happy one, for she seems to have been largely ignored, while her husband and Gaveston spent their time "fully making up for earlier absence by their daily sessions of intimate conversation."[143]

When Parliament met in February 1310, its mood was ugly—the barons appeared once more in arms, in defiance of the King—so Edward sent Gaveston back north for safety,[144] while he and Isabella remained at Westminster.[145]

The King was now in a weak position, and he knew it. Parliament's condemnation of his rule was shattering.[146] He was accused of corruption and extortion, heeding evil counsel, losing Scotland, and dismembering the Crown without the lords' assent, this last being a direct reference to Gaveston, whom the barons described as "their chief enemy, who was lurking in the King's chamber."[147] But there was worse to come: on 16 March, the barons demanded that he agree to the appointment of a controlling committee comprised of twenty-one "Lords Ordainers," whose brief would be the drawing up of Ordinances, or regulations, for the reform of abuses within the government and the royal household; their real agenda, however—and Edward was well aware of this—was the undermining of the royal prerogative and the placing of restraints upon the King.

Edward protested strongly, but the barons held firm, telling him that unless he cooperated, "they would no longer hold him as their King, nor keep the fealty they had sworn to him, since he himself would not keep the oath which he had sworn at his coronation." Edward had no choice but to capitulate.[148]

The names of the Ordainers were announced the next day in the Painted Chamber: foremost among the hard-liners were Warwick, Hereford, Arundel, Lancaster, and Archbishop Winchelsey, yet the moderates Pembroke, Lincoln, Surrey, and Gloucester were also of their number, and even the royalist Richmond.[149] Within forty-eight hours, these lords had issued six preliminary Ordinances regulating taxation and customs dues.

By the end of April, Edward was trying desperately to reassert his authority and undermine the Ordainers. Gaveston returned to his side before 11 May,[150] and in June, Edward began seeking the support of Surrey, Richmond, and Gloucester.[151] That month, to sweeten the barons, who were grieved that he had not seized the initiative three years earlier when the chances of success were greater, he announced his intention of leading a campaign against the Scots. His real motive for going north, however, was the establishment of his court away from Westminster, where the Ordainers now held sway. Significantly, on 6 July, he appointed his loyal supporter, Walter Reynolds, who was not an Ordainer, to the office of Chancellor; Reynolds, he informed the Pope, was "not only useful, but indispensable";[152] thus, the King was able to resume control of the Great Seal, the prime instrument through which he could wield executive power.[153]

Isabella was at Westminster with Edward when, in July, he formally accepted the preliminary Ordinances. That month, Gaveston again went north, this time to prepare for the Scottish campaign.[154] During the next four months, Edward unheedingly made a series of further grants to Piers.[155] But he also continued to make grants to Isabella throughout 1310 and 1311, in the form of writs and warrants issued under the Privy Seal through the Royal Wardrobe.

The Queen was to go north with the King; she left London at the beginning of August and traveled in slow stages via Nottingham and Beverley.[156] Edward himself, having appointed Lincoln Keeper of the Realm,[157] followed in September and on the eighteenth was reunited with Gaveston at Berwick,[158] whence the English army marched into Scotland. Yet it was an army largely without baronial support, for although all the earls had been summoned to attend the King, only Gloucester, Richmond, and Surrey showed up; the rest stayed at home "because they hated Gaveston more than the others."[159] Furthermore, the campaign proved a humiliating failure, for Bruce had laid waste the Scottish Lowlands, destroying crops and moving livestock north. Faced with starvation, the English were forced to retreat.[160]

By the beginning of November, Edward and Piers were back at Berwick, where Isabella joined them before the sixteenth.[161] The King and Queen decided to winter at Berwick and actually stayed there until the following July. Gaveston went to Roxburgh in November and joined them later on.[162] After Christmas, Gaveston surrendered a rich wardship, that of Thomas Wake, which he had been granted in October 1308, to Isabella.[163] This must be interpreted as a conciliatory gesture toward the Queen; Gaveston was now constantly in her company and needed her goodwill, so it was imperative that relations between them be as cordial as possible. Edward would also have wished King Philip to know of Piers's generosity toward Isabella.

In February 1311, there was bad news from London. The well-respected Lincoln had died on the fifth at his house, Lincoln's Inn, in Holborn.[164] His death removed the last moderate influence on the chief Ordainers. It also made his son-in-law, Lancaster, the richest and most powerful of the magnates, for Lancaster now inherited two more earldoms, those of Lincoln and Salisbury. However, when the Earl went north to pay homage to the King for them, he humiliated Edward by forcing him to cross the River Tweed to come to him, rather than cross it himself, as courtesy demanded, and then pointedly ignored Gaveston.[165]

Lancaster typified the "over-mighty subject" of the Middle Ages; his mission now was to become a second Simon de Montfort,[166] ostensibly to save the country from misgovernment, but the chief aim of this grasping and ambitious aristocrat was to control the King; there was little political integrity or foresight in him. This was the man who emerged as the natural leader of the Ordainers, by virtue of his birth and wealth alone, and who would soon be Edward's most dangerous enemy.

Gloucester was appointed Keeper of the Realm in Lincoln's place.[167] At this time, the King was experiencing increasing financial difficulties; he had even pledged the crown jewels as security against a loan.[168] He had also lost support and credibility as a result of the humiliating Scottish fiasco; a further campaign, led by Gaveston in May and June 1311, was equally unsuccessful.[169]

This all played right into the hands of the Ordainers, who had nearly completed work on their proposed reforms and who now required the King's presence in the capital. Reluctantly, on 16 June, Edward summoned Parliament to London,[170] and at the end of July, he left Berwick with Isabella, having appointed Gaveston his Lieutenant in Scotland.[171] After Edward had gone, however, Piers was unable to make any inroads against the enemy, and after a series of savage Scottish raids into the north of England, withdrew to Bamburgh in Northumberland.

Meanwhile, the Lords Ordainers had drawn up their full list of forty-one Ordinances,[172] and on 3 August, a copy was sent to the King for inspection. To his utter dismay, he could see that the Ordainers meant to limit his power severely: he was not allowed to grant land, go to war, or even leave the realm without the consent of the barons in Parliament; his bankers, the Frescobaldi, were banished—and ruined—and his financial privileges curtailed. He was to "live more wisely and avoid oppression of the people." "The King must not . . . ; the King must not. . . ." The list of prohibitions went on and on. This was all shocking enough; but Edward was far more distressed by Ordinance 20,[173] which demanded that, because Piers Gaveston had "misled and ill-advised our Lord the King, and enticed him to do evil in various deceitful ways," he be exiled "for all time and without hope of return" as "a public enemy of the King and his people."

Parliament met at Blackfriars in London on 8 August, and the King arrived in the capital a day or so later.[174] On the sixteenth, Parliament formally presented the Ordinances to the King for his consent. A desperate Edward tried to bargain with them, offering to agree to all their provisions on condition that his "brother Piers" be allowed to remain with him. But the barons were implacable. Even though the King went on relentlessly "coaxing them with flattery" or "hurling threats," "they could in no way be brought to agree."[175]

So far, the records have afforded us only occasional glimpses of Isabella, but fortunately, her *Household Book* for the year 1311–12 has survived. This provides a great deal of information about her daily life at this time, which is why there are more detailed references to her in the period covered by the rest of this chapter.

Isabella had traveled south at a slower pace than Edward.[176] She moved south via Morpeth (27 July), Durham (29 July), Darlington (30 July), Northallerton (1 August), Pontefract (5 August), Doncaster (6 August), Nottingham (9 August), Northampton (16 August), and Saint Albans (19 August) and joined the King in London around the twenty-first. Her possessions were transported on carts supplied by northern monks.[177]

During her journey, Isabella dictated letter after letter to a number of people, including the Bishop of Durham; the Abbot of Thornton; the Abbot of Newburgh; William Melton, Keeper of the King's Wardrobe and of the Privy Seal; and one Brother William de Caverce of the Minorite Order.[178] As will be seen, this correspondence was to continue after her return to London. All these letters are lost, but, looking at the number sent, we may speculate that some of them at least were written in an attempt to win support for the King.

Isabella brought in her train a Scottish orphan boy, "little Thomelinus," and when she got to London, "moved by piety of heart by his miseries," she charitably gave him alms in the form of "sustenance and clothing, in the amount of four ells of blanket cloth and one hanging, purchased for the bed of the said Thomelinus by the hands of John de Stebenhethe, merchant of London, at Westminster," for 6s. 6d. (33p.). Once in London, Isabella sent the child to live with Agnes, the wife of Jean, one of her French musicians, "to learn his letters from her," and provided 40s. (£2.00) for his keep for the next year. She also paid 12s. 8d. (63p.) "for small necessities, purchased for his use, along with getting rid of the sores on his head."[179] Another instance of her thoughtfulness occurred when, on 4 September, she sent one William Bale "to see the condition of John de Moigne, ill at St Albans"; both men were employed by her as messengers.[180]

On her arrival in London, Isabella, who had been brought up to regard kings as virtual autocrats, cannot have been pleased to learn that her husband's royal prerogatives had been usurped by his barons, and she must have had very mixed feelings as she watched him agonizing over approving the Ordinance that demanded Piers's banishment. Yet both he and she knew that he really had no choice. The alternative, with which he had already been threatened, was civil war, and he was in no position to win it. Isabella may well have confided her anxieties in a letter she wrote to Queen Marguerite, then at Devizes, on 4 September.[181]

The Ordinances were publicly proclaimed on 27 September in Saint Paul's Churchyard in London,[182] and Archbishop Winchelsey threatened to excommunicate anyone who dared to violate them.[183] Three days later, Edward was finally forced to agree to them all, without exception. It may be significant that, on 5 October, Isabella wrote to John de Insula, a prominent judge, at York;[184] was she seeking legal advice regarding her husband's position?

The King was determined to see Piers one more time before their parting, and on 8 October, he issued a safe-conduct to "our chosen and faithful one" so that he could "come to the King at his command."[185] But their time together was brief: they had until All Saints' Day, 1 November, by which time Piers was to have left England forever.[186] This time, the barons were determined to ensure that the absent favorite was not given any kind of office by the King, and they had specified that he was not to set foot in any of Edward's dominions, that is, not in England, Ireland, Scotland, Wales, or Gascony. On 9 October, Edward wrote to his sister Margaret and her husband, Duke John, in Brabant, asking if they would receive Piers.[187] Then, in accordance with the Ordinances, the King stripped Gaveston of the earldom of Cornwall but defiantly placed it in the hands of Piers's cousin, Bernard de Calhau.

On 9 October, Isabella left London to go on another pilgrimage to Becket's shrine; it is interesting to note that her expenses for this short trip came to an astronomical £140,000.[188] She arrived at Eltham on the eleventh and there received a messenger from her father, for whom a bed was provided by her Officer of the Hall. She was in Rochester on 13 October, Ospringe on the fourteenth—where her apothecary, Odinet, paid 3s. 8d. (18p.) for no less than five hundred Galloway pears for her use—and reached Canterbury on the fifteenth. That day, she went as a pilgrim to the cathedral and prayed at the shrine of Saint Thomas, offering there a gold nugget worth £4 6s. 8d. (£4.33).[189]

The Queen stayed in Canterbury only one night. While she was there, she sent a messenger, John de Nauntel, "to parts of France" with letters for her brother Charles "and to various other magnates and ladies of those parts."[190] She returned via Ospringe, Sittingbourne, Rochester, and Dartford—here, on 18 October, she purchased wine from "George, an innkeeper"—and was back at Eltham on 19 October, on which day she dispatched a letter to the Earl of Surrey "with great haste," which suggests that she was again building bridges on the King's behalf. She wrote to her friend Isabella de Vesci, on 27 October, and to the King at Windsor, again "with haste," on the twenty-eighth. On the twenty-ninth, she sent a letter to Adam Osgodby, the Vice-Chancellor.[191] Her *Household Book* lists many more letters sent by the Queen during the weeks prior to Christmas; some of these letters were clearly only concerned with domestic issues, but, given the names of some of the recipients, others are likely to have been related to the current political crisis.

Meanwhile, Edward had sent envoys to ask King Philip for support against the Ordainers,[192] and it was to sweeten Philip, and "comfort" Isabella, that he joined the Queen at Eltham before 29 October[193] and, in late October and early November, granted her the manors of Bourne and (Market) Deeping in Lincolnshire, and Eltham, with further land in Kent.[194]

Eltham Palace, where Isabella stayed both before and after her pilgrimage, was now her own, Bishop Bek having died and bequeathed it to the King, who had immediately granted it to the Queen.[195] During the next few years, with financial assistance from her husband, Isabella would make various improvements and alterations. In 1312, lead, "estricheboard," and plaster of Paris were purchased for minor works. Then, on 12 May 1315, Isabella ordered a new stone wall, with fifty-six buttresses, to be built around the moat, at a cost of £305 15s. 7d.; but the work turned out to be seriously defective and the wall had to be demolished, while the three London masons responsible were tried by the Exchequer Court and thrown into prison.[196] In 1317, however, after providing sufficient sureties and undertaking to rebuild the wall, they were released, and the work was subsequently completed. The foundations of this wall still survive on the northwest side of the Great Court. The timber drawbridge was rebuilt in stone around the same time as the wall. In 1315, the royal apartments were refurbished; they were probably timber-framed on stone foundations and were one hundred feet above sea level; from the windows, Isabella could see the spire of Saint Paul's Cathedral. These apartments included at least two halls, chapels for the King and Queen, "a long chamber next to the King's great chamber," and a "bath house."[197] The extended palace was built round three courtyards, the inner Upper and Lower Courts, and the outer Green Court, beyond which was the wooded hunting park.[198]

On 29 October, perhaps in gratitude for her new properties, or at the King's instance, Isabella wrote to her receiver in Ponthieu "for the affairs of the Earl of Cornwall,"[199] which suggests either that she had agreed to shelter Piers in her domains or that she was willing to transfer funds to him through her officers there.

The continuing favor shown by Edward to Isabella now bore fruit, for Philip agreed to issue a safe-conduct through France for Gaveston, should he need it.[200] In November, John de Nauntel returned from France with replies to Isabella's letters, and in December, the Queen was again in contact with her father through another messenger, John de Moigne,[201] who was now recovered from his sickness. These exchanges of messengers prove that the Queen was keeping Philip IV closely informed of events in England and was receiving advice from him. It may be that her own reports of her husband's recent generosity helped to influence Philip's decision to give Gaveston the safe-conduct.

On 3 November, Gaveston left England under guard, sailing down the Thames[202] on a ship probably bound for Brabant.[203] The next day, Parliament met at Westminster and the Ordinances were promulgated. The Queen arrived at Westminster on the sixth and stayed nine days. Thus, she was present when her friends Henry de Beaumont and Isabella de Vesci and several officers of the royal household and her own household were dismissed from court in accordance with the Ordinances.[204] Both Beaumonts had been censured for having given evil counsel to the King; Lady de Vesci, who now returned to her home in Yorkshire, was accused of illegally securing the issue of writs.

Then the lords demanded "that Piers' friends and partisans should leave court, lest they should stir up the King to recall Piers once more. At this, the King's anger knew no bounds, so out of hatred for the earls, he recalled Piers, swearing on God's soul that he would freely use his own judgement."[205]

Gaveston came at once, secretly returning to England at the end of November. He came "by way of Flanders, because he suspected the King of France. But though France might be dangerous for him, England was going to be more so."[206] On the thirtieth, hearing rumors that he had been sighted, now in Tintagel and other places in the west country, now at Wallingford, or was hiding in the royal apartments at Westminster, the barons obliged the King to institute a search for him.[207] The next day, Edward once again begged Philip for support, and on 18 December, he retreated in a temper to Windsor, complaining bitterly that the Ordainers were treating him like an idiot.[208]

Isabella, already in residence in the castle, was a witness to his fury. She may well have been angry herself with the Ordainers for dismissing the Beaumonts. On 27 November, she had sent letters to her father, her three brothers, her uncles, Evreux and Valois, "and to various other magnates and ladies of parts of France,"[209] possibly expressing her indignation. Her *Household Book* also records that, on 26 December, she paid 27s. (£1.35) to the clerks of the King's Chancery to make her a copy of the Ordinances for her own use;[210] was she looking for ways to circumvent them?

By 21 December, the King and Queen had arrived at Westminster, where they were to spend Christmas. Isabella wrote to Queen Marguerite on that day; the Dowager Queen was keeping Christmas at Berkhamsted, which Edward had deemed it politic to restore to her. On Christmas Eve, Isabella instructed her Treasurer and Wardrobe Keeper, William de Boudon, to give Edward 100s. to wager at dice.[211]

Gaveston had remained in hiding, but on 23 December, Edward received a message from him, and by Christmas, Piers had joined the King and Queen at Westminster, where he showed himself openly at court.[212] Isabella was "greatly moved" to see him back, but she held her peace.[213] There were now greater issues at stake than the defiance of the favorite.

Edward was utterly determined to throw off the yoke imposed on him by the Ordainers, and on 30 December, he secured control of the Great Seal of England, having resolved to reassert his authority, build up his own party, and "escape bondage."

Isabella stood with the King. She might not have approved of Gaveston's role in her husband's life, but, thrown into his company as she often was, she had perhaps come to find him an amusing companion, and not such a threat to her own position as she had at first feared. More pertinently, she certainly would have applauded Edward's determination to stand up to those who were doing their best to strip him of his sovereign powers. In January 1312, demonstrating that she was not to be dictated to, she sent New Year's gifts of wild boar meat not only to Lancaster and Hereford but also to Isabella de Vesci, who received more wild boar meat and some Brie cheese worth 27s. 6d. (£1.38), which was brought to her, wrapped in canvas, by the Queen's messenger, Gafiot de Laenville.[214]

Another lady who benefited from Isabella's generosity was Margaret de Clare, Gaveston's wife. Margaret was pregnant, and at the end of December, Isabella sent her man, John de Marny, from Westminster "with various precious foods to give on behalf of the Queen to the Countess as her New Year's gift."[215] The singling out of Gaveston's wife is further proof that Isabella had thawed toward Piers or was at least making an effort to please her troubled husband.

After Christmas, Edward and Piers had gone to Windsor, leaving the Queen in London. On 1 January 1312, Isabella sent William de Boudon to the King with "certain precious objects" as her New Year's gifts to him. Little Thomelinus was also in the Queen's thoughts at this time, and on 3 January, she sent him alms in the form of "four ells of mixed cloth from which to make one robe for himself," at a cost of 8s. 2d. (41p.). On 4 January, Isabella left Westminster for Windsor; she stayed that night at Isleworth, where ale was purchased for her use, and joined Edward at Windsor on 5 January. From here, she sent letters to Hugh le Despenser, Isabella de Vesci, and Joan de Genville, Roger Mortimer's wife, and dispatched William de Boudon to London to obtain for her goblets and "various other precious objects." She was still at Windsor on 25 January but had returned to Westminster by 2 February.[216]

The King had decided that he would be better able to assert his authority, and protect Gaveston, if he moved the seat of government to York. Leaving Isabella behind, he and Piers left London on 7 January, Edward having given orders that the Great Seal be brought to him at York and that the officers of Chancery, who communicated the monarch's wishes by means of writs, attend him there.

Then Edward conceived a "stupid scheme" to seek a safe refuge for Piers in Scotland—he was even prepared to ask his archenemy, Robert Bruce, to give him sanctuary. Bruce, however, refused, saying, "If the King of England will not keep faith with his own people, how then will he keep faith with me?" "Thus was the King's hope shattered."[217]

Edward and Gaveston reached York by 18 January,[218] and two days later, the King returned Gaveston's forfeited estates to him, then defiantly sent orders to London that public proclamation be made at the Guildhall that his "good and loyal" Piers Gaveston had now returned at the royal command, having been exiled contrary to the laws of England.[219] Edward also restored Bamburgh Castle to Isabella de Vesci and the Isle of Man to Henry de Beaumont; both properties had been confiscated at the time of their dismissal from court. On 27 January, the King announced that only the Ordinances that were not prejudicial to his prerogative were to be observed.[220] Then he began preparing for the war that was now inevitable.[221] He sent orders to the Lord Mayor to hold London for him against the barons[222] and also sought support from the Pope.

On 31 January, Isabella was given £400 for the expenses of her journey north[223] and set off soon afterward. Again, her *Household Book* details her route, which took her via Saint Albans, where she made her oblations in the abbey on 5 February, Dunstable (6 February), and Newport Pagnell (7 February), where Odinet, her apothecary, paid 6s. 8d. (33p.) for apples, pears, and cherries for the Queen; then it was on to Northampton (8 February), Leicester (11 February), Nottingham (making further oblations on 13 February), and Blyth (16 February). From Doncaster, on 17 February, Isabella sent the King "one basket of lampreys," then continued her journey via Pontefract (18 February), Sherburn and Tadcaster (19 February), and Thorpe (21 February). There her baggage was loaded onto a boat to be taken up the River Ouse to York. During this journey, Isabella kept in touch with the King through her messenger, John de Moigne.[224]

Gaveston had brought his pregnant wife, Margaret de Clare, to York with him, and there, in late January or early February, she gave birth to her second child, a daughter who was named Joan, after Margaret's mother, Joan of Acre.[225] The Countess underwent the customary ceremony of postpartum purification (known as "churching") on 20 February in the Franciscan friary at York, and after the Queen had arrived—she was in York by 24 February[226]—the infant was christened, and at the King's expense, the court was entertained by one "King Robert" and his minstrels.[227] While staying in York, Isabella gave cloths of gold to the Friars Minor, on 8 March, and to Saint Mary's Abbey, on 14 April. She must also have ordered new clothes for herself from her tailor, John de Falaise, who was with her in York. On 3 April, she gave 10s. (50p.) in alms to "Little Walter, the courier of the Queen's great wardrobe, for buying one robe for himself."[228]

By this time, Edward and Isabella had finally consummated their marriage, for in March, the Queen discovered she was pregnant. Soon afterward, Edward wrote to King Philip, informing him that his daughter was "in good health, and will (God propitious) be fruitful."[229] This, incidentally, is the only reference the King is known to have made to Isabella in his correspondence with her father.

Isabella sent letters, too, probably announcing her happy news, to Queen Marguerite, the Countess of Pembroke, and Edward's sister, the nun Mary.[230]

The latest date for the consummation of the royal marriage would have been the previous Christmas, by which time Isabella would have reached her sixteenth birthday. Of course, the consummation could have taken place before then, for it was usual for married couples to begin cohabiting when the wife was fourteen, or even before that; it could therefore have happened as early as 1308, during Gaveston's exile, when Edward began paying proper attention to Isabella and was intent on winning the goodwill of her father. If so, intercourse must have been infrequent, as the Queen did not become pregnant for at least three years. The fact that the births of her children were to occur at widely spaced intervals (four, two, and three years), and that there were four-year gaps both before and after these child-bearing years, suggests that Edward never visited her bed regularly.

It is possible, however, that the King chose to mollify Isabella by timing the consummation of their marriage to coincide with Piers's unauthorized return at Christmas 1311, in order to win her support and that of her father and also reassure them that Gaveston was no threat to her position; as we have seen, she readily gave that support. Was she demonstrating her grati-tude at being given at last a chance to bear an heir and thus consolidate her position as Queen? Was she also pleased that her handsome husband had at last played the man and paid her the kind of attentions that she regarded as being due to her alone? We can only speculate.

Whenever it took place, the consummation of Isabella's marriage may well have contributed to the improvement of her relations with Gaveston.

It was not an auspicious time to be expecting an heir to the throne. Gave-ston's recall by the King had been tantamount to a declaration of war, and by March, the barons had taken up arms, ready to force the issue over the favorite. Five earls—Lancaster, Warwick, Pembroke, Arundel, and Here-ford—all swore to kill Piers if they laid hands on him. Even the moderate Gloucester offered his support against him. That month, the lords assem-bled at Saint Paul's to witness a wrathful Archbishop Winchelsey "seize his sword and strike Piers with anathema" for having contravened the Ordinances.[231] Meanwhile, Isabella was busying herself, probably on her husband's behalf, writing endless letters, including what were perhaps conciliatory ones to Lancaster, Gloucester, Hereford, Surrey, Richmond, and Pembroke; she even wrote to the Countess of Lancaster at nearby

Pickering.[232] Given that she would soon earn a reputation as a peace-maker, she may well have been trying to mediate with the opposition.

On 6 March, the King ordered the powerful northern baron, Henry Percy, to hand over Scarborough Castle to his own custodian,[233] and by the seventeenth, Gaveston had left York[234] and was ensconced there, surveying the fortifications. For the King and Queen, there was a brief respite from care at Easter, with much revelry at court on Easter Monday. Knowing that the King was a great lover of horseplay, the Queen's damsels burst in upon him as he lay late in bed in the morning, dragged him out of it and made him their prisoner, forcing him to pay a ransom before they would release him. Amid much laughter, he paid them a generous sum. This tomfoolery had its origins in an old custom celebrating the resurrection of Christ.[235]

Gaveston returned to York on 31 March and was granted Scarborough Castle, with orders to hold it against all comers and relinquish it to no one but the King.[236] Isabella's *Household Book* records that she sent letters from York to the King on 1 and 4 April; at that time, he was in Scarborough with Gaveston, overseeing the repairs to the castle that were then being put in hand and trying to win the support of the burgesses.[237]

But Lancaster and his private army were now closing in on York, and on 5 April, after issuing a hurried summons to Gascony for troops,[238] Edward fled northward with Gaveston to Newcastle, which they reached on the tenth, leaving the Queen to follow at a more leisurely pace; she reached Thirsk on 16 April and stayed four nights, which suggests that she needed to rest on account of her pregnancy; then she lodged at Darlington on 20–21 April, where she dictated a letter to her husband.[239] She arrived at Newcastle before the twenty-second, but her Wardrobe had had to be left behind at York, and she was evidently anxious about some of her possessions, because she sent her messenger, John de Nauntel, back to York "to look for certain secret things pertaining to the chamber of the Queen there."[240]

In leaving Isabella to make her own slow way north, Edward may have reasoned that she had little to fear from her uncle of Lancaster, although she would of course have made a valuable hostage, a fact of which her husband must have been aware. However, Edward's first priority was to protect Gaveston. On 23 April, only a day or two after Isabella had arrived in Newcastle, he sent her to Tynemouth Priory for safety, whence she could escape by sea if necessary. She was in residence there by 26 April, when she presented a cloth of gold to the priory church.[241] The next day, she wrote to her father and various French lords,[242] doubtless to tell them of her plight.

Tynemouth Priory, perched upon a cliff top overlooking the Tyne estuary and the North Sea, dated from the seventh century but had been refounded and rebuilt by the Benedictine Order between 1090 and 1130. A nearby Norman church had since been converted into one of the largest castles in England, and both castle and priory were surrounded by a curtain wall.[243] Yet fortified though it was, Tynemouth was highly vulnerable to Scottish raids or attack from the sea—the priory had once been destroyed by Viking invaders—so Isabella was by no means safe there. Nor, in such spartan and antiquated surroundings, could she have been very comfortably housed.

On 4 May, having taken York, Lancaster's army surprised Edward and Gaveston at Newcastle, whence they managed to escape with barely any time to spare, leaving behind their baggage, clothes, jewels, and horses.[244] Meeting no resistance, Lancaster and his men occupied Newcastle and seized not only Gaveston's wife and baby but also all his goods, among which were many luxurious items, including precious ornaments given to Edward by Isabella,[245] which took the Earl four days to catalog. While he was doing so, King and favorite had made their way down the River Tyne to Tynemouth,[246] whence, on 10 May, fearing with good reason that Lancaster meant to lay siege to the castle and priory, they fled by boat to Scarborough.[247] The King left Gaveston there to hold the castle and made for York, where he was hoping to raise an army.[248]

Perhaps because she was in the difficult early stages of pregnancy, Isabella did not accompany them on the sea voyage. She had begged her husband in tears not to leave her, but he insisted that she remain behind at Tynemouth. Lancaster sent a secret message to her there, reassuring her that the barons intended her no harm and that "their sole object was to secure the person of the favourite." He would not rest, he told her, until Gaveston had been driven from the King's society.[249] This is the sole piece of evidence on which the theories of Lancaster's support for Isabella during Gaveston's ascendancy have been based. However, it is unlikely that Isabella received his reassurances, since her *Household Book* shows that she left Tynemouth in a hurry, leaving most of her possessions at South Shields so that she could make speedier progress; they were not retrieved for several weeks.[250] There is no evidence that she went to Scarborough, so she probably fled the priory shortly after Edward and Gaveston had sailed away and traveled via Darlington and Ripon to York, where she rejoined the King on 16 May. On this day, Edward reimbursed her controller, John de Fleet, for the expenses of her household.[251] Isabella could not have felt very kindly disposed toward her husband, who had twice fled and left her behind, all in order to keep his favorite safe, and with little thought for her own safety, even though she was carrying his child.

The Ordainers' army, under the command of Pembroke, now laid siege to Scarborough, ignoring the King's commands to desist.[252] Unable to hold out due to lack of provisions, Gaveston surrendered to Pembroke on 19 May, on very generous terms. Gaveston was to be held under house arrest at his own castle of Wallingford until he could present his case before Parliament and give an account of his actions. If Parliament had not decided his fate by 1 August, or he disputed its verdict, he should then be free to return to Scarborough with fresh supplies; in the meantime, his own men could hold the castle for him. Pembroke himself swore on the Gospels, on pain of forfeiture of his estates, to keep his prisoner safe until 1 August.[253]

Piers was then taken by Pembroke in honorable captivity to York, where he had a brief (and final, although neither knew it) meeting with the King,[254] and thence, at the beginning of June, southward toward Wallingford.[255] On 9 June, he and his escort arrived at the market town of Deddington, ten miles south of Banbury in Oxfordshire, where Pembroke arranged for Piers to lodge in the rectory. Pembroke's wife was staying just twelve miles away at Bampton, and, wishing to spend the night with her, he rode off, leaving his prisoner—as he thought—safely under guard.[256] Warwick, however, had learned of Gaveston's whereabouts, and early in the morning of 10 June, he had the rectory surrounded with a large force of soldiers, then cried out in ringing tones from the courtyard, "I think you know me; I am the Black Dog of Arden. Get up, traitor, you are taken!" In his bedchamber, Piers began pulling on his clothes, but Warwick's men burst in and hustled him out half-dressed and without his hat, hose, and shoes.[257]

Gaveston was taken under guard to Warwick Castle that same day. Barefoot, stripped of his belt of knighthood like a common thief, and deafened by "blaring trumpets and the horrid sound of the populace," he was compelled to walk through the town, running the gauntlet of the jeering, taunting mob. Only when the grim procession had left Deddington behind was he allowed to mount a mule, a sorry steed for one who had been such a great earl and the King's beloved.[258] But Edward was far away. On reaching Warwick, Gaveston was immediately thrown into a dungeon. "He whom Piers had called Warwick the Dog has now bound Piers with chains."[259]

The King was distraught to hear that Piers was taken and dashed off frantic letters to Philip IV and the Pope, beseeching them to intervene with the barons and even offering them joint possession of Gascony if they could save Gaveston's life.[260] Isabella, meanwhile, had left York sometime after 5 June and had moved south to Selby and eastward to Howden by the eighth. Here, she probably lodged in the bishop's palace. She left Howden by 11 June, and by the fifteenth, she had traveled farther east to Beverley (the roof boss in the cathedral may commemorate her visit) and was in Burstwick on the eighteenth.[261] Thus, she was far removed from the events taking place in Deddington and Warwick and was in no way involved in them.

Presently, Lancaster, Hereford, Arundel, and other magnates arrived at Warwick[262] and debated with Warwick what to do with Gaveston; all agreed that he should be put to death, but they were concerned to cloak their proceedings with a semblance of legality. Warwick did not want to be implicated at all in the killing of Gaveston, so Lancaster, "being of higher birth and more powerful than the rest, took upon himself the full peril of the business."[263] "While he lives, there will be no safe place in the realm of England, as many proofs have hitherto shown us," he declared.[264] There was a travesty of a trial, in the presence of two hastily summoned royal justices.[265] Probably coincidentally, one was William Inge, to whom Isabella had written four letters between 17 January and 4 February.[266]

Gaveston was not allowed to speak in his own defense. Lancaster presided over the hearing "and ordered Piers, after three terms of exile, as one disobedient to three lawful warnings, to be put to death."[267] Later, the earls were to claim, on questionable grounds, that, having proceeded against Piers for having contravened the twentieth Ordinance, they were unaware at the time that the King had revoked that Ordinance.[268]

Meanwhile, Pembroke, whose honor was at stake because he had given his oath to keep Gaveston safe, and who stood to lose his estates if that oath was broken, was desperately trying to persuade the other Ordainers to order Gaveston's release. But no one, not even Piers's brother-in-law, Gloucester—who coldly advised him "to learn another time to negotiate more cautiously"—nor the University of Oxford, to which Pembroke appealed in desperation, was willing to listen to him.[269]

In the small hours of 19 June, "Warwick sent a sharp-tongued messenger to Piers, telling him to look to his soul, because this was the last day he would see on Earth." With sighs and groans, the condemned man pitiably lamented his fate, but he knew that there could be no reprieve and was fatalistic. "Let the will of the earls be done," he said. At three in the morning, he was bound, dragged from his dungeon, and handed over by Warwick to Lancaster, who told him that he was to be beheaded "as a nobleman and a Roman citizen," a concession to his status as Gloucester's brother-in-law; it would have shamed the Earl if Piers were hanged or made to suffer the full horrors of a traitor's death.[270] On hearing of his fate, Piers threw himself on his knees before Lancaster and begged for mercy, but Lancaster merely said, "Lift him up, lift him up. In God's name, let him be taken away." Those watching, seeing him brought so low, "could barely restrain their tears."[271]

Then Gaveston was "hastened to the place where he was to suffer the last penalty," to Blacklow Hill, which lies a mile or so north of Warwick and was just beyond the boundary of Warwick's estates, on Lancaster's land; Warwick had stayed behind in his castle, again dissociating himself from what was to happen, but Lancaster, Hereford, and Arundel followed the prisoner at a distance. Crowds had gathered to watch the hated favorite pass, and they blew horns and shouted for joy to see him brought so low. At Blacklow Hill, at Lancaster's command, Piers was handed over to two Welsh soldiers, both Lancaster's men, and the earls withdrew a short way off. Then Piers was dragged up the hill by the Welshmen. Ignoring his pleas for mercy, one pierced him through the heart with his sword, and the other cut off his head and showed it to Lancaster.[272]

The earls then rode off, satisfied that the odious reign of the favorite had come to an end. The body lay where it had fallen until four shoemakers found it, and the head, and conveyed both on a ladder to Warwick Castle. But Warwick came to the gate and refused the corpse admittance, ordering that it be carried off his land. So they took it back again and left it on Blacklow Hill, where they had found it. Soon, some Dominican friars of Oxford came upon the remains and conveyed them to their convent. They sewed the head back on with twine and had the body embalmed with balsam and spices and dressed in cloth of gold, but they could not give it Christian burial because Gaveston had died excommunicate. So they kept it in their friary until such time as its fate should be decided.[273]

In the opinion of one chronicler,[274] Gaveston had been "wicked, impious and criminal, and as such deserved to die; but the manner of his death was equally impious and criminal." As another observed, "They had put to death a great earl, whom the King had adopted as brother and cherished as a son and friend."[275] Whatever Gaveston had been, what happened at Blacklow Hill was little better than murder, and the repercussions from it were to overshadow Isabella's life for many years to come.

CHAPTER THREE

All That Is Prudent,
Amiable, and Feminine

When they brought the news of Gaveston's murder to the King, although he was "saddened," his first reaction appeared callous.

"By God's soul, he acted like a fool!" he cried angrily to those standing by. "If he had taken my advice, he would never have fallen into the hands of the earls. What was he doing with the Earl of Warwick, who was known never to have liked him?"

When this "flippant utterance became public, it moved many to derision." But of course, Edward was devastated by grief. His biographer wrote, "I am certain the King grieved for Piers as a father grieves for his son. For the greater the love, the greater the sorrow." And to grief was added deadly rage, as Edward vowed to destroy those who had killed Gaveston and thus avenge his murder.[1]

Edward's need for vengeance was to dominate his life in the years to come. He could not bring himself to forgive those who had committed this final atrocity. "Because of Gaveston's death, there arose a mortal and perpetual hatred of the King for his earls," observed a chronicler.[2]

Nor did he neglect to do all honor to Gaveston's remains. Both he and Piers's widow paid for waxed cere cloths and a coffin in which to lay the dead man's unburied body and funded men to watch over it;[3] Edward also made generous financial provision for Margaret de Clare and her daughter, and for Gaveston's former servants,[4] and he gave gifts to the Dominicans at Langley in return for prayers for Piers's unhallowed soul.[5]

Gaveston's murder split the barons' party and undermined the opposition, removing the threat of civil war. It brought an angry Pembroke, "full of rage" and still smarting at that broken oath, over to the King, and Surrey and Hugh le Despenser the Younger with him.[6] It also led to the emergence of the Elder Despenser, whom Lancaster loathed, as leader of the court party that supported Edward.[7] There were, of course, many who rejoiced in the fall of the favorite[8]—"the death of one man had never before been acceptable to so many"[9]—but others were shocked and of the opinion that the Lords Ordainers had acted unlawfully. Consequently, there was considerable sympathy for the King.[10] Edward was now in a stronger position than he had been since his accession.

Isabella was at the royal manor house at Burstwick on the day of Gaveston's beheading; she moved to Beverley the next day and had returned to York before 29 June, when she gave the chaplain of "the chapel of the Temple, next to York Castle, material for one chasuble"; the next day, she made her oblations before the altar of Saint Mary's Abbey.[11] Isabella must have learned of Gaveston's death by then, because on 29 June, she wrote to the King, almost certainly to express her sympathy, and perhaps her outrage, at his loss.[12] There is no suggestion anywhere that Edward ever entertained any notion that Isabella had been involved in Gaveston's death.[13]

The King had already hastened south, but the Queen stayed in York until the end of July, when her husband sent an escort to conduct her to Westminster.[14] He himself was then in London, taking counsel of his loyal advisers as to what action he should take against Gaveston's murderers. Pembroke and Surrey were urging him to declare outright war on these "traitors,"[15] and certainly for a time it appeared that Edward was preparing for a military confrontation. Late in June, he called on the Lord Mayor of London to hold the City for him,[16] and he spent July and August securing his position, summoning levies, fortifying castles, and putting his defenses in order.[17] During August, he sent Pembroke to King Philip and the Pope to inform them of the critical situation in England and ask for help.

However, when Parliament met at Westminster on 20 August, its main concern was to establish a peace process. But on 3 September, in defiance of the King, Lancaster, Warwick, and Hereford marched on London in arms[18] and unrepentant, determined to face down their master; they were stopped at Ware and forbidden to enter the City.[19]

As far as Lancaster in particular was concerned, the removal of Gaveston had been merely the first step toward limiting the King's power to the extent that he would become Lancaster's puppet. The Earl was determined to force Edward to observe the Ordinances, be he ever so hostile to them. Edward, for his part, wanted Lancaster and Warwick tried, condemned, and executed.[20] Only the mediation of Gloucester averted a military confrontation.[21] Isabella was not there to support Edward through this contretemps; she had to travel slowly because of her pregnancy and did not return to London until 9 September.[22] This was the first time she had seen the King since Gaveston's death, and it cannot have been an easy reunion.

Philip IV, spurred on by news of the murder of the favorite and hope that Isabella was carrying a prince, responded to Edward's request by sending Evreux once more to England, with a team of lawyers, to help bring about a peace between the King and his barons. The Pope, too, sent legates to assist in this process. After Evreux arrived in the middle of September[23]—he dined with Isabella on the fifteenth[24]—negotiations were opened. Isabella played her part, supporting Gloucester, the legates, and the bishops in their efforts to bring about a reconciliation,[25] but progress was slow, since feelings ran high on both sides, and the parleying went on for many weeks.[26] Amid this uproar, various rumors were "flying hither and thither, as one man foretold peace, his neighbour war."[27]

When Isabella was seven months pregnant, she retired to Windsor, where her child was to be born.[28] There she was joined by Queen Marguerite, who stayed to be present at the birth.[29]

Windsor Castle was the largest royal stronghold in England; there was "no finer castle in the whole of Europe."[30] The original fortress had been built by William the Conqueror in the late eleventh century to protect the Thames Valley, but it had been enlarged and rebuilt by several kings since. In Isabella's time, Windsor was both a mighty castle surrounded by massive stone walls and a sumptuous palace. There were two wards within the castle walls: the Lower Ward, in which stood the great hall erected by Henry I, and the Upper Ward, where were to be found the private royal apartments and chapels in "the King's House" as well as a lesser hall and the King's kitchen. The Upper Ward was sited at the top of the escarpment on which the castle stood and commanded fine views of the surrounding countryside.

As at Westminster, the royal apartments had been extensively refurbished and improved under Henry III. The Queen's lodgings, which had been rebuilt in 1256 following the destruction of an earlier range by light-

ning, were on the first floor and overlooked the herb gardens in the clois-
tered kitchen court. They featured an oriel window and a turret. The
rooms were brightly decorated: archaeological evidence shows that the
stonework in the windows was painted vermilion, red ocher, and black and
that there were extensive murals of biblical subjects; in Isabella's chamber,
there was a wall painting depicting the Wise and Foolish Virgins, while the
wainscot was painted green with gold stars. There were marble pillars,
stained-glass casements in the windows, ceilings of traceried wood, and
tiled floors. Isabella's private chapel was two-storied, her pew being on the
upper gallery, which was accessed directly from her apartments; her household worshipped below.[31]

In the Lower Ward was the chapel dedicated to Saint Edward the Confessor, founded by Henry III in 1240. This was demolished, along with the great
hall, in the late fifteenth century, when Saint George's Chapel was built on
the site. Henry III's chapel had a timber vault painted to look like stone, and
six columns of Purbeck marble; the west doors, with their splendid iron
scrollwork, still survive in Saint George's Chapel. On the altar was a silver-
gilt image of the Virgin Mary and another of Saint George in armor.[32]

The King joined Isabella at Windsor in the middle of September, probably
bringing her uncle of Evreux with him, and departed on 25 October. He did
not stay away long but returned on 30 October, presumably expecting the
birth to be imminent; however, when nothing happened, he went away again
on 9 November. Three days later, Isabella's labor began, and he came hurrying back.[33] At 5:40 the next morning, Monday, 13 November 1312,[34] which
was Saint Brice's Day, the Queen gave birth to a strong, "handsome and long-
looked-for son."[35] The King was so delighted that he bestowed £20 and a substantial life pension of £80 per annum from London rents on the Queen's
squire, John Launges, and his wife, Joan, who brought him the joyful news.[36]

Hours after the birth, following the custom whereby the Queen herself
announced the birth of an heir, a triumphant Isabella had the glad tidings
proclaimed in London:

> Isabella, by the grace of God, Queen of England, Lady of Ireland and
> Duchess of Aquitaine, to our well-beloved the Mayor and aldermen and
> the commonalty of London, greeting. Forasmuch as we believe that
> you would willingly hear good tidings of us, we do make known to you
> that our Lord, of His grace, has delivered us of a son, on the 13th day of
> November, with safety to ourselves, and to the child. May our Lord pre-
> serve you.
>
> Given at Windsor, on the day above-named.[37]

Evreux and the other French lords in his train wanted the boy to be called Louis after Saint Louis, himself, and the Queen's brother,[38] but the King and the nobles overrode them, insisting that the heir be named Edward, after his father and grandfather,[39] a decision that greatly pleased Edward's subjects, who were rejoicing jubilantly over the birth.[40] London erupted in celebration; the Mayor himself, with his aldermen, led the dancing in the street, and tuns of free wine were set up so that the citizens could drink to the health of the royal mother and child; the festivities continued "day and night" for a week.[41]

On 17 November, the Prince was baptized with much pomp in Henry III's chapel, in the presence of an august company that included Evreux and his sister, Queen Marguerite. Cardinal Arnaud Novelli of Saint Priscia, one of the papal legates, officiated, and the child had no less than seven godfathers: Louis, Count of Evreux; the Earls of Richmond and Pembroke; Richard, Bishop of Poitiers; John Droxford, Bishop of Bath and Wells; Walter Reynolds, Bishop of Worcester; and Hugh le Despenser the Elder; no godmother is recorded.[42] Nor was Lancaster, or any of the Lords Ordainers, present. On 24 November, the proud father created his son Earl of Chester,[43] a title he had himself borne before his accession, and which is still borne by the Prince of Wales today; the infant was also granted the counties of Flint and Chester, saving the manor of Macclesfield, which Edward had given to Isabella,[44] and in December, he was granted Knaresborough Castle, which had once been Gaveston's.

It was not until 9 December that Isabella left Windsor for Isleworth, where her churching was to take place. Even then, this ceremony was further deferred until 24 December.[45] In the case of queens, this ritual was usually an occasion of great splendor. However, the lapse of six weeks between birth and churching suggests that Isabella had not had an easy labor and that her recovery had been slow.

Several chroniclers testify that the birth of the Prince helped somewhat to mitigate Edward's dreadful grief for Gaveston, "and it provided a known heir to the throne; for if the King had died without issue, the crown would certainly have been disputed."[46] It also boosted public support for the King and put a stop for the time being to any intent on the part of Lancaster to undermine Edward's authority. On 20 December, thanks to the continuing efforts of Evreux and the papal legates, King and magnates agreed "a final peace," whereby Gaveston's killers were humbly to beg the King's pardon and return to him all Gaveston's treasure, which they had seized at Newcastle; in return, he was to grant them a free pardon.[47] This must have tasted like gall to Edward, who wanted nothing better than to wreak a bloody vengeance on those who had deprived him of Piers; nevertheless, two days later, it was proclaimed that King and lords were now at peace, and on that evening, in a politic public display of reconciliation, Edward dined with Lancaster. "And so, on this occasion, the dispute died down, but neither party had obtained what it had sought."[48]

The Queen's churching followed two days later, on 24 December, and immediately afterward, she and the King left for Westminster.[49] They spent Christmas at Windsor; according to Walsingham, the season of goodwill was marred by a brief clash between the barons and the French envoys, but it is not known what gave rise to this, as the chronicler does not elaborate further.

Peace had been proclaimed, but beneath the surface, tensions and enmity simmered, and much work needed to be done before the King and the barons could truly live in amity. As early as January 1313, cracks were appearing in the fragile facade of friendship, as Lancaster and Warwick published a list of twenty objections to the "final peace," and Lancaster declared that he would not hand over Gaveston's treasure unless the King acknowledged that Gaveston was a common felon and undertook to maintain the Ordinances. This led to further negotiations, with Hereford acting as a go-between and Edward vehemently refusing to accede to Lancaster's demands.

On 29 January, the royal family left Windsor for Westminster, for further celebrations to mark the Prince's birth. On 4 February, "a noble pageant" was staged in the Queen's honor in London by the Fishmongers' Guild. "They caused a boat to be fitted out in the guise of a great ship, with all manner of tackle that belongs to a ship; and it sailed through Cheap[side] as far as Westminster, where the fishmongers came, well mounted and costumed very richly, and presented the ship to the Queen." The guild members were wearing a livery of linen shot with gold and embroidered with the arms of England and France; the Mayor and aldermen were there, too, all in their ceremonial robes, as were the guilds of the Drapers, Mercers, and Vintners.

After the pageant, the members of the Fishmongers Company escorted Isabella and the Prince with appropriate solemnity to Eltham Palace. The Queen then traveled to Canterbury, to give thanks to Saint Thomas for her safe delivery of a son.[50]

As mother of the heir to the throne, Isabella's position was now established and secure, and her influence with the King considerably greater. At seventeen, she was blossoming into a beautiful and charming woman. Always conscious of her status as a princess of France, she was to be diligent in promoting friendly relations between the two kingdoms—until things went badly wrong, far in the future.

There can be no doubt that Isabella was a proud and ambitious woman, nor that she was materialistic, acquisitive, and jealous of her dignity and the benefits and privileges attached to her high status. The records show her to have been active and often successful in exercising patronage, particularly in the bestowal of grants and honors and the preferment of her servants, and in obtaining for herself lands, castles, manors, towns, honors, boroughs, wardships, knights fees, sheriffdoms (in which she had the right to appoint sheriffs), and fines paid to the Chancery and Exchequer.[51]

Isabella was tenacious, resolute, strong-willed, and intelligent—"all that is prudent, amiable and feminine," according to one chronicler; others repeatedly praised her sagacity, one even calling her "very wise," a phrase not often applied then to a female.[52] Time would prove her to be a capable woman who, in a later age, would have early on obtained recognition of her talents. We have also seen that she could be kind and thoughtful, and she was extremely generous to her servants.

Isabella was healthy and energetic, too: she was forever on the move, and yet suffered no known miscarriages or stillbirths; at least four of her children survived into adulthood. This was something of a feat in an age in which approximately one-third of children died in childhood, and the average age of life expectancy for a man was thirty-five; for women, it was even less, given that many of them perished in childbed.

Whereas previous consorts had been served by no more than a hundred persons, Edward generously provided his Queen with a magnificent household of about 180. At least 70 of these were servants of the upper ranks, and they included a physician, Master Theobald, and two apothecaries, Peter of Montpellier, who had transferred from the King's service, and Master Odinet, who purchased his supplies, namely, "various cordials and other medicinal things for the Queen's use," from another apothecary, Thomas de Buckingham;[53] there were also three cooks, Richard de Glamorgan and Hugh de Hoperton, who both cooked for the household, and Robert de Snodhill, who was "cook for the Queen's own mouth"; a chaplain, "Lord" Thomas Burchard; and an almoner, John de Jargeaux, who dispensed alms on his mistress's behalf each day and also on feast days and holy days, using a wheeled alms boat and "the Queen's great silver alms dish, with the engraving of her coat of arms on the bottom, impaling the arms of

England with the arms of France." Then there was the Queen's confessor, the Franciscan Father John de Chisoye; Isabella was especially kind to one of his brethren, Brother Richard: when Richard's mother died, she sent a very costly pall of cloth of gold to lay upon the body.

The most important servants were the senior officers: the Queen's steward, Eubulo de Montibus, and her Wardrobe Keeper, or Treasurer, William de Boudon, who was answerable to the Exchequer; these two were responsible for the running of the Queen's household and the supervision of expenditure, and they were assisted by the comptroller, Hugh de Leominster, and the cofferer, John de Fleet. These four officers formed the core of the Queen's council, which dealt with legal matters and the administration of her household and estates. The Queen's wardrobe supplied these officers with ink, parchment for her household books and miscellaneous memoranda, a checker board for reckoning, and a pair of scales for weighing silver.

All four officers were experienced administrators.[54] In 1312, Edward II granted Montibus some manors that had been confiscated from the Templars, "on account of his good service to the late King and that he may the more becoming serve Queen Isabella, in whose train he is by the King's command."[55] Montibus officially retired in February 1314 but continued to be active in Isabella's service for some time after that.[56] William de Boudon had transferred around 1308 from the King's employ to that of the Queen, having been usher and Wardrobe Keeper to Edward when he was Prince of Wales. He served as Isabella's Treasurer until at least 1316 and appears again as her comptroller in 1325.[57] Hugh de Leominster had been Edward I's Chamberlain of North Wales from 1295 to 1302; in 1313, when that King set up a separate household for Prince Edward, Hugh was appointed Keeper of his Wardrobe. John de Fleet, the cofferer, may perhaps be identified with three men of that name who were employed at different times in the wardrobes of Edward I, Edward II, and Thomas of Brotherton and Edmund of Woodstock, Edward I's sons by Marguerite of France.[58]

The Queen's household was divided into several departments or offices: hall, chamber, pantry, buttery, kitchen, scullery, ewery, napery, and saucery. The office of the Marshalsea was responsible for her chargers and palfreys. Among the lower servants were a butler; a pantler, John de Freyn; a clerk of the spicery; a waferer, John Brye; a saucerer, John de Marthe; two sergeants at arms, Peter de Monte Ozeri and Arnold Sanx; an usher of the Queen's hall, Thomas de Chetyngdon; a marshal of the Queen's hall, Nicholas de Chilham; a chandler called William; five messengers, John Moigne, John de Nauntel, William Bale, John de Noyun, and Gafiot de Laenville; two watchmen, Richard de Burwardesle and Robert Chauncellor; ten junior clerks; a smith, William de Bath; six carters; thirty-nine grooms and harbingers; twenty-five palfreymen; a keeper of the Queen's horses and chargers, Laurence de Bagshot; twenty-two sumptermen; porters; outriders of the Queen's carts; three keepers of the hackneys; pages; scullions; a fool called Michael (who received in alms from his mistress 4s. 4d. [22p.] "for shoes and other small necessities for himself"); a courier of the Wardrobe known as "Little Walter" (who also got a charitable grant from Isabella); and laundresses and washerwomen.

Joan, the woman who laundered the Queen's napery and chapel vestments, was paid an allowance for firewood and ashes; Matilda, Isabella's personal washerwoman, received 4¼d. (2p.) a day. Most of the Queen's other servants were paid between 7d. (3p.) and 15d. (7p.) a day, plus allowances or expenses where appropriate; even the Treasurer and the physician received only 15d. The mysterious William de Mily received 2s. (10p.) a day "when in court"—in 1313–14, he was only there on thirty-five days—but there is no record of what he did to earn this princely sum. It was, however, sufficiently important for Isabella to take him to France in her train in 1313.[59]

The Queen employed several household knights, including Sir John de Sully, Sir William de Sully, Sir John de Wynston, and Sir William Inge, a respected lawyer who had served Edward II as Prince of Wales.[60] The role of these knights was to protect the Queen; they received fees and livery allowances amounting to £7 18s. per annum.[61] There were also twenty-eight squires in the Queen's household.

Isabella also had a receiver, who collected her revenues, and many officials who administered her estates: stewards, bailiffs, castellans, and the keepers of her manors and forests. Sir Henry Green was her advocate; she later granted him the manor of Brigstock, Northamptonshire.[62] Like the King, the Queen enjoyed the right of purveyance, that is, the right to buy a wide selection of goods below market price, and to do this, she employed a number of purveyors, including William atte Putte, who was her purveyor for wine and ale.[63] Understandably, this practice was not popular with merchants, nor with local people who had to pay higher prices, and it was easily open to abuse.

Isabella's personal attendants numbered several highborn ladies, including Isabella de Vesci. Her principal lady-in-waiting, though, was the King's niece, Eleanor de Clare, the wife of Hugh le Despenser the Younger;[64] she was a great favorite with the King. Eleanor was sufficiently important to have her own retinue, headed by her chamberlain, John de Berkhamsted.

Then there was Alice Comyn, Countess of Buchan in her own right and the wife of Henry de Beaumont; Ida de Odingsells, the widow of John de Clinton; and Margaret de Abrenythy, who may have been Welsh. These ladies received no wages or fees but were entitled to allowances for ceremonial winter and summer robes. Since most of them had families and feudal responsibilities, they attended on the Queen on a shift system.

Isabella was waited on by at least eight "damsels of the Queen's chamber," who were of lesser birth; some were the wives of male members of her household. These ladies did not just wait on their mistress; at least two of them were sent to London to attend to business matters for her, and four had pages to assist them in their duties.[65] Isabella's old nurse, Théophania de Saint-Pierre, was one of her damsels, and Alice de Leygrave, the King's former nurse, was another, as was Alice's daughter Cecilia, to whom the Queen once gave a gown made by John de Falaise.[66] The tailor's wife, Joan de Falaise, was another damsel. The others were Joan Launges, the wife of the Queen's squire; Joan de Villers, to whom Isabella generously gave a length of cloth of gold,[67] and whose son Guy was also in the Queen's service; her daughter, Margaret de Villers, whose marriage to Odin Bureward, one of the Queen's squires, prompted a rich gift of £300 from Isabella "for their sustenance";[68] Katherine Brovart; Mary de Saint Martino; and Juliana de Nauntel, who was probably the wife of the Queen's messenger.

There were ten senior clerks in the Queen's household, among them Peter de Collingbourn, who sometimes doubled as the King's Wardrobe Keeper.[69] There was also a "writing clerk," John de Gifford, who acted as Isabella's secretary. He wrote out all her letters on parchment, probably at her dictation, then validated them by attaching her seal imprinted in red wax; the seal still survives and shows the full-length figure of the Queen standing beneath a canopy.[70] No signature was required: this was normal procedure, and we should not infer from it that Isabella was unable to write. This was a skill that was beginning to be expected of royal ladies—Eleanor of Castile had bought tablets for her daughters to write on—and there is every reason to believe that Isabella herself was fully literate.

Isabella had been very well educated and was developing into a cultivated person with refined tastes. She shared with her husband a love of "minstrelsy" and paid for Walter Hert, one of her watchmen, to go to London during Lent to receive musical training. Together, she and Edward spent vast sums on musical entertainment.[71] There is evidence also that the Queen was interested in art, since she owned exquisitely illuminated manuscripts in the latest taste, and three panels of Lombard work, which were presumably paintings or sculptured reliefs.[72]

The Queen owned several books and once paid 14s. (70p.) for one to be made, with an extra payment to Richard the Painter for some azure paint to be used in the illumination. In June 1312, her office of the chamber paid for "books for the Queen's chamber" when she was staying at Beverley.[73] Her library[74] included "a great book covered in white leather, concerning the deeds of Arthur" and other manuscripts of the Arthurian legends; all her life, Isabella seems to have been fascinated by the chivalric legends of King Arthur. She also possessed eight romances, among them tales of the Trojan War and Charlemagne, and of Aimeri of Narbonne, which must rival that of Patient Grizelda as a marriage guidance textbook for medieval wives, for when Aimeri beat his wife, Lady Ermengarde, for protesting at his sending their seven sons out into the world to seek their fortune, she meekly called on God to "bless the arm which has so well recalled me to myself. What I said was folly. Do what you will."[75]

The inclusion of three missals, a breviary, a book of homilies, two graduals,[76] a martyrology, and an ordinal, or service book, among these volumes testifies to Isabella's piety. One psalter, the Isabella Psalter,[77] dating from 1303–08, has been identified through its heraldic emblems as having belonged to her and was perhaps made as a wedding gift.[78] It has also been credibly suggested that the so-called Queen Mary's Psalter, a vividly illuminated English manuscript produced around 1310–20, was Isabella's, too; it may be significant that it has many prominent illustrations of biblical queens and noblewomen.[79] We do know, again from heraldic evidence, that Isabella owned a French Apocalypse, which was perhaps given to her by her father.[80]

Isabella owned several sacred relics, including a ring made by Saint Dunstan, the tenth-century Archbishop of Canterbury. Every day, she offered 7d. (3p.) in oblatory money, or "set obligations," which was redeemed by her chaplain, except on the Feast of the Assumption of the Virgin Mary, when the Queen offered £10 10s. (£10.50) in gold florins.[81] When Isabella attended Mass in one of the great cathedrals or abbeys, she usually offered 4s. 8d. (23p.) in oblatory money. For the Easter service of Tenebrae, the clerk of the Queen's chapel acquired a large wooden figure of Judas to hold the twelve Paschal candles that would be snuffed out, one by one, to symbolize the disciples abandoning Jesus. At this time, the chapel was adorned with embroidered altar cloths and hangings and curtains trimmed with corded ribbon and suspended by iron rings on rails, and there was a font for making holy water on the eve of Easter.[82]

Isabella gave gifts of clothing and jewelry to various churches, and in January 1312, she sent some cloth to a hermit, Brother John, who lived in

Windsor forest, so that he could make himself a chasuble. She and Edward donated a great window depicting Becket, their favorite saint, to Canterbury Cathedral; it was set up in the North Transept.[83] As we have seen, both King and Queen frequently went on pilgrimage to the shrine of Becket, and Isabella also visited the shrine of Our Lady of Walsingham, where the Virgin Mary's milk was venerated. This shrine was especially popular with mothers-to-be and those wanting a child.

The royal couple were great patrons of the Dominican Order, but Isabella, in common with her aunt, Queen Marguerite, had a special affection for the Franciscans, who, by their emotive preaching, were promoting the involvement of the laity in devotional practices and attracting the interest of many important and talented people. The Order, which had been active in England and increasingly successful since 1224, was inspired by the life and teachings of Saint Francis of Assisi; the friars were forbidden to own property and had to earn their living by work or begging. All Isabella's confessors were Franciscans,[84] and among her books were several "for the use of the Friars Minor."[85] The Queen was a great benefactor of the Franciscan houses at King's Lynn, Coventry, and from 1327, Newgate in London.[86]

By the fourteenth century, the English court was becoming a more stable institution and was expanding in size and expenditure. Although the population of the royal household fluctuated from ruler to ruler, it was usual for several hundred persons to be residing at court at any given time. Both the King and Queen had their separate households and staffs. The court was a social as well as an administrative and political center and had its own elaborate code of courtesy and etiquette. Its language at this time was Norman-French, a bastardized version of the tongue spoken by the Conqueror and his companions; Latin, however, was the traditional language of the government and the royal secretariats.

By any standards, Edward II's court was a disorderly hotbed of jealousies, intrigues, and tensions. The chroniclers complained that it was "full of ruffians, parasites and ribalds, [who] spent the night in jesting, playing and banqueting, and in other filthy and dishonourable exercises." The King was no great judge of character and employed many persons of questionable probity, who became bitterly hated. Take, for example, Robert Lewer, who had been ordered out by the Ordainers but who defiantly stayed on, building up a fortune by dubious methods and murdering his mistress's husband along the way; when arrested for "trespasses, contempts and disobediences," he threatened to cut up his captors limb by limb—and in the King's presence, if necessary.[87] In 1317, Gilbert de Middleton, a household knight, gained lasting notoriety by mugging the Bishop of Durham and two cardinals as they were riding north. And in 1326, another member of the household, a felon called Roger Swynnerton, who already had a record for violent intimidation, was indicted for murder.[88]

Edward's court was essentially a masculine world, and very few women were permitted access to it. Early on in his reign, the King decreed that no member of his household, "of what condition so ever he be, keep a wife at court, nor elsewhere as a follower to the court; but only such women to be there which are in chief with the King." That included the Queen and her ladies, of course, and female members of the royal family. It was certainly not misogyny that dictated such a ban, for it is clear that Edward very much enjoyed the society of some women; he was probably more concerned about the onerous cost of maintaining unauthorized persons in his household.

Three times a year—at Easter, Whitsuntide, and Christmas—the King held court and gave a great feast, at which he and the Queen wore their crowns, a custom dating from Norman times. There was much revelry after these feasts, with games, theatricals, and disguisings. At other times, the court was entertained by minstrels, jesters, acrobats, and tumblers, while gambling was rife. Isabella and her ladies enjoyed games of chess, draughts, or "tables" (backgammon) and at quieter times would have sat together at their embroidery, telling stories and riddles for one another's amusement, or playing charades. Isabella inherited the set of crystal and jasper chessmen that had been made for Eleanor of Castile; it is mentioned in an inventory of her goods taken at her death. The Queen also regularly partnered her husband at gambling and games of chance.

Isabella shared her husband's enthusiasm for hunting and hawking[89] and owned eight greyhounds, who each got one bone a day, a falcon-gentle—a bird suitable for a prince—some hawks and lanners, and a tercel. There is a picture of a noblewoman hunting in Queen Mary's Psalter, which, as has been noted, may well have belonged to Isabella. There were plenty of opportunities for indulging in this traditional royal sport, for most royal residences either had their own hunting parks or were situated in or near the royal forests, which were specifically reserved for the King's hunting.

Medieval courts were essentially nomadic; state business and the need to have houses cleansed and freshened after a large number of people had been staying for some time meant that the royal households were kept constantly on the move. During his reign, Edward II lodged at more than four thousand places in England.

But travel in the Middle Ages could be arduous. No decent roads had been built since Roman times, those that did exist were rarely well kept, and it was easy to get lost in remote areas, for there were no signposts and very few milestones. Wise travelers hired local guides to see them to their destination; Isabella's officers paid for guides "for leading the Queen on the right and best roads with her chariots on her travels throughout parts of England." An average day's journey on horseback was twenty to thirty miles. Sometimes it made more sense to go by river, with baggage being transported by barge; boat hire was the responsibility of the office of the scullery.

Most people traveled on foot, but for noblewomen, there were three preferred forms of travel. Most ladies rode either on horseback—usually pillion behind a manservant—or in a horse-drawn litter. For the very rich, there were carriages known as "charettes" (chariots) or "chairs," which resembled elaborately decorated wagons and were pulled by chargers; some were large enough to seat the Queen and her ladies. Litters and chariots were unsprung but were well upholstered and liberally provided with cushions to buffer passengers from the jolts. In 1311–12, Isabella thoughtfully provided her tailor with some cloths of gold to be made into cushions for the chariot used by her ladies, and in 1318, the King's *Household Book* records a payment to one Vanne Ballard for pieces of flame-colored silk and gold tissue for making cushions for the chariots of the Queen and her ladies.

Litters and chariots were purchased for the Queen by the office of the hall. Isabella's *Household Book* records repairs to her chariots, including the fitting of an axle, and, in August 1311, the payment of £120 to a foreign merchant for three black chargers to pull the Queen's chariot. A bay charger costing £20 was purchased as a palfrey "for the person of the Queen"; it is clear that Isabella loved riding and did not always travel by litter or chariot. The Queen's horses were looked after by grooms of the Marshalsea, who purchased mown hay, oats, barley, horsebread, bran, horseshoes, tallow for the candles that burned in the cressets on the stable walls, saddlecloths, stable equipment, and carts.

When a queen traveled, meticulous organization and hard labor were involved, for her household and most of her movable goods, even the furniture, went with her, packed in coffers and boxes that were stacked onto carts and covered with waxed canvas to keep the rain out. Smaller items were packed in saddlebags, which were carried by sumpter horses. Isabella's *Household Books* reveal that sumpter horses frequently died in her service and had to be replaced at a cost of at least 40s. (£2) each. Boys rode as outriders beside the Queen's baggage train to keep it safe from robbers.

The Queen's harbingers would ride ahead to warn the keepers of her manors and castles that she was on her way, often precipitating a frenzy of repairing and cleaning. When her servants arrived, they would unpack everything and put it in its place. If the Queen needed to make an overnight stop, she would usually lodge in the guest house of an abbey; if there was insufficient room for her retinue, they would be housed in tents or wooden huts or might even have to sleep out in the open.

Tucked away into the Queen's litter or chariot would be two small barrels bound with iron, one containing wine, the other water to dilute it, "for her own drinking." During her frequent journeying, her almoner would distribute money to "various paupers through various parts of England, each day at 2s" (10p.).

When Isabella ventured to sea, she would have sailed in a ship with fore- and sterncastles and a mast with a square sail, and been accommodated in a cabin fitted out with every comfort. But a Channel crossing could last any length of time from a few hours to a month, depending on the wind and the weather. Isabella made nine such sea crossings during her lifetime.

In Edward II's reign, there were twenty-five royal residences scattered all over the country, and within their walls, Isabella lived lavishly, thanks in part to Henry III's great program of improvements in the middle years of the previous century. At this period, castles were still used primarily for defense, but palaces and manor houses were being built with only minimal fortifications, and there is evidence of a new accent on domestic architecture and comfort, and also on privacy, which was a luxury in an age of communal living. The life of a medieval household centered upon the hall, where most people lived, ate, and slept, but the wealthier had for some time now been building themselves suites of private rooms adjoining the hall, often at right angles to it. By the thirteenth century, most manor houses were built to an L-shaped ground plan, and brick was the most commonly used building material; timber and thatch were also favored.

The halls in royal residences usually had two aisles of stone pillars stretching along their length. Architecturally, these halls were built in what the Victorians called the Decorated style and followed a trend set by Henry III when he began rebuilding Westminster Abbey in 1245 and embellished the older Early English style with less rigidly defined lines, frivolous floral ornament, and the introduction of the double curved or ogee arch. Halls were lofty and usually dwarfed the two-story blocks of apartments at each end. Until circa 1340, halls were heated by a fire on a central hearth, the smoke escaping through a louver in the roof. At the end of the hall nearest the chamber block would have been a dais, where the King and Queen held court, seated on carved chairs beneath a canopy of estate. They also dined here. At the opposite end of the hall, there was usually a decorated screen with arched doorways set into it, and above it a galleried area where minstrels might play. Beyond was the screens passage, which led to the kitchens and service area. Some royal halls were centered upon courtyards, around which other ranges of lodgings were beginning to be built. Access to the courtyard was via a fortified gatehouse.

Until the thirteenth century, English queens lived in the King's household. Separate lodgings for a queen consort were first built for Eleanor of Provence, who married Henry III in 1236, and it was she who set new standards in comfort and style. Since her day, every queen had been allocated her own spacious suites of rooms in each royal residence. Isabella's apartments normally comprised a chamber, a bedchamber, and a chapel. What would strike us most today about these rooms would be their vibrant color schemes and sumptuous decor.

The Queen's chamber usually featured a great hooded fireplace of stone or marble, in which logs were burned in winter. Smaller rooms without fireplaces were heated by charcoal braziers. Firewood and charcoal were supplied by the offices of the hall and scullery. No fires were lit after Easter Sunday, when the hearths were cleared and adorned with floral displays.

Beside the fireplace was set a heavy wooden chair, resembling a bishop's throne, for the Queen and settles, stools, or benches for her attendants, as well as a table and chests. Cushions and bench covers made by John de Falaise afforded Isabella and her ladies greater comfort. Windows, which had painted mullions and transoms, and perhaps sculptured moldings and linen curtains, were usually built into deep embrasures, with upholstered window seats. Large oriel windows had been introduced in many royal houses during the previous century, and they made rooms lighter. Glass was still a luxury only available to the rich and featured prominently in royal palaces. Lesser rooms or the service quarters merely had wooden shutters or glass panels above the shutters.

The walls in the royal chambers were often brightly painted with murals, chivalric emblems, or decorative borders and were normally hung with tapestries or hangings of silk, wool, damask, or extremely costly and rare velvet, which came from Florence. The floors were laid with tiles that were often embossed with heraldic designs. It was customary for floors to be strewn with herb-scented rushes or rush mats, which were provided by the office of the hall, but Turkey carpets, which were very expensively imported from Italy, had been introduced by Eleanor of Castile in the thirteenth century and were used extensively by her as floor coverings; carpets might also be thrown over tables or utilized as wall hangings.[90] Isabella's *Household Book* refers to her carpets being repaired. Queen Eleanor had also embellished her apartments with jeweled plate, Venetian glass, and metalwork of Damascus, which must have still been in evidence when Isabella was queen.

Rooms were lighted with candles in decorative sconces or torches set into iron cressets on the walls. Oil lamps were also used. Candles might be fixed onto spikes on a metal hoop that was hoisted to the ceiling by means of a pulley.

The Queen's bedchamber would be dominated by her canopied bed with its rich hangings. The canopy would have been similar to the carved canopies seen on fourteenth-century tombs. Beds were fitted with a rope-mesh base that supported a feather mattress; Isabella's feather bed might have been covered with dimity, as Marguerite of France's was. Her pillows were stuffed with feathers and made of dyed fustian. John de Falaise made hangings of various colors and two scarlet covers for Isabella's beds. At least two of the Queen's demoiselles slept in her bedchamber on truckle beds that were stored beneath her own during the daytime; her *Household Book* records payments for cloth for coverlets for their beds.

The clothes for the Queen's immediate use would be hung from "perches" on the wall, but the rest would be kept in the room known as her Wardobe, which was either downstairs or next to her bedchamber. Here, her clothes were stored in chests, presses, and covers and cases of rawhide.

Each of the principal rooms would have had its own privy, or garderobe, built into the wall. Sanitary facilities were primitive; there was rarely any system of flushing, and an open chute discharged waste into the moat below. Rags were used as toilet paper. Sometimes clothes were hung in garderobes (hence the name), because it was believed that the stench of human urine and excrement kept off the moths. During the thirteenth century, Henry III had made strenuous efforts to improve royal sanitation. One of his privy chambers was twenty feet long and was built above a deep pit that served as a sewage tank. He had white glass inserted in the windows of other privies, to stop the drafts, and at Westminster, after someone had tried to assassinate him by climbing up one of the privy vents that discharged into the Thames, he had bars fixed across them all. At Woodstock, to contain the stink from the privies, Henry had double doors fitted to them. In 1234, when a new water system was installed at Westminster, it fed a garderobe near the lesser hall.

Prior to the Black Death of 1348–49, very little attention was generally paid by the English to hygiene. Bathing did not become fashionable until Eleanor of Castile popularized the practice in the thirteenth century. Eleanor's bath was a wooden tub lined with linen sheets, cushioned with sponges, and covered with a circular linen canopy. Following Eleanor's example, aristocratic ladies bathed fairly regularly in hot water scented with flowers or sweet herbs; their attendants scrubbed them with sponges and used rose water for rinsing. Isabella seems also to have bathed frequently, for there are various entries in her *Household Book* mentioning the transportation by cart of "tubs for the Queen's baths" as she moved from place to place, and the repair of those bath tubs, which suggests that they were used quite often; there are also payments for mending the garments that the Queen wore when bathing.

Water for washing was piped into the King's Wardrobe at Westminster from a cistern below his and the Queen's chambers, but it did not extend to the Queen's lodgings. By 1324, Edward II had his own bathroom at Westminster, with a canopied oak tub set on a slab of Reigate stone. The floor had 2,250 paving tiles and was strewn with mats "on account of the cold." Customarily, the royal children had baths on the eves of the great festivals of Easter, Whitsunday, and Christmas.

At most of the royal residences, the Queen's apartments included a private chapel. It is recorded that, among the furnishings for her chapel, which accompanied Isabella wherever she went, were two alabaster statues, one of the Virgin and another, broken, of Saint Stephen. She also had cushions and kneelers embroidered with monkeys and butterflies, a dorsal of worsted painted with a Nativity scene, and a painted wall hanging showing the Apocalypse.

Usually, the Queen had her own private gardens; in castles, these might be laid out within the bailey; in manor houses, her rooms would look out onto them. These gardens variously had lawns, fishponds, herb beds, fruit trees, vines, aviaries, fountains, and arbors and were flanked by covered paths, pleached alleys, cloisters, or iron trellises. Outdoor areas, stairways, and courtyards were lit at night by lanterns.

Sadly, hardly any of the rooms used by Isabella survive in their original form today, and where they do exist, any trace of their decoration or contents has long disappeared; to obtain an idea of what they might have looked like, we should look at the reconstructed royal apartments in the Tower of London or the Queen's rooms at Leeds Castle.

Each royal residence had its service area, with its kitchens and scullery, a buttery (where drinks were bottled and stored), a pantry (where bread was made and kept), a ewery, and a saucery. In castles, the kitchens were often built in the bailey because of the risk of fire; in manor houses, they were frequently in a block at the opposite end of the hall to the chamber block. Food for the King and Queen was on many occasions prepared in separate kitchens by their own personal cooks.

Dinner, the main meal of the day, was taken between nine and ten in the morning; a lighter repast, or supper, was served around five o'clock. Trestle tables were set up in the hall and spread with linen cloths. A fanfare of trumpets heralded the arrival of the King and Queen, who would emerge from their lodgings and take their places on the dais. Important guests would sit with them on the dais, above the saltcellar according to their degree; this cellar was always placed in front of the most important person present, and only he or she could use it; there were smaller saltcellars for everyone else. The rest of the household would eat at tables set at right angles to the dais, along the walls of the hall. Before the meal started, pages would enter with basins, ewers, and napkins, so that everyone could wash their hands. Then a Latin grace was said by one of the household chaplains; there would be another grace after the meal.

Before the meal began, the nef, a gold model of a ship studded with jewels, which contained precious spices for flavoring the food, was brought in with much ceremony and set before the King and Queen. Both Edward and Isabella owned such nefs.[91] At the high table, the royal couple were served by squires on bended knee; the squires also carved the meats. The King and Queen ate off gold and silver plates, using beautifully crafted knives and spoons. Forks were rare, although Piers Gaveston had owned some for eating pears, and it is likely that Edward II did, too. The royal couple would have drunk from cups and goblets of precious metal or from mazers, covered cups that were often used for drinking toasts. On the lower tables, food was served onto bread chargers, and men used their hunting knives to spear and serve it. Table manners were refined: men and women often shared chargers and cups, and it was up to the man to let his lady take the finest morsels.

Several different dishes were served at each course, the choicer ones being reserved for the high table. Much of the food served was spicy, highly flavored, or smothered in sauces, especially in winter, when most meat was salted or smoked. There was a great deal of game, and many varieties of meat and fish, but few vegetables. Meat was not allowed to the devout during Lent. Judging from entries in her *Household Book,* Isabella's favorite dishes were oysters, pigeons, venison, "pickerels," and pottage with beans (a kind of thick soup or stew); she particularly enjoyed cheese, and her gift of Brie to Isabella de Vesci indicates that she had it sent to her from France. Bread was served at every meal; it was the staple of everyone's diet, but a more refined form would be offered to the King and Queen and their guests in the form of white manchet rolls, wrapped in napkins. Mustard and sauces, both savory and sweet, were served in saucers. As much care was taken with appearance and presentation as with taste; the Flemish chronicler Jean le Bel, who visited England in 1327, was very impressed with the standard of the food at court.

A variety of sweet dishes and fruits comprised the dessert course. Sugar was very expensive but had been used in the royal kitchens since the thirteenth century; honey was still used by most people as a sweetener. We know from entries in her *Household Book* that Isabella loved fruit; Eleanor of Castile had enjoyed oranges, lemons, pomegranates, dates, figs, and raisins, and some of these fruits were still being imported for the royal table by Italian merchants, who in addition brought spices from the East. Isabella liked tablets of sweetmeats, which were made for her by her apothecary, who supplied pounds of cloves as well; these were for flavoring and probably for medicinal use. The apothecary also mixed cordials for the Queen to drink.

The wine served at the royal table had usually been imported from Gascony, France, or the Rhine area and had to be drunk young; ale was the drink of the masses, for water was generally considered to be suspect, and the *Household Book* reveals that the Queen and her retinue drank gallons of it. Isabella did drink water, for she owned two silver water pitchers, but it was probably boiled first. Hippocras, or spiced wine, was sometimes served at the end of a meal.

Isabella liked to dress fashionably and introduced French styles of costume that were so widely copied that her influence on fashion could still be detected in the middle of the fourteenth century. Details of Isabella's clothes appear in her Wardrobe accounts, which survive for the period 1314–15. Her tailor, John de Falaise, employed sixty workmen for making, maintaining, beating, cleaning, and repairing her clothes; the Queen's *Household Books* record payments to him for such items as four pounds of silk of various colors for stitching robes, fourteen pounds of thread, silk fastenings, and four dozen hooks for robes and mantles. In 1311–12, he supplied fifteen robes, thirty pairs of stockings, thirty-six pairs of shoes, three cloaks, another cloak of tiretaine (or linsey-woolsey, a blend of wool and linen imported from Florence), six hoods, six bodices, a pelicon of triple sindon (heavy satin or linen), and a tunic of silk stuff known as Tartarin cloth of Lucca. He also made all the hangings for the Queen's chapel. Small wonder, then, that he and his busy team were supplied with thirty pounds of candles so that they could work through the dark winter evenings.

Isabella popularized the sideless cyclas, or surcoat, which was worn over the undergown and was trimmed with fur or other decoration round the edges. She also affected the pelicon, a voluminous fur-lined mantle with slits in front for the arms; Isabella wore hers with a great cowled hood falling over her shoulders, as depicted in a manuscript illustration of her with her son Edward in the Bodleian Library, Oxford. This same picture shows her wearing a crown and a diaphanous gauze veil over netted cauls; she has abandoned the chin-barbe shown in other representations of her. Isabella and her ladies also set a trend for gowns that were lower cut than had been seen for centuries.

Isabella needed little excuse to order new clothes or jewels, and each notable occasion was marked by the purchase of a new chaplet of gold. One particularly beautiful example was set with rubies, sapphires, emeralds, diamonds, and pearls. When she attended the wedding of one of her demoiselles, Katherine Brovart, the Queen wore a new golden circlet and a girdle of silk that was studded with silver and encrusted with three hundred rubies and eighteen hundred pearls; together, these items cost £32. In 1311, among precious objects from the King's store delivered into the Queen's Wardrobe were three gold brooches studded with rubies and emeralds, worth £40. On 2 February 1312, the Feast of the Purification of the Virgin Mary, the Queen appeared in a beautiful cloak adorned with fifty gold "knots," which were decorative bows or loops. Five hundred silver-gilt knots were attached to other garments made for Isabella.

The Queen's goldsmiths were Thomas de Westminster and John de Saint Florentino; they made jewelry for her, melted down her old plate and refashioned it anew, and repaired damaged plate and cutlery. When not in use, the Queen's plate, rich robes, and other valuables were locked up in great leather strongboxes and coffers bound with iron and kept in her treasury, or wardrobe, which was housed in a turret in the Tower of London. John de Falaise may have been in charge of this treasury, or at least used it as a workroom, for he was constantly repairing articles found there.[92]

Isabella could never be accounted a major political figure in the years prior to 1325, but her surviving *Household Books* contain evidence that she worked indefatigably behind the scenes, writing an endless stream of letters on both domestic and political issues, many of them to influential people.

For the rest of the time, she lived the traditional life of a medieval queen, gracing state and ceremonial occasions, managing her household and estates, bearing heirs to the throne, looking after her financial interests, and dispensing alms and charity. Among several benefactions, as joint overlord of Coventry with the cathedral prior, she gave the ground on which the collegiate church of Saint John the Baptist was built and handsomely endowed it. Like many queens before her, Isabella was patroness of the Royal Hospital of Saint Katherine by the Tower of London, which had been founded in the twelfth century by Matilda of Scotland, wife of Henry I.[93]

Above all, Isabella supported her husband. Even though he had done much to forfeit her love and respect, she was exemplary in her devotion and loyalty to Edward, and for this, and her many other evident qualities, she earned the respect and love of the barons and people.

There can be little doubt that relations between Edward and Isabella improved after Gaveston's death. No longer did she have to compete with a third party for her husband's attentions, nor endure the humiliation of other people's pity. Neither did she have to suffer in silence the usurpation of her high position, which may have hurt her more than being forsaken for another man; young as she had been during the years of Gaveston's supremacy, she had perhaps thought more of the slights to her pride and her birth rather than to her burgeoning womanhood. Now that she was maturing, both physically and mentally, she was perhaps becoming more aware of how Edward had failed her on a personal level and looking to him for more than he had hitherto been prepared or able to give—later evidence suggests that she was a sensual, even highly sexed, woman. Fortunately, for some time to come, Edward would be hers alone, and their marriage much happier and more harmonious, for there is no evidence that he made any effort in the next few years to replace Gaveston. During this period, it might have seemed to onlookers that Isabella had filled the void left by Piers.

There is no record of any discord between the King and Queen during the next decade. Edward treated Isabella with honor and provided very well for her; his Wardrobe was responsible for her household finances,[94] and he himself provided the jewels, cloths of gold, and Turkey carpets that she gave as gifts and offerings; it was William de Boudon's responsibility to look after them and ensure that they reached the correct recipient. The only gift that Isabella paid for herself during her marriage was the gold nugget she offered at the shrine of Becket. Thanks to Edward, she lived in luxury and wanted for nothing in a material sense; her husband even allowed her to overspend by up to £10,000 each year. With her vast landed assets scattered throughout north Wales and seventeen English counties, and her generous income, which would in time be augmented by her dower, she was as great a feudal magnate as any of the earls.

Edward seems to have respected and appreciated Isabella's intelligence, good judgment, and loyalty to himself, and he was happy for her to mediate in political affairs from time to time, especially after it became clear that this usually proved beneficial to him. Whenever circumstances found them apart, husband and wife corresponded frequently; Edward's letters were sent under his secret seal, so few survive. The King and Queen had also established a sexual relationship, although as has been postulated, it may have been only occasional. However, if they were not lovers in the truest sense, they at least enjoyed an amicable partnership with shared mutual interests and were supportive of each other. To all intents and purposes, theirs was a successful royal marriage, and in the years to come, Isabella's support would prove invaluable to her husband and win her golden opinions.

CHAPTER FOUR

His Dearest Companion

On 23 February 1313, after much persuasion by Hereford and the papal legates, Lancaster and Warwick at last handed over Gaveston's treasure to the King, which slightly improved relations between Edward and his cousin. But the Earl still wanted Gaveston declared a felon, and that Edward would never agree to.

On 1 March, Isabella, returning from her pilgrimage, joined the King at Windsor.[1] They left soon afterward for Westminster, where Parliament met on 18 March. But some of the barons declined to attend, furious that the King was still refusing to recognize that Gaveston's execution amounted to lawful punishment for a felon.[2] Yet Edward could count on at least one loyal supporter. Roger Mortimer was at Westminster at this time, having returned from Ireland in January and then having spent some weeks in Gascony on the King's affairs; Mortimer would remain at Westminster for much of the year.[3]

Philip IV, delighted at news of the birth of his grandson, had no intention of supporting the English barons any further; from now on, his relations with his son-in-law would be far more cordial. In the spring, Isabella must have been delighted when her father sent a messenger, Louis de Clermont, to invite Edward and her to Paris for the ceremonial knighting of her brothers.[4] Her uncle of Evreux and the other French envoys were still in

England, and on 1 May, Isabella entertained them to dinner at Westminster.[5] Thereafter, she was busy with preparations for the coming journey.[6] But many of the barons were concerned that the King had decided to leave England at such a critical juncture, what with the Scottish raids and the issues with Lancaster still unresolved.[7] Mindful of these criticisms, Edward protested that both the Pope and King Philip were insisting he make the trip, since there were pressing Gascon affairs to be dealt with.[8]

On 11 May, the magnates' party was weakened by the death of that "passionate"[9] and inflexible adversary of the King, Archbishop Winchelsey; during Edward's absence abroad, the Chapter of Canterbury was due to hold an election to decide his replacement. The King wanted a new Primate who would be more loyal to himself, and far more accommodating, than Winchelsey had been.

Edward and Isabella sailed from Dover to France on 23 May with a splendidly appointed retinue of 220 persons, leaving Gloucester as Keeper of the Realm.[10] Edward had spent nearly £1,000 on his clothes and jewels, and doubtless Isabella was royally garbed, too. The royal couple first traveled south to Gascony, being "received with very great honour as they passed through the country,"[11] and then returned north to Paris, arriving there by 1 June.[12] They lodged at Saint-Germain-des-Prés, to the west of the city.[13]

Two days later, on Pentecost Sunday, in a magnificent ceremony, Isabella's three brothers, Louis, Philip, and Charles, along with many other young noblemen, were knighted by King Philip. The event was marked by weeks of pageants and feasts, with the two Kings and Evreux acting as hosts; Edward's wine bill for the whole visit came to £4,468 19s. 4d. For the English King's delight, a morality play was staged, entitled *The Glory of the Blessed and the Torments of the Damned*.[14] Edward was particularly impressed with the skills of Philip's minstrel, Hurel, and rewarded him with 40s. (£2.00).

The visit provided the two Kings with an opportunity to discuss business, and Edward found Philip most accommodating over Gascony[15] and also openhanded when it came to lending money.[16] The fact that Isabella was now the mother of the heir to England and no longer had any rival had something to do with this, but Philip was also keen to underline the diplomatic and dynastic importance of his daughter's marriage: She was mentioned in every document detailing her father's concessions to her husband.[17] During this visit, Philip gave Isabella many gifts.[18] Edward, too, was lavish in his giving—his present bill came to £3,016 13s. 8d.

On 6 June, both monarchs declared publicly their intentions of going on a crusade to free the Holy Land from the Turks; in token of their vows, they solemnly took the Cross from Cardinal Nicholas of Saint Eusebius, the papal legate.[19] Carried away by a sudden enthusiasm for the venture, Edward used his persuasions on Isabella, who, on 13 June, herself took the Cross at Pontoise, whither Philip had conducted her and Edward three days earlier. It appears, however, that Isabella was not particularly enthusiastic about fulfilling her vow, and neither was her sister-in-law, Jeanne of Burgundy, who had taken the Cross with her at her husband Philip's insistence. Isabella had sworn to go on crusade only on condition that she do so in company with her husband, who she probably realized would never make the effort, and that she be not required to donate any more money to the crusade than "her own devotion" obliged her to offer.[20]

While Edward and Isabella were staying at Pontoise, their silken pavilion and all their possessions were destroyed in a fire, and they barely managed to escape with their lives, after fleeing in their nightclothes.[21] This must have been a terrifying experience, and Isabella suffered burns to her hand and arm that took a long time to heal.

On 2 July, Philip accompanied the King and Queen to Poissy, a seat of monarchs since the fifth century, with a twelfth-century church in which Saint Louis had been baptized. Edward and Isabella may have lodged in the eleventh-century royal abbey to the west of the town. After saying farewell to Philip on 5 July, the King and Queen traveled toward Wissant via Maubisson, Beauvais, and Boulogne. They docked at Dover on 15 July,[22] then rode to Westminster.

According to two chroniclers, soon after she returned home, Isabella became troubled about the conduct of her sisters-in-law, Marguerite, Blanche, and Jeanne of Burgundy. At least four chroniclers[23] assert that, during her visit to France, Isabella attended a satirical puppet show given by her brothers Louis and Charles, and that she afterward gave silk purses that she had herself embroidered to her sisters-in-law as gifts. In July, to celebrate their return home, the King and Queen gave a feast at Westminster, which was attended by some knights of the French court who had accompanied the royal couple back to England. Two of the knights were Norman brothers, Philip and Gautier d'Aulnay, and Isabella was disconcerted to see hanging from their belts the purses she had given to Marguerite and Blanche. The chroniclers state that she confided her concerns to her father,[24] but she cannot have done so immediately, since nothing was done about the matter until the following May. Probably she kept her suspicions to herself until further proof was forthcoming. After all, the purses could have been given as knightly favors, a practice that was entirely acceptable in courts that took the game of courtly love seriously. And the knights were wearing these favors openly.

Much had happened during the King's absence. The monks at Canterbury had elected the well-qualified Thomas Cobham as Archbishop, but Edward had decided to push for the appointment of his friend Walter Reynolds and promptly appealed to the Pope to annul the election. And Parliament had assembled at Westminster on 8 July, expecting the King to have returned; by the time he had reached England, the impatient and exasperated barons had dispersed.[25]

Meanwhile, while Edward had been squabbling with his barons in England and going on a pleasure jaunt to France, Robert Bruce had been scoring success after success in Scotland:[26] by the summer, Stirling was the only important Scottish castle left in English hands, and Bruce's men had been laying siege to it since October 1312.[27] Fearing that his sovereign would not trouble himself to come to Stirling's defense, the castle's governor reached an agreement with Bruce's brother, Edward, that if the English had not relieved Stirling by 24 June 1314, he would surrender the castle to the Scots.

There was, of course, no guarantee that Edward would go to Stirling's aid—he was more concerned with triumphing over the earls—and there were many to murmur at the King's continuing failure to counteract the advances made by Bruce and put a stop to the savage raids that were terrorizing the North. "Our King has now reigned six full years, and has till now achieved nothing praiseworthy," observed one chronicler succinctly, "except that he has married royally and has thereby raised up for himself a handsome son and heir to the throne."[28]

Isabella left Westminster on 26 July and went via Henley and Wallingford to Bisham, where her baby son was staying, probably in the thirteenth-century preceptory of the Knights Templar, which had now reverted to the Crown. She remained there until 17 August, when she moved to the Benedictine abbey at Chertsey, renowned for extending hospitality to itinerant royalty. While there, she wrote a most affectionate letter to Edward about her affairs in Ponthieu, which is reproduced in full here since it gives some interesting insights into her relations with her husband:

My very dear and dread Lord, I commend myself to you as humbly as I can. My dear Lord, you have heard how our seneschal and our controller of Ponthieu have come from Ponthieu concerning our affairs; the letters they had to bring can remain in the state they are at present until the Parliament,[29] except one which will concern your inheritance in Ponthieu and the Count of Dreux, which should be acted upon immediately in order to keep and maintain your inheritance. I beg you, my gentle Lord, that by this message it may please you to request your chancellor by letter that he summon those of your council to him and take steps speedily in this matter, according to what he and your said council see what is best to do for your honour and profit. For if action is not speedily taken, this will do you great harm, and be of much benefit to the said Count, your enemy, as I have truly heard by my council. May the Holy Spirit keep you, my very dear and dread Lord.

 Given at Chertsey, 11 August.[30]

This letter shows that the Queen had her finger on the pulse of affairs, was able to prioritize matters of urgency, and could use her political judgment shrewdly and to her husband's advantage. There is also a suggestion that she was rather bossy and dictatorial, and accustomed privately to giving Edward advice for his "honour and profit"; it appears, too, that he had come to rely on it. Furthermore, we may deduce that Isabella was far more quick-witted than he, and a stronger and more forceful character, as events would indeed prove.

The Queen stayed at Chertsey for some weeks before returning to London in September.[31] Even then, the King and the barons had still not reached a lasting concord, and on 28 August, Edward had asked Philip IV to send Evreux back to England to act as a mediator.[32] In September, the earls met in London and appealed to the King to remit his rancor toward them. "He did not immediately yield, but dragged out the business as usual."[33] During the Parliament that met on 23 September and sat until 15 November, Evreux, Gloucester, and representatives of the Pope all did their best to forge a peace.

In October, news came from Avignon that Thomas Cobham's election had been quashed and that the Pope had appointed the King's own candidate, Walter Reynolds, as Archbishop of Canterbury. The chroniclers of the day were in little doubt that the sin of simony had been committed—"my lady Money transacts all business in the curia!"—and sneered at the new Archbishop for being "a mere clerk and scarcely literate,"[34] which may be an exaggeration, but however his preferment had been achieved, Edward now had what he wanted, an ally in Canterbury, which considerably strengthened his support.

On 13 October, perhaps at the instance of Evreux or Gloucester, Isabella herself became a mediator between her husband and his barons, urging the latter publicly to crave the King's forgiveness for Gaveston's murder. "The Queen anxiously interceded, striving to calm the feelings of both parties and strenuously attempting to make peace."[35] It was this, as well as the prayers of Cardinal Arnaud and Evreux,[36] that finally helped to bring about an agreement. The next day, Isabella was present at a formal ceremony of reconciliation in Westminster Hall, in which Lancaster, Warwick, and Hereford knelt before Edward in submission; then he gave them the kiss of peace and told them that their pardons, and those of five hundred of their supporters, had been granted "through the prayers of his dearest companion, Isabella, Queen of England." On 15 October, the King confirmed the pardons by his Letters Patent, and soon afterward he rescinded the Ordinance censuring the Beaumonts. The reconciliation was marked by two banquets, one given by Edward, the other by Lancaster,[37] but this display of amity was little more than a veneer. Behind the masks of courtesy, the two men were still determined to destroy each other.

At this time, Isabella was suffering from "an infirmity of the hand and arm,"[38] probably caused by burns sustained during the fire at Pontoise, which may have become infected. While staying at Westminster, she was attended by two English physicians, as well as two French ones sent by her father. On their instructions, her apothecary, Peter of Montpellier, made up some herbal plasters and a lotion of rose water and olive oil, which he mixed on a lead plate; during November and December, her second apothecary, Master Odinet, treated the Queen with ointments, more plasters, and enemas.[39]

Isabella's illness must have incapacitated her for a time. The King, doubtless impressed with her diplomatic and successful intervention in his negotiations with the magnates, had intended to send her to the Paris *Parlement* on 19 November to put forward his case in a dispute over Gascony,[40] but her injuries were so painful that she was unable to travel and her visit had to be postponed. Her sufferings were such that on 18 November, she sent an offering to the shrine of Saint Thomas at Canterbury; she had meant to go in person on her way to France but had had to postpone it because of her infirmity. The fact that Isabella was to be treated for her injuries for at least the next two years suggests that they were quite serious.[41]

She did, however, send a letter interceding with her father on behalf of her husband's nephew, Edward, Count of Bar, who had been wrongfully imprisoned by the Duke of Lorraine, one of Philip's vassals; the Count was released the following June.[42] The Queen also wrote to King Philip and many other French lords on 8 December;[43] these letters may well have been connected to the short trip that Edward himself made to France on 12 December, which purported to be a pilgrimage but was doubtless to discuss difficulties over Gascony with Philip.[44] Nothing much is known about this meeting, which took place at Montreuil, but matters were probably not resolved when the King returned to England on the twentieth. He and the Queen spent Christmas at Westminster, then went to Eltham for the New Year.[45]

Late in 1313, the King had belatedly resolved to mount a military campaign to relieve Stirling, and in January 1314, he began assembling a mighty army. He was in a strong position now, and a victory in Scotland would go further than anything to cement his peace with the barons; when he returned home in triumph, they would be able to gainsay him nothing.

Isabella's hand was now presumably better, because in the middle of January, she resumed her preparations for a visit to France and sent William de Boudon to the council in London to ask for money to defray her expenses. At the council's request, the King's banker, Antonio di Pessagno, paid to the Queen £3,995 plus £948 13s. to defray her traveling costs.[46] The King's councillors, aware of her influence with her father, and impressed by her efforts at peacemaking, had themselves urged Edward to send her at this time to present his case at the imminent Paris *Parlement,* in the hope that King Philip would be unable to resist the pleas of his beloved daughter. Ostensibly, the reason for Isabella's journey would be her desire to undertake a private pilgrimage to the shrines at Boulogne, Amiens, Chartres, "and other places in France."[47] Nevertheless, she would go in great state, as the Queen and official emissary she was.

In February, the Earl of Surrey was forced to surrender the High Peak to the Queen, and from March onward, Edward arranged for Isabella to be endowed with a greater permanent source of income, since her future dower was still in Queen Marguerite's hands; in order to do this, he borrowed heavily from Genoese bankers, who virtually supported Isabella's household for an entire year.

Before she went to France, Isabella accompanied the King to the enthronement of Archbishop Reynolds in Canterbury Cathedral. They left Eltham on 10 February[48] and arrived in Canterbury on the fifteenth;[49] the impressive ceremony took place two days later.[50] The royal couple had returned to London by 23 February,[51] where, on the twenty-sixth, the King commissioned Gloucester, Henry de Beaumont, William Inge, and Bartholemew de Badlesmere, a Kentish baron, to accompany the Queen to France and help safeguard his French interests.[52] Since January, Isabella had been receiving briefings from William Inge and from one Thomas de Cambridge, who were both very knowledgeable about Gascon affairs.[53]

Isabella and her advisers immediately traveled down to Sandwich, where they boarded a magnificent vessel under the command of William de Montacute; it had been hired by Antonio di Pessagno, along with twenty-six other ships and thirteen barges for the Queen's household.[54] The flotilla sailed for France on 28 February and landed at Wissant on 1 March.[55] Isabella de Vesci, Eleanor le Despenser, and the Countess of Surrey were among Isabella's entourage. She also took with her a team of fifteen greyhounds, intending to enjoy some hunting during her visit; a man was paid to look after them on the journey.[56]

As soon as she landed, Isabella dispatched a messenger to Edward with a letter from her informing him of her safe arrival.[57] Journeying through her county of Ponthieu, she came first to Boulogne, where on 3 March she prayed at the shrine of Our Lady in the cathedral where she had been married. The next day saw her at Montreuil, and the day after that at the village of Crécy-en-Ponthieu. On 6 March, she reached Saint Riquier, where she made her devotions in the beautiful abbey church of the Benedictines, which dated from the seventh century, and on the seventh and eighth, she stayed at Amiens, on the banks of the Somme, where she made an offering at the shrine of Saint Firmin in the city's great cathedral. Traveling southward, Isabella reached Poix-de-Picardie on 9 March, before proceeding through Normandy and visiting Gerberoy, Neufmarché, Gisors, Chars, and Pontoise.[58]

The Queen entered Paris on 16 March and took up residence at Saint-Germain-des-Prés, where she had stayed with Edward the previous year. As soon as she arrived, she visited the nearby Benedictine abbey and made an offering; during her stay in Paris, she made her devotions in several churches and sent offerings to other holy places, notably the shrines of Saint James at Compostela in Spain and Saint Brieuc in Brittany.[59]

On the night before Isabella arrived in Paris, King Philip and his court had witnessed the burning of her godfather, Jacques de Molay, last Grand Master of the Knights Templar, and his associate, Geoffrey de Charnay. The executions took place on the Île de la Seine in Paris. As Molay was slowly consumed in the fire, he famously cursed King Philip and his descendants to the thirteenth generation and summoned him and Pope Clement to meet him at God's tribunal before the year was out.[60] This chilling event must have overshadowed Isabella's reunion with her father.

Soon after arriving in Paris, not only as Queen of England but also as a humble daughter, Isabella presented seven petitions on the subject of Gascony to Philip IV on behalf of her husband and asked him to respond favorably and graciously to them, so that the land would gain profit and Philip honor, and she would be able to return more happily to her lord. It is made clear in the rolls of the *Parlement* that it was her personal intervention that prompted King Philip to grant most of her petitions and hold others over for further consideration; however, his refusal of the rest shows that he was not so besotted a father that he would prejudice his own interests.

Isabella's initial success paved the way for further negotiations to be entered into by Edward's commissioners, in which the Queen was not directly involved, although of course she may have tried to influence her father in private. It was not her fault that some of these negotiations ultimately ended in failure or stalemate.[61]

On 18 March, Isabella wrote another letter to her husband, presumably concerning Philip's reception of her petitions. The next day, resuming her pilgrimage, she left Saint-Germain for Palaiseau, southeast of Versailles, and the following day arrived at Saint Arnoult-en-Yvelines. Leaving the greater part of her retinue in the fortified town of Gallardon, in its great priory, from 21 to 24 March, she and a few attendants visited Chartres Cathedral and then moved south to make offerings to the image of the Virgin in the basilica at Cléry-Saint-André on the Loire. At each shrine she visited, Isabella presented gifts of rich cloths. She also paused on her travels to purchase a fur and a hanging embroidered with pictures of baboons.[62]

The Queen was back at Saint Arnoult on 24 March and moved to Longpont-sur-Orge the next day. She sent more letters, to King Edward and to several English magnates, on 27 March and had returned to Paris by 30 March. This time, she lodged at Saint-Germain-en-Laye, staying in the favored summer residence of the kings of France, set in the vast forest of Saint-Germain, a royal hunting ground for centuries.[63] Here she remained until 16 April. During this period, she made frequent visits to her father, who was staying at his palace of the Cité in Paris; on 6 April, money was paid to ten torchbearers who lit her way each evening from Saint-Germain.[64] On 11 April, in gratitude for the good work she had done, Edward made a generous award to Isabella and confirmed to her the reversion of the dower held by Queen Marguerite.[65]

On 16 April, Isabella left Paris for Ponthieu. That night, she stayed at Boissy-l'Aillerie, near Pontoise; here, she wrote to Edward, announcing that she was making her way back to England.[66] But she was back in Paris on the eighteenth, to reimburse Elias de Johnstone, who had traveled to France in January to assist her with her mission; her household waited for her at Bonvillers, where she rejoined it the next day.[67] On that same 18 April, as if in fulfillment of Jacques de Molay's curse, the Pope died. It was a superstitious age, and on hearing the news, Isabella may well have remembered that curse and feared that she had said farewell to her father for the last time.

The Queen now revisited her own domains. She was at Poix-de-Picardie on 20 April, Airaines on 21 April, and Abbeville on 23 April, where she entertained her brother Charles and her uncle, Charles of Valois.[68] The next day, she sent letters, which may have concerned a matter of dreadful significance (as will shortly become clear), to King Philip, Louis of Navarre, and other lords and ladies of France.[69] Three days later, having ridden north via Montreuil and Boulogne, she arrived back at Wissant and took ship for England. On landing at Dover, she was given the strange gift of a porcupine, which was doubtless sent straight to the royal menagerie in the Tower; in May, payment was made for apples for it, but it is not mentioned again and may have died soon afterward.[70]

Isabella now rode to the shrine of Saint Thomas at Canterbury, where she made an offering.[71] Was she just giving thanks for her safe return and the partial success of her mission, or was she praying for her father's preservation? Or did she have something darker on her mind that prompted the need for spiritual comfort?

The likelihood is that Isabella came home greatly disturbed, for in April, scandal and tragedy had hit the French royal family, and she herself perhaps had been involved with it. They called it the affair of the Tour de Nesle, for it was in that tower in Paris, on the banks of the Seine, that Marguerite and Blanche of Burgundy had been wining, dining, and carrying on adulterous affairs with the brothers d'Aulnay; their sister-in-law, Jeanne, had been a witness and had pleaded with them to desist but had not thought fit to reveal their treason. As we have seen, Isabella had already been nursing her own concerns about these young people; according to the chronicles, prompted by her observation of their suspicious behavior, she now informed her father of what she had seen the year before; some go as far as to say that she was one of the chief witnesses against her sisters-in-law.

There is no reason to disbelieve this, despite much of the evidence coming from later chronicles. For all the embroideries and inaccuracies in some accounts, there is a certain consistency in what they say. Isabella was indeed in Paris at the time the affair was brought to light and had ample opportunity to make her suspicions known and to testify against her sisters-in-law: the Exchequer records show that she was having prolonged private discussions with her father, and it is likely that it was during the course of these that she made her accusations. After she left Paris for the first time, on

19 March, she wrote three letters to her brother, Louis of Navarre, from Palaiseau, Chartres, and Gallardon,[72] and, as we have seen, she kept in touch with her father, uncle, and brothers after her departure. Writing around 1317, the French chronicler Geoffrey de Paris states that, through Isabella, many things were disclosed and revealed in France, "to our royals," which were proved and found true by many people.[73] He does not say what these revelations were, but there is little else they could relate to other than the Tour de Nesle affair. Furthermore, "it was generally rumoured among the common people" that Isabella had revealed the affair to the King, although there were many who did not believe that.[74]

Adultery in a queen or the wife to the heir to the throne placed the royal succession in grave jeopardy, and any man committing adultery with such royal ladies was guilty of treason. Philip had the five suspects watched for a period, then ordered an immediate inquiry; when it found against the lovers, his vengeance was terrible. All were arrested. The *Scalacronica* states that one of the knights fled to England but was recaptured and sent back to face his fate. After merciless torture, the d'Aulnay brothers confessed to their crimes and were condemned to death. In a trial held in camera before the Paris *Parlement* in April, Marguerite and Blanche also admitted their guilt. In May, both were sentenced to life imprisonment.[75]

Marguerite's marriage to Louis of Navarre was immediately annulled; it had never been very happy anyway, for he had often neglected his feisty and shapely wife to play tennis, for which he felt more passion, so it was not surprising that she had looked elsewhere for love. Now, weeping constantly with remorse, she was made to wear the cowled garb of a penitent, and her hair was symbolically shorn;[76] then she was shut up in a dark, damp dungeon in Château Gaillard in Normandy, a grim fortress built in the late twelfth century by Richard the Lion-Hearted; here, she appears to have been subjected to a regime of systematic ill-treatment. Her two-year-old daughter, Jeanne, her only surviving child, was disinherited on suspicion that Louis was not her father, a suspicion that was probably unjustified, since Marguerite's adulterous liaison does not appear to have begun until after Jeanne's birth in 1311.

Blanche of Burgundy also had her head shaved and was immured in Château Gaillard, in a cell below ground, yet despite the pleas of her husband, Charles, the Pope refused to annul their marriage. Ten years later, after Blanche had borne a bastard child to her jailer, the Pope proved more cooperative, and she was allowed to take the veil at the Abbey of Maubisson. But her health had been broken by the severity of her imprisonment, and she died a year later, in 1326. Prince Philip did not repudiate his wife,

Jeanne of Burgundy, because he believed her innocent of adultery, but despite having been acquitted by the Paris *Parlement,* she was kept under house arrest at Dourdan for some months as a punishment for not having revealed what had been going on; however, she was treated with far more leniency and respect than Marguerite and Blanche and in 1315 was received back at court. Later, she bore her husband two more children.

The unfortunate d'Aulnay brothers fared far worse: after being publicly castrated, with their genitals thrown to the dogs, they were partially flayed alive before being broken on the wheel and then mercifully decapitated at Montfaucon in Paris; afterward, their broken bodies were displayed on gibbets.[77]

If Isabella felt any remorse for the dreadful fate of these stupid, promiscuous girls and their lovers, there is no record of it. And if she had given evidence against them, she doubtless would have accounted it a signal service to the House of Capet, for no bastard strain could be allowed to pollute such a sacred royal bloodline. It has been suggested that she was at the center of a plot to discredit the issue of her brothers so that her son could in time succeed to the French throne,[78] which is stretching credibility rather too far, since the French Princes were young men who could easily remarry and have other heirs. Nor is there evidence of any such plot; Isabella went to France at Edward II's behest, not with the purpose of denouncing her sisters-in-law.[79]

Furthermore, the *Chronicum Comitum Flandriae* asserts that the accusations against the Princesses and their knights were "without cause" and that they had all been framed by Philip's chief councillor, Enguerrand de Marigny, but we know that the King placed the lovers under surveillance, and it seems that the guilty lovers were all condemned on good evidence. King Philip would hardly have allowed the French Crown to be tainted by such a scandal without sufficient justification.

Isabella's actions argue a certain ruthlessness in her nature, which, given that she was the daughter of Philip IV, was perhaps only to be expected; they also provoked a backlash, at least in France, where she was vilified for betraying her sisters-in-law, and for a time, this had a detectable effect on diplomatic relations with England.[80]

Edward II's preparations for his campaign against the Scots were now complete, and on 10 June, an immense English army assembled at Wark in Northumberland. The next day, it marched for Berwick. Pembroke and Mortimer were among those who attended on the King. Although Lancaster, Warwick, Arundel, and Surrey had also been summoned, all were conspicuous by their absence, which they were to justify on the grounds that the King had gone to war without the consent of Parliament and thus disregarded the Ordinances.[81]

On arriving in London after her return from France, Isabella had obtained her traveling expenses and immediately ridden north to join her husband; passing through Doncaster, Pontefract, and Boroughbridge, she arrived at Berwick on 14 June[82] and was lodged in the castle, which had been heavily fortified by Edward I. She was involved to a degree in the preparations for the campaign and lent Gloucester equipment for his field kitchen; it was never returned.[83] On 17 June, the great army marched forth from Berwick. Five days later, it reached Falkirk.

Robert Bruce was ready and waiting for the English, his forces drawn up before Stirling at a place called Bannockburn. There, the two armies met. Bruce was heavily outnumbered—he had seven thousand men, and Edward had twenty thousand—but he knew the terrain and had deliberately chosen a site surrounded by boggy ground and in the enclosed area had dug concealed pits, which were to prove lethal to the invading army. The battle was fought over two days, on 23 and 24 June, and its outcome was a devastating defeat for the English. The young Earl of Gloucester was among four thousand killed, Hereford was captured,[84] and King Edward, despite having "fought like a lion," was forced to flee the field. With the aid of Despenser, he made his way home by stealth via Dunbar and Berwick, having left all his possessions, including his seal, behind. Chivalrously, the victorious Bruce sent them after him.[85]

Isabella was waiting at Berwick when her husband returned, crushed, angry, and humiliated. She was supportive, lending him her seal to replace the one he had abandoned and supervising the cleaning of his armor. She also bought clothes for three knights who had lost everything when they fled the battlefield,[86] and she later secured the release of a royal messenger, Robert le Messager, who was imprisoned after Bannockburn for speaking "irreverent and indecent words" about his sovereign: he had said "it was no wonder the King couldn't win a battle, because he spent the time when he should have been hearing Mass in idling, ditching, digging and other improper occupations." Isabella persuaded Archbishop Reynolds to stand surety for the man's good behavior;[87] presumably, she had had the wisdom to realize that he had been punished only for uttering sentiments that most people were thinking or saying in private.

The dreadful import of the defeat is reflected in the words of the author of the *Vita Edwardi Secundi:* "O day of vengeance and disaster, day of utter loss and shame; evil and accursed day, not to be reckoned in our calendar!"

Bannockburn was a disaster for Edward in many ways. It effectively ended England's hopes of ever establishing political supremacy over Scotland and essentially secured Bruce's crown and Scotland's independence. It left the north of England more vulnerable than ever to Scottish raids and protection rackets. And it also shattered Edward II's credibility with his barons and put Lancaster in an impregnable position, determined to enforce the Ordinances.

Almost immediately, the Lords Ordainers gathered in York, where the disgraced King faced his Parliament in September. Isabella also attended,[88] no doubt dismayed and shamed by her husband's humiliation. Stiff-faced, they sat there, King and Queen, as Lancaster blamed England's defeat on the King's failure to observe the Ordinances, refused to heed Edward's demands to press on with the war, and demanded a purge of the royal household and the administration that would lead to the expenses of the King's household being cut to £10 per day. And Edward was forced to capitulate: he "refused nothing to the earls";[89] there was no redress, for it was clear that from now on, it was to be Lancaster, and not Edward, who ruled England. Edward would be merely a cipher, a puppet, in Lancaster's hands.

Isabella, staunch as ever, supported her husband. There was now every reason for Lancaster to regard her as an enemy. She had been close to Gloucester, with whom he had fallen out, and she had continued to befriend the Beaumonts, whom he hated, and had welcomed them back to court after their dismissal by the Ordainers. In soliciting pardons without reference to Parliament, she had ignored the provisions of the Ordinances. Moreover, she was influential with her father, who had already sent lawyers to help Edward circumvent the Ordinances.[90]

In retaliation, Lancaster saw to it that Isabella's revenues were drastically cut; this slump is evident in records of her finances between October 1314 and March 1316;[91] fortunately, the King was able to supplement her reduced income by small grants from his own Wardrobe.[92] Lancaster's spite may not have been the only reason for the cuts, for the weather was now mirroring the political situation: during the late summer and autumn, there were torrential rains that led to a ruined harvest, which heralded the great famine that was to ravage Europe over the next two years.

Then Isabella, back at Westminster, received the sad news of the death of her father, King Philip, who died on 29 November at Fontainebleau, cut down by a stroke while out hunting. Now it truly seemed to many that the Grand Master's curse had been fulfilled, for both the Pope and the King of France had died before the year was out. And, given the dynastic scandal that had overtaken Philip's sons, it is hardly surprising that he and they quickly became known as "les Rois Mauduits"—"the accursed Kings." As for Philip's daughter, it may very well have seemed to her at this time that that curse extended to both her and her husband, as Philip's daughter and son-in-law.

Philip IV was succeeded by his eldest son, who became Louis X and was nicknamed "le Hutin," which has been variously translated as "the Stubborn," "the Quarrelsome," or "the Headstrong." With his Queen in prison and his daughter disinherited, he did not enjoy an auspicious start to his reign. He was a somewhat frivolous young man with little interest in government, and the real ruler of France during his reign was his uncle, Charles of Valois.

In Avignon, also, there was change, with the election of a new Pope, the shrewd and clever John XXII, who was to play an influential role in Isabella's life during the years to come. In December 1314, to mark his election, the Queen sent him two copes that had been embroidered with coral and large pearls by Rose de Burford, the wife of a London merchant. They were purchased through an intermediary called Katherine Lincoln. Through her almoner, Isabella also sent the Pope an incense boat, a ewer, and a gold buckle set with pearls and precious stones. These three gifts cost £300, which the King paid.[93]

By now, Edward had been successful in his bid to have the ban of excommunication on Piers Gaveston overturned by the Pope, and on 2 January 1315, he had the corpse of his late lamented "intimate friend"[94] wrapped in cloth of gold and buried with great pomp in the Dominican church at Langley; Archbishop Reynolds officiated, assisted by four other bishops and thirteen abbots. The Queen attended, as did Pembroke, Norfolk, Mortimer, Hugh le Despenser the Younger, Henry de Beaumont, the Lord Mayor of London, and fifty knights. Hereford, who had been instrumental in having Piers condemned to death, but who had now made his peace with the King, was also among the mourners. But most other magnates stayed away.[95] Edward paid for Masses for Gaveston's soul to be offered in churches all over England and later established a chantry at Langley, where prayers could be said for Piers in perpetuity. His Wardrobe accounts show that every year, for the rest of his life, on Gaveston's birthday and the anniversary of his death, the King would have Masses said and offer gifts, including rich cloths, at his tomb.[96]

Parliament was in a bullish mood when it met at Westminster on 20 March; it confirmed the Ordinances and demanded the dismissal of several more of the King's supporters, including the Elder Despenser and

Henry de Beaumont.[97] On 23 February, the day before Beaumont left the King's household, Isabella defiantly demonstrated her solidarity with her husband by including Henry de Beaumont among the guests at a feast she gave, at which several other leading royalists, including the Earls of Richmond and Norfolk, were present. Isabella de Vesci was also ejected from the court at this time, but Isabella kept in touch with her regularly by letter or messenger.[98] During this period, there is no record of Isabella's communicating with Lancaster or his supporters.[99]

In April, the King himself hosted a great banquet at Westminster for the Archbishop of Canterbury and the nobility, but it was to be the last for a long time. Not only was the hall damaged by fire soon afterward, but there was also, that spring, more torrential rain and widespread flooding across Europe, which would continue unceasing until the autumn and lead to another failed harvest and the worst recorded famine in European history.

To add to Edward's troubles, there were rumors of a Scottish invasion of Ireland; at the end of April, he sent Roger Mortimer back there as Lieutenant,[100] and not a moment too soon, for in May, in the interests of building up a Celtic alliance against England, Robert Bruce sent his brother Edward to free the Irish from English rule. In June, Dundalk fell to Edward Bruce, and in September, he took Ulster.

Between June 5 and 23, Edward and Isabella visited the new town of Winchelsea in Sussex, which had been built by Edward I on a grid plan, much like his continental bastides, to replace the old town that had been swept away into the sea during a storm; the royal couple perhaps stayed at the newly founded Franciscan priory. There was no sign of famine here, for the town was prosperous, and the King and Queen were plied with food and wines. Isabella attended Mass in the parish church, which was dedicated to Thomas à Becket, and her chaplain made offerings in her name. Then she and Edward moved south to Hastings, where they stayed in the castle and made gifts to the chapel there, in which they were entertained by two harpists and a fiddler.[101] The royal couple then made yet another pilgrimage to Canterbury, before returning to Westminster, where they stayed until at least 7 July.[102]

By now, the dread famine held England in its grip.[103] The price of grain had soared to an unprecedented level, and it was reported that, on 9 August, Saint Laurence's Eve, even the King and Queen found it hard to obtain bread when they passed through Saint Albans.[104] Because of the scarcity of food, the council ordered that no one below the rank of earl was to have more than two dishes at each meal, but this only resulted in lords' reducing their households and casting out unneeded servants to starve. Because there was so little fodder for cattle, disease spread, and herds had to be culled; it was not uncommon to see the bodies of animals lying dead and rotting in the flooded fields. This led to further shortages of meat and dairy products and "misery such as our age has never seen"[105] for many of the King's subjects; "in Northumbria, dogs and horses and other unclean things were eaten,"[106] and there were reports of desperate people committing murder to get food, and even of instances of cannibalism. The evidence suggests that, in some parts, the death rate from starvation was as high as 10 percent. In the towns, trade suffered and many people lost their livelihoods. Edward passed statutes to lower the price of provisions, but he could do nothing to relieve the serious dearth that was now affecting the land.

On 12 August, Warwick died, greatly lamented. His friends claimed he had been poisoned, probably in an attempt to discredit the King. Warwick's passing left Lancaster in a position of unchallenged supremacy. Only four days earlier, on 8 August, Edward had appointed him King's Lieutenant in the North. Lancaster had now replaced most of the royal officials and sheriffs with his own men and was enjoying widespread support as the self-proclaimed champion of the Ordinances. He controlled the administration, issued orders and pardons, granted petitions, and made appointments. Before the King acted, he was obliged to seek Lancaster's advice, but as Lancaster preferred to hold himself aloof from the council, Edward was forced to treat with him almost as another sovereign prince, sending envoys to him at Kenilworth or Donnington.[107] Isabella, the daughter of the autocratic Philip IV, cannot have relished seeing her husband's royal authority thus subverted.

Soon afterward, there came news from France that Marguerite of Burgundy had died in her prison on 14 August. Rumor had it that she had been strangled, smothered, or starved to death, and rumor may not have lied, for it was imperative that King Louis have an heir, and on 19 August, only five days after his wife's demise, he married his distant cousin, Clemence of Hungary, who rivaled Isabella in being reputed the most beautiful princess in Europe. She was crowned with him ten days later at Rheims.

September found Edward and Isabella at the twelfth-century Augustinian priory at Barnwell in Northamptonshire, which boasted an important royal hospice. Later that month, they visited Lincoln and in October were at Clipstone, the royal hunting lodge in Sherwood Forest. In December, Isabella stayed behind while Edward went to meet his barons at Doncaster.[108] They were also apart at Christmas, which the King spent "rowing in the Cambridge Fens with a great concourse of simple people, to refresh his spirit" and even swimming with this "silly company" in the cold weather, which only aroused the derision of the barons, who openly expressed their scorn for such "childish frivolities."[109]

That December of 1315, there was dire news from Ireland: Mortimer had been utterly defeated by Edward Bruce at the Battle of Kells in Meath. English rule had now virtually collapsed in Dublin, and Mortimer came hurrying back to England to obtain reinforcements, arriving at court by 17 January.[110] But the King, needing his support against Lancaster, kept him in England.

Mortimer was therefore present[111] when Parliament assembled at Lincoln late in January, but Lancaster did not deign immediately to grace it with his presence, despite pressing concerns over the famine and the Scots; instead, he arrived three weeks late, on 12 February. Nevertheless, a compliant Parliament appointed him chief councillor to the King—much against Edward's will—for the lords had agreed that "the King should undertake no important matter without the consent of the council."[112] At this time, Edward and Isabella were staying at Somerton Castle at Navenby, eight miles south of Lincoln. The castle had been built in 1281–82 and had been visited by the King before his accession. While staying there, Edward granted £50 and lands in Ponthieu to Isabella's nurse, Théophania de St. Pierre, perhaps on her retirement.[113] He also rewarded his own nurse, Alice de Leygrave, for her good service to Isabella.[114] Around this time, Lancaster also gave £92 in gifts to Théophania and the Queen's French servants.[115]

By February, Isabella knew herself to be pregnant again. On 27 March, a new litter was delivered to her so that she could travel in comfort, for breeding women were not supposed to ride.

In April, Parliament met again, at Westminster, but soon afterward, Lancaster withdrew from the King's council. From now on, he would spend most of his time on his estates in the north, keeping state like a king but doing very little to maintain effective government. He was proving to be a reluctant, indecisive, and not particularly able ruler and was losing support, thanks to his own inertia and incompetence, and Edward's relentless intrigues. It did not help that the famine was still raging, the Scots were still raiding the North with impunity, the Welsh were rebelling, and the kingdom was generally in a ferment of unrest, with private wars breaking out among the barons. But Lancaster repeatedly neglected state business in order to attend to his own interests. He had muzzled his king but had failed to offer a credible alternative; the principles he had claimed to uphold had been seemingly cast aside, and his sole purpose, it now appeared, was to control and humiliate the King.

Mortimer, who had crushed the rebellion in Wales, which had been led by a patriot called Llywelyn Bren,[116] had returned to court by 21 April but was back in the West between May and August. Then came the unwelcome news that Edward Bruce had had himself crowned High King of Ireland on 1 May.

There were more bad tidings when Isabella's brother, King Louis, died on 5 June at Vincennes of pleurisy or pneumonia, contracted through drinking iced wine after getting overheated playing tennis. He left his widow, Queen Clemence, pregnant. Until her child was born, France would be without a king, the first time this had occurred since 987, when the Capetian dynasty was founded; hence, Isabella's second brother, Philip, Count of Poitou, was appointed Governor of France during the gestation and minority of the future sovereign. By 20 June, Isabella had heard of Louis's passing and retired to Mortlake in Surrey to nurse her grief.[117]

With Lancaster out of the way, and public discontent with his misrule mounting, the King was beginning to reassert himself. In June, he began to restore the victims of the Lancastrian purge, including the Elder Despenser, who now returned to court, and on 1 July, he replenished Isabella's income, confirming all grants of land made to her since 1314[118] and increasing the allowances he made for her household.

The King was also planning to lead a new campaign against the Scots in October, and on 20 and 21 July, he arranged for the Bardi to pay the Queen's expenses during his coming absence.[119] In the hope of further reasserting his authority, he wrote to the Pope, asking if he might be crowned again with holy oil brought to England by Thomas à Becket; the Pope, a wiser man than Edward, could foresee how provocative such an act would be and refused.

Late in July, Isabella went to Eltham to rest before her confinement, while the King went north to Lincoln for the next session of Parliament. He was now doing his best to woo Lancaster back to court, hoping to enlist his support for the coming Scottish campaign, but after Parliament had met at Lincoln on 29 July, he and Lancaster engaged in a furious quarrel over Scotland that scuppered all hopes of an invasion.[120]

On 15 August, Isabella bore a second son, John, at Eltham. The King had resolved to make this happy event an occasion for reconciliation with Lancaster, and immediately after the birth, the Queen dispatched her valet, Goodwin Hawtayne, with letters to Lancaster and John Salmon,

Bishop of Norwich, "requesting them to come to Eltham to stand sponsors for her son John." The gesture had been made, but the response was an unforgivable snub, for there is no record of Lancaster's turning up for the christening.

The infant Prince was baptized on the twentieth in the Queen's chapel at Eltham,[121] where the font was specially draped with cloth of gold and a costly and rare piece of Turkey carpet. These cloths had been acquired by John de Fontenoy, the clerk to the Queen's chapel, and came from the King's Wardrobe, which also supplied the Queen's tailor, Stephen Taloise, with five pieces of white velvet to make her a robe for her churching; Edward gave Isabella some jewelry and paid £40 for the ceremony.[122]

The King rewarded Sir Eubulo de Montibus, Isabella's steward, with £100 for riding to York and bringing him the joyful news of the "happy delivery" of John of Eltham, as the Prince would be known.[123] He also rewarded Isabella, bestowing on her various grants of land and precious items supplied on credit by the Bardi,[124] and arranged for prayers to be said for her and John in the house of the Dominicans in York. On 9 September, fearing an armed confrontation with Lancaster, the King ordered Isabella to join him in York with all speed.[125] She left Eltham before 20 September, was at Buntingford in Hertfordshire on the twenty-second, and arrived in York just five days later. Edward, who had waited anxiously for news of her coming, rewarded the messenger who heralded her imminent arrival.[126] The King and Queen stayed in York until October, when they returned south.[127] By now, Edward's trust in Isabella's judgment was such that he allowed her to attend council meetings.

On 9 October, the Bishop of Durham died, and both Edward and Isabella put forward their own candidates for the vacant see. Edward wanted Henry de Stanford, the Prior of Finchale, and Isabella, influenced by Henry de Beaumont and Isabella de Vesci, chose their brother, the "lavish" and "gleeful"[128] Louis de Beaumont, a choice that seemed deliberately calculated to anger Lancaster.

There were other contenders, too, nominated by Lancaster himself and Hereford, but on 19 October, the King commissioned Pembroke to ensure that either his own or the Queen's man was appointed; Pembroke sent a number of barons to Durham Cathedral to ensure that the King's wishes were complied with. But the Queen was angry to learn that, on 6 November, the monks of Durham had chosen Henry de Stanford, and, hastening to the King, she fell on her knees and begged him to secure the see for Louis de Beaumont, urging that Louis would "be a stone wall" against the Scots.[129] Ignoring the protests of the Chapter of Durham that Louis was illiterate, Edward capitulated to his wife, refused to sanction the appointment of Stanford, and made a complaint to Avignon.[130]

That autumn, the Mortimers, uncle and nephew, were riding high at court. At the beginning of October, Mortimer of Chirk had been reappointed Justiciar of North Wales, with almost sovereign powers, and in November, having persuaded Edward to allow him to deal with Edward Bruce, Roger Mortimer was made King's Lieutenant of Ireland and began preparations to return there with an army.[131]

There was more sad news from France. On 14 or 15 November, Queen Clemence had given birth to a son, King John I "the Posthumous," but the precious infant died at the age of only seven or eight days and was buried near his father in the abbey of Saint-Denis. He was succeeded by his uncle, Isabella's second brother, who now ascended the throne as Philip V.

Philip V, nicknamed "the Tall" or "the Fair," was another king such as his father had been, good-looking, intelligent, decisive, harsh, and ruthless. Predictably, there was talk that he had hastened his little nephew's death, which may not have been without justification.

At the beginning of December, the King ordered the Exchequer to pay Isabella a further £366 13s. 4d. (£366 67p.) a year, less the income from her English lands; however, the barons of Exchequer were tardy in making payments, and twice in January, the King and Queen had to chase them.[132]

Christmas that year was spent at Clipstone. Roger Mortimer was present and stayed until after the Feast of the Epiphany.[133] But it was a Christmas overshadowed by conflict, for Lancaster was making trouble, and England seemed once again to be on the verge of civil war.

On 9 January 1317, Philip V was crowned with Jeanne of Burgundy at Rheims, but there were still those who asserted that his niece, the dispossessed Jeanne of Navarre, had a better title to the throne than he. The next month, therefore, he summoned an assembly of the three estates and invoked what he was pleased to call the Salic law (which allegedly dated from the time of the early Frankish kings), declaring that "a woman cannot succeed to the kingdom of France." This law was of dubious legality and certainly contravened the normal feudal laws of inheritance; it was in time to have far-reaching implications for Isabella and her heirs. As for Jeanne, who was only six, Philip placated her supporters by agreeing that she could succeed her father as Queen of Navarre.[134]

Robert Bruce himself landed in Ireland in January, and in February, he and his brother established themselves in Ulster. But when they pressed south and came within five miles of Dublin, Mortimer halted their advance.

That same month, the King and Queen moved to the palatial royal hunting lodge at Clarendon, which stood on a hill in the midst of a forest near Salisbury and dated from the eleventh century. Like most of the other royal residences, it had been improved by Henry III. There were Gothic windows with gable heads in Isabella's chambers, and one window sported a stained-glass depiction of the Virgin and Child. In the Queen's Wardrobe, which was beneath her private chapel dedicated to Saint Catherine, there were murals showing Richard I fighting with Saladin and scenes from the history of Antioch. In the Queen's hall, the marble-columned mantel was sculpted with a relief of the twelve months of the year.[135]

Isabella attended the council meeting that took place at Clarendon on 9 February,[136] during which Edward and his supporters accused Lancaster of plotting with the Scots against him. Lancaster denied it, but there were many who had noticed that, during their repeated northern raids, the Scots had left his estates untouched and who openly speculated that he meant to enlist Robert Bruce's help against Edward, which would have been treason of the first order.[137]

On that same 9 February, in response to the Queen's pleas, and also, it appears, some hefty bribes, including gifts worth £1,904 from the King and Queen, the accommodating Pope John provided Louis de Beaumont to the see of Durham, Louis having obligingly agreed to take reading lessons.[138] Nevertheless, when he was enthroned on 26 March 1318, he was still barely able to understand the Latin.[139]

Later that month, another bishopric, that of Rochester, became vacant, and again, Isabella involved herself in a contest to fill it, competing with the King in providing candidates. Edward wrote to Pope John in support of Hamo de Hethe, and Isabella made her plea to the Pontiff on behalf of her own confessor, John de Chisoye. She also enlisted the support of her brother, King Philip, and Pembroke. On hearing how she had set herself up in opposition to her husband, the Pope and his cardinals "marvelled" but put it down to Edward's "inconsistency." This time, however, Isabella did not get her own way, and on 18 March, Hamo de Hethe was elected Bishop of Rochester.[140]

In April, the King and Queen visited Ramsey in Huntingdonshire,[141] where they stayed in the abbey guesthouse dedicated to Saint Thomas of Canterbury, which had been built around 1180. The famine had now abated, and England was once more becoming "fruitful, with a manifold abundance of good things."[142] And there was encouraging news from Ireland, for that spring, Robert Bruce returned to Scotland, and soon afterward, Mortimer defeated his old enemies, the treacherous Lacys. He then set about rebuilding the English administration and persuading the King's Irish subjects to return to their obedience.

April saw the four-year-old Prince Edward's first public appearance. Very little is known about the Prince's childhood, apart from the fact that he spent much of it at Eltham with his brother John in "the Princes' tower,"[143] and that one of his noble companions was a Griffin of Wales, but we do know something about his education. He was taught by royal clerks, the most celebrated of whom was Richard de Bury, who was made Bishop of Durham by his former pupil in 1333. Bury was a great bibliophile and scholar, and in his time served as an ambassador to France, Hainault, and Germany. Under his auspices, the Prince learned to read and write—his is the first surviving autograph of an English king—and became fluent in Norman-French, French, Latin, and English. He also developed a working knowledge of German and Flemish. There is abundant evidence that he acquired proficiency in the admired aristocratic skills of riding, swordsmanship, jousting, hunting, hawking, coursing, dancing, singing, and shooting with a longbow. He was brought up to be articulate, courteous, and affable with all. No king could have asked for a more promising son and heir.

Parliament met at Westminster on 15 April. On the same date, £20 was paid to one Brother Richard de Brumfield "for three days' entertainment for the Lord the King, the Lady the Queen and the Lord Edward, their son."[144] On 22 April, Edward granted Isabella the manors of Wallingford, which had belonged to Gaveston, and Saint Valery.

Then scandal erupted. In May, Lancaster's Countess, Alice de Lacy, eloped with her lover, Eubulo Lestraunge, a squire in the service of the Earl of Surrey, Lancaster's enemy, whose knight, Sir Richard de Saint Martin, had "abducted" her from her unfaithful and unprepossessing husband. Alice immediately claimed Surrey's protection, while Lestraunge lost no time in proclaiming to the world that he had slept with her before her marriage and in so doing severely compromised her reputation. There had been bad blood between Lancaster and Surrey for years, but the abduction of Lancaster's wife, who was irrevocably and publicly shamed, was a deadly insult that the Earl was determined to avenge, and he now entered into a destructive and futile struggle with his rival to retrieve his wife and his lost honor. He began by ravaging and plundering Surrey's lands and castles in Yorkshire, in the process plunging them both into a bloody and disruptive private war.[145]

To make matters worse, Lancaster suspected that the King and Queen had actually encouraged his wife to leave him and that they had plotted her abduction at the council held at Clarendon in February. Edward feebly forbade Lancaster to resort to violence and advised him to "seek a remedy in law only,"[146] but this made no difference whatsoever, even though the Earl was warned that, if he persisted in his private war, "the King would either have his head or consign him to prison."[147] Lancaster, in turn, declared that he would not come to court because he feared treachery. It now seemed unlikely that Edward and his cousin would ever be reconciled.

At Whitsun, as was customary, the King and Queen held court at Westminster, but as they were feasting, a mysterious woman "adorned with a theatrical dress" entered the hall "on a fine horse" and, "after the manner of players, made a circuit round the tables" before approaching the dais and presenting the King with a letter. Before he could respond, she bowed, turned her horse, and left the hall. Thinking this was some kind of courtly game, Edward commanded that the letter be opened and read aloud for the amusement of the company. But he was mortified and embarrassed when it proved to be a damning indictment of his rule. The woman was quickly arrested and revealed that a certain knight had set her up to deliver the letter; when questioned, this knight insisted that he had acted in the interests of the King's honor and in the sincere hope that his sovereign would heed "the complaints of his subjects"; however, he emphasized that he had meant the letter to be read in private. Edward was impressed with the man's sincerity and integrity; he rewarded him "with abundant gifts" and set the woman free.[148] But he paid little or no attention to their grievances.

On 7 July, Edward II effectively founded what later became known as King's Hall at Cambridge, which was refounded by Henry VIII as Trinity College in 1546. Edward's foundation was for the education of twelve scholars, who he probably hoped would become loyal servants of the Crown. In 1318, the Pope granted King's Hall the status of a university college.

In July, the King and Queen set out for Nottingham. They spent some days at Saint Albans Abbey, where Edward blessed and touched twenty-two scrofulous persons suffering from "the King's Evil," in the hope of curing them, a royal duty that would be faithfully carried out by every future sovereign until the time of Queen Anne. After this, the King and Queen moved on to Bedford, then to the royal manor of King's Cliffe in Northamptonshire.[149]

Parliament met at Nottingham on 18 July. On the twenty-fifth, the King granted Isabella Gaveston's old county of Cornwall.[150] Later in the year, in November, the Queen would also be assigned revenues from London.

In September, after visiting Lincoln, the royal couple stayed at Tickhill Castle in Yorkshire.[151] On the tenth, at Isabella's request, the King confirmed charters that had been granted to the Order of Premontré at

Blanchelande in the Côtentin in Normandy.[152] Then it was on to York, where the royal couple stayed once more with the Franciscans.[153]

There now arose a property dispute that was to have an immense bearing not only on Isabella's future but also on national politics and the lives of the King's subjects.

When Gilbert de Clare, Earl of Gloucester, had been killed in 1314 at Bannockburn, he had left no child to succeed him, and hence, the great and ancient earldom of Gloucester looked set to be divided up among the Earl's coheirs, his three sisters. However, his Countess immediately announced that she was pregnant, so the matter was left in abeyance until such time as she should bear her child. Three years later, even she had to concede that there would be no baby, and in November 1317, the earldom was divided up among the Earl's sisters, all of whom were now married to men high in the King's favor.

The eldest sister, Eleanor, now twenty-five, was married to Hugh le Despenser the Younger, a fine figure of a man[154] who was at least three years younger than the King and had been a member of his household when he was Prince of Wales. He had fought at Bannockburn in 1314, had been first summoned to Parliament in 1315, and had again served in Scotland in 1317. While his father had been a consistently loyal supporter of the King, the younger Despenser had aligned himself with the baronial party, which had long been hostile to the elder Hugh. He was proud, cunning, aggressively acquisitive and self-serving, and extremely capable. He could be brutal when provoked: in 1315, he had illegally seized Tonbridge Castle, thinking that it belonged to Gloucester's widow, and then had to give it back when it transpired that it was actually held by the Archbishop of Canterbury; and in 1316, for reasons that are not clear, he physically attacked one of the lords at the Lincoln Parliament.[155]

The royal Wardrobe accounts show that Despenser's wife, Eleanor de Clare, was clearly a favorite of her uncle, the King, who paid her living expenses throughout his reign,[156] a privilege not extended to her two sisters.

The second sister, Margaret de Clare, aged twenty-four, had been married to Piers Gaveston but was now the wife of Hugh de Audley, one of the King's household knights. The third sister, Elizabeth, aged twenty-two, had just married her third husband, Roger d'Amory, another household knight, who had served with distinction at Bannockburn.

Normally, where there was more than one heiress, an estate was divided into equal shares, but in November 1317, Hugh le Despenser was allowed to claim Glamorgan, the largest and richest share of the Clare inheritance, ostensibly because he was married to the eldest sister. The truth was that he was already embarked on a meteoric rise to royal favor, thanks no doubt to the influence of his wife, and was rapidly becoming skilled at manipulating the King. Audley had to be content with Newport and Netherwent, and d'Amory got Usk.

But Despenser was not satisfied with his share. He meant to have the rest of the Gloucester inheritance, and he now set out to get it, by fair means or foul. In 1317, he attempted unsuccessfully to seize from Audley the lordship of Glennllwg, which had once been part of Glamorgan. He "set traps for his co-heirs; thus, if he could manage it, each would lose his share through false accusations, and he alone would obtain the whole earldom."[157]

For nearly four years now, Lancaster had been in the ascendant, and he and the King had wrangled and struggled for power, with barons siding behind one or the other—mostly, to begin with, behind Lancaster. But Lancaster had proved that he was no more capable than Edward of good government. Meanwhile, the King had been steadily building up his own court party, which included d'Amory, Audley, Surrey, the Despensers, and William de Montacute, another loyal household knight. Lancaster would certainly have regarded Isabella as being affiliated to this court party, since she had recently extended her patronage to several men who were dependents of Edward's principal supporters.[158]

Roger d'Amory, who was naturally anxious to receive his proper share of the de Clare inheritance, was gaining rapidly in favor with the King and became especially close to Edward at this time. But again, Edward displayed poor judgment in allowing such a man to influence him. In September 1317, thanks to the efforts of two emissaries from the Pope, Lancaster had grudgingly agreed to return to court. But the King, egged on by d'Amory, who had been ousted from the constableship of two royal castles by Lancaster, had raised an army at York and marched provocatively in full battle order past the Earl's castle at Pontefract. Although Lancaster ignored the challenge, the King's action effectively scuppered any chance of a reconciliation between them. In fact, civil war appeared to be a very real possibility.

Pembroke, remembering Gaveston, now realized the necessity for controlling d'Amory, and on 24 November, he entered into a compact with the new favorite, and with an influential baron, Bartholemew, Lord Badlesmere, with all agreeing that they would support and consult one another when advising the King.[159] Their alliance has been erroneously described as a "Middle Party," but it was more of a damage-limitation exercise; nevertheless, it did moderate the King and provided an alternative to Lancaster's misrule. And d'Amory's influence ensured that, by the spring of 1318, Pembroke and Badlesmere had gained greater credit with Edward. By then, others—including Arundel, Hereford, Surrey, the Mortimers, and Archbishop Reynolds—had tired of Lancaster's complacency and aligned themselves with Pembroke.

The King and Queen kept the Christmas of 1317 at Westminster. Isabella was once again pregnant.

There was more sad news for the Queen in the new year of 1318, for on 14 February, her aunt, Queen Marguerite, died at Marlborough Castle.[160] Isabella was probably present with the King at her funeral later that month;[161] wrapped in a Franciscan habit, Marguerite was buried before the high altar in the unfinished choir of the Grey Friars in Newgate, London, the church she had herself partially rebuilt, enlarged, and endowed, and in which the heart of Eleanor of Provence, Edward's grandmother, had been interred in 1291. A beautiful tomb would be raised to the memory of Queen Marguerite, but it was defaced and then lost after the Reformation.

Isabella, too, had a special affection for this church, and not just because of her affinity with the Franciscan Order. It seems that Marguerite had asked for the new building to be modeled on the lines and scale of the Franciscan Church of the Cordeliers in Paris, which had been founded by Saint Louis around 1250, and in which Isabella's own mother, Jeanne of Navarre, had been laid to rest. It is no coincidence that there was a chapel dedicated to Saint Louis at Newgate. It was Isabella who would pay handsomely toward the completion of the London church, which, when finished in 1348, would measure a grand three hundred feet long by eighty-nine feet wide by sixty-four feet high, making it second only to Saint Paul's in size. It was a beautiful light and spacious building, having fifteen bays with two clerestory windows in each, and several chapels leading off the aisles, which had slender piers with octagonal bases supporting a tall arcade of pointed arches.[162] Isabella herself paid for the glazing of the window at the east end, behind the altar; in all, she spent about £70 on Grey Friars. Thanks to the patronage of Isabella, Marguerite, and other royal ladies, Grey Friars at Newgate remained the most prestigious Franciscan house in England, and the most fashionable church in London, for the next two centuries, and many notable persons chose to be buried there.

The death of Marguerite at last released the dower lands and manors of the queens of England, which now reverted to Isabella. On 23 February, the King commanded the Exchequer to list all the late Queen's properties,[163] and that same day, Isabella surrendered all her holdings to the Crown pend-

ing the new settlement. On 5 March, thanks to the efficiency of William de
Montacute, she was granted her permanent dower lands,[164] and on the sixth,
Ponthieu and Montreuil were restored to her, but she would have to wait
until 30 October to receive back the county of Cornwall.[165] On 20 March,
when the royal couple were at Clarendon, the King arranged for the arrears
of the Queen's income to be paid to her and ordered the Bardi to cover her
expenses in the interim.[166] Her Treasurer was ordered to keep close watch
on the expenditure of her servants from now on. Edward also made a grant
to the priory of Ivychurch at Isabella's instance.

There was good and bad news from beyond England's borders. In Ireland, by March 1318, Roger Mortimer had stamped out most of the resistance to English rule; but on 26 March, Bruce delivered a crushing blow to
the English by seizing the strategic fortress of Berwick, thus depriving his
enemies of their traditional bridgehead into Scotland. The Scots followed
up this triumph by impudently raiding as far south as Yorkshire. At this
time, the King was in no position to attempt to recover Berwick, having
insufficient money or men.

It was at this perilous juncture that, thanks to Pembroke's conciliatory
influence, Edward reached a preliminary settlement with Lancaster. But it
was to be systematically sabotaged by Edward's new court favorites,
d'Amory, Audley, and Montacute, who objected vehemently to Lancaster's
insistence that the Crown resume all grants and gifts made since 1310.[167]
Had the King agreed to this, it is likely that some of Isabella's dependents
would have been considerably worse off, for it is clear that Lancaster meant
to stem the flow of gifts to her servants; therefore, it would be fair to
assume that the Queen, who had already suffered financially at Lancaster's
hands and had since been most generously compensated by the King, was
on the side of the court party;[168] after all, she had no reason to love Lancaster and had been his enemy for at least four years now.

Early in the summer, the King and Queen were guests of honor at weddings at Havering-atte-Bower in Essex, Windsor, and Woodstock. Edward's
household roll records the provision of coins that, at the King's order, were
thrown over the heads of the happy couples as they made their vows at the
chapel doors.

Isabella, whose confinement was approaching, retired to the royal manor of
Woodstock in Oxfordshire before 11 June. Woodstock, which stood in
Wychwood Forest and had been recently settled on the Queen as part of
her dower,[169] had been a royal retreat and hunting box since before the Conquest, but the present house, with its aisled hall, had originally been built by

Henry I in the early twelfth century. The stone wall surrounding the hunting park extended for seven miles, and within its precincts was a royal menagerie that housed "strange beasts from far countries," notably, lions, lynxes, leopards, and porcupines. Henry III had remodeled the royal apartments in the thirteenth century. Isabella's chambers overlooked a garden with a maple tree by a pool, and she could take the air in open cloisters or walk to the spring at nearby Everswell, where there was a garden with a hundred pear trees.[170]

On 13 June, the King visited Canterbury alone.[171] Five days later, back at Woodstock, the Queen bore a daughter, who was christened Eleanor, after the King's mother. Edward hastened to his wife's side and paid out £333 for a feast given to celebrate her churching.[172] After this, on 28 June, the royal couple traveled together to Northampton,[173] where Parliament assembled in July.

While they were there, Isabella became very disturbed about growing rumors that the King was a changeling. Considering the disasters of his reign and his inept rule, it is hardly surprising that people were beginning to believe such rumors.[174]

They had started when a tanner's son, John Deydras, also known as John of Powderham, who may have been mentally unbalanced, suddenly appeared at Beaumont Palace, the old royal residence in Oxford, and claimed possession of it, insisting that he was "the true heir of the realm, as the son of the illustrious King Edward, who had long been dead. He declared that my Lord Edward was not of the blood royal, nor had any right to the realm, which he offered to prove by combat with him."[175] Deydras was tall and fair, and uncannily resembled Edward, but he was missing an ear.

He claimed that, when he was a baby, he had been mauled by a sow who had ripped off his ear, and that his nurse, too terrified to tell Edward I what had happened, had substituted a carter's son in his place; he himself had been reared by the carter, and the changeling as the King's son. As additional proof of Edward's humble origins, Deydras cited his notorious love of rustic pursuits and "other vanities and frivolities" that were unbecoming in a king's son. But he could offer no proof to support his tale.

Edward had the imposter arrested and brought before him at Northampton. "Welcome, my brother," he said, with some irony.

But Deydras was in no mood to be trifled with. "Thou art no brother of mine," he retorted, "but falsely thou claimest the kingdom for thyself. Thou hast not a drop of blood from the illustrious Edward, and that I am prepared to prove against thee."

This was outrageous, and Deydras was put on trial for inciting sedition. At length, he admitted that he was an imposter but that he had been put up to it by the Devil appearing to him in the form of a cat. But that did not save him from the gallows, nor from the fire that afterward consumed his body. His cat was put to death in the same way.

And that, as far as the King was concerned, was an end to the matter. But the rumor that he was a changeling had "run through all the land," and Isabella had been "troubled beyond measure" by it.[176] Emotionally vulnerable after childbirth, she was evidently profoundly humiliated and unsettled by Deydras's very public claims; there is no evidence, however, that she ever thought there was any truth in them.

Even though he was now more or less politically isolated, Lancaster was again making difficulties, insisting on the removal of the new favorites, who he warned were "worse than Gaveston"; naturally, he saw d'Amory and his colleagues as a dangerous threat to his position. But the King refused to send them away, and Parliament spent much of its time negotiating with Lancaster, sending emissaries as if he were the actual sovereign. On 29 July, a second delegation returned from the Earl, having made encouraging progress, at which point the Queen herself joined Pembroke and Hereford and the bishops in seeking a peace.

Did Isabella, at this juncture, visit Lancaster to make a personal plea for his cooperation? In the records of the Duchy of Lancaster in the Public Record Office, there are three references to preparations for the Queen's visit to the Earl at Pontefract. They belong to 1319 but are undated. Lancaster went to considerable trouble to receive Isabella with due state: hangings were put up in the hall, streamers were attached to the instruments of his trumpeters, and four men spent six days making trestles and benches for the hall,[177] which suggests that the Queen was bringing a large retinue with her. However, there is no record of the visit ever taking place.

Whether it did or not, as a result of the Queen's intervention, a third embassy was sent to Lancaster on 1 August. Isabella certainly played a vital part in bringing about the settlement embodied in the Treaty of Leake, which was signed on 9 August 1318;[178] Trevet attests that she had vigorously orchestrated the concord for the purpose of making peace. No doubt she also had in mind her own financial interests.

The treaty bound Edward to observe the Ordinances and dismiss his favorites but released him from his odious tutelage to Lancaster, who had been bribed into standing down from his position of power; instead, however, the King would have to obey the will of a council of masters under

Pembroke rather than just one. But Pembroke was a fair man, and some of his associates were loyal to Edward. The King, however, was still determined to shake off all restraints on his royal authority and was by now a past master at playing one man off against another. As his wife, Isabella must have been aware of the King's true feelings and intentions.

Five days after the treaty was signed, Edward met Lancaster on a bridge over the River Soar near Loughborough and went through the charade of giving his cousin the kiss of peace, having granted him a full pardon for all the offenses he had committed against the peace of the realm; this effectively brought to an end the Earl's private war with Surrey. Notwithstanding Lancaster's humiliation, Edward was still utterly determined to be revenged on him for Gaveston's death but had probably reasoned, like him, that a peaceful settlement with the moderates was the best way forward, considering how weak his position was.

Edward took up residence at York on 28 September and stayed there until November. Isabella was staying in the vicinity and made two visits to Beverley Minster, on 8 and 18 October.[179] Soon afterward, there arrived the welcome news of the death of Edward Bruce at the Battle of Faughart, near Dundalk. By the end of the year, the Scots had left Ireland for good, and the Irish crisis was at an end.

When Parliament met at York on 28 October, it endorsed the Treaty of Leake and set up a standing council of seventeen headed by Pembroke. In recognition of his great achievements in Ireland, Mortimer, who was back at court by this time, was nominated to be a member, as was the Elder Despenser, who was now allowed to return to the King's service, despite having stood alone against the Treaty of Leake. The King had agreed not to act without this council's consent, and Mortimer was among those who stood surety for him. Mortimer was also chosen to sit on a commission set up by Parliament to reform the King's household;[180] these are the first instances of his acting against Edward, and they indicate that he had now allied himself with Pembroke's party.

Hugh le Despenser the Younger was also appointed to the permanent council, Parliament being under the impression that he, too, was with Pembroke. Parliament approved the recent appointment of the Younger Despenser as chamberlain of the King's household. But Despenser's allegiance was no longer to be counted upon, for with d'Amory out of the way, the younger Hugh rapidly took his place in the King's confidence and affections. Despenser's preferment to the influential post of chamberlain marks the beginning of his notorious reign as royal favorite, while a succession of grants tracks the growth of the King's regard for him. As a man of far greater ability than Gaveston, the grasping and politically ambitious Despenser was to prove a more dangerous favorite in every way, and a far worse threat to the barons, who would come in time to fear him.

As chamberlain, Despenser had the final say on who gained access to his royal master and consequently controlled patronage. Thus, he was easily able to wield power and command huge bribes. Soon, he was suspected of subverting every other influence on the King, including Pembroke's, and it was whispered that he led Edward "like a cat after a straw."[181] At this stage, however, there is no evidence that Isabella regarded Despenser as a rival, nor that there was tension or friction between them, although Isabella surely cannot have welcomed Hugh's growing ascendancy over her husband. Even if the Queen did not realize it, Despenser, by virtue of his unique position, was already a threat to her position and her influence.

Although Froissart baldly states that Despenser "was a sodomite, even, it was said, with the King," there is very little other direct evidence that Edward's relationship with Hugh was of a homosexual nature. Nevertheless, circumstantial evidence makes it likely. Otherwise, Despenser could hardly have exercised such a mesmeric influence over Edward. And in 1321, Pembroke was to warn the King that "he perishes on the rocks that loves another more than himself." He was certainly not referring to Edward's love for Isabella.

Like his son, the Elder Despenser profited greatly by his son's rise and came to enjoy greater political power than ever. Together, with the son as the driving force, the Despensers gradually gained a dominant hold upon the King. They hired and fired household officials as they pleased, and their rapaciousness soon became legendary. Let a man displease them or own something they coveted, and he might find himself in prison or dispossessed.

The York Parliament also dealt with the contentious issue of the resumption of royal grants, but Lancaster's original comprehensive demands were sidestepped, and in the end, only one yeoman of the Queen's household had his grant cut. Lancaster's sole contribution in Parliament was to insist that, as hereditary Steward of England, he had the right to nominate a new steward of the household to replace William de Montacute, who had been given a post in Gascony; but, demonstrating how far the mighty Earl had fallen, Parliament disagreed and, to Lancaster's fury, approved the King's appointment of Badlesmere, who had once been Lancaster's partisan; thereafter, there was bad blood between Lancaster and Badlesmere.[182]

Civil war had been averted, and the Treaty of Leake had heralded a fragile peace that was to last for the next two years. The King and Queen stayed on in the North through November 1318, and it was now that a reenergized Edward resolved to recover Berwick and began making plans to launch an all-out attack on the Scots the following June. Then the royal pair returned south, spending Christmas at Baldock in Hertfordshire.

On Twelfth Night, 6 January, the King and Queen distributed lavish gifts, which they could ill afford, and presided over the revelry at court. Edward generously presented a silver-gilt ewer with stand and cover to the courtier who was lucky enough to be "King of the Bean" for the evening; his role was similar to that of the Lord of Misrule, except that he held sway only on Twelfth Night.

Edward returned to York in January 1319, leaving the Earl of Norfolk as Keeper of the Realm. Isabella was in York by March, as was Despenser's wife, Eleanor de Clare, who had been summoned by Edward to wait on her.[183] Roger Mortimer, who had spent Christmas at Wigmore, also joined the court at York. On 15 March, the King appointed Mortimer Justiciar of Ireland; he would go there in June to keep order.

It was probably during her journey north that Isabella helped to end a dispute between the Abbot and townsfolk of Peterborough over who should meet the cost of repairing the town's bridge. When word was sent in the King's name that the Queen and her younger son, Prince John, would be coming to stay at the Abbey, the Abbot hastened to repair the bridge, ready for the royal visit. Then he was put to the further expense of presenting the Queen with a gift of £20 and outlaying another £400 for more presents and for entertainments during her visit.

Isabella spent most of the year in York and, according to Robert of Reading, gave birth to a daughter, Joan, while she was there. It has usually been assumed that this chronicler made an error and was in fact referring to the daughter of the same name whom the Queen bore in 1321; yet it is just possible that she did indeed bear a child, another Joan, in 1319, and that the infant died young. Nevertheless, no other chronicler mentions this second Joan.

Since 1317, Isabella had been urging Edward to address problems in her county of Ponthieu, where a French royalist party in Abbeville was steadily undermining English authority and threatening to turn the fief over to Philip V.[184] But the King had had other, more pressing, concerns on his mind, and he had also neglected affairs in Gascony, which had earned him the censure of the Pope and the French King.[185]

Apart from needing to sort out these problems, there was another reason why it was politic for Edward to go to France. It was customary for each new king to receive the homage of all his vassals for the lands they held of him, and for some time now, Philip V had been pressing Edward II to come to France to perform this feudal duty in respect of Gascony, Ponthieu, and Montreuil. It was also customary for English kings to resist such demands for as long as possible, since they regarded the act of homage to be incompatible with their royal dignity. Before, Edward had been able to plead the unrest in his kingdom as being responsible for the delay, but there was now no reason why he should not go to France in the near future and every reason why he needed Philip's goodwill; so in May 1319, he reluctantly sent Walter Stapledon, Bishop of Exeter, to the French court to make the necessary arrangements.

Stapledon was also to make a detour to Hainault to inspect one of the Count's daughters, who had been suggested as a possible bride for Prince Edward. The Count, William V, was married to Isabella's cousin Jeanne, the daughter of Charles of Valois, and they had five girls, Sybella, Margaret, Philippa, Jeanne, and Isabella. Stapledon's description of the princess selected still survives but does not mention her name; it is likely that she was the eldest, Sybella, who died soon afterward, which was probably why the negotiations proceeded no further. Some historians suggest that it was Philippa who was described, but it is hardly credible that the third daughter would take precedence before the first and second.

Parliament met at York on 6 May. Isabella was probably present with the King. The time for the muster was now drawing near, but it was postponed until 22 July. The King left York on 14 July and in August met up with Pembroke, Surrey, Hereford, Arundel, Despenser, Lancaster, and Lancaster's brother Henry at Newcastle, where eight thousand men were waiting for him. Then he led them north and, on 7 September, laid siege to Berwick. Although Lancaster was cooperating with the King in this venture, his support was halfhearted at best—it was commented on that none of his men attempted to scale the walls—and an angry Edward was still bent on destroying him; during the siege, he told the Despensers, "When this wretched business is over, we will turn our hands to other matters. For I have not yet forgotten the wrong that was done to my brother Piers."[186]

Isabella, meanwhile, was staying with her children in "a little rural dwelling near York,"[187] possibly at Brotherton, or at the Archbishop of York's palace at Bishopsthorpe; as both of these houses were more than a hundred miles from the siege, she must have reasoned that she would be safe. But while Edward was at Berwick, the Scots were raiding the north of

England with impunity, and the legendary Black Douglas[188] had penetrated as far as Yorkshire with ten thousand men, having conceived the daring plan of kidnapping the Queen of England and holding her to ransom. "Had the Queen at that time been captured, I believe that Scotland would have bought peace for herself," observed the author of the *Vita Edwardi Secundi*. Indeed, with Isabella held hostage, King Edward would have little choice but to acknowledge Bruce as King of Scots; in fact, he would have had to agree to everything Bruce demanded.

"Douglas marched into England with great secrecy and nearly arrived at the village where Queen Isabella and her children resided." But by great good chance, one of his scouts fell into the hands of William Melton, the saintly Archbishop of York. Threatened with torture, "the man promised him, if they would spare him, to confess the great danger their Queen was in." Melton and his colleagues "laughed his intelligence to scorn, until he staked his life that, if they sent scouts in the direction he pointed out, they would find Douglas and his host within a few hours' march of the Queen's retreat. Alarmed by the proofs given by the man," the Archbishop and John Hotham, the Bishop of Ely, "went forth from the city with their usual retinues and the sheriffs and the burgesses and their followers, the monks and canons and other regulars, as well as anyone else who could handle a weapon." They "marched on a sudden to the Queen's residence with the tidings of her great danger, and brought her back to the city. Thence, for her greater security, she was taken by water to Nottingham,"[189] where she probably sought refuge in the castle.

Then Melton hurriedly gathered together an army of monks and old men and bravely marched to confront the Black Douglas. But they were no match for the Scots and, on 12 September, were savagely defeated at the Battle of Myton-in-Swaledale; because so many clergy were slaughtered, this battle became known as the Chapter of Myton.[190]

If the plot to abduct Isabella was a decoying tactic, it worked, because on 17 September, once news reached the King of how narrowly she had escaped capture, he abandoned the siege of Berwick and hurried back to York, just as the victorious Scots were making their way home unopposed through Lancaster's lands and then north via Westmorland, burning the harvest as they went.[191] On 22 December, Edward had no choice but to make a two-year truce with Bruce.[192] By now, his reputation was in the dust, and from this time forward, according to Robert of Reading, his infamy began to be notorious, not to mention his torpor, his cowardice, and his indifference to his crown and his realm. Again, there was popular speculation that he was a changeling.

The failure of the Scottish campaign led to further bad feeling and angry accusations. The jealous barons pointed the finger at the Younger Despenser as the man who had betrayed the Queen—which is perhaps indicative of ill feeling on his part toward her—but "in his defence," he and his father blamed Lancaster, alleging that Bruce had bribed the Earl to create a diversion by threatening Isabella, a charge that was believed by many.[193] There was no escaping the fact that someone with knowledge of the whereabouts of the King and Queen had passed that information to the Scots. It is hard to see what motive Lancaster or Despenser could have had in sabotaging the siege; nor did Isabella ever accuse Despenser of doing so, even when, later, she had good cause and opportunity. As for Lancaster, "rumour alone was active, and there was no evident crime."[194]

Furthermore, there is evidence that the real culprit was possibly Sir Edmund Darel, "a certain soldier of the King's chamber," who is named as the traitor by both Robert of Reading and the *Annales Paulini*.[195] Darel was a Yorkshire knight who had been in the service of the Percies, and a known opponent of the King. In 1313, he had been arrested as an accessory to Gaveston's murder; in 1322, he would again be apprehended for taking up arms against the King and spend two years in the Tower as punishment.[196] Darel may have been prompted by financial hardship to pass his information to the Scots. We know that he had raided and looted his neighbor's property, which suggests he had fallen on hard times; moreover, there was talk that the Scots had paid large bribes for information leading to the kidnapping of the Queen.[197] The *Annales Paulini* state that, back in May, while Parliament was sitting at York, Darel had been arrested for betraying the Queen, but that he had been released for lack of evidence. The King, however, had dismissed him from his service.[198] This suggests that the plot to capture Isabella had been conceived months earlier and that, angry at his dismissal and still badly in need of money, Darel made a second attempt in September.

Edward spent Christmas that year at York, having invited the scholars of King's Hall to join him. Isabella had rejoined Edward at York by 1 January 1320, for on that day, he gave her expensive gifts, including jewelry.[199] Edward had now finally arranged to go to France to pay homage to Philip V, and the Queen was no doubt looking forward to their trip, for which preparations began early in the New Year;[200] it was six years since she had visited her homeland.

Lancaster now capitalized on Edward's unimpressive showing at Berwick. When Parliament met at York on 20 January, he refused to attend on the grounds that "the King and his associates were suspect by him, and he had openly proclaimed them his enemies."[201] There can be little doubt that he was referring to the Despensers.

Without Lancaster to restrain it, Parliament arranged a reshuffle of offices and promoted members of the court party, men high in the King's favor—and in Despenser's. On 27 January, Robert Baldock, a clerk of the Wardrobe, was appointed Keeper of the Privy Seal. Baldock owed his preferment not so much to his brilliant administrative talents but to the patronage of the Younger Despenser, whose "brain and hand" he was reputed to be.

Walter Stapledon, Bishop of Exeter, was made Treasurer. He was a learned man, who founded Stapledon Hall, later Exeter College, in Oxford, and he was utterly loyal to the King, but he would soon be detested for his extortions and his perceived alignment with the Despensers, to whom he probably owed his appointment as Treasurer. It is clear that Isabella came to hate and distrust Stapledon, and this enmity on her part was in time to have deadly consequences for him.

At the end of January, Edward and Isabella returned to Westminster,[202] whence, in February, they departed for Dover. But having got as far as Canterbury, they suddenly made their way back to London; it seems that Philip had failed to issue a safe-conduct, or it had not arrived.[203]

Around this time, Thomas Cobham, Bishop of Worcester, noticed an improvement in the King's conduct, which was signified by his rising earlier than hitherto in the mornings to face his duties and "respectfully, wisely and with discernment listening patiently to all who wished to speak to him, contrary to his wont."[204] Edward also won praise for banning from his court entertainers who were notorious for their insolence and greed.[205]

The King was apparently feeling the need to get away from all his troubles, for around this time, he began converting a hut or shack within the precincts of Westminster Abbey as a private retreat. The hut was known as "Burgundy," and the King let it be known that he preferred "to be called King of Burgundy" than use "the magnificent titles of his famous royal ancestors."[206]

Edward was back in Kent in March and visited Canterbury on the twelfth.[207] On 24 March, Philip V issued the King and Queen a safe-conduct to travel through France,[208] but again, on 7 April, Edward returned to Westminster.[209]

Edward and Isabella finally sailed to France on 17 June,[210] leaving Pembroke as Keeper of the Realm. The Younger Despenser and Roger d'Amory were in Edward's train, while Pembroke's countess, Beatrice de Clermont, daughter of the Constable of France, was among the Queen's chief attendants; Beatrice was to die that year. The Elder Despenser, Bartholemew de Badlesmere, and Edmund of Woodstock, Earl of Kent, the younger son of Edward I by Marguerite of France, joined the royal entourage in France.[211]

Edward paid homage to Philip before the high altar in Amiens Cathedral on 20 June, and in return, Philip took steps to ensure that the French party in Ponthieu would no longer pose a threat to Isabella's authority there.[212] Philip also promised Edward military aid against Lancaster.[213] During this summit, Isabella presented a petition to her brother on behalf of an English merchant who had asked King Edward to intercede for him. Edward obviously thought that the man stood a better chance of success if the Queen put his request to her brother.[214]

The King and Queen lingered in France for a further month. On 20 July, they attended the consecration of the newly elected Bishop of Lincoln, Henry Burghersh, in Boulogne Cathedral. Burghersh, an avaricious and unscrupulous prelate[215] who was related to both the Mortimers and Bartholemew de Badlesmere, was not yet thirty but was already riding high in the King's favor, thanks to his championing of Edward at the papal court, which had contributed to the Pontiff's releasing the King from his vow to obey the Ordinances; Edward had paid no less than £15,000 in bribes to the Holy See for Burghersh's appointment, which created a scandal and led many to question its legality.[216] Later evidence strongly suggests that Isabella also thought highly of Burghersh.

Two days after the new Bishop's enthronement, the royal couple returned to England[217] and on 2 August made a state entry into London, where they had a warm reception, the Mayor and citizens, in their robes of office, riding out to meet them "in fine style."[218]

September found the Queen at Clarendon and then at her manor of Banstead in Surrey, which she had inherited from Queen Marguerite.[219] The manor house, which had been in royal hands since 1273, was a large timbered building with a tiled roof and stood east of the churchyard, in a hunting park. Isabella ordered repairs to the roof but did little to restore the crumbling walls that enclosed the house.

A new conflict was looming on the horizon.

The Despensers were by now a political force to be reckoned with, and Edward was using them to create a new court party. The younger Hugh had become "the King of England's right eye and his chief counsellor against the earls and barons, but an eyesore to the rest of the kingdom. His every desire became a royal command."[220] He had "gained so much influence over the King and had so moulded his opinions that nothing was done without him, and everything was done by him. The King paid more attention to him than to anyone." More alarmingly, "Sir Hugh and his father wanted to gain supremacy over all the knights and barons of England," and it looked as if they were succeeding in this objective. Unsurprisingly, "bitter hatred and discontent arose between the barons, and the King's council especially, against Sir Hugh le Despenser,"[221] who was, it was said, "even worse than Gaveston."[222] Unlike Gaveston, Despenser understood the nature of the baronial opposition and was ready to champion the King against his enemies, particularly Lancaster.

It is likely, too, that by now, the Queen had also come to regard Despenser as a sinister influence and that relations between her and the new favorites had become strained, for in 1320, the Elder Despenser suddenly ceased paying the Queen the considerable dues owed to her from his manor of Lechlade. It seems he had been infected by the contempt in which his son undoubtedly held Isabella, for up until recently, there had apparently been nothing but goodwill between the Queen and the Elder Despenser; indeed, back in 1312, he had been chosen as one of Prince Edward's godfathers.

Capitalizing on his influential position, and "fired by greed,"[223] Hugh the Younger was concentrating all his formidable efforts on getting his hands on the whole of the Gloucester inheritance and on building up a vast power base in south Wales. In May 1320, he had "deceitfully" wrested Newport and Netherwent from Audley, in return for lesser manors in England.[224] He had also been granted Lundy Island, which gave him control over the Bristol Channel. The Mortimers and the other Marcher lords felt threatened by Despenser's aggrandizement; they realized that he meant to build up a large lordship for himself in what had hitherto been their power base, and they feared that their independence, and even their own lands, were at risk. The Mortimers in particular had good reason to fear Despenser, for a Mortimer had killed his grandfather during the barons' wars of the 1260s, and Despenser, whose family had borne a bitter grudge against the Mortimers ever since, was determined to avenge him.[225] Already, he was doing his aggressive best to appropriate certain estates that had been granted to Roger Mortimer, and he was probably responsible for Roger's recall from Ireland in September.

But the lordship that Despenser now coveted most was Gower, which lay alongside his lands in Glamorgan, and which had recently been purchased by John Mowbray from his penurious father-in-law, William de Braose, whose daughter and heiress was Mowbray's wife. As was the time-honored custom with the Marcher lords, Mowbray did not obtain the King's licence to take possession of Gower, but this omission was exploited by Despenser, who insisted it was illegal and urged Edward to declare the land forfeit and grant it to himself. This was a direct attack on Marcher privileges, but the King did not recognize it as such.[226]

On 26 October, Edward, a willing tool in Despenser's hands, confiscated Gower from John Mowbray, who adamantly refused to surrender it. Furious, Edward sent men to take it from him by force on 14 November. The Marcher lords were outraged, and Hereford formed a confederacy against the Despensers, which included Mowbray, Audley, d'Amory, and the Mortimers; Lancaster also promised his support. Effectively, there now occurred "a great schism" between the King and most of the nobility, all on account of his overweening affection for Despenser.[227] Roger Mortimer was at court at Westminster in November, but by January 1321, having failed to persuade the King to agree to any compromise, he and most of the other Marchers had withdrawn from court and gone home to fortify their castles and rally the rest of the barons. "Deeply moved by [Despenser's] abuse, the barons unanimously decided that [he] must be pursued and utterly destroyed."[228] As Isabella realized that she was once again pregnant, civil war seemed a certainty.

CHAPTER FIVE

The Displeasure of the Queen

On 27 February 1321, the Marchers met with Lancaster, hoping to enlist his support. They were well aware that they now faced an almost impossible choice between rising against their lawful King, which was treason, or countenancing the depradations of the Despensers. There was really no contest, for the latter were proving ruinous to the Marchers and their time-hallowed privileges, and so the Marchers resolved to force the King to dismiss his favorites, as he had Piers Gaveston.[1] Lancaster agreed with them that the best way forward would be to mount an offensive on the Despenser lands in south Wales.

The King, warned by Despenser, had anticipated this, and on 1 March, at Westminster, began mobilizing troops and gave orders that all the royal castles in Wales be prepared for war. By so closely identifying himself with the Despensers' interests, he was effectively placing the fundamentally royalist Marchers in open rebellion against the Crown, making reluctant traitors of most of them and losing the support of other barons who also resented the influence of the favorites. On 27 March, and again on 13 April, the King commanded all his subjects to keep the peace and forbade any assemblies.[2] The next day, he summoned the Marcher lords to convene at Gloucester on 5 April.[3] But Hereford and Mortimer refused to come into the King's presence while the Younger Despenser remained in his company and demanded that Hugh be placed in Lancaster's custody while their grievances were aired in Parliament. Edward refused to listen. Three days later, he confiscated Audley's estates in the Marches.

Isabella herself was known to be no friend to the Despensers; her support was enlisted at this time in a dispute in which they had involved themselves. This quarrel, between the Abbot of Saint Albans and his subordinate, William de Somerton, Prior of the abbey's cell at Binham in Norfolk, was in itself relatively unimportant—that is, until the Abbot called upon Despenser to support him. Resorting to his usual brutal methods, Despenser dispatched his men to arrest Somerton and drag him to the Abbot, who summarily cast him in jail. Some of the Marchers eager to discredit Despenser, notably Mowbray and Mortimer, now appealed to the Queen to intervene with the King in order to secure Somerton's release. Clearly, Isabella was ready and willing to defy the favorites, and so persuasive was she that Edward granted her request—much to the annoyance of the Despensers, who must have added another notch in their reckoning against Isabella.[4]

Yet whatever she might have felt about the Despensers, Isabella's loyalties at this time lay firmly with the King. Certainly, she had no sympathy for Lancaster, and she may even have come to regard the Marchers' hostility to Despenser as an attack on the King, as did Edward himself. On 20 April, in demonstration of her loyalty, Isabella turned over her castle at Marlborough to the Elder Despenser; at Easter, she appointed a prominent royalist, John de Trejagu, to her shrievalty of Cornwall; then, on 3 May, she put her castle at Devizes in the custody of another of Edward's supporters, Oliver de Ingham.[5]

The King had now raised a strong force and marched westward, reaching Bristol by Easter. From here, he issued a further summons to the Marchers to meet with him on 10 May. On 1 May, as they took up battle stations, he warned them not to attack the Despensers.[6] But they paid him no heed and, on 4 May, launched a devastating attack on the Despenser lands. By 12 May, Newport, Cardiff, and Caerphilly had fallen to Mortimer and the vast Marcher army, which thereafter swept across Glamorgan and Gloucestershire, seizing castles, burning, looting, destroying crops, and leaving in its wake a trail of devastation.[7] Having accomplished their objective, the Marchers then rode north to meet once more with Lancaster.

On 24 May, Lancaster held what was effectively a private parliament at Pontefract. The result was an alliance between the Earl and the Marchers, who all swore to defend their own lands and one another's.[8] This was followed by a baronial convention at Sherburn-in-Elmet on 28 June, at which the rebels—henceforth to be known as the "contrariants"—were loud in their condemnation of the Despensers and swore to see them disinherited.[9]

Edward, meanwhile, had returned to London. The Queen was now nearing her confinement, and for safety, it was decided that her child should be born in the Tower of London, which was committed to her custody on 14 June. That the King should place such a strategically crucial fortress in her care is a measure of his trust. On 5 July (or a week or so later), Isabella bore a second daughter, Joan, in the palace within the fortress.[10] The Queen's apartments there were in a sad state of disrepair, and as Isabella lay in labor, rain dripped through the ceiling, soaking the bedclothes. When this was reported afterward to the King, he reacted furiously and instantly dismissed the constable, John, Lord Cromwell, from his post.[11]

On 14 July, as a further mark of trust, the Great Seal was entrusted to the joint custody of the Queen (who was still recovering from her confinement in the Tower), William Airmyn, and Roger de Northburgh,[12] two prominent royal clerks.

The next day, Parliament met at Westminster.

The King had done little to counteract the threat from the contrariants, and Mortimer was now marching on London with an armed force clad in green livery bearing the royal arms, underlining their loyalty to the King.[13] Mortimer was at Saint Albans on 22 July, and on the twenty-ninth, he left Waltham with the intention of entering London and forcing the expulsion of the Despensers. Finding that the citizens had closed their gates to him, he ordered his men to surround the walls with a ring of steel, effectively placing under siege the Tower, where Isabella lay with her newborn infant.

By 1 August, Lancaster and other aggrieved barons had joined Mortimer, and all demanded that the King hear their complaints concerning the Despensers. They cited eleven articles against them, accusing them among other things of usurping the royal authority, inciting civil war, perverting justice, barring the magnates from the King's presence, committing acts of violence and fraud, and alienating the King from his people. If Edward did not banish the favorites, they warned, they would renounce their homage and set up another in his place.[14] Notwithstanding this, Edward stubbornly refused to accede to their demands, and Despenser sailed menacingly up and down the Thames in a borrowed ship, only stopping when the barons threatened to burn to the ground all the royal buildings between Charing Cross and Westminster Abbey.

Isabella had left the Tower by 24 July but was still in London on that date.[15] She, Airmyn, and Northburgh retained custody of the Great Seal until at least 24 August.

Pembroke, meanwhile, had just returned from Paris, where he had married Marie de Châtillon, daughter of Guy IV, Count of Saint Pol by Mary of Brittany, a granddaughter of Henry III. Count Guy's half sister, Blanche of Artois, was Isabella's grandmother, so the Queen and Marie were cousins; they were also related through Marie's sister, Matilda, who had married Charles, Count of Valois, Isabella's uncle. Not surprisingly, Isabella and Marie soon became close friends. A well-educated woman and a great patron of letters, the Countess Marie was to found Pembroke College at Cambridge in 1347.

On 1 August, the King, panicking at the barons' demands, summoned Pembroke to Westminster; the Earl arrived the next day, met first with Edward and subsequently with the Marchers, then did his best to persuade the King to agree to the Marchers' demands. But the King would not hear of it.[16]

Then Pembroke suggested that the Queen intervene in the hope of achieving a settlement; she had been so successful in the past that she had now earned a reputation as a peacemaker.[17] Isabella was willing to do her best, and, supported by Pembroke, Richmond, and the bishops, she went to the King and "begged on her knees for the people's sake" that he would show mercy to his subjects by banishing the Despensers and making peace with his lords.[18] It was now that Pembroke warned Edward, "He perishes on the rocks that loves another more than himself."[19] The Queen's intervention allowed the King to capitulate to his opponents without too much loss of face, and at length, on 14 August, he reluctantly summoned the Marchers to Westminster Hall and icily informed them that he had agreed to send away his favorites within the month. Five days later, the Despensers were sentenced to exile and forfeiture and forbidden to return to England without the consent of Parliament. On the following day, 20 August, pardons were issued to Lancaster, the Mortimers, and the other Marcher lords who had risen against the King.[20]

"Reluctantly," the Despensers "left their native soil and splendour." The Elder Hugh went first to Flanders, thence to Bordeaux, while his son embarked upon a successful career as a pirate in the English Channel, where he became a sea monster, lying in wait for the merchants as they crossed his path. He was master of the seas, their merchandise, and chattels, and no ship got through unharmed. His greatest prize was a Genoese ship; having boarded it, he slew its crew and stole more than £5,000 worth of treasure.[21] Many years later, King Edward III had to repay that amount, with interest, in compensation to the owners of the vessel.[22]

Edward had no intention of being parted from the Despensers for long and was resolved to be revenged on those barons who had forced him to have them exiled.[23] With a cunning scheme in mind, he went to Rochester on 30 August and to Gravesend by 19 September. Some sources claim that he and Isabella then went on yet another pilgrimage to Canterbury, but this is unlikely, since the city was packed with the armed retainers of the powerful Kentish baron, Lord Badlesmere, and Badlesmere, despite being steward of the royal household, had recently thrown in his lot with Lancaster and the Marchers; his daughter Elizabeth was married to Mortimer's heir, Edmund. It is almost certain that the King was in contact with Despenser at this time, because he and Isabella met with him when the latter's ship put in at the Isle of Thanet later in September.[24]

When Edward returned to London on 23 September and lodged in the Tower, Isabella was probably with him. But then, on 1 October, Edward went to Sheen, then on to Byfleet in Surrey the next day,[25] and Isabella traveled back to Kent, ostensibly on yet another pilgrimage to Canterbury. However, the real purpose of her journey seems to have been to force a confrontation with Badlesmere. Badlesmere's chief seat was at Leeds Castle, which until 1318 had formed part of the dower of the queens of England, having been the favored residence of Eleanor of Castile and Marguerite of France. But on Marguerite's death, notwithstanding the fact that the reversion of the castle had been promised in 1314 to Isabella, the King granted Leeds to Badlesmere in return for the manor of Adderley in Shropshire.[26]

But Badlesmere was now a marked man, having angered the King by supporting his enemies, and in September, he had prepared all his castles for war and stored his treasure for safety at Leeds, which he placed in the care of his wife, Margaret de Clare.[27] Clearly, he was expecting an attack. In sending Isabella to Leeds at this time, Edward was almost certainly springing a trap for Badlesmere, a trap he may well have plotted with Despenser during their meeting at Thanet. Its purpose was to provide a just cause for the King to move against the contrariants.[28]

On 2 October,[29] Isabella approached Leeds Castle and told her retinue that she purposed to rest there for a night. Accordingly, her harbingers and purveyors were sent ahead to make the necessary arrangements. They found, however, that Badlesmere was away and that his wife was in charge of the castle. Understandably, Lady Badlesmere was alarmed, for if the Queen were indeed on a pilgrimage to Canterbury, she had gone consider-

ably out of her way to visit Leeds, since the usual route was through northern Kent;[30] moreover, she had brought with her a military escort. So Lady
Badlesmere told the Queen's officers that her husband had left her strict
instructions not to allow anyone to enter the castle and "insolently" suggested "that the Queen might seek some other lodging, for she would not
admit anyone within the castle without an order from her lord."

The shocked harbingers rode back to Isabella to inform her of the position, and, indignant at what she was pleased to call treason, she insisted on
confronting Lady Badlesmere herself. But when the Queen and her retinue
drew up before Leeds Castle, Lady Badlesmere remained obdurate, and
when Isabella instructed her marshals to force an entry into the castle, Lady
Badlesmere ordered the archers of the garrison to open fire on them. Six
men fell dead before Isabella's appalled eyes, and the Queen prudently
retired to seek shelter in a nearby priory.[31] She had no doubt expected some
opposition, but nothing as violent and contemptuous as what she had just
witnessed, and her anger was genuine.

On 3 October, Isabella sent an urgent and indignant message to Edward,
now at Witley, complaining bitterly about the affront to her dignity, asking
him to send soldiers to her assistance, and begging him to avenge the murder
of her servants and punish Lady Badlesmere for her defiance of all the laws of
courtesy and hospitality.[32] The King must have been secretly delighted at the
outcome of his little scheme but nevertheless showed himself incandescent
at such an outrageous slight to "his beloved consort," using it as a pretext to
take up arms against Badlesmere, which he almost certainly intended as a
preliminary to netting the bigger fish.

On 4 October, Edward moved to Portchester for a second clandestine
meeting with Despenser. Then, on the seventh and eighth, the King began
to hire mercenaries and ordered "a general muster of all persons between
the ages of sixteen and sixty." After nine days at Portchester, he was back at
the Tower by 14 October.[33]

Edward had written to Badlesmere, complaining of his wife's conduct,
and Badlesmere played right into Edward's hands when he sent an insulting
letter in reply, declaring he "approved of this misconduct of his family in
thus obstructing and contumeliously treating the Queen."[34] On 16 October,
the King declared that he would make an example of Badlesmere, and the
very next day, he sent Pembroke at the head of the vast army he had summoned to lay siege to Leeds Castle, "to punish the disobedience and contempt against the Queen committed by certain members of the household
of Bartholemew de Badlesmere."[35] Lady Badlesmere, realizing that she

could not withstand a siege for long, sent a frantic message to her husband, who had by now joined the retiring Marcher forces at Oxford.

By 23 October, the day Pembroke drew up his forces before Leeds, Isabella had moved to Rochester, where, jointly with William Airmyn, she was again given custody of the Great Seal.[36] Meanwhile, at Badlesmere's urging, Mortimer and Hereford had marched south, aiming to relieve Leeds. In so doing, they were placing themselves in direct opposition to the King, which would prove a fatal mistake. By 27 October, their army had reached Kingston-upon-Thames,[37] where Pembroke came to persuade them not to advance into Kent. Then they received a message from Lancaster, who had had no time for Badlesmere since he had been made steward of the household against Lancaster's will; he made it clear that he did not approve of Mortimer and Hereford's going to Badlesmere's aid.[38] The Marchers therefore stayed at Kingston, waiting upon events. Two chroniclers claim that they had refused to go to the relief of Leeds out of respect for the Queen.[39] Yet, at Badlesmere's entreaty, they tried to mediate with the King on his behalf. Edward, however, refused to heed their pleas.

In avenging the insult to his popular Queen, the King had stirred up a great deal of public support; many barons, including Arundel, Richmond, Surrey, and the King's half brothers, Thomas of Brotherton, Earl of Norfolk, and Edmund of Woodstock, Earl of Kent, had hastened to join Pembroke before Leeds Castle, as had many Londoners, for Isabella had always been highly regarded in the capital. The besieging forces now numbered thirty thousand. Heartened by this sudden surge of support, the King went personally to take charge of the siege.[40]

Leeds finally surrendered to the King on 31 October. Edward exacted a savage vengeance: ignoring their pleas for mercy, he summarily hanged the constable of the castle and thirteen of his men before the castle gates. Lady Badlesmere and her children (among whom was the young wife of Mortimer's son), along with Badlesmere's sister and her son, Bartholemew, Lord Burghersh (whose brother Henry was the Bishop of Lincoln), were all taken prisoner and sent first to Dover Castle, and thence to the Tower of London, the first women to be held in custody there.[41] The King was determined to make an example of them all, "so that no one in future would dare to hold fortresses against him."[42]

Although many at the time applauded his punitive measures, his first successful military operation since his accession, these punishments in fact mark the beginning of Edward II's tyranny. No longer could he be dismissed as a weak and inept apology for a king, for he had made it terrify-

ingly clear that any person who rebelled against him or defied him might
not just suffer imprisonment or a fine, as before, but might lose his life as
well as his goods and have his womenfolk and kinsmen clapped into jail—
and all without proper process of law. The seeds of political violence sown
with the murder of Gaveston were bearing a bitter harvest, one that would
set precedents for the centuries to come.

Isabella left Rochester on 4 November and joined her victorious husband at
Tonbridge Castle, where she surrendered the Great Seal into his custody.
The King had brought with him provisions that he had seized from Leeds
Castle and gave them to Isabella, as compensation for her ordeal there.[43] It
appears that he also gave her Leeds Castle itself, which had now reverted to
the Crown. Although there is no record of any grant of it to Isabella before
1327, a roll of her receiver's receipts for Easter 1322 records that victuals in
Leeds Castle were sold by the Queen's command,[44] which suggests that the
castle was in her possession. The royal couple returned to Westminster on
the ninth.[45] That month, with the terrifying example of Leeds before them,
all Badlesmere's castles surrendered to the King.[46]

    Knowing he now occupied a strong position, Edward was determined to
press home his advantage and reclaim his royal prerogative. To achieve this,
he was determined to deal once and for all with the Marchers and Lancaster. After learning what had happened at Leeds, Mortimer and Hereford
had fled north to meet with Lancaster, knowing that "the King was a man
without mercy, and would destroy them."[47] On 29 November, Lancaster
held another private parliament, this time at Doncaster, which Mortimer
and Hereford attended, in defiance of an order from the King. Here, Lancaster assured them of his support in their quarrel with Edward and the
Despensers.

In light of the events just recounted, the assertions of Agnes Strickland and
Denholm-Young[48] that Isabella began an affair with Roger Mortimer in the
autumn of 1321 are incredible. Mortimer was in opposition to the King
throughout most of this period, and Isabella was loyally supporting her
husband against both Lancaster and the Marchers. It is also hard to see what
opportunities the Queen and Mortimer could have had to conduct such an
affair, since he did not attend court other than in a confrontational role.
There is no evidence that either had any special regard for the other at this
time.

    Strickland's whole theory is based on her misdating the birth of Princess
Joan to 1322, when Mortimer was in the Tower of London. She asserts that

PHILIP IV OF FRANCE WITH HIS CHILDREN AND HIS BROTHER, CHARLES OF VALOIS
Isabella *(third from left)* was born into the most illustrious royal house in Europe.

JEANNE OF NAVARRE
Isabella's mother was a dignified and
pious woman who twice defended
her own territories with great vigor.

ISABELLA OF FRANCE
"One of the fairest ladies in the world"
and "the fairest of the fair."

PHILIP IV
"He is neither a man nor a beast,
but a statue."

LOUIS X
He was a frivolous young man with
little interest in government.

PHILIP V
He was another such as his father,
handsome, intelligent, and ruthless.

CHARLES IV
A clever and subtle man, he could be
severe to those who opposed him.

THE WEDDING OF EDWARD II AND ISABELLA OF FRANCE, 1308
Although Edward's good looks cannot have failed to make a good impression on
his young bride, it is unlikely that the marriage was consummated at this time.

EDWARD II

Edward did not personify contemporary ideals of kingship: he didn't even seem
to want to be king and cared little for his royal duties.

EDWARD II

Edward's "excessive love" for Piers
Gaveston "surpassed the love of
women," and he was accused by
a contemporary of desiring
"wicked and forbidden sex."

ISABELLA OF FRANCE
"A most elegant lady, and a
very beautiful woman."

ISABELLA OF FRANCE
The Queen was "all that is prudent,
amiable and feminine."

ISABELLA OF FRANCE
Isabella proved herself to be a capable
woman of above average ability and
soon gained a reputation
as a peacemaker.

MARGUERITE OF FRANCE
Isabella's aunt was "good withouten lack," yet her frequent absences from court deprived the young Isabella of the support she so badly needed.

CHARLES IV WELCOMES ISABELLA TO PARIS, 1325
"We will find some remedy for your condition," Charles assured his desperate sister.

ISABELLA SAILS WITH HER INVASION FLEET TO ENGLAND, 1326
"God was merciful and helped them. He altered their course by a miracle."

toft ke menees en hollande =
zeellande · A moult grant
messause passa la royne et sa
plente · Car moult trouuerct
le pape riche et bien pourueu
pour tant que riens neftoit

ISABELLA RIDES WITH ROGER MORTIMER TO OXFORD, 1326
Wherever the Queen went, "she found favour with all."

ISABELLA ARRIVES
AT BRISTOL, 1326
"When the people of the
town saw that almost all
England was on her side,"
they "joyfully" opened
their gates.

Isabella's enmity toward the Despensers was on account of their hostility toward Roger Mortimer and that it was her love for Roger that came to alienate the King. Neither claim is supported by the facts, as we will shortly see.

Capitalizing on his new ascendancy, Edward persuaded his friend Archbishop Reynolds to summon a convocation of the clergy to Saint Paul's Cathedral on 1 December and formally annul the sentence of banishment on the Despensers, on the grounds that it had not had the unanimous support of the bishops.[49]

In the absence of the Mortimers, the Welsh, who hated their oppressive rule, had taken up arms against them. Now the King gave orders for his levies to meet with him at Cirencester on 13 December, ready to march on the lands of those contrariants who were still in open opposition. At the beginning of December, Mortimer and Hereford hurriedly returned to their estates, prepared to defend them.

Edward was displaying unwonted energy and decisiveness. On 8 December, armed with Reynolds's decree of nullity, he invited the Despensers to return to England under his protection. At the same time, Lancaster was doing his best to undermine the King's support in London, sending the citizens a copy of the so-called Doncaster Petition, in which Edward's perfidy in supporting Despenser in acts of piracy was spelled out for all to see, and Lancaster himself was portrayed as a second Simon de Montfort, a guardian of the public interest whose sole objective was to rid the realm of the evil influence of the favorites.[50]

During this tense period, the Queen had been lodging in the Tower,[51] but by 10 December, she had joined the King at Langley. On that date, Edward commanded his Treasurer to "provide sixteen pieces of cloth for the apparel of ourselves and our dear companion, also furs against the next feast of Christmas, and thirteen pieces of cloth for corsets for our said companion and her damsels, with napery."

Edward summoned more troops on 13 December, unaware that Lancaster had now resorted to treason. The Earl was actively seeking the aid of England's archenemy, Robert the Bruce, against his lawful sovereign; proof of this is to be found in the safe-conduct granted to his messenger by the Black Douglas on 16 December.

Accompanied by his half brothers, Norfolk and Kent—"both active soldiers, considering their youth"—the King and his forces now chased after the Marchers, reaching Cirencester by Christmas;[52] Isabella appears to have stayed behind to keep the festival at Langley. On 31 December, Edward was at Worcester, planning to cross the Severn there and force a confrontation with the Marchers, who had retreated beyond the river; but the rebels had burned the bridge. The same thing happened on 5 January at Bridgnorth, where the King was prevented from crossing the great river.[53] As he moved north, the Marchers panicked, and men began deserting in droves. Mortimer's only hope now was that Lancaster would come to relieve them; but for all his assurances of support, Lancaster was conspicuous by his absence, having deliberately remained holed up in Pontefract. On 14 January, the King crossed the Severn at Shrewsbury, and for the Marchers, all was lost. The next day, Edward ordered the arrest of the Mortimers. He had already issued a safe-conduct so that they could come to him in safety.[54]

From Pontefract, Lancaster had continued to treat with the Scots; his emissary received a further safe-conduct from them on 15 January, and the Earl was still negotiating with Bruce during February, using the pseudonym "King Arthur," and thus investing himself not only with a royal identity but also with the qualities of the legendary hero.[55] Before long, he was joined by Hereford, who had managed to flee from the path of the vengeful King Edward, who had to be content with seizing his lands and those of Audley and d'Amory.[56]

For the Mortimers, however, there was no escape. They did their best to make terms with Edward, but he would promise nothing. They had committed treason by rising in arms against him and in defying his commands and supporting his enemies; what did they expect? The only concession he made was twice to extend their safe-conducts, until 20 and 21 January.[57] On that latter date, when the Mortimers failed to appear, Pembroke stepped in as a mediator, rashly taking it upon himself to assure them that, if they submitted, their lives would be spared and they would be pardoned. Realizing they had no choice, uncle and nephew came to Shrewsbury on 22 January and surrendered to the King. But instead of receiving clemency at his hands, they were put in chains and cast into jail.[58]

Edward now took a sweeping revenge on the Mortimers. On that same day, he confiscated all their lands and property, and the next day, he ordered the arrest of Lady Mortimer, who was imprisoned in Hampshire.[59] Her husband and Chirk were taken to the Tower of London on 13 February.[60] A Hainault chronicle, the *Chronographia Regum Francorum,* claims that they were sent there because Despenser had planted suspicions in Edward's mind that the Queen and Mortimer had become involved in a clandestine liaison, but this was written later with the benefit of hindsight, and no other chronicler mentions it; and if the King had thought that his wife had betrayed him with his enemy, he would surely have punished her for it, given his vengeful mood at this time.

The sons of Mortimer and Hereford were also apprehended and confined at Windsor, and Mortimer's three unmarried daughters were incarcerated in different nunneries, while his mother, loudly protesting, was stripped of some of her property.[61] After this, as the King moved southward, castle after castle fell to him, the last being Berkeley in Gloucestershire. Its owner, Thomas, Lord Berkeley, was cast into prison at Wallingford with his son Maurice,[62] who was married to Mortimer's daughter Margaret; both had sided with the Marchers. Berkeley's lands were later given to Despenser.

By then, the Despensers were back in England. On 22 January, Edward had appealed to Philip V to support him in the matter of their recall,[63] not knowing that Philip had died on 3 January and, leaving only daughters, been succeeded by his brother, Charles IV, the last surviving brother of Isabella. Charles was crowned at Rheims on 21 February and soon afterward had his ill-fated union to Blanche of Burgundy annulled; in September, he married Marie of Luxembourg, who bore him two daughters in rapid succession.

Although the Despensers had returned in secret in the middle of January,[64] the King did not issue the official writ sanctioning their return until 11 February. Inspired by his success against the Marchers, and encouraged by his favorites, who were urging him to use force to repress the power of the barons,[65] and also by Isabella, who was deeply offended by the failure of Lancaster and his allies to support the King against Badlesmere, Edward now resolved to make an end of Lancaster. At the end of February, he ordered a general muster of men at Coventry, ostensibly "for the Scots"; but when they were assembled, he marched north in pursuit of Lancaster, crossing the Trent before 10 March and taking the Earl's castle of Tutbury, where evidence of Lancaster's dealings with Bruce was discovered, along with Roger d'Amory, who was hiding in the castle, badly wounded. He was tried and condemned to death, yet "because the King loved him much," he was reprieved. However, he died three days later.

As Edward was ransacking Tutbury, a detachment of the royal forces defeated Lancaster's army at Burton-on-Trent. On 12 March, the Earl was publicly proclaimed a rebel, and the King gave orders that he and his adherents were to be hunted down. Lancaster fled north, probably hoping to seek sanctuary in Scotland or to take refuge in his castle at Dunstanburgh. But he was trapped at Boroughbridge between the royal army and a force led by Andrew Harclay, the Sheriff of Westmorland, who had gained a heroic reputation fighting the Scots. According to Robert of Reading, Queen Isabella had personally sent messages to Harclay, and to Simon Ward, the Sheriff of Yorkshire, urging them to move southward in order to prevent Lancaster from penetrating farther north. Both responded with alacrity. The Queen also had supplies for the King sent to York and Carlisle, in case he might need them.

The battle of Boroughbridge took place on 16 March. Lancaster's men deserted in droves. An unhorsed Hereford was mortally wounded by a pike thrust from below that pierced him "through the fundament" as he raced across the bridge that spanned the River Ure; it was not "the custom of knights to protect their private parts," and he died horribly with his bowels hanging out.[66] An overnight truce was arranged, but the next day, knowing that it was fruitless to offer further resistance, Lancaster surrendered to the King, who was now determined finally to avenge the murder of Piers Gaveston.

The disgraced Earl was taken in manacles to his own castle at Pontefract, and there, on 20 March, in the great hall, tried as a rebel under martial law before the King and several magnates, including the Elder Despenser. He was not permitted to speak in his own defense, since, ten years before, he had not permitted Gaveston to do so.[67] The lords found him guilty of treason,[68] and he was sentenced to be hanged, drawn, and quartered as a traitor, but in consideration of his royal blood, the King commuted the sentence to beheading. *The Brut* claims that this was at the intercession of the Queen, but Isabella was in London at this time, lodged in the Tower, and it would have been impossible for her to have received news of Lancaster's capture and then got a message back to the King in three days. It took four days for a fast messenger to ride from London to York.

Few had anticipated that Edward would go so far as to put Lancaster to death; not only was the Earl his kinsman, but no English nobleman been executed for treason since the time of William the Conqueror. But as far as the King was concerned, death was the only fitting penalty for the man who had ordered Gaveston's murder, a death that would in many respects mirror Gaveston's own.[69]

"Violent deeds bring their own punishment," observed one of Lancaster's critics. On 22 March, in the midst of a snowstorm, the once proud Earl, now wearing the somber robes of a penitent and a tattered old hat, was led trembling out of the castle on a "worthless mule" to Saint Thomas's Hill, a mound about a mile off, and forced to pass through a jeering mob, which flung stones, offal, and handfuls of snow at him. At the place of execution, he was made to kneel facing in the direction of Scotland, whence he had so treacherously appealed for aid. After his head had been roughly hacked off "with two or three strokes," it was shown to the King, then buried with his body in Saint John's Priory at Pontefract.[70]

With Lancaster dead, Edward was now free to rule without opposition. He exacted a bloody and unprecedented vengeance on those who had supported Lancaster and, in so doing, made a clean sweep of all his enemies. On 22 March, twenty-four of the Earl's followers were executed in various places; the next day, a further six were drawn and hanged at York. Others were hunted down and slaughtered. The bodies were quartered, and the quarters exhibited in public places all over the land for the next two years.[71] On 14 April, Badlesmere, who had been discovered hiding in the house of his nephew, Bishop Burghersh, at Stow Park, was hanged and beheaded at Canterbury.[72] The King's wrath extended even to Lancaster's estranged wife, Alice de Lacy, and her elderly mother, the Dowager Countess of Lincoln, both of whom he committed to jail.[73] In all, 118 persons, many of them barons and knights, suffered execution, rigorous imprisonment, or exile, and many more faced crippling fines.

Nor did Henry Burghersh, Bishop of Lincoln, escape the King's vengeance. Edward felt Burghersh had betrayed his trust and favor by harboring Badlesmere and seized his temporalities—the financial and material mainstays of his episcopal office. He also wrote several letters exhorting the Pope to depose him from his see. But the Pope refused, protesting that it was unreasonable to ask him to visit unproven offenses with severe penalties.[74]

The chroniclers, like most of the King's subjects, were horrified. "Oh calamity!" cried the author of the *Vita Edwardi Secundi*. "To see men, so recently clothed in purple and fine linen, now tied in rags, bound and imprisoned in chains. The harshness of the King has increased so much that no one, however great or wise, dares to cross his will. The nobles of the realm are terrified by threats and penalties. The King's will has free play. Thus today might conquers reason, for whatever pleases the King, though lacking in reason, has the force of law." The Pope begged the King to desist from his tyrannical course, but he refused to listen. Of those apprehended, only fifteen men escaped punishment. Andrew Harclay's loyalty was well rewarded: on 25 March, the King created him Earl of Carlisle.[75]

After Lancaster's execution, Edward stayed at Pontefract, having summoned Isabella to join him there.[76] She had been kept well informed about the judicial bloodbath that was taking place, and when she arrived, she did her best to mitigate the King's savagery. One rebel for whom she successfully interceded was Bewes, Lord Knovill, whose wife, Joan, had petitioned

the Queen for her help: he was allowed to save his life and his lands on payment of a huge fine and later received a pardon.[77] But Edward was rarely as
willing to be merciful, while Despenser certainly resented Isabella's intervention, and "when he saw the displeasure of the Queen," he deliberately
continued to encourage the King in his bloody reprisals.[78]

In May, Isabella and Edward arrived at York, where the Parliament that
would finally repeal the Ordinances as prejudicial to the Crown met on
the second.[79] That the Queen had proved loyal and supportive throughout
the rebellion and its aftermath, despite her undoubted antipathy toward the
Despensers, is evident from her letters to Harclay and Ward, and another
that she wrote to Pope John around April, vigorously condemning Lancaster's actions.[80] Yet she was shocked by the Earl's execution; he was, after
all, her uncle and of royal blood. Even though she herself had urged
Edward to rise against him, she blamed Despenser for his death,[81] for which
he "earned the deep hatred of the whole country, and especially of the
Queen."[82] "Small wonder if [the Queen] does not like Hugh, through
whom her uncle perished," observed the author of the *Vita Edwardi
Secundi*. Not only did Isabella blame Despenser for the ignominious
butchering of her kinsman, but she must also have considered him responsible for a deed that had undermined the very fabric of monarchy and set a
dangerous precedent.

Now Parliament had without a quibble finally repealed the Ordinances
that Lancaster had forced on Edward, and whatever her feelings about Lancaster's execution, Isabella must have rejoiced to see her husband restored
to his proper authority.

Yet there was a price for this, to be exacted not only from Edward's subjects but also in time from Isabella herself. That price would be the breakdown of her marriage and all its tumultuous consequences, which were
directly attributable to the Despensers' influence over the King. "From that
time on," says Higden, "the power of the Despensers began to increase,
and the power of the Queen decreased."

The creation of the Elder Despenser as Earl of Winchester on 10 May
signals the beginning of the tyranny of the favorites; henceforth, they ruled
the King with scant regard for law or justice and were firmly in control of
both state affairs and royal patronage—or out of control, as many feared.
The King's recent purges had left all their chief opponents either dead or in
prison, and of the remaining magnates, not one was strong enough to
oppose them or curb their power. Even Pembroke was unable to keep them
in check: not only was he ailing, but Edward was aggrieved with him for

urging the Despensers' exile and had made him pledge his body, land, and goods to obey the King and not ally with anyone against him;[83] consequently, Pembroke was slavishly lending his support to the new regime.

From now on, "King Edward II truly governed his country with great cruelty and injustice, by the advice of Sir Hugh le Despenser."[84] He might have ennobled the father, but it was the son who came to dominate the King. Edward began by showering the younger Hugh with many large grants and most of the confiscated lands and honors of the contrariants, including those of d'Amory and Audley, which effectively made him the unopposed ruler of South Wales.[85] Thereafter, the Younger Despenser was to appropriate everything he could lay his hands on, exploiting the King's generosity, intimidating people into selling him property at vastly reduced prices, and extorting cash from his victims by violence, bullying tactics, outright fraud, and cunning manipulation of the machinery of law. By such unscrupulous methods, he built up a vast landed estate and a huge fortune that rivaled even that of the late Earl of Lancaster.[86] This was all done with the full cooperation and the blessing of the King, and it would not be too much of an exaggeration to say that, between them, Edward and Despenser subjected the country to a reign of terror. As Hugh grew ever more rapacious and oppressive, his arrogance became more and more insufferable. He was far cleverer, and much more vicious, than Piers Gaveston.

Despenser's ruthless brutality extended even to women. It was probably he who had prompted Edward's harshness toward Mortimer's wife, mother, and daughters. He himself had imprisoned the wife and children of the Welsh rebel Llywelyn Bren, and in 1326, he was accused of having committed extortion and violent crimes against the widows and children of executed Lancastrians.[87] He intimidated his sister-in-law, Elizabeth de Clare, d'Amory's widow, into giving him Usk in return for the lesser lordship of Gower and then persuaded Edward to confiscate Gower, thus effectively dispossessing Elizabeth of her rightful inheritance. Later on, Despenser harassed Pembroke's widow, the friend of the Queen, in a similar manner, extorting from her £20,000 as well as lands and livestock, and forcing her to sell him the latter at a grossly debased price. He kidnapped a wealthy heiress, Elizabeth Comyn, and held her hostage for a year until she signed over £10,000 and two valuable estates to him. Eager to get his hands on more knights' fees, castles, and manors, Despenser persecuted Lancaster's widow, Alice de Lacy, accusing her of being the chief cause of her husband's execution and threatening to have her burned alive, which was the penalty for murdering a husband. In terror, she handed over her lands and also paid a massive fine, of £20,000.[88] Then there was Elizabeth Talbot, a widow who was forced by Despenser to surrender her manor of Painswick, Gloucester-shire, and other lands to him. He even had another widow, Lady Baret, tortured so that her four limbs were broken and her other injuries were so horrific that she went insane.[89] It seemed that Despenser took a perverted pleasure in seeing his victims crushed. Isabella may well have been behind the accusations against the Despensers made in 1326, which suggests that she was revolted by his cruelty to innocent women and children.

The Despensers made many enemies. Of the Younger Hugh, it was said, "The whole land has turned to hatred of him, and few would mourn his downfall."[90] People grumbled that one king was bad enough, but three were intolerable. The fateful result of the Despensers' tyrannical ascendancy was a gradual erosion of sympathy for the King, who did little to check their excesses, and whose wishes no one now dared withstand.[91]

There is no denying, however, that the Despensers were both able and efficient administrators. They solved the King's financial problems by introducing innovative fiscal reforms and made him very rich—it was soon said that, although many of his forefathers had amassed money, "he alone exceeded them all."[92] In collaboration with their staunch allies and clients Robert Baldock, who was Keeper of the Privy Seal from 1320 and Chancellor from August 1323, and Walter Stapledon, Bishop of Exeter, who was Treasurer, they brought about significant reforms in the Chancery and the Wardrobe, and reorganized the Exchequer records. The Despensers also boosted the wool trade by instituting a series of staples, or markets, in England, so that merchants did not have to go abroad to buy wool for export. However, their motive behind this was not concern for the prosperity of the realm but to raise the King's revenues.[93]

There can be little doubt that the Despensers resented the Queen's influence over Edward; they knew she had been instrumental in securing their exile and the release of William Somerton. The Younger Hugh may have been jealous of her in a sexual sense, but the overriding perception of both father and son was surely that Isabella was the one remaining threat to their political dominance and must be neutralized. We have seen that relations between the Queen and the favorites had been strained since 1320, when the Elder Hugh had failed to pay her her dues, and they must now have all but broken down when, in July 1322, the Younger Despenser suddenly ceased paying her the £200 he owed her annually out of the farm of Bristol. From now on, neither would pay Isabella the rents due to her nor enter into any recognizance for the payment of arrears.[94] They also ensured that her castles at Marlborough and Devizes were not returned to her. To a queen who was jealous of her financial privileges, this was a most potent slight, leaving her in no doubt as to where she stood with the favorites. Furthermore, it was clear that she stood alone, for there was no one left to act as her champion, and it had become starkly manifest how ruthless the Despensers could be and how far the King had fallen in thrall to them. Yet Isabella was not one to be easily intimidated. She dissembled, put on a smiling face toward the favorites, and quietly set about undermining them.

Despenser had a blood feud to settle—he had vowed to despoil Mortimer and "revenge the death of his grandfather upon him,"[95] and encouraged by him, Edward now dealt with the Mortimers. The Welsh, who had resented their harsh rule, had petitioned him to show no grace to either man.[96] On 13 June, the King issued a commission for the trial of the Mortimers and ordered the seizure of their followers' lands. On 13 July, he commanded a review of Mortimer's rule in Ireland, anticipating that some treachery or financial irregularities might be uncovered. The next day, justices were appointed to pass sentence on both uncle and nephew. The Mortimers were tried "for notorious treasons" on 21 July in Westminster Hall and sentenced to forfeiture and death;[97] the next day, for reasons that are unknown, and to many people's astonishment, this sentence was commuted to perpetual imprisonment in the Tower.[98]

It has been argued that the passing of the death sentence on the Mortimers was merely a formality, since the King had intended all along to show mercy because they had surrendered to him without further resistance. Pembroke had told them as much back in January, but Pembroke was now out of favor and it is unlikely that Edward would have heeded any request from him to honor the undertakings that he had given then. Nor is it likely that the vengeful Despensers would have approved of or permitted such clemency. There has been more plausible speculation that some highly influential person interceded on the Mortimers' behalf, possibly the Queen. Less plausibly, it has been suggested that she pleaded for Mortimer's life because she was in love with him, but there is no evidence for this. Nor is there any evidence that Lady Mortimer's French relatives intervened for him.[99]

If Isabella did intercede, she was probably acting on behalf of Lady Mortimer, to whose plight she is known to have been sympathetic; she may also have felt some latent sympathy for the Mortimers themselves, who had after all lost everything in making a stand against the very family that was now threatening her own position. Of course, it must have given her great satisfaction to pit her influence against that of the favorites, whose power at this time may not have extended beyond the door of the royal nuptial chamber; after all, Edward had heeded Isabella's pleas in the Somerton case and was probably mindful of the support she had given him during the recent rebellions. Nevertheless, it would have been obvious that Isabella was once again deliberately acting in opposition to the Despensers on behalf of their enemies and in so doing demonstrating that she was an opponent to be reckoned with.

The Mortimers' lives had been spared, but they faced spending the rest of their days in what was probably the Lanthorn Tower, in a lofty, narrow cell in conditions that were "less elegant than were seemly," with barely enough to eat—their keepers were allocated only 3d. (not quite 2p.) a day for their maintenance;[100] as nobly born prisoners, they could have expected to have been relatively comfortably housed, with certain privileges, but there were limits to the King's clemency, and the Despensers had to be placated.

Back in May, knowing that his truce with the Scots was about to expire, the King had announced his intention of mounting a new campaign against Bruce and had ordered a muster at Newcastle for 22 July. In June, once the truce ended, Bruce again began raiding the North. When Edward finally did march into Scotland in August, with his bastard son Adam among his company,[101] it was to find that the land had been laid waste. The only sustenance that his men could find was an aged cow in Lothian, which Surrey described as "the dearest beef I ever saw." On 6 September, Edward optimistically reported that there was no resistance, and on the eighteenth, he was still hopeful of success,[102] but by the beginning of October, his army was demoralized, starving, and racked with dysentery—his son Adam, who died during this campaign,[103] was probably one of those who succumbed to it—and the King had no choice but to retreat south toward Yorkshire, where he hoped to raise more troops.[104]

Intent on surprising and capturing Edward, Bruce now crossed the Solway Firth and swept down to Northallerton in Yorkshire, which he reached on 12 October. During the campaign, Isabella had stayed in Northumberland;[105] Edward had sent her to the fortified priory at Tynemouth,[106] which proved to be an unwise decision in light of what was shortly to happen. On 13 September, he addressed a letter there to his niece, Eleanor de Clare,[107] the Queen's principal lady-in-waiting, who was in attendance on her at that time. When the King reached York, he sent Isabella twenty pieces of sturgeon, which was evidently a favorite dish of hers, and thirteen to Eleanor.[108]

On 14 October, Isabella was still at Tynemouth, while the King and the Despensers were staying only fourteen miles east of Northallerton, at the Cistercian monastery at Rievaulx. Here, they received an urgent warning that the Scots were fast approaching. Just in time, Edward, "being ever chicken-hearted and luckless in war,"[109] fled to Bridlington and thence to York, abandoning his treasure, his state papers, and his baggage. He was well aware that his flight would leave his wife isolated at Tynemouth and vulnerable to attack or capture by Bruce's army, which now commandeered most of the North, but he found time to write a hurried letter to Thomas de Grey, the constable of nearby Norham Castle, warning him to be vigilant and placing the Queen under his protection; should the Scots approach, the constable was to enlist the support of all the castellans on the eastern March of the border and take steps to safeguard her. Edward also sent orders to the Earls of Richmond and Atholl, and the seneschal of his household, commanding them to raise a troop of men from Despenser's forces and fortify Tynemouth Priory. Then he wrote to Isabella, telling her that he was sending Richmond and Atholl to rescue her, but without referring to Despenser. Nevertheless, it seems that she did find out about the plan to send Despenser's men, for in a second letter to her, Edward wrote that he had ordered a French knight, Henry de Sully, to go to her defense at Tynemouth, since he understood that Sully "would be more agreeable than others to her."[110] This is almost certainly an oblique reference to Despenser, whose name Edward seems to have been reluctant to mention to his wife. Evidently, her hatred and fear of Hugh were such that she would rather have faced the Scots than entrust her safety to him.

Isabella was aware of her peril and realized that she had not the resources to withstand a siege. Nor could she afford to wait for the earls and Sully to arrive, for the Scots were already closing in on Tynemouth. In this crisis, she had to rely on the expertise and bravery of her young household squires, who made strenuous efforts to make good the priory's crumbling fortifications, then, when it became clear that they could never hold it against the invaders, commandeered a ship so that the Queen could escape by sea to a safer place farther south; later, she would reward them for these services.[111] But for the present, she had to endure a hazardous voyage in violent tempests, suffering great hardships and discomfort and dodging hostile Flemish ships that were policing the North Sea on behalf of their allies, the Scots. Tragically, one of her ladies was drowned while at sea, and another died soon after disembarking.[112] Four years later, Isabella was to blame Despenser publicly for what had happened, claiming that he had persuaded Edward to take flight and ignored the consequences for herself. But the accusation was hardly justified, because Despenser's own wife had been at Tynemouth with her, and it was his men who were to have gone to relieve it. But at the time, shattered by her experiences and the realization that

Edward had put his own safety, and that of his favorite, above hers, it was understandable that Isabella should have held Despenser responsible. And by 1326, she was ready to blame all her misfortunes on him.

Afterward, when the Queen had thankfully reached dry land at Scarborough, and was preparing to travel to York to rejoin her husband, the King's messengers came to Isabella[113] and informed her that, after Edward's flight, Bruce had seized all his effects at Rievaulx and had then gone on to defeat soundly the royal forces at Byland, where he captured the Earl of Richmond.[114]

Apparently, the Queen's patience snapped at this point.

CHAPTER SIX

Then Let Her Live
Abandoned and Forlorn

Until the autumn of 1322, there is no suggestion in any source that Isabella was anything but supportive of her husband, nor that he held
her in anything other than high esteem. To every appearance, in the ten
years following the death of Gaveston, theirs had been a strong and successful royal marriage. She had proved herself a loyal and devoted wife, and he
had treated her with honor, respect, and generosity. Now all that was to
change. Between 1 November 1322 and 18 September 1324, there is barely
a mention of Isabella in the Chancery Rolls and the household accounts;[1]
she virtually ceased to exercise any patronage, and only a few minor gifts to
her are recorded.[2] Taken together, these are strong indications that she had
fallen from favor. There can be little doubt that her indignation at her plight
at Tynemouth had led to a falling-out between her and Edward.

More to the point, she must have given vent to her fury and resentment
against the Younger Despenser, whose pernicious influence was gradually
eroding her own power and had also, she was adamant, placed her in dire
peril. Even discounting this, she naturally resented his hold over her husband, and if she knew that he was a rival in a more personal sense, there
was even more reason for her jealousy. In the years when Edward had been
emotionally and probably sexually involved with Gaveston, she had been a

virtual child, too young to deal with the situation; now, however, she was a confident, beautiful woman of twenty-seven, the mother of four children, one of them the heir to the throne, and would not so meekly tolerate this insult to her position, or her femininity.

Later evidence suggests that Isabella's revulsion was triggered by the knowledge that Despenser's power over the King was rooted in a perverted sexual dominance.[3] It may well be significant that she bore Edward no more children after 1321. Paul Doherty has pointed out that, in her later letters to the King, it is the Younger Hugh she singles out for bitter criticism, while making no mention of the Elder Despenser. Since it is clear that most of the political establishment regarded the latter as being almost as responsible as his son for the tyranny of these years, it is likely that Isabella's hatred for the son was born of personal jealousy and resentment. She had no real quarrel with the Elder Despenser: he was not her rival in her husband's bed, nor is there any evidence that he ever treated her vindictively. One chronicler states that he was in fact a worthy man who was led astray and ultimately destroyed by his devotion to his son. But he was deeply unpopular nevertheless.

Several writers have speculated that the rift between Edward and Isabella occurred so suddenly that there was perhaps another, more sinister reason for it. Later on, Isabella bitterly accused Despenser of being an "intruder" in her marriage and alienating the King's affections from her: "Someone has come between my husband and myself, trying to break this bond."[4] This, of course, could either refer to Despenser's attempts to poison the King's mind against the Queen or be an allusion to a homosexual relationship between Edward and Despenser. But in February 1326, Isabella complained that Hugh had wished to dishonor her by every possible means,[5] an assertion repeated in the accusations made against Despenser in November 1326[6] and by most chroniclers. In light of this, it has been suggested[7] that the Queen was the victim of some sexual offense committed by Despenser. The words "by every possible means," while they perhaps to a degree refer to Despenser's vicious campaign to discredit Isabella, the disrespectful and injurious way in which he was to treat her, and his possible homosexual relationship with her husband, are also suggestive of some serious sexual misconduct toward the Queen herself with the intent of humiliating and intimidating her. Had Hugh thrust himself into her marriage bed, with Edward's connivance, or even raped her? It is not beyond the bounds of possibility, considering his cruelty toward other women.

Edward responded to Isabella's accusation by protesting, both to her and to her brother Charles IV, that "never, in the slightest instance, has evil

been done to her by [Despenser]" and that "he could never perceive that
Hugh, privately or openly, in word or deed or in countenance, did not
behave himself on all points towards the Queen as he ought to have done
to his lady." Furthermore, he stressed, she had had no cause to allege that
she had gone in fear of her life from Despenser.[8] Clearly, Edward was blatantly twisting the truth, or his memory was very short.

There are other factors that possibly contributed toward Isabella's anger
with her husband. Foremost among them may have been pent-up exasper-
ation and bitterness that had been mounting over the years when she had
put up with his weaknesses, and fury that, having striven so dutifully to play
her part as his wife and queen, sometimes in the face of extreme provocation, he was now prepared to supplant her with Despenser. It may be that
she had long secretly despised him for failing to live up to the ideal of kingship personified by her father, Philip IV, and that any respect she had had for
him had now been shattered.

The *Chronographia Regum Francorum*—never very reliable—asserts that
Edward was involved at this time in an affair with his niece, Eleanor de
Clare,[9] as well as with her husband, Hugh,[10] which would certainly have
accounted for Isabella's disillusionment. Not only did he correspond with
Eleanor, but he had also given her some of the property confiscated from
Lancastrian traitors after Boroughbridge, while Isabella received nothing.[11]
None of this, however, is proof of any sexual relationship between Edward
and Eleanor, and it is probably merely evidence of an uncle's affection for a
favorite niece, albeit one whose husband was an enemy of the Queen.

Was Isabella also angry because she had learned that her husband was
being promiscuous with lowborn men? In one of Edward's chamber books
of 1322, there is a record of substantial payments made by the King to
Robin and Simon Hod, Wat Cowherd, Robin Dyer, and others for spending
fourteen days in his company. Of course, they may have joined him in innocent pastimes such as digging ditches, but this is not mentioned, and the
words "in his company" sound euphemistic, while the substantial sums
paid to these men were perhaps hush money. And as they stayed for two
weeks, the Queen would surely have got to hear of it.

Whatever the reason for this falling-out between the royal couple, Isabella had probably betrayed her true feelings, and Despenser—who had for
some time regarded her as a threat to his own influence—was ready to cap-
italize on it. He now did everything in his power to create a serious rift
between husband and wife. Froissart states that he "maliciously caused
such discord between [them] that, for a long time, the King would neither
remain in the Queen's company, nor even see her at all." On 23 December,

Edward announced to his sheriffs and bailiffs that, after Christmas, which they were to spend together at York, the Queen would depart on an extended pilgrimage throughout England that would last for no less than nine months, until Michaelmas 1323; the royal officials were commanded to offer her every assistance on her journey.[12] Since there is no evidence that Isabella ever went on such a pilgrimage, we may perhaps infer from this announcement either that Despenser had so effectively succeeded in poisoning Edward's mind against her that he was ready to banish her from his side, as Froissart asserts, or that Isabella had angrily withdrawn from the King's company; in either case, Edward would have had to come up with a diplomatic explanation for her absence.

On 12 January 1323, when the King and Queen arrived back in London, Isabella took up residence in the Tower with Prince Edward and stayed there until 17 February or later.[13] It is recorded that on 3 February, she dined with her ten-year-old son in the Tower.

Matters between the royal couple cannot have improved when, in February, Edward launched an attack on Louis de Beaumont, the Bishop of Durham. After Byland, Beaumont, despairing that the King would ever succeed in protecting his northern subjects, had attempted to negotiate a peace with Bruce. The King angrily reminded him of his promise to be "a stone wall against the Scots" and complained that the Bishop had not kept his word.[14] Naturally, Despenser exploited this quarrel; he may even have fostered it, as a means of discrediting the Queen, who had secured Beaumont's election. As a result, Henry de Beaumont and Isabella de Vesci, who had long been friends of both the King and the Queen, also lost Edward's favor.

On 7 February, the Queen and Eleanor de Clare lent their weight to petitions submitted by John de Sadington.[15] Ten days later, they both wrote letters to the acting Treasurer, Walter de Norwich, asking him to show all the favor he could in paying out the modest amount that the King had allocated for the sustenance of the imprisoned Lady Mortimer, to whom Isabella now referred as "our dear and well-beloved cousin."[16] The Queen was undoubtedly sympathetic to this lady's plight, but she was aware that her own influence had been eroded and knew that, in enlisting the support of Despenser's wife, she was ensuring that her plea stood a greater chance of success.[17]

It may be no more than a coincidence that these letters were written in the Tower, where Lady Mortimer's husband and his uncle were incarcerated. It is highly unlikely that Isabella visited them during her stay: they had, after all, been convicted of treason against her husband. But it is possible that Roger had managed to get a message to the Queen, pleading with her to help his wife. Six months later, it became clear that he had won the sympathy of Gerard d'Alspaye, the Sub-Lieutenant of the Tower, a process that might not have happened overnight. In February, this man's loyalty to the King may have been so far subverted that he agreed secretly to pass a plea to the Queen.

The outcome of the petitions of the Queen and Eleanor de Clare is unknown. Lady Mortimer remained in prison in Hampshire until April 1324, when she was moved to the royal castle of Skipton-in-Craven in Yorkshire, where she was permitted four female servants and a pittance of only one mark per day for her food and expenses.[18]

Between 7 February and 10 June, Isabella's movements cannot be easily traced. Perhaps she did go on a private pilgrimage to various shrines. Certainly, she was maintaining a low profile, or being made to do so.

After a few months of the Despensers' tyranny, people began to forget Lancaster's treason and self-interest and remembered only that he had striven to mitigate royal oppression and misgovernment. Already, he was being venerated not only as a popular hero but as a martyr for English liberties and even as a saint.[19] The cult of "Saint" Thomas quickly flourished among the credulous: his tomb at Pontefract became a place of pilgrimage, as did Saint Paul's Cathedral, where attached to a pillar was a tablet that bore his effigy and commemorated the Ordinances he had made it his mission to enforce. Before long, there was talk of miracles taking place at his tomb—it was said that a dead child had been brought back to life and cripples made whole—and songs comparing him to Thomas à Becket and Simon de Montfort became widely popular. By 1325, Lancaster was being linked in the popular imagination to Saint George,[20] and there were calls for his canonization.

Lancaster was proving almost as much of a threat in death as he had been in life. In some alarm, the King had the tablet removed and forbade the pilgrimages, placing a guard over Lancaster's tomb to keep the people away, but many defied him and continued to flock to the priory at Pontefract and also to the denuded pillar in Saint Paul's.[21] In 1323, two thousand people, finding themselves barred from leaving offerings at the tomb, attacked the King's guards and killed two of them.[22] This is some measure of the strength of feeling against the Despenser-led government and a weak and vicious King.

On 3 March 1323, Andrew Harclay was executed for treason. Shaken and disgusted, like Beaumont, by what had happened at Byland, he had taken it upon himself to make terms with the Scots, with a view to recognizing Bruce as their king, something that Edward would never countenance. But Harclay was more of a realist than the King—the Pope himself recognized Bruce's sovereignty that year—and his crime had been committed in the interests of peace, for he was convinced that this long and grueling war could not be won; later it transpired that Queen Isabella herself held similar views. Harclay's punishment was to suffer the full horrors of a traitor's death, although he died protesting he was no traitor.[23] Thereafter, Pembroke and Despenser were active in negotiating the thirteen-year truce with Bruce that was concluded on 30 May.[24] There would be no more fighting for the rest of Edward's reign.

That same day, Parliament assembled at Bishopsthorpe near York, and Henry de Beaumont, the Queen's old friend, was arrested. Angry at the King's censure of his brother, the Bishop of Durham, he had refused to give any advice on negotiating the Scottish truce, and when he appeared in Parliament, he was told to leave. "Nothing would please me more!" he retorted, at which he was apprehended for contumacy.[25] Isabella may have been a witness to this scene; she and Edward were at Selby on 10 June and at York on 3 and 4 July.[26] Possibly there had been a patching up of sorts between them, but the arrest of Beaumont would have been cause for further resentment on both sides, especially when Beaumont refused to swear an oath of loyalty to Despenser and was consequently cast into prison.[27] After his removal from court, Isabella would have felt even more isolated.

On 1 August 1323, Roger Mortimer made a dramatic escape from the Tower, a feat that had been achieved only once before, by Ranulf Flambard in 1101. That day was Roger's birthday and the feast day of Saint Peter ad Vincula, the patron saint of the Tower garrison. Evidently, the rigors of Mortimer's imprisonment had been relaxed, for by now he had won over the sympathies of Gerard d'Alspaye, the Sub-Lieutenant of the Tower, who had brought him a crowbar and a pick so that he could bore a hole in the stone wall of his cell. It was with d'Alspaye's connivance that, on this night, Mortimer hosted "a great feast, inviting there Sir Stephen de Segrave, Constable of the Tower," and his own guards. But the wine was drugged, and the guests were soon in a comatose state. Once it was safe to do so, d'Alspaye helped Mortimer to escape through the hole in his cell, which appears to have been located in the Lanthorn Tower;[28] this building stood next to the Hall Tower (now the Wakefield Tower), which had a guardroom downstairs and royal chambers upstairs. Beyond were the great hall and the Queen's apartments.

Once through the hole, Mortimer and d'Alspaye found themselves in the King's kitchen. They climbed up the great chimney to the roof of the Hall Tower, from which they apparently crossed to the leads of the adjacent Saint Thomas's Tower. Using rope ladders, they managed to scale down the stout wall of the outer bailey to the wharf. D'Alspaye had ensured that a boat was waiting to take him and Mortimer across the Thames to the Surrey shore, where some of Roger's friends were waiting with horses. The small party then galloped through the night to Netley on the Hampshire coast. A boat carried them out to a waiting ship, which had been provided by a London merchant called Ralph de Botton; it sailed for France the next day, landing in Normandy.

Mortimer and his friends then made straight for Paris to seek the protection of the French King,[29] who received him "with great honour," provoking a bitter complaint from Edward II.[30] Charles's warm reception of Mortimer must have been particularly galling to Despenser, who had been driven out of France and placed under sentence of banishment in 1321 during his pirating days, and consequently had no love for the French.[31] Even more galling was Charles's response to Edward's complaint: he said he would banish all the English exiles from France if the King would in turn banish any French exiles from England—meaning, of course, Despenser.[32]

Strickland quotes "an old chronicle" that asserts that "the sleepy drink" was provided by the Queen for Mortimer's use and incorrectly claims that Mortimer swam across the Thames to the Surrey shore, "the Queen doubting much of his strength for such an exploit, as he had been long in confinement." No other original source claims that Isabella was involved in Mortimer's escape, and there is no evidence that she was even in London, let alone residing in the Tower, at this date. In fact, the first English writer to assert that Isabella helped Mortimer to escape was the dramatist Christopher Marlowe in *Edward the Second*, written in 1593. He was followed by Michael Drayton, whose claims appear in three plays written between 1596 and 1619.[33]

Nevertheless, many writers still follow Strickland in asserting that Isabella was Mortimer's accomplice. It has been argued that d'Alspaye, who had a responsible post, would not have put his career and even his life on the line to aid a landless traitor who could offer him nothing in reward unless he had been promised the patronage of some important person, possibly Isabella.[34] But that is perhaps to underestimate the convictions of both Mortimer and d'Alspaye. It may be that when Mortimer had finished cozening him, d'Alspaye was indeed prepared to risk all if it would help to bring down the Despensers, or he might have had reasons of his own for wishing to do so.

Yet we cannot discount the possibility that Charles IV's warm reception of Mortimer was extended not just as a result of his antipathy toward the Despensers and his concerns about the way in which they were slighting his sister but also on the basis of Isabella's own private recommendations. Charles cannot but have been aware of the Despensers' tyranny, and he must have seen in Mortimer, their deadly foe, a means of somehow counteracting it and thus aiding Isabella. England was not then at war with France,

so what other reason could Charles have had for welcoming such a notorious traitor? As for Isabella herself, she had probably been instrumental in the
commuting of the death sentence on Mortimer, and she had certainly tried
to assist his wife, possibly at his request. She had probably realized by now
that Mortimer was the only person capable of resisting the tyranny of the
Despensers and that, as such, he could prove very useful to her. By using her
influence with her brother, she perhaps indirectly assisted in his escape, and
if this is so, then she must have known about it in advance.

Michael Drayton also claimed that Mortimer's ally Bishop Orleton helped
him to escape, a claim that is well supported by contemporary evidence.
Adam Orleton had been born on one of Mortimer's Herefordshire manors,
had been elected Bishop of Hereford in 1317, and before that had spent
most of his hitherto distinguished career at the papal Curia. In recent years,
he had become a close friend and ally of Roger Mortimer, his patron. He
had sent men to assist Mortimer in the offensive on the Despenser lands and
had staunchly supported the Mortimers in their attack on the Despensers in
Parliament. Even now, when they lay in prison, convicted traitors, he did
not withdraw his support. On the contrary, he remained one of the most
active opponents of the Despensers.

Orleton's reputation has suffered because of a piece of character assassination by the chronicler Geoffrey le Baker that is demonstrably untrue. Far
from being as unscrupulous as Baker claims, Orleton was a clever politician,
lawyer, and diplomat who took his ecclesiastical responsibilities seriously and
genuinely deplored the misgovernment of Edward II and the Despensers
and the embarrassment this caused him in European diplomatic circles. He
also had an inflated respect for the dignity of popes and bishops and was a
friend of the astute John XXII.[35] Archbishop Reynolds held a high opinion of
Orleton's capabilities, but Orleton's overt approval of Mortimer's acts of
rebellion now made him a natural target for the King's wrath.

In February 1324, in an unprecedented action against a bishop, Despenser accused Orleton in Parliament of treasonably having aided and counseled the enemies of the King and of having provided the weapons and
horses that had enabled Mortimer to escape. Relying on his episcopal
immunity, Orleton refused to answer the charges, declaring that he was
only responsible to the Pope, the Archbishop of Canterbury, and his fellow
clergy, and when Edward ordered that he be committed into the custody of
the Archbishop of Canterbury, he provoked a furor in the ecclesiastical
nation, which led to Archbishops Reynolds and Melton, and Alexander
Bicknor, Archbishop of Dublin, placing Orleton under their protection and

threatening with excommunication anyone who dared lay violent hands on him.[36] This was the first time that Reynolds, who had hitherto been a staunch friend, had defied Edward, and it must have come as a shock to him. Nevertheless, he had his justices declare Orleton guilty, confiscated his estates and personal property, and kept him in custody.[37]

In April 1324, the King complained to the Pope about Orleton's treason, and in May, he demanded that he be deposed from his bishopric,[38] but, as in the case of Burghersh, the Pope refused to cooperate because of the lack of evidence to support the charge of treason.

Edward had also called for the deposition of John of Drokensford (now Droxford), Bishop of Bath and Wells, a worldly and unscrupulous liberal who had also shown himself a friend to Mortimer and was a close associate of Orleton and Burghersh. Burghersh, however, had been so frightened by the King's stern treatment of Orleton that he had made his groveling (and insincere) peace with Edward, offering his unconditional loyalty and obedience. This ploy helped him regain some of his former favor and the restoration of his temporalities.

Yet it is unlikely that Orleton himself arranged Mortimer's escape, although he may have solicited the Queen's help. Ian Mortimer, in his biography of his namesake, has put forward a compelling argument that it was Mortimer himself who masterminded it, relying for the practicalities on d'Alspaye and his own contacts in the City of London, where he enjoyed great popularity;[39] among the latter were two prominent citizens, Richard de Béthune and John de Gisors.[40] It later emerged that, through them, Mortimer had been in contact with a number of influential supporters, including Orleton, and that his escape had been part of a broader master plan to raise the Despensers' opponents. And if it had been Isabella who had interceded for Mortimer the previous year, then it was perhaps Orleton who, knowing of this, had told her of the planned escape attempt and solicited her intercession with King Charles. Some chroniclers, sickened by the oppressive regime of the Despensers, regarded Mortimer's escape as an act of God, claiming that he had, like Saint Peter, been guided by an angel from his cell.[41] Isabella may have viewed it in the same way.

Now that he was at liberty, Roger was potentially the focus for a concerted opposition. In a panic, the King made strenuous efforts to find and recapture him, alive or dead, raising the hue and cry all over England, but he sent his officers to look in all the wrong places. Until the end of August 1323, Edward was convinced that Mortimer would have gone to either Wales or Ireland.[42] It was only in late September that he learned that his quarry was staying with his kinsfolk in Picardy,[43] beyond the King of England's reach.

Even in exile, Mortimer was to prove a deadly threat to the Despensers. In November, he sent an assassin from Saint Omer to England to murder them and their closest associates. The attempt failed—the man got as far as London but was then arrested and questioned[44]—but it proved just how far Roger was prepared to go to be revenged upon these most hated enemies, and it gave rise to fears on Edward's part that Mortimer, succored by Charles IV (who by then had quarreled with Edward II), might even invade England for the purpose of destroying the Despensers. Edward now accused Charles and his uncle, Charles of Valois, of having assisted Mortimer in his escape.[45] This has sometimes been cited as evidence that Isabella was also involved, but if Edward—and, more to the point, the Despensers—had suspected as much, as a result of the comprehensive official investigations into the escape, they would surely have accused her of treason.

Thereafter, Edward received conflicting intelligence of Mortimer's whereabouts. On 6 December, he was informed that Roger was in Hainault and making his way to Germany; then, around 13 December, came a report that he had gone south to Toulouse with the Count of Boulogne.[46]

Isabella again disappears from the records until 13 October 1323; possibly she had resumed her pilgrimage. She was with Edward at Lichfield on 19–20 December and then traveled south with him to Sutton Coldfield[47] before going to Kenilworth Castle, formerly owned by Lancaster, where the court celebrated Christmas with great magnificence. In January, the King and Queen were guests of Despenser at his castle on the River Trent at Hanley, and in February, they visited Gloucester and nearby Berkeley Castle before returning to London.[48]

Edward had now plunged into a fierce dispute with Charles IV. In September, Charles had summoned his brother-in-law to pay homage, a summons Edward managed to avoid complying with on the grounds that he could not at present safely leave his kingdom—in other words, the Despensers did not want him to go, fearing that their enemies would pounce in his absence. Although Charles agreed to postpone the homage until July 1324, his harboring of Mortimer had led to mistrust and resentment on Edward's part. There was already a lot of ill feeling on both sides when, in October, a dispute broke out over a bastide, or fortified town, that the French had begun building on the site of the priory of Saint Sardos in the English-held Agenais; Edward's Gascon subjects reacted with hostility to this possibly illegal encroachment and attacked the bastide, killing a French sergeant. Although Edward had not sanctioned the attack, indeed, had known nothing about it, there were fears that this incident might lead to war between England and France—the very thing that Isabella's marriage had been intended to prevent. The French, however, were outraged, and Mortimer, seizing his opportunity, promptly offered his sword to Charles IV, traitorously volunteering to fight against his liege lord, Edward II, in Gascony.[49]

In January 1324, Charles made it clear that he accepted Edward's protestations of innocence in the Saint Sardos dispute. But in February, when it became clear that Edward was doing very little to rectify the situation and was also proving dilatory about paying homage, the French King threatened to seize Gascony. A crisis was looming, and Parliament met on 23 February at Westminster to discuss it.

In March, Edward suddenly ceased to pay certain of his debts to Isabella.[50] Did he—perhaps encouraged by the hostile Despensers—fear that her sympathies lay with Charles IV? In April, he made Isabella send a plea to her brother not to seize Gascony, instructing her to remind Charles that her marriage had been contracted to secure a lasting peace between the two kingdoms.[51] The implication was that, if war broke out, the marriage would have failed. It may be significant that, during that spring, an unidentified person wrote to Isabella, advising her to instruct a French knight, who had been sent to England by Charles IV, to tell his master upon his return that the matter of the dispute over Gascony should in the first case be dealt with by Despenser and Pembroke in council. Was this a warning to Charles not to involve Isabella further in the matter?

We know very little of Isabella's activities or movements at this time, other than that, on 27 June, she wrote to Chancellor Baldock to request the appointment of Pembroke and others as justices of oyer and terminer for her forest of Havering. It seems likely that she was still out of favor and wisely, in view of her husband's unpredictable behavior and the fear and confusion it engendered,[52] keeping her head down.

Pembroke had been sent to France to mediate with Charles IV over Gascony, but he died there suddenly, probably of apoplexy, on 23 June. There were rumors that he had been "murdered suddenly on a privy seat,"[53] but whatever the cause of it, his death removed the last moderate restraining influence on Edward, who was now hopelessly in thrall to the Despensers. In July, reneging on his word, he instructed his envoys at the French court to refuse to hand over to Charles IV those English subjects who had offended at Saint Sardos. Then, to add insult to injury, he again asked for his homage to be postponed. At this point, Charles lost patience and declared Gascony forfeit. The next month, he sent an army into the duchy to take possession of it.

In response, Edward appointed his inexperienced and unpopular twenty-two-year-old half brother Edmund, Earl of Kent, King's Lieutenant in Gascony. This did not prove a wise choice, since Kent, although a magnificent young man of great stature and strength, was also a feeble and gullible individual who thought nothing of sanctioning acts of brutality or violating the laws of sanctuary. He immediately alienated the Gascons by extorting money from them, allowing his household officials to plunder at will, and abducting a young girl who took his fancy.[54] When Charles of Valois led an army against Kent, the latter proved disastrously ineffective in a military capacity and, after several losses, was tricked by Valois into signing a six months' truce, in a desperate effort to save what was left of Gascony. However, its terms left the French in possession of the greater part of the duchy.[55]

The outbreak of hostilities between England and France had a devastating impact on Isabella's life, for it gave Despenser the chance to treat her as an enemy of the state, further undermining her position as Queen and annihilating what little influence she had left. At first, he insisted she swear an oath of loyalty to him personally, but she refused,[56] just as Henry de Beaumont had done. Then, on 18 September, the Queen's estates were suddenly sequestered and taken back into the King's hands, depriving her of much of her income.[57] Allegedly, Bishop Stapledon had advised the King that this was necessary for security reasons,[58] reminding him that the Queen's lands in Cornwall, with their valuable tin mines, were particularly vulnerable to invasion.[59] But this was, at bottom, an overt attack upon the Queen, for Stapledon was hand in glove with Despenser,[60] and there can be little doubt that Despenser had maliciously persuaded the King that Isabella, as a Frenchwoman, was quite capable of plotting treachery against him with her brother. Back in 1317, Queen Marguerite's estates had been briefly sequestered when war with France had seemed imminent, creating a precedent. But Marguerite had been compensated with a substantial allowance; not so Isabella. On 25 and 26 September, Edward changed the arrangements he had made for the financial support of his wife, and on 28 September, her allowance for her personal expenses was cut from 11,000 marks to a miserly 1,000 marks per annum.[61]

Isabella was outraged. She was not a woman to countenance such affronts to her dignity and her regal position, and she blamed both Despenser and Stapledon for the loss of her dower—Despenser was charged with this in 1326.[62] In medieval times, money was no fair exchange for property, which conferred its own special status, and Isabella was more than ordinarily acquisitive. But there was worse to come. On 28 September—again, purportedly on Stapledon's advice—Parliament ordered the banishment of all subjects of the King of France from the King's household and that of "our dearest consort,"[63] which effectively deprived Isabella of the loyal service of those French servants who had been with her for many years, some since she had first come to England as a bride of twelve. On 9 October, the King ordered a general levy of all gold due to the Queen, which went straight into his own coffers, along with money that he owed her; and on the fourteenth, the payment of her daily expenses was made the responsibility of the Exchequer.[64] In practice, however, the Despensers "sent her from the King's coffers what they would." In effect, Isabella, one of the greatest landowners in the realm, had been reduced to the status of a humble pensioner.[65]

But Despenser was by no means finished with her. She might be the mother of the heir to the throne, but around Michaelmas, her three youngest children were removed from her custody on the grounds that, as a Frenchwoman, she might encourage them to commit treason against their father. The children were initially given into the care of Eleanor de Clare and Despenser's sister Isabella, Lady Monthermer, who was married to Ralph de Monthermer, the King's brother-in-law.[66] John of Eltham, now eight, seems to have remained with Eleanor de Clare, but the two Princesses, Eleanor, six, and Joan, three, were shortly afterward sent to live with the Monthermers at Pleshy and Marlborough.

There is a consensus of opinion among historians that Isabella was not overly maternal and was even guilty of neglecting her children, but there is no evidence that she was less devoted than any other royal mother in an age in which it was customary for heirs to the throne to have their own households from infancy. Prince Edward had been given his at the age of five, but his three younger siblings had remained with their mother, which suggests that Isabella was actively involved in their upbringing. In fact, she seems to have been determined to play a controlling role in their lives, rather than a passive one, and to have been ambitious for her children, which argues that she cared very much about what happened to them. Her great joy at being reunited with her younger children in 1326 is surely evidence as to how devastated she must have been at being forcibly parted from them and how she must have suffered during the long separation. Any neglect seems to have been the fault of those who had had care of them in the interim period. Furthermore, all Isabella's children, particularly the young Edward, remained devoted to her all their lives, which would surely not have been the case had she been a distant and uncaring mother and the "Jezebel" that later generations made her out to be.

Isabella was now a virtual prisoner. She had lost her status, her husband, her children, her influence, her income, her friends, and her freedom and had suffered extreme anguish as a result.[67] In a letter smuggled out to Charles IV, she protested bitterly about the sequestration of her lands and the loss of her French servants, accused Despenser of depriving her of her husband's love, and complained that "she was held in no higher consideration than a maidservant in the palace of the King, her husband," to whom she referred disparagingly as "a gripple miser," or one who had been mean to her but lavish toward another.[68] Eleanor de Clare was now in constant attendance on her as her "housekeeper" or "chaperone," whether she wanted her there or not; Despenser and the King were using Eleanor as both jailer and spy and had given her instructions to carry the Queen's seal with her at all times and to read all Isabella's letters before they were sealed. Isabella, "greatly enraged,"[69] managed to circumvent this supervision and smuggled out yet another letter to her brother, complaining about these new indignities. But when a shocked Charles IV reacted with angry demands for fairer treatment for Isabella,[70] Edward chose to ignore him.

Instead, on 18 November, he gave orders that only 2,920 marks per annum, or £1.00 per day, was to be allocated to the Queen for her food and drink. He was more generous when it came to the maintenance of her household, for which 1,000 marks per day were allocated,[71] but he also ordered that any Frenchmen left in England were to be arrested and imprisoned and their property confiscated.[72] By this time, a number of Isabella's French servants had already fled to France, but some twenty-seven persons had stayed behind, including her clerks; her two chaplains, Thomas Burchard and Peter de Vernon; her physician, Theobald de Troyes; and the Launges. All were now apprehended and shut up in scattered religious houses.[73] Nor was Isabella allowed to secure their freedom by giving sureties for their good behavior, a concession extended to other persons of rank.[74] In France, Charles IV erupted in astonishment and fury at the arrest of his subjects, much to the embarrassment of the English envoys at his court.[75]

Like Isabella herself, the Lanercost chronicler believed that it was Despenser who was chiefly responsible for the sequestration of the Queen's lands and the arrest of her servants. Lanercost also states that, around this time, Despenser persuaded the King to petition the Pope for an annulment of his marriage to Isabella and himself sent Robert Baldock and an "irreligious" Dominican friar, Thomas Dunheved, to Avignon to present this petition. Lanercost's statement is to some extent corroborated by the fact that Dunheved was sent to the papal Curia on secret business at this time, while the *Annales Paulini* refer to rumors of an annulment.

What must have been so shocking to the Queen was not so much the vindictiveness of Despenser and his desire to humiliate her—she had learned to expect that—but the naked malice of her husband, which she had only ever experienced as an onlooker. Now, as a result of Edward's anger with Charles IV, and Despenser's whispering campaign, it was directed at her. She had done nothing to deserve such intolerable treatment. She had been a patient, loyal, and dutiful wife; a good mother; and a conscientious consort who had earned a widespread reputation as a peacemaker. Before 1325, there is no hint in any source of any infidelity on her part. But now her marriage had been destroyed, for "the King had driven out the Queen at [Despenser's] incitement,"[76] and she was being unjustly vilified and cruelly punished for crimes she had not committed. This was all because of her hatred of the corrupt favorite and her husband's weakness in permitting that favorite to treat her so unjustly. Baker, who is hostile to Isabella, accuses her of denying her company (and no doubt her bed) to her lord, but if this is true, was it not understandable in the circumstances? All things considered, there can be no doubt that Edward II must bear the lion's share of the blame for the breakdown of the marriage and that, by his own carelessness, he sowed the seeds of future tragedy.

Despenser's cruelty toward the Queen was apparently well known in diplomatic circles. Before long, Pope John heard of it in Avignon and himself wrote to Despenser, reprimanding him for his harsh treatment and his misgovernment and for causing bitterness between princes.[77] When Despenser, deeply perturbed by an attempt to murder him and the King by using black magic on wax effigies,[78] wrote craving the Pope's special protection, John XXII tartly recommended him "to turn to God and make a good confession and such satisfaction as shall be enjoined. No other remedies are necessary."[79] Clearly, the Pope had got the measure of Despenser, and this may be one reason why nothing more is heard of the King's petition for an annulment. Another reason may be that the marriage of Edward and Isabella had been contracted at the instigation of the Papacy in the interests of forging a lasting peace between England and France, and that it was now more than ever necessary to uphold that alliance as a cement in diplomatic relations. Furthermore, the only possible grounds for an annulment could have been consanguinity, and a dispensation had already been granted to allow for this; moreover, it would have been dynastically catastrophic for the legitimacy of the heirs of the marriage to be impugned.

In the absence of any further information, we must conclude that, if Edward II had indeed asked the Pope to annul his marriage, he either met with a categorical—and confidential—refusal or withdrew his petition for reasons that will shortly become clear. This would explain why, when

Stephen Dunheved reported to the King from Avignon on 7 October 1325, he made no reference to any matrimonial proceedings.[80]

Edward now knew for certain that he faced not only the prospect of a war with France but also the threat of an invasion led by Mortimer; Despenser had learned in the autumn that Mortimer was in Hainault trying to raise troops, with the intention of sailing with an army from Holland or Zeeland for the East Anglian coast.[81] Diplomatic relations between England and Hainault were already frosty on account of disputes over trade, and on 24 October, Edward wrote to Count William V of Hainault protesting about his harboring of English traitors.[82] The Count, however, took no notice. Mortimer's next move was to raise a force of German mercenaries, financed by his wife's French relatives, the Joinvilles.[83]

The situation was critical, but the Pope was convinced it was not irretrievable; around December, on his instructions, his two nuncios in Paris, the Archbishop of Vienne and the Bishop of Orange, suggested that Queen Isabella be sent to France to use her renowned powers of mediation in the interests of defusing the crisis and settling the dispute over Gascony. This may have been the Pope's way of making it clear to Edward II that his marriage was a valuable diplomatic tool and that its dissolution would spell political disaster at this time, and it perhaps prompted Edward to withdraw his nullity suit.

Baker claims that the suggestion that the Queen go to France originated with Isabella herself and that, after receiving her appeals for aid, Charles IV took steps to facilitate her escape from England. Froissart also states that Isabella "secretly did purvey to go into France." There may be some truth in their statements, but Baker's assertion that Charles enlisted Orleton and Burghersh to let the Queen go can hardly be correct, for the disgraced Orleton was in no position to plead for the Queen.

It is certainly possible that, at Isabella's prompting, or at the very least in response to her pleas for help, Charles IV had originally suggested to the Pope that she come on a peace mission to France.[84] And once this escape route miraculously opened up before her, Isabella was undoubtedly more than eager to take it. By her own later admission, she was so desperate to get away that she made every effort to appear friendly toward Despenser so that he would not veto the idea.[85] Going to France as England's ambassador extraordinary would not only restore her status as Queen but would also afford her a respite from the miseries she had to endure at home and remove her from the orbit of the hated Despensers. There is no evidence, however, that the Pope, sympathetic though he undoubtedly was toward Isabella, ever intended her mission to have any purpose other than to negotiate a peace.[86]

In January 1325, first the royal council, then Parliament debated the Pope's suggestion. Despenser was against Isabella's leaving England; although she was managing to dissemble her anger and loathing, and behaving toward him with studied courtesy, he knew he had made a bitter enemy of her and had every reason to fear that she might plot some mischief against him while she was in France. Yet Edward himself feared to go to France and leave his favorites unprotected, so sending Isabella seemed a sensible solution, and the King was tempted to consider it seriously.

His envoys in Paris were ready to put pressure on him. On 13 January, John Salmon, Bishop of Norwich, intervened with Despenser on the Queen's behalf. He was supported by his fellow envoys, the Earl of Richmond, who had recently been freed by the Scots, and Henry de Beaumont, who had apparently made a superficial peace with the King and regained a degree of favor. On 17 January, John Stratford, Bishop of Winchester, who had been on the same embassy and was newly returned from France, reiterated Salmon's plea; he added that Charles IV had promised that, if Edward would create his son Duke of Aquitaine and send him to France with the Queen to pay homage, then Charles would restore all the lands he had taken, and that this offer had been approved by the French royal council.[87]

In the end, the bishops' intervention, backed by the persuasions of Charles IV and the Elder Despenser, proved decisive:[88] Parliament decided that any expedient was preferable to pursuing the war,[89] and by 7 February, the King had consented to Isabella's going to France, with Prince Edward following as soon as a satisfactory settlement was reached. On that date, the English council sent Thomas de Astley to the envoys in France to inquire whether it would be acceptable to the French if the Queen came alone to negotiate peace terms. The answer was in the affirmative.[90]

Edward's decision to send Isabella to France turned out to be the most foolhardy and tragic mistake he made in his entire life. It was to have devastating consequences for him. Yet the fact that he gave his consent suggests that Isabella had dissembled so cunningly, hiding her rage and humiliation at the treatment meted out to her by himself and the Despensers, that he really believed that he had nothing to fear from her and that she would loyally uphold his interests, as in the past. His sanctioning of her mission also gives the lie to the assertions made the previous September, in justification of the sequestration of her estates, that she was a threat to the security of the realm, and corroborates Isabella's own conviction that she had lost her lands chiefly as a result of Despenser's malice.

Some historians have expressed surprise at Despenser's permitting Isabella to leave England, but he was in fact more fearful of the consequences of the King's going to France and leaving him unprotected. Isabella's own submissive and outwardly courteous conduct toward Despenser, and Edward's evident belief in her faithfulness, could have persuaded Despenser that she was harmless. Moreover, he would assuredly have been glad to have her out of the way for a spell and unable to exert any influence on Edward. Almost certainly, he underestimated her in every way that counted.

Edward, too, had been fatally mistaken in his assumptions about Isabella. Robert of Reading commented on "the insane stupidity of the King, who, condemned by God and man [for] his infamy and his illicit bed, should never have put aside his noble consort and her soft wifely embraces, [nor been] contemptuous of her noble birth." Much had happened to turn Isabella against Edward in the weeks since September, and already, it seems, she had begun to conspire against him.

More than two years of suffering Despenser's cruelty and her husband's callousness certainly changed Isabella; it hardened her and brought out in her latent strengths and faults that even she herself may not have suspected she possessed. More than ever now, she was her father's daughter. The humiliations imposed upon her had not humbled her but had made her even more aware of her pride in her rank and her dynastic connections. The insults she had endured had awakened a desire for vengeance and a ruthless determination to recover all that had been so cruelly taken from her. Living in constant fear had taught her to be courageous, resourceful, and cunning. Her innate kindness and thoughtfulness had apparently been subsumed by the realization that she must act to end this intolerable situation. No longer was she prepared to accept a passive, compliant role. For seventeen years, she had striven to be a loyal and dutiful wife, and she now felt she had no choice other than to embark on a perilous course of defiance. To allow matters to continue as they were would have exposed her to further degradation and danger, her children to a motherless existence, and England to the unbridled tyranny of the Despensers.

In light of later events and circumstantial evidence, it has been suggested that an embryonic opposition party was forming around the Queen before she left England. Some historians assert that it had been in existence as early as 1322, as a reaction to the Despenser ascendancy; although there is no evidence for this, many people certainly did resent the favorites and were ready to plot their downfall, but it is unlikely that anyone would have viewed the Queen as the focus of a cohesive opposition party until after the sequestration of her estates, when it became plain to everyone that she had good cause for grievance.

Isolated and spied upon as she was, Isabella would have found it difficult to establish and maintain links with disaffected persons at court, but she apparently did find opportunities secretly to enlist the sympathy and support of others—we know she had managed to smuggle out letters to Charles IV, and in February, she had a private meeting with the Prior of Christ Church, Canterbury. Yet before her departure for France, there is no hard evidence that she was actively involved in forming an opposition party in England, nor that she had begun intriguing with the men who later became her allies. However, given the secret nature of underground political movements, one would not expect to find much in the way of evidence. Certainly, the enemies of the Despensers would have been more than willing to involve the Queen in their intrigues and to pass on messages or letters for her. Walsingham, writing much later, asserts that Edward had not considered it safe to allow Isabella's dower to remain in her hands, "as she maintained a secret correspondence with the enemies of the state." Had the King really suspected this, it is hardly likely that he would have sanctioned her going to the Continent, where Mortimer, the deadliest enemy of all, still plotted against him.

That is not to say, however, that Isabella was not already in league with the Despensers' opponents. She must have been sympathetic toward those who, like herself, had suffered at the hands of the favorites, and they may now have been looking to her to deliver the realm from the Despensers. With her visit to France in view, the Queen had determined on "securing revenge and satisfaction,"[91] but that would surely have depended on her counting on the support of others. At the very least, she was planning to reveal all to her brother, King Charles, in a bid to enlist his sympathy and his help in ridding England of the Despensers. Isabella may well have believed that, if, from the safety of France, she threatened to desert Edward, his desire to avert a worse public scandal might drive him to dismiss his favorites. This is corroborated by the author of the *Vita Edwardi Secundi*, who, soon after the Queen had left England, expressed this opinion: "Small wonder if she does not like Hugh, through whom her uncle [Lancaster] perished, and by whom she was deprived of her servants and all her rents; consequently, she will not (so many think) return until Hugh le Despenser is wholly removed from the King's side." This chronicler was almost certainly expressing contemporary opinion, for he apparently died soon afterward and so was not writing with the benefit of hindsight. Whatever the extent of Isabella's schemes—and we do not know exactly what, at this stage, was in her mind—she was going to need substantiation of her suffering and support on both sides of the Channel.

Isabella could number among her allies, or potential allies, Adam

Orleton, Bishop of Hereford, Henry Burghersh, Bishop of Lincoln, and John de Drokensford, Bishop of Bath and Wells, who are together referred to by Baker as "disciples of Isabella"; all three were close associates of Roger Mortimer. Then there was her uncle, Henry of Lancaster, the late Earl's brother, John de Stratford, Bishop of Winchester, William Airmyn, a prominent churchman, and even the King's own half brothers, Norfolk and Kent. Richmond, now in France, had shown himself to be sympathetic, and Henry de Beaumont was as dependable as ever.

Baker says that Orleton fueled the Queen's anger against the Despensers, exploiting her resentment at the loss of her estates. But although he was in a position to understand exactly how she felt, Orleton was still very much in disgrace at this time[92] and is unlikely to have been in any position to influence Isabella. It was only later that he emerged as one of her strongest allies.

Henry of Lancaster was a kind and honorable man in his midforties, who was known for his courtesy and balanced judgment. Having taken no part in his brother's rebellion, he had been bitterly disappointed when, after petitioning the King for the earldoms of Lancaster and Leicester, to which he was the rightful heir, since Thomas had left no children, Edward refused him, and then, suspecting his loyalty, had him kept under close observation. After two years, however, the King was satisfied that Henry was loyal and allowed him to take possession of just one of his brother's earldoms, that of Leicester. But Leicester had all along blamed the Despensers for his brother's death and wanted not only his revenge upon them but also Lancaster's name rehabilitated. He had defiantly assumed the late Earl's arms rather than his own, even though they had been declared forfeit, and had built a stone cross to Thomas's memory near Leicester.[93]

That Leicester was sympathetic to Orleton is proved by his having sent a comforting and supportive letter to the Bishop in 1324, after Orleton, accused of treason for assisting in Mortimer's escape, had written to Leicester begging him to help him make peace with the King. But before Leicester could do so, Edward got to hear of his warm response to Orleton's plea and accused him, too, of treason. Thanks, however, to Leicester's able defense and his position as the foremost magnate in the realm, he escaped conviction.[94]

Leicester would be moved to offer the Queen his support because he wanted to rid the realm of the Despensers and, more important, recover his rightful inheritance. There is no evidence that he ever intended any harm to his cousin the King.

John de Stratford, a worldly wise statesman,[95] had no love for the Despensers, who hated him and had forced him to pay them £1,000 as the price of making his peace with the King after angering Edward the previous year. He had failed to press the case for the election of the King's candidate, Robert Baldock, to the see of Winchester at Avignon, and had himself accepted that see from the Pope without first receiving royal permission. Edward's fury was such that he withheld Stratford's temporalities for over a year.[96] Stratford's intervention in pressing for Isabella to be sent to France may have been made purely out of a desire for peace, but there is always the possibility that he had another agenda entirely and that the Queen had somehow enlisted his support. Stratford may well have been one of the first to perceive her potential as a focus for the opposition to the Despensers.

Kent, being of royal birth, particularly resented Despenser's influence; both he and his brother Norfolk, another wild young man, voiced criticism of the King for allowing it. Kent's spectacular failure in France had lost him royal favor and left him vulnerable to the blandishments of Edward's enemies. While in Gascony, Kent came to rely on the advice of Sir Oliver Ingham, who had gained a reputation as a King's man but would soon emerge as a staunch ally of Mortimer, who may well have used Ingham to subvert Kent's loyalty and enlist him in the coalition against the Despensers.

It is also possible that Despenser came to harbor suspicions of Kent and took steps to neutralize him. Froissart stresses how much Kent feared Despenser and asserts that he and Isabella were both "secretly told of the danger they were in from Sir Hugh, and of their probable destruction, unless they took good care of themselves." Coming in the wake of Despenser's recent moves against the Queen, such warnings could not easily have been discounted. If Froissart's story is true, and it is seemingly corroborated by Edward's later refutation of Isabella's claim that she went in fear of her life from Despenser, then it proves that others were able to pass secret messages to the Queen and suggests that a network of intrigue did in fact exist.

In 1326, Isabella revealed her fears that Edward, too, had intended to murder her; in a sermon given at Wallingford, Bishop Orleton publicly stated that "the King carried a knife in his hose to kill the Queen, and had said that, if he had no other weapon, he would crush her with his teeth." There is no way of verifying the truth of this, but it sounds like a threat that had been uttered in the heat of the moment during a marital row; alternatively, Despenser, using his customary bullying tactics, might have threatened as much to Isabella to spell out the consequences if she proved difficult. Having been warned that both Despenser and the King wanted to kill her, Isabella must have been desperate to leave England.

There is no direct evidence that Roger Mortimer was at this time part of any opposition party forming around the Queen. Had the King entertained the slightest suspicion of this, Isabella would never have gone to France. As it was, Edward ordered Thomas de Astley, one of his envoys in France, to obtain assurances from Charles IV that "Mortimer and the other traitors and enemies of the King had left the realm of France before the coming of my lady," for the avoidance of any "perils and dishonour" that might ensue, "which God defend!"[97] Yet, as we have seen, it is more than likely that Isabella had long since come to regard Mortimer as a victim of the Despensers, like herself. She had known him, probably quite well, for about sixteen years and must have been aware of his unblemished record of loyalty to the Crown in the years before the Despensers had forced him into rebellion. Isabella must have known that, in Mortimer, she could have her greatest potential ally against the favorites. Here was a man who had tried to have them assassinated, who wanted his revenge upon them, and who was prepared to plot an invasion of England in order to achieve that end. Had Isabella already thought of joining forces with Mortimer, once she escaped abroad? It is inconceivable that it would not have crossed her mind.

Early in February, the Queen held a private meeting with Henry Eastry, the Prior of Christ Church, and confided certain secret concerns to him, chief of which might well have been the parlous state of her marriage and her fear and loathing of Despenser. Whatever it was, she not only won Eastry's sympathy but also filled him with foreboding. On 8 February, he wrote to Archbishop Reynolds, urging that "it would be quite right that the Lady Queen, before she crosses over, should have restored to her her accustomed and dignified state."[98] Reynolds may have repeated this advice to the King, for Edward would shortly take steps to ensure that Isabella departed for France with full royal accoutrements; he did not, however, go as far as to restore her estates or her income.

On 18 February, the King officially notified his envoys in France that the Queen was coming and stated that he wanted a prolongation of the truce successfully concluded by 26 May, or 24 June at the latest, so that Isabella could return home to prepare to accompany him on a visit to Gascony.[99] On 20 February, the King issued letters of protection for Isabella's retinue.[100] Charles IV also sent a safe-conduct for his sister, which arrived before 5 March, when Edward drew up a list of instructions for Isabella's guidance.[101]

Preparations for the Queen's journey were now almost complete. She was to travel in some state with a train of thirty persons, as befitted her position as Queen and formal emissary. Edward himself carefully selected all those who were to accompany Isabella, choosing only those whom he believed to be loyal to himself; some were probably set to spy on her. Her retinue was headed by John, Lord Cromwell, and four knights.[102] There were no French persons on the King's list, but he did include William de Boudon, the Queen's former treasurer, as her comptroller, and he also appointed two high-ranking noblewomen as her chief female attendants: Joan of Bar, Edward's niece and Surrey's ex-wife, and Alice de Toeni, the Dowager Countess of Warwick.[103] The King was determined that Charles IV should have no excuse to say that his sister was slighted, and if she complained about the treatment she had received in England, her words would hopefully be given the lie by her entourage and equipage.

Despite his friendship with Archbishop Reynolds having cooled after Reynold's championing of Orleton, Edward had asked him to accompany Isabella to France. But Prior Eastry, evidently still fretting over what the Queen had said to him, dissuaded Reynolds from going and supplied him with a plausible excuse, which the King apparently accepted at face value.[104]

While in France, Isabella's expenses were to be paid by grants from the Exchequer—William de Boudon was initially given £1,000 and was also authorized to withdraw any funds that the Queen needed from the Bardi's branch in Paris; in total, they are known to have paid out to her £3,674 13s. 4d.[105]

On 5 March, the King informed his envoys in France that the Queen was on her way;[106] accompanied by Despenser, he and Isabella then traveled down through Kent to Dover. At Canterbury, Isabella left her huntsmen and hounds in the care of Prior Eastry, who later complained to Despenser that they were eating him out of house and home.[107]

Meanwhile, the Pope had written to the Queen to congratulate her on having once again assumed the role of peacemaker.[108] Clearly, he had been kept closely informed of developments—and not by Edward II, for the King did not officially inform John XXII of the Queen's forthcoming peace mission until 8 March.[109]

Isabella looked to the land of her birth as a place of refuge and succor. At last, on 9 March 1325, just after Easter, her day of freedom dawned, and she finally boarded the ship that would take her to France. "The Queen departed very joyfully, happy with a twofold joy: pleased to visit her native land and her relatives, and delighted to leave the company of some whom she did not like."[110]

"On her departure, she did not seem to anyone to be offended," Edward later wrote, remembering how Isabella even bade a courteous farewell to Despenser—"towards no one was she more agreeable, myself excepted." He recalled also "the amiable looks and words between them, and the great friendship she professed for him on her crossing the sea."[111]

He had no idea that he would never see her again.

PART TWO

Isabella and Mortimer

Sweet Mortimer,
the life of Isabel

CHAPTER SEVEN

⚜

Mortimer and Isabel Do Kiss
When They Conspire

Isabella disembarked at Wissant that same day, 9 March,[1] and with her company of thirty-one persons,[2] rode to nearby Boulogne, where "she gave thanks to Our Lord" for her safe arrival "and went on foot to the church of Our Lady, and made her offering and her devotions. And the captains of the town and the Abbot welcomed her with joy and gave her lodging and hospitality, and they rested and refreshed themselves there for five days. On the sixth day, they left Boulogne, riding on horses and donkeys, which they had brought from England. The Queen was escorted and accompanied by all the knights of the surrounding country, who had come to see her and entertain her, since she was the sister of their lord the King." This is according to Froissart, who wrote many years later. His account is full of omissions and courtly embellishments, but this part of it seems sound enough.

Where did Froissart get his information about Isabella? Probably during his sojourn at the English court in the 1360s, when he was in the service of Philippa of Hainault, Isabella's daughter-in-law. Isabella was dead by then, but Philippa had known her for more than thirty years and would doubtless have heard the tale of her adventures on the Continent many times. Froissart must have also picked up information in his native Hainault, much of it from the Flemish chronicler Jean le Bel.

Accompanied by her enlarged retinue, Isabella traveled via Montreuil, Crécy, Pois, and Beauvais to Pontoise, where, on 21 March, she was received by fifteen-year-old Jeanne of Evreux, the young woman whom Charles IV had chosen as the future Queen of France; his second wife, Marie of Luxembourg, had died in childbirth the previous year, along with her premature infant, Louis. As the daughter of Louis of Evreux, Jeanne was Isabella's first cousin.

On 10 March, Isabella arrived at Poissy to meet the English envoys, whom she entertained to dinner for two successive nights. There, she began preliminary talks with representatives of King Charles, only to discover that the peace negotiations were already in deadlock.[3]

King Edward had stayed in Kent "so that it would be easy for messengers to pass swiftly between himself and his wife."[4] By the thirty-first, Isabella could report to him that, after King Charles had arrived at Poissy, she had been able to persuade his commissioners to resume talks.[5]

Charles IV was an intelligent and subtle man who had inherited the good looks of his race and was called "the Fair" like his father. He had also inherited Philip IV's severity with those who opposed him. His driving ambition was to be elected Holy Roman Emperor, and to this end, he pressured the Pope into excommunicating his rival, Louis of Bavaria. This suggests that John XXII was Charles's puppet, which would explain his support for Isabella; but the Pope was also shrewd and nobody's fool.

Both Baker and Froissart give touching accounts of the meeting between Isabella and Charles. Baker describes how the Queen "at last saw the dear face of her beloved brother, and embraced him." According to Froissart, "when the King of France saw his sister, whom he had not seen for a long time, he went up to her as she came into his chamber, took her right hand and kissed her, and said, 'Welcome, my fair sister!' The Queen, who had little joy in her heart except at being near her brother the King, tried to kneel down two or three times at his feet, but the King would not allow her, and kept hold of her right hand, and inquired most kindly how she was. The Queen answered him calmly," but she could not contain her misery "and told him sadly of all the injuries and felonies committed by Sir Hugh le Despenser, and asked his aid and comfort. And when King Charles heard his sister's troubles, he took great pity on her, and comforted her most kindly, and said, 'Fair sister, stay with us; do not be distressed or downhearted. We will find some remedy for your condition.' The Queen knelt down and thanked him deeply."

But the problem of the Despensers had to be shelved, for the avoidance of war was a more pressing priority. Isabella's task was not easy, and she later confessed to Edward that she was veering from day to day between hope and despair. Stratford had assured the King that her mediation would almost certainly secure the return of the Agenais, that part of Gascony that lay between the Dordogne and the Garonne, and other lands that the French had conquered the previous year, but Charles was reluctant to relinquish any of these territories. The papal legates who had suggested the Queen's mission were there to lend her their support, and on 31 March, a peace treaty was finally drawn up, and the Bishops of Orange, Winchester, and Norwich, along with Henry de Sully, were commissioned to take it to England for the King's approval.[6] By the terms of this treaty, Edward was to surrender Gascony, Ponthieu, and Montreuil to Charles pending his paying homage to the French King at Beauvais by August; after the homage, Charles would restore all these lands to Edward except the Agenais, the tenure of which was to be the subject of arbitration by French judges.

Until any treaty could be signed and ratified, however, the English were demanding a new truce in place of the humiliating one that had been agreed by Kent and Valois. But the French were not prepared to sanction anything but a prolongation of that truce. Isabella told Edward that, by 29 March, matters had reached such a deadlock that she was contemplating returning home. Instead, she made one final appeal to her brother and was able to report that the French had agreed to a new truce, which would last until 9 June. She closed her letter with an apology for not having informed her husband sooner of all these developments and said that she would stay on at the French court until the treaty and the truce had been successfully concluded, provided this met with Edward's approval.[7]

Accompanied by the English envoys, the Queen made a state entry into Paris on 1 April.[8] She rode astride her horse, wearing a gown of black velvet with such voluminous skirts that only the toes of her checkered black and white leather riding boots could be seen. Her unplaited hair was confined on each side to cylindrical crespinettes of gold fretwork suspended from a narrow fillet, the very latest in headdresses.[9] "Many of the nobles came out to welcome her. She was escorted to the palace by Lord Robert of Artois [her cousin], the Count of Dammartin, the Lord of Coucy, the Lord of Montmorency and several others."[10] Froissart places her first meeting with Charles here, but it is clear from her letter of 31 March that it had already taken place at Poissy. "And afterwards she stayed with all her company with the King at Paris."[11]

A week later, Edward issued safe-conducts for the Bishop of Orange's embassy to come to England,[12] Stratford and his colleagues having returned home by 10 April.[13]

On 18 April, Edward ordered the promulgation of the new truce.[14] The draft treaty reached him on 29 April; its terms were by no means acceptable, but Charles IV was demanding a prompt response, and on 2 and 3 May, Edward reluctantly agreed to them, asking only to be informed when the Agenais would be returned to him.[15] On 6 and 8 May, he granted Stratford, Airmyn, and the other English envoys further powers to treat with Charles IV.[16]

Matters had not turned out anywhere near as well as the King had hoped, and on 14 May, he complained to the Pope that the Queen had not been granted all that she had requested and that this was the fault of the legates, who had suggested her mission and held out false hopes of her success.[17]

Doherty outlines a convincing theory that the unsatisfactory terms of the treaty were the outcome of a deliberate attempt by Charles IV, Isabella, Stratford, Airmyn, and the legates to discredit the Despenser administration and give Isabella a pretext for staying on in France; however, he also cites Isabella's letter of 31 March as proof that she had made every effort to reach an acceptable settlement. Furthermore, in this letter, she asked Edward's permission to remain in France, and we know that he gave it because he sent her funds for her support.[18]

By 18 May, Stratford and Airmyn were back in France. That evening, Airmyn dined with Isabella in the royal palace at Vincennes.[19] Soon afterward, Charles IV appointed commissioners to treat with the English envoys.[20]

Isabella was present when the peace treaty was drawn up on 30 May at the Palace of the Cité in Paris; it was substantially the same as the draft sent to Edward and contained only an imprecise reference to the King of England's one day receiving justice concerning the Agenais. The treaty was ratified by Charles IV the next day and by Edward II on 13 June, although Edward can hardly have found its terms congenial and must have wondered whether it had been worth his while to send Isabella to France: she had been "no more successful than any other ambassadors, except that her brother, out of affection for her, prolonged the truce."[21] Indeed, for all his fine words, Charles had been largely impervious to her persuasions, granting only a few financial concessions "for the love of the Queen of England." There was nothing more for Isabella to do in France, and it was probably around now that Edward began to agitate for her return, writing to her frequently of his desire to have her with him.[22] But Isabella had no wish to go back and live under Despenser's tyranny. She may well have decided to prolong her stay in France for as long as possible.

Isabella's expenditure in Paris was heavy: up until 29 September alone, it amounted to £2,841 17s. 7d.; after that, the accounts are incomplete.[23] Prior to 17 June, these expenses were met by the Exchequer, the money being taken out of the Queen's confiscated revenues, but on 17 June, these payments abruptly ceased,[24] possibly because Edward saw no need for his wife to stay in France any longer.

In July, Charles IV married Jeanne of Evreux. Shortly after the wedding, doubtless embarrassed by her dwindling funds, Isabella left Paris and took up residence in the royal castle at Châteauneuf, some forty miles west of Paris. King Charles came to her rescue and, from 18 July to 1 September, subsidized her living expenses.[25] During this period, she lodged at various places near Paris, including Sainte Hilaire, Poissy, Mantes, Saint-Germain, Corbeil, and Fontainebleau, and spent her time visiting churches and entertaining; among her guests were the new Queen of France, the Abbot of Saint-Denis, the Earl of Richmond, Louis de Clermont, the Countess of Foix, and the papal legates.[26]

John Salmon, the Bishop of Norwich, died on 6 July, and as soon as she heard, Isabella put forward the name of her friend William Airmyn (or Ayermine) to the Pope. Airmyn, a canon of Saint Paul's Cathedral, had been Keeper of the Privy Seal until January 1325, when he had been elected to the See of Carlisle; however, his election had been quashed a month later. Airmyn knew Isabella well: they had worked closely together in 1321, when sharing custody of the Great Seal. John XXII now proved most accommodating and expeditious, providing Airmyn to the vacant See of Norwich on 19 July. However, in England, four days later, King Edward's candidate, Robert Baldock, was elected by the Chapter of Norwich as their bishop; he received his temporalities from the King on 25 August.

Edward's intention of going to France to pay homage had been implicit in his ratification of the new treaty. By 15 August, arrangements had been made for the ceremony at Beauvais,[27] and the King began to prepare for his journey. But the Despensers were filled with trepidation at the prospect of his going abroad and leaving them at the mercy of their enemies[28] and were also unwilling to afford Isabella any opportunity of regaining her influence with her husband. Thus, when the proposed visit was debated in council, opinion was divided as to the wisdom of the King's leaving his realm at this time. But Leicester, who was in favor of his going, carried the day.

On 23 August, Edward arrived in Dover with his eldest son, ready—for all intents and purposes—to depart.[29] But the Despensers continued to urge him not to leave England.[30] The next day, Edward suddenly announced that he was too ill to travel and that he was sending a new embassy, headed by Richmond and Stratford, to France to make different arrangements.[31]

Knowing that Despenser would be left behind in England, Isabella may have been looking forward to Edward's visit as an opportunity to lay before him her grievances about Hugh and the treatment she had suffered. She might even have planned to offer him an ultimatum, that either the favorites were dismissed or she stayed in France, and she may have counted on, or been promised, the support of Charles IV in these negotiations. But Edward was not coming now.

It must have been at this point that Isabella conceived a scheme whereby the terms of the treaty could be met, and she herself would, at the very least, be able to wield the upper hand in any confrontation with Edward over the Despensers. It would also remove her eldest son from the orbit and control of the favorites. On 1 September, the Queen returned to Paris to meet with Richmond and Stratford.[32] The following evening, she entertained the Bishop to dinner and suggested to him that Prince Edward be given all his father's continental possessions and be sent to pay homage in his stead. This, as we have seen, was not a new idea but one that had been mooted the previous winter by Charles IV. Presciently, on the same day that Isabella was dining with Stratford, Prince Edward was being invested as Count of Ponthieu and Montreuil, as his mother's heir, at Langdon Abbey near Dover. In France, Isabella was to protest against this, whereupon Charles IV assured her that "the homage done by the Prince her son" for these counties would not "in any way prejudice her interests therein."[33]

Stratford and Isabella put the Queen's suggestion to Charles IV, who, on 4 September, issued letters patent in which he agreed to accept the homage of the Prince, whereupon Stratford hastened back to England to obtain the King's approval. Some of Edward's advisers "were of the opinion that his son would be vulnerable to all manner of misfortunes if he were exposed to the wily and avaricious French without the protection of his father. Those who argued thus were indeed justified."[34] But the Despensers were greatly in favor of the idea,[35] for "they dared neither to cross the Channel with King Edward, nor to remain behind in England in his absence."[36] Rashly, therefore, Edward II agreed to send his son to France in his stead, little realizing that, by allowing his heir to go overseas to his mother, he was placing in Isabella's hands a hostage to fortune.

On 10 September, the twelve-year-old Prince was created Duke of Aquitaine. Two days later, in the company of Bishops Stratford and Stapledon, Henry de Beaumont, and a number of lords and knights, he boarded a vessel for France.[37] Before it sailed, his father made him promise that he would not accept any guardian nor enter into any marriage alliance without the King's permission.[38] Negotiations were well advanced for the Prince's marriage to the Infanta Eleanor of Aragon; at the same time, Edward was planning to marry one of his own daughters to Pedro, the heir of James II, King of Aragon, and applications had already been made to the Pope for the necessary dispensations.[39] Naturally, the King did not wish to prejudice this hoped-for alliance. The Prince told his father that it should be his pleasure to obey his commandments, as far as he could, all his days.[40]

When young Edward's ship dropped anchor at Boulogne on 14 September, his mother was waiting to greet him and take him with her to Paris. Isabella must have been overjoyed to see her son, but not so pleased to discover that Stratford had brought with him a safe-conduct for her from the King, who had commanded her to return home "without delay" as soon as the Prince had performed his homage.[41]

Evading this issue, Isabella turned her attention to the imminent consecration of the new Bishop of Norwich. A few days earlier, much to Edward's chagrin, Robert Baldock had been obliged by the Pope to resign from the See of Norwich in favor of William Airmyn; twice now, thanks to Isabella's influence, Baldock, that close associate of the Despensers, had been deprived of high episcopal office, despite being the King's nominee. Isabella was well aware how furious Edward and the Despensers would be at the success of her candidate, William Airmyn, and to ensure that no further obstacles were placed in his way, she arranged for Airmyn to be consecrated Bishop of Norwich at a ceremony in France on 15 September, "for which the King was angry."[42] By then, however, it was too late for Edward to do anything about it, apart from vengefully refusing to allow Airmyn the temporalities of his see.

On 22 September, the Queen and her son arrived in Paris, and Isabella witnessed the young Duke of Aquitaine's first audience with his uncle, Charles IV, who "received him kindly."[43] Two days later, the Prince did homage to Charles at the royal hunting lodge at Bois-de-Vincennes, "in the presence of the Queen his mother" and many English lords.[44] Immediately afterward, Charles ordered the withdrawal of French troops from Gascony.

Edward was now hoping that the Agenais would soon be returned to him, but shortly afterward, Charles informed him that he intended to retain that territory as indemnity for French losses suffered during the war. Strickland suggests that Isabella had deliberately arranged this in order to give herself a further pretext for staying on in Paris, but it may be that King

Charles himself had conceived it as a strategy for keeping the heir to England in France and wresting every advantage out of Edward.

During her stay in France, Isabella had earned the support of several men at her brother's court, notably her cousin, Robert of Artois.[45] She also became a magnet for a group of disaffected Englishmen, among them "exiles who were the enemies of the King of England, but who had gained the Queen's favour."[46] It is not known exactly when these men switched their allegiance to Isabella, but it is probable that her support expanded over a period of months. Some of her new adherents, such as Sir John Maltravers, had escaped from England after Boroughbridge;[47] the rest, such as John, Lord Ros, had other scores to settle with Edward and the Despensers. Both the Queen and these men had one thing in common: their loathing of the favorites.

Isabella's chief supporter at this time appears to have been the Earl of Richmond, who had served as the principal English envoy in France since the previous year. He had been greatly offended by the Despensers and was now "one who was of the affinity of the Queen"[48] and was often in her company, both before and after the homage. The King recalled him many times,[49] but he repeatedly ignored these summonses.

Another who had attached himself to the Queen's party was the King's own brother, the Earl of Kent. Kent had returned to France on 25 August, in company with Surrey, who had been appointed captain of the English forces in Aquitaine. On 6 October, Kent was to obtain from the Pope a dispensation permitting him to marry Margaret, the daughter of John, Lord Wake, and a cousin of Roger Mortimer: her mother and his were sisters. The marriage took place in December 1325. Margaret's brother, Thomas, Lord Wake, had once been the Queen's ward and was now with Isabella in Paris.

Bishop Airmyn, who owed his see to Isabella, became another member of this cabal. "A prudent and circumspect man, efficient and experienced,"[50] he was a natural ally of the Queen, not only on account of her earlier intervention with the Pope on his behalf but also because he was seriously out of favor with the King after Baldock's expulsion from Norwich.

Henry de Beaumont had long been Isabella's friend and, like her, a victim of the Despensers' spite. He had his finger on the pulse of political opinion in the north of England and was able to tell her that a majority of Edward's subjects there had turned against him, many having been irrevocably alienated by Edward's failure to deal effectively with the Scottish raiders. In time, Beaumont would return to England to sound out the northern lords as to where their loyalty really lay.[51]

Beaumont's fellow envoy, Bishop Stratford, was also sympathetic toward the Queen, as was John, Lord Cromwell, who had accompanied her to France in March. Both were men whom Edward had obviously thought he could trust, so it must have come as a shock when Cromwell repeatedly defied his orders to return. Stratford was more subtle, and there was no open breach between him and the King, but the evidence suggests that his true loyalties lay with Isabella.

Someone who joined the Queen later in Paris was the Prince's former tutor, Richard de Bury, who, in his capacity as young Edward's official receiver in Gascony, had been illicitly diverting revenues to the Queen, for which he only narrowly escaped arrest by fleeing to the French court.[52] Bury had long since discovered in Isabella a kindred spirit with a love of books, and his first loyalty was to her and the Prince, who was always to look on him with great favor.

Judging by how promptly they were to come to Isabella's support the following year, Leicester and Norfolk, Earl Marshal of England and a young man "of a wild and wicked character,"[53] must have been in secret communication with her for some time. Although both were close kin to the King, neither was prepared to endure the tyranny of the Despensers for any longer than necessary, while Lancaster had his own deadly score to settle, for he wanted revenge for the execution of his brother and restitution of the Lancastrian inheritance. In Isabella, both he and Norfolk saw an ally who was well placed to take action against the favorites.

According to Ian Mortimer, earlier intelligence reports sent back to England show that some of the exiles had in the past kept company with Roger Mortimer as he moved around the Continent. It is possible, therefore, that they were still in touch with him. Perhaps, too, they were in contact with Mortimer's partisan Adam Orleton, Bishop of Hereford, who was to prove himself a staunch supporter of Isabella in 1326. It is not unfeasible that the exiles were also negotiating with Mortimer himself, with a view to securing his support for the Queen.

Isabella now began to hold "secret conferences"[54] with her supporters and came to rely on their counsel; in so doing, she gave offense to those officials who had been sent by Edward to give her guidance[55] and who now expressed surprise at the Queen's conduct in consorting with her husband's known enemies. Charles IV must have known about these secret talks, at which the chief topic was doubtless the dilemma in which Isabella found herself. Should she go home, as her husband was commanding, and risk incurring the fury of Despenser; or could she contrive to stay in France?

For more than a year, Isabella was to insist that her quarrel was with the Despensers alone. Yet there is evidence, as we will see, that the exiles surrounding her were bent on targeting the King as well, and it seems that they did their utmost to persuade the Queen that she would be justified in lending her support to the overthrow of a weak and tyrannical regime. Isabella initially may well have resisted this scheme and apparently spent weeks agonizing over what course she should take, which would explain why she did not deliver Edward any ultimatum regarding the Despensers until November and why she continued to send cordial letters to the favorite.[56] Avoiding any criticism of Hugh, or an open breach, would make life easier for her if she was forced to return to England.

Charles's retention of the Agenais left Edward seething with rage. Too late, he attempted to reassume the rights he had just devolved upon his heir, but Charles was having none of it and declared the whole duchy forfeit, much to the King's horror; later, the French King was to send a force into Gascony to defend the Prince's tenure. As far as the peace was concerned, Isabella's mission had been in vain, but it was to serve another, more sinister purpose.

Edward was also simmering with anger against his envoys in France, Airmyn and Richmond, who he was convinced had betrayed him over the treaty. He ordered their arrest and brought a case against the absent Airmyn in the Court of King's Bench.[57] The King was now beginning to be perturbed by Isabella's failure to return home and the fact that she had his heir in her custody, a circumstance of which he seems to have feared—and with good reason—that Charles IV might take advantage. Now that the treaty had been concluded and the homage performed, he saw no reason for Isabella and Prince Edward to stay in France.

Isabella, on the other hand, had every reason to keep her son with her. Having the heir to England in her control gave her every advantage. Not only was he Edward's heir, but Edward was also very fond of the boy, and Isabella was aware that the threat of his being kept in France would be a powerful bargaining counter in forcing her husband to banish the Despensers. Edward might regard her as dispensable, but he could not do without his son and heir. Moreover, the Prince was a valuable asset in the dynastic marriage market and could be used by his mother as a means of forging an alliance that would assure her of political and military support in her quarrel with Edward. That Isabella came to contemplate going to such lengths to get rid of the Despensers shows how deadly was her hatred of them. But it makes even more sense in the context of her considering another agenda entirely, in the event of Edward's failing to cooperate: in which case, she would endeavor to bring about the deposition of the King himself, in favor of his son. For if Isabella defied Edward to the extent of allying with his enemies and marrying off his heir against his father's will, how could she ever hope to be reconciled to him? The Prince was the key to the success of such a daring scheme, and with him in her possession, and the backing of Charles IV, Isabella was in a very strong position.

It has been suggested that Isabella also kept the Prince in France because she was aware that Charles IV had as yet no male heir and was hopeful that he might name this promising boy, his nephew, as his successor, in the event of Queen Jeanne's failing to bear sons. This is possible. It is certain, too, that the presence of the heir to England in France crystallized the ambitions of the English exiles.

Soon after Michaelmas, Edward wrote to Isabella, "advising that she should escort her son back to England as soon as possible. Isabella replied that the King of France was treating them with great kindness and all but keeping them there against their will."[58] Not satisfied with this, Edward began sending Isabella further commands and entreaties to come home[59] and ordered Stratford to broach the matter with the Queen and Charles IV. During their discussions, Isabella expressed her anger over the sequestration of her estates and her fears that she would not be safe in England. The Bishop insisted that she would come to no harm, but she was evidently not reassured by this and tried again to put Edward off with a succession of flimsy and frivolous excuses.[60]

On 18 October, the King complained to the Pope about Charles's retention of the Agenais. He also expressed his mounting concern about the unwonted prolongation of the Queen's visit to France.[61]

Isabella was now spending much of her time with King Charles and Queen Jeanne, "and the news she told them from England gave them little pleasure."[62] Much of it concerned the activities of Walter Stapledon, Bishop of Exeter.

Bishop Stapledon had known that he was not welcome in France: it was said that, because he was closely associated with the Despensers, if he ever set foot in that kingdom, he would be tortured.[63] Before he left England, he had confided his fears for his safety to the King, who had asked Isabella for an undertaking that the Bishop would come to no harm, which she readily gave. Despite this, he was treated by French courtiers and officials "as if he were guilty of some crime,"[64] which seems to have made him somewhat paranoid.

Prior to his departure, Stapledon had been commanded by Edward to raise a loan to help meet the expenses of Isabella's household, but the money was only to be given to her once she had agreed to return with Stapledon to England.[65] Clearly, Edward had from the first been edgy at the prospect of Isabella's being in France with his heir in her custody.

Stapledon had so far failed to raise the loan.[66] He did not like what he saw of the Queen's activities in Paris, especially the favor shown by her to the English exiles who were now clustering around her, and he was greatly perturbed by the intelligence that had come to him concerning the intrigues of this group, who were apparently plotting nothing less than the murder of the King, an act of the most heinous treason. This is the earliest evidence for this being the ultimate aim of Edward's enemies.

Stapledon was never to accuse Isabella directly of being a party to such treason, but it is hard to believe that she was unaware of what was being discussed by the members of her circle. That she should sanction, or engage in, discussions concerning the regicide of her husband the King, which was then regarded as one of the most dreadful and sacrilegious crimes that could be committed and carried with it terrible penalties, is testimony to the virulence of her anger against Edward, and to the change in her character that had been brought about by his and the Despensers' ill-treatment of her during the past years. Above all, her actions at this time must have been dictated by her fear of returning to face the wrath of the Despensers and the King, who she knew from bitter experience could not be trusted to keep his word. And doubtless she was being pressured by those who were convinced that the removal of Edward II was a political necessity after years of his inflicting misgovernment and rapacious favorites upon his subjects.

Stapledon was so horrified at what he had learned that he was desperate to return to England without delay and was seeking a way to do so without alerting anyone to his suspicions.

Without a doubt, Isabella did not like Stapledon: he was too closely associated with the Despenser administration to be any friend to her, and he had a reputation for being "unreasonably avaricious; during his term of office [as Treasurer], he had become remarkably rich, whence it seemed that he had made his wealth by extortion rather than by honest dealing."[67] Unsurprisingly, he was "excluded from [the Queen's] secret conferences,"[68] and she refused to entertain him[69] or receive any letters from him, sending them back unread through Stratford.[70] But she could not let his failure to raise the loan pass and summoned him to her presence. This must have been before 22 October, on which date she left Paris to visit Le Bourget and Rheims with her son; she would not return until 12 November, by which time Stapledon would be back in England.[71]

Their interview must have left her more convinced than ever that the Despensers must be removed and him painfully aware that she was impervious to any influence he might try to exert over her.

Isabella began by reminding Stapledon that he had been commanded by the King to help finance her stay in Paris but had done nothing. He, in turn, lied to her that the King had written summoning him home, whereat Isabella demanded to see the letter. Of course, Stapledon could not produce it, although he said he would do so. By now, he must have made it obvious to Isabella that he was fearful of staying in France and wanted to return to England forthwith, but she forbade him to do so without her permission.[72] Undoubtedly, she was concerned about her funds and expected him to obey his orders, but she was also almost certainly alarmed at what he might have found out.

It is significant that, soon after this interview, Stapledon received a death threat. This suggests that Isabella knew exactly what the English exiles were plotting and that, before she left Paris, she warned them they might be exposed. The consequence of this was that someone threatened Stapledon, not dreaming that he would defy the Queen's order to stay in Paris.

On 31 October, Bishop Stapledon suddenly arrived back in England[73] and hastened to the royal headquarters at Portchester Castle in great distress. Certain of the King's banished enemies, he warned Edward, were plotting to kill him. His own life had been threatened, and he had secretly escaped from France under cover of darkness, disguised "as a merchant or pilgrim." It was claimed that he had left behind his household "to pretend he was there," but his expense account shows that every one of his retinue of forty-nine men, along with thirty-two horses, accompanied him, and that they traveled in three ships.[74] This suggests that his flight had been planned carefully in advance.[75] Stapledon now urged the King to demand the immediate return of the Queen and the Prince.[76]

Evidently, Stapledon felt embarrassed about the precipitous and undoubtedly rude manner in which he had deserted the Queen and left the French court, for he had the grace to write to her excusing his conduct, taking care not to apportion any blame to her.[77]

On 14 November, probably as a result of Stapledon's revelations, Edward apparently ceased paying Isabella's expenses, for her accounts come to an abrupt end on that date.[78] Evidently, he was not prepared to finance her self-imposed exile any longer. It was probably this that hardened Isabella's resolve against him and forced her to declare her defiance.

The *Vita Edwardi Secundi* states that "when the King sent his son to France, he ordered his wife to return to England without delay" and then refers to messengers laying this command before the Queen in the presence of Charles IV. In fact, given that Isabella had not yet declared her reasons for staying in France, it is more likely that Edward sent his demand in November rather than September and that he sent it via Stratford, who was the messenger in question. Isabella was evidently prepared for this.

"When this command had been laid before the King of France and the Queen, she replied: 'I feel that marriage is a joining together of man and woman, maintaining the undivided habit of life, and that someone has come between my husband and myself, trying to break this bond. I protest that I will not return until this intruder is removed, but, discarding my marriage garment, shall assume the robes of widowhood and mourning until I am avenged of this Pharisee.' " This last word meant an opponent of Christ, or one who separates. Charles IV, seeing Isabella's distress and "not wishing to detain her, said, 'The Queen has come [to France] of her own will, and may freely return when she so wishes. But if she prefers to remain in these parts, she is my sister, and I refuse to expel her.' "[79]

From now on, Isabella made a point of wearing only simple black mourning garments, with a nunlike veil and a barbe above the chin, "like a doleful lady who has lost her lord."[80] We may imagine that, far from concealing her charms, this severe attire enhanced her famous beauty to striking effect and aroused men's sympathy, as she had certainly intended.

At the end of November, Stratford arrived back in England "and reported all this to the King."[81] He also gave him a letter from Isabella, in which she declared that neither she nor her son would return to his court until the Despensers had been dismissed from his presence, for she believed that "it was the[ir] intention to cause her to be put to death if she returned to England." She also insisted on reaching an agreement with Edward regarding her status and her income.[82] In another letter, Isabella warned that she and her brother, with the aid of her supporters in France, intended to do "that which will turn out not to the prejudice of the lord King, but to the destruction of Hugh alone."[83] This could mean only one thing: a show of armed force against England with the intention of removing the favorite.

At face value, Isabella's demands and threats indicate that she was still willing to return to Edward, but on her own terms. Her ultimate aim at this time must have been the assassination of the Despensers. Given Edward's long history of breaking his word and putting the interests of his favorites before all other considerations, he could hardly be counted on to send them away forever for her sake. Nor could she have expected them to remain meekly in exile, causing no trouble. She must have known that to return to England and trust to Edward to keep his word would be foolish in the extreme. How many times had he been constrained to banish his favorites and then secretly recalled them? And Despenser, she must have known, would not hesitate to take a brutal revenge on one who had so opposed him, while Edward had already demonstrated that he was hardly likely to intervene on Isabella's behalf.

But did Isabella really believe that Edward would accede to her demands? If she did, she was less of a realist than her other deeds proclaim her to be. No, it is far more likely that Isabella made those demands in the full expectation that Edward would refuse them and thus give her a pretext for remaining in France until her future could be safely assured through the intervention of her brother and her supporters. As for her threats against Despenser, she had given Edward due warning, and Hugh's fate would now be his responsibility.

Edward, thick-skinned and self-centered as he was, and not well endowed with great powers of perception, was shocked by his wife's ultimatum. On 18 November, Parliament had met at the Tower of London, and before it rose on 5 December, having been transferred to Westminster, the King appeared before the magnates and prelates "and began to rehearse what had happened in a short speech," which amounted to a public complaint about the Queen's conduct, which now appeared not only disloyal and undutiful but menacing and scandalous. He told the assembly:

> You know how providentially, as then it seemed, the Queen crossed to France to make peace, being told that when her mission was accomplished, she should at once return. And this she promised with a good will. And on her departure, she did not seem to anyone to be offended. As she took her leave, she saluted all and went away joyfully. But now someone has changed her attitude. Someone has primed her with inventions. For I know that she has not fabricated any affront out of her own head. Yet she says that Hugh le Despenser is her adversary and hostile to her. It is surprising that she has conceived this dislike of Hugh, for when she departed, towards no one was she more agreeable, myself excepted. For this reason, Hugh is much cast down, but he is nevertheless prepared to show his innocence in any way whatsoever. Hence I firmly believe that the Queen has been led into this error at the suggestion of

someone, and he is in truth wicked and hostile, whoever he may be. Now therefore deliberate wisely, that she whom the teaching of evil men incites to guile may be led back to the path of unity by your prudent and kindly reproof.[84]

Who was the "someone," the man who had led Isabella astray? Edward's reference to "evil men" probably refers to the group of exiles that had attached itself to Isabella in Paris, and clearly, he did not know which one of them to blame most. If anyone had influenced Isabella, it was perhaps Richmond, who had also refused to obey an order to return home, and who certainly held great sway with the Queen.

Edward's defense of Despenser cannot have impressed his listeners, most of whom would have known that Hugh had indeed given Isabella many causes for offense and had repeatedly proved himself hostile to her. Yet the refusal of the Queen of England to return home was creating a major scandal as well as undermining national security, and the lords, however sympathetic they were toward her, were anxious to put an end to this situation as soon as possible.

In response to the King's appeal, Despenser made a public declaration to the Lords that his intentions toward the Queen had always been innocent of malice. Edward then began to put pressure on the bishops, who reluctantly agreed to write collectively to Isabella, as "fathers" to a "dear daughter," exhorting her to set aside "her baseless ill-feeling" and return home to her husband. Their letter, which was dated 1 December 1325, read:

> Most dear and potent lady, the whole country is disturbed by your news, and the answers which you have lately sent to our lord King; and because you delay your return out of hatred for Hugh le Despenser, everyone predicts that much evil will follow. Indeed, Hugh le Despenser has solemnly demonstrated his innocence before all, and that he has never harmed the Queen, but done everything in his power to help her; and that he will always in future do this, he has confirmed by his corporeal oath. He added moreover that he could not believe that these threats ever proceeded from your head alone, but that they come from some other source, especially as before your departure, you showed yourself gracious to him, and afterwards sent him friendly letters, which he produced in full Parliament.

The phraseology in this letter so closely mirrors that in the King's speech that preceded it that one cannot avoid the suspicion that these words had been dictated to the bishops by either Edward himself or Despenser.

The letter continues:

Wherefore, dearest lady, [we] beseech you as [our] lady, [we] warn you as a daughter, to return to our lord King, your husband, putting aside all rancour. You who have gone away for the sake of peace, do not, for the sake of peace, delay to return. For all the inhabitants of our land fear that many evils will result from your refusal to return. They fear the arrival of foreigners and that their goods will be plundered. They do not think that this comes from due affection, that you should wish to destroy a people so devoted to you, through hatred of one man. But as for what you have written, that what your brother the King of France and your other friends of their country intend to do on your behalf, will turn out not to the prejudice of the lord King or anyone else, but to the destruction of Hugh alone. Dearest and most powerful lady, refuse to give an opening to such a business, as its furthering can in all probability bring irreparable loss. The English people predict from these threats the coming of foreigners, and say, if the French come, they will plunder the land. It is impossible that the innocent should not suffer equally with the guilty [was this a Freudian slip, an admission that Despenser *was* guilty?], and what the innocent do not snatch away they shall lose. Alas! If things turn out thus, it may happen that we shall regard as a stepmother her whom we had hoped to have as a patron. Alas! Clergy and people with complaining voice reiterate their fear that they and theirs will be utterly destroyed through the hatred felt for one man. Wherefore, lady Queen, accept wise counsel and do not delay your return. For your longed-for arrival will restrain the malice of men and restrict all opportunities for evil.[85]

This was a clever letter, constructed so as to put Isabella firmly in the wrong and place upon her the responsibility for any hostilities that resulted from her action. "But notwithstanding this letter, mother and son refused to return to England."[86]

Meanwhile, Isabella had begun to find herself seriously short of money and unable to maintain the state required of a queen and pay all her servants, so she sent some of her people home.[87] At the end of November, members of her entourage and Prince Edward's began arriving back in England.[88] Hamo de Hethe, Bishop of Rochester, met some of them while he was traveling through Kent, and they told him that the Queen had sent them back because Stapledon had fled from France without giving her any money with which to pay them.[89]

The Queen was now relying on loans from the Bardi,[90] but there was no guarantee that these would continue, so Charles IV again came timely to her rescue and lent her 1,000 Paris livres.[91] According to Froissart, he told her, "We have enough for you as well as for ourselves," and "he had everything necessary supplied to her." This was no purely altruistic or fraternal gesture, for Charles had every intention of exploiting the bad relations between his sister and her husband with a view to recovering Gascony. He wrote firmly and unequivocally to Edward "that he could not permit her to return to him unless she were guaranteed from the evil that was meditated against her by her enemies, the Despensers."[92]

On 1 December, the day on which he obliged the bishops to write to the Queen, Edward himself sent her a letter ordering her to come home forthwith.

> To the Queen.
>
> Lady [he wrote], oftentimes we have sent to you, both before and after the homage, of our great desire to have you with us, and of our great grief of heart at your long absence; and, as we understand that you do us great mischief by this, we will that you come to us with all speed and without further excuses. Before the homage was performed, you made the advancement of that business an excuse, and now that we have sent, by the honourable father the Bishop of Winchester, our safe conduct to you, you will not come for the fear and doubt of Hugh le Despenser. Whereat we cannot marvel too much, when we recall your flattering deportment towards each other in our presence, so amicable and sweet was your manner, with special assurances and looks, and other tokens of the firmest friendship, and also, since then, your very especial letters to him of late date, which he has shown to us.

In his next sentence, Edward demonstrates that he was a liar of the first order or capable of the greatest self-deception or perhaps extraordinarily stupid.

> And certes, Lady, we know for truth, and so know you, that he has always procured from us all the honour he could for you, nor to you hath either evil or villainy been done since you entered into our companionship; unless, peradventure, as you may yourself remember, once when we had cause to give you secretly some words of reproof for your

pride, but without other harshness. And doubtless both God and the law of Holy Church require you, both for your honour and ours, for nothing earthly to trespass against our commandments, or to forsake our company.

As a woman subject to her husband, Isabella was in an impossible situation. If she obeyed his commands and returned to him, having declared her hatred of Despenser, she would almost certainly be placing herself in danger. Yet if she defied her lord and stayed where she was, she ran the risk of incurring the censure of the Church and society in general. Edward was clearly aware of this, yet he was too blind to see that most people regarded his wife as more sinned against than sinning, even in detaining their son. Only able to see that he was a wronged husband, and believing that the sympathies of many were with him rather than his wife, he had no compunction about occupying the high moral ground. He went on:

And we are much displeased, now the homage has been made to our dearest brother, the King of France, and we have such fair prospect of amity, that you, whom we sent to make the peace, should be the cause (which God forfend!) of increasing the breach between us, especially by things which are feigned and contrary to the truth.

Edward did not pause to ask himself why Isabella should feign hatred for Despenser. It was plain to most people that she had enough cause to hate him, and it was not in her interests to foment trouble with the French. Had she not been given extreme provocation, she would have had no reason to seek her brother's support, nor to remain in France. But the King chose to make out that, for unfathomable reasons of her own, she was deliberately creating a breach between the two countries. He concluded:

Wherefore we charge you as urgently as we can that, ceasing from all pretences, delays and false excuses, you come to us with all the haste you can. Our said Bishop [Stratford] has reported to us that our brother the King told you in his presence that, by the tenor of your safe-conduct, you would not be delayed or molested in coming to us as a wife should to her lord. And as to your expenses, when it shall be that you will come to us as a wife should to her lord, we will provide that there shall be no deficiency in aught that is pertaining to you, and that you be not in any way dishonoured by us. Also, we require of you to suffer and cause our dear son Edward to return to us with all possible speed, as we have ordered him, and that you in no way let [prevent] him. For we much desire to see him and to speak with him.[93]

That same day, the King wrote also to Charles IV, attempting to sweeten him with falsehoods:

We have received and understood your letters, delivered by the Bishop of Winchester, and have also understood what the Bishop has told us by word of mouth.

It seems that you have been told, dearest brother, by persons whom you consider worthy of credit, that our companion, the Queen of England, dare not return to us, being in peril of her life, as she apprehends, from Hugh le Despenser. Certes, dearest brother, it cannot be that she can have fear of him or any other man in our realm, since, by God, if either Hugh or any other living being in our dominions sought to do her ill, and it came to our knowledge, we would chastise him in a manner that should be an example to all others. And this is, and always will be, our entire will, as long as, by God's mercy, we have the power. And, dearest brother, know certainly that we have never perceived that he has either secretly or openly, by word, look or action, demeaned himself otherwise than he ought in all points to do to so very dear a lady. And when we remember the amiable looks and words between them that we have seen, and the great friendship that she professed for him on her crossing the sea, and the loving letters which she has lately sent him, which he has shown to us, we have no power to believe that our consort can, of herself, credit such things of him; we cannot in any way believe it of him, who, after our own person, is the man of all our realm who would most wish to do her honour, and has always shown good sincerity to you. We pray you, dearest brother, not to give credence to any one who would make you otherwise suppose, but to put your faith in those who have always borne true witness to you in other things, and who have the best reason to know the truth of this matter.

Wherefore we beseech you, dearest brother, both for you honour and ours, but more especially for that of our said consort, that you would compel her to return to us with all speed; for certes, we have been ill at ease for want of her company, in which we have much delight; which truly we would have in no wise suffered, but for the great trust which we had that she should return at our will. And if our surety and safe conduct is not enough, then let her come to us on the pledge of your good faith for us.

We also entreat you, dearly beloved brother, that you would be pleased to deliver up to us Edward, our beloved eldest son, your nephew; and that, of your love and affection to him, you would render to him the lands of the duchy, that he be not disinherited, which we cannot suppose you wish. Dearly beloved brother, we pray you to suffer him to come to us with all speed, for we have often sent for him, and we greatly wish to see him and to speak with him, and every day we long for his return.

And, dearest brother, at this time, the honourable father in God, Walter [Stapledon], Bishop of Exeter, has returned to us, having certified to us that his person was in peril from some of our banished enemies; and we, having great need of his counsel, enjoined him on his faith and allegiance to return forthwith, leaving all other matters in the best way he could. We pray you, therefore, to excuse the sudden departure of the said Bishop, for the cause before said.

Given at Westminster, the first day of December.[94]

It is noticeable that Edward does not categorically deny that Despenser has treated Isabella badly, only that he himself has never perceived that he has, or could not believe it, or that, if Despenser did do her ill, he would be punished. There is too much repetition and emphasis in this letter, too much protest. The King's plea to Charles to be mindful of Isabella's honor shows that he knew already that her reputation was at stake. Medieval society frowned upon women who dared to desert their husbands, however provoked they had been; a wife was her husband's property, and his honor was vested in her. Public opinion and the law would almost always be on his side, especially when that wife had also deprived her husband of his son and heir; and how much more opprobrious would such conduct be when her husband was also her king? But Edward grossly underestimated the extent of public sympathy for Isabella.

On 2 December, Edward sent a third letter, this time to his son. In it, he shows that he was aware of the wider implications of the boy's being in his mother's hands and the danger to himself from any alliance she might make.

Very dear son, as you are young and of tender age, we would remind you of that which we charged and commanded you when you left us at Dover, and you answered then, as we know, with good will, that you would not trespass or disobey any of our injunctions in any point for anyone. And since that your homage has been received by our dearest brother, the King of France, your uncle, be pleased to take your leave of

him and return to us with all speed, in company with your mother, if so
be that she come quickly; and if she will not come, then come you without further delay, for we have great desire to speak with you; therefore
stay not for your mother, nor anyone else, on our blessing.

Given at Westminster, the 2nd day of December.[95]

For Isabella, Edward's letters only confirmed what she had long
believed, that he was deaf to her complaints and resolved only to put
Despenser's interests first. The young Prince found himself placed in an
impossible position, torn between his duty to his father and sovereign, and
his obedience to his mother, that wounded figure in mourning. It is clear
that he loved both his parents, but he was only thirteen; how could he defy
his mother when he was in her custody in a foreign kingdom where her
brother ruled? All he could do was reply to his father that, yes, he did
remember the promises he had made at Dover, but he could not return
home because of his mother and felt he should stay with her on account of
her great unease of mind and unhappiness. Isabella herself, however,
assured her husband that, if the Prince wished to return, she would not prevent it.[96] But of course, she did her best not to encourage it.

Charles IV discussed the contents of Edward's letters with Isabella, who
asked him to reply to her husband that she did desire to be with him as a
wife ought to be; indeed, "she could wish for nothing better than to live and
die in the company of her dear lord" and would be with him but for her fear
of Despenser. She also asked Charles to explain why she had feigned friendship with Despenser.[97]

Aware now of what Stapledon had told Edward, Isabella wasted no time in
embarking on what appears to have been a damage-limitation exercise with
a view to blaming Stapledon's actions on Despenser and thus deflecting
scrutiny from her own supporters; on 8 December, she wrote reprovingly
to the Bishop:

We have understood what you have told us by your letters and your
excuses for leaving us in the way you did. Know that, since our very dear
lord, the King of England, sent you with Edward our son into the
regions of France, and we promised faithfully to keep you from harm
and to take good and safe care of you; and our said lord the King commanded you to make a money loan for the expenses of our household,
but—as we understand it—you have done nothing. And we forbade you
to leave without our permission, and you gave us to understand that you

had orders by letter from our very dear lord the King to leave, but you have never been able to show his letters to this effect, as it appears to us, and we are certain of it.

In spite of our very dear lord and brother [Charles IV] and ourselves, in disobedience, and despite our prohibition, and to the great dishonour of our said lord of England and ourselves, and to the advantage of Hugh le Despenser, you left us in an ill-intentioned way, so that we can see clearly that you are in league with the said Hugh, and more obedient towards him than towards us. We would therefore have you know that we do not consider you in any way excusable, though this is what it is our duty to do.

Given at Paris on 8 December.[98]

It was probably at this point that Roger Mortimer came back into Isabella's life.

The Queen's uncle, Charles, Count of Valois, had recently died, and in December, his relatives gathered in Paris for his funeral. His daughter Jeanne, Countess of Hainault, had traveled from the Low Countries to be there.[99] During her visit, she met with Isabella and Charles IV for talks, and they doubtless discussed the poor relations between England and Hainault, the abortive negotiations for Prince Edward to marry one of Jeanne's daughters, Count William's anxiety to have the maritime dispute with England resolved, and the potential for an alliance between the two countries. Doherty plausibly suggests that Jeanne came armed with the firm offer of an alliance with Isabella: the terms were the amicable resolution of the dispute and the marriage of her son to a princess of Hainault, in return for aid from the Count.[100]

Jeanne probably brought with her in her train Roger Mortimer, who was certainly in Paris that December. For more than a year now, he had been in Hainault endeavoring, with the Count's full approval, to raise troops for an invasion of England, and it would not be surprising if Jeanne had contrived a meeting between him and Isabella, now that Isabella was known to be in open opposition to the Despensers. Before this date, there is no record of Mortimer's being in France at the same time as Isabella, so it is unlikely that he was the third party referred to by Edward II the previous November.

The likeliest scenario is that, urged on by Charles, Mortimer, Jeanne, and her own supporters, Isabella accepted in principle the offer of an alliance with Hainault. Because of the war over Gascony, Charles was reluctant to provide Isabella with an army, and she herself must long since have realized that invading England with French backing would not help to win her popular support, France being regarded as England's ancient enemy. But a pact with the increasingly prosperous county of Hainault would offer many trading advantages to the English.

Certainly, this alliance was being mooted in diplomatic circles as a very real possibility during the weeks that followed. Most historians assert that, until the autumn of 1326, Isabella's aim was purely the removal of the Despensers, but her intention to form an alliance with Hainault in defiance of her husband's expressed wishes is strong evidence that, fired up by the resolve of her allies, she was seriously contemplating the deposition of her husband in favor of her son. This, of course, was a momentous and controversial proposition, and in order to win and retain popular support, Isabella was prudently to keep up the pretense that her quarrel was with the Despensers only.

Whatever the Countess Jeanne's role in bringing them together, Isabella and Mortimer certainly met in Paris that December, were attracted to each other, and plunged headlong into an adulterous affair[101] that flouted every convention of the medieval Church and state and ultimately caused a scandal of epic proportions.

Adultery was normally regarded then as a necessary evil in men but as a vile sin in women, especially the wives of landed men, for it endangered dynastic bloodlines. When a woman was the Queen of England, therefore, it was an even more serious crime. Isabella could not have forgotten the cruel fates of her sisters-in-law but probably felt that they had not been as bitterly provoked as she had, nor as deserving of sympathy. And indeed, it is clear that many people were sympathetic toward her plight and were prepared to turn a blind eye to the adulterous nature of her relationship with Mortimer, as long as their alliance remained advantageous in other ways. Nowadays, of course, many people would applaud Isabella's courage in breaking away from an unendurable marriage and would regard her liaison with Mortimer as an opportunity for self-fulfillment and the chance to take control of her own destiny. But we cannot apply modern values when judging the actions of one who lived seven hundred years ago. Isabella must have known that she risked incurring the condemnation of society at large and that a woman flouted the conventions of the age only at her peril.

Although Isabella and Mortimer patently did not flaunt their sexual relationship, it would soon become abundantly clear that they were locked in much more than a political alliance; although it was certainly that, too, for both were victims of the Despensers, and both were driven by their determination to be revenged upon them and their ambition to be restored to greatness.

The English chroniclers of the day are infuriatingly reticent in writing about the affair between Isabella and Mortimer, apart from their tacit acceptance that it existed. Baker, for example, says euphemistically that "at that time, Mortimer secretly came first in the private household of the Queen." He and some continental chroniclers hint that Mortimer was not the only man to share Isabella's bed in Paris, but this probably reflects merely malicious gossip; had she taken other lovers, someone would have found out, and it would have given rise to talk in diplomatic circles, as did this affair with Mortimer.

We are left, therefore, to speculate as to the nature of the personal relationship between Isabella and Mortimer. He appears to have been everything that Edward II was not: strong, manly, unequivocally heterosexual, virile, courageous, audacious, and decisive. It is easy to understand why Isabella was attracted to him and why, after surrendering herself to his embraces, she could feel nothing but profound revulsion for her husband.

Mortimer's marriage had apparently been one of mutual interest, affection, and physical satisfaction,[102] but he had been parted from his wife for nearly three years now. He may well have maneuvered himself, or been maneuvered, into Isabella's orbit for political reasons, if indeed he had not been in secret communication with her and her friends in Paris for some time. She was beautiful, intelligent, and well born, and in her widow's weeds, she presented a tragic figure. In forming an attachment to Isabella, Mortimer was certainly motivated in part by a lust for power, but the chance to seduce the wife of the King who had condemned him to a terrible punishment and forced him into exile must have been an irresistible form of vengeance and probably added piquancy to the affair. Furthermore, Mortimer apparently seized every opportunity to poison Isabella's mind against Edward, and he probably had little difficulty in convincing her that, if she returned to her husband, "he [Edward] would kill her with a poignard or other weapon." Thereafter, Isabella was resolved never again "to afford him her bed."

For her part, Isabella, at twenty-eight, had probably suffered emotional and sexual frustration for years and was doubtless all too willing to succumb to this strong and virile adventurer, with whom she shared many bonds. He was in a unique position to understand her alienation and her fear of Despenser, and what was more, he was a powerful ally who was ready to protect her and take decisive action to rectify her situation.[103] For

Isabella, going to bed with Mortimer may well have been a means of getting back at Edward and his favorites. Thus, the affair may have been born partly out of a desire for revenge on both sides.

But the union of Isabella and Mortimer was also a meeting of minds and shared interests. Both were fascinated by the Arthurian legends;[104] both loved fine objets d'art and the luxuries of life. Yet this appears to have been no equal relationship. By all accounts, Mortimer dominated Isabella, probably because of the sexual hold he had over her, and also because he was a jealous, possessive man. He seems to have made the decisions, while she, by virtue of her position, helped him to implement them. It seems, too, that, after their early days together, she did not venture to question what he did but willingly complied. Modern women might conclude that she had sold out, but few females enjoyed any autonomy in the Middle Ages, and after all she had suffered, Isabella was probably greatly relieved to have a strong and domineering man take up her cause.

Although, in private, Mortimer was reportedly very familiar with the Queen, in public, the couple seem to have taken care to be discreet. But royal courts were hotbeds of gossip, and their servants would have been in a position to spread some very revealing items of information. Within two months, the affair was notorious in diplomatic circles, even in England. Their becoming lovers in so short a time suggests either an upflaring of sudden passion or a previous understanding. It has been claimed[105] that Isabella gained the dubious distinction of being the only English queen to live in open adultery, but in fact, a century earlier, Isabella of Angoulême, the wife of King John, had taken lovers, whom her husband had had hanged from her bed frame.

Several medieval sources[106] assert that the breakdown of the royal marriage occurred at the same time as Isabella's liaison with Mortimer, and some even state that her true purpose in going to France was to meet up with him there, but there is no evidence prior to December 1325 that there was any emotional bond between them, and if there had been, the Queen and her lover would for years have had very few opportunities for dalliance. It is possible that Isabella had been in secret contact with Mortimer through intermediaries, but if so, it is more likely to have been in connection with their joint aim to unseat the Despensers than with any intimate understanding. What we will never know, but which is certainly possible, is whether there had long been a mutual undeclared attraction between them.

Through her valet, Gawain Cordier, Isabella was still in regular communication with the wise and perceptive Prior Eastry, and on Christmas Day, Eastry commented on her hatred of Despenser to Archbishop Reynolds. No one, he wrote cautiously, could be liked by everyone, and some, through no malice and evil on their own part, are always disliked. The Queen, he added, had stressed that "no real or personal calumnious charge should be instituted against our lord the King of England, or any people subject to him."[107] Except, of course, Hugh le Despenser. Isabella was well aware that any attempt to oust the favorite would meet with popular support; a move against the King was another matter entirely and was better kept secret for the present.

Mortimer was not the only man able to influence the Queen at this time, for Richmond still rode high in her counsels. At Christmas, at Isabella's instance, the thirteen-year-old Prince Edward, as Duke of Aquitaine, received the "faith and homage" of Richmond, who agreed to surrender to young Edward all his lands in England in return for 10,000 Tournai livres petites from the revenues of Aquitaine.[108] This contract was subject to the approval of both Charles IV and Edward II, but it was primarily an alliance between Isabella and Richmond and also perhaps a means of raising funds for the invasion.

In England, at the beginning of January, Despenser, aware that the threat of an invasion from Hainault was no idle rumor, moved the bulk of his treasure to his stronghold at Caerphilly.[109]

But the threat of invasion was not just from Hainault. By 2 January, Archbishop Reynolds had learned from the well-informed Prior Eastry, who had again got his information from Gawain Cordier, that Charles IV had formally proposed a marriage between Prince Edward and one of the daughters of William V of Hainault and Jeanne of Valois; more alarmingly, the French King had also asked the Count to lend his assistance to a French offensive against England. This scheme was almost certainly the result of the talks that had taken place between Charles IV, Isabella, the Countess Jeanne, and Mortimer during December, and the very nature of the alliance betokened a plot against Edward II himself. In some alarm, Reynolds immediately alerted the King.[110]

The next day, a concerned Edward ordered watches set up along the south coast to prevent troops, arms, and letters from being smuggled into England.[111] Evidently, he feared that France might now join forces with Hainault in an offensive on England. That same day, he ordered that Mortimer's mother be seized and shut up in a convent for life for holding seditious meetings; fortunately, the indomitable old lady had gone into hiding and thus managed to evade arrest.[112] On the thirteenth, restrictions were imposed on anyone trying to leave England, while on the twentieth, the

King's worst fears appeared to be realized when Reynolds told him he had heard from Eastry that France and Hainault had formed a secret alliance and would indeed mount a joint invasion of England soon after Candlemas; there were reports that an invasion fleet was already gathering in Normandy and the Low Countries. Eastry, however, was at pains to stress that these were rumors and expressed the opinion that King Charles was merely trying to intimidate Edward on Isabella's behalf, to make him dismiss the Despensers, and that he had no real intention of declaring war on England.[113]

Eastry's opinion was founded probably on reports that claimed the Pope had urged the French King to use caution in his support of his sister, for the rift between her and Edward was having a destabilizing effect on European politics and might well plunge England into a bitter civil war.[114]

Nevertheless, Edward took the invasion threat seriously. On 22 January, he wrote a placatory letter to Count William, offering to come to some friendly agreement, but this met with no response.[115] He also wrote letters to Charles IV and sixteen French peers, asking that the Queen and the Prince be sent back to him forthwith. Again, his plea was ignored. Meanwhile, the King continued to put his defenses in place and to take precautions against any attack.[116]

During January and February 1326, some of the remaining members of the Queen's depleted retinue deserted her to return to England;[117] most of them abandoned her because they were shocked at her liaison with Mortimer and her disloyalty to the King.[118] It may well have been from these retainers that Edward II learned the truth about his wife's activities in Paris, which would explain why he rewarded them.[119] The King and the Despensers must have been appalled to learn that the Queen was consorting with Mortimer, his chief enemy and a convicted traitor. It was intolerable enough that she was refusing to return to him and detaining their son, but that she should cuckold him with Mortimer, of all people—it would make him an object of derision and mockery in the eyes of Christendom.

Throughout February, Isabella was in correspondence with the Countess Jeanne,[120] doubtless in connection with the planned alliance and invasion. That month, Edward was staying at Barnwell Priory, discussing his collegiate foundation, King's Hall. But he was more preoccupied with his wife's betrayal and the threat from abroad, and on 3 February, he ordered that Henry de Beaumont's lands be seized.[121]

Isabella was still maintaining the pretense that her quarrel was only with Despenser. In a letter written to Edward on 5 February, she insisted that no one must think she had left him "without very great and justifiable cause."

That cause, she stated, was Hugh le Despenser, who had "wished to dishonour us by all means in his power." She admitted that she had, for a long time, held secret her hatred, but only as a means of escaping from danger. She concluded, "We desire above everything else, after God and the salvation of our soul, to be in the company of our said lord, and to die with him."[122]

But the moral emphasis was now shifting, for Edward knew she was lying to him. On 8 February, in a proclamation ordering a general commission of array, the King made his first reference to Isabella's having deserted him for Mortimer: this commission had been issued, he declared, "because the Queen will not come to the King, nor permit his son to return, and the King understands that she is adopting the counsel of the Mortimer, the King's notorious enemy and rebel, and that she is making alliances with the men of those parts and with other strangers, with intent to invade." The King instructed that, if the Queen, the Prince, and the Earl of Kent returned, they were to be honorably received, but if they arrived with banners unfurled, bringing foreign soldiers, they were to be taken prisoner and the foreigners hanged as hostile invaders.[123] Four days later, the King began raising men to defend the Southeast.

Fearful that his heir would be used as a pawn in an alliance that was distasteful to him, Edward wrote to the Pope, begging him not to issue any dispensation for the boy's marriage without first obtaining the King's consent.[124] Actually, Pope John was becoming concerned about the reports that had been reaching him from Paris. Aware that he himself had suggested Isabella's mission, he must have felt to a degree responsible for what had happened. On 15 February, in an attempt to put matters right, he commissioned two nuncios, the Archbishop of Vienne and the Bishop of Orange, to mediate between Edward and Isabella, in the hope of effecting a reconciliation.[125] Two days later, he wrote to Despenser, suggesting that, since his interference had been cited by the Queen as the reason why she could not return to the King without danger to herself, he should retire from court at once and devise a way whereby she would no longer fear to rejoin her husband.[126]

The invasion of Isabella and Mortimer had initially been planned for February 1326. Doherty has suggested that it did not take place then because the Pope had persuaded Charles IV to adopt a less aggressive stance, and that the negotiations with Hainault were put on hold pending the outcome of the nuncios' mission. But even without the active support of Charles and Hainault, Isabella was clearly determined to press on with her plans. That she was preparing for an invasion may be inferred from the likelihood that, before 25 February, she, Mortimer, and Kent were making astonishing overtures to Robert the Bruce, almost certainly promising him recognition as King of an independent Scotland in return for an undertaking that he would not, once the Queen's forces landed, invade England through her northern border and thus prejudice the success of Isabella's offensive. In making such an offer, Isabella showed herself to be aware that the war with Scotland could never be won, and that it was better to bow to the inevitable, since a pragmatic solution was to everyone's advantage. These negotiations were conducted through Bruce's envoy to France, Thomas Randolph, Earl of Moray, who was in Paris at this time but was ordered home by the Pope on 25 February.[127]

The Queen knew for certain that Edward II would never have agreed to recognize Bruce as King of Scots, so these negotiations, together with the mooted marriage alliance with Hainault, offer compelling evidence that her husband's deposition was now her ultimate goal. It is significant that these developments all took place soon after Isabella teamed up with Mortimer, which suggests that Mortimer was now making the decisions; up until December, Isabella seems to have been unable to see her way clearly to committing herself to any decisive course of action. Now, "on the advice of her lover, she [had] finally made firm her resolve."[128]

March arrived with no sign as yet of any invasion, and Prior Eastry expressed the view that it would only happen if Charles IV stood to gain some profit from it. Charles could hope for little material advantage from the removal of the favorites. But there were others, notably, Isabella, Mortimer, and William V, who stood to gain a great deal. The question was, would Charles go so far as to back them?

On 3 March, Edward ordered that the Tower defenses be strengthened[129] and gave instructions that all letters leaving the kingdom were to be inspected in case they were treasonable communications. Shortly afterward, he summoned Airmyn and Richmond home from France to appear before him and account for why they had misled him over the peace treaty of 1325, giving him to believe that Charles would restore the Agenais.[130] Edward also had a score to settle with Airmyn over the bishopric of Norwich, but the official reason for the summons may have been a pretext to remove these influential men from Isabella's orbit.

The King still believed that any invasion force would come from France. On 10 March, the constable of Portchester was ordered to be especially vigilant, and the Mayor of London was commanded to inform the citizens of all that had happened in the current conflict between their King and

Charles IV and to demonstrate to them that the King was not at fault; the sheriffs were served with a similar order on the fifteenth.[131]

By March, the affair between Isabella and Mortimer was gaining notoriety in both France and England. Seemingly, Isabella was not unduly troubled about the effect of this on her reputation. Later evidence strongly suggests that her son the Prince disliked and resented Mortimer, but Isabella either did not realize this or was determined to ignore it. She even went so far as to make Mortimer young Edward's adviser, thus ensuring that the two of them were often in each other's company. It was fortunate for her that the boy's innate courtesy prevented him from revealing his hostility to this man who had supplanted his father. Isabella must have been well aware that Edward would regard it as highly inappropriate for the heir to England to be associating with his father's declared enemy, a convicted traitor, but she was almost certainly of the opinion that Mortimer had been forced into opposition by the Despensers and was no traitor at all: his previous record of service and loyalty to the Crown proved that and eminently qualified him to act as a counselor to her son, the future King. Again, her defiance of Edward's known wishes strongly suggests that she was plotting his overthrow.

By now, the papal envoys had arrived in Paris and were doing their best to convince Isabella that she should become reconciled with her husband. On 12 March, Eastry reported to Reynolds that they had persuaded her and Charles to agree to a plan that would result in her peaceful return to Edward. The Prior knew no details but advised the Archbishop that, if the Queen returned peacefully, she should be honorably received. He warned him, however, that matters might not turn out as well as they were hoping, since the Pope openly favored the French.[132]

Apparently, Isabella had agreed to return to Edward on two conditions: first, that the Despensers withdraw from court, and second, that Edward offer sworn guarantees concerning her status as queen and the restoration of her estates.[133] Again, it was unlikely that Edward would agree to the first and most crucial of these demands, but Mortimer was apparently incensed at the prospect of Isabella's going back to her husband and dramatically threatened to kill her if she set foot in England.[134] This was probably said in the heat of the moment, for Isabella seems to have ignored his threat, but it reveals his jealousy and his fear that she would abandon the plans upon which he was so set.

Kent, who apparently disliked Mortimer, and whose conscience was troubling him on account of his intended treason, was also alarmed at the prospect of returning to England and explaining his conduct to the King, his brother, who had cut off his allowance at the end of January;[135] in a panic, Kent sent a member of his household to Edward to assure him that, while staying in Paris with Isabella, he had done nothing prejudicial to the King's interests.[136]

Isabella also asked the nuncios to negotiate the safe return of Richmond and Cromwell to England.[137] The King had repeatedly ordered them home, but they had merely sent him feeble excuses. It may be that they needed to go back now to attend to urgent business, or perhaps Isabella wanted them to make contact with her friends in England. If so, she was expecting Edward to turn down the proposals for a reconciliation and was broadening her network of supporters. In so doing, she may have been placating Mortimer, having had to convince him that she must appear to be complying with the Pope's desire for her and Edward to be reconciled. But he remained implacably opposed to such a prospect.

The nuncios were now due to go to England to urge the King to receive his wife kindly, but, having learned how far he felt they had let him down during the peace negotiations in 1325, they were too scared to cross the Channel.[138] Their failure to arrive led to unfounded rumors of intimidation on Edward's part,[139] which were damaging in the extreme, since Isabella's refusal to return had led many people in England to conclude that he had behaved badly toward both her and their son, and rumors to this effect were proliferating throughout the kingdom.

On 14 March, Edward again commanded Richmond to return and give an account of his conduct, but again, Richmond defied him.[140] The King continued to take defensive measures, on 18 March, ordering that any suspicious-looking persons entering the kingdom be arrested.[141]

In a fever of agitation, he wrote again to the son he had not seen for more than six months now. He was still perturbed by the unconfirmed reports of a projected marriage alliance between the Prince and a princess of Hainault but even more horrified by the knowledge that the boy was being exposed to the inappropriate influence of the traitor Mortimer and risked being tainted by the adultery of that traitor with his mother. Evidently, the King no longer wanted his wife back, but he was determined to have his son and heir. Somehow, the Prince must be extricated from this situation, by his own wits if necessary, but first, he must be made aware of the enormity of his mother's conduct, and his duty to his father. The King's letter therefore amounted to an attack on Isabella and was written in a stern tone. It read:

Edward, fair son, we understand by your letters written in reply to ours that you remember well the charge we gave you; among other things, not to contract marriage, nor to suffer it to be contracted for you, without our knowledge and consent; and also that, at your departure from Dover, you said that it should be your pleasure to obey our commandments, as far as you could, all your days.

Fair son, if thus you have done, you have acted wisely and well and according to your duty, so as to have grace of God, of us and all men; and if not, then you cannot avoid the wrath of God, the reproach of men and our great indignation, for we charged you so lately and so strictly that you should remember well these things, and that you should by no means marry, nor suffer yourself to be married, without our previous consent and advice; for no other thing that you could do would occasion greater injury and pain of heart to us.

And inasmuch it seems, as you say, you cannot return to us because of your mother, it causes us great uneasiness of heart that you cannot be allowed by her to do that which is your natural duty, the neglect of which will lead to much mischief. Fair son, you know how dearly she would have been loved and cherished if she had timely come, according to her duty, to her lord. We have knowledge of much of her evil doings, to our sorrow; how that she devises pretences for absenting herself from us on account of our dear and faithful nephew, Hugh le Despenser, who has always so well and loyally served us, while you and all the world have seen that she openly and notoriously, and knowing it to be contrary to her duty, and against the welfare of our crown, has attached to herself and retains in her company the Mortimer, our traitor and mortal foe, proved, attainted and adjudged; and him she accompanies in the house and abroad, despite of us and our crown and of the right ordering of the realm—him, the malefactor whom our beloved brother, the King of France, at our request, banished from his dominions as our enemy. And worse than this, if worse than this can be, she has done in allowing you to consort with our said enemy, making him your counsellor, and you openly to associate and herd with him, in the sight of all the world, doing so great a villainy and dishonour, both to yourself and to us, to the prejudice of our crown and of the laws and customs of our realm, which you are supremely bound to hold, preserve and maintain. Wherefore, fair son, desist you from a part which is so shameful, and may be to you perilous and injurious in too many ways.

We are not pleased with you, and neither for your mother nor for any other ought you to displease us. We charge you, by the faith, love and allegiance which you owe to us, and on our blessing, that you come to us without opposition, delay or further excuse. For your mother has written to us that, if you wish to return to us, she will not prevent it, and we do not understand that your uncle the King detains you against the form of your safe-conduct. In no manner, then, either for your mother, or to go to the duchy, nor for any other cause, delay to come to us. Our commands are for your good and for your honour, by the help of God. Come quickly, then, without further excuses, if you would have our blessing, and avoid our reproach and indignation.

Fair son, trespass not against our commands, for we hear much that you have done of things you ought not.

Given at Lichfield, the 18th day of March.[142]

The King also wrote again to Charles IV, reiterating much of what he had said in the past: he evidently believed that constant repetition would make it the truer, but in fact, he was protesting rather too much to be convincing. The knowledge of his wife's adultery gave him all the more reason to occupy the high moral ground and take the stance of a wounded and wronged husband; Charles, however, would have known that this was a gross perversion of the truth. He would not, however, have been pleased to read the final passages of the letter, in which Edward implies that Charles has been remiss in not chastising his sister and that this matter reflects on his honor. The King wrote:

Dearest brother, we have considered well your letter wherein you signify that you have spoken with good diligence to your sister touching the things of which we have replied to you, and that she has told you that it is her desire to be with us and in our company, as a good wife ought to be in that of her lord, and that the friendship between her and our dear and faithful nephew, Hugh le Despenser, was but feigned on her part because she saw it was expedient for her support in past time, and to secure herself from worse treatment. Certes, dearest brother, if she loved us, she would desire to be in our company, as she has said. She who ought to be the mediatrix between you and us of entire and lasting peace should not be the cause of stirring up fresh strife, as she has done, when she was sent to nourish peace and love between you and us, which we intended in all good faith when we sent her to you. But the thought of her heart was to devise that pretence for withdrawing from us. We have already shown you that what she has told you is, saving your reverence, not the truth, for never (so much as she has done against us) has she received either villainy or evil from us or from any other. Neither has she had any occasion for feints to support herself in times past, nor to escape from worse; for never, in the slightest instance, has evil been done to her by him. And since she has departed from us and come to you, what has compelled her to send to Hugh letters of such great and especial amity as she has been pleased to do from time to time?

But truly, dearest brother, it must be as apparent to you as to us and to all men, that she does not love us as she ought to love her lord, and the cause why she had spoken falsehoods of our nephew and withdrawn herself from us proceeds, according to my thoughts, from a disordered will, when she so openly, notoriously and knowingly against her duty keeps in her company the Mortimer. If you wished her well, dearest brother, you would chastise her for this misconduct and make her demean herself as she ought, for the honour of all those to whom she belongs.

Then our son, dearest brother, is made also by his mother, your sister, the companion of our said traitor and foe, who is his counsellor in delaying his return in our despite. We entreat you to restore our son, who is of too tender an age to guide and govern himself, and therefore ought to be under our paternal care, to the duchy. And that you will be pleased to do these things, dearest brother, for the sake of God, reason, good faith and natural fraternity, without paying regard to the wilful pleasure of a woman, is our desire.

Given at Lichfield, the 18th of March.[143]

Prince Edward was surely disturbed when he read his father's letter, which must have left him in little doubt—if he were not already aware—of the nature of his mother's relationship with Mortimer. He wrote back protesting that he was indeed bearing in mind the things with which the King had charged him at Dover and that he had not transgressed his commands in any point that was in his power to avoid.[144] But clearly, there was much that he could not avoid, such as the company and advice of Mortimer, the whispers about that man and his mother, and the fact that both were using him as a bargaining counter and making him set his signature to documents concerning Gascony without reference to his father. Yet his father apparently expected him to surmount these obstacles, defy his mother, take the initiative, and return on his own to England.

Persisting in his efforts to gain the support of the French nobility, Edward wrote to Philip, Count of Valois, heir of the late Charles of Valois, asserting that Isabella's complaints about Despenser were but a pretense:

> When the King sent to seek her, she then showed the feigned matter for the first time, which was never heard or suspected by anyone, unless by her: wherefore, the matters being considered, one ought not to give faith to such feigned invention against the truth. But indeed, the King fully perceives, as the King of France and everybody may, that she does not love the King as she ought to love her lord, and that the matter that she speaks of the King's said nephew [Despenser], for which she withdraws herself from the King, is feigned and is not certain, but the King thinks it must be of inordinate will when she, so openly and notoriously, knowingly, against her duty and the estate of the King's crown, which she is bound to love, has drawn to her and retains in her company of her council the King's traitor and mortal enemy, the Mortimer, and others of his conspiracy, and keeps his company in and out of the house, which evil-doer the King of France banished from his power at another time as the King's enemy, by virtue of the alliance between his and the King's ancestors.[145]

Edward is here obviously implying that Charles should banish Mortimer again!

On 24 March, the King confiscated Richmond's lands and also those of John, Lord Cromwell, who, he had heard, had offered his sword to Mortimer. Another who refused to obey Edward's commands to return was Thomas, Lord Wake, Kent's brother-in-law and Isabella's former ward.[146]

In April, Edward was forced to admit to the King of Portugal that he could not at present continue with negotiations for his son's marriage.[147] On 15 April, he wrote to the Pope, defending his own conduct in respect of Isabella and the nuncios and appealing for support; he had, he protested, done everything in his power to bring the Queen home and had not intended any ill toward her.

> And as for our said son, indeed, he has not offended us, nor does his youth allow either that he could do any harm, or that it should be imputed to him. Wherefore it would be inhuman and unnatural to treat them with so much rage and cruelty.[148]

He may well have enclosed a bribe, because on 1 May, John XXII replied to Edward, thanking him for his gift of 5,000 florins. (On 21 June, the Pope would thank Stapledon for another monetary gift, which was probably another bribe[149].) But John XXII proved impervious to bribes. He sent again to Despenser, reminding him to continue his good offices to promote agreement between the King and Queen,[150] an injunction that Despenser ignored. Meanwhile, on 18 April, Edward had publicly condemned those who were spreading malicious gossip and thus prejudicing the success of the nuncios' mission.[151] He had the Archbishop of Canterbury offer up prayers for the Queen's safe return and the clergy deliver sermons emphasizing that the King had not banished his wife and son and was not threatening the nuncios.[152] On 2 May, Bishop Stapledon was commanded to strengthen the defenses of the realm against the expected invasion.

On Whitsunday, 11 May, Jeanne of Evreux was crowned Queen of France at the Sainte Chapelle in Paris. Isabella and her son were present as guests of honor, while Mortimer was given the honor of carrying the Prince's robes.[153]

On 19 May, Edward ordered that elaborate preparations be made for the reception of the papal envoys,[154] who arrived at Dover soon afterward and rode to Saltwood Castle in Kent to meet with the King and Despenser. No one else was permitted to be present, and the Archbishop and his entire episcopate were banned from even entering Kent and making contact with the nuncios.[155] In this atmosphere of paranoid secrecy, the nuncios laid before Edward the Queen's proposals for a reconciliation and asked him to pardon Richmond and Cromwell and permit their return.

Edward was in frequent communication with the Pope at this time, and in May, he sent to Avignon a messenger called William Weston, whose mission was probably connected with the reconciliation process. After speaking with Weston, the Pope made a point of speedily informing Isabella that Weston had said nothing derogatory concerning her,[156] which suggests she had rather feared he would.

In June, the King ordered an investigation into illicit meetings in East Anglia. These may have had some connection with the projected invasion, for Mortimer's plan had all along been to land in East Anglia.

On 6 June, at the intercession of the Bishop of Orange, Edward agreed to pardon Cromwell on condition that he return within two weeks.[157] Richmond, however, was another matter: he had consistently refused to obey Edward's summonses and, as Edward informed the Pope on 18 June, was still in France conspiring with his enemies.[158]

By 10 June, it was clear that the nuncios' mission had failed; as Isabella had no doubt anticipated, neither Edward nor Despenser would agree to the latter's withdrawing permanently from court. This meant that, effectively, her marriage had irretrievably broken down and that, if she wished to get rid of the Despensers, she would now have to use force. On the tenth, Edward wrote to the Pope, but his letter contained nothing about the reconciliation proposals. It was left to the envoys, who departed from England the next day, to explain the disappointing outcome of the talks to the Pope.[159]

Isabella was still in Paris on 10 June, when she commissioned her proctors to meet with a delegation from Ponthieu, who had been summoned to discuss raising money so that the Queen could hire ships in Hainault and buy provisions.[160] Negotiations with Hainault must therefore have been resumed; clearly, Isabella was not prepared to wait until the outcome of the nuncios' visit to England was known but was pressing on with her plans for the invasion.

On 15 June, Edward and Despenser visited Rochester,[161] where, in a long discussion with the Bishop, Hamo de Hethe (which was reported verbatim by an eyewitness, William Dene), they revealed something of what had gone on at Saltwood. The Bishop inquired as to how the talks had progressed, whereat Despenser angrily remarked that the Queen should return home forthwith and that she had no right to demand his withdrawal from court or to ask for sworn guarantees regarding her status. He added that she would have returned a long time ago but had been prevented from doing so, not by himself but by Mortimer, who had threatened to kill her if she returned to England.[162] This information almost certainly came from the nuncios, who would probably have witnessed Mortimer's outburst in March.

Edward reminded Hethe of the example of a notorious Saxon Queen, Eadburh, the wife of Beorhtric, King of Wessex; she had been a cruel, domineering woman who undermined her husband's regal standing and, legend claimed, tried to poison him, for which she was ultimately set aside, stripped of her title, and exiled. "Is it not true that a queen who once upon a time wilfully disobeyed her lord was set aside and deprived of her royal dignity?" Edward asked, revealing plainly what was in his mind.

Hethe, who owed his bishopric to Isabella but was by no means her creature, immediately caught the King's meaning, but he did not approve and replied tartly, "Whoever has told you that has given you bad advice!" He emphasized his point with a quote from Scripture about Haman, the evil counselor who tried to drive a wedge between Ahasuerus, King of Persia, and his Jewish wife, Esther, but was hanged for his pains. The allusion to the favorite was blatant, but the King and Despenser refused to rise to the bait.[163] The conversation proves that Despenser was leaving no stone unturned in pursuing his vendetta against the Queen.[164]

Edward's allusion to the fate of Queen Eadburh suggests that he was again contemplating seeking an annulment of his marriage. The chances are that he had learned much about the affair between Isabella and Mortimer from the nuncios. It was almost certainly they who had revealed to the King, to his outrage and disgust, that Mortimer had publicly appeared in company with the Queen and her son at the coronation. This prompted Edward, on 19 June, to make one final and futile attempt to persuade Prince Edward to return to England. He wrote:

> Edward, fair son, we have seen by your letters lately written to us that you well remember the charges enjoined you on your departure from Dover, and that you have not transgressed our commands in any point that was in your power to avoid. But to us it appears that you have not humbly obeyed our commands as a good son ought his father, since you have not returned to us to be under government, as we have enjoined you by our other letters, on our blessing, but have notoriously held companionship, and your mother also, with Mortimer, our traitor and mortal enemy, who, in company with your mother and others, was publicly carried to Paris in your train to the solemnity of the coronation at Pentecost just past, in signal despite of us, and to the great dishonour both of us and you. For truly, he is neither a meet companion for your mother, nor for you, and we hold that much evil to the country will come of it.
>
> Also we understand that you, through counsel which is contrary both to our interest and yours, have proceeded to make divers alterations, injunctions and ordinances without our advice and contrary to our orders, in the duchy of [Gascony], which we have given you. But you ought to remember the conditions of the gift and your reply when it was conferred upon you at Dover. These things are inconvenient and must be most injurious.
>
> Therefore we command and charge you, on the faith and love you ought to bear us, and on our blessing, that you show yourself our dear and well-beloved son, as you have aforetime done, and, ceasing from all excuses of your mother, or any like those that you have just written, you come to us here with all haste, that we may ordain for you and your estate as honourably as you can desire. By right and reason, you ought to have no other governor than us, neither should you wish to have.

> Also, fair son, we charge you by no means to marry till you return to
> us, or without our advice and consent; nor for any cause, either go to
> the duchy or elsewhere, against our will and command.

The King then added a postscript with some stern fatherly advice:

> Edward, fair son, you are of tender age. Take our commandments ten-
> derly to heart, and so rule your conduct with humility, as you would
> escape our reproach, our grief and indignation, and advance your own
> interest and honour. Believe no counsel that is contrary to the will of
> your father, as the wise King Solomon instructs you. Understand cer-
> tainly that, if you now act contrary to our counsel, and continue in wil-
> ful disobedience, you will feel it all the days of your life, and all other
> sons will take example to be disobedient to their lords and fathers.[165]

There is an implicit threat in the final sentence of this letter; perhaps
Edward is hinting that he might have his marriage annulled and disinherit
his son. This is the second indication that he was considering divorce at this
time, but if so, we hear no more of it. Possibly the King feared, given the
Pope's censorious letters to Despenser, that John XXII would again prove
uncooperative.

There is no evidence that the Prince replied to this letter. Later evidence,
which will be examined in due course, strongly suggests that the young
Edward did indeed suffer from a guilty conscience concerning his father "all
the days of [his] life." Yet it is clear that he also felt chivalrously protective
toward his mother. He hated the Despensers as much as she did,[166] doubtless
on her account, and probably also because of the shameful hold they had
over the King. The poor boy was at an impressionable age and must have felt
outraged at the disruption the Despensers had caused in his own life and in
the world he inhabited. Yet he did not like Mortimer either and perhaps felt
that, in keeping company with him, he was betraying his father. All in all, it
was an impossible situation for a boy of thirteen to cope with.

At the same time as he wrote to his son, Edward also sent further letters
of appeal to the Bishop of Beauvais and to Charles IV. The latter, which
reeks of desperation, sought to apportion to Charles some of the blame for
Isabella's behavior and called upon him to display solidarity with a brother
monarch. It read:

> Most dear and beloved brother, we would wish to remind you that we
> have at different times signified to you by our letters how improperly

your sister, our wife, has conducted herself in withdrawing from us and refusing to return at our command, while she so notoriously has attached to her company, and consorts with, our traitor and mortal enemy, the Mortimer, and our other enemies there, and also makes Edward, our son and heir, an adherent of the same, our enemy, to our great shame, and that of everyone of her blood. And if you wish her well, you ought, both for your own honour and ours, to have these things duly redressed.

Edward here begs Charles once again to send back Prince Edward,

who is of too tender an age to guide and govern himself, and therefore ought to be under our paternal care.

But these things are as nothing; it is the herding of our said wife and son with our traitors and mortal enemies that notoriously continues, insomuch that the said traitor Mortimer was carried in the train of our said son publicly to Paris at the solemnity of the coronation of our very dear sister, the Queen of France, at the Pentecost last past, to our great shame, and in despite of us.

Dearest brother, you ought to feel for us, and so should all men of our estate, for much we are, and much we have been, grieved at the shameful despites and great injury which we have so long endured. Nay, verily, brother-in-law, we cannot bear it longer.

The Holy Spirit have charge of you.[167]

Frantic now to have his son back and the threat of invasion removed, the King sent copies of these letters to the Pope, advising him that the Queen was sharing her lodgings with Mortimer and beseeching him to intervene with King Charles on his behalf. He also complained of Richmond, who, he said, had been consorting with and aiding his enemies.[168]

From now on, in order to save face and avoid the humiliating admission that the Queen had left him, Edward and his advisers maintained the pretense that the French King was detaining Isabella against her will.[169] But around this time, Edward granted some of the Queen's lands in Cornwall to Bishop Stapledon,[170] a sure sign that he no longer expected to be reconciled with her. Gawain Cordier's pension was cut off,[171] and on 28 June, the King was present when Isabella's treasury in the Tower was broken into and ordered that money be taken from it for his own use.[172]

In July, in order to preempt his enemies, and as an expression of disapproval at Charles's harboring of Isabella, Edward declared war on France.

On the fifth, his arrayers in East Anglia were ordered to recruit three thousand men to man the fleet on the east coast.[173] On the sixth and the eighteenth, he issued a command to his fleet to intercept and attack French vessels in the Channel,[174] and on the twenty-first, he arranged for a surveyor of French goods to be appointed in every shire.[175] Several orders were issued for the arrest of any Frenchman found in England.[176] At the end of the month, the King established a system of array in every county and commanded that his castles in Wales be refortified.[177] Mortimer's Welsh enemy Rhys ap Gruffydd was ordered to raise troops against him.[178]

In England, the Despensers were now more unpopular than ever, and there were vicious attacks on their adherents,[179] yet the Younger Hugh was rising ever higher in the King's favor: "the influence of Sir Hugh le Despenser, and the affection the King felt for him, increased every day. He had such a hold on the King that the whole country was amazed. Nor could anything be done at court without the agreement of Sir Hugh. And he behaved cruelly and wickedly, for which he was well hated. But nobody dared to mention or raise any complaint."[180]

Edward's favor extended also to Despenser's wife, Eleanor de Clare, whom Knighton describes as being treated like a queen. William Cappellani, a chronicler writing in Hainault, claims that Eleanor was now Edward's mistress, which echoes a similar assertion relating to 1322–23 in the somewhat unreliable *Chronographia Regum Francorum*. The King's household accounts for 1326 show that he was visiting Eleanor frequently and sending her gifts of jewels and golden chaffinches.[181] These rumors emanate only from hostile and uncorroborated Flemish sources. Furthermore, not only was Eleanor clearly Edward's favored niece, but the period of her ascendancy corresponds exactly to that of her husband, who was the dominant influence in the King's life. It is only to be expected, therefore, that, as a tribute to Hugh, and out of his own natural affection, Edward should treat Hugh's wife with excessive consideration and accord her disproportionate importance. And it is also easy to see how such treatment could have been misconstrued by those who wished to believe ill of him. The alternative scenario is that Edward was involved in a weird sexual triangle with Hugh and Eleanor and had been for some time. If so, it is strange that there was no gossip about it in the English chronicles and that Isabella and Mortimer made no political capital out of it, as they were to do with every other aspect of Despenser's life.

Information about Isabella's activities in France had been steadily filtering through into England, where many people had been feeling "disturbed" that the Queen was "delaying and keeping her son in France against his father's wishes. Some maintained they were being held against their will, others argued that the Queen had been seduced by the illicit embraces of Roger Mortimer and that she had no wish to return, preferring to stay with him and others who had been exiled from England and who were now in France."[182]

News of the Queen's alliance with Mortimer gave encouragement to those who were heartily sick of Despenser's regime. "All the barons and thoughtful people in the country saw that it was not to be endured, and that they could no longer tolerate his wicked, outrageous behaviour." Isabella was soon secretly corresponding with many of these disaffected persons; she had already secured the support of several nobles and bishops, prominent among whom were Lancaster and Norfolk,[183] and had also sent agents to England to foment unrest. In June, the King panicked when he was informed that "secret conventions" were being held in East Anglia,[184] which was Norfolk's territorial power base. By the summer, thanks largely to the covert efforts of Mortimer's friend Bishop Orleton, there had emerged in England a rapidly expanding Queen's party that was committed to the overthrow not only of the favorites but also of the King.

Around this time, Isabella received an urgent communication from some barons of England, who had been "debating amongst themselves secretly and decided to send for her and ask her to return. They wrote and put it to her that, if she could by any means contrive to raise an armed force, even a thousand men, and if she would bring her son and all her company to England, they would rally to her side and place him on the throne to govern under her guidance. For they could not, and would not, endure any longer the general disorder and the misdeeds of the King, which were all inspired by the advice of Sir Hugh and his followers."[185]

Upon reading this, Isabella must have become more than ever convinced of the rightness of her cause and justified in moving against a weak and tyrannical regime: in so doing, she would be liberating an oppressed and resentful people from tyranny and herself from a hateful marriage and the persecution of the vengeful Despenser. Armed with her convictions, she consulted with King Charles, "who willingly listened to her and advised her to press on boldly, for he would help her and lend her as many men as she wanted, and he would also lend her all the silver and gold she needed."[186] But Charles's offer cannot have been more than halfhearted: he had no desire to fight a war with England on two fronts, for he was heavily committed in Gascony and was already uncomfortable about sheltering his sister now that her relationship with Mortimer was becoming notorious.

Unconscious of Charles's dwindling support, Isabella continued to "make what provision she could for the future. And she secretly sought the help of the greatest barons in France whom she trusted most, and who would voluntarily support her—the ones, that is, whom she thought she could depend on. Then she sent a message to the barons in England who had communicated with her. But this could not be kept secret from Sir Hugh le Despenser," and there would be repercussions for Isabella.[187]

In July, it was rumored in France that, on the advice of the Despensers, Edward had outlawed the Queen and the Prince as rebels and traitors and had them proclaimed as such in London, declaring that, if they returned to England now, they faced execution. Another rumor claimed that the King had ordered Richmond to murder Isabella and her son, but that God had restrained him from doing so. There was no foundation for these stories, but it is true that the King had warned that, if Mortimer returned to England, he faced certain death.[188] On top of this, Isabella was soon to receive the crushing news that the Pope had abandoned her; Edward's appeal had moved him, and given the scandal that the Queen's affair with Mortimer was causing, he decided to make a stand in the interests of ortho-dox morality. To this end, he wrote to Charles IV, censoring him for harbor-ing adulterers and commanding him, on pain of excommunication, not to countenance their sin nor offer them shelter any longer.

The arrival of the Pope's edict prompted Charles to take decisive action. There is some evidence that his sympathy for his sister had been waning for some time now, and he may well have been reaching the conclusion that events were spiraling out of control as a result of his support of Isabella. First, his conscience may have begun troubling him after he read Edward II's letter. Not only was Isabella's continued presence in France prejudicing any hope of a settlement with England over Gascony, but Charles also probably held strong personal views on queens who committed adultery; his first wife had been imprisoned and divorced for that crime, and he must have felt deeply uncomfortable about Isabella's relationship with Mortimer.[189]

Second, according to Froissart, Despenser, aware that Isabella's dealings with the English dissidents and exiles spelled disaster for himself, had used bribes (sent through a wine merchant) to subvert the loyalty of Charles IV's advisers to her and tried to persuade them to force her to return to England; he had even written to Charles himself, warning him that the Queen was plotting treason against her lord. This was one of the accusa-tions later laid against Despenser by Isabella.[190] That Edward was a party to Despenser's bribes is suggested by an angry complaint he made to the Count of Hainault late in May, which possibly concerned the recent capture of a ship carrying Despenser's silver to France.[191] Most chroniclers believed that Despenser managed to persuade Charles IV to withdraw his support from Isabella and send her back to England; Froissart says that, "in a short space, the King of France and all his privy council were as cold to help the Queen in her voyage as they had before great desire to do it."[192] However, Charles's later behavior suggests that he was playing a far more complex game.

Third, Charles had perhaps learned how two of Mortimer's agents had been arrested in England and had confessed to being involved in a plot to murder Edward II and the Despensers by means of witchcraft: they had already paid a magician in Coventry to stick pins in waxen images of their intended victims;[193] nor was this the first time that Mortimer had sent assassins to England.

And now the Pope had spoken out against Isabella.

"When King Charles had read these letters he was greatly disturbed" and "withdrew his countenance from his sister," ordering "that she be made acquainted with their contents, for he had held no conversation with her for a long time." Then, abruptly, he summoned her to him and told her, "as definitely and clearly as he could, to stay quiet and abandon her project. When the Queen heard this, she was naturally amazed and astounded, and she saw that the King was now disposed against her, for nothing that she could say would alter his decision or help her case. And so she left him, sadly and sorrowfully, and returned to her lodging. But she did not abandon her plans, and the King was angry that she ignored his words," and sent a message "commanding her to leave his kingdom immediately, or he would make her leave it with shame.

"When the Queen received this stern and contemptuous message from her brother, she was greatly troubled." Her turmoil increased when she heard that Charles had decreed "that whoever should speak in behalf of his sister, the Queen of England, should forfeit his lands and be banished from the realm. When the Queen heard this, she was sadder than before, and with reason. She did not know what to think or do, because everything was, and had been for so long, against her, and those who should have come to her help were failing her, through wicked advice. She became desperate, she had no comfort, and she did not know what to do or what would become of her. And she often prayed and beseeched God to give her help and guidance."[194]

Immediately, nearly all Isabella's French supporters abandoned her. The only one to stay faithful was "her dear cousin, Robert of Artois," who came secretly "in the middle of the night to warn Isabella of the peril in which she stood," telling her "in all truth, that if she did not behave discreetly, the

King her brother would have her sent back to her husband, and her son with her, because it did not please the King of France that she should stay away from her husband. At this, the Queen was more appalled than ever, because she would rather have been dead and dismembered than fall again into the power of her husband and Sir Hugh."

Robert "strongly urged her to enter the imperial territories and to throw herself upon the protection of some of the independent German princes, especially William, Count of Hainault, whose consort was Isabella's cousin," and who had shown himself so friendly to Mortimer. "So she decided to leave France and go into Hainault to see Count William and his brother, Sir John, who were the most honourable knights of the highest reputation. She hoped to find in them every comfort and good advice." The Queen "informed her people of her decision, ordered her baggage to be made ready as secretly as possible and, having paid for everything she had had, she left her lodging as quickly and quietly as she could, with her son, her husband's brother, the Earl of Kent (at this time decidedly her partisan), Roger Mortimer and other English knights."[195]

It may be that there had been some prior arrangement for Isabella to seek refuge in Hainault if her remaining in France became untenable. It had been agreed by now that Hainault would be the springboard for the projected invasion, and as soon as they had left Paris, Mortimer went straight there, while Isabella, accompanied by Kent, made for her dower lands of Ponthieu, where she began raising money.[196] She was obviously aware that, after leaving Ponthieu, she would be welcome in Hainault; furthermore, her presence would assist Mortimer in his preparations for the invasion.

Some chroniclers assert that Isabella was warned by Richmond to flee from France after the Earl received a letter from King Edward in which the latter "privily" urged that both the Queen and Prince Edward should be "slain." In view of Edward's anxiety for his son, this claim sounds absurd, although it is quite possible that threats were made at this time against the Queen's life. We have seen that, even before she left England, she had been warned that the Despensers wanted her dead, and she was later to assert that the King himself had threatened to kill her.

Strangely, Charles IV made no attempt to pursue Isabella, nor did he denounce her to Edward II or divulge her plans or her whereabouts. Instead, he deliberately built up an invasion fleet along the Norman coast in order to divert Edward from the real threat that was to come from Hainault;[197] we may be sure that Charles knew all about the revived alliance between Count William and the Queen and would have been aware there-

fore that his sister would not lack for practical support. He need consequently do very little himself on her behalf.

It would appear, therefore, that after being seen to heed the Pope's commandments and deflecting both excommunication and scandal, Charles
continued secretly to lend Isabella his support. His measures against her
were probably a bluff to appease the Pope and mislead Edward II, and it
was probably he who sent Robert of Artois to suggest that she now go to
Hainault.[198] And we may infer from what happened soon afterward that she
was left in no doubt as to the role Charles was playing and that they
remained secretly in communication with each other.

It had seemingly been agreed that Isabella should attend to the details of
policy while Mortimer looked after the practical arrangements for the invasion.[199] By 24 July, Mortimer was in Zeeland "in the service of Queen Isabella"; on that day, Count William ordered his harbor masters to give him
every assistance in gathering provisions and hiring a fleet of ships that was
to be assembled by 1 September between Rotterdam and Dordrecht, ports
that offered excellent facilities.[200]

From Ponthieu, Isabella traveled east through Vermandois to Cambrai
in the fertile and prosperous county of Hainault. "When she found that she
was in the teritories of the [Holy Roman] Empire, she was more at her
ease." She then rode north to Ostrevant, where she lodged at the castle of
Brigincourt, near Valenciennes. It belonged to "a poor knight called Sir
Eustace d'Ambreticourt, who gladly received and entertained her in the
best manner he could, insomuch that afterwards the Queen and her son
invited the knight, his wife and all his children to England and advanced
their fortunes in various ways."[201]

Count William and his brother, Sir John of Hainault, who were at that
time staying at Valenciennes, were soon apprised of Isabella's arrival in
Hainault. Sir John was "a married man and also a valiant knight,"[202] but he
was "at that time very young and panting for glory like a knight errant," so
he "mounted his horse and, accompanied by a few persons, set out from
Valenciennes and arrived in the evening to pay the Queen every respect and
honour." Froissart, who gives a highly romanticized version of this occasion, states that Isabella was feeling very dejected; at the sight of Sir John,
she burst into tears and made a lamentable complaint to him of her griefs.

Hearing her, Sir John chivalrously resolved to champion the cause of
this damsel in distress. "Lady," he said, "see here your knight, who will not
fail to die for you, though everyone else should forsake you. Therefore I will

do everything in my power to conduct you safely to England with your son, and restore you to your rank, with the assistance of your friends in those parts. And I, and all those whom I can influence, will risk our lives on the adventure for your sake, and we shall have a sufficient armed force, if it please God."

Overcome with gratitude, Isabella tried to kneel at Sir John's feet, but he raised her up, saying, "God forbid that the Queen of England should think of kneeling before her knight! But be comforted, Madam, and all your company, for I shall not break my promise. You shall come and see my brother and your cousin, the Countess his wife, and all their fine children, who will be rejoiced to see you, for I have heard them say so."

"Sir," replied Isabella, "I find in you more kindness and comfort than in the whole world beside; and I will give you five hundred thousand thanks for all you have promised me with so much courtesy. I and my son shall be forever bound unto you, and if in time we are restored, as I hope, by the comfort and grace of God and yourself, you will be richly rewarded." Sir John then withdrew to the nearby abbey of Denain. The next day, after Mass, he returned to Brigincourt to escort Isabella to Mons. Upon leaving with her company, she told Sir Eustace and Lady d'Ambreticourt "that she trusted a time would come when she and her son could acknowledge their courtesy and ask them to their court."[203]

Sir John and the Queen arrived at Mons by 3 August, when she confirmed an agreement between Mortimer and Count William, whereby William undertook to lease to the invaders 140 ships, and Isabella promised to pay out of her revenues of Ponthieu financial compensation for any that were lost; Charles IV had agreed to act as her guarantor.[204]

On that day, Mortimer of Chirk died in the Tower. Rumor had it that he had starved to death in his grim cell. Adam Orleton conducted the funeral service at Wigmore Abbey on 14 September.[205] Roger Mortimer should have inherited his uncle's lands, but of course, they had been declared forfeit. Mortimer now had even greater cause to seek vengeance on the Despensers.

Count William hastened to invite Isabella and her son to Valenciennes, "where they were gladly and gallantly welcomed" by their hosts and the citizens. The Count received the Queen in the great galleried hall of the Hôtel de Hollande, which was a magnificent room with a paved floor, six tall glazed Gothic windows, and splendid red hangings. When Isabella was installed in her lodgings, the Countess Jeanne came to visit her "and did her all honour and reverence"; she also paid all the Queen's expenses throughout her stay in Hainault.[206] The Count came to visit, too, despite suffering from gout and being able to ride "only with difficulty."[207]

Isabella's visit lasted eight days (not the three weeks that Froissart claims), during which time she was "honoured and feasted nobly." The Count was delighted when Isabella formally asked for the hand of one of his daughters for her son,[208] and care was taken to ensure that Prince Edward, "a youth of great charm and much promise,"[209] spent as much time as possible in the company of the Count's four surviving girls, Margaret, Philippa, Joan, and Isabella. Soon, according to Froissart, it became apparent that the lad was "devoting himself most and inclining with eyes of love to Philippa rather than the rest. And the maiden knew him best and kept him closer company than any of her sisters. So I have heard from the mouth of the good lady herself."

When the time came for the Queen and her son to leave Valenciennes, and Isabella and Edward "embraced all the damsels in turn, the Lady Philippa, when it was her turn, burst into tears." Asked what was the matter, she replied, " 'My fair cousin of England is about to leave me, and I had grown so used to him.' Then all the knights who were there present began to laugh,"[210] and perhaps to smile knowingly, aware that this youthful attachment had been just what was intended. Not only was this marriage a political necessity for Isabella, it was also a means of binding her son to her, and that bond would be all the closer if he was grateful to her for securing him a bride he could love. The promise of Philippa might also help the boy to forget that, in marrying with Hainault, he was disobeying his father's commands.

On 4 August, King Edward, still expecting an invasion from France, appointed searchers to comb every coastline. He himself was busy touring his realm, visiting cities and castles, and attempting to raise support among the nobility. On the tenth, a system of warning beacons was put in place, and two days later, the King ordered a number of large ships to assemble at Portsmouth.[211] But Edward was not as foolish or as ill-informed as Charles IV believed, for a watch was also set on the east coast, and on 16 August, preparations began for ships to assemble at Orwell by 21 September. Edward's intelligence must have been sound, for it had pinpointed with uncanny accuracy the date and place of the invasion.

On 26 and 29 August, Edward ordered the imprisonment of any French persons remaining in England, on account of the King of France's "detention" of the Queen and Prince Edward and his "cherishing" of English exiles.[212] Despenser, meanwhile, had prudently withdrawn £2,000 in cash from his bankers.

Back in Mons, on 17 August, Isabella drew up an agreement with her subjects in Ponthieu, whereby they would provide her with financial assistance to help fund the invasion; this would be sealed on 5 September at Ostrelte, with Charles IV again acting as the Queen's guarantor.[213] The Queen was now busily involved in raising money and men for the invasion, preparing for her journey to England, and putting her affairs in order. Notable people who joined her at this time included Sir Wiliam Trussell, Mortimer's client Simon de Beresford, and the celebrated Flemish chevalier Walter de Manny. Several Gascons came, and the city of Bayonne sent the Queen thirty-five sailors, much to the disapproval of many in the duchy.[214]

On 27 August, again at Mons, Isabella took the irrevocable step of signing a treaty providing for the betrothal of Prince Edward to a daughter of the Count of Hainault. The princess's dowry was to be in the form of troops, money, and ships, which were to be delivered in advance of the marriage and put at the Queen's disposal; in return, Isabella promised that the wedding would take place within two years and that, once she gained power in England, she would settle its maritime dispute with Hainault to everyone's satisfaction.[215]

The Queen then departed on a tour of Brabant, seeking to raise men for her cause. Meanwhile, mercenaries from all over northern Europe were converging on Dordrecht, the main embarkation point. Their appearance owed as much to Mortimer's sustained efforts over the past three years and the recent entreaties of Sir John as to Isabella's presence in Hainault. The latter certainly proved effective, for Sir John was not the only one to see her as a damsel in distress: the burghers of Malines (Mechelen) and Diest were also touched by her plight and sent mercenaries, arms, and supplies for her army. When the Queen was able to, she would reward them for it.[216]

While Isabella was in Brabant, she learned that her husband's envoy William Weston had arrived there on his way home from Avignon. Perhaps fearful of what he might report to Edward, she seems to have persuaded John III, Duke of Brabant, to detain Weston for the time being, which prompted several puzzled complaints from Edward II.[217]

True to his word, Sir John of Hainault had exerted himself indefatigably on Isabella's behalf. He had written to all the knights of his acquaintance in Hainault, Brabant, and Bohemia, and many had responded to his call to arms "for love of him; though many refused, for all his entreaties." Sir Eustace d'Ambreticourt was one of those who did respond to his summons. But Sir John's determination to accompany the invading army earned him a rebuke from his brother, the Count, who thought this notion too "bold and perilous, in view of the prevailing discord among the barons and the common people of England, and since the English are generally ill-disposed towards foreigners who gain the advantage over them and invade their country." Sir John might, warned William, never return home. But he "would not be dissuaded."

"I believe for certain that this lady and her son have been driven from their kingdom wrongfully," he told his brother. "If it is for the glory of God to help the afflicted, how much more is it to help and succour one who is daughter of a king, descended from royal lineage, and to whose blood we ourselves are related?" He insisted "that he could only die once, and that it was in the hands of Our Lord. He had promised this noble lady to escort her back to her kingdom, and he would support her to the death. And he would just as soon die with that noble lady, who had been forced to leave her country, as anywhere else, for it was the solemn duty of every knight, especially when appealed to, to help ladies in distress." He added dramatically, "I will renounce everything here and go and take up the Cross in heathendom if this good lady leaves us without comfort and aid."[218]

Hearing this, the Count gave up arguing.

Edward arrived at Portchester, where his fleet was gathering, on 30 August. The next day, he sent orders to Oliver Ingham, recently appointed Seneschal of Gascony, to refuse all aid to the Queen, but Ingham defied him and hastened north to join her, for which she would later reward him. From now on, Ingham would be regarded chiefly as Mortimer's man.[219]

On 2 September, Edward ordered his half brother, Norfolk, and his other commissioners of array in East Anglia to raise two thousand men by 21 September to defend the Suffolk port of Orwell against invasion. Again, his instincts were accurate, but strangely, he did not follow up these orders, and the muster never took place; this may in part be due to Norfolk's covert operations on the Queen's behalf. Around this time, the King launched a naval attack on the French fleet in Normandy, but his ships were driven back.[220]

On 7 September, Isabella joined William V's court at Dordrecht and was entertained there by the Count and his wife the following day.[221]

Meanwhile, Bishop Airmyn had returned to England and gone into hiding. Learning of his whereabouts, the King attempted to lure him to London, but Airmyn continued to elude him.[222] He had still not received the temporalities of his office and, having failed to respond to Edward's earlier summons, could not expect a warm reception.

On 10 and 12 September, Edward ordered a squadron to take up battle stations at Hunstanton on the north Norfolk coast and sent small flotillas to guard the approaches to Orford and Thanet. He left Portchester for London on 16 September and took up residence in the Tower with the Despensers.[223]

On 11 September, Isabella promised to pay for the upkeep of the ships that were being loaned to her.[224] She had accompanied Count William and his court to Rotterdam and was still with him and the Countess when they left on 13 September and traveled fourteen miles westward to the port of Brielle on the River Maas, arriving there on the sixteenth. Here they were joined by Sir John of Hainault and a host of knights. In the Countess Jeanne's account books, Isabella is last recorded at Brielle on 20 September, but she was probably still there when Mortimer arrived on the twenty-first.[225] By now, the Queen had apparently successfully concluded her secret agreement with Robert the Bruce.[226]

Froissart says that Isabella bade farewell to Count William and his family on 22 September at Valenciennes, but that is more than 110 miles south of Dordrecht and Brielle: the Hainault court could not have got there in a day, and there is no reason why Isabella should have traveled with them so far from Dordrecht. The farewells were doubtless said at Brielle on the twenty-first, Isabella taking her leave of the Count and Countess, kissing them, and thanking them "deeply, humbly and graciously for their kind and noble hospitality."[227]

Although Froissart states that Sir John of Hainault then escorted Isabella's party to Mons, which is about fifteen miles from Valenciennes, he in fact took them to Dordrecht, where the invasion force had assembled. The Queen was attended by the Countess of Garonne and the other noble ladies who were to accompany her to England. At the port, men, baggage, horses, and provisions were being loaded onto the ninety-five waiting ships.[228]

Various figures are quoted for the size of the Queen's army, which was comprised mostly of Flemish, German, and Bohemian mercenaries: Walsingham says it numbered 2,757 men; Lanercost, 1,500; Froissart, 700; and the *Chronicle of Meaux,* 500. *The Brut* just says that the invasion force was very small: clearly, Isabella and Mortimer anticipated a substantial level of support once they arrived in England. The Hainaulters, 700 in number according to most estimates, were under the command of Sir John; Mortimer was in charge of the rest, who included the Queen's men-at-arms, the other mercenaries, and the English exiles, among them Kent, Richmond, and Henry de Beaumont.[229]

On 22 September, "when they had a fair wind," the invaders "entrusted themselves to Our Lord," weighed anchor, and sailed from Dordrecht into the North Sea.[230]

CHAPTER EIGHT

Welcome, in God's Name, Madam and Your Son

They sailed with a good wind, meeting no resistance from English ships, for Edward's sailors were either elsewhere or had mutinied and refused to fight "because of the great wrath they had towards Sir Hugh le Despenser."[1] Then their fleet ran into a storm "that sent them off their course, so that for two days they did not know where they were. And in this, God was merciful and helped them: He altered their course by a miracle. So it happened that, at the end of two days, the storm was over, and the sailors sighted land in England. They made for it gladly, and landed on the sands on the open seashore,"[2] just before noon on 24 September 1326. Contemporary accounts state that the landing was made at either Orwell or Harwich, but it is more likely to have been on the Suffolk side of the River Orwell,[3] given that the invaders went to nearby Walton for the night.[4]

"The Queen being got safely ashore, her knights and attendants made her a house with four carpets, open in the front, where they kindled her a great fire."[5] At first, "they did not know what part of England they were in, nor whether they were in the power of their friends or their enemies,"[6] but local inquiries established, to their relief, that they were in the territory of Thomas of Brotherton, Earl of Norfolk. During the three hours that it took for men, horses, and provisions to be unloaded,[7] the Queen wrote letters to the citizens of London, and to other cities and towns, stating that she had come to avenge the murder of Lancaster and to rid the realm of the Despensers and Robert Baldock, the enemies of the kingdom, and asking for their assistance in this enterprise.[8]

The reference to Lancaster was probably made at the behest of Isabella's uncle, Leicester, whose support had been offered as a means not only of overthrowing a hateful regime but also of avenging his brother's death. He was an important ally, one the Queen could not afford to lose, and from the first, his influence was paramount. Isabella might have withdrawn her support from Thomas of Lancaster, but she had been shocked by the manner of his trial and execution—he was, after all, her uncle, and a prince of the blood royal—and she was well aware that he was now revered in England as a virtual saint and martyr. The political value of her cause's being associated with such a powerful legend was immense and was another reason why the invaders identified themselves so closely with the Lancastrian cause.

Once the unloading had been completed, the invasion fleet sailed back to Hainault.[9] In the afternoon, Norfolk arrived to escort Isabella to his seaside castle at Walton-on-the-Naze,[10] where she spent the night. Here, she was joined by many barons, knights, and gentlemen of East Anglia and by secret supporters of the contrariants.[11]

Thomas of Brotherton had done his work well: in the three days after the invading forces landed, only fifty-five men rallied to the King in Norfolk.[12] It was a foretaste of what was to come and the beginning of one of the most dramatic episodes in English history.

The next morning, still clad in her widow's weeds, "as if on a pilgrimage," the Queen marched her forces, "with banners displayed," to Bury Saint Edmunds, thirty miles away. In "the next country town" she came to, which could have been Ipswich, "she found all the houses amply and well-furnished with provisions, but all the people fled."[13] In Bury, she was given lodgings in the Dominican abbey, where she discovered 800 marks that had been deposited there by Hervey de Staunton, one of the King's justices, of which she immediately took possession.[14]

Meanwhile, the Queen's "advance guard had spread themselves all over the country, and seized all the cattle and food they could get; and the owners followed them, crying bitterly, into the presence of the Queen, who asked them what was the fair value of the goods. And when they named the price, she paid them all liberally in ready money. The people were so pleased with this conduct that they supplied her well with provisions."[15] This was just one of many examples of Isabella's skill at public relations, a skill she was to bring into play many times during the coming weeks.

News of the invasion spread rapidly, provoking different responses. "Some declared that [the Queen] was the betrayer of the King and the kingdom, others that she was acting for peace and the common welfare of the kingdom."[16] It was not long, however, before popular opinion polarized in her favor.

After visiting the shrine of Saint Edmund, and allowing her soldiers time to rest, the Queen moved another thirty miles west to Cambridge. Wherever she went, she "found favour with all," and the common people flocked to her banner.[17] The news of her arrival had rapidly "spread over the country until it reached those who had communicated with the Queen and invited her back. And they immediately prepared to come and see her, and her son, whom they wanted as their sovereign."[18]

At Cambridge, Isabella spent three days at Barnwell Priory, the principal royal hospice in the city.[19] The Queen was joined at Cambridge by many magnates and several bishops, including Orleton of Hereford, Burghersh of Lincoln, Hotham of Ely, and Beaumont of Durham, as well as Alexander Bicknor, the Archbishop of Dublin.[20] Orleton made Isabella a substantial donation of funds toward her expenses, while Burghersh persuaded his fellow bishops to give generously for the Queen's cause, and Hotham helped to raise men.[21] Baker, whose loyalties lay firmly with Edward II, later scathingly referred to these bishops as "priests of Baal, the accomplices of Jezebel."

The bishops had elected Orleton as their spokesman, and he reassured the Queen and her lords as to the rightness of their cause, "saying that it was to the advantage of the kingdom that the King should be forced to submit to the counsel of the great gathering of noblemen assembled there."[22]

By 27 September, word of the Queen's invasion had reached London.[23] The King and the Despensers were seated at table in the royal apartments of the Tower when some of his sailors came hurrying with news that the Queen had landed with a great army. This provoked little reaction; indeed, it was gratifying for Edward to hear that the Queen was apparently having to rely on the assistance of foreign mercenaries to achieve her aims; but when subsequent, better-informed messengers reported that Isabella had only seven hundred men with her, he was struck with consternation, and the Elder Despenser cried aloud, "Alas, alas! We be all betrayed, for certes, with so little power, she had never come to land but folk of this country had to her consented."[24]

The King immediately issued a general summons of array,[25] wrote letters begging for aid from the Pope and the King of France, and appealed to the Londoners to resist the Queen. Only four people responded.[26] The crucial factor was that Isabella had always been popular in the capital, while Edward had lost the love of its citizens in 1321, when he had rashly tried to curtail their jealously guarded liberties. Thus, they were demonstrably reluctant to assist him and would have preferred to have sent aid to the Queen, but they were obliged to ignore her letter "for fear of the King."[27]

The next day, Edward summoned men from the Home Counties to join him "wherever they found him," which indicates that he was already thinking of leaving London.[28] He also appealed to the Welsh for support and even offered pardons to prisoners and outlaws if they would rally to his cause; a hundred convicted murderers immediately offered their services.[29] He issued a proclamation proscribing all who had taken up arms against him and urging all men to rise and destroy the Queen's power, sparing only her life, her son's, and Kent's.[30] He then sent one Robert de Wateville to East Anglia to raise a force to repel the invaders, but Wateville could muster only sixty men, whom he promptly led to the Queen.[31]

The King also offered £1,000 to anyone bringing him Mortimer's head,[32] and on 30 September, he had Archbishop Reynolds read a papal bull against "invaders" at Paul's Cross: it had in fact been intended for use against the Scots some seven years earlier. The Londoners listened in hostile silence.[33] Meanwhile, members of the royal household and secretariats had begun to desert Edward. The only lords to stay loyal were Arundel, whose son was married to Despenser's daughter, and Surrey.

That day, full of consternation at the news that the invaders were making for Oxford, the King appealed to the town and university for assistance against them, offering generous privileges in return; the next day, he committed Mortimer's three sons to the Tower and ordered Oxford to close its gates to the Queen.[34] But when she arrived there, probably on 2 October, the burghers of Oxford came in procession and welcomed her joyfully, presenting her with a silver cup;[35] this must have been a relief, as she had been anxious about her reception.[36] After all, Oxford was the first major city she had approached, and Edward II had been the first monarch to extend his patronage to the university.

Yet the university offered Isabella its wholehearted support. From Saint Mary's pulpit, Bishop Orleton preached an incendiary sermon in the presence of the Queen, the Prince, and Mortimer, taking his text from Genesis: "I will put enmity between thee and the woman, and between thy seed and her seed: she will bruise thy head." He explained that this referred not to the King but to Despenser, that snake in Eden and "the seed of the first tyrant, Satan, who would be crushed by the Lady Isabella and her son, the Prince," who had come to put an end to misgovernment.[37]

At Oxford, the Queen lodged in the house of the Carmelites, while Mortimer stayed with her other captains in Oseney Abbey, to the west of the city.[38] This suggests that Isabella and Mortimer were deliberately maintaining a discreet distance from each other, wishing to avoid scandal. There were far wider and more important issues involved in Isabella's enterprise than complicated personal relationships, and no scandal was to be allowed to prejudice the success, or the rightness, of her cause.

On 2 October, realizing that he could not count on any support in the capital, and believing that "the whole community of the realm" would declare for the Queen, Edward left London with a small company, which included the Despensers; Arundel; Surrey; the Chancellor, Robert Baldock; and some of the royal clerks. The King took with him £29,000 in ready cash and a force of archers.[39] They fled westward toward Wales, where Despenser held vast territories and was confident of raising support;[40] Edward himself was optimistically hoping that the Welsh would rise in his favor, for, as their former Prince, he had enjoyed a degree of popularity with the people. The King left Stapledon as guardian of the City[41] and Despenser's wife in custody of the Tower.[42] That night, he and Hugh stopped at Acton.[43]

The Earl of Leicester had also risen in arms for the Queen, and on 3 October, he marched on Leicester, gathered a great force, and seized Despenser's treasure, which had been deposited in the abbey for safety. Then he marched south to rendezvous with the Queen.[44]

Edward was at Ruislip on 4 October and at Wycombe on the fifth. By the time he arrived at Wallingford on the sixth, he had decided to take a stand against the invaders at Gloucester. But he was greatly overestimating the support he would receive.

By then, Isabella had marched south to Baldock, where she had the Chancellor's brother Thomas arrested and his house ransacked. From there, on 6 October, she sent a second letter to the Londoners; this was of a vastly different tone from the first, for it was a summons to all good citizens to come to her aid in securing the destruction of Despenser or suffer punishment for defaulting.[45] Doubling Edward's price for Mortimer, she offered £2,000 for Despenser's head.[46] She then moved to Dunstable,[47] only thirty miles from London, where she planned to muster her forces before advancing on the capital.

On 7 October, Edward was at Faringdon and, on the eighth, at Cirencester. The next day, he reached Gloucester,[48] where he issued an order for Leicester's arrest and tried, without success, to rally men to his cause.[49] No one, it was becoming clear, was prepared to fight for him,[50] and the relatives and friends of the contrariants, whom he had punished so savagely, were actively moving against him.

The Queen's letter arrived in London on 9 October and was posted on the Eleanor Cross in Cheapside; its contents were widely circulated, and copies were soon being displayed in the windows of private houses to proclaim the support of their owners for the Queen. On the tenth, Edward learned to his dismay that Leicester, "with a great company of men-at-arms," had joined the Queen at Dunstable. "And after him, from one place and another, came earls, barons, knights and squires, with so many men-at-arms that the Queen's men thought they were out of all danger. And as they advanced, their numbers increased every day."[51]

The King was still at Gloucester on the eleventh, when, in desperation, he announced that he would offer free pardons to any who would join him. He then rode on to Westbury-on-Severn in the Forest of Dean, arriving on 12 October, and to Alnington on the thirteenth. By the time he had reached Westbury, he had only twelve archers left and was reduced to making a pathetic appeal to them not to desert him.[52]

On 13 October, Archbishop Reynolds urgently convened a conference of bishops at Lambeth to discuss plans for a peace summit at Saint Paul's Cathedral. Among those present were Stratford, Stapledon, Airmyn, Hethe, and Stephen de Gravesend, Bishop of London. On 14 October, it was proposed that two of the bishops go to intercede with the Queen, but only Stratford was willing to volunteer. By then, it was becoming obvious that the Londoners were in an ugly mood, and Hethe warned the Archbishop not to cross the Thames or enter the City because the people believed him to be the King's man.[53]

This was no longer the case. Reynolds had been out of favor for some time, having quarreled with Edward over the vexing question of liturgical precedence, and had already secretly sent large sums of money to the Queen.[54] Eastry had advised Reynolds not to offend the King but to lie low and wait upon events or to work for a compromise; to this end, he might perhaps "reverently go and meet" the Queen and her son, but if he failed to achieve a settlement, he should take sanctuary in his cathedral.[55] The Archbishop would have liked to declare openly for Isabella, but he was reluctant to do so in case Edward emerged triumphant from this present struggle. Therefore, he heeded Hethe's warning, and the meeting broke up, whereupon he and most of his colleagues, abandoning their plans to launch a peace process, fled the capital. Reynolds shut himself up with Hethe in his palace at Maidstone, and Stratford rode off in search of the Queen.[56]

The King was at Tintern Abbey on the River Wye on 14 October, with Baldock and the Younger Despenser, the Elder having gone to occupy Bristol, where he received a less than enthusiastic reception.[57] That day, Wallingford surrendered without resistance to Isabella. On coming to the castle,[58] she liberated Sir Thomas de Berkeley, who, with his father, a fellow contrariant who had since died, had been imprisoned there in 1322.

From Wallingford, on 15 October, Isabella issued a proclamation against the Despensers, which was at once a savage indictment of their misrule and a call to arms:

We, Isabella, by the grace of God Queen of England, Lady of Ireland, Countess of Ponthieu; and we, Edward, elder son of the lord King of England, Duke of Guienne [Gascony], Earl of Chester, Count of Ponthieu and Montreuil; and we, Edmund, son of the noble King of England, Earl of Kent: to all those to whom these letters may come, greetings.

Whereas it is well known that the state of the Holy Church and the kingdom of England is in many respects much tarnished and degraded by the bad advice and conspiracy of Hugh le Despenser; whereas, through pride and greed to have power and dominion over all other people, he has usurped royal power against law and justice and his true allegiance, and through the bad advice of Robert Baldock and others of his supporters, he has acted in such a way that the Holy Church is robbed of its goods against God and right, and in many other ways insulted and dishonoured, and the Crown of England brought low in many respects, through the disinheritance of our lord the King and of his heirs. The magnates of the kingdom, through the envy and wicked cruelty of the said Hugh, have been delivered to a shameful death, many of them blamelessly and without cause. Others have been disinherited, imprisoned, banished or exiled; widows and orphans have been unlawfully deprived of their rights, and the people of this land much hurt by many taxes, and held to ransom by frequent, unjust demands for money and by divers other oppressions, without any mercy; by virtue of which misdeeds, the said Hugh shows himself to be a clear tyrant and enemy of God and the Holy Church, and of our very dear said lord the King and the whole kingdom.

And we, and several others who are with us and of our company, who have long been kept far from the goodwill of our said lord the King through the false suggestions and evil dealings of the aforesaid Hugh and Robert and their supporters, are come to this land to raise up the state of Holy Church and of the kingdom, and of the people of this land, against the said misdeeds and oppressions, and to safeguard and maintain, so far as we can, the honour and profit of the Holy Church and of our said lord the King and the whole kingdom, as is stated above. For this reason, we ask and pray you, for the common good of all and each of you individually, that you come to our help well and loyally, whenever the time and place are right, and by whatever means lie within your power, so that the above matters may be speedily put right. For be assured that we all, and all those who are in our company, intend to do nothing that does not redound to the honour and profit of the Holy Church and the whole kingdom, as you will see in the course of time, if it please God.

Given at Wallingford on 15 October in the 20th year of the reign of our very dear lord the King.[59]

There was no hint in this letter of any criticism of the King, to whom the Queen constantly referred as her "very dear lord," as became a loving wife. Yet almost as soon as it was written, encouraged by her welcome in England, she was emboldened to make clear her true intentions, which were revealed in another inflammatory sermon that Bishop Orleton preached at Wallingford that same day, taking his text from 2 Kings, 4:19, "My head, my head acheth."[60]

"When the head of a kingdom becometh sick and diseased," he told his congregation, "it must of necessity be taken off, without useless attempts to administer any other remedy." In other words, a feeble king should be removed "and not be protected by the support of flatterers."[61] The rest of the sermon was devoted to a scathing attack on Edward and to justifying the Queen's invasion. Referring to the ill-treatment of Isabella, and the reason why she had been forced to leave her husband, the Bishop revealed "that the King had carried a knife in his hose to kill Queen Isabella, and he had said that, if he had no other weapon, he could crush her with his teeth." As he had intended, his words incited much ill feeling against Edward.[62]

That day, the Londoners had erupted in violence against the King and his favorites, the rioting citizens shouting their support of the Queen and viciously turning on all who had supported Edward and the Despensers. In the name of the Queen and Prince Edward, they seized the Tower from Eleanor de Clare, wresting the keys out of the Constable's hands, and liberated all the prisoners, including Mortimer's sons.[63] Finding the ten-year-old Prince John in residence in the royal apartments—he had been in Eleanor's care—the Londoners proclaimed him Warden of the City and the Tower. Then they marched their unpopular Mayor, Edward's man, Hamo de Chigwell, who was "crying mercy with clasped hands," to the Guildhall and forced him to declare his allegiance to Isabella and to warn that any enemies of the Queen and the Prince would remain in London at their peril. To demonstrate that this was no empty threat, the mob seized and butchered Despenser's clerk, John the Marshal, whom they believed to be his spy.[64]

After the abortive Lambeth conference, Bishop Stapledon, mindful of the King's having left him as guardian of the City, had decided to return to London.[65] His arrival coincided with the outbreak of the riots on 15 October, and he immediately fell foul of the Londoners, who identified him with the Despensers' rule and detested him for his rapacity;[66] they had already sacked his house in the Temple, stolen his valuables, and burned his episcopal registers. After spotting him, clad in armor, riding into the City attended by only two squires, a baying mob chased him nearly to Saint Paul's. Before he could reach the sanctuary of the cathedral's north door, they dragged him from his horse and manhandled him through the churchyard and all the way to the Eleanor Cross in Cheapside, where they pulled off his armor and brutally hacked off his head with a butcher's knife. His squires were dispatched in the same gruesome way. The Bishop's head was speedily conveyed to the Queen as a trophy, while his body was stripped and left naked in the street. Later, after being refused burial in Saint Clement Danes Church on the Strand, it was interred under a rubbish dump "without the office of priest or clerk."[67]

The mob then went on to plunder and ransack properties owned by Arundel, Baldock, the Bardi, and other associates of the King and the Despensers. They would have lynched their own Bishop, Gravesend, too, but he managed to escape.[68] Deprived of any effective government, London descended into near anarchy, with orgies of violence and looting raging unchecked for weeks to come, and its citizens terrorized and even forced into hiding. Trade, of course, came to a standstill, and normal daily life ceased.[69]

Edward arrived in Chepstow in Monmouthshire on 16 October. Here, he optimistically appointed the Elder Despenser guardian of all the southwestern counties of England.[70] The next day, in London, at the insistence of the mob, the tablet commemorating Lancaster and the Ordinances was set up again in Saint Paul's Cathedral.[71]

By then, Isabella, after learning of the unrest in London, had taken counsel with her barons and swung westward, aiming to intercept Edward and Despenser. Her pursuit of them, however, turned into a triumphant progress. "In every town they entered, they were honoured and feasted, and new supporters joined them from every side."[72] During their march, the Queen's soldiers "did no harm to the country, but only devastated the manors of the Despensers."

At Gloucester, the Queen lodged in the castle, the city's chief royal residence, which stood between the cathedral and the quay; its massive twelfth-century keep had been remodeled by Henry III in the thirteenth century with a great hall, a great chamber, and private chapels.[73] Here, Isabella was joined by northern forces led by Henry, Lord Percy, Thomas, Baron Wake, and Henry de Beaumont, and by some Marcher barons and Welsh contingents.[74] Isabella appointed Wake marshal of her army,[75] which was now a formidable fighting force.

Here also, apparently without flinching, she received the head of Stapledon, which was presented to her "as if it were a sacrifice to propitiate Diana."[76] According to a sixteenth-century source, she suppressed her distaste and dismay, for she could not approve of this sacrilegious murder,[77] and expressed her thanks to the Mayor for "his late bloody act," which she termed "an excellent piece of justice."[78] She then marched on to Berkeley Castle, which had been held by Despenser since 1322 and which she now restored to its rightful owner, Sir Thomas de Berkeley.[79]

In the absence of firm, centralized government, the kingdom was descending rapidly into chaos. "Thieves, murderers and all manner of criminals did great damage, knowing that no one would stand in their way or bring them to justice. Rapacity raged unchecked, so that any friend of the King, if found, would at once be stripped of his possessions or his life, and those responsible would suffer no punishment. It was enough for the conspirators that the victim had been of the King's party."[80]

By 18 October, Isabella had arrived before Bristol,[81] with an army that now numbered two thousand. Bristol was then "a good town, large and rich and well enclosed, with a good seaport. And there is a very strong and powerful castle there, with the sea beating all round it."[82] The Queen's army, under the command of Mortimer, immediately laid siege to the town and castle, which were held by the Elder Despenser.[83]

Meanwhile, the King's efforts at Chepstow to secure military aid had proved futile.[84] On 21 October, he and Despenser, "seeing the terrible situation they were in, and not knowing of any relief that might come to them from any quarter," set sail from Chepstow "in a small boat."[85] They were perhaps making for Despenser's island of Lundy in the Bristol Channel, which could afford them a safe refuge, being well fortified by the "very steep and rugged cliffs" that rose above its coastline and "rendered attack impossible";[86] they might alternatively have been hoping to reach Ireland, whence they could bribe the Scots for reinforcements, which was what Isabella greatly feared.[87] But in the event, they were tossed for four days by storms in the Bristol Channel before being driven back to Cardiff on 25 October.[88]

On her way to Bristol, Isabella had received alarming reports of the situation in London. Knowing that Prince John was there, and fearing for his safety, she had first written to the citizens, asking them to send her son to her, but they had effectively refused, for they wanted him in London, as their nominal leader.[89] Isabella next wrote to Archbishop Reynolds, asking him to go to the capital and look to the Prince's well-being. But, as Reynolds reported to Prior Eastry on 21 October, he was too terrified to enter London.[90] For the time being, the Queen had therefore to trust the Londoners to keep her son safe, for she had too many pressing matters on her hands to go to London for the present, nor was she certain that it was safe for her to do so. The mood of its ever-mercurial citizens was bullish, and when the Queen had attempted to intercede for a German merchant who had fallen foul of them, she was bluntly told that no enemy of London could be a friend to her and that she should not meddle in the City's business.[91]

On 25 October, Isabella ordered Roger Martival, Bishop of Salisbury, to hand over some treasures that Despenser had left with him to keep safely.[92] Despenser, she was determined, should never profit from his illegal gains.

Edward was still at Cardiff on 26 October. On that day, Bristol fell to Isabella. Froissart says that "when the people of the town saw how powerful the Queen had become, and that almost all England was on her side, and clearly understood the danger they were in, they took counsel to give themselves up, and the town as well, in order to save their lives and their possessions." In fact, public opinion in Bristol was so overwhelmingly in Isabella's favor that Despenser, "overcome with despair," was obliged to surrender to her without offering any resistance or negotiating any favorable terms for himself.[93] Then the citizens joyfully "opened their gates, so that the Queen, Sir John and all the barons, knights and squires entered and lodged in the city.[94] Those who could not get in stayed outside. Sir Hugh the Elder was taken and brought before the Queen, for her to do what she liked with him."[95] Isabella, observed Baker, who scathingly calls her "that harridan" or "that virago," "had now attained a position of great power."

Waiting for the Queen in Bristol were her "two little daughters," eight-year-old Eleanor and five-year-old Joan, who had been living there under the guardianship of the Elder Despenser. When the Princesses were brought to her, "the Queen was overjoyed, since she had not seen them for a long time."[96]

Isabella had now learned of the King's departure from Chepstow, which she and her advisers deemed to be tantamount to abandoning his kingdom. This was an ideal opportunity to establish an alternative government, and later that day, 26 October, the Queen presided over a council that was attended by Mortimer, Kent, Norfolk, Lancaster, Wake, Beaumont, William, Lord Zouche, Robert de Montalt, Robert Wateville, Archbishop Bicknor, Stratford, Hotham, Burghersh, and Orleton. This council acted, it was claimed, by the consent of the community of the realm, and it proclaimed Prince Edward "custos" or Keeper of the Realm in the King's absence, on the grounds that Edward had deserted his people.[97] Isabella's clerk, Robert Wyville, was appointed Keeper of the Prince's Privy Seal, which gave the Queen control over her son's acts. The council also acknowledged Leicester's right to succeed to his brother's inheritance, and that very day, he began styling himself Earl of Lancaster.[98]

Mortimer was noticeably absent from this council, which was a foretaste of things to come. He evidently preferred to exert his formidable power behind the scenes, through Isabella. In future months and years, Mortimer was to shun a formal role, which meant that he could easily dissociate himself from unpopular decisions and avoid being challenged. But his power was very real, nonetheless.

Bishop Stratford caught up with the Queen at Bristol,[99] and on 26 October, Archbishop Reynolds finally switched his allegiance and wrote to her, begging for her protection.[100]

On 27 October, the Elder Despenser was tried at Bristol. "The Queen had him brought before her son and the barons that were there," prominent among whom were Mortimer, Lancaster, Wake, Kent, and Norfolk, "and told him that she and her son would see that law and justice were done to them, according to their deeds."

"Madam," said Despenser, clearly expecting the worst, "may God give me a good judge and a good judgement. And if I may not have that in this world, may I have it in the next."[101]

The proceedings against him mirrored exactly what had taken place at Thomas of Lancaster's trial in 1322. The articles against Despenser were read out by Lord Wake, who asked the lords "to say on oath what judgement should be passed on those who were guilty of such crimes." They conferred together "and reported it as their definite opinion that the defendant deserved death for the many horrible crimes with which he had been charged, and which were believed to be clearly proved."[102] Murimuth states he was found guilty "by clamour of the people," or rather, by the ancient doctrine of "manifest ill-fame," which disposed of the requirement to offer any evidence.

Sentence was passed by Sir William Trussell, who had been with Isabella in France. "Sir Hugh," he said, "this court denies you any right of answer because you yourself made a law that a man could be condemned without right of answer, and this law shall now apply to you and your adherents." The silencing of Despenser had probably been insisted on by Lancaster, whose brother had been condemned unheard in 1322, a victim of this alleged law.

Trussell went on, "You are an attainted traitor, for you were formerly banished as such, by the assent of the King and the whole baronage, and have never been reconciled. By force, and against the law of the land, and accroaching to yourself royal power, you counselled the King to disinherit and undo his lieges, and notably Thomas of Lancaster, whom you had put to death for no cause. You are a robber, and by your cruelty you have robbed this land, wherefore all the people cry vengeance upon you. Wherefore the court awards that you be drawn for treason, hanged for robbery, beheaded for misdeeds against the Church, and that your head be sent to Winchester, of which place, against law and reason, you were made earl. And because your deeds have dishonoured the order of chivalry, the court awards that you be hanged in a surcoat quartered with your arms, and that your arms be destroyed forever."[103]

It was a degrading and shameful punishment, and Isabella did her best to spare the old man,[104] but she was overruled by Lancaster and his faction, who reminded her that she had undertaken to destroy the favorites, and Despenser suffered that same day, on the common gallows at Bristol. Afterward, his decapitated corpse was displayed like that of "any common thief," tied by the arms to a forked gibbet, before a mob that screamed, "Traitor!" After four days, it was taken down, chopped up, and fed to the dogs.[105]

In happy ignorance of these events, the King and Despenser had been traveling through Glamorgan, trying to raise support among Despenser's tenants,[106] but most were hostile to him and refused to fight. On the day the Elder Despenser perished, the King and Despenser sought refuge in the latter's massive stronghold at Caerphilly.[107] They were well aware now that "the greater part of the country was won over to the side of the Queen and her elder son, and drawn up in opposition to the King," and naturally, they "were worried and frightened and distraught."[108] But the King was still issuing useless commissions of array and writs of summons.[109]

On 28 October, writs were issued in the name of Prince Edward, summoning Parliament to meet at Westminster on 14 December and stating that, as the King would be absent from the kingdom, "Isabella, Queen Consort, and Edward, son of the King, the Guardian of the Realm, and the lords might treat together."[110]

The King was still at Caerphilly Castle on 29 October, but two days later, his household accounts come to an abrupt end, doubtless as a result of his servants and clerks deserting him.[111] Effectively, his reign was over and he was a fugitive.

At the end of October, aware that she held the country in her grip and no longer needed his services, Isabella sent John of Hainault and eight of his mercenaries to London to take possession of the Tower in her name and to act as a bodyguard for Prince John.[112] Sir John was in receipt of an English pension from 9 November 1326 to 10 March 1327.

On 1 November, the Queen went to Hereford, where she was received "most respectfully and joyfully" by the people. Here, she kept the feast of All Saints "with great solemnity and ceremony, out of love for her son and respect for the foreign nobles who were with him."[113] The Queen took up residence as Orleton's guest in his episcopal palace, which boasted an aisled Norman hall and stood on the south side of the cathedral.[114] For the time being, she was sharing a household with her son, and on 1 November, a new household roll, listing the joint expenses of Isabella and Prince Edward, was drawn up.[115] Writs were issued at Hereford in their joint names on 5 November,[116] and on the sixth, the Prince nominated Stratford as Treasurer in place of Melton.[117] His appointment would smooth the transfer of the Exchequer and Treasury to Isabella's control.

The King had moved to Morgan on 3 November, and thence to Gower, where he was still desperately trying to raise troops on the fifth.[118] He then moved to Neath, where he remained until 10 November; his last writs were issued there on the sixth and seventh.[119] On the tenth, realizing that any further attempts at resistance were futile, Edward sent the Abbot of Neath and Rhys ap Gruffydd to open negotiations with Isabella.[120] Her response was to send Lancaster, William, Lord Zouche, and Rhys ap Hywel (a Welsh clerk who had been released from the Tower by the Londoners and was to act as Lancaster's guide) with an armed force to take the King.[121]

Meanwhile, in the hope of restoring law and order in the City of London, Isabella had sent Bishop Stratford to the citizens with a letter autho-

rizing them to elect a new Mayor in place of the unpopular Hamo de Chigwell. Stratford's arrival on 15 November heralded an end to the violence
and anarchy of the past weeks. The Londoners chose as their Mayor
Richard de Béthune, the merchant who had helped Mortimer escape from
the Tower in 1323; his election would cement London's loyalty to the
Queen and Mortimer. John de Gisors, who had also assisted in Mortimer's
escape, was made Constable of the Tower.[122]

The circumstances surrounding the King's capture are cloaked in obscurity.
Apparently, his whereabouts were revealed to Lancaster either by the
Welsh, in return for a bribe,[123] or by the steward of the royal household, Sir
Thomas Blount, and on 16 November, in torrential rain, the Earl apprehended Edward, Despenser, Baldock, and six other men, who were all that
remained of the King's supporters, in open country near Llantrissant, and
escorted them under guard to the castle there.[124] Many years later, however,
Orleton, on being accused of having incited the people to seize the King,
testified that it was well known that, by the time of their apprehension,
Despenser was holding his master captive and that Edward "came of his
own will to the Earl of Lancaster, his kinsman."[125] This is not an unlikely
scenario: Edward had approached Isabella about a settlement, and
Despenser would not have needed to be a genius to realize that she would
demand nothing less than his death as the price of her agreement. He may
well have used force to remove Edward to a place where the Queen's messengers could not find him, and Edward could have sent Blount to seek
them out. Blount could have told him that they were approaching, and he
perhaps mistakenly assumed that they were coming to negotiate with him.
Instead, Lancaster placed him under arrest and immediately escorted him
to Monmouth Castle.

Five of those arrested by Lancaster were immediately released, but
Despenser, Baldock, and Despenser's marshal, Simon of Reading, who had
appropriated the lands of one of Mortimer's clients[126] and even now had
the effrontery to speak insultingly of the Queen, were entrusted to the vig-
ilance of Lord Wake and sent in chains to Isabella at Hereford.[127]

That same day, Arundel was arrested in Shropshire by John de Charlton,
who had been Edward's chamberlain before being ousted by Despenser and
was now high in favor with Isabella and Mortimer; his son was married to
Mortimer's daughter Matilda. Charlton brought his prisoner to the Queen
at Hereford, where, on Mortimer's express orders, Arundel was summarily
beheaded[128] without trial on 17 November, in company with his henchmen,
Thomas de Micheldever and John Daniel. These executions without trial

were acts of tyranny on the part of Mortimer, who had many reasons to regard Arundel "with a perfect hatred," not the least because he had appropriated Chirk's estates and some of Mortimer's, too;[129] and Isabella was a party to them.

On the journey to Hereford, Despenser's jailer went out of his way to humiliate him. "Wake had Sir Hugh tied onto the meanest and poorest horse he could find, and he had him dressed in a tabard over his clothes, embroidered with the coat-of-arms that he bore, and so conducted him along the road as a public laughing stock. And in all the towns they passed through, he was announced by trumpets and cymbals, by way of greater mockery, till they reached the good city of Hereford." Despenser, notes Froissart, "was not popular in that district,"[130] and when they reached Hereford on 20 November, the crowds were waiting to greet him with savage mockery and screams of hatred, while Sir John of Hainault, that mirror of chivalry, with two other men, joined Wake in roughly dragging him through the streets.[131]

At the Bishop's palace, Despenser and Baldock were delivered to the Queen as her prisoners, and she duly paid the £2,000 reward to their captors. Baldock, who was in holy orders, had claimed benefit of clergy and was given into the custody of Bishop Orleton, who kept him under house arrest in his London residence, Saint Mary Mountshaw in Old Fish Street Hill, near where the monument now stands.

That same day, Orleton was sent to Monmouth to demand that Edward II surrender the Great Seal of England. Now that the King had been found, he could in theory be restored to power, but of course, that was the last thing that Isabella and the majority of his subjects wanted. The Queen was also sensible of the fact that, with the King now indubitably resident in his realm, there was no longer any need for the Prince to act as its Keeper. So Orleton's task, which he carried out successfully, was to persuade Edward to surrender the Great Seal to the Queen[132] so that she could claim that she was acting in his name and her rule would have some semblance of legality. From the first, Isabella had been careful to win and retain the goodwill and approval of the people, and her anxiety to be seen to be acting within the law was to be repeatedly made manifest.

Isabella wanted to have Despenser tried and executed in London,[133] not only to show that she had accomplished what she had come to do but also as an example to the riotous citizens and to achieve maximum publicity for the event. But Despenser was no fool, and realizing what fate surely awaited him, he had been refusing food and drink since his arrest, in an attempt to starve himself to death.[134] After a week of this, he was so weak that it was feared that the journey to London would kill him and that he would thereby escape the punishment he deserved. So it was decided to try him in Hereford.

On 24 November, so faint with hunger that he was almost insensible, Despenser was brought before a "tribunal" consisting of the Queen and the same magnates who had condemned his father.[135] A list of his misdeeds was read out to him by Sir William Trussell, "to which he made no reply."[136] Like his father, he was forbidden to say anything in his defense.

Despenser was accused of a whole catalog of crimes, including several committed against Isabella: unspecified cruelty shown toward the Queen; dishonoring and disparaging her and damaging her noble estate; maliciously interfering between her and her husband, to the detriment of their marriage (this is the closest the indictment came to a charge of sodomy with the King); advising the King to abandon the Queen at Tynemouth, to her life's peril, in 1322; depriving the Queen of her dower and "ousting her from her lands"; attempting by bribery to turn members of the French court against her and even to procure her murder and that of the Prince; making it impossible for her to return from France with her son; procuring the murder of the late Earl of Lancaster; illegally confiscating the property of Bishops Orleton, Hotham, Burghersh, and Airmyn; incarcerating the Mortimers "in a harsh prison to murder them without cause, except for his coveting of their lands"; ill-treating the widows and children of the contrariants; and dishonoring the King by inducing him, after the Queen's invasion, to abandon both his kingdom and his wife.[137] The bitter grievances of both Isabella and Mortimer rang out loud and clear.

The lords and knights wasted no time in reaching a guilty verdict, and Trussell delivered the dread sentence of death handed down to those convicted of treason: Despenser was to be hanged as a thief, drawn and quartered as a traitor, beheaded for violating his sentence of exile, "and, because you were always disloyal and procured discord between our lord the King and our very honourable lady the Queen, you will be disembowelled and then your entrails will be burnt." This was the usual penalty for treason, but there was to be another refinement, as yet unrevealed to any.

"Go to meet your fate, traitor, tyrant, renegade!" Trussell concluded vehemently. "Go to receive your own justice, traitor, evil man, criminal!" Did Isabella gloat in triumph, to see her enemy brought so low? Or did she sit there, glacially impassive? We do not know, because no chronicler records her reaction. But the lords and commons present made their feelings apparent, shouting, "Traitor! Renegade! Traitor!"

Immediately after the hearing, the condemned man, wearing a crown of nettles and with his skin roughly tattooed with verses from Scripture on arrogance and retribution,[138] was "dragged in a chest through the streets of Hereford, to the sound of trumpets and clarions; then he was taken to the market-place, where all the people were assembled" and baying for his blood. The Queen watched,[139] with Mortimer, as Despenser was stripped naked, swung up in the air by a noose round his neck, and, half-hanged, tied to a tall ladder, fifty feet high, "so that all the people could see him; and a large fire was lit. When he was thus bound, they cut off his penis and testicles because he was a heretic and a sodomite, and guilty of unnatural practices, so it was said, even with the King himself, whose affections he had alienated from the Queen. After his private parts had been cut off, they were thrown into the fire and burned." Despenser, we are told, at first suffered with great patience, asking forgiveness of the bystanders, but then a ghastly, inhuman howl broke from him. The castration of Despenser was perhaps Isabella's particular revenge, and it was widely regarded as a most apt punishment for his crimes.

"Then his belly was split open and his heart and entrails cut out and thrown on the fire to burn, because his heart had been false and treacherous and he had given treasonable advice to the King, so as to bring shame and disgrace on the country, and had caused the greatest baron in England to be beheaded. And he had encouraged the King not to see his wife. When the other parts of his body had been disposed of, Sir Hugh's head was cut off and sent to London. His body was then hewn into quarters, which were sent to the four next largest cities in England."[140]

With Despenser was hanged, ten feet below him, Simon of Reading.[141] After the executions, Isabella and Mortimer held a feast to celebrate their triumph.

Surrey now hastened to make his peace with Isabella; how he achieved this is not recorded. He would be the only one of Edward's noble supporters to escape with his life. Knighton claims that Isabella had determined upon the destruction of the whole Despenser family, "root and branch," so that never again would a Despenser rise to power, but he was rather overstating the case, for the lives of Despenser's two sons were spared; even though the elder, another Hugh, defended Caerphilly Castle against the Queen's besieging forces, he received a pardon only two months after it fell and would live to be summoned to Parliament as a baron. His younger brother, Edward, became a distinguished soldier. Despenser's widow, Eleanor de Clare, had been imprisoned in the Tower on 17 November,[142] on the Queen's orders, and spent two years there, after which her lands were returned to her, which proves that Isabella did not long harbor vindictive feelings toward this woman who had caused her so much grief. Despenser's five daughters were placed in convents while their mother was in the Tower; three later became nuns, one returned to her husband, Arundel's son, and the other made a good marriage to Lord Berkeley's heir.[143]

"So the Queen won back the whole kingdom of England." Although her company had been initially few in number, they had, for love of her, "acted boldly and bravely" and, reinforced by the multitudes who flocked to her banners, "they conquered as mighty a country as England, in spite of the King and all his men."[144] The success of the enterprise was due also to widespread hatred of the Despensers,[145] bitter resentment arising from years of Edward's misrule, the majority of bishops declaring for the Queen, the support of the City of London for her, and the wholesale desertion of the King by his civil servants. Isabella's was the first successful invasion of England since the Norman Conquest of 1066, and it was also one of the most successful coups in English history. "Thus ended this bold and noble enterprise; and Queen Isabella reconquered her entire kingdom and destroyed her enemies, at which the whole country rejoiced together."[146]

Orleton delivered the Great Seal to the Queen on 26 November at Hereford.[147] Once this was in her possession, she began governing in her husband's name, and many writs were issued "by the King" or "by the King, on the information of the Queen."[148] Furthermore, although the Chancery was with the Queen, its writs were dated at Kenilworth, as if Edward had issued them.[149] All of this gave Isabella's rule a veneer of legality. Not since the time of Eleanor of Aquitaine, who governed in the absence of Richard I in the twelfth century, had an English queen consort exercised such power.

On 27 November, Lancaster was appointed constable of Kenilworth Castle, and soon afterward, on the advice of Orleton, Edward was moved to that luxurious stronghold and placed under armed guard, with Lancaster as his custodian. Kenilworth, which had been formerly a seat of Simon de Montfort and Thomas of Lancaster, seems to have been deliberately chosen because it was indelibly associated in the popular consciousness with the champions of good government. Lancaster proved a considerate jailer, and the King was well and honorably treated, "spending the winter in reasonably comfortable conditions as befits a king in captivity."[150]

Isabella was now faced with the perplexing problem of what to do with her husband. There was no doubt that, after twenty years of appalling misgovernment and tyranny, Edward II had to go. Yet he was an anointed king, and it was essential that any proceedings against him were seen to be legal. From the time of the Norman Conquest of 1066, no precedents had been set for deposing an English king, and there was no known process of law

through which it might be done. Yet it was clear that most of Edward's subjects would no longer tolerate his rule and wanted his son to sit in his place,
and it was also clear that achieving this was going to require a degree of violation of established constitutional principles. But the alternative—the
return of Edward II to power—was unthinkable.

How far was Isabella responsible for the violence and degradation of the
executions of the Despensers? Not at all in the case of the Elder Hugh, for
she had interceded for him but been overruled by Lancaster. And it is likely
that she was obliged to bow also before Mortimer's dictates, for Murimuth
states that the associates of the favorites were executed "at the instance of
Mortimer, who hated them, and whose counsel the Queen followed in all
things." In the case of the Younger Despenser, however, she was apparently
more than willing to do so. Baker says that "the Queen, whose anger could
not be assuaged, was to have her wishes concerning the two Despensers
carried out; thus would her goodwill be assured." Baker is a hostile source,
and is demonstrably incorrect in the case of the Elder Despenser, but probably very near the truth with regard to the Younger. In her terrible
vengeance on him, Isabella proved herself to be a true daughter of the ruthless Philip the Fair and a pragmatist who did what was necessary, however
distasteful.

The fact remains that Hugh was a traitor and suffered the punishment
prescribed by the law; no one protested against this or criticized the Queen
or her advisers for their severity; no contemporary even censured Isabella,
as a woman, for sanctioning such a cruel death, for nothing less would have
satisfied the people. The execution was greeted with popular approval as
the means of ridding the realm of a dangerous and detested tyrant. And
given Despenser's crimes, it was fully justified.

The dreadful punishment of drawing, hanging, beheading, and quarter-
ing had first been introduced into England by Henry III in 1238, when it
was meted out to a man who had tried to murder the King. Edward I had
revived its use against Welsh and Scottish rebels, and to punish traitors, with
the added refinement of disemboweling. So far, the most famous victims
had been Dafydd ap Gruffydd, brother of the last native Prince of Wales, in
1283, and William Wallace, in 1305. During the reigns of Edward I and
Edward II, only two English gentlemen had been executed in this way.
But until 1326, the penalty for treason had not included castration. Castration by itself had been a routine punishment in Norman times, but it was a
practice that had long since fallen into disuse. The Queen, however, would
have recalled that, in 1314, the d'Aulnay brothers had been publicly cas-

trated as part of their punishment for having dishonored her sisters-in-law, and it is possible that it was she who suggested that castration was a peculiarly apt penalty for sexual crimes. Certainly, Froissart and other chroniclers viewed Despenser's punishment as such. That the Queen should sanction such a cruel torture is testimony to the virulence of her loathing of Despenser and perhaps further evidence that he had indeed had a sexual relationship with her husband. In a wider context, the Queen would have intended the ferocity of his punishment to reflect the magnitude of his crimes, and that, in her eyes at least, would have justified it.

It should, however, be emphasized that, apart from the six executions of the Despensers, Arundel, Micheldever, Daniel, and Simon of Reading, and the lynching of Stapledon and others in London (which was none of the Queen's doing), Isabella's was a bloodless coup that could easily have been otherwise. Only the guilty were punished, while many associates of the Despensers were left unmolested. Far from being bloodthirsty, as she has often been portrayed,[151] the Queen was in fact merciful and anxious to justify her deeds by due legal process. The fact that Mortimer had ordered Arundel and others to be executed without trial undermined this intention, but in the climate of the times, no one was interested in such niceties. Furthermore, during the course of the Queen's rebellion, only the goods of the Despensers and their associates were plundered—indeed, most of the Younger Despenser's estates were laid waste; yet the property of others was left unmolested.[152]

It is unclear how far, or how often, during the invasion and its aftermath, Isabella had taken the initiative in making decisions and shaping policy. The Queen was undoubtedly a formidable woman, a seasoned diplomat who was skilled at wooing people to her cause and making allies, and one who had very definite goals in mind. However, it is likely that she left matters of strategy to Mortimer and the other lords, who were experienced in military matters. Undoubtedly, it was Mortimer who had planned the invasion in Hainault; he had been doing so for a long time before Isabella became his ally. He was one of its commanders and had great experience in the field of warfare and campaigning, and so it is probable, too, that, once in England, he was largely responsible for planning strategy. In this respect, Isabella could only have been a figurehead.[153]

Clearly, Mortimer exercised tremendous power through Isabella. He could not have done so had it not been for his intimate relationship with her, for he was never accorded an official position in the government and enjoyed great influence solely because he was her lover; this backstairs role seems to have been his choice, for reasons that have been noted. The likeli-

hood is that, in the privacy of the Queen's chamber, Mortimer made decisions and shaped policy and that Isabella, by virtue of her position as
queen, was able to implement those decisions. This suggests that Mortimer's was the dominant character in the relationship, an assumption
borne out by Murimuth.

It has been suggested that the references to Hugh's ill-treatment of
women and children, both in his indictment and in the proclamation issued
at Wallingford, reflect the Queen's personal views, but Mortimer's own
wife and children had been victims of Despenser's spite, and he may have
been keen to underline this.

Nevertheless, the invasion was undertaken in the Queen's name, and its
success left her effectively the ruler of England; her influence and authority
can be detected in the orders she issued and inferred from official documents
and her own acts, as will be seen. Her status, her popularity, and the acclaim
she received would have obliged her male companions to defer to her in
many things, but as a woman, she must necessarily have remained at a disad-
vantage, for Mortimer especially was far more experienced than she in governing and shaping policy, and her sex would always brand her as inferior in
such matters. Women, it was held, were born to be ruled by men, not to rule
over them. Lancaster's determination to execute the Elder Despenser in
spite of Isabella's protest, and Mortimer's decision to execute Arundel without trial, show that the Queen's opinions were not always taken into account
and that the men around her found it relatively easy to overrule her.

But Isabella was nevertheless an intelligent and perspicacious woman
whose skills lay in public relations and the subtle manipulation of human
beings. It has been claimed that her hitherto hidden talent for plotting,
which emerged in the buildup to the invasion, was out of keeping with her
earlier career,[154] yet this talent had been manifestly evident early on, on several occasions: during her inexperienced efforts to undermine Gaveston's
influence; in the course of several episcopal elections; and most notably, in
the Tour de Nesle scandal of 1314, and the Queen's covert efforts on
Edward II's behalf in his struggle with the Ordainers.

Isabella's subtlety in successfully concealing her loathing for Despenser
and her growing resentment of her husband over a sustained period of
time demonstrate great inner strength and tenacity. In Paris, she had built
up her party discreetly and with circumspection, capitalizing on her role as
a wronged wife to win more support. In England, she had marshaled all her
formidable skills in public relations to ensure the success of her cause, and
she had won many hearts and minds. In all these things, she was able to
demonstrate her considerable ability in statecraft.

———

Isabella and Mortimer left Hereford for London on 26 or 27 November; traveling "by easy stages,"[155] they reached Newent on the twenty-seventh and Gloucester on the twenty-eighth. By now, a great number of lords and ladies were in attendance on the Queen, and at this time, Isabella gave many of them leave "to return to their country seats, except a few nobles whom she kept with her at her council. She expressly ordered them to come back at Christmas, to a great court which she proposed to hold."[156]

On 30 November, in a ceremony that took place before the Queen, Prince Edward, and Mortimer at Cirencester, Airmyn was appointed Chancellor in place of Baldock.[157] That day, Isabella, Prince Edward, and Airmyn were formally made joint Keepers of the Great Seal, which they were to hold until 20 January, and which the Queen was to keep firmly under her personal supervision.[158] From this point, the pretense that the King was personally governing his realm began to be abandoned, and some writs were issued "by the Queen and the King's first-born son," "by the council," or even "by the Queen."[159]

At Isabella's command, Despenser's treasury in the Tower was broken into and its contents delivered to her;[160] she also obtained Arundel's confiscated goods.[161] She doubtless considered it fitting that these ill-gotten gains should come into her possession: they represented financial reparation for all that she had suffered at the hands of Despenser and his followers.

Isabella was anxious to recover everything that had been unjustly taken from her. Between 1 December and 13 January, she awarded herself a series of large grants, amounting to £11,843 13s. 4d.[162]

Some sources claim that Isabella and Mortimer were at Lichfield on 1 December,[163] but as they were at Cirencester the day before, and Witney the day after, this seems highly improbable. On the first, determined to ensure the obedience of the City, the Queen granted the custody of castles surrounding London to her own nominees.[164] The court lodged at Witney in Oxfordshire on 2 December, then moved to Woodstock on the third. That day, because the City was not yet quiet, it was decided that the coming session of Parliament should be postponed, and a new summons was issued for it to meet on 7 January "to treat with the King, if he were present, or else with the Queen Consort and the King's son, Guardian of the Realm."[165]

On 4 December, in the presence of the Mayor and Corporation, the rotting head of Despenser was set up on London Bridge, amid "much tumult and the sound of horns."[166] Around this time, the Queen, "desirous to show that [Stapledon's] death happened without her liking, and also that she reverenced his calling, commanded his corpse to be removed from the place of its first dishonourable interment under a heap of rubbish, and caused it to be buried in his own cathedral" at Exeter.[167]

On 6 December, the Queen was busy arranging transport for the returning Hainault mercenaries.[168] "The companions of Sir John were anxious to return home, for their task was accomplished and they had won great honour. They took leave of the Queen and the nobles, who begged them to stay a little longer, to consider what ought to be done with the King. They implored Sir John to stay at least until after Christmas. The gallant knight courteously agreed to stay as long as the Queen wanted. And he kept as many of his companions with him as he could, but these were only a few, for the rest refused to stay, which displeased him very much. Even when the Queen and her council saw that nothing would induce his companions to stay, they were still shown every mark of respect, and the Queen ordered a large sum of money to be paid to them for their expenses and for their services, and jewels of great price, to each according to his rank. And she had them all paid in ready money for their horses, which they decided to leave behind, accepting their own estimate of the value without question. Sir John stayed on in England, at the Queen's earnest request," enjoying the attentions of her ladies, who were all competing for the favors of this amiable hero.[169] Isabella was to reward him handsomely for his services.[170]

On 9 December, the Tower garrison was reinforced, and on the eleventh, a proclamation condemning lawlessness in London was issued. The Tower was entrusted to Lord Wake on 12 December, along with Hertford Castle.[171] The City was now returning to normal, but there was still some residual unrest.

On 21 December, the court moved to Wallingford for Christmas, pausing at Oseney Abbey on the way. Isabella at last had all her children with her, as well as Mortimer.[172] As she had promised, the Queen "held her court, and it was very fully attended by all the nobles and prelates of the realm, as well as the principal officers of the great cities and towns."[173] A mandate for a new government could not have been more clearly proclaimed.

At Wallingford, Isabella was joined by Archbishop Reynolds, whose plea to be placed under her protection she had willingly granted,[174] and who had come to make his submission. Now that her victory was assured, Prior Eastry had also declared himself her partisan and had written wishing her "good and long life, grace on Earth and glory in Heaven." He also praised Reynolds for having switched his allegiance to the Queen.[175]

The Archbishop was present at a meeting of the council summoned by the Queen to debate what was to be done with the King. Also present were

Lancaster, Kent, and many bishops. There had been rumors that the King and Queen were to be reconciled,[176] but this was certainly not Isabella's intention. In fact, she and her advisers were determined upon his deposition and debated in council how this could be achieved.[177] Some unnamed persons wished to go further and have the King put to death, on the grounds that he had deserved it on account of his misrule and, moreover, if left alive, would always be a focus for dissidents who might try to restore him to the throne; if that happened, they warned, those who had overthrown him could expect no mercy. However, there was no legal process for trying and executing a king, and most people were of the opinion that a king could not technically be guilty of treason. Opinions were acutely divided on this issue until John of Hainault settled the matter by expressing the view that it would be impossible to execute an anointed monarch and that the best course would be to depose him and keep him in custody in a secure fortress for the rest of his life.[178]

This led to a discussion of the delicate question of whether Isabella should honor her marriage vows and go to live with her husband in captivity, for Edward had already begged, weeping, to be reunited with his wife and children,[179] and some people had expressed the view that the Queen's rightful place was with her husband. Clearly, Isabella had no wish to return to Edward, nor to relinquish Mortimer, and few were willing to press her, although some of the churchmen present were clearly uncomfortable about this issue. In the end, considering the threats that Edward had made against her life, it was agreed that it was unthinkable that she rejoin him, whatever public opinion might demand.[180]

True to his word, Robert the Bruce had made no move against England during the invasion and the fraught weeks that followed, but all that was over now, and the Queen was anxious to have the problem of Scotland settled once and for all. She was aware that she had enough on her hands without a conflict on the northern border and was realistic enough to see that there was no point anyway in pursuing a war that could never be won and had for years drained the Exchequer and taken a heavy toll in human suffering. On 26 December, Isabella appointed commissioners to treat with the Scots for peace.

On the thirty-first, the court left Wallingford for Windsor.[181]

At the beginning of January, Caerphilly Castle, the last bastion of Despenser power, finally surrendered.[182] More of Despenser's treasure was found in the castle, and on the third, Isabella appointed Thomas of London, one of her clerks, to receive it on her behalf.[183]

The court was now moving toward London, staying at Chertsey Abbey and Merton Abbey on the way. On 2 January 1327, in advance of the arrival of the royal party, a proclamation was issued as a final warning to the Londoners to maintain the peace; and just in case they were planning to do otherwise, it stipulated that all those accompanying the Queen were commanded to bear arms in the City.[184]

Isabella and Prince Edward entered Westminster two days later.[185] "And when they arrived, great crowds came out to meet them, and received the Queen and her son with great reverence. And the citizens gave handsome presents to the Queen" and hailed her as their deliverer. During the next few days, there were "entertainments and feasts,"[186] and Isabella discovered that Edward had left £60,000 in his Treasury.

Parliament was due to meet in Westminster Hall on 7 January 1327. But the Queen and her advisers were aware that there were serious doubts as to whether a parliament held without a king was a legal assembly, and they were anxious to act within the law as far as possible. On Eastry's advice,[187] a deputation led by Stratford and Burghersh was sent to the King at Kenilworth to invite him to attend, but he declined. Lanercost states that Stratford and Burghersh asked him to appear before Parliament in order to abdicate voluntarily, but that Edward "utterly refused to comply therewith; nay, he cursed them contemptuously, declaring that he would not come among his enemies, or rather his traitors."[188]

Several historians have expressed doubts that these bishops really did invite the King to attend Parliament, on the grounds that the Queen would not have wanted him there in case his presence incited sympathy or he publicly refused to cooperate. But this is unlikely, because there is good evidence that, being apparently unsatisfied with the outcome of the bishops' mission, Isabella and her advisers sent a second deputation, headed also by two bishops (who are not named), with a further invitation for the King to attend Parliament.[189] They were obviously anxious to secure the King's cooperation because it was important that what they were planning be seen to be done with Edward's consent and approval.

Parliament met in the King's absence on 7 January. One otherwise reliable source[190] states that it proceeded at once to the business of deposing the King, but according to several others, that matter was postponed until after the return of the second deputation from Kenilworth on 12 January.[191] In the meantime, Parliament dealt with routine matters, such as petitions.[192] On 8 January, in the name of Edward II, Isabella was granted all Despenser's movables, plate, and jewels,[193] and £20,000, a huge sum of money then, to pay her debts overseas. Two days later, the lands seized in 1324 were restored to her.[194] On 22 January, she would be granted all the arrears of revenues due from her duchy of Cornwall.

On the evening of the twelfth, the second deputation returned from Kenilworth and informed the Queen of the King's response to their requests.[195] Isabella now acknowledged the necessity of proceeding without him. The legality of a parliament held in the absence, and without the sanction, of the King was dubious indeed, however widely it represented the political nation, yet Isabella was well aware of the strength of public feeling and was to take scrupulous care to ensure that the wishes of the people were taken into consideration at every turn, and that not only the three estates of the realm, but also representatives of every national institution, were involved in the deposition process. This served the additional purpose of distributing responsibility for what was about to happen as widely as possible. For what the Queen and her associates were proposing to do was revolutionary, insofar as no anointed English sovereign had been deposed since the Conquest; yet it was not so extreme as to encompass the destruction of the monarchy or the overthrow of the royal House. Nor was the monarchy to be stripped of any of its powers or privileges. Nevertheless, the deposition of Edward II was to set a precedent that would have far-reaching consequences for several future sovereigns.

That night, Isabella met with the magnates to discuss the King's refusal and debate what was to be done with him. The lords were unanimous in agreeing that he should be deposed, and a strategy was agreed. Mortimer seems to have played a prominent role at this meeting.[196]

Given that the deputation had only returned the previous evening, it must have been on the morning of 13 January that it was announced that Edward had refused to attend Parliament and had cursed all involved as traitors. Thereafter, events moved swiftly. Mortimer had already enlisted Lord Wake to secure the support of the Londoners,[197] and it was almost certainly due to Mortimer's influence that his friend Lord Mayor Béthune, when told of the King's refusal to come to Parliament, promptly sent a respectful letter to the three estates, asking them to come to the Guildhall to join the City in swearing not only to maintain the cause of the Queen and her son but also to depose Edward II for his frequent offenses against his coronation oath and his crown and to crown the Prince in his stead.[198]

Later that day, 13 January, Mortimer led the lords, bishops, and commons in solemn procession to the Guildhall, where, under the eagle eye of Kent, they all swore a modified version of the oath the Lord Mayor had requested, namely, to uphold the Queen's cause to the death, to rid the realm of the King's favorites, to observe the Ordinances, and to maintain the liberties of the City.[199] The other matters raised by Béthune were reserved for Parliament.

Aware that he was regarded as a turncoat by the people, and nervously mindful of the fate of Stapledon, Archbishop Reynolds took advantage of this visit to the Guildhall to distribute fifty tuns of free wine to the Londoners. This did not, however, stop them from assaulting him as he left the Guildhall.[200] Fortunately, it was only his pride, rather than his person, that was injured.

The Queen was present,[201] a silent figure in black, when Parliament reassembled in Westminster Hall to hear an address by Mortimer on the reasons for the King's necessary overthrow; he spoke, he said, only for the lords, for he knew their minds; he could not, however, speak for the commons. The deposition of the King, he reminded everyone, could only be brought about "if the people gave their consent."[202] At this, Wake rose, held up his hand, and declared that he, for one, would never again accept Edward II as king. There was a general murmur of assent.[203]

Thanks to Wake's efforts, crowds were now conveniently gathering outside, and his words were the signal for Bishop Stratford to invite them to come in, saying that the lords were resolved to make Prince Edward king but that this needed their assent. Soon, Westminster Hall was packed with restive Londoners, who had fought their way in, eager to have their say in deposing the King. Many had been among those citizens who had orchestrated the October uprisings and riots, and their presence was undoubtedly intimidating.

Orleton now preached a sermon to the assembled lords and commons.[204] "A foolish king shall ruin his people,"[205] he warned, and then spent some time in utilizing the text "Woe to thee, o land, when thy king is a child" to expound on Edward II's childish behavior.[206] He spoke out in favor of granting the wishes of the Londoners, and, mindful of those who now expected Isabella to return to her husband, warned of the consequences that might befall her if Edward II were allowed to return to power: her life, he declared, would never be safe in the King's hands, and she would surely suffer death. The Bishop concluded by asking the estates to consider whether they would have the father or the son for king and urged the estates to accept the Prince and depose Edward II.

"Away with the King!" shouted lords and people alike.

Stratford preached next,[207] asking what happened to a body politic "whose head is feeble"[208] and enlarging on Orleton's earlier text, "My head, my head acheth."[209] When he had finished, Wake stood up again, stretched out his arms, and gesturing with his hands, asked the people if they would agree to the deposition of the King.[210]

"Let it be done! Let it be done!" the people cried. "The son shall be raised up! We will no more have this man to reign over us!"[211] Only Archbishop Melton and the bishops of London, Rochester, and Worcester spoke up in favor of the King. Edward's other remaining friends were intimidated into silence.

The people had spoken, and now all that remained was for the King to be formally deposed. This ceremony began with Archbishop Reynolds' preaching a sermon before Parliament, based on the text "Vox populi, vox Dei!" ("The voice of the people is the voice of God!").[212] He reminded the assembly that the King's subjects had suffered oppression for far too long and declared that, if it was their will that the King be deposed, then it was also God's will, and the reign must come to an end.

"Is this the will of the people?" cried Wake.

"Let it be done!" they roared again in noisy approval, with a great show of hands.[213]

"Your voice has clearly been heard here," said the Archbishop. Then he formally announced that, by the consent of the magnates, clergy, and people, Edward II was deposed in favor of his son.[214] The assembly erupted in tumultuous acclaim.

The Articles of Deposition, which apparently had been drawn up under the auspices of Stratford,[215] doubtless on instructions from the Queen and her council, were then read out to Parliament, to great acclaim. They accused Edward of many offenses: being incompetent to govern and unwilling to heed good counsel; allowing himself to be controlled by evil counselors; giving himself up to unseemly works and occupations; persecuting the Church; executing, exiling, imprisoning, and disinheriting many great men of his realm; losing Scotland, Ireland, and Gascony; violating his coronation oath to do justice to all; plundering the realm; and showing himself incorrigible through his cruelty and weakness, and beyond all hope of amendment.[216]

It was probably after Reynolds had finished speaking that Prince Edward was brought into the hall to cries of "Behold your King!"[217] At the sight of the handsome youth, the Londoners unanimously and vociferously acclaimed him as their sovereign, crying, "Ave, Rex!" Then the lords, with greater dignity, knelt to pay him homage. It was noticed that Melton and the three bishops who had declared for Edward II did not join in.[218] Afterward, the whole assembly rose for the hymn "Glory, Laud and Honour."

Witnessing all this, Isabella "seemed as if she should die for sorrow" and broke down in tears.[219] Was this a politic gesture, maintaining the fiction that she was still a loyal wife to her husband? Or was she overcome by the occasion and the realization that all she had fought for had come to pass and that she was now safe at last? It was probably a combination of the two; assertions that she was merely crying crocodile tears are far too simplistic. As for Mortimer, after this momentous session, he hurried off to order his sons' robes for the coming coronation.[220]

But there was one obstacle to the successful conclusion of the matter. Prince Edward's conscience was certainly uneasy about the turn events had taken; Baker says he had been "led astray by his elders to join in the revolt against his father," and certainly, he had had little choice in the matter. He was fond of his mother and sympathetic toward her, had hated the Despensers, and had probably been convinced that there were good reasons for deposing his father. Nevertheless, he was extremely reluctant to accept the crown while his father still lived. Consequently, seeing his mother weeping, and misinterpreting the cause, he tried to comfort her by vowing that he would never accept the crown unless his father freely offered it to him.[221] Over the next three days, no one could persuade him to change his mind.

Throughout, there had been concerns that the recent proceedings were not entirely lawful, so in order to give them some semblance of legality and reassure the Prince, it was necessary to persuade the King to renounce his crown in favor of his son, to demonstrate that he sanctioned Parliament's decision. On 16 January, a new deputation of thirty persons, headed by Orleton[222] and representing all the estates and institutions of the realm, was sent to Kenilworth to announce the decision of the people to Edward II and persuade him to abdicate formally. At the Queen's request, the Franciscans were excused from sending one of their Order, so that they should not have to bear such dolorous tidings to the King who had always professed such a special devotion for them.[223] This gives the lie to those historians who assert that Isabella had by now lost all her finer feelings; indeed, it is in keeping with earlier instances of her kindness and suggests that, even now, she felt some pity for her husband.

The deputation arrived at Kenilworth by 20 January,[224] when Orleton, Stratford, and Burghersh had a preliminary private audience with Edward, who was brought to them "gowned in black." Despite the fact that Edward was clearly in a very emotional and fragile state, Orleton took great pleasure in venting his hatred for the King in bitter insults.[225] Addressing Edward harshly, he recited the damning catalog of the King's crimes, "invited" him to abdicate, and warned him that the people would repudiate the claims of his children to succeed and set up some other person not of the blood royal if he proved obdurate; the implication was that Parliament might well choose Mortimer to be king. However, he went on, if the King cooperated, his son would succeed him and he himself would be permitted to continue to live honorably. Edward was apparently too distressed or too stupid to perceive that Isabella would never permit the Prince to be disinherited and that the threat was merely a bluff; and even if he did realize this, he was in no position to take any chances. Weeping bitterly, he capitulated without further argument, for the sake of his son.

Then it was time for him to enter the presence chamber to face Lancaster and the rest of the deputation to convey to them his decision. He looked to be on the verge of collapse as, sobbing, he appeared before them. Then he suddenly fainted dead away, but, "as piteous and heavy as the sight was, it failed to excite the compassion of any of the Queen's commissioners."[226] It was left to Lancaster and Stratford to hasten to Edward's aid, tenderly raising him in their arms and doing everything in their power to bring him round. But as soon as Edward had come to his senses, Orleton brusquely demanded that he now renounce his crown, as he had agreed to do. In "a fresh paroxysm of weeping," the King meekly complied, saying "he was aware that for his many sins he was thus punished, and therefore he besought those present to have compassion upon him in his adversity. Much as he grieved for having incurred the hatred of his people, he was glad that his eldest son was so gracious in their sight, and gave them thanks for choosing him to be their king."

The next day, Sir William Trussell, "on behalf of the whole kingdom," formally renounced the nation's homage to the deposed monarch. Then Sir Thomas Blount, the steward of the royal household, symbolically broke his staff of office to signify the termination of the household's service. The former King was advised that, from henceforth, "ye shall be held a singular man of the people" and known as "the Lord Edward, sometime King of England." The deputation then hastened back to Westminster, bearing with them the crown and the royal regalia.[227]

In the fourteenth-century Holkham Bible in the British Library, there is a picture of a queen turning a wheel of fortune. At the top appears a crowned king with a scepter; to the left, a figure hands him a crown. But to the right, the king is shown falling headlong, losing his crown, and dropping the scepter; and at the bottom, he is lying bareheaded and naked, covered only by a cloak, and ruefully gazing up at his former self. Almost certainly, the queen shown turning the wheel is meant to represent Isabella, and the picture is a comment on the fall of Edward II. Rarely in the annals of British royalty have the political consequences of a broken marriage been so clearly manifested.

By 24 January, Isabella had taken up residence in the Tower. On the morning of that day, when she rode through the City toward Westminster, members of the guilds, wearing their best hats and cloaks, hastened to greet her. That evening, when she returned, the heralds were out in the streets, proclaiming "Sir Edward's" abdication and the new King's peace.[228] Soon, Isabella was surrounded by crowds of cheering, rejoicing citizens.

Edward III's reign officially began the following day, 25 January 1327.[229] Of course, as the King was a minor, the real rulers of England were Isabella and Mortimer.

CHAPTER NINE

✣

Plots and Stratagems

Late January 1327 found Isabella and Mortimer busily establishing their new government. The Great Seal of England was delivered into Edward III's hands on 28 January, and that same day, Hotham was appointed Chancellor and Orleton, Treasurer. On the twenty-ninth, the new King formally announced his father's abdication, and new justices and barons of the Exchequer were appointed. At this time, Isabella settled half her debts to the Bardi.[1]

Edward III was crowned in Westminster Abbey on 1 February 1327 by Archbishop Reynolds; Bishops Stratford and Segrave assisted, while Burghersh, Hethe, and Airmyn sang the litanies. Before the ceremony began, the fourteen-year-old King was knighted by Lancaster, the senior male member of the royal House. The crown of Saint Edward the Confessor "was of vast size and a great weight," but Edward III "bore it like a man."[2] Isabella wept throughout the long ritual of crowning,[3] but Walsingham says that, although she had the face and bearing of a sorrowful widow, this was just a pretense. He was probably right, for she had every reason to rejoice, having accomplished all that she had set out to achieve. Sharing in her triumph was her lover Mortimer, a prominent presence at the coronation, during which three of his sons were knighted by the new King.[4] After the ceremony, gold coins depicting a child's hand reaching out to save a falling crown were scattered among the people—a pretty piece of propaganda.

It appears that Isabella also had a say in the design of Edward III's Great Seal, which shows him seated on a throne carved in the Decorated style. Two fleurs-de-lis are prominently displayed, which signify his connection to the royal House of France through Isabella, and historians have noticed similarities with the seal of her brother, Louis X.[5]

On his coronation day, King Edward returned Isabella's dower to her, with substantial additions, so that, instead of the £4,400 per annum she had formerly been assigned, she was now to receive the unprecedented sum of £13,333,[6] which would make her one of the greatest landowners in the kingdom. Murimuth and Baker both assert that her dower amounted to about two-thirds of the royal income, so that Edward III was left with only one-third of his revenues to live on, but this is a gross exaggeration. No one at the time complained of the size of the award, which is understandable in view of her popularity both as the destroyer of the Despensers and the mother of the young King. One chronicler enthusiastically refers to her as "Mother Isabella, our royal, noble, prudent, beautiful and excellent star,"[7] a view echoed by the Pope himself,[8] while Parliament was at pains to acknowledge the country's debt to Isabella and to emphasize that she was to continue to reign all her life in consideration of the great labors she had undertaken and the anguish she had suffered.[9]

Isabella may have been acquisitive and materialistic, yet the securing of such a great landed interest was probably due less to mere greed than to her need to exercise extensive patronage in the interests of consolidating her position and that of the regime she had established, which she was aware had been founded on a shaky constitutional basis. Both she and Mortimer recognized the wisdom of rewarding their supporters with grants, offices, and perquisites. Another reason for Isabella's apparent greed was undoubtedly the desire to be compensated for what she had lost, in terms of both money and status, and the determination that she should never again suffer the financial insecurity and humiliation that had been imposed on her by the Despensers.

The lands of Isabella's enlarged dower were scattered throughout every English county except the four northernmost ones, and in parts of Wales. Among them were many important properties, including a number owned by Edward II, notably, his favorite house at Langley and the royal Thames-side manor of Sheen, which Isabella would hold until her death; it was a moated house dating from the twelfth century, with upper and lower courts, and had been used occasionally by Edward.[10]

Then there was Leeds Castle,[11] the scene of the siege of 1321 and a property that had belonged to earlier queen consorts. Built in a stunning setting on two connected islands on a large and beautiful lake, the original Norman keep had been extensively altered by Edward I to form a luxurious fortified palace for his wives. A stone "gloriette" (Spanish for "pavilion") enclosing a courtyard garden with a fountain had been raised on the smaller island for Eleanor of Castile and a second castle built on the larger island for Marguerite of France. A bridge connected the two. A chantry for Queen Eleanor had been established in the chapel. The chambers Isabella used were those built for Eleanor in the gloriette, and they included a bathroom.[12]

Other properties granted to Isabella included the royal manor of Havering-atte-Bower in Essex, which had been built by Edward the Confessor, remodeled in the thirteenth century, and then held by Eleanor of Provence and Marguerite of France; the royal castle and adjacent palace at Guildford in Surrey; other royal castles at Portchester in Hampshire, Saint Briavel's, Gloucester, and Tickhill, Yorkshire; Odiham Castle in Hampshire, which had once belonged to Roger d'Amory; the royal manors of Byfleet in Surrey (another place favored by Edward II), Gravesend in Kent, Isleworth in Middlesex, and Burstwick and Cowick in Yorkshire; Hadleigh Castle in Essex; the castle of the Peak in Derbyshire; Rockingham Castle in Northamptonshire; Builth in Wales, which the Queen passed on to Mortimer; Bristol Castle; and Langley Marish in Buckinghamshire, an exceptionally attractive property that had been visited often by Edward II; Isabella's chamber there opened onto a garden, and there were vines growing by the door of the great hall.[13]

The Queen also received much of the Lincoln inheritance, including Pontefract Castle, which had been appropriated by Despenser and should by rights have gone to Lancaster. This was probably the main reason why she arranged for her dower to be assigned before Parliament reassembled, for she dared not risk the grant's being openly challenged by the powerful Lancastrian faction.[14]

In 1327, Isabella purchased Castle Rising in Norfolk, a house that was in the future to be indelibly associated with her, from Emma, the widow of Robert de Montalt, in exchange for an annuity. Montalt, who had been one of the first to join the Queen the previous autumn, had since died without heirs and left Isabella his manor of Framsden in Suffolk. Hertford Castle also came into Isabella's hands in 1327, surrendered to her by Pembroke's widow; it had been given to Pembroke by Queen Marguerite, but Isabella evidently felt it should revert to her.[15]

It was probably at this time also that Isabella acquired her London residence in Lombard Street. This street was thus named because, since the twelfth century, Lombard bankers had based their London operations there, but the house Isabella took was leased from the Benedictine priory of Saint Helen in Bishopsgate, one of the wealthiest religious houses in the City. When in London, Isabella stayed either here or at Westminster Palace; between 1327 and 1330, "by order of the Queen Mother," various improvements were made to her apartments at Westminster.[16]

There can be no doubt that, during the period of her rule, Isabella lived more lavishly than any English queen before her. Not until the heyday of Henry VI's wife, Margaret of Anjou, in the fifteenth century, did a consort again enjoy such wealth, luxury, and power.

On the day after the coronation, the Queen made an overnight visit to Eltham.[17] She returned on 3 February, when Parliament met again at Westminster,[18] and her influence is plainly detectable in its proceedings, as is Lancaster's. That first day, a regency council was formed, with Lancaster as its president and the King's official guardian. Most sources agree that there were twelve members: the rest were Archbishops Reynolds and Melton; Bishops Stratford and Orleton; the Earls of Norfolk, Kent, and Surrey; Lords Wake and Percy; Sir Oliver de Ingham; and John de Ros, who was steward of the joint household of Edward III and Queen Isabella, and Lancaster's son-in-law.[19] No official roles were assigned to the Queen or Mortimer: the Rolls of Parliament are alone in stating that there were fourteen members of the council, but this may be an error, as they do not name the other two. Doherty[20] thinks Mortimer was one of them, because Froissart refers to him as one of the great men who ruled the kingdom after the coronation, but Froissart does not specifically say that Mortimer was a member of the council, and if he had been, contemporary chroniclers would surely have included him in their lists.

Although the fiction was maintained that Edward III was in control of his government, Isabella effectively "practised on [him] in his minority" and ruled in his name with Mortimer as unofficial regents, while Mortimer's interests were represented on the council by his friends Orleton and Ingham, and later by Hotham and Sir Simon Bereford. Isabella and Mortimer "entirely governed" both King and administration and dictated policy, and power was firmly in their hands.[21] The Queen controlled the great offices of state through the men she had nominated to them, and the Chancellor, Treasurer, and Keeper of the Privy Seal accompanied her everywhere she went.[22] She controlled access to the King, a state of affairs that before long would "inspire a great deal of envy."[23]

There can be little doubt, however, that Isabella was motivated also by ambition for her son, whom she undoubtedly loved very dearly. It was fortunate that her ambitions for him coincided with those she cherished for herself and that she was able, quite legitimately, to identify the latter with those of the Crown. The relationship between mother and son was epitomized in an illuminated manuscript illustration in a treatise by Walter de Milemete, which was probably executed at this time and was presented to Edward III; it shows the young, beardless King enthroned beside his mother, both wearing their crowns.[24]

Baker claims that Orleton formed the third part of a triumvirate with Isabella and Mortimer, but this is grossly to overstate his role. In fact, he was abroad on a diplomatic mission for much of 1327, and when he did return, it was to find himself out of favor with Isabella and Mortimer for having accepted the bishopric of Worcester from the Pope to the detriment of their own candidate.

Since Isabella and Mortimer shared power, and exercised it unofficially, it is hard to determine whose was the dominant influence. Everything was done in the name of the King, or of the Queen and her son, and although it was said that "the Queen ruled,"[25] many people believed that both Isabella and Edward were dominated by Mortimer. However, there is plenty of evidence that it was Isabella, rather than Mortimer, who was the real power behind the throne at this time. Nevertheless, she relied on Mortimer's military strength and expertise, and there are examples of his taking the initiative in important matters without reference to her. It seems, therefore, that each trusted the other to act in a way they would approve of and that both exercised authority in different spheres.

Isabella's power was founded upon the formidable bastions of her status as Queen Mother and her son's affection and loyalty. She kept the boy with her as much as possible and exerted considerable influence over him. Mortimer's power, however, was founded mainly upon his intimate relationship with the Queen, although he himself liked to stress his descent from King John, as several contemporary documents referring to him as "the King's kinsman" bear witness.[26] Yet many other lords could claim kinship to the King, and Mortimer's present preeminence was due entirely to the fact that he was the Queen's lover.[27] Knighton claims they shared one lodging wherever they went, but in view of the golden opinions of Isabella voiced at this time by the Pope and others, it appears that the lovers were at pains to be discreet.

Parliament proceeded to issue pardons, redress Lancastrian grievances, reinstate the contrariants in their lands, and reward those who had supported the Queen.[28] Henry of Lancaster's substantial contribution to the success of the Queen's invasion was handsomely recognized. The sentence on Thomas of Lancaster was reversed, enabling his brother to succeed him formally,[29] and soon afterward, Edward III, at the prompting of his mother, sent a request for Thomas's canonization to the Pope, extolling his virtues,[30] which she knew would earn her popularity and keep Lancaster loyal. John XXII was to refuse this request, and three more made in the name of Edward III, probably because he was aware that Thomas's motives had been more self-interested than saintly.

Another popular move promoted by the Queen was the passing of an act limiting the areas in which the harsh forest laws could be enforced.[31] Edward II's proceedings against Orleton were annulled, and on 6 February, Airmyn at last received the temporalities of Norwich. At this time, the Queen was granted all seigneurial rights in her estates.[32] On 15 February, at the request of his mother, Edward III granted two of Despenser's manors to Henry de Beaumont and his wife.[33]

Isabella saw to it that Mortimer was lavishly rewarded "in consideration of his services to the Queen and the King, here and beyond seas."[34] On 15 February, the lucrative wardships of the heirs of Warwick and Audley were restored to him, and he was granted that of Lord Hastings (in October, he would also receive the wardship of Pembroke's heir),[35] and on 20 February, he was appointed Justiciar of the diocese of Llandaff. On the twenty-first, Parliament reversed the sentence on both Mortimer and Chirk, formally pardoned Mortimer for escaping from the Tower and for "other offences," and restored his father's estates to him. He was then appointed Justiciar of Wales for life, with jurisdiction over all the Crown lands there.[36] The Queen also ensured that Mortimer received Chirk's estate.[37]

In late February and early March, grants of lands, tenements, and revenues were made to Lancaster, Kent, Norfolk, Wake, Orleton, and Burghersh in consideration of their good service rendered to Edward III and Queen Isabella,[38] while Sir John of Hainault was rewarded with a pension.[39] Edward III confirmed the grants made to his mother during the Epiphany Parliament and granted her another 1,000 marks for provisions;[40] in March, she finally took possession of her lands and chattels.[41] By then, Isabella had set up her own household once more, which was from now on to be independent of that of the King.

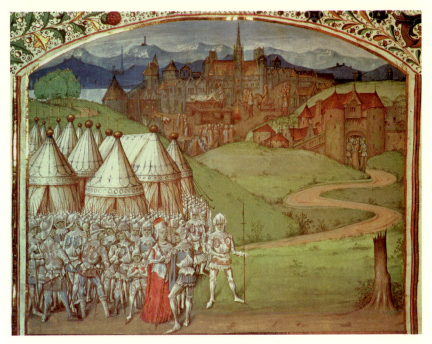

ISABELLA AND HER ARMY BEFORE HEREFORD, 1326.
IN THE BACKGROUND CAN BE SEEN THE EXECUTION OF HUGH LE DESPENSER.
At Hereford, the Queen was received "most respectfully and joyfully,"
and the town was to be the scene of her triumph.

THE EXECUTION OF
HUGH LE DESPENSER, 1326
Despenser at first suffered
with great patience, but then
a ghastly, inhuman howl
broke from him.

EDWARD II ABDICATES IN
FAVOR OF HIS SON, 1327
"As piteous and heavy
as the sight was, it failed
to excite the compassion
of any of the Queen's
ministers."

THE WHEEL OF FORTUNE
Almost certainly the queen
turning the wheel is meant to
represent Isabella. Rarely have
the political consequences of a
broken royal marriage been
so clearly manifested.

THE CORONATION OF
EDWARD III, 1327
Isabella wept throughout
the long ritual of crowning.

BERKELEY CASTLE
Edward II was allegedly
murdered here in 1327.

THE CELL AT BERKELEY CASTLE
IN WHICH EDWARD II IS SAID
TO HAVE BEEN IMPRISONED
A well shaft that was originally in
this cell is the subject of one of
the more lurid chroniclers' tales.

ISABELLA WITH HER SON, EDWARD III
The Queen "practised on the King in his minority"
and ruled in his name with Mortimer
as unofficial regents.

A QUEEN AT PRAYER
It has been suggested that Isabella commissioned the Taymouth Hours as a wedding gift for her daughter, Joan of the Tower, in 1328. If so, the Queen in these miniatures may represent either Isabella or Joan.

THE VIRGIN PRESENTING A QUEEN
TO THE ENTHRONED CHRIST

A KING AND A QUEEN KNEELING

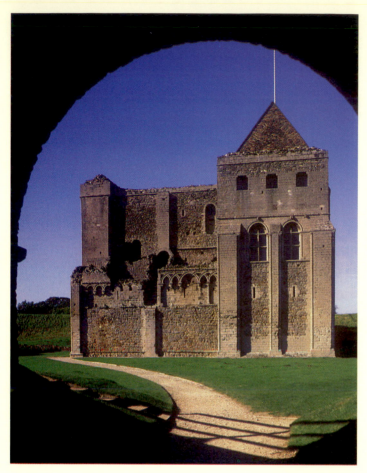

CASTLE RISING, NORFOLK
Here, during her retirement,
Isabella maintained a
considerable degree of state.
The castle is the setting for
many legends about her.

JOHN OF ELTHAM, EARL OF CORNWALL
The loss of her son was deeply painful to
Isabella and left her preoccupied
with her own mortality.

ISABELLA OF FRANCE
Despite her enforced retirement, kings
still had respect for Isabella's undoubted
political skills, and she came to be regarded
as a kind of elder stateswoman.

PHILIPPA OF HAINAULT
The Pope commended Philippa for the
sympathy and consolation she showed
to Isabella in her tribulation.

ISABELLA OF FRANCE (?) IN OLD AGE
The year before she died, Isabella
became a lay member of
the Franciscan Order.

THE FIESCHI LETTER
No satisfactory explanation has ever been advanced to show how the writer came by some of his information, unless it was from the mouth of Edward II himself.

Parliament also issued pardons to the City of London, which received a new charter of liberties, and to many of the Despensers' former adherents. Isabella's treasurer, William de Boudon,[42] was promoted, while her clerk, Robert Wyville, was relieved of the Privy Seal and, through her influence, made a canon of Lichfield. Its long program of rewards and restorations completed, Parliament finally adjourned on 9 March.

Meanwhile, during February, a London mob had broken into Orleton's London house and savagely assaulted Robert Baldock, who was still living there under house arrest. They dragged him off to Newgate prison and had him locked up, but his injuries were so serious that he died there soon afterward.[43] Orleton was later to be accused of maltreating Baldock but successfully protested his innocence.[44]

It has been claimed that Isabella had no real policy apart from consolidating her position. She certainly made efforts to achieve the latter through rewarding her supporters, keeping the Lancastrian faction sweet, and compensating those who had suffered under the Despenser regime. To begin with, her overriding preoccupation was to redress the catastrophes and injustices of the previous reign and so maintain her popularity.

Yet she was also a realist who understood that popularity did not come at any price and that unpopular measures were sometimes necessary. She knew she faced daunting problems, especially concerning Scotland and France, which had eluded solutions for decades past. Her foreign policy with regard to these kingdoms would amply demonstrate her pragmatism and show that she recognized the limitations within which she had to operate and did not shrink from implementing commonsense policies that would bring long-term benefits rather than short-term glory and plaudits.

Mortimer, on the other hand, was more preoccupied with self-aggrandizement, building himself a vast power base in the Marches, and accumulating great wealth. Wider issues did not concern him so greatly, unless they interfered with his own ambitions. It was ambition that drove him—that and the need to maintain his position.

Isabella's secret peace negotiations with Robert the Bruce had ended in deadlock, and on the day of the coronation, the Scots attacked Norham Castle in Northumberland.[45] Thereafter, there were unnerving reports that Bruce, despite encroaching old age and a disease that many thought was leprosy, was building up his forces, and on 4 March, the Queen sent a second set of commissioners to negotiate a peace.[46] On 22 February, she had also opened peace negotiations with France,[47] in an attempt to resolve the problem of Gascony. These were successful to a degree, and on 31 March, a peace treaty would be signed in Paris, providing for the restoration of part of Gascony on payment of a war indemnity of 50,000 marks. The treaty was unpopular in England, however, because it left Charles IV in possession of the Agenais.[48] But Isabella knew she was in no position to contemplate a war with France, nor did she want one. Her policy for the period of her rule would be pro-French.

During these early months of the year, Isabella was still writing charming and flattering letters to Edward II, inquiring after his health and comfort, and preserving the fiction that she would be happy to visit him if only Parliament had not forbidden it. She also sent him gifts of fine clothes, linen, edible delicacies, and other little luxuries[49] and in so doing displayed her essential thoughtfulness and perhaps a sense of guilt. But her husband's pitiful requests to see her and their children[50] were ignored. Baker claims that Edward was suffering "so much for love"—which is surely a gross exaggeration—that Lancaster took pity on him and sent a message to Isabella, "whose heart was harder than stone, to tell her that the noble knight was languishing for love of his wife. But that woman of iron was moved not to love but to anger." If this story is true, her reaction would be entirely understandable, for Edward had shown no love or concern for her when Despenser was wrecking their marriage and depriving her of her income, her liberty, and her children. Moreover, "as she turned the matter over in her mind, she began to be fearful lest the Church might compel her to return to her repudiated husband and share his bed." This was a very real concern, and one that was to surface in April at a council meeting.

Baker says that Isabella, "that fierce she-lion of a woman," asked advice of "that priest of Baal," Orleton, who recommended that Edward be removed from Lancaster's care. This is pure fantasy, for, as we will shortly discover, there would soon emerge far more pressing reasons for effecting this. But of course, Baker was writing many years later, at a time when attempts were being made to canonize Edward II and tales of his sufferings could invest him with an aura of sainthood.[51] Baker was to make up other lies about Orleton, who emerges in his history as even more of a villain than Mortimer, and this story is almost certainly another fabrication, designed to show the Bishop and Isabella in the worst possible light.

It is easy to see why Baker should have a low opinion of Isabella, who had left her husband for her lover, overthrown that husband, and then, Baker believed, ordered his ill-treatment and murder—assumptions that, as will be shown, have no basis in fact. But why the savaging of Orleton? The answer perhaps lies in the attitude of Baker's patron, Sir Thomas de la More, who had witnessed, and possibly been shocked by, Orleton's harshness toward Edward at Kenilworth and perhaps later jumped to the false conclusion that the Bishop was responsible for the other miseries that befell the fallen King.

There can be little doubt, though, that Isabella did not wish to return to Edward. Her reluctance was compounded by her very natural fears: fear of his anger and coldness, fear of being deprived of her lover and the company of her son, and fear of living in isolation and virtually losing her liberty. And it is certain that Mortimer had a say in her refusal to see Edward. Mortimer had already proved himself to be a jealous man and would have welcomed another chance to have his revenge on Edward.

If the poems that are attributed to Edward II, which are believed to have been written at this time, are genuine, he apparently saw through Isabella's duplicity. Written in Norman-French, they are bitter reflections on the vicissitudes of Fortune and the perfidy of his wife, and they speak volumes about his state of mind at this time.

One is entitled "The Song of King Edward, that he himself made" and, loosely translated, reads:

> *My winter has come; only sorrow I see.*
> *Too often, too cruel, Fortune has spoken.*
> *Blow after blow she rains upon me,*
> *Heart, hope and courage, all, all she has broken.*
> *Be a man fair or be a man wise,*
> *Perfect in courtesy, honoured in name,*
> *If Fortune forsake him, if his luck flies,*
> *To the blast he stands naked, a fool come to shame.*
> *The greatest grief my heart must bear,*
> *The chiefest sorrow of my state*
> *Springs from Isabeau the Fair,*
> *She that I loved but now must hate.*
> *I held her true, now faithless she;*
> *Steeped in deceit, my deadly foe*
> *Brings nought but black despair to me,*
> *And all my joy she turns to woe.*

In his grief and isolation, the King apparently sought solace in religion. Concluding the poem, he dwells upon his sins and expresses his hopes for redemption:

To Him I turn my contrite heart,
Who suffered for me on the Cross.
Jesus, forgive my baser part,
Bend Thou to me in my dire loss.
For all my sins and treacherous deeds . . .
That she beseech the Child she bore,
The Son that on her knee she sat,
His tender grace on me to pour
And grant me mercy yet.

Another poem laments that, in adversity, the writer is losing his looks and his courtly accomplishments:

On my devoted head
Her bitterest showers,
All from a wintry cloud,
Stern Fortune pours.
View but her favourite [i.e., himself],
Sage and discerning,
Graced with fair comeliness,
Famed for his learning;
Should she withdraw her smiles,
Each grace she banishes,
Wisdom and wit are flown
And beauty tarnishes.

In winter, woe befell me,
By cruel Fortune threatened.
My life now lies a ruin.
But once I was feared and dreaded,
But now all men despise me
And call me a crownless king,
A laughing stock to all.[52]

Around the first week of March, a plot to free the former King Edward from Kenilworth was apparently uncovered. Inquiries were ordered into affrays caused by several men, namely, Stephen Dunheved, a Dominican friar; William Aylmer, parson of Doddington and a former trusted clerk of Despenser; another William Aylmer, parson of Beadwell; William de la Russell; Thomas de la Haye; Edmund Goscelyn; William atte Hull; and

John Norton.[53] Since these same men would be indicted in July for another conspiracy to liberate the King, it is reasonable to conclude that these inquiries concerned an earlier attempt that proved abortive.

Stephen Dunheved, who appears to have been the driving force behind these plots, was particularly dangerous. He had loyally served Edward II as his confessor and had been an adherent of the Despensers. It was he who had been sent to Avignon by Despenser to procure an annulment of the King's marriage to Isabella. For this, as much as his close association with Despenser, he was a marked man, but he had gone to ground after the Queen's invasion.

Knighton says simply that this plot was organized by some who privately favored the former King, but the author of the *Annales Paulini* specifically states that Dunheved was supported by some of the magnates. In view of his later defection, and the fact that he unquestionably felt guilty about his betrayal of his half brother, it is possible that the unstable Kent was one of them. It is perhaps too much of a coincidence that Stephen Dunheved was to be involved, three years later, in Kent's own conspiracy against Isabella and Mortimer.[54]

After all that had happened, Isabella apparently felt the need to visit once more the shrine of Becket at Canterbury, and on 13 March, the court left London to travel down through Kent, arriving in Canterbury the next day. On the fifteenth, the King and the Queen Mother went to Rochester, where they were entertained by Bishop Hethe, who presented Isabella with expensive gifts.[55] Mother and son returned to Canterbury the following day and, on 21 March, were back at Westminster, where they stayed for nine days,[56] addressing concerns that had arisen in the wake of the conspiracy to free Edward II.

Security at Kenilworth was immediately tightened, but Lancaster made it clear that he did not relish the responsibility of guarding the former King while there were plots to free him,[57] and there were fears that Edward had too many partisans in Warwickshire. Isabella and Mortimer therefore decided to relieve Lancaster of his duties as jailer and move their prisoner some way south, to Berkeley Castle, which was situated near Mortimer's Marcher estates. On 21 March, Thomas de Berkeley, now restored as Lord Berkeley, and John Maltravers were appointed Edward's new keepers, with equal liability;[58] both were members of Mortimer's affinity, and Berkeley had served in his household. This all suggests that it was chiefly Mortimer who was responsible for these appointments and Edward's change of prison.

Thomas de Berkeley was Mortimer's son-in-law, having married the latter's daughter Margaret in 1319. Berkeley had no reason to love Edward II,
having suffered under the Despensers' regime. He and his father had been
imprisoned for four years as supporters of Thomas of Lancaster, and his
father had died in captivity.

John Maltravers, who came from a wealthy Dorset family and was married to Berkeley's sister Ela, was aged about thirty-seven. He had served
under Mortimer in Ireland and Scotland[59] and had also fought for Lancaster
at Boroughbridge. After the Earl's defeat, he had fled the country in fear of
his life and attached himself to Mortimer, whose trusted captain he
became. Later, he joined the group of exiles who had surrounded Isabella
in France. In February 1327, his lands had been restored to him by Parliament. Like Berkeley, he can have felt little affection for the former King.

Now that Edward III was established on his throne, the Queen and Mortimer turned their attention to fulfilling the treaty made with Hainault for
his marriage. In the last week of March, Orleton and Burghersh (who now
replaced Orleton as Treasurer) were chosen by the council to go to Count
William to ask formally for the hand of one of his daughters; once he had
consented, they would then travel south to Avignon to seek a papal dispensation, which was necessary as the mothers of the bride and groom were
first cousins. The embassy finally left England in late April.[60]

Isabella took all her children with her when the court set out on 30 March
for Stamford, where a council was to be held to decide how to tackle the
Scots.[61] She was at Ramsey in the Fens on 4 April[62] and probably lodged in
the guesthouse of the great Saxon abbey there.

That month, Lancaster was formally reinstated in much of his inheritance, although Isabella still retained the de Lacy estates that had been
granted to her on coronation day,[63] which was a matter of some grievance to
Lancaster. Then there was a serious riot at Abingdon, followed by more bad
news from Scotland, where Bruce was assembling an army for a new offensive into Northumberland: this was in actuality a tactical exercise to force
the English to accept his sovereignty. Isabella and Mortimer responded on
5 April by ordering a general muster against the Scots,[64] which proved a popular move with both King and people, who hoped that the new reign would
afford an opportunity to reverse the ignominious defeat of Bannockburn
and reestablish English sovereignty over Scotland. However, given the number of attempts she made to forge a peace settlement, this was not a view
shared by Isabella, who regarded the Scottish war as already lost, as well as
being an unnecessary drain on finances. In her view, the sooner these facts

were recognized and a peace concluded, the better it would be for both sides. Several northern barons were of like mind, for they owned estates north of the border and hoped to recover them by means of a peace treaty. But Isabella was aware of the necessity of not only defending England's borders but also of maintaining the popular appeal of her regime and realized that, at this point, a war would meet with far greater public approval than a peace. It might also serve to demonstrate that finding a peaceful settlement would be an infinitely preferable alternative.

The custody of Edward II was formally transferred to Lord Berkeley and Sir John Maltravers on 3 April.[65] That night, they escorted the former King from Kenilworth. Accompanying them was a third custodian, Sir Thomas Gurney (or de Gournay), a Somerset knight of Mortimer's affinity who had been in prison with him in the Tower.[66] One of the guards who accompanied the ex-King was William Bishop, who had served as a soldier under Mortimer in 1321.[67]

On the day after the King was moved, Berkeley and Maltravers were assigned the princely sum of £5 a day from the Exchequer for his keep and the expenses of his household, which implies that he still had servants in attendance.[68] They took their prisoner on a circuitous route to Berkeley, initially heading westward; on the night of Palm Sunday, 4 April, the little party stayed at the remote Augustinian priory at Llanthony in Monmouthshire, then traveled southeast and crossed the Severn, arriving at Berkeley Castle on 5 or 6 April.[69]

Murimuth and Baker both assert that Edward's captors took him on an even more roundabout route, as far south as Corfe Castle in Dorset and then back to Gloucestershire via Bristol. Here, says Baker, the citizens made plain their intention of delivering the King from his captors, so Maltravers and Burney hurried him on to Berkeley. This is all pure fiction. Traveling from Kenilworth via Llanthony to Corfe, Bristol, and Berkeley would not have been possible in three days, the longest time the journey could have taken. Nor would it have been worth the security risk to have moved the ex-King so far, giving more people the opportunity to see him and learn of his whereabouts.

Baker, who says he got his information from William Bishop after the Black Death of 1348–49, also claims that the former King was subjected by his jailers to many indignities on the way from Bristol to Berkeley. He states that they would only travel at night and would not let him sleep when he was weary, and that, despite the cold, he was left to shiver in flimsy garments; they also gave him poisoned food that made him ill. They contradicted him, made out he was mad, and jeered at him, Gurney mockingly crowning him with straw. Then, so that he should not be recognized, they made him shave off his beard, forcing him to sit on a molehill in a field and to use cold, muddy ditchwater from an old helmet. Weeping, he is said to have retorted, "Whether you will or no, I will have warm water for my beard," referring to the tears that were streaming down his face. But again, Baker is apparently guilty of resorting to lurid fabrication, for, as we have seen, Edward could not have gone to Bristol at this time, which casts doubt on the whole story, a story that is not corroborated by any other source. Nor would Berkeley have sanctioned such ill-treatment, for we know from other evidence that he behaved well toward his prisoner. Furthermore, Baker says that Edward's jailers subjected him to these cruelties because they were hoping he would "succumb to some illness and thus languish and die," but Isabella and Mortimer had gone to great lengths to ensure that Edward's abdication and the establishment of their rule were attended by a semblance of legality and the maximum of publicity, so it is hardly likely that they would now try to kill the former King by such clumsy and ill-thought-out methods. Furthermore, it would take three rescue attempts before any move was made to dispose of Edward. It is possible that Bishop colluded with Baker in fabricating a tale that would show Edward II in a more saintly light or that Baker just made it up for propaganda purposes.

Berkeley Castle, which commanded the main Bristol-to-Gloucester road and the Severn estuary, had been built in the twelfth century by one of Thomas de Berkeley's ancestors and is still owned by the family today. In the middle of the fourteenth century, it was much improved and altered. The domestic ranges and remodeled great hall that we see today are largely of that period. When Edward II was there, Berkeley consisted mainly of the mighty Norman keep with rose stone walls fourteen feet thick, towering on a high mound, inner and outer baileys encircled by high curtain walls that were bisected by towers and a gatehouse, and a moat.

Edward was apparently lodged in one of the keep towers, the Thorpe Tower. The cell he is traditionally said to have occupied, which is now known as "the King's Gallery," is still shown to visitors today. Just outside it is a well-like shaft, twenty-eight feet deep, which extends down to the level of the courtyard below; this shaft was originally in the corner of the cell and is nowadays linked to one of Baker's more inventive tales, as we shall see.

Baker says that Edward II "was welcomed kindly" at Berkeley "and treated well by Thomas, Lord Berkeley." Murimuth corroborates this, stating that Berkeley treated the King well but that Maltravers behaved toward him with much harshness. It may have been during a period when Maltravers was in charge that a workman in the castle heard Edward moaning and groaning, although this story, which comes from an unnamed chronicle, may be spurious.[70] Both Berkeley and Maltravers were often away from the castle on official business in the western shires, so they shared custody of their prisoner or delegated their custodianship to others. The evidence of Froissart, who visited Berkeley in 1366 in the hope of finding out more about the fate of Edward II, corroborates that of Murimuth. He says that Lord Berkeley "was ordered to serve the King and look after him well and honourably, with proper people in attendance on him, but on no account to let him leave the castle. Those were his orders." This is in keeping with Lancaster's treatment of Edward at Kenilworth, and, as has been noted, Edward's daily allowance was for the maintenance of such "proper people in attendance on him." Furthermore, the Berkeley accounts show that plenty of victuals, including capons, beef, cheese, eggs, and wine, as well as other necessities were purchased for the former King,[71] which corroborates Baker's statement that his jailers gave him delicacies. It seems, therefore, that we may discount claims that Isabella deliberately ordered that her husband be ill-treated at Berkeley. On the contrary, it appears that he was honorably housed and served there.

On 8 April, the Queen arrived at Peterborough Abbey (now the cathedral), where she probably stayed either in the King's Lodging by the gateway or in the Abbot's palatial house, with its luxurious hall, chamber, and chapel. Here, at Peterborough, Edward III formally ratified the new peace treaty with France.[72] On the eleventh, the royal family celebrated Easter in the abbey, and they were still there on the fourteenth, but had arrived at Stamford in Lincolnshire two days later. Much to the Abbot's dismay, Isabella left her younger children at Peterborough for eight weeks, at his expense, which proved a severe strain on the abbey's finances.

At Stamford, during a council meeting held by the Queen on 19 April, the sensitive subject of Isabella's relations with Edward II was discussed. Her letters and gifts were probably mentioned, and the possibility of her joining him was again brought up by some of the bishops, whose consciences were exercised over her illicit relationship with Mortimer.[73] As we have seen, the Queen was reluctant to go back to her husband,[74] but as she did not wish to incur public censure, she left the decision as to what she should do to the council. Mortimer, however, was well aware of her fears and violently opposed to her returning to Edward, and after he had done some hard talking behind the scenes, Orleton reminded the council that it had already forbidden the Queen ever to return to Edward, "owing to his cruelty." At this, the matter was quietly dropped, but it must have left Isabella feeling somewhat perturbed.[75]

The government was still doing its best, without any success, to track down the conspirators who had tried to free the former King, and on 23 April, the council ordered the arrest of William Aylmer, on the pretext that he had been an ally of Despenser, which was nonsense, since Parliament had pardoned the favorite's more important adherents back in March.[76] In fact, the council was reluctant to publicize the fact that there had been a conspiracy to free Edward II, in case other malcontents had the same idea.

The court left Stamford on 25 April. The next day, Isabella was granted further arrears of revenues due to her from her dower lands.

On 28 April, Lancaster asked for a warrant to be issued for the arrest of another Dominican friar, John Stoke. Although he was not listed with the rest of Dunheved's gang, the fact that he was based in Warwickshire suggests that he was connected with their conspiracy. The order for his arrest was issued on 1 May; it contained the unusual instruction that, if found, he was to be brought immediately before the King.[77]

The court arrived at Nottingham on 29 April. Although Isabella had commissioned new peace talks with the Scots on 23 April,[78] the outlook for a settlement now seemed dismal, and war appeared inevitable. In anticipation of an invasion by Bruce, a general evacuation of the northern shires was ordered, and, at Isabella's behest, the young King sent a "most affectionate" request to Hainault for Sir John to return with his mercenaries[79] (he had gone back to Hainault after the coronation, loaded with gifts from the Queen and an annuity of 400 marks from her son).[80] Henry Eastry criticized Isabella for hiring foreigners to fight the Scots, prophetically foreseeing trouble ahead.[81]

On 4 May, a warrant was issued for the apprehension of Stephen Dunheved, who was to be conveyed to the Queen's castle at Wallingford.[82] But Dunheved, like Stoke, proved elusive.

The next day, "with the assent of Queen Isabella," Edward III granted privileges to the inhabitants of her city of Winchester, which he had assigned to her for life.[83]

The question of the Queen's return to her husband was still unresolved, at least in the mind of the Pope, who, on 9 May, wrote urging that every effort be made to bring about a reconciliation between Edward and Isabella.[84] The timing of this letter suggests that it was written in response to an appeal from one or more of those who had attended the council meeting at Stamford, perhaps one of the ecclesiastics who were privately scandalized at Isabella's liaison with Mortimer. It has been suggested also that the Pope's letter was solicited as a ploy, by those who felt she had too much influence, to neutralize Isabella,[85] but this was unlikely, as it would not have accounted for opposition on the part of Mortimer, who, as we have seen, would not have countenanced Isabella's returning to her husband.

The Pope's injunction was conveniently ignored. Isabella and Mortimer and their associates were too preoccupied with the imminent confrontation with the Scots. On 23 May, Isabella and the young King reached York,[86] where a large army was gathering. There, they took up lodgings in the house of the Black Friars (Dominicans), "keeping their households separate: the King with his knights, [who were] lodged in the hall and cloisters, and the Queen with her ladies, of whom there were a great number."[87] The friary, which had been founded by Henry III in 1228, stood in King's Tofts, between Tanner Row and the city walls.[88]

On 27 May, Sir John of Hainault arrived with five hundred Flemish mercenaries, "and they were splendidly feasted by the King and his mother and all the barons. They were given the best quarters in the city, and Sir John was given the abbey of Whitefriars as his headquarters."[89] Unfortunately, this cordial welcome was to be marred by the appalling events of Trinity Sunday.

On that day, 7 June, Isabella hosted a banquet in the house of the Black Friars, where

> the young King held court. The King had six hundred knights, and he created fifteen new ones. The Queen held her court in the dormitory, where at least sixty ladies sat at her table, whom she had assembled to entertain Sir John and the other knights. A large number of nobles were seen there, well served with many ingenious dishes, so disguised that no one could tell what they were. And the ladies were superbly dressed, with rich jewels, taking their ease.
>
> But there was to be no continuation of the feast, or dancing, for immediately after dinner, a violent quarrel broke out between the servants of the army of Hainault and the English archers, who were lodged with them. When these servants began fighting with the English, all the other archers who were in the same quarters as the Hainaulters assembled together, with their bows strung. A cry of alarm went up, and they started shooting at the Hainaulters. Most of the knights and their masters were still at court and knew nothing of the matter, but as soon as they heard of this affray, they hurried back to their quarters. Those who were left outside were in great danger, for the archers, who were at least two thousand in number, were quite beyond control, and were shooting indiscriminately at masters and servants alike.

Some people were of the opinion that this had all been planned as an act of revenge by friends of the Despensers, but in fact, the English archers were merely expressing their usual xenophobic hatred of foreigners. During the riot, many Hainaulters were wounded, and the violence was only curbed when three knights "took great oak staves from the house of a carter and dealt such fierce blows that nobody dared approach," knocking down sixty men. In the end, Isabella made the King and Lord Wake mount their horses and ride through the streets, proclaiming that anyone caught attacking the Hainaulters would be instantly beheaded. At this, the archers retreated, leaving three hundred dead bodies in and around the Blackfriars. Even now, the Hainaulters were not completely safe and were warned of violent reprisals, "for the surviving archers hated them more than the Scots, who all this time were burning their country!" None of the foreigners dared leave their lodgings for the next four weeks, "except to join the lords who went to see the King and Queen and their council."[90]

In the King's name, on 14 June, an inquiry into the riot was ordered. Ultimately, it blamed the English archers, which only exacerbated the bad feeling against the Hainaulters and made the latter feel even more threatened.[91]

On 8 June, the day after the riot, Mortimer's judicial jurisdiction was extended to cover the counties of Hereford, Stafford, and Worcester, which suggests that the government was still disturbed about the activities of dissidents in those parts. On the twelfth, Roger received the lavish grant of the Despenser lands in Glamorgan, which he was to hold "during pleasure."[92] By now, so much of the property of the former favorites had been appropriated or reassigned by Isabella that their descendants complained to Froissart that she had been "an evil queen who took everything from them." By contrast, Mortimer, through her influence, was now a very wealthy man.

On 10 June, negotiations with the Scots again broke down,[93] and on the fifteenth, Bruce sent new raiding parties across the border. Norfolk and Kent were now appointed to captain the royal army, with Lancaster in overall command, and more levies were summoned.[94]

Edward III marched north from York, at the head of his army, on 1 July.[95] After he had left, the Queen vacated the Blackfriars monastery for the greater security of York Castle, where she remained with her younger children; £28 was spent on fitting out a tower for her.[96] She kept in touch with the King by letter and deployed measures to ensure that York was adequately defended against the Scots.[97]

In the middle of July, as the English envoys were leaving Hainault for Avignon after receiving Count William's formal consent to the proposed marriage, Bruce launched an attack across the border. The King's train reached Durham by the fifteenth,[98] when Mortimer joined it.

The campaign was farcical. On 19 July, the English, who had no idea where the Scots really were, pushed south toward Stanhope in Weardale, hoping to force a confrontation. The Scots were waiting for them and preparing for battle, but the English thought they were about to flee and rushed away to cut off their retreat at the River Tyne. Of course, the Scots did not appear. Thereafter, they continually outmaneuvered the English and employed maddening evasion tactics. On 27 July, the exhausted English army was stranded between Haydon and Haltwhistle, and by the thirtieth, having failed repeatedly to engage the enemy, they had returned dejectedly to Stanhope. The next day, the Scots cunningly foiled an attempt to ambush them, and early in August, the Black Douglas daringly raided the King's own camp in Stanhope Park before vanishing back to Scotland on the sixth. The young King felt so deeply humiliated by the failure of his first campaign that he burst into tears of frustration.[99]

It was probably in mid- to late June that a party of conspirators led by the Dominican friar Stephen Dunheved managed to free Edward II from Berkeley Castle. The whole episode is shrouded in secrecy because Isabella and Mortimer did not want it publicized,[100] but it can be dated to this time thanks to a number of measures taken by the council.

As we have seen, the government had long regarded Stephen Dunheved as a very dangerous man and was anxious to apprehend him. These fears were justified, for while in hiding, he had continued plotting to restore Edward II and, to this end, had formed a band of outlaws. It included a murderer, a thief, a monk from Hailes Abbey in Gloucestershire, an Augustinian canon, and Stephen Dunheved's own brother Thomas, lord of the manor of Dunchurch in Warwickshire. There must have been others and, indeed, a network of conspirators throughout the southwest, or the group would never have succeeded in their mission.

How they did it is not clear, but the Dunheved "brigands" successfully stormed Berkeley Castle, that supposedly secure fortress, ransacked and looted it, and, overcoming his guards, carried off the King. They possibly took advantage of the building work being carried out in the castle at the time or had accomplices among the workforce.[101] It may have been now that Edward was taken to Corfe Castle in Dorset "and other secret places."[102] Berkeley and Maltravers were away from Berkeley at the time and had left a royal clerk, John Walwayn, as their deputy. Evidently, he was incompetent.

The news of the King's escape was urgently transmitted to the council in York, 250 miles away, where it seems to have provoked near panic. The first indication that something was wrong may lie in an order issued to the Sheriff of Shropshire on 26 June, instructing him to arrest all troublemakers on the Welsh border. Then, on 1 July, a warrant was issued for the arrest of Stephen Dunheved.[103] That same day, Berkeley and Maltravers were appointed commissioners of the peace for Dorset (where Corfe was situated), Somerset, Wiltshire, Hampshire, Herefordshire, Oxfordshire, and Berkshire, which gave them the authority to track down and deal with offenders; and on 3 July, Berkeley was excused from military service against the Scots and "charged with the special business of the King [Edward III]."[104]

Then the records are silent until 27 July, when a letter was sent from Berkeley Castle to the Chancellor, John Hotham; it was written probably by Lord Berkeley in his capacity as commissioner of the peace,[105] although the sender could also have been John Walwayn, the royal clerk. Whoever it was reported that Dunheved and his accomplices had been indicted for forcing an entry into the castle, abducting "the father of our lord the King out of our guard, and feloniously plundering the said castle."[106] But there was little comfort for the council in this because none of the twenty-one conspirators listed in the letter had been seized, and Berkeley's custodians were now begging for greater authority to pursue them. In response to this, on 1 August, Lord Berkeley was granted special powers for this very purpose.[107]

Although several theorists have argued otherwise, there can be little doubt that Edward II had been quickly recaptured and brought back to Berkeley by 27 July, for Lord Berkeley's (or Walwayn's) letter does not mention tracking down the King, only his abductors, and refers to fears of another plot to liberate him: "I understand, from a number of sources, that a great number of gentlemen in the county of Buckingham and in adjacent counties, have assembled for the same cause."[108] We may infer from this that Edward was back in custody. Had he not been, Berkeley would have been far more preoccupied with recapturing him than with catching those who had freed him. And even if Edward was still at liberty at this time, he was certainly back in prison by 7 September, when yet another attempt was made to free him.

Stephen Dunheved managed to elude capture,[109] but his brother Thomas and most of their fellow conspirators were taken, Thomas being imprisoned on Isabella's orders in Newgate, where he died of a fever soon afterward or was murdered.[110] The rest were never heard of again, apart from William Aylmer, who was apprehended at Oxford the following month and charged with conspiring to free Edward II; but the Queen ordered him to be released on bail,[111] and he was found innocent at a hearing in October and released. This is astonishing, given Aylmer's links with Despenser and his having given judgment against some of Mortimer's Welsh supporters in 1324–25, but Doherty plausibly suggests that he had turned King's evidence and betrayed his fellow plotters, a role he appears to have undertaken in a murder case in 1329–30.[112]

At Stanhope, on 7 August, Edward III, devastated by the humiliation of the Weardale campaign, summoned Parliament to meet at Lincoln on 15 September to discuss the next moves against the Scots.[113] The following day, he returned, very dejected, to Durham. He left for York on 10 August, and on the thirteenth, he was reunited there with Isabella, "who welcomed him with great joy, as did the ladies of the court and the burgesses of the city."[114] With the King were Sir John of Hainault, Roger Mortimer, and the other lords who had led the campaign. For the next week or so, Isabella was busy entertaining Sir John and his company.[115]

The English envoys had arrived at Avignon early in August, and on the fifth, they had put forward their request for a dispensation. But it was refused because John XXII was unhappy about the way Edward II had been treated. Hearing this, Edward III himself wrote to the Pope on 15 August, begging him not to delay granting his request. His letter prompted the Pontiff and his College of Cardinals to issue the dispensation "most benignantly" on 3 September without further prevarication.[116] Philippa of Hainault is first named as Edward III's future bride in this document. The young King had already expressed a strong preference for marrying Philippa, "for she and I accorded excellently well together, and she wept when I took leave of her."[117] After secretly observing her and her sisters at Valenciennes, Orleton, too, had thought Philippa "a young lady most worthy to be Queen of England."[118]

The court was now moving south toward Lincoln and was at Doncaster on 26 August.[119]

The English army was finally disbanded on 27 August[120] and the Hainaulters sent home a few days later; when Sir John and his men took their leave, the King, the Queen, and all the lords "paid them great honour," doubtless trying not to dwell on the huge bill for nearly £55,000 with which Sir John had just presented them.[121] This money was raised from Exchequer funds, the pledging of the crown jewels, and loans from merchants. The Queen did not contribute a penny out of her vast revenues.[122] Nor did she offer any financial assistance to the King, who was desperately short of money after the Weardale campaign, although she had at various times throughout the year implemented measures to raise funds for him.[123]

On 7 September, a third plot to liberate Edward II was uncovered. Its apparent leader was Mortimer's avowed enemy, the Welsh knight Rhys ap Gruffydd, who had been with Edward at Neath in November and wanted to "forcibly deliver the said Lord Edward" and perhaps set him up as a champion of Welsh liberties. "Rhys ap Gruffydd and others of his coven had assembled their power in south Wales and in north Wales." However, there were others involved, namely, "certain great lords of the land of England";[124] again, we might suspect the Earl of Kent, for the Fine Rolls show that Rhys ap Gruffydd was another who supported his later conspiracy. Another likely ally was Robert the Bruce's nephew, Donald, Earl of Mar, an expatriate Scot who had been brought up with Edward II and had helped the Elder Despenser to hold Bristol Castle; after its fall, Mar had fled north to Scotland, but in June 1327, at Bruce's behest, he was in the Welsh Marches, not far from Berkeley, trying to raise a force to rescue Edward and creating considerable disturbances in the process.[125]

Whoever they were, Rhys ap Gruffydd's conspirators must have been finalizing their plans in late August and early September, but on 7 September, they were betrayed to Mortimer's lieutenant in south Wales, William de Shalford.[126]

Mortimer had left court by then and was on his way back to Wales. He was with Isabella at Nottingham on 31 August and also on 3 September, when the court arrived at Lincoln.[127] The next day, he was ordered to resume his duties as Justice of Wales and inquire into conspiracies there and apparently left court that very day for south Wales.[128] Since he did not yet know of Rhys ap Gruffydd's conspiracy, it is reasonable to assume that his mission was connected with the government's hitherto unsuccessful attempts to apprehend Stephen Dunheved and the remaining members of his gang, as well as those persons who were causing unrest in the Marches. On the eighth, instructions were sent after him to arrest all those breaking the peace in Wales.[129] On the thirteenth, Mortimer was granted lands worth £1,000 per annum, including Denbigh Castle, which had formerly been held by the Elder Despenser, Oswestry Castle, and all Arundel's forfeited manors.[130]

Mortimer was at Abergavenny in 14 September when William de Shalford wrote from Rhosfair in Anglesey to inform him of Rhys ap Gruffydd's conspiracy to free Edward II. Shalford "also made clear in the letter that, if the Lord Edward was freed, that Lord Roger Mortimer and all his people would die a terrible death by force and would be utterly destroyed, on account of which Shalford counselled the said Roger that he ordain such a remedy in such a way that no one in England or Wales would ever think of effecting such deliverance." Shalford's original letter does not survive, but its contents were revealed in 1331, when Hywel ap Gruffydd accused Shalford of being a party to Edward II's murder, and Shalford challenged him to a duel. Hywel refused to take up the challenge and took his complaint to the Court of King's Bench, citing many witnesses, but he conveniently fell ill—or was intimidated—and failed to appear on the appointed day, so the case was dismissed.[131]

According to the Meaux chronicler and the *Annales Monastici,* the discovery of this third plot sealed Edward II's fate. The former King had now been the focus of three conspiracies to liberate and restore him, and clearly, he was a dangerous threat to the new government, to Isabella, and to Mortimer in particular, as Shalford had pointed out. The safest and most expedient course would therefore be to have him quietly disposed of. But in 1327, there was no precedent for murdering a deposed king.

Hywel ap Gruffydd claimed that Mortimer's response to Shalford's communication was to show it to William Ockle (or Ockley), a trusted retainer who had been in the household of Mortimer's wife during her captivity. He "commanded him to take the said letter and to show it to those who were guarding Edward. And Mortimer charged him to tell them to take counsel on the points contained in the letter and to quickly remedy the situation in order to avoid great peril."[132]

Ockle carried out Mortimer's orders. Berkeley was later to protest that he had had nothing to do with any plot to murder the former King, and indeed, he may well not have been at Berkeley when Ockle arrived. But Maltravers and Gurney were apparently left in no doubt that Edward was to be disposed of in any way they thought fit. This chain of events makes it clear that any orders for the murder of Edward II came from Mortimer acting on his own initiative and not from Isabella, who, more than 130 miles away in Lincoln, could have had no knowledge of Rhys ap Gruffydd's plot or its consequences and could not have been an accessory before the fact to the murder of her husband. Even in the unlikely event of Mortimer's sending a messenger with a letter informing her of his intentions, she would not have had time to respond.

In the meantime, Mortimer's soldiers were sent to round up Rhys ap Gruffydd and his compatriots. Rhys and some of his men sought refuge in Scotland,[133] but thirteen others were caught and imprisoned at Caernarvon.

Baker ignores the rescue plots entirely and asserts that it was Isabella and Orleton who plotted Edward's murder. His account suggests that, because of Isabella's fears that she might have to return to Edward, Orleton had the former King ill-treated by his jailers on the way to Berkeley in the hope that he might die. But this had been in April, and the King had survived. Indeed, since then, Baker says, Edward's jailers "had been too lenient with him and fed him delicacies," an assertion that is corroborated by other evidence.

This apparently went on throughout the summer, then suddenly, Baker says, "Isabella was angered that [Edward's] life, which had become most hateful to her, should be so prolonged. She asked advice of the Bishop of Hereford, pretending that she had had a dreadful dream, from which she feared, if it was true, that her husband would at some time be restored to his former dignity, and would condemn her as a traitress, to be burned or given into perpetual slavery. The Bishop of Hereford feared greatly for himself, just as Isabella did, conscious that, if this should come to pass, he was guilty of treason." The fact that Orleton had been out of the country since April does not seem to have registered with Baker, and it is highly improbable that Isabella would have committed such a sensitive matter to paper or to a messenger in order to communicate with Orleton at the papal court.

Baker says that letters were duly sent to Edward's keepers, censuring them for their lenience and hinting that their prisoner's death would cause "no great displeasure, whether it were natural or violent," and that Orleton sent the jailers a Latin message that, thanks to the omission of a comma, could be read in two ways: either

> Edwardum occidere nolite, timere bonum est.
> Kill not Edward, it is good to fear the deed.

> Edwardum occidere nolite timere, bonum est.
> Fear not to kill Edward, it is a good deed.

Of course, the jailers were meant to interpret it in the latter way. It was a clever story, but an utter fabrication, since Orleton was at this time far away in Avignon. Furthermore, Baker plagiarized the tale from the pages of the great thirteenth-century chronicler Matthew Paris, where it appeared in relation to the murder of a queen of Hungary in 1252.[134] In 1334, Orleton issued an "Apologia" insisting that he was not a party to, and had had no hand in, Edward II's death,[135] and indeed, he was never formally charged with it. Moreover, Baker's whole tale is clearly a fiction, since it takes no account of the real circumstances in which the instructions for Edward's murder were given, nor of the role of Mortimer, the real culprit, who is barely mentioned, even though his guilt was public knowledge at the time Baker was writing.

Parliament met in the chapter house of Lincoln Cathedral on 15 September.

Edward II is said to have been murdered at Berkeley Castle on 21 September. There are various versions of how he met his end, hardly any of which are strictly contemporary or based on firsthand knowledge. Most come from monastic chronicles, the writers of which relied on information and gossip brought by travelers or in other chronicles.

The author of the contemporary *Annales Paulini*, writing in London probably in 1328, states simply that "King Edward died at Berkeley Castle, where he was held prisoner."

Another contemporary, Adam Murimuth, also a canon of Saint Paul's, and a royal councillor who was very well informed through his connections with the court and the higher clergy, and who was based in Exeter at the time of Edward's death, wrote his account of events around 1337, basing them on notes he made at the time.[136] He claims that "it was commonly said" that the King had been "killed as a precaution" on Mortimer's orders and that he had been suffocated by Maltravers and Gurney, who had put him to death in this way so that no one would suspect foul play. Murimuth adds that many people adhered to this view.

In his life of Edward II, written between 1327 and 1340, the anonymous canon of Bridlington in Yorkshire wrote that the King "died in Berkeley Castle, where he was held in custody." Then he adds, "Of his death, various explanations are commonly suggested, but I do not care for such things as now are written. I myself prefer to say no more about the matter, for sometimes, as the poet says, lies are for the advantage of many, and to tell the whole truth does harm." This reads as if the canon discounted most of the tales he had heard as distasteful fabrications and gave them little credence, but we may infer that sensational and far-fetched rumors as to how Edward met his end were now gaining currency. The canon seems to be implying that writing what he believes to be the truth might get him into trouble and that many people were being protected by the tissue of lies that shrouded the real circumstances of Edward II's murder.

In 1331, Hywel ap Gruffydd's testimony against William de Shalford asserts that Edward II "was feloniously and traitorously slain by murder" but gives no details of the method used. He accuses "William Ockle and others who were guarding the Lord Edward" of killing him.[137]

Two versions of *The Brut* chronicle were written in the 1330s. The one that was probably compiled in London says merely that soon after Edward II was moved to Berkeley Castle, he "became ill there and died on the day of St. Matthew the Apostle."[138] The other version, which may have been partially written in the North, and was certainly penned by a Lancastrian adherent, accuses Berkeley, Maltravers, and Gurney of being the murderers, and states, "Roger Mortimer sent orders as to how and in what manner the King should be killed. And when the aforesaid Thomas and John had seen the letter and the order, they were friendly towards King Edward at supper-time, so that the King knew nothing of their treachery. And when he had gone to bed and was asleep, the traitors, against their homage and fealty [which had in fact been renounced], went quietly into his chamber and laid a large table on his stomach, and with other men's help pressed him down." At this point, Edward woke up and managed to turn over—no mean feat when a heavy table is being pressed down on one on all four corners. But there was no escaping his tormenters, who spread his legs and inserted "a long horn into his fundament as deep as they might, and took a spit of burning copper, and put it through the horn into his body, and ofttimes rolled therewith his bowels, and so they killed their lord, and nothing was perceived." This is the earliest account of Edward's being murdered in this revolting and sadistic manner, and it may be one of the stories to which the canon of Bridlington was referring.

In the far North, the Lanercost chronicler, writing around 1346, either had not heard the colorful rumors or was skeptical about them, recording only that "the deposed King died either by a natural death, or by the violence of another." But another northern chronicle, the *Historia Aurea,* also dating from around 1346, asserts that Edward II "was killed by the introduction of a hot iron through the middle of a horn inserted into his bottom."[139]

Ranulph Higden, the monk of Chester who wrote his highly successful (and highly unoriginal) *Polychronicon* in the North around 1347, echoes the northern *Brut,* asserting that Edward was "ignominiously slain with a redhot rod piercing his anus."

But the French *Chronicle of London,* which derives from the London *Brut* and can be dated to the 1340s, says nothing of this and asserts only that Berkeley and Maltravers, "abetted by certain persons, falsely and traitorously murdered [Edward]." No details of the method used are given.

The most detailed account of Edward II's murder, and the one most often quoted, is that of Geoffrey le Baker, which was written between circa 1350 and 1358. But it is seriously flawed. To begin with, it is said to be based on the accounts of witnesses, one of whom was William Bishop, yet we have no idea who the others were. By the time Baker wrote his account, Mortimer and Gurney were dead, Maltravers had been living in Europe for several years, and Ockle had long since disappeared, probably having fled abroad. William Bishop was apparently a guard at Berkeley Castle, but since the information he gave Baker about Edward's journey there is patently suspect, we should not place too much reliance on his credibility as a witness.

According to Baker, when Ockle arrived with Shalford's letter and Mortimer's instructions, Berkeley felt his authority was being undermined and, complaining that he was no longer master in his own house, took his leave of the King and went to stay elsewhere. We know, from Berkeley's own testimony, that he was not at Berkeley on 21 September but was staying at one of his manors.[140] Baker says that, once he had gone, Maltravers, Gurney, and Ockle first tried employing various cruelties in an attempt to bring about Edward's death by natural causes. These included starving him of food, depriving him of light and sleep, and placing him "for many days" in close proximity to a pit in which the stinking corpses of animals had been left to rot, so that he nearly suffocated from the stench. Nowadays, it is claimed that this was the pit that was once in the corner of "the King's Gallery." But since Edward was only forty-three, his constitution was so strong that he survived this ill-treatment. Apart from the fact that Baker was much given to lurid fabrication, and that there is no evidence to corroborate these allegations, it would surely have been unrealistic for Edward's jailers to have expected him to have succumbed to starvation and stench within five days, which was the longest time that could have elapsed between Ockle's arriving at Berkeley and the date on which the King is said to have been put to death.

Drawing heavily on the northern *Brut,* Baker asserts that, when "his tyrannous warders," Maltravers and Gurney, realized that they could not kill him in this way, they decided to kill him in a way that would leave no discernible outward marks of violence. They "made the King in good cheer at his supper," so that when he went to bed, "he fell soundly asleep." Then, with four stout men, they crept into his chamber and, as he lay "sore afraid" and "grovelling," they suffocated him with "cushions heavier than fifteen strong men could carry"—surely an exaggeration, this, especially as there were only six men present. Then they laid "a great table" across his belly, their four assistants holding it down firmly at the corners; they lifted the

King's legs, took a horn and pushed it into his rectum as far as possible, then they thrust up it "a plumber's soldering iron, heated red hot," driving it through "the privy parts of the bowel, and thus they burnt his innards and vital organs" and "in the end" murdered him "in such wise that, after his death, it could not be perceived how he came by his death." Baker claims that later, it was said that, if the King's body were to be opened up, burn marks would be found "in those parts in which he had been wont to take his vicious pleasure." Thus, we are to infer that, as with Despenser, the mode of Edward II's death was devised by vindictive men as a punishment for his homosexuality, which reflected a contemporary belief that he had been the passive partner in sexual acts.

If we are to believe Baker, Edward was already dead when the red-hot iron was applied, for he had been suffocated first with those extraordinarily heavy cushions. But no, Baker would have us believe that, as "this brave knight was overcome, he shouted aloud, so that many heard his cry both within and without the castle, and knew it for a man who suffered a violent death. Many in both the town and castle of Berkeley were moved to pity for Edward, and to watch and pray for his spirit as it departed this world."

Would Mortimer and his henchmen have risked others' hearing their prisoner screaming in agony? It is unlikely. And if those weighty pillows had been suffocating him, how could he have screamed out anyway? It would surely have been easier to poison Edward or just suffocate or strangle him.

Baker's embellishments of the account in the northern *Brut* render his story full of inconsistencies; like his tale about Orleton's commaless message, much of what he wrote was undoubtedly fictitious. Modern medical opinion holds that, even if Edward did have a red-hot spit thrust into his rectum, he would probably have taken several days to die an agonizing death, because perforation and scorching of the rectum can lead to peritonitis and the gradual breakdown of other internal organs, such as the bladder.

The *Meaux Chronicle* and the somewhat unreliable Leicester chronicler, John of Reading, both recount the red-hot-spit story given in the northern *Brut*, the latter claiming that Edward's murderers had confessed to killing him in this way.

In the 1380s, John Trevisa, who had been a child at Berkeley when Edward II was held there, and was now its vicar, wrote his translation, with additions, of Migden's *Polychronicon*. In his version, the King was partially smothered, then killed "with a hot brush put through the secret place posterial," but Trevisa makes no comment as to the veracity of this tale. Trevisa had been a chaplain to Thomas de Berkeley before the latter's death in

1361, and it has been asserted[141] that he therefore must surely have known the truth about Edward II's fate, but this was not necessarily so, for if Berkeley had had anything to confess, he would have done it years before Trevisa appeared. In fact, as he later publicly stated, he was not at his castle on 21 September and knew nothing of the King's death until he was told about it in 1330.[142]

Froissart, who gleaned his information when he stayed as the guest of Despenser's grandson Edward at Berkeley in 1366, says that "an ancient squire" told him that Edward II "had died within a year of coming to Berkeley, for someone cut his life short." He does not mention the red-hot-spit story, but other later chroniclers, including Knighton and Walsingham, all report it as fact.

We have now established that this notorious version of Edward's end is not strictly contemporary. Nevertheless, it is repeated by several chroniclers and has long been accepted by several historians, so where, then, did it originate? It is noticeable that none of the London chroniclers mentions it, which suggests that the story may have originated in the North or the Midlands, and that its emergence in these areas reflects Lancastrian propaganda designed to discredit the regime of Isabella and Mortimer. The circumstances in which this propaganda may have been produced will be recounted in due course, when we come to look at the events of 1328–29, but there is a strong possibility that the red-hot-spit story emerged at this time and that its dramatic nature ensured its spread. In London and the South, however, there were less lurid theories as to what fate had befallen Edward II.[143]

We can be almost certain that, given this evidence, and the obvious flaws in the red-hot-spit story, Edward II did not perish in this dreadful manner. If he was murdered at all, he was probably suffocated.

It is worth noting at this point that not one chronicler accuses Isabella of being an accomplice in the murder of her husband, nor is there any other evidence to link her to it. As to her being an accessory after the fact, that is another matter that will be discussed later.

None of the above accounts is entirely reliable because what happened at Berkeley Castle that September remained shrouded in secrecy, and very few people would have known the truth. However, the truth may not be concerned with a murder, for there is dramatic evidence that Edward II was not murdered but managed to escape from the castle.

It was probably in early 1337 that a Genoese priest, Manuele de Fieschi, who was a senior clerk or notary to Pope John XXII, sent Edward III a long, undated letter, written in Latin, from Italy, where Fieschi was then living. The letter contained a startling, and very convincing, account of how the King's father had escaped from Berkeley Castle,[144] which reads:

In the name of the Lord, amen.

Those things that I have heard from the confession of your father I have written with my own hand, and afterwards I have taken care to be made known to Your Highness.

First, he has said that, feeling England in subversion against him after the threat from your mother, he departed from his followers in the castle of the Earl Marshal [Norfolk] by the sea, which is called Chepstow. Later, driven by fear, he boarded a barque together with Lord Hugh le Despenser and the Earl of Arundel and several others, and made his way by sea to Glamorgan on the coast. There he was captured, together with the said Lord Hugh and Master Robert Baldock, and they were taken by Lord Henry of Lancaster. And they led him to Kenilworth Castle, and the others were taken to various other places. And there, many people demanding it, he lost the crown. Subsequently, you were crowned at the feast of Candlemas next following.

Finally, they sent him to the castle of Berkeley. Afterwards, the servant who was guarding him, after some little time, said to your father, "Sire, Lord [*sic*] Thomas Gurney and Lord Simon Barford, knights, have come with the purpose of killing you. If it pleases you, I shall give you my clothes, that you may better be able to escape." Then, wearing the said clothes, at twilight, he [Edward] went out of the prison. And when he had reached the last door without resistance, because he was not recognised, he found the porter sleeping, whom he quickly killed. And, having got the keys out of the door, he opened it and went out, with his keeper.

The said knights who had come to kill him, seeing that he had thus fled, and fearing the indignation of the Queen, for fear of their lives, thought to put that aforesaid porter in a chest, his heart having been extracted and maliciously presented to the Queen, as if they were the heart and body of your father; and, as the body of the King, the said porter was buried at Gloucester.

After he [Edward] had escaped from the prison of the aforesaid castle, he was received at Corfe Castle together with his companion, who had guarded him in prison, by Lord Thomas, the castellan of the said castle, without the knowledge of Lord John Maltravers, lord of the said Thomas, in which castle he remained secretly for a year and a half.

Afterwards, hearing that the Earl of Kent, for maintaining that he was alive, had been beheaded, he took a ship with his said keeper and, with the consent and counsel of the said Thomas [de Berkeley], who had received him, crossed into Ireland, where he remained for nine months. Afterwards, fearing lest he be recognised there, and having taken the habit of a hermit, he came back to England and proceeded to the port of Sandwich, and in the same habit crossed the sea to Sluys.

Afterwards, he turned his steps in Normandy, and from Normandy, as many do, crossing through Languedoc, he came to Avignon, where he gave a florin to a Papal servant and sent, by the same servant, a note to Pope John. The Pope summoned him and kept him secretly and honourably for more than fifteen days. Finally, after various deliberations, all things having been considered, and after receiving permission to depart, he went to Paris, and from Paris to Brabant, and from Brabant to Cologne, so that, out of devotion, he might see the [shrine of] the Three Kings. And, leaving Cologne, he crossed over Germany and headed for Milan in Lombardy.

In Milan, he entered a certain hermitage in the castle of Milasci [Melazzo], in which hermitage he remained for two and a half years; and because war overran the said castle, he moved to the castle of Cecima in another hermitage of the diocese of Pavia in Lombardy. And he [has] remained in this last hermitage for two years or thereabouts, always the recluse, doing penance or praying God for you and other sinners. In testimony of which I have caused my seal to be affixed for the consideration of Your Highness.

Your Manuele de Fieschi, notary of the Lord Pope, your devoted servant.[145]

The authenticity of the Fieschi letter itself is not in doubt, but that of its contents has been disputed by many historians, even though they can find little to say to discredit them. Yet its veracity is crucial in determining whether or not Isabella was a party to the murder of her husband. If Edward II was not murdered, then posterity has wronged her, which would allow us to judge her in a very different light. It is therefore necessary to scrutinize Fieschi's account in detail.

The letter begins very abruptly, as if there had been some previous communication informing Edward III that his father was alive and living in Lombardy and offering him proof that this was no imposter. The phrase "In the name of God, amen" is a customary salutation in ecclesiastical letters of the period and an implied assurance that what follows is the truth.

The information divulged to Fieschi was given in the form of a confession, but Fieschi does not say that Edward had given him permission to reveal it, either because that is perhaps implicit in the letter anyway or this was not a sacramental confession. As Doherty points out, there is nothing very sinful in this confession apart from the murder of the porter, and that, surely, would have been confessed by Edward long before this. The letter would certainly have been sent by a messenger who could verbally furnish the King with any sensitive details that Fieschi had not seen fit to commit to paper. Who this messenger was will be discussed shortly.

A strong argument in favor of the letter's authenticity is the accuracy and authenticity of the narrative that takes us from the King's flight from Chepstow up until his alleged escape from Berkeley. It corroborates the known facts and reveals details that very few people could have known other than those who actually shared Edward's flight to Wales. As has recently been noted,[146] no single chronicle written before 1343 (the latest date for the Fieschi letter to have been written) contains all these details, and not one refers to Edward's putting to sea from Chepstow and landing in Glamorgan; this information was recorded only in the chamber accounts, which Fieschi could not have seen.[147] Whatever else may be said about the letter, no satisfactory explanation has ever been advanced to show how he came by this information, apart from his having heard it from Edward II himself or from one of those who had accompanied him. But Despenser, Arundel, and Baldock were dead, so whom did that leave—royal clerks? Men-at-arms? Is it likely that Fieschi would really have got his facts from such lowly sources or would have known whom to question?

There are errors in the letter, such as the reference to "Lord" Thomas Gurney, when it should be "Sir." This can be put down to Fieschi's lack of familiarity with English titles. "Simon Barford" is perhaps to be identified with Mortimer's lieutenant, Sir Simon Bereford (or Beresford), who was later described as Mortimer's accomplice "in all his crimes,"[148] although there is no other evidence that he was at Berkeley at this time, and he was never specifically accused of regicide. Ockle is not mentioned, but then Edward might not have seen him, and even if he had, he probably would not have known who he was. He would certainly have known Gurney and Bereford, who *are* mentioned by name.

We do not know the name of the warder or servant who helped Edward and escaped with him, but he was apparently in the confidence of his superiors. The fact that he knew that they were planning to kill Edward suggests that the escape, if it happened at all, probably took place after Ockle had arrived with Mortimer's instructions and Shalford's letter. It is highly unlikely, in my view, that Edward escaped with Mortimer's collusion, as has recently been suggested by Ian Mortimer.[149] Roger Mortimer had no motive for keeping Edward alive, and every reason to want him dead; as had been made abundantly clear, living, the former King posed an ever-present threat, as the focus of plots to free him and restore him to his throne or as a potential figurehead for dissidents who opposed Isabella's rule. While Edward lived, Mortimer, whose power depended on that of the woman who controlled the young King, could never feel secure. Should Edward ever return to power, Mortimer would face a bloody end.

It has been claimed that a change of clothes would not have disguised Edward II, but middle- and lower-class men of the period often wore brimmed hats, hoods, and/or coifs, which could completely cover the hair and, in some cases, shade the face. And if the warder had been of a similar height, few would have given Edward a second glance.

It is indeed difficult to believe that Edward got past his guards and as far as the porter's lodge without being challenged; after all, there had recently been two more plots to free him, one of which had temporarily succeeded, and security had presumably been tightened. However, not only was he in disguise, but he had also probably been kept in such close captivity that few people in the castle would have seen or recognized him, and anyway, no one could have anticipated that he would just walk out of his prison. Any-one encountering him would simply have assumed he was the warder. Fur-thermore, the warder would almost certainly have had a set of keys. It is likely, too, that the escape took place at night, when there were fewer guards on duty, and that the warder went on ahead and left Edward to fol-low. Edward was perfectly capable of swimming the moat, and once out-side the castle, the warder, who was probably a local man, would have known his way through the surrounding marshland and woodland.

A telling point in the letter is the reference to the jailers' fear of Isabella's reaction when she found out that Edward had escaped his killers. Edward himself could have had no means of knowing that the order to kill him had come just from Mortimer, and not from Isabella, who, far away in Notting-ham, could not have known of the latest plot to free him—just as the per-son who gave Fieschi this information assumed that it had been Isabella who had ordered the murder. However, by the time this letter was written, it was common knowledge that Edward III held Mortimer responsible for his father's murder.

If Edward had escaped, why did he not show himself and proclaim his restoration? First, he knew he could count on very little support, since most of his adherents had been seized. Second, very few people would believe his story, as the majority assumed he was dead and buried. Third, it had been proved to him just how ruthless Mortimer could be: were he to publicize his whereabouts, Mortimer would not hesitate to hunt him down and do away with him. Fourth, as Doherty suggests, he was a man broken in body and spirit, as had been made manifest at his abdication at Kenilworth in January. Since then, he had suffered the miseries of imprisonment. He had lost his throne, his wife, his children, and his liberty, and he was doubtless still grieving for Despenser. And last, in adversity, his thoughts may well have turned to the solace of religion, which perhaps prompted a desire to abandon earthly things and withdraw from the world. Support for this theory might be found in the poems attributed to Edward, which are preoccupied with contrition for his sins, the abandonment of a "baser part," and the hope of redemption through Christ.

Fieschi is not the first writer to connect Edward with Corfe. Both Baker and Murimuth erroneously allege that the King was taken to Corfe on his way to Berkeley, and the Dunheved plotters are alleged to have installed him there after abducting him from Berkeley, while yet another plot, some way in the future, would also place him there. It is perhaps significant that Dorset was the first county on the list of those of which Berkeley and Maltravers were appointed commissioners of the peace.

Corfe Castle was a massive Norman fortress that commanded—and still commands—a spectacular position on a high ridge overlooking a ravine and valley. The Saxon King, Edward the Martyr, had been murdered there in 979, but the present castle had been built by the Normans and steadily enlarged over the centuries. It was a royal stronghold, technically under the control of Isabella and Mortimer, but the evidence we have suggests that it was a hotbed of dissidents who cared little for their oaths of allegiance and were affiliated to the Dunheved group. Furthermore, there is so much that links Edward II to Corfe that there is a strong possibility that he must have been there at some time, perhaps after his alleged escape in September.

However, the reference to "Lord Thomas," the castellan of Berkeley, is puzzling. There is no record of any "Lord Thomas" being appointed the custodian of Corfe; a John Deveril held the post in 1329, but the date of his appointment is not known. It is likely, therefore, that Fieschi has confused him with Thomas de Berkeley. Maltravers was indeed appointed custodian of Corfe Castle, but not until 24 September 1329. Whoever the castellan was, he must have been a party to the escape plot, and he could easily have concealed Edward's presence after Maltravers became custodian in 1329, because no one would have been looking for the former King, since most people believed him dead; anyway, who would have taken much notice of a lowly hermit, even if he did show himself in public?

If Edward did go immediately to Corfe and remained there a year and a half, he would have arrived probably in the late autumn of 1327 and left in the spring of 1329. But, according to Fieschi, he did not leave Corfe until after he heard that Kent had been executed, which was in March 1330. It is possible that either Edward or Fieschi got their dates or time spans wrong, or that Edward did not go directly to Corfe but remained in hiding in various places to begin with. His being at Corfe in March 1330 would account for Fieschi's reference to Maltravers's being its custodian.

If he left Corfe in the spring of 1330, then spent nine months in Ireland, Edward would have returned to England in the early months of 1331, at which time he would have known that it was now safe to do so. And if he arrived at Sluys in the spring of that year, then traveled down to Avignon via Normandy and the Languedoc, a distance of about 650 miles, the shortest time it could have taken him would have been just over two months, assuming that he traveled about ten miles each day and did not linger. He was therefore in Avignon in the summer or early autumn of 1331. He then traveled north to Paris, a distance of approximately 380 miles, and on to Cologne, another 250 miles. Given that travel in winter was very difficult in the Middle Ages, it would be safe to say that he did not reach Cologne until the early spring of 1332 at the earliest. Edward then traveled at least 375 miles south to Milan, arriving there perhaps in the late summer of 1332. He stayed in the first hermitage for two and a half years, until early 1336, and the second for two years, until early 1338. The timings given above for Edward's journey are purely conjectural, of course, and do not allow for his staying for long at certain places or taking a more leisurely pace. They are merely to demonstrate that the earliest date on which the Fieschi letter could have been written was in early 1336.

The last dated document in the episcopal register in which the Fieschi letter was found is from 1337, and there are further undated documents that could belong to a later period, so it is perfectly possible for the Fieschi letter to belong to 1336 or later.[150] Although it could have been written as late as 1343, the year in which Fieschi became Bishop of Vercelli, the likeliest date, as we will see, was early 1337.

Who brought Edward III this letter? In 1336, when Edward II could have been living at Melazzo, Cardinal Nicolinus de Fieschi, a kinsman of Manuele, brought the King letters from Genoa. One contained a request for compensation for the booty stolen by Despenser in his pirating days. The Genoese had tried without success to obtain this in 1329, yet it may be significant that their request was now granted—Edward III paid out 8,000 marks in July 1336.[151] Could it be that the Cardinal had also brought the King information as to the whereabouts of his father and the hope of making contact with him? This would account for the abrupt opening of the Fieschi letter and the lack of any explanatory preamble or attempt to convince Edward III that the man who had made the confession was really his father. And it may have been Nicolinus who came back early the following year with Manuele's letter, after Manuele had had time to visit Edward II and hear his confession, which may have been divulged in the course of several meetings.

Why did Edward visit the Pope? Obviously, he would have wanted the spiritual leader of Christendom to know the truth, and he may well have sought spiritual guidance and advice as to his future.

The locations in Lombardy mentioned in the letter have been identified as Melazzo d'Acqui and Cecima sopra Voghera, and the second hermitage as the abbey of Sant' Alberto di Butrio.[152] The castle of Melazzo is a small, hilltop fortress forty-five miles north of Genoa, and modern plaques there record Edward II's escape and Fieschi's letter. Cecima is a walled Apennine village, about fifty miles northeast of Genoa. The Romanesque abbey of Sant' Alberto, built around 1065, is nearby in an isolated spot,[153] an ideal retreat for someone wishing to withdraw from the world and keep his identity secret. Sadly, most of its medieval records were lost before the sixteenth century.

Why should Edward II choose these places for a refuge? First, they were remote and a long way from England. Second, he may have heard of them from Fieschi when he visited Avignon, probably in 1331. Or third, the Pope might have suggested that he go there.

It is noticeable that Fieschi does not say whether Edward II is still alive, only that he had been in the last hermitage for two years. Possibly he was still there when the letter was written, for in the penultimate paragraph, the text could be translated either as "he remained in this last hermitage for two years" or as "he has remained," etcetera. A local tradition persists that an English king sought refuge at Cecima and was buried in the nearby abbey, but it cannot be traced back further than the nineteenth century. In the church of Sant' Alberto di Butrio, there is an empty tomb carved out of rock that is alleged to be Edward's. A modern plaque above it proclaims that this was

THE FIRST TOMB OF EDWARD II, KING OF ENGLAND.
HIS BONES WERE TAKEN BY EDWARD III AND
TRANSPORTED TO ENGLAND AND REBURIED
IN THE TOMB AT GLOUCESTER.

However, the carvings on the tomb that gave rise to this identification, which are said to depict Edward II, Isabella, and Mortimer, have been proved to date from the early thirteenth century or earlier, and the tomb itself is probably eleventh-century.[154] This is not to say, however, that it did not at one time hold the body of Edward II.

Of course, if Edward II was buried in Italy, who, then, was buried in his tomb in what is now Gloucester Cathedral? The obvious candidate, as Fieschi says, was the porter he slew on his way out of Berkeley Castle. How did Edward know about the substitution of the porter's body? He probably guessed, for he surely would have got to hear of the inspection of a body by local officials and its burial at Gloucester. The tomb there was opened for two hours in October 1855. Immediately below the base of the chest, there was an outer wooden coffin, "quite sound." This was partially opened, revealing an inner one of thick lead, encasing a body, which was left undisturbed, so that the body was not seen.[155] There were no signs of any earlier interference with the tomb, but that does not rule out the possibility of its having been opened before, to facilitate yet another substitution of a body. The likelihood of this having happened will be discussed in due course, in chapter 11.

What do we know of Fieschi? A scion of a powerful Genoese family and a career clergyman, he was a distant but acknowledged relative of the English royal House, had long enjoyed close links with England, and held several English benefices. He was known to, and was perhaps a friend of, Richard de Bury, Edward III's former tutor. Fieschi was granted his first benefice, at Salisbury, in 1319[156] and another, at Ampleforth, in June 1329. Soon afterward, he became a canon of Liège in the Low Countries. In December 1329, he was appointed a canon of Salisbury Cathedral and Archdeacon of Nottingham. By August 1330, he was working at the papal Curia at Avignon and at some stage served as the Pope's collector of taxes in Lombardy. In December 1331, he exchanged his archdeaconry at Nottingham for a more lucrative benefice in the diocese of Lincoln. His attestations of letters of attorney show that he was in England from 1333 to 1335, when he returned to Italy. In April 1342, Edward III authorized his retention of the benefices at Salisbury and Ampleforth. In 1343, the Pope appointed Fieschi as Bishop of Vercilli in northern Italy, which gave him ecclesiastical jurisdiction over the region in which Melazzo and Cecima were situated. He died in 1348. Given his distinguished career, and the positions of trust he occupied, he does not appear to have been the type of man who would fabricate such a story, nor the kind of person who could have been deceived by an imposter or madman, however extraordinarily well informed.[157]

Tout, who could detect in the Fieschi letter none of the usual characteristics of a medieval forgery, suggested that it was an attempt on the part of a Francophile clergyman to discredit Edward III after he had scored victories over France in the Hundred Years' War. But if the letter was written in early 1337, Edward III had yet to claim the French Crown, and he would win no victories until 1340.

Doherty points out that Fieschi received three of his church appointments from Isabella and Mortimer but asks why they should show such exceptional favor to a foreign clergyman. The answer probably lies in Fieschi's ties of kinship to Edward III and in the Queen's desire to maintain her good relations with the Papacy. I am not convinced that these appointments were bribes to persuade Fieschi to support Isabella and Mortimer's case against Kent at the papal court, as Doherty suggests, because when Ampleforth was granted to Fieschi in June 1329, Kent's conspiracy was several months in the future, and no one could have predicted the outcome. Furthermore, Edward III continued to patronize Fieschi after he assumed power in 1330, although that patronage ceased after there was an outcry over the granting of benefices to absentee foreigners, which is probably why Fieschi left England in 1335. Doherty has suggested that Fieschi's letter was an attempt to blackmail Edward into restoring his revenues: if he did not pay up, Fieschi would make public the contents of Edward II's confession.

But his letter, sent "in the name of God," does not read like a blackmail threat. Nor did Edward III apparently respond to it as such, for there is no record of Fieschi's receiving any further church appointments in England in the years left to him; all Edward did, in 1342, was confirm him in the two benefices he already held. The evidence we have looked at, and some that will be scrutinized later, overwhelmingly suggests that the Fieschi letter was written in 1337. So if it was an attempt at blackmail, why did Edward III wait five years before responding? And what did Fieschi gain from it?

It is significant that Fieschi had lived in England and had actually seen Edward II, his kinsman. Had they met in Italy, he would surely have recognized the King. Edward III was also his kinsman, and Fieschi would have been ideally placed to be chosen by the father as an emissary to the son. His background and the blood tie were impeccable credentials. These are compelling reasons for believing that the Fieschi letter was genuine, and we should not discount the possibility that it was sent simply because Edward II wanted his son to know that he was alive and was praying for him, and had therefore forgiven him. It was in no way a threat to Edward III's security as King.

All things considered, we cannot just dismiss the evidence in the Fieschi letter as being of no consequence, because so many factors point to its being genuine that there must therefore be a strong possibility that it is. In which case, there can be no question of Isabella's being held responsible for the murder of her husband, because no murder actually took place. And, as we will discover in due course, there is even more evidence to support this theory.

From 21 September until its burial on 20 December, a man called William Beaukaire watched over the body at Berkeley.[158] This suggests that the corpse was eviscerated, embalmed, and wrapped in waxed linen cerecloth within hours of the death. This task was carried out not by a royal physician or apothecary, as was usual, but by a local wise woman, probably a midwife— who was perhaps the only person available, and who would probably not have recognized Edward II if she saw him. The heart was removed and placed in a silver casket costing 37s. 8d., which would be sent by Berkeley to the widowed Queen as a memento mori, a practice that was by no means unusual in those days. Berkeley charged the cost of the embalming and the casket to the Royal Wardrobe.[159] Once it had been cered, the corpse was probably laid on a bier in the tiny chapel of Saint John within the castle, where Berkeley, on his return, arranged for Masses to be sung for the soul of the departed.[160]

William Beaukaire was a royal sergeant at arms who had been an adherent of the Despensers and had helped to defend Caerphilly Castle against Isabella's forces. After its fall, he had become reconciled to the new regime, and, perhaps because of his earlier affiliation to Edward II, and the fact that he had yet to prove his loyalty to Edward III, he had been chosen to watch over the body to ensure that no one inspected it too closely for marks of violence. What is remarkable about this is that Beaukaire was at Berkeley on the day of the murder, which suggests that Mortimer had sent him there, knowing that Edward would be killed that day. Beaukaire had probably accompanied Ockle and been furnished with instructions to guard the body and let no one inspect it until the embalming process had been completed.[161]

Assuming that Edward II had escaped, and that Maltravers and Gurney knew about the substituted body, how did they hoodwink Beaukaire? They may have risked taking him into their confidence, for Beaukaire had once been Despenser's man and might have rejoiced to learn of Edward's escape. Or, more probably, they made sure that the body was embalmed and wrapped in cerecloth before he saw it. There was, however, to be no rush to bury the body with unseemly haste. As was normal when a royal personage died, there would be a considerable time lapse between the death and the funeral.

Of course, when Lord Berkeley returned—and there is no record of when this was, although he was probably summoned urgently—he must have been told by Maltravers what had happened, since he was later to deny all knowledge of Edward II's having died.[162] Because the escape of his important prisoner reflected so badly upon him, and would probably have led to severe reprisals if discovered, he kept quiet.

Although "friends and kin of the dead King were kept well away" from Berkeley,[163] Murimuth states that "many persons—abbots, priors, knights, burgesses of Bristol and Gloucester—were summoned to view the body, and indeed superficially examined it, standing far off." There has been much speculation as to what the word *superficially* indicates. It may mean that these people were not allowed to get close enough to the body to see it properly. Or, which is more likely, it meant that the body had already been embalmed and, as Ian Mortimer convincingly argues, even had its face covered with cerecloth, as Edward I's was proved to have had when his tomb was opened in 1774.[164] We do not even know how long after the death this inspection took place. Whatever the truth, it is certain that no one who "inspected" that body would have been able to pronounce definitively on the cause of death and likely that few of these local dignitaries would have been able to recognize the dead man, even if his face had been exposed. "Nevertheless," continues Murimuth, "it was commonly said that [Edward II] was cunningly slain as a precaution by the orders of Sir John Maltravers and Sir Thomas Gurney."

Edward II's murder or escape must have taken place in the early hours of 21 September, because less than three days later, during the night of 23 September, Sir Thomas Gurney arrived at Lincoln, 130 miles away, and privately informed Edward III and Queen Isabella that the former King had died.[165] Isabella probably received the news with mingled sadness, regret, and overwhelming relief, for any threat to her son's rule and her own power had now been removed, as well as the fear that public opinion might one day force her to return to her husband.

We have no means of knowing whether she asked herself how a strong man of forty-three had so conveniently died, and who might have been responsible. If so, she did not voice any of these concerns in public. Yet there is some evidence, which will be examined in the next chapter, that she was perturbed about the nature of her husband's death. It is very unlikely that Mortimer would have entrusted to a messenger or letter details of his plot to murder the King, so the Queen would have had no means as yet of knowing what was supposed to have happened at Berkeley. Nor is it certain that Mortimer ever did reveal to Isabella his part in Edward II's fate. There was undoubtedly a conspiracy of silence surrounding the events of 21 September, and he certainly felt that the fewer people who knew about it, the better. Edward had been the father of Isabella's children, and there was always the risk that she might feel that Mortimer had gone too far this time. Regicide was a terrible crime, and the knowledge that Mortimer had committed it might conceivably serve to alienate Isabella from him.

Soon after hearing the news of his father's death, Edward III wrote an unemotional letter to his cousin, John de Bohun, Earl of Hereford, stating only that Edward II had been "commended to God."[166] We may infer from later evidence, however, that he was shocked and horrified to hear of his father's death and that he immediately suspected that the absent Mortimer had in some way been responsible.[167]

Gurney was sent back to Berkeley with instructions to withhold any information about the fate of Edward II until 1 November.[168] This in itself suggests that Isabella wanted time in which to establish what had really happened. Had Mortimer found some way of informing her, they would surely have had a strategy planned already. In the meantime, Edward III was allowed a few days to grieve in private while the Queen debated what to do next. It was not until 28 September, the last day of the Lincoln Parliament, that the former King's death was publicly announced; it was claimed that his demise was "an accident destined by fate"[169] and that he had died on the feast day of Saint Matthew the Apostle and Evangelist, 21 September. This may have been as much as Mortimer was prepared to tell Isabella, at least in a message carried by a third party. The last day for which Berkeley and Maltravers claimed the daily allowance for Edward's maintenance was 21 September. Thereafter, until 21 October, they were allocated the same amount for taking care of the corpse.[170]

On 28 September, after Parliament had adjourned, the court left Lincoln for Nottingham, arriving there two days later.[171] The next day, 1 October, Edward II's death was officially proclaimed. Mortimer had rejoined the court before 4 October, when he witnessed a charter at Nottingham.[172]

In October, the envoys arrived back in England with the papal dispensation. Orleton returned to a row with Isabella and Mortimer, because, in defiance of their orders, he had accepted from the Pope the vacant See of Worcester, for which they had already approved a candidate. Orleton seems to have presumed on their friendship and gratitude but been sadly mistaken. For several months, he was to be out of favor.

On 8 October, a new embassy headed by Roger Northburgh, Bishop of Lichfield, was sent to Hainault to draw up the marriage contract and perform the proxy ceremony.[173] The Bishop was also empowered to inform Count William officially of Edward II's demise and to assure him that he had "died naturally." Throughout October and November, Isabella and Edward III were busy making preparations for Philippa's arrival. Edward commanded "his beloved Bartholemew de Burghersh, Constable of Dover, to receive and welcome into his kingdom that noble person, William, Count of Hainault, with the illustrious damsel Philippa, his daughter; and he charges all and singular his nobility and people of the counties through which [they] may pass, to do them honour and give them needful aid."[174] Several modern historians assert that the marriage had been arranged to divert the young King and his subjects from dwelling on Edward II's murder, but of course, it had been arranged long before September. Certainly, the prospect of welcoming his bride would have helped to ease Edward III's grief and, perhaps, his conscience.

On 9 October, a fourth set of commissioners was appointed to negotiate a peace with the Scots. Robert the Bruce was dying, and he knew it. His heir was a child of three, and he feared his kingdom would descend into anarchy after his death. He therefore needed to make peace with England on terms favorable to Scotland, and on 18 October, he responded positively to the overtures made by Isabella and Mortimer but stipulated that any settlement would depend on the English recognizing him as King of Scots "without any kind of subjection." He also demanded that Isabella's daughter Joan be married to his heir, David; that no Englishman lay claim to any land in Scotland; and that England would give military aid to Scotland if another country attacked her. In return, he offered £20,000 as compensation for his raids in the North, and Scottish aid against any enemy of England except France, his ally.[175]

These were draconian terms, and totally unacceptable to Lancaster, Henry de Beaumont, Lord Wake, and many of the anti-Scottish Lancastrian faction, who regarded them as being utterly dishonorable and humiliating to the English Crown. And while Isabella was concerned about the loyalty of these and other lords who stood to lose their Scottish lands, the young King was unhappy about the sovereignty issue; yet he approved of the offer of compensation and the marriage proposed for his sister, and on 20 October, the Queen sanctioned further peace talks with the Scots at Newcastle. Between November and the following February, both sides worked hard at hammering out a treaty that was mutually acceptable.

We have an insight into Isabella's state of mind at this time in a letter that she wrote on 10 October to John de Bohun, which is preserved in the Public Record Office. Bohun had evidently responded to the King's missive of 21 September with letters of condolence to both Edward and Isabella. The Queen's reply reveals that she had been deeply affected by her husband's death:

Most dear and beloved nephew,

We have well understood what you have sent us word of by letter, and as to our estate, we give you [to] know that we are even in great trouble of heart; but, considering the condition we are in, we were in good health of body at the setting forth of these letters, which Our Lord ever grant to you.

Dearest nephew, we pray you that you will leave off all excuses and come to the King our son in the best manner you can, and as he commands you more fully by his letters. For you well know, dearest nephew, if you come not, considering the necessity that now exists, it will be greatly talked of, and will be a great dishonour to you. Wherefore, make an effort to come at this time as hastily as you can, and you well know, dearest nephew, that we shall ever be ready to counsel you as well as we can in all things that shall be to your honour and profit.

Most dear and beloved nephew, Our Lord have you in His keeping.

Given at Nottingham, the 10th day of October.

If Isabella had been in any way responsible for the death of Edward II, she would hardly have confessed to being "in great trouble of heart" to Edward's own nephew. Anyone with a modicum of sensitivity would have realized that a queen who had led a rebellion against her husband and overthrown him, then kept him a prisoner and deprived him of her company and that of their children, however sound her motives, would have had good cause to suffer "great trouble of heart" on hearing of his death. Moreover, there is reason to believe, as we will discover, that Isabella had her own suspicions about Edward's fate and her lover's possible involvement in it. No wonder she was troubled.

Her letter reveals also her concern for her son, who was apparently grieving deeply for his father and had asked his cousin John to come to him. Isabella, well aware of the "necessity" of keeping up the boy's spirits and diverting him with good company, was virtually pleading with Bohun to attend her son, knowing that, although Bohun was well-meaning, he was also headstrong and not entirely reliable, having recently defied a royal ban on holding tournaments. Hence her pleas to him to come not only for the King's sake but for his own honor.

Several abbeys in the vicinity of Berkeley—notably, Saint Augustine's at Bristol, Saint Mary's at Kingswood, and Saint Aldhelm's at Malmesbury— refused to receive the body at Berkeley for burial, "for fear of Roger Mortimer and Queen Isabella and their accomplices,"[176] which suggests that monastic heads were fearful of receiving the corpse in case it was thought that they were still loyal to the former regime. Nor was the Queen willing to grant the petition of the monks of Westminster for Edward to be laid to rest with his forefathers in Westminster Abbey because he had not deserved it, having made too many errors as a ruler.[177] More to the point, perhaps, Westminster was too near London, London was still simmering with unrest, and the funeral would be too high-profile and excite too much interest. In the end, Mortimer's kinsman, Abbot Thoky of the Benedictine abbey of Saint Peter in Gloucester (now Gloucester Cathedral), which had been founded in 1070, offered to bury the King's body in his church.[178] According to local tradition, Edward had expressed a wish to be laid to rest here. Isabella was adamant that this was the best solution; in her view, Edward did not deserve to be buried at Westminster, and his interment at faraway Gloucester would serve to underline the fact that he had renounced his throne.[179]

On 21 October, Berkeley and Maltravers released the body to the Abbot of Gloucester, who came that day with his brethren to collect it. The corpse had been dressed in the late King's coronation robes, including his shirt, coif, and gloves,[180] and presumably encased in its two coffins. The monks covered the top coffin with a rich pall, then they placed it on a chariot lined with black canvas and conveyed it in solemn procession to Gloucester. The official escort was headed by a royal clerk, Hugh de Glanville,[181] and Berkeley, Maltravers, and members of their household rode behind the chariot, which was received at the city gates by the Mayor and burghers, who escorted it to the high altar of the abbey.[182] Here, the body was laid in state, and from now on, it would be guarded not just by William Beaukaire but also by four "knights of honour," the late King's chaplains and sergeants at arms, Andrew his candlemaker, and John de Eaglescliffe, Bishop of Llandaff.[183] The latter had been chosen by Isabella because he belonged to the Dominican order that Edward had so greatly favored, a kind gesture that, along with her gifts to Edward and her refusal to involve the Franciscans in his abdication, shows that she still retained some vestiges of affection for her husband.

On 21 October, Hugh de Glanville joined the knights who were watching over the bier; he would remain with them until 20 December. Glanville had been given responsibility for paying those staying with the corpse and also the funeral expenses; among his purchases were palls of expensive Turkey cloth and cloth of gold embroidered with the leopards of England, which were draped across the coffin.[184]

On 10 November, instructions were issued for the funeral of the late King, who was to be buried with full honors and ostentatious pageantry. A great deal of care and planning went into his funeral, and Isabella must have been fully involved. On the tenth, the court left Nottingham for Coventry.[185]

Baker claims that Isabella and Orleton planned to make Maltravers and Gurney scapegoats for the assassination of Edward II, so that they themselves would appear innocent. He says that the jailers, fearing this, produced Orleton's ambiguous letter, protesting that they had acted on his instructions. The Bishop, however, insisted that the letter had been "perfectly innocent and loyal in its meaning," and "it was the keepers who had misinterpreted it." He seems to have conveniently forgotten the other incriminating letters that Baker says had been sent at the same time. In fact, "he so terrified them with his threats that they fled." Maltravers, Gurney, and Ockle did not flee the country until Mortimer had been overthrown but were well rewarded for their services at Berkeley, probably at Mortimer's instigation. The Queen made a grant to Maltravers specifically for his services to her,[186] and it was at her request that Gurney was appointed Constable of Bristol Castle,[187] while Ockle became a squire in the young King's household.[188] Isabella later submitted a petition on Ockle's behalf, in an attempt to ward off his creditors.[189] It might be inferred from this that Isabella was now aware of the fate of Edward II and was eager to reward his assassins, but there is no proof that Mortimer had divulged to her that he had been murdered, and these rewards, which are not excessive by any means, could simply have been for good service to the deposed King.

On 16 November, Archbishop Reynolds died, "of grief and horror of mind," it was said, for having abandoned the cause of Edward II and helped to depose him.[190] This may be a fantasy, for in his will, the Archbishop left gifts to the Queen and John of Eltham.[191] Isabella and Mortimer now put forward to the Pope their loyal supporter Henry Burghersh, who had succeeded Hotham as Chancellor in July, as their candidate for the vacant primacy, but Lancaster and his faction were wary of the Queen and her lover controlling Canterbury as well as everything else and practiced on the cathedral chapter to choose the weak and undistinguished Simon Meopham. To the Queen's chagrin, Meopham was elected on 11 December.[192] The rigging of this election is the first sign of a growing rift between Lancaster and Isabella and Mortimer, and it had probably been sparked by the ignominious defeat in Weardale and the Queen's determination to make peace with the Scots. There is no evidence that, at this time, there was widespread outrage at the supposed murder of Edward II and that Lancaster shared it.

On 20 November, Bartholemew, Lord Burghersh, and William, Lord Clinton, who had recently been rewarded for his services to Queen Isabella,[193] were commissioned to escort Philippa of Hainault to England; they left for the Low Countries on the twenty-eighth.[194] On 22 November, Mortimer received yet another grant, of the manor of Church Stretton in Shropshire, "in consideration of his services to Queen Isabella and the King, here and beyond seas."[195]

The court was still at Coventry on 10 December, when writs were issued for Parliament to meet at York on 7 February,[196] and arrived at Gloucester on 19 December for the late King's funeral.[197]

On 20 December, the body believed to be that of Edward II was buried in Saint Peter's Abbey, Gloucester, with such pomp and circumstance that it would have been easy to forget the King had been overthrown. The true purpose of this royal and extremely public funeral was probably to underline how very properly Isabella and Mortimer had behaved toward the deposed King, to help restore the status of the monarchy, and to preempt the claims of any would-be pretenders, and possibly one pretender in particular.

The body was carried through the streets of Gloucester on a magnificent hearse drawn by horses displaying the royal arms of England. The canopied hearse, which had been specially made in London, bore a carved and painted wooden effigy of the King in his royal robes and a copper-gilt crown, the first such effigy ever to have been recorded at a royal funeral. This was an innovation, because prior to 1327, it was the embalmed body, rather than an effigy, that was borne on the bier,[198] which in itself suggests that something was now amiss. The conveyance rested on the backs of gilded wooden lions and was decorated with carved images of the four Evangelists and eight angels, all painted with gold leaf. Edward III and

Queen Isabella followed the coffin as chief mourners, Isabella making, it was said, an excessive show of widowhood. Mortimer also walked in the procession, wearing a black tunic he had ordered for the occasion.[199] The streets were packed with crowds, which had been anticipated, for solid oak barriers had been erected to hold them back. Before and after the committal in the north aisle by the high altar in the abbey, the funeral and requiem Masses were respectively celebrated.[200]

By now, the whole country knew of the death of Edward II, yet not one voice had publicly challenged the official claim that he had died of natural causes nor protested about the treatment meted out to him since his abdication. He had been deeply unpopular, and his few supporters had either been neutralized or gone to ground.

After 1330, Edward III ordered a magnificent tomb of Purbeck marble carved in the Decorated style to be built in memory of his father. On it was laid a beautiful effigy of precious alabaster that was perhaps modeled on the wooden effigy carried at the funeral and that may be a stylized attempt at an actual portrait, for the sculptor was almost certainly the same man who was responsible for John of Eltham's tomb in Westminster Abbey, and both effigies have a protruding lower lip. The use of the same sculptor for father and son suggests that it was the Queen who ordered both effigies. Edward II's, which depicts him wearing his crown and holding a scepter, was almost certainly intended to emulate the French royal gisants at Saint-Denis, and in this also we can perhaps detect Isabella's influence, for she would certainly have been familiar with them. Above the tomb was raised a pinnacled double canopy of ogee arches, the first one ever raised above an English royal tomb.

As with Thomas of Lancaster, Edward II's reputation was gradually rehabilitated after, and perhaps because of, his supposed death; during the abbacy of John de Wigmore, who was elected in 1329, there began to be reports of miracles being performed at Edward's tomb and calls for this distinctly unsaintly man to be made a saint.[201] The Meaux chronicler observed tartly that no amount of visitors to the tomb, or miracles performed there, could make Edward a saint because of the wickedness of his life.

Nevertheless, with the numbers of visitors increasing, Edward's tomb was designed primarily as a shrine, and niches were provided for praying pilgrims. Multitudes flocked there, and so much money was raised through offerings that the Abbot was able to rebuild the south transept in the new

Perpendicular style.[202] In 1343, Edward III and Philippa of Hainault visited the tomb as pilgrims,[203] and their grandson, Richard II, whose white hart badge appears on Edward II's tomb, petitioned the Pope several times for Edward II's cannonization. He was unsuccessful, but the cult of the "murdered King" persisted for more than two centuries and was only suppressed at the Reformation.

CHAPTER TEN

Now, Mortimer,
Begins Our Tragedy

Isabella did not linger long in Gloucester after the funeral. The court left the next day for Tewkesbury and spent Christmas at Worcester, staying there until at least 28 December. During the festive season, Isabella made over Wallingford Castle to Mortimer.

According to the account he later submitted to the Exchequer, Hugh de Glanville remained at Gloucester for four days after the funeral, then traveled north to Worcester, arriving there on 26 December. With him was the woman who had embalmed the late King, whom he had secretly brought to Worcester on the Queen's orders. Glanville stayed for one day only at Worcester, then went on to York. We know about this episode because the Exchequer clerks later queried why Glanville had taken as long as seven days to travel from Gloucester to York, at which point he had to tell them that he had gone via Worcester, and why.[1]

Isabella's desire to meet the embalmer suggests that there were doubts in her mind concerning the fate of Edward II and that she suspected that Mortimer had not told her the whole truth about it. An alternative theory, that she did know about the murder and was worried in case the woman knew too much and might talk, is less likely since Isabella also would have known that Maltravers, Gurney, and Ockle were in possession of the same sensitive information. Furthermore, they received rewards for their services—

rewards, it should be pointed out, that were a matter of public knowledge, yet hardly generous enough to buy their silence. Of course, it is possible that Isabella wished to thank this woman in person for her discretion, and perhaps to intimidate her into keeping her mouth shut, but there is no record of her benefiting.

Isabella probably summoned the woman because she had private doubts that her husband really had died a natural death and hoped to be reassured by the one person who would have had good reason to know. It was doubtless to avoid Mortimer's finding out what she was doing that she ordered Glanville to bring the woman secretly to her. If the body she had embalmed had been the real Edward II, the likelihood is that he had been suffocated, which would have left hardly any mark. Yet the corpse could have been that of the unfortunate porter, and while we do not know how Edward is supposed to have killed him, it could well have been by suffocation, to prevent him from crying out and thus bringing the guards running. It is highly unlikely that the embalmer would have found burn marks inside the body because the stories about the red-hot spit were almost certainly invented. Therefore, we may assume that, on all counts, the woman was able to reassure the Queen that the King had died naturally.

Glanville also brought Isabella the silver casket containing what she believed to be her late husband's heart. It was reported later that she received it with sorrow.

Meanwhile, on 23 December, Philippa of Hainault had arrived in England and the next day made a state entry into London, where she was received with "great rejoicings" and "rich display," and lodged at Ely Place, Bishop Hotham's town residence in Holborn.[2] The citizens were impressed with this "full feminine" thirteen-year-old girl,[3] who represented a lucrative trade treaty with the prosperous Low Countries. For three days, they feasted her, danced, caroled, and jousted, then presented her with a gift of plate worth 300 marks, and the celebrations in London went on for three weeks after her departure on 28 December.[4] Escorted by the King's cousin, John de Bohun, Earl of Hereford and High Constable of England, Philippa began the long journey north, along roads deep in snow and mud, to meet up with her bridegroom. She was at Peterborough on 1 January 1328. Four days later, the court was at Nottingham. It then moved north via Rothwell and Knaresborough[5] to York, arriving there on 20 January.[6]

Three days later, the King rode out of the city to greet his new Queen. Isabella looked on as he took Philippa "by the hand, and then embraced and kissed her." Side by side, the happy young couple led the cavalcade back into York to the joyous sound of "great plenty of minstrelsy," to be greeted by many lords "in fair array." Then Edward escorted Philippa to the Queen Mother's lodgings, where she was to stay in Isabella's care until the wedding.[7] In the midst of a blizzard, the young couple were married in York Minster on 30 January, with Archbishop Melton officiating and Hotham assisting. It was freezing cold, as the choir was only partially roofed, but the ceremony was splendid and well attended.[8]

Afterward, the young couple returned to the lodging that had been made ready for them in the Archbishop's palace,[9] which stood on the site now occupied by Dean's Park. Because it would soon be Lent, a season during which the devout were supposed to abstain from sexual intercourse, Edward and Philippa delayed making any "display of marriage" but remained quietly in York until after Easter, when they consummated their union and celebrated it with three weeks of feasting, dancing, jousting, and revelry. Strickland claims that these marriage festivities were an attempt by Isabella to divert public attention from the death of Edward II, but if this was so, why had Edward been accorded such a lavish state funeral? Moreover, it would have been natural for the Queen to wish to bring some cheer to her son after he had lost his father.

Despite Edward's later passing infidelities, this was to be one of the most successful of royal marriages. Philippa was kindly, amiable, and maternal; she also dressed royally and looked every inch a queen, despite being inclined to plumpness. Edward evidently adored her. Like Isabella before her, she was to gain a reputation as a peacemaker and remained hugely popular with the English. Never, wrote Froissart, "since the days of Queen Guinevere," had so good a queen come to England, "nor any who had so much honour. And as long as she lived, the realm enjoyed grace, prosperity, honour and all good fortune."

For the time being, however, Philippa's role would be largely subordinate to that of her mother-in-law. She was not given an independent household as Queen of England but was expected to share the King's. Nor was she assigned any dower, since the Queen Consort's dower lands, which were meant to be held by her only during the lifetime of her husband, were firmly in the hands of Isabella. Nor were arrangements made for Philippa's coronation.

By any standards, Philippa had been slighted, and one may speculate that the root cause lay in Isabella's resentment or jealousy of the young girl who had supplanted her as Queen Consort. Philippa had everything Isabella had lost, or never enjoyed—youth, a handsome husband who loved her, and what looked set to be a glorious life ahead—whereas Isabella was now thirty-two, which was quite middle-aged in the fourteenth century, and her famous beauty was probably fading. At Philippa's age, she had been married to a man who ignored her, and her youthful efforts to establish a happy marriage had come to nothing, while that union had ended in cruelty, rebellion, and death. She had Mortimer's love, or at least shared his bed, but she could not acknowledge him publicly as her lover, and as his wife was still living, she could not marry him. But what probably mattered to Isabella most now was her relationship with her son, which was so essential for the maintenance of her power, and Philippa represented a threat to that, for as Edward's beloved wife, she would be able to influence him in ways that his mother never could. The solution, therefore, was to keep Philippa firmly in the background and deprive her of any means of exercising patronage.

On 1 February, Charles IV died prematurely at Vincennes. His death brought to an end the male line of the Capetians, which had descended from father to son since 987, but he left a pregnant widow, and until the sex of her child could be known, Charles's cousin, Philip of Valois, acted as regent of France.

Mortimer joined Isabella at York on 4 February.[10] Just over a week later, the regency council was meeting daily in the interests of promoting accord between the magnates,[11] which was necessary because tempers were rising high over the proposed peace with Scotland, which was proving deeply unpopular. Yet Isabella and Mortimer were determined to have their way.

On 1 March, because his mother insisted on it, a glowering Edward III appeared in Parliament in York and publicly acknowledged Scotland's independence. Afterward, a new embassy was commissioned to treat with Robert the Bruce in drawing up a peace treaty.[12] That same day, Hotham resigned as Chancellor, and news of Charles IV's death reached the English court. The latter must have occasioned Isabella much sorrow, for now all her siblings were dead, and Charles had been a constant support to her over the years. His death meant that Isabella was the last surviving child of Philip IV, and grief did not blind her to the fact that her son was now Charles's nearest male relative. In her view, should Jeanne of Evreux bear a daughter, the French throne should go to Edward III.

Orleton was now back in favor; the Queen and Mortimer had realized they valued his support too much to lose it, and early in March, after he had satisfactorily answered questions in Parliament about his acceptance of the See of Worcester, he at last received its temporalities.

The kingdom now seemed to be settling down at last, and Isabella seized this first opportunity she had had of snatching a few weeks away with Mortimer. On 2 March, the King ordered the sheriffs to render his mother all possible assistance during her coming progress throughout the realm,[13] and from 3 March to 21 April, Isabella and Mortimer were absent from court.[14] There is no record of where they went. On the day of their departure, Mortimer's nominee, Sir John Maltravers, was appointed Steward of the Household to the Queen in place of Lancaster's man, John, Lord Ros.[15] The fact that Maltravers held the post for just over a week suggests that his appointment was merely a means of ousting the Lancastrian. This was another crack in the facade of friendship between Isabella and Lancaster.

On 17 March, Robert I sealed the formal peace treaty with England at Edinburgh. Despite lengthy negotiations, the claims of English lords who held land in Scotland were expressly excluded, which led to these unfortunate peers' becoming known as "the Disinherited."

Charles IV's widow had not yet given birth, but on 28 March, doubtless primed by Isabella but needing no encouragement, Edward III announced that he intended "to recover his rightful inheritance," the Crown of France, which he would be claiming through his mother.[16] Both Edward and Isabella were to argue that the Salic law did not prevent a woman from transmitting a claim, and that, rather than going to a cousin of the late King, the Crown should pass to his nephew, who was nearer in blood. But on 8 April, after Queen Jeanne had borne a daughter, the French peers assembled at Paris chose Philip of Valois as their king. He was proclaimed Philip VI on 14 April.

Isabella and Mortimer had arrived at Stamford by 21 April,[17] and Mortimer went ahead the same day to Northampton,[18] where Parliament assembled three days later. Isabella was still in Stamford on the twenty-sixth and held a council meeting there at the end of the month, which Mortimer attended. Then they both traveled to Northampton, arriving before 3 May.[19]

Meanwhile, Parliament had approved the Treaty of Northampton, which Robert I had sealed in Edinburgh.[20] This treaty conceded to the Scots everything they had fought for—chiefly, the right to sovereign independence and recognition of Robert the Bruce as King of Scots. It also renounced any claims to English overlordship over Scotland, claims that had been pressed by nearly every English king since the Conquest, and the rights of any English lords to lands in Scotland. The treaty was to be cemented by the marriage of the Princess Joan to David Bruce. In return, as he had promised, Bruce undertook to give England aid against any enemy except the French and to pay compensation of £20,000 for the losses caused by his savage raids of the North. The treaty was ratified by a reluctant Edward III on 4 May, and the next day, the peace with Scotland was proclaimed in London.[21]

There was an outcry. People called it "the shameful peace," whereby Edward III, "through the false counsel of traitors," had been "fraudulently disinherited" of Scotland.[22] The young King, who had been powerless to resist the determination of his mother and Mortimer, was outraged at having been forced to agree to this humiliating settlement, and horrified at the selling of his sister,[23] while Lancaster objected that the treaty had been passed without the consent of the King or the realm.[24] The Disinherited were particularly appalled.

The King made no secret of the fact that he was passionately opposed to making peace and wanted nothing to do with the treaty, even publicly declaring that "the Queen and Mortimer had arranged the whole thing."[25] Through their counsel, he had been obliged to give up "the kingdom of Scotland, for which realm the King's ancestors had full sore travail, and so had died many a nobleman for the right."[26]

Because of the Treaty of Northampton, the popularity of Isabella and Mortimer evaporated virtually overnight. How, people asked, could they have conceded so much to a man whom most Englishmen regarded as a war criminal? There were even wild rumors that Mortimer had made concessions to the Scots in exchange for their aid in setting him up as King of England.[27] The Lanercost chronicler was nearer the mark when he claimed that Edward III, "acting on the pestilent advice of his mother and Roger Mortimer," had been forced to agree to the treaty in order to pursue his claims to France.

Yet in major respects, the Treaty of Northampton was a successful piece of policy making, for it released England from a hopeless and expensive war and brought peace to the North. Although the King and most of his subjects would have infinitely preferred one decisive push to conquer Scotland, bitter experience had shown that this was a fast-receding possibility, and the government could not afford it anyway, since Isabella and Mortimer had spent so lavishly that Edward II's treasure was now virtually exhausted. And as they had both argued in Parliament, peace was essential if there was to be a war with France.[28]

It was the Treaty of Northampton, rather than rumors that she had colluded in the murder of Edward II, that cost Isabella the goodwill of the people and lost her her allies. In fact, there is very little evidence that there was an upsurge of public feeling against Isabella after Edward's death or funeral. Certainly, there had been mounting disillusionment with her regime since the autumn of 1327, but it is clear that this resulted from the ignominious failure of the Weardale campaign.

It is clear, too, that, in 1328, Isabella and Lancaster became involved in an increasingly bitter rivalry for control of the King and the government. They had never been natural allies, despite their kinship, and had only been drawn together to make common cause against the Despensers. But from the time that Isabella had appropriated the Lincoln inheritance, relations between them had rapidly deteriorated. The Queen seems to have gone out of her way to provoke Lancaster and undermine his authority, and he, in turn, was to become one of her severest critics and would have ousted her from power if he could.

The affair of Sir Robert Holland graphically illustrates the impasse that was developing between the Queen and Lancaster. Originally a trusted adherent of Thomas of Lancaster, and much beholden to him for his wealth and advancement, Robert Holland had abandoned the Earl in 1322 and gone over to the King, a betrayal for which the present Earl of Lancaster had never forgiven him, for Holland's desertion had deprived Thomas of crucial support in the Midlands and led directly to his defeat. Even the royalists were appalled at such treachery, and Edward II had imprisoned Holland and confiscated his lands. In the Parliament of February 1327, in which Isabella and Mortimer were amicably collaborating with Lancaster, it had been decreed that he should not be restored to his estates, although he was pardoned for escaping from jail. In September 1327, Holland petitioned for the return of his lands at a time when Isabella was beginning to regard Lancaster as a threat to her position, and his petition was finally granted by Edward III, at her instance, in December.[29]

This was a sure indication that the alliance between Isabella and Lancaster was crumbling by the end of 1327. Lancaster resented being marginalized by Mortimer, and Isabella was aware that Lancaster, who was both influential and popular, had the potential and means to become a powerful and effective opponent. Determined to retain her monopoly of power, she dared not risk further eroding her popularity by forcing an open breach with the Earl, but she began to subvert his authority by subtle means and by excluding him and his faction from government.[30] After Holland's restoration, she deliberately extended her patronage to him and "did love him wonder much,"[31] a policy that was probably calculated not only to win over one of Lancaster's chief enemies but also to provoke the Earl to a quarrel and thus give her a pretext for ousting him from power.[32]

But Lancaster had other reasons for disapproving of Isabella's rule. She was greedy and avaricious—there can be no doubt about that. As we have seen, there were compelling reasons for her to seek financial security and the trappings of her status, but by any standards, her acquisitiveness was excessive and deserving of censure. It is also clear that, from the passing of the Treaty of Northampton in 1328, her integrity as a ruler became increasingly compromised and that this alienated most of her former allies.

But Isabella was in an impossible position. She had not led an invasion, overthrown a king, reestablished her authority, and set up her own government only to have it snatched away from her. What mattered to Isabella was retaining control over her son, with whom she certainly had a close relationship, as well as maintaining her status and influence, and keeping her lover; and doubtless she anticipated that she would remain the power behind the throne after the King had come of age. But with Lancaster and his faction maneuvering against her, she was in danger of losing all three. Therefore, her policies had of necessity to be directed toward bolstering her regime and discrediting her enemies. And that included controlling access to the King, appointing her own nominees to the high offices of state, and amassing enough wealth and territory to ensure that her power extended throughout the realm and that she was well equipped to cope with any crisis or threat to her political supremacy.

It also meant that the Queen resorted to underhanded measures such as excessive use of the King's Privy Seal in exercising patronage,[33] in order to maintain an affinity of support that could be called upon if necessary, and to the occasional subverting of justice in the interests of undermining her enemies.[34] And it meant building up the power of Mortimer, her chief ally and staunchest supporter, however unpopular he might be, and sidelining Lancaster and the rest of the regency council. Isabella was well aware that the Earl was the King's official guardian, while she herself was just his mother and had no formal role in the government. Lancaster could, if he wished, legally seize control of the King. And while Isabella was faced with that appalling and intolerable prospect, she was compelled to look to her own interests, and—as she doubtless sincerely believed, as a loving, possessive, and certainly manipulative mother—her son's, before the welfare of the kingdom.

In a bid to win approval, Isabella sponsored a statute to curb the endemic lawlessness in the country, a legacy of the weak rule of Edward II and the revolution that had overthrown him, and a matter of great grievance to many. Lancaster's influence can be detected in some of its provisions. Henceforth, the use of the Privy Seal would be restricted, and pardons and grants, which the Queen and Mortimer had certainly issued far too liberally,[35] would not be so easily obtainable; accused men would not be allowed to bring armed followers to court with them; justices of the peace had their powers extended; royal officials were to exercise fairness in the execution of their duties and maintain the King's peace at all times, and they would be under the supervision of justices invested with the power to punish those who defaulted.[36] These were eminently sensible measures, and Isabella was plainly determined to ensure that they were implemented.

Already she had made stringent efforts to curb unrest in London, through a subtle combination of threats, conciliatory gestures, and punitive measures such as temporarily removing the Exchequer and the Court of King's Bench to York for a time. The citizens were fierce defenders of their liberties and well aware of their power to influence the rest of the kingdom. Isabella knew that, although they had vigorously supported her in 1326–27, their allegiance was fickle and they might turn against her at a whim. Already, in October 1327, they had reelected the pro-Lancastrian Hamo de Chigwell as their Mayor. It had been necessary therefore to retain their approval while at the same time making it clear that violence and unrest would not be tolerated and in the process establishing the supremacy of the Crown.

Now, bending before public opinion, the Queen had shown herself zealous to reestablish law and order throughout the realm. For the next two years, she would issue a steady stream of commissions of oyer and terminer to her circuit judges, to assist them in their task of implementing the new statute. She had also instructed the sheriffs to forbid armed assemblies of men.[37] Isabella knew that a regime that could not enforce law and order was in danger of falling and that, having suffered years of misgovernment and unrest, the people of England would surely be grateful to those who had restored justice and peace within the realm. Again, she was demonstrating her understanding of the need to cultivate public opinion, and this statute was probably intended to counterbalance the catastrophic effects of the Treaty of Northampton. Unfortunately, for all the Queen's orders and fine words, within six months, there would be complaints that it was not being properly enforced, although this may not have been entirely her fault. Yet, as we will see, she herself was to undermine the integrity of the statute when she blatantly contravened its provisions.

Twice, before Parliament rose on 14 May, the King undertook to dower his wife within one year with lands and rents worth £15,000 per annum.[38] How he was to do this was problematical, since the Crown was virtually impoverished.

Of greater import was the Queen Mother's announcement that she intended to pursue her son's claim to the French throne, a resolve enthusi-

astically supported by Edward III and calculated to placate the English people, who felt their national honor had been disparaged by the peace with
Scotland. She had already had Edward write a letter to the Pope, in which
he acknowledged that his mother could not succeed to the French throne,
"as the kingdom of France was too great for a woman to hold by reason of
the imbecility [that is, weakness] of her sex," but that he wished to claim it
himself as Charles IV's nearest male relative. Isabella would have realized
that, if she had pressed her own claim, those of her brothers' daughters
would take precedence.

On 16 May, Bishops Orleton and Northburgh were sent to France to
demand officially that Edward III be recognized as its king.[39] Orleton
argued that Isabella could legitimately transmit her claim to her son since
no woman had ever been legally excluded from the French throne, for it
had never yet had occasion to pass to a female; furthermore, it could not be
denied that every feudal lordship in France could be inherited by a woman,
so why not the Crown? Nor, however, could it be denied that a thirty-five-
year-old man with experience in statecraft was infinitely preferable as a
ruler to a boy of fifteen in tutelage to his mother and her lover, and the
twelve peers of France, who were well aware of Isabella's dubious private
life, and utterly averse to the prospect of any English king sitting on
France's throne, "clean put out" Edward's claim, insisting that the throne of
France "was of such great noblesse that it ought not by succession to fall
into a woman's hand."[40] Nor did Isabella's efforts to secure the support of
the Gascon nobility bear fruit. The French lords prevailed, and Philip VI
was crowned on 29 May.

An incensed Isabella, who was still bent on pressing her son's claims but
was in no position to resort to military force, focused instead on seeking
allies in an attempt to undermine Philip, to whom she was thereafter to
refer disparagingly as "the foundling king," a nickname bestowed on him by
his enemies, the Flemings. She began cultivating the friendship of France's
neighbors, with Brabant, Gueldres, Bruges, Navarre, and Castile, and on
21 May, she opened negotiations for the marriage of her younger son, John,
now nearly twelve, and the daughter of the Castilian Lord of Biscay.[41]

On 24 May, Edward III arrived at Warwick, to be greeted by Lancaster, who
had come to discuss possible strategies for a war with France.[42]

Isabella had probably accompanied Mortimer to Hereford for the double wedding of his daughters, Joan and Katherine, to Audley's heir, James,
and Warwick's heir, Thomas de Beauchamp, respectively, which took place
on 31 May.[43] Afterward, Mortimer escorted his wife back to Ludlow. He

hardly ever saw Joan nowadays, and it appears that they were more or less estranged, although he did send her gifts of romances from time to time, and he did continue to have her arms engraved on his plate.[44] Isabella's movements are unrecorded at this time, so we may assume that she attended the wedding, for she was at nearby Worcester on 10 June. If so, it was probably at this time that she stayed as Mortimer's guest at Ludlow, either in the luxurious new chamber block adjoining the great hall, which he had built before 1320, or in the late thirteenth-century solar palace at the other end of the hall.

Ludlow Castle had come into Mortimer's hands through his marriage to Joan de Genville. Built in the twelfth century, it occupied a lofty position above the River Teme. Originally a great Marcher fortress, it was now a palatial residence offering the latest in domestic comforts. Mortimer could have shown Isabella the chapel he was building to Saint Peter ad Vincula in the outer ward of the castle, in thanksgiving for his escape from the Tower on the saint's feast day in 1323.[45] How Lady Mortimer reacted to the Queen's presence in her home is a matter for speculation.

From Warwick, the young King and Queen intended to make a leisurely progress south toward Woodstock, which would become one of Philippa's favorite residences. Their removal there represented a tactical withdrawal from the arrangements that were being made for the marriage of Edward's seven-year-old sister Joan to David Bruce, with which Isabella was now greatly preoccupied. Edward wanted nothing to do with the marriage and had already publicly announced that it did not have his blessing and that he would not be attending it.[46] Instead, he would remain with Philippa at Woodstock. This rare act of defiance testifies to the strength of his objections to the treaty. Isabella tried to persuade him to change his mind, even arranging a spear fight in Berwick as an incentive, but Edward was adamant, and she did not press the matter.

First, however, the King went to Worcester to meet up with his mother and Mortimer, who had arrived there by 10 June. The council was due to meet to discuss raising troops to send to Gascony in pursuance of the King's claim to France, but Lancaster, perhaps fearing that the views of the Queen would prevail, adamantly refused to proceed, on the grounds that insufficient councillors were present, and insisted that the discussion be postponed until the full council could be assembled. After five days of wrangling, the Queen conceded defeat on this issue, and the King summoned the lords to meet at York on 31 July.[47] Isabella arrived in York on 1 July.[48]

The Treaty of Northampton had provided for the return of the Stone of Scone to Scotland. Despite Edward's opposition, Isabella had every intention of taking it north with her when she went to Berwick for Joan's wedding, and at her insistence, on 1 July, the King reluctantly sent the Abbot of Westminster an order to deliver up the stone to the sheriffs of London, who were to "have it carried to the Queen of England, our very dear lady and mother, in whatever part of the north of England she may be."[49] Edward was being deliberately awkward and unhelpful, since he must have known full well where Isabella could be found. But the London mob were on his side and staged a demonstration, refusing to allow the Abbot to surrender the stone. Edward must have been delighted to receive his letter stating that he would not release it until the matter had been discussed further. So the Stone of Scone stayed at Westminster; Isabella evidently did not wish to further alienate her son by pressing for its removal.[50]

The Queen appointed her staunch ally Bishop Burghersh Chancellor on 2 July. At this time, nearly every high office was in the hands of her supporters,[51] but Burghersh was one of the most deserving, being "noble and wise in counsel, of great boldness, yet of polished manners, and singularly endowed with personal strength."[52] Furthermore, he would remain loyal to Isabella through crisis after crisis.

Early in July, Isabella and Mortimer, accompanied by a great retinue that included the Queen's younger children, Chancellor Burghersh, Bishops Airmyn and Orleton, and the Earl of Surrey, escorted the Princess Joan north to Berwick, where on the sixteenth, they witnessed her marriage to David Bruce, which was celebrated with considerable splendor.[53] Isabella financed her stay in the North by appropriating provisions that were meant for the Tower of London and the services of her son's purveyors;[54] this was just one example among many of her misuse of public funds.

On 22 July, after attending the magnificent entertainments hosted by the Scottish lords,[55] Isabella presented her daughter with numerous farewell gifts before formally handing her over to the Scots. Among these gifts was probably a precious manuscript, the Taymouth Hours, which dates from circa 1325–35[56] and has illustrations that are similar to those in Queen Mary's Psalter. The Taymouth Hours has four pictures of the Queen who either commissioned it or owned it: she is depicted at prayer during Mass, kneeling beneath a purple canopy in front of an open book that lies on a prie-dieu; at prayer before a vision of the Holy Ghost, with a bearded man beside her; kneeling with a king, keeping vigil as Christ agonizes in the Garden of Gethsemane; and, wearing her crown, being presented by the Virgin to the enthroned Christ.[57] This queen has been identified with either Isabella or her daughter Joan.[58] It has been suggested that Isabella commissioned the Taymouth Hours, with its French prayers, as a wedding gift for Joan.[59] If so, she must have hoped that her daughter would benefit from the spiritual and moral guidance it offered and follow the role models of the Virgin Mary and the chaste Diana the Huntress, as exemplified in its pages.

After the feasting was over, the Scottish lords took Joan and David to Cardross Castle to meet King Robert, who extended to Joan "a fair welcoming."[60] Hearing that Edward III had refused to attend the wedding, he, too, had stayed away,[61] so Isabella never met him.

Escorted for part of the way by Thomas Randolph, Earl of Moray, and Sir James Douglas, "the Black Douglas," who had famously tried to abduct her on two occasions, Isabella returned south with Mortimer, knowing that it would be a long time before she saw Joan again. It was being said in England that the Queen had "disparaged" the Princess by this "vile marriage,"[62] while the Scots gave their dowerless little Queen the derisory nickname "Joan Make-peace."[63]

On 28 July, at Isabella's plea, Robert I made concessions to some of the Disinherited, including Wake, Beaumont, and Henry, Lord Percy,[64] which incensed those whose claims had been passed over. Percy received other marks of favor from Isabella and remained her loyal ally, unlike Wake and Beaumont.[65] Wake was Lancaster's son-in-law, and Isabella had deprived him of his office of Justice south of the Trent on 9 May and replaced him with William, Lord Zouche, who owed his advancement to his "good service to Queen Isabella."[66] As for Beaumont, who had long been a good friend, Isabella would never forgive his disaffection.

The Queen and Mortimer were at Pontefract on 25 July[67] and arrived in York a day or so after Parliament had met there on the thirty-first.[68] Immediately, they summoned a meeting of the council to discuss sending troops to Gascony, but Lancaster, Norfolk, Kent, and Wake failed to show up.[69] The significance of this would not have been lost on Isabella and Mortimer, who must have realized that a conflict was looming. All talk of war was therefore shelved until the next Parliament.[70]

It was now painfully clear that, as a direct result of the "disgraceful peace" of Northampton, Isabella's and Mortimer's former allies had lost faith in them and were ready to desert them. Matters were only made worse when most of the first installment of Bruce's compensation money disappeared into Isabella's coffers rather than going to replenish the empty Exchequer.[71] She had also appropriated taxes raised at Lancaster's behest for fighting the

Scots. Soon, it was being said that she and Mortimer had arranged the treaty and compromised England's honor purely for their own personal gain.

In this general climate of disapproval, other resentments had begun to surface. There had long been a growing undercurrent of feeling that Mortimer was getting above himself, and many had begun to resent his and Isabella's monopoly of power, which, it was said, they meant to hold on to at any price.[72] Mortimer's increasing arrogance and presumption earned him much disapproval. He dispensed patronage like a king, for grants to his followers were made in the King's name, under the Privy Seal, effectively under Isabella's control, which had led to complaints in Parliament that it was being misused.[73]

Lancaster had been irrevocably alienated from Isabella and Mortimer by the passing of the Treaty of Northampton, which starkly exposed how far his own power and influence had been eroded. Norfolk, Beaumont, and many of the Disinherited also felt outraged and humiliated, and by August, Kent, whose loyalty to Isabella had long been wavering, had aligned himself with Lancaster.

Hence, Lancaster, Norfolk, Kent, and others had deliberately absented themselves from the council meeting at York out of utter indignation at the peace with Scotland, the undermining of their own influence, and the increasing autocracy of Isabella and Mortimer. Furthermore, they were publicly claiming that the Queen had usurped the sovereign's authority under the pretense of reforming the abuses of Edward II's rule and asserted that, in a little over a year, she and Mortimer had committed more crimes than Edward and his favorites had in twenty years.[74] This was a vast exaggeration, but Lancaster was a driven man, spurred on by his anger over the treaty, his desire to retrieve the Lincoln inheritance from the Queen, and his determination to reassert his authority, which Isabella and Mortimer had subverted at every turn. He was well aware that he was the only person able to coordinate effective opposition against them, but he also knew that, once he openly proclaimed himself their enemy, they would be bent on destroying him.[75]

As for Kent, he desperately wanted an opportunity to redress the wrongs he had done Edward II, while he and Norfolk felt that Mortimer had usurped their positions as Princes of the Blood. Both must have felt that the rewards given them for supporting Isabella were paltry compared to those that she and Mortimer had awarded themselves.[76]

Another who had deserted Isabella was Bishop Stratford, who was to act as Lancaster's public mouthpiece in the coming conflict. Almost alone among the Queen's chief supporters, he had received no substantial reward or public office, which had apparently rankled greatly.

Thanks to the efforts of Hamo de Chigwell, many Londoners also sympathized with Lancaster, and on 12 August, the Mayor sent a tentative letter of support to him, Kent, Wake, and Stratford, thanking them for their favor shown to the City in the past and wishing them long continuance.[77]

On 18 August, the court left York, and on the twenty-second, the day before it reached Doncaster, Isabella sent Thomas Garton, controller of the King's Wardrobe, to Lancaster, probably to invite him to talks. Garton rejoined the court at Nottingham four days later.[78]

Isabella and Mortimer were together at Nottingham on 2 August.[79] Soon afterward, Mortimer lost two of his sons, Roger, who died shortly before 27 August, and John, who was killed in a tournament.[80] These tragedies appear to have had a profound effect on Mortimer, whose grief seems to have found its outlet in aggression.

On 7 September, the court was at Barlings Abbey near Lincoln when Lancaster came to parley at the head of an armed force, having decided that there was no other way of emphasizing his grievances. This provoked an uproar, with Isabella and Mortimer angrily protesting against such defiance and refusing to listen to Lancaster's complaints, and Lancaster furiously threatening to turn his troops on them. In the end, the King was compelled to command the Earl to lay his complaints before Parliament, which had been summoned to meet at Salisbury.[81]

Isabella was badly shaken by this scene. The specter of civil war had once again raised its grimacing head, and the government reacted accordingly, issuing contingency plans for dealing with Lancaster to the sheriffs. At Wisbech, on 16 September, Isabella and Mortimer banned all public assemblies and moved to replace any sheriff whose loyalty was questionable.[82] Shortly afterward, they left Wisbech and made for Gloucester,[83] where Mortimer began to muster troops from the Marches. With some truth, the pro-Lancastrian *Brut* claimed that this open rift with Lancaster marked the beginning of the tyranny of Isabella and Mortimer.

The row at Barlings had driven Lancaster to seek openly the support of the Londoners. On 14 September, Wake and Stratford had gone to the Guildhall and, in an address to the citizens, publicly declared their grievances. They demanded that the King should live off his own revenues so that he would have at his disposal sufficient treasure to fight his enemies; that his mother should surrender her vast dower and live on the traditional income of a queen consort; that she should avoid abusing the privilege of purveyance, which she had used to obtain goods for Mortimer as well as herself, and cease oppressing the people with her extravagance; that Mortimer be banished from court and made to remain on his own lands, since he had disinherited many in order to acquire them; that there should be an inquiry as to why the Weardale campaign had failed; that the regency council should be permitted to function without obstruction or interference and not be neglected; and that law and order should be properly enforced. The Londoners loudly voiced their approval and called for these matters to be discussed in a Parliament at Westminster, not at Salisbury.[84]

After leaving Wisbech, Edward III had progressed through East Anglia, probably making for London by a roundabout route; at Thetford on 24 September, he received a letter from Isabella.[85] By now, however, Lancaster had learned that the King was on his own and marched his forces from Higham Ferrers in Northamptonshire to intercept and take custody of him.[86] On 27 September, when Edward arrived at Cambridge, he was warned of Lancaster's intentions and "turned aside," probably to join his mother and Mortimer at Gloucester,[87] a journey that meant swinging southward to avoid meeting Lancaster. On the day Edward left Cambridge, Hamo de Chigwell wrote to inform him of the proceedings at the Guildhall.[88]

Isabella and Mortimer had arrived at Gloucester by 4 October.[89] Edward III must have arrived soon afterward, to be shortly followed by news of the proceedings at the Guildhall. Isabella was devastated when she heard and fell weeping into her son's arms, crying that Lancaster was his enemy and meant her evil by his false and cruel accusations. Edward was appalled at her distress and took it upon himself to send Sir Oliver Ingham and Bartholemew, Lord Burghersh, to the Mayor with a demand that he explain his conduct to the King.[90]

When the royal party arrived at Salisbury, they received the shocking news that Lancaster's men had murdered Sir Robert Holland. Yet this had not been without provocation, for once he had been reinstated in his lands, Holland, a thoroughly unpleasant character, had dared to raid Lancaster's estates.[91] In retaliation, in June 1328, William Bradshaw, one of Lancaster's adherents, had accused Holland of the murder of one Adam Banastre in 1326. Almost certainly this was a ploy on Lancaster's part to discredit Holland and remove him from the political arena. An indictment had been brought against Holland, but the Queen, contravening the provisions of the Statute of Northampton, issued a writ under the Privy Seal prohibiting any justice from proceeding against him.[92]

On 23 August, Edward III had written to Holland from Doncaster, probably summoning him to take up arms against Lancaster.[93] But Lancaster was determined to get his hands on Holland first. On 15 October, Lancaster's men seized him at Borehamwood in Hertfordshire and chopped off his head, which they sent to the Earl.[94] When news of the murder reached the Queen, she took steps to bring the killers to justice, but Lancaster took them under his protection and ensured their immunity.[95]

Parliament met at Salisbury on 16 October.[96] Fearing that Lancaster would arrive at the head of an army intent on declaring war, Isabella had sent the King and Queen to the safety of her castle at Marlborough, instructing Chancellor Burghersh to open Parliament in the King's name.[97] In the event, Lancaster and his allies stayed away and sent transparent excuses for their absence, which were not accepted. But the situation still looked ugly, and on the opening day, Mortimer came to Parliament at the head of his own forces, silencing the protests of the bishops by forbidding them, on peril of life and limb, to oppose his interests.

Presently, Stratford, Lancaster's spokesman, arrived and announced that the Earl was refusing to attend because of his fear of Mortimer, whom he had no reason to trust and who had made peace with the Scots with the intent of destroying him. Whereupon Mortimer hotly defended himself and swore on Archbishop Meopham's crucifix that he intended no harm to Lancaster. The bishops then sent a message inviting Lancaster to come to Parliament, and Isabella made the King send a private note to the Earl, personally guaranteeing his safety and saying that he was welcome but that Henry de Beaumont was not. Never again did she want to have anything to do with Beaumont.

Lancaster still would not come to Salisbury. He sent the bishops a message stating that he was acting not in his own interests but in those of the King, the realm, and the Church. Then, according to the official records, he reiterated the demands that Wake and Stratford had listed at the Guildhall. *The Brut* claims that he also accused Isabella and Mortimer of removing Edward II from his custody at Kenilworth, "without consent of any Parliament," and placing him in Berkeley Castle, where "none of his kindred could see or speak to him, and afterwards they had traitorously murdered him."[98] That Lancaster made such accusations is unlikely, because no other source refers to his making such momentous charges, and if he had made them publicly, it would surely have caused a sensation and been commented on elsewhere. If Lancaster believed that Edward had been murdered, why wait until now to bring it up? After all, it was more than a year since Edward II's death had been announced, no new evidence is known to have emerged, and Lancaster was certainly not privy to Mortimer's actions

at Abergavenny in September 1327. The story in *The Brut* is probably propaganda calculated to discredit Mortimer and Isabella. This ties in with the
theory that the red-hot-spit tale, which apparently emerged at this time in
the Lancastrian heartlands of the North, and was soon afterward recounted
in this same chronicle, was also Lancastrian propaganda, put about to justify an uprising against the government that could, given that Isabella and
Mortimer had control of the King, be construed as treason.

It is also significant that Lancaster made no complaint about the private
relationship between the Queen and Mortimer, a scandal out of which he
could have made immense political capital. The chroniclers, too, as has
been noted, are very reticent about this matter, although they say enough
to confirm the sexual nature of the relationship. In fact, there is so little criticism of the affair in contemporary sources that we must conclude that, far
from being notorious, as many historians claim, it was conducted with the
utmost discretion, so that few outsiders could have guessed what was going
on. Isabella was no fool; she knew her enemies were waiting to pounce and
gave them no grounds for accusing her of immorality.

In his message, Lancaster concluded that he was willing to come to Parliament if the King would permit him to bring an armed retinue to protect
him from those persons "who are notoriously anxious to do me wrong."[99]

While these demands were being considered, Stratford did his best to
enlist the support of the bishops, inviting them to his own lodgings to discuss the matter, but Mortimer found out and sent armed men to break up
the meeting. Prudently, Stratford hastened from Salisbury and, on receiving
a warning that Mortimer was plotting to murder him, sought sanctuary
with the nuns at Wilton Abbey.[100]

Carefully briefed by his mother, Edward III wrote a letter in response to
Lancaster's demands. He protested that he could not live "of his own"
because the present crisis had drained his resources, "but if any man knew
how to make the King richer, it would give the King and his advisers great
satisfaction." As for the Queen's living off her own revenues, that was a
matter between the King and his mother, and no one else. If Lancaster had
been apparently sidelined, that was his own fault for failing to attend council meetings; in his absence, the King, quite properly, had taken counsel of
the other magnates, an allusion no doubt to Mortimer. As for law and
order, the King had done his best to maintain it. And although there was no
precedent, he would grant Lancaster a safe-conduct to attend Parliament.
However, the Queen and the lords had stipulated that this be conditional
upon Lancaster's being prepared to prove, if need be, that it was in accor-

dance with Magna Carta.[101] The obvious downside of this was that, if a safe-conduct was issued, and Lancaster failed to attend Parliament, it would offer him no protection from prosecution in any other circumstances, and when Lancaster read the King's letter, he decided he would stay away from Parliament rather than risk being arrested for inciting rebellion or abetting Holland's murderers.

Both Isabella and Lancaster had parties of supporters in London, and on 28 October, the citizens elected a neutral Mayor, John de Grantham, to replace Chigwell, who had shown himself such an enemy to Isabella and Mortimer.

On the closing day of Parliament, 31 October, Edward III created his brother John Earl of Cornwall; that county, however, would remain under their mother's control. Next, "by the procuration of the Queen," the King raised Mortimer to the highest echelon of the peerage as Earl of March, a new creation, and himself buckled on the belt and spurs of nobility.[102] "Such a title had never before been heard of in England," wrote one chronicler, but Mortimer evidently intended it to reflect his supremacy in the Welsh Marches and also perhaps his dynastic connections with the Lusignans, who were Counts of La Marche in France.[103]

The raising of Mortimer to the dignity of an earldom proved too much for many to stomach, especially Lancaster, who immediately marched on Winchester. The new Earl was hated enough as it was for his ruthless ambition and as the architect of the shameful peace of Northampton, and that hatred now also extended to Isabella. Furthermore, Mortimer's title had an ominous ring to it, for it was only two years since the removal of another royal favorite who had carved out for himself a Welsh principality on the scale of Mortimer's.

Mortimer's ennoblement made him more arrogant and insufferable than ever. He began to conduct himself like a king, bearing himself so haughtily, it was said, that he was a wonder to watch. On 6 October, Isabella, in the King's name, had granted him permission to travel with an armed retinue, and everywhere he went now, he was accompanied by 180 "wild" Welsh men-at-arms, to protect him and doubtless to intimidate his enemies; later, there were complaints that no woman was safe from them. On an income of £8,000 a year, Mortimer lived in sybaritic luxury, sleeping in silken sheets and wearing "wondrously rich" clothes of costly satin and velvet. The inventory of his goods drawn up after his death records lavish furnishings, exquisite fabrics and embroideries, rare carpets, fine armor, and vessels of silver and gilt.[104] Isabella doubtless appreciated such expensive taste.

She must have been aware of her lover's self-aggrandizement, but she apparently did nothing to counteract it. All the evidence suggests that love, infatuation, or lust blinded her to Mortimer's baser characteristics. There can be no doubt that both were of a rapacious nature, but it must be said that both had known adversity and penury and were determined to retain their hold on power for as long as possible so that they might continue to enjoy the privileges it brought them. Isabella would have been horrified at the prospect of her son's loyalty being subverted by Lancaster and his allies and must have privately feared that, if they got the King into their clutches, she stood to lose her child, her power, and her lover at a stroke. With such a threat hanging over her, Mortimer's arrogance bespoke strength and authority, and she was increasingly coming to rely on him as her champion against these hostile forces. From this time forward, it appears that Mortimer was the dominant partner in their relationship, both politically and privately. Isabella's growing tendency to devolve power upon him undoubtedly helped to foster his arrogance.

Parliament adjourned on 1 November, intending to reassemble at Westminster.[105] But Lancaster had occupied Winchester, through which the court meant to pass on its way back to the capital, so the sheriff of Southampton was sent to negotiate and, after warning the Lancastrians that they risked being charged with treason for rising against the King, secured Lancaster's withdrawal.

Meanwhile, Isabella and Mortimer had ridden to Marlborough, where Mortimer insisted that Edward III accompany him to Winchester, so that he could confront Lancaster in the name of the King and then accuse him of treason if he refused to lay down his arms. Isabella warned Edward that Lancaster, Kent, and Norfolk were bent on dethroning him, whereupon Edward agreed to go with them on condition that Philippa could accompany him, to which Mortimer and the Queen agreed. But when they arrived at Winchester on 3 November, the Lancastrians were already riding out of the city.[106]

Two days later, Lancaster wrote to inform the new Mayor of London of what had happened at Winchester, claiming that Parliament had been suspended before he could get a fair hearing and complaining that his powers as the King's guardian had been infringed. Curiously, he added that Kent had told him of certain matters in confidence, but that he could not commit them to paper and had instructed the bearer to impart this information by word of mouth. He concluded by saying that Kent and some of the bishops had advised him to retire to his estates for the present.[107]

So what had Kent told Lancaster? Some historians think that he had somehow found out or guessed that Edward II was still alive.[108] But this is unlikely. Had Lancaster learned of Edward's survival, he would surely have acted upon this information or at least exploited it for political purposes to justify his rebellion. But Lancaster never again mentioned this matter. Furthermore, there were no repercussions from Kent's revelations, and the subject apparently never surfaced again.

Whatever it was, it was a sensitive issue, and it might have concerned the sexual relationship between Isabella and Mortimer, about which Kent, who had been in France when it began, could probably have revealed a great deal. Mindful of the effect on the young King, and aware that a scandal such as this would prejudice any claim that Edward might make to the French throne, Lancaster probably preferred to keep this matter confidential while at the same time wishing the Londoners to know what kind of people they were dealing with. Whatever the matter was, the Mayor was perhaps too fearful of a royal backlash to repeat what he had heard, nor would he have wished to provoke the displeasure of the King.

The court left Winchester for London on 7 November. The next day, the Mayor, anxious not to appear too partisan, wrote to Edward III, thanking him for holding the next Parliament in London and begging him not to credit rumors that the City was disloyal to him.[109]

After lodging at Wallingford, where Isabella, responding to Lancaster's criticisms, instructed the sheriffs to send the King lists of all those who had infringed the Statute of Northampton,[110] the King and his retinue moved to Windsor by 14 November.[111]

Mindful of the imminent arrival of the Queen in London, Mayor Grantham wrote to the King on 18 November, disclaiming any responsibility for those Londoners who had joined Lancaster.[112] The King and his mother arrived in London on 21 November[113] and stayed for nearly two weeks. During this time, Lancaster sent two messengers to Isabella in an attempt to reach a settlement, asking to have their differences debated at a full meeting of the council. But she replied that he had offended the King and that nothing but his submission would suffice.[114]

Mortimer had deemed it wise to remain in the background at this time and did not join Isabella at Westminster until 25 November.[115] However, when he did appear in the City, he was warmly received, for he still enjoyed great popularity with many Londoners.[116] While the royal party was at Westminster, the envoys of Philip VI arrived to demand that Edward III pay homage for his continental possessions, as was customary when a new king ascended the French throne.

But Isabella was having none of it. "My son, who is the son of a king, will never do homage to the son of a count," she declared fiercely. Hearing of this, Philip VI retaliated by seizing the revenues of Gascony, and the alarmed English magnates counseled the Queen to be prudent.[117] She had enough to worry about without inviting a war with France.

Kent and Norfolk were now emerging as the most extreme of Lancaster's allies. In December, they dared to issue a circular letter to the magnates and bishops, complaining that the King had violated Magna Carta and his coronation oath and urging them to meet at Saint Paul's to debate what should be done about it. The real target of their complaint was clear, as several, including Bishop Hethe, ignored the letter,[118] but others, including Stratford, Wake, and Archbishop Meopham, whose election Isabella had opposed, went to meet with the royal Earls.[119]

On 2 December, Isabella, Mortimer, and the King left London for Gloucester. They arrived there on the tenth, immediately began to raise more soldiers, and departed on the twentieth.[120] On 15 December, Mortimer made one of his very few endowments to religious foundations, to Leintwardine Church, providing for nine chaplains who were to say Mass daily for the souls of the King and Queen, Queen Isabella, and Lady Mortimer, among others.[121] Presumably, the chaplains did not find it strange to be praying for Mortimer's mistress as well as his wife.

Word of Kent's circular letter had soon reached the Queen, and to counteract its effects, she made the King write on 16 December to the City of London, begging for aid against his enemies and giving a full, but somewhat biased, account of the conflict with Lancaster.[122]

The Archbishops of Canterbury and York were both sympathetic toward Lancaster, and on 18 December, Archbishop Meopham dared to preach against Edward III at Saint Paul's Cathedral. The next day, the disaffected lords met there and began lengthy discussions as to how next to proceed.[123]

On 21 December, the King's letter arrived in London and was read out at the Guildhall. Some Lancastrians were present and, realizing that public opinion was veering away from them, protested that Lancaster could not respond without taking counsel of his friends. But the citizens reacted by proclaiming their loyalty to the King and urged that neither side take up arms until the matter could be debated in Parliament,[124] a plea that both parties ignored.[125]

On 23 December, Meopham sent a brisk letter to King Edward, threatening Isabella and Mortimer and anyone else of their party who disturbed the peace, apart from the young King and Queen, with excommunication.[126] It was this offensive letter, together with rumors that Lancaster was marching on London, that precipitated civil war.

On 29 December, Mortimer was with the King at Worcester, leading their army toward Warwick with the intention of attacking Lancaster's lands in his absence. While they were at Worcester, Edward III declared war on Lancaster but offered an amnesty to all who submitted to him before he reached Leicester.[127] The next day, the royal army arrived at Warwick. It left on 1 January 1329 for Lancaster's stronghold at Kenilworth, to which the King was refused access by the garrison, an unforgivable act of lèse-majesté.

That day, Lancaster arrived in London. Within twenty-four hours, six hundred men had flocked to his banner, and it appeared that he was at the center of a powerful confederacy, which had resolved to seize the King and impeach Mortimer and Isabella for concluding the "shameful peace" with Scotland.[128]

Mortimer and the King marched through Coventry on 2 January, and by the sixth, Mortimer had gone ahead, ravaged Lancaster's lands, and seized his town of Leicester. That day, the King arrived with Queen Isabella to take possession of it.[129] They left Leicester on 11 January and were in Bedford on the twelfth. Lancaster was marching north to confront them there when he learned to his dismay that further opposition was futile.[130]

The taking of Leicester by the King's forces had proved a powerful deterrent, driving Lancaster's allies to abandon him. When Kent and Norfolk deserted him and made their submission to the King, he knew that his cause was lost and that he must make his peace with Edward and, more pertinently, with Isabella and Mortimer.[131] Another reason for this decision may have been the realization that he was slowly going blind.

At Bedford, Lancaster dismounted; knelt on the ground before the King, Isabella, Mortimer, and their entire army; and surrendered, swearing on the Gospels that he would in future do nothing to harm "our Lord the King, my ladies the Queens, nor any great or small of the council."[132] Thanks to the mediation of Archbishop Meopham, his life was spared and he was left at liberty, but he was ordered to pay a fine equivalent to the value of half his lands and was stripped of all his offices save that of Seneschal of England. Effectively, Mortimer and Isabella had crushed him, and while they remained in power, he would play only a minor role in public affairs.

The court left Bedford on 21 January and went to Woburn Abbey, whence Edward sent an order to the Mayor of London and leading citizens to meet with him at Saint Albans on 23 January. Here, for the next three days, the City's representatives were locked in talks with the Queen and the council, Mortimer then being absent.[133] Significantly, Richard de Béthune and John de Gisors, who had helped Mortimer escape from the Tower, were among the delegates. On 28 January, the London deputation arrived back at the Guildhall, where they proclaimed the King's commission to deal with breaches of the peace and to search out and punish Lancaster's followers. The commissioners began their investigations the following day.[134]

On 29 January, Isabella joined Mortimer at Windsor, where they stayed until at least 3 February.[135] On 1 February, the Mayor came there for further talks with the King, who the next day appointed justices to sit in the Guildhall to deal with offenders. Among them were Ingham and Maltravers, who could be relied upon to act in Mortimer's favor, in case the Londoners could not be trusted. These justices wasted no time, for the first miscreants were tried in London on 6 February; on the thirteenth, Hamo de Chigwell was indicted and sent to the Tower.[136]

A few of Lancaster's followers, among them Henry de Beaumont, had fled to France. The rest were punished with forfeitures or stiff recognizances, whereby they were bound to keep the peace on penalty of a large fine.[137] Isabella and Mortimer were surprisingly merciful, and most of these forfeitures were later reversed and the fines—even Lancaster's—pardoned.[138]

On the day before the trials began, Edward III and Queen Isabella had arrived in London and taken up residence at the Tower;[139] Isabella perhaps intended their presence there to be a warning to any justice inclined to leniency toward the Lancastrians.

Parliament met at Westminster on 9 February, and during this session, new French envoys arrived with Philip VI's final demand for Edward III to pay homage. The realization that she was in no position to risk the consequences of a further refusal prompted Isabella to swallow her pride and change her policy toward France, and the envoys were informed that the King would come to France after all and then sent home with rich gifts.[140] It was decided, however, that in order not to commit himself to performing military service for Philip, Edward would perform only conditional homage, not liege homage, and he would do so without prejudice to any future claim he might make to the Crown of France.[141] Baker later strongly criticized Isabella for betraying her son's rights to the French throne, but it is difficult to see what else she could have done under the circumstances.

When Parliament adjourned on 22 February,[142] the court left Westminster for Eltham. While Isabella was there, she appointed Maltravers as Steward of the Household to Edward III, a post he would hold until 9 July 1330.[143]

The court arrived at Guildford on 7 March and lodged in Isabella's castle and nearby palace. Here, the King hosted a two-day tournament, at which Mortimer, at the Queen's instance, was presented with rich gifts as a reward for his defeat of Lancaster.[144] Throughout the spring, the court perambulated at its leisure through Buckinghamshire, Oxfordshire, and Berkshire, staying at High Wycombe around 15 March; Woodstock Palace, from at least 19 to 22 March; Thame Abbey; Islip, where Edward the Confessor had been born in 1004, although little can have remained of the Saxon palace in Isabella's day; Abingdon Abbey; Wallingford Castle, from at least 12 to 16 April; and Reading Abbey.[145]

Isabella was exercising all her considerable diplomatic skills. On 14 April, Edward III wrote to Philip VI explaining that the delay in his paying homage had been caused by the recent rebellion and promising that he would be setting out from England very soon.[146]

We might detect at this time a certain restiveness in the young King's attitude toward his mother and Mortimer, for on 16 April, at Wallingford, Queen Philippa was granted 1,000 marks per annum for her chamber expenses, "till some better provision be made for her estate";[147] this may have been a ploy to mollify Edward. Another possible sop to the King was the retaining of his friend Sir William de Montagu "to stay with the King with twenty men-at-arms for life,"[148] an appointment that Isabella and Mortimer would have cause in time to regret.

William de Montagu, an intelligent and chivalrous man of twenty-eight, was from a noble Anglo-Norman family that had settled in Somerset soon after the Conquest. His late father had served Edward II faithfully and well as Steward of the Household and Marshal of Gascony, and in 1325, young William had been in the retinue that accompanied Prince Edward to France. Thereafter, he quickly rose in Edward's favor and in 1328 became a Knight Banneret. Despite William's eleven years' seniority, he and the young King were the closest of friends and would remain so until death.[149]

On 28 April, the court was at Windsor but had moved to Eltham before 11 May,[150] when Edward's envoys returned from France to inform him of the arrangements that had been made for the ceremony of homage. The evil moment could be put off no longer: on or after 15 May, the royal entourage left Eltham and traveled down through Kent, staying at Canterbury from 20 to 22 May, and reaching Dover by the twenty-fifth.[151]

The next day, Edward III sailed for France, leaving John of Eltham as nominal Guardian of the Realm in his absence.[152] Isabella and Mortimer returned to Canterbury, where they remained at least until 16 June.[153]

On 6 June, Edward, wearing robes of crimson velvet embroidered with leopards and a gold crown atop his long fair hair, and supported on either side by his uncles of Norfolk and Kent, paid homage to Philip in Amiens Cathedral.[154] All was cordiality between the two Kings, but Knighton says they were "friends only according to the outside of their faces." It is said that, while in France, Edward heard salacious gossip about his mother and Mortimer that both shocked and embarrassed him.[155]

Bishop Burghersh had accompanied the King to Amiens and was alarmed to hear whispers that Philip was plotting to kidnap Edward. Realizing that any delay might expose his charge to danger, he insisted that they all return home immediately.[156] Their departure was so precipitate that Edward had no time to say a proper farewell to Philip. He returned home on 11 June and rejoined Isabella and Mortimer at Canterbury,[157] to be met with the news that Robert the Bruce had died and that David II had succeeded at the age of five to the throne of Scotland—which meant that Isabella's daughter Joan, now eight, was its Queen.

Edward III left the court behind at Canterbury shortly after 14 June and hastened off to Windsor to rejoin his beloved Philippa, who conceived her first child three months later.

Mortimer had left for Windsor by 18 June,[158] but Isabella stayed on at Canterbury until 20 June, when she, too, departed for Windsor. There, in a lavish ceremony on 20 July, the King—doubtless at the instance of Isabella—presented Mortimer with valuable jewels.

Eight days later, the court rode off to the west country to attend the weddings of Mortimer's daughters, Beatrice and Agnes, to the heirs of Norfolk and Pembroke. After Lancaster's disgrace, Norfolk had been reconciled to Isabella and Mortimer, doubtless fearful of losing the forfeited Despenser estates that they had granted him. This marriage of his ten-year-old heir, Edward, to Beatrice Mortimer, and his presence at the coming wedding, probably demonstrate his eagerness to ingratiate himself with Isabella and Mortimer rather than any genuine desire to be identified with their regime.[159] For Mortimer, the marriage represented the pinnacle of his success, for it would ally him with the royal House and forever enhance his status and that of his family.

On 2 September, Isabella did an unusual thing: she appointed Mortimer heir to several of her properties and gave her executors control over her revenues from Ponthieu for three years after her death.[160] She had drawn up similar documents only once before, prior to the birth of her first child, so, since she is not known to have been ill, it is possible that she was now pregnant by Mortimer and making provision for the future in case she did not survive the birth. The wonder is that she had not conceived earlier than this, for she had borne Edward four healthy children, while Mortimer and his wife had a dozen.

Because the birth of an illegitimate child to the Queen would cause a scandal throughout Christendom, secrecy would have had to be maintained, for Isabella and Mortimer were not so popular that their enemies would have refrained from making political capital out of such an event. Moreover, there was the reputation of the Crown to be considered and the effect on the young King.

The court reached Leominster on 3 September. The next day, the King and the Queen Mother led their retinues to Wigmore Castle,[161] where, over the next three days, Mortimer held a spectacular Round Table and tournament as a preliminary celebration of his daughters' nuptials, he himself entering the lists as King Arthur. The theme of this celebration was highly significant, since Mortimer was stressing his descent from the mythical King Brutus the Trojan, the hero who, according to twelfth-century chroniclers, gave his name to Britain, founded London as a second Troy, and was the first king to hold a Round Table in the Arthurian tradition. Mortimer was also re-creating a Round Table held by his grandfather in 1279 at Kenilworth, in the presence of Edward I and Eleanor of Castile. Isabella must have enjoyed this event immensely, as she had a particular fondness for the legends of King Arthur, and since she is known to have presided with Mortimer over these proceedings, it is not impossible that she assumed the role of Guinevere.[162]

But was there a subtext? Was Mortimer cunningly emphasizing his royal blood and his right to rule? Certainly, from now on, he was to seize every opportunity to assert his supremacy in the realm.

The court left Wigmore on or after 6 September, then went to Hereford on 9 September for the Mortimer weddings.[163]

The King granted Mortimer £1,000 toward the cost of his cousin of Norfolk's nuptial celebrations,[164] but he himself cannot have greatly enjoyed the festivities. By now, and with good reason, Edward III had become disturbed by Mortimer's rampant self-aggrandizement and was evidently concerned that the decisions taken by his mother and her lover in his name did not reflect his own views and, in some cases, were in direct opposition to them. Because he was still a minor, there was little he could do about it, but he was determined to circumvent Mortimer's power. He decided to enlist the assistance of the Pope. On 12 September, he sent William de Montagu to Avignon to speak to John XXII on his behalf. The fact that Bishop Burghersh's brother Bartholemew went with him suggests that Mortimer had his suspicions about this mission.

Montagu, however, managed to secure a private audience with the Pope, and between them, they devised a coded signal that the Pontiff would recognize on genuine communications from the King: Edward was to write "Peter Sancte" in his own hand at the bottom of his letters. Anything else would be from Isabella or Mortimer and could be dealt with accordingly.[165]

In the autumn of 1329, Kent, who was supposed to be "on the King's business,"[166] was also at Avignon, informing a startled Pope John of his conviction that Edward II was still alive and that he intended to liberate him.[167] According to a statement he made later, he told the Pontiff that a Dominican friar of London had come to him at Kennington Palace and informed him that he had "conjured up a spirit" (Murimuth says it was a devil) who assured him that the former King yet lived. Lanercost states that this friar was none other than Stephen Dunheved, the Dominican who had twice tried to free Edward in 1327. It is likely that Kent had been one of the great magnates who had backed Dunheved then, and it would therefore have been natural for Dunheved to have approached Kent now. Of all people, Dunheved was the one most likely to have learned of Edward II's survival. The warder who, according to Fieschi, helped Edward to escape, was possibly a member of Dunheved's group or had helped them gain entry on the day they ransacked Berkeley Castle and spirited the King away. After his recapture, Dunheved had gone to ground, but it is possible that either he or his remaining coconspirators had helped Edward after his escape or had at least heard about it.

Whoever the friar was, Kent had soon become convinced that his story was genuine. It lent credence to the rumors, which were now rampant throughout the realm, that Edward II had survived, rumors that Kent apparently believed.[168] His conscience had never ceased to trouble him with regard to his betrayal of Edward, and one suspects that he wanted to believe that his brother was alive; he certainly leaped at this chance to redress the wrongs he had done him. The Pope, he later claimed, gave this scheme his blessing, "charged him that he should use his pains and diligence to deliver Edward," and promised his moral and financial support; but John XXII was later to deny this.[169]

On his way back through Paris, Kent had a meeting with Henry de Beaumont and Thomas Rosselin, another Lancastrian exile, and discussed with them the restoration of Edward II. They promised him they would make contact with Donald, Earl of Mar, another conspirator from 1327, and endeavor to invade England from the northeast coast.[170]

Kent then returned to England to enlist support for his plans.

On 16 September, the court was at Gloucester, and Edward again asserted himself, appointing his own man as Treasurer in place of Mortimer's; he also promoted Thomas Garton, who had been recommended by Montagu, to be Controller of the Household. Then, on 24 September, he made his former tutor and loyal secretary, Richard de Bury, Keeper of the Privy Seal. Since Bury was still being referred to as Isabella's "dear clerk" in June 1330,[171] she must have been happy about this appointment and had perhaps suggested it. At the end of September, Sir John Maltravers was appointed custodian of Corfe Castle,[172] although he remained Steward of the Household until 29 July 1330 and probably divided his time between his different responsibilities.

Between 8 and 16 October, the court was at Dunstable[173] for a tournament that lasted for four days, before traveling to Northampton. It then moved to Kenilworth on 29 October and stayed for more than three months, until 3 January 1330, an unusually long sojourn.[174]

Kenilworth Castle, which was built of red sandstone and lay four miles north of Warwick, had until recently belonged to Lancaster. It was one of the greatest and strongest fortresses in England. It had originally been built in 1112 but soon afterward had been taken over by the Crown because of its strategic importance. King John had strengthened its defenses and added the vast artificial lake that surrounded the castle on three sides, but in 1244, Henry III had granted it to Simon de Montfort. Later, it had become part of the earldom of Lancaster. Edward II had been held prisoner there in 1327, but there is no evidence that the castle held unhappy associations for his consort. In Isabella's time, Kenilworth consisted of a massive keep surrounded by a curtain wall intersected by towers.[175]

Ian Mortimer has suggested that Isabella secretly gave birth to Mortimer's child during their prolonged stay at Kenilworth,[176] but although it is possible that she conceived in the early spring, it is unlikely that she carried the infant to term. She was in the public eye for most of the year and could not possibly have concealed her condition. Women's costume of the period skimmed the body or fell in soft folds, and any pregnancy would have been noticeable. According to the calculations below, Isabella would have been eight months pregnant when she arrived at Kenilworth, which would not have escaped the notice of a great household full of lords, ladies, and servants.

Kent arrived at Kenilworth around 3 December, on which date Mortimer left to visit his Marcher estates. He went to Ludlow on 5 December and Clun on the eighth, and was back at Kenilworth on the twelfth.[177] It has been suggested that Mortimer took the child with him and left it with a wet nurse at Montgomery Castle, which is not far from Clun. This theory rests on two pieces of possible evidence: first, Isabella made over her interests in Montgomery Castle to Mortimer the following April; and second, there is an effigy of a knight in Montgomery parish church about which there is some mystery. The tomb is supposed to be that of Sir Edmund Mortimer, Mortimer's great-grandson, who supported the Welsh rebel Owen Glendower and died during the siege of Harlech between 1409 and 1411. Yet although Edmund was born in lawful wedlock, the Mortimer shield on this tomb bears a bend (or baton) sinister, which denotes bastardy and in the Middle Ages was often used for royal bastards. The inference is that this knight was a royal bastard and that he was perhaps Isabella's son by Mortimer, who had spent much of his life at Montgomery. Yet he could also have been the natural son of any one of a number of Mortimer males who lived in the fourteenth century; furthermore, it should be pointed out that, by 1400, the Mortimers had long been linked by marriage and blood to the royal House and were considered to have a good claim to the throne. Any Mortimer bastard would have been considered blue-blooded enough to merit the bend sinister.[178]

Furthermore, had Mortimer left Kenilworth with Isabella's child on 3 December, it must have been born at the end of November at the latest and conceived around the beginning of March. That meant that, when she was presiding over the Round Table at Wigmore, the Queen would have been six months pregnant, and seven months when she attended the tournament at Dunstable. Again, people would surely have noticed and her condition been remarked upon.

Ian Mortimer has pointed out that, in February 1330, Mortimer added the name of the "Earl of Lincoln" to the list of benfactors at Leintwardine Church[179] and has implied that this could have referred to the newborn son of Isabella and Mortimer. Yet at that time, there was no Earl of Lincoln. The title had come to Thomas of Lancaster through his marriage to Alice de Lacy, who was still alive, and it should have passed to Henry of Lancaster, but the lands had been divided among Isabella, Mortimer, and the latter's son Geoffrey. It is possible that Mortimer was anticipating that Geoffrey might get the earldom. A bastard could not inherit, and any new creation would automatically have attracted publicity, which, if Isabella and Mortimer had had a child, they had already gone out of their way to avoid.

If Isabella had become pregnant in 1329, which is quite likely, she had probably lost the baby early in the pregnancy. After all, it was eight years since she had last borne a child, and she was now thirty-four, middle-aged by medieval standards. The reason for the extended stay at Kenilworth was probably Queen Philippa's pregnancy, not Isabella's. Philippa had conceived around September, so by the end of October, when she arrived at Kenilworth, she could have been experiencing the nausea, sickness, and tiredness that are so typical of the first trimester of pregnancy. By the thirteenth week, such symptoms usually abate, so by the end of December, Philippa was probably well enough to move on, which would account for the court's leaving Kenilworth on 3 January 1330.

Isabella spent most of January and February at Eltham.[180] That month, Mortimer was granted yet more of Despenser's possessions as well as custody of the heir to the earldom of Kildare. In Ireland, he now held the honor of Trim and enjoyed palatine status in his lands in Meath and Uriel (Louth).[181]

On 25 January, Parliament was summoned to Winchester to discuss England's future policy toward France.[182] Two days later, Orleton was dispatched to Philip VI to negotiate a new peace treaty that would be cemented by the marriages of Prince John and Princess Eleanor to the daughter and son of Philip VI, matches that had first been suggested at Amiens the previous summer.[183]

For more than two years now, the coronation of Queen Philippa had been postponed. Nor had she received her rightful dower, because Isabella had no intention of relinquishing it. Once Philippa was crowned, Isabella stood to lose her status, her income, and her privileges. Now Philippa was visibly pregnant with a possible heir to the throne, and it was unthinkable that she give birth to him without first having been consecrated as Queen. The King was evidently growing increasingly angry at the way she had been slighted, and on 12 February, to pacify him, Isabella and Mortimer surrendered some of their lands to Philippa,[184] and arrangements were at last put in hand for her coronation. But Isabella had not the slightest intention of ceding anything else to her daughter-in-law.

On 28 February, at Eltham, the King formally summoned his estates to Westminster for the coronation of "his dearest Queen Philippa."[185] That day, the court left for the Tower, where the royal couple, following tradition, were to lodge prior to the ceremony.[186]

Amid great rejoicings, Philippa was crowned on 4 March 1330, in Westminster Abbey, by Archbishop Meopham.[187] Because she was nearly six months pregnant, the ceremony was shortened so as not to tire her.

After the coronation, the court went via Windsor and Guildford to Winchester, where Parliament had been summoned.[188] At Winchester, it took up residence in the castle that had been built by Henry II in the twelfth century on the site of an earlier wooden keep. Henry III, who had been born there, had extended the defenses and converted the royal lodgings into a palatial residence with a magnificent great hall that housed the reputed Round Table of King Arthur, which had in fact been made for Henry III or Edward I. Unfortunately, these royal chambers had been largely gutted by fire in 1302 and never restored. Since then, visiting monarchs had used the Bishop's Palace by the cathedral, but Isabella and Mortimer wanted to stay in a more secure place for this particular visit and had had some repairs to the royal apartments put in hand before their arrival.[189]

Since the previous autumn, Kent had been actively plotting to restore Edward II.[190] He had enlisted the support of several opponents of Isabella and Mortimer, notably, William Melton, Archbishop of York; Stephen Gravesend, Bishop of London; and William, Lord Zouche, who had recently abducted and married Despenser's widow, Eleanor de Clare, and then become embroiled in a bitter struggle with Mortimer over her lands in Glamorgan, which Mortimer held.[191] Gravesend had always been loyal to Edward II, but the support of the saintly Melton suggests that this was more than just a plot to overthrow an unpopular regime, and that it was based on credible and convincing evidence.[192]

Isabella's former close friend Lady de Vesci took sides with her brother, Henry de Beaumont, and sent her confessor to act as Melton's messenger to Kent. The news of Lady de Vesci's betrayal must have been a bitter blow to Isabella, for she had championed the Beaumonts in the years when the Ordainers had ousted them from court.

We know that Stephen Dunheved joined Kent's conspiracy,[193] and of course, he could have been the friar who instigated it. Two other Dominicans, Edmund and John Savage, were also involved—Edward II had always had a special affection for their Order—and a number of Dunheved's original gang of conspirators as well as one or two former adherents of the Despensers.

Abroad, Henry de Beaumont and Thomas Rosselin, now in Brabant, were in league with Kent, as was the exiled Rhys ap Gruffydd, whose plot to free Edward II in 1327 had prompted Mortimer to order the King's assassination. Donald of Mar was also involved. As conspiracies went, this one was formidable, since it had drawn together a host of Edward II's most active supporters.

In January, the government was alarmed to learn that, at the instance of certain magnates, aliens were entering the realm.[194] They could have been go-betweens acting for Kent and Beaumont, and it is likely that at least one of them broke under interrogation and revealed all. Several months later, Mortimer was to confess that he had led Kent into committing treason, and many historians are of the opinion that it was he who originally sent the friar to Kent, but contemporary sources are generally agreed that he discovered an existing plot and then set a trap, hoping to ensnare and then destroy the Earl.[195] Given the time frame involved, this probably happened in January, and the reason why Lancaster was dispatched on an embassy to France that month may have been to get him out of the way.[196] The surviving evidence makes it clear that Isabella was also deeply implicated in the framing of Kent. He might have been her brother-in-law and the son of her aunt, Queen Marguerite, but now he had become dangerous and had to be liquidated.

It was probably after the court had left Kenilworth that the two friars, Edmund and John Savage, approached Kent and told him that they had discovered that Edward II was living at Corfe and offered to act as intermediaries between Kent and his brother.[197] Kent sent them off to Corfe to establish that Edward was still there. They reported back that many people in the village had told them that the former King was being held in captivity in the castle. The friars added that they had gone up to the castle to check this story and met with two members of the garrison, John Deveril and Bogo de Bayouse,[198] who had not denied that Edward was there but had told the Savages that they could not allow them to speak with him. They did, however, permit them to come into the dimly lit great hall at night and observe from a distance a tall man seated at the dinner table on the dais; he bore, they would claim, a great resemblance to Edward II.

When Kent heard of this from the returning friars, he resolved to remove Edward from Corfe and take him to his own castle at Arundel in

Sussex. He wrote to Deveril and Bayouse, demanding an interview with the prisoner. Receiving no response, Kent rushed off to Corfe, offered a bribe to Deveril, and demanded "to be conducted to the apartment of Sir Edward of Caernarvon, his brother." This time, permission was firmly refused. So Kent wrote a letter to Edward, outlining his plot, and asked the custodians of the castle to give it to him. They sent it at once to Isabella and Mortimer, and on 10 March, an order was issued for the arrest of Kent and several others on charges of treason.[199]

Once Mortimer had been made aware of the conspiracy, it would have been easy to enlist the help of Maltravers, the governor of Corfe Castle, who was also to be accused of ensnaring Kent.[200] Whether Maltravers actually did arrange for his subordinates to spread rumors in the vicinity about Edward's being held captive there and then put on that little charade with a look-alike imposter are matters for conjecture, for it is also probable that the two Dominicans acted as agents provocateurs on behalf of Mortimer. Despite being described by Kent as "the chief dealers in the matter," they were the only two named conspirators who were never arrested.[201] The choice of Corfe was an obvious one because Edward had probably been taken there before, by the Dunheveds, in 1327; it was also in the custody of Maltravers, who was loyal to Isabella and Mortimer and had been Edward's jailer before, which lent credibility to the fabricated story. After these measures were put in place, it was only a matter of waiting for Kent to walk into the trap.

Those who question the veracity of Fieschi's letter point out that it would have been impossible for the real Edward II to pass unnoticed at Corfe with all this going on. However, we must remember that until now, most people had believed Edward to be dead and buried. Since rumor apparently had it that he was a prisoner in the castle, no one would have identified him with an unshaven, shorn, and tonsured hermit, wearing a hooded homespun habit, and anyone who by an unlikely chance had noticed a resemblance to the former King would probably have dismissed it as pure coincidence. Besides, in view of the rumors flying about, Edward was probably keeping out of sight. Soon, if Fieschi's account is to be believed, he would prudently leave Corfe and escape to Ireland.

The accused were apprehended on 11 March, the very day on which Parliament assembled. Kent was hauled before Mortimer and Robert Howell, coroner of the royal household. Mortimer produced three letters and asked Kent if the seal was his. It was, but Kent pointed out that his Countess had written one of these letters. Mortimer then read them out, and they proved to be those that had been written to Deveril, Bayouse, and Edward II. Faced with such incriminating evidence, Kent capitulated and confessed everything. Later, he was made to repeat his confession before a deputation from Parliament.[202]

The young King was all for pardoning his uncle,[203] but since the Queen had sworn, on the soul of her father, that she would have justice, the outcome was a foregone conclusion, and on the twelfth, Kent's property was taken into the King's hands.[204] On 13 March, Isabella and Mortimer put pressure on a reluctant Edward III to proceed against Kent: "all that day, the King was so beset by the Queen his mother and the Earl of March that it was impossible for him to make any effort to preserve his uncle from the cruel fate to which he had been so unjustly doomed." Isabella "bade him with her blessing that he should be avenged upon him as upon his deadly enemy."[205] In the end, it was Mortimer who bullied Edward into submission.[206] Later that day, Kent, who was not present, was impeached by Parliament, which found him guilty in his absence and condemned him to death. These proceedings were illegal, since Kent, as a peer of the realm, had the right to be tried by the lords in open Parliament.

The Queen was nervous that Edward III would pardon his uncle or at least commute his sentence, so without his knowledge, she gave orders to the bailiffs of Winchester to have the sentence carried out without delay. In the meantime, she kept Edward busy with state business.[207]

At noon on 14 March,[208] Kent, wearing only his shirt, was led to a scaffold that had been erected outside the gates of Winchester, only to find that the public executioner had slunk off, unwilling to decapitate one of such high rank. The wretched prisoner was kept waiting until Vespers, since no one willing to behead him could be found. At length, in the early evening, a convicted murderer agreed to dispatch him in return for a pardon, and Kent was made an end of, at only twenty-nine years old. He was buried in the church of the Franciscan friars in Winchester.[209]

It was only on 16 March, after his death, that Kent's confession was finally read out to Parliament.[210] During the following week, forty arrests were ordered, then on 21 March and 13 April, commissioners (Maltravers was one of them) were appointed to search out and punish more of Kent's adherents.[211] On 24 March, at the behest of Isabella and Mortimer, the King wrote to the Pope with a full account of Kent's treason, explaining that his punishment had been intended as an example to other would-be traitors. He pointed out that Kent had known that Edward II was dead because he had been present at his funeral at Gloucester and implied that the tale of the friar conjuring up a spirit was a piece of nonsense.[212]

Perhaps it was, for Kent's confession, as it has come down to us, could easily have been censored or doctored by the government and may not be a true account of what really happened. The tale about the friar's conjuring up a spirit sounds suspect and may have been invented in order to discredit Kent and Dunheved. It may be significant that the messenger chosen to carry the King's version of events to Avignon was John Walwayn, the royal clerk who had been at Berkeley at the time of the Dunheved plot. Edward had charged him to supply the Pope with further details of the conspiracy by word of mouth.[213] It is almost certain, therefore, that the full truth about this strange affair will never be known.

Kent had never been popular,[214] but there was outrage and revulsion at his death, and the manner of it.[215] It was said, with truth, he had been denied a proper trial and executed only on the strength of his confession.[216] Even though Kent had certainly been guilty of treason, such a violation of justice amounted to nothing less than tyranny. Lancaster, who had returned from France in February, was irrevocably alienated by these proceedings. Kent had been a king's son, and executing him seemed almost an act of sacrilege. Now no one, certainly not Lancaster and maybe not even the King, was safe. And no man, according to Knighton, "durst open his mouth for the good of the King or his realm."

Isabella and Mortimer had gone too far this time. To most people, it seemed that the chief result of the revolution of 1326–27 had been the replacing of one tyrannical regime with another. Their rapacity equaled or exceeded even that of the Despensers, and their policies seemed to be dictated only by self-interested opportunism. They had undermined the reputation and prestige of the monarchy, ruthlessly eliminated their enemies, and alienated every stratum of society.[217]

Mortimer was especially resented, for his presumption had become insupportable. "Roger Mortimer was in such glory and honour that it was without all comparison." He "honoured whom he liked, let the King stand in his presence, and was accustomed to walk arrogantly beside him," refusing to cede precedence; he insisted on sharing Edward's plate at table, as well as the royal chariot, and he was attended by a greater following than the King.[218] Isabella's passive toleration of Mortimer's lèse-majesté is surely proof of how deeply in thrall she was to her lover.

Mortimer was now "so proud and high that he held no lord of the realm his equal."[219] He insisted that everyone had to refer to him as "my lord Earl of March." This was the cause of "great contention" among both the nobility and the common people, who called Mortimer "the Queen's paragon and the King's master, who destroys the King's blood and usurps the regal majesty." Even Mortimer's own son named him "the King of Folly."[220]

Public sympathy for Isabella as a wronged wife had long since evaporated, but because she was the King's mother, she never attracted the opprobrium that extended to Mortimer, although she did come in for her share of criticism for her acquisitiveness, her unpopular policies, and her subversion of the law. One of the petty things objected against her was that she had confiscated books on canon and civil law, worth £10, that Edward II had granted to the Master of his foundation at King's Hall, Cambridge.

Because she did so much in partnership with Mortimer, it is impossible to determine how far Isabella herself was responsible for the disasters of the regency. She was certainly accountable for them all insofar as that she allowed Mortimer free rein and used her power to build up his. Without her collusion, he could not have monopolized the government so extensively. Thus, if she was tainted by association with him and his misdeeds, it was her own fault. Blinded by her lust or love for him, and driven by her need to maintain the status quo, she seems gradually to have lost all sense of reality and proportion.

Had Isabella felt oppressed by Mortimer's dominance, there were any number of people who would have been willing to help her free herself from it. The fact that she made no effort to dissociate herself from this destructive and much-hated man and his repressive approach to government is proof of his hold over her and perhaps of her deep feelings for him.

After Parliament had adjourned on 23 March, the court had moved east to Reading, then, on the twenty-ninth, to Woodstock Palace, where Queen Philippa was to remain until the birth of her child. Isabella stayed with her for at least a month.[221]

Mortimer was now closing in on his other enemies. On 4 April, the arrest of Kent's brother-in-law, Lord Wake, was ordered, but he, along with many others, had already fled the country.[222] Bishop Gravesend and several others were imprisoned,[223] but Gravesend was later released on sureties, while Archbishop Melton, after being indicted for high treason in the Court of King's Bench, was surprisingly acquitted of all complicity in Kent's plot.[224] Deveril and Bayouse were later rewarded for helping to uncover the conspiracy.[225]

On 5 April, Kent's treason was publicly proclaimed, and it was announced, in response to rumors to the contrary, that he had confessed before Parliament and then received judgment, which was rather twisting the truth.[226] Two days later, his widow gave birth to a second son, John, at

Arundel Castle. Because Kent's property had been declared forfeit, his elder son, Edmund, aged four, was not allowed to succeed to the title. The Countess had been implicated by Kent in his treason, and so, as soon as she had recovered, she and her sons and two daughters, Margaret, three, and Joan, two, were sent to live under house arrest at Salisbury Castle.[227]

On 10 April, a new embassy was sent to France to conclude a lasting peace treaty; a settlement with Philip VI was reached on 8 May.

On 12 April, Queen Philippa formally petitioned the King to grant her more revenues, since the income she had to live on was insufficient. All she got for her efforts was one manor.[228] In April, however, she was finally given her own household, although she remained heavily dependent on the King for provisions.[229] That month, Isabella, never willing to give up an iota of her wealth, granted herself lands of greater value than those that she had surrendered to Philippa on 12 February.[230]

On 13 April, a second proclamation concerning Kent's treason was issued, ordering the arrest of those who claimed that he had been unjustly condemned and of those persons who were continuing to spread rumors that Edward II was still alive,[231] for there was mounting panic at the prospect and "almost all the commons of England were in sorrow and dread" in case the deposed King really had survived.[232] Now that these rumors had served their purpose, they were to be quashed once and for all.

By the middle of April, William de Montagu had returned from Avignon and informed Edward III of the code to be used in his letters to the Pope. One of them is extant, bearing the earliest surviving signature of an English king,[233] but there is no evidence that Edward ever used this device to complain of his mother or of Mortimer to the Pope.

On 16 April, through Isabella's influence, her clerk, Robert Wyville, was made Bishop of Salisbury, despite being illiterate.[234]

Mortimer had now built up a vast landed estate, but what he and Isabella needed was money. Should there be an uprising against them, or an invasion, ready cash would buy them soldiers and the wherewithal to bribe their way out of a crisis. Already, Kent's goods had been sold and the money put in the Exchequer.[235] During the last Parliament, Mortimer had demanded money for an expedition to Gascony and had ordered Convocation to raise it, but Archbishop Meopham had objected, clearly—and doubtless correctly—suspecting that Isabella and Mortimer would appropriate it for themselves.[236] But there were other ways of raising cash.[237] On 20 April, all Mortimer's debts to the Exchequer were forgiven.[238] Five days later, grants were made to him and his son Geoffrey, the latter receiving the

lion's share of Kent's estates.[239] Further grants were made to Isabella and
Mortimer on 12 July,[240] and to Mortimer in August, and a loan offered by
the City of London was haughtily accepted as a gift.[241]

Around May and June, Isabella and Mortimer were busily granting the
rest of Kent's property to their remaining supporters, the Earl of Surrey,
Hugh de Turpington, Oliver Ingham, Simon de Bereford, Maltravers, Berkeley, and the Burghershes, in return for undertakings to attend the King with
an armed following in the event of war.[242] One man who was definitely not
to be bought was Arundel's dispossessed heir, Richard FitzAlan, who was
arrested at the beginning of June for plotting Mortimer's downfall.[243]

After 4 May, Isabella went to stay at Eltham,[244] and on the nineteenth, aware
that the birth of her grandchild was imminent, she wrote to Bishop Stratford, reminding him to pay Philippa arrears of the allowance that the King
had granted her for her chamber. Stratford had been a very vocal opponent
of the government during Lancaster's rebellion, but he had been reconciled
to the King early in 1330,[245] and the tone of the Queen's letter is unexpect-
edly warm, suggesting that she was prepared to forgive and forget the past:

> Greetings and true love.
>
> We pray you from the depths of our heart to make immediately
> available to our very dear daughter the Queen those Letters Patent
> under the Great Seal in which the King our son assigned her 10,000 [*sic*]
> marks for her chamber, to be received from the Exchequer of our said
> son, and which—as you know—his father agreed to. And in addition to
> this, please also cause writs of liberate to be issued for 500 marks for the
> term of Easter last past, and for the remaining 500 marks for Michael-
> mas next coming, for the whole year, and have these delivered to Sir
> William Colby, his clerk, for the love of us.
>
> May the Lord keep you.
>
> Given at our manor of Eltham on 19 May.[246]

The reference to Edward II's agreeing to the settlement on Philippa is
strange, since he was believed to be dead by the time she came to England,
and he had not been involved in the marriage negotiations. It probably
refers to arrangements he had discussed years before for a settlement on
any future bride for his son. The fact that Isabella mentions him at all to
Bishop Stratford suggests that his name was not taboo but that Isabella
referred to him openly, something she might not have done had she had a
guilty conscience.

———

The Queen Mother was back at Woodstock when, at ten o'clock in the morning of 15 June, Queen Philippa gave birth to a beautiful healthy son, an heir to England.[247] Named Edward, like his father, grandfather, and great-grandfather, this boy was to win lasting renown as the "Black Prince" in the decades to come. He was Isabella's first grandchild, and the surviving evidence suggests that there was always a close bond between them.

Isabella and Mortimer stayed at Woodstock for three days after the birth, then went to Gloucester from 20 to 23 June,[248] which meant that they were absent from Philippa's churching and the great banquet that followed it.

On 8 July, Edward III sealed the new treaty with France.[249] The next day, the council met at nearby Oseney Abbey[250] and found itself dealing with yet another crisis, for a warning had just been received from Count William of Hainault that Henry de Beaumont, Rhys ap Gruffydd, and other exiles were planning to invade England from Brabant, and that their friends in Wales were poised to attack Mortimer's lands.[251] Immediately, the council sent a message summoning Isabella and Mortimer urgently back from Gloucester, then ordered a general muster of troops throughout the realm and forbade all tournaments, in case they served as a pretext for armed men to gather.[252] On 11 July, the Mayor of London was ordered to meet with the King at Woodstock.

Isabella and Mortimer were back at Woodstock by 15 July,[253] to hear that the Mayor had begged to be excused from waiting upon the King since he was needed in London to deal with the mounting unrest there, which had no doubt been precipitated by the invasion scare. But the Queen would brook no excuses, and he was commanded to present himself and two dozen leading citizens at Woodstock on 27 July for talks on how to deal with the present emergency, during which the Londoners would declare their loyalty to the King, and Isabella, in return, would graciously solicit a pardon for Hamo de Chigwell.[254] Mortimer immediately canceled plans he had made to go on a pilgrimage to the shrine of Saint James at Compostela in Spain, for he dared not leave the country at this juncture, and throughout July and August, various measures were deployed for the defense of the realm.[255] They were sufficient to deter the invaders but not to stop their plotting, from their safe distance, the destruction of Isabella and Mortimer.

On 17 July, at Isabella's request, the King made a grant to Saint Peter's Hospital in York, which had been founded before the Conquest and later became known as Saint Leonard's Hospital. That month, Isabella again made Mortimer the heir to several of her properties,[256] which lends substance to Froissart's assertion that, some time after Kent's execution, "great infamy fell on the Queen Mother (whether justly or not I do not know) because it was reported that she was with child by Mortimer." It is indeed possible that Isabella was pregnant at this time, but the "great infamy" did not fall upon her until later in the year, as will be seen.

By 29 July, the court had moved to Northampton.[257] On that day, Maltravers was replaced by Mortimer's man Sir Hugh de Turpington as Steward of the Household.

The court was at King's Cliffe on 6 August, Stamford on the tenth, Bourne in Lincolnshire on the fourteenth, Lincoln on the twenty-fourth, and Clipstone on 1 September. On 6 September, the council was summoned to meet at Nottingham, where the King and his train arrived four days later.[258]

On 15 September, the Pope wrote to Edward III and Queen Isabella in response to Edward's letter of 24 March. With perhaps more than a touch of irony, he expressed his deep surprise at Kent's claim that Edward II was still alive, especially since the late King had been given a state funeral: "the Pope believes and holds firmly that those who were present could not possibly have been deceived, and did not attempt to deceive. If the funeral had been in secret, there would have been some grounds for suspicion, but as it was public, there were none." He protested, rather too vehemently, that he had not believed in Kent's incredible claims, and that, if he had, he would not have dealt directly with the Earl but would have warned the King and the Queen Mother immediately.

Perceptive, shrewd, and well informed, John XXII evidently realized that Isabella and Mortimer were on a headlong course to disaster, for he concluded by offering the Queen some sage advice: "Whatever you do, do prudently, and keep an eye on the end; and put up with minor irritations lest worse be thrust on you."[259] Unfortunately, it was advice that came all too late.

Nottingham Castle had originally been built on the orders of William the Conqueror in 1068 on a high sandstone crag that towered 130 feet over the town and the River Trent; it had been rebuilt by Henry II a century later and was now a mighty stronghold that held "no peer in the kingdom." The royal apartments boasted a mural depicting scenes from the life of Alexander the Great, and the chapel, dedicated to Saint Catherine, was richly furnished and decorated with wall paintings of the saint's life.[260]

Security was tight for the meeting of the council, which reflects Mortimer's increasing paranoia. He was attended as always by his 180 armed followers, and guards were posted all around the castle. The Queen and Mortimer took up lodgings in the most secure part, the "old tower," as the keep was known, and each night, every door and gate was locked and barred, and the keys brought to Isabella, who slept with them under her pillow.[261]

By now, the King had had enough. His uncle's execution, the birth of a son and heir, the mounting catalog of his grievances against Mortimer, the slights to his wife, the realization that his mother was pregnant with a bastard child—Froissart says that the rumors had "finally reached the ears of the King"—and the approach of his eighteenth birthday, when he would attain his majority, had all had a deep psychological effect on Edward III. He no longer wished to be associated with the factional squabbles and general unrest that had been the consequences of Isabella and Mortimer's rule, and he had grown increasingly resentful of his mother's tutelage. His dealings with the French would have reinforced the conviction he undoubtedly shared with most of his contemporaries that women were not born to rule nor to wield dominion over men. Edward may also have heard the rumors that were apparently gaining currency in Nottingham, that Mortimer "thirsted for the destruction of the royal blood and the usurpation of the royal majesty."[262]

It was Edward himself who, by his own admission, conceived a "secret design" against Mortimer,[263] probably around late September or early October, since there is no evidence of his coup's being planned earlier, although the King had probably been growing ever more desperate to get rid of Mortimer for at least a year, since Montagu's secret visit to the Pope. Now he realized it had become imperative that he do so, for the man was dangerous and, even if he did not have designs on the Crown, was dragging the monarchy into disrepute.[264] Edward himself later informed John XXII that the only persons to whom he initially confided his plans were William de Montagu and Richard de Bury, his devoted friends, in whose discretion he had every confidence.[265]

Edward seems to have had no clear idea as to how his design was to be carried out, but he knew that any plan had to be foolproof, since the consequences of failure did not bear thinking about. It was Montagu who came up with a workable but daring scheme. He had befriended William d'Eland of Basford, the deputy constable of the castle, who was in charge in the absence of the constable, Lord Grey of Codnor. Eland was no friend to

Mortimer and was willing to divulge the existence of a secret passage that had been cut through the massive rock on which the castle was built;[266] this passage still survives today and is known as "Mortimer's Hole,"[267] although evidently neither Mortimer nor Isabella knew of its existence. Entry to it was gained via a postern gate near the "Trip to Jerusalem," an inn that dated from 1189, the year in which Richard the Lion-Hearted departed on the Third Crusade. The tunnel was between six and ten feet wide and had rough steps where the gradient was at its steepest. It led up to the kitchen in the keep, which was next to the great hall. Upstairs were the chambers occupied by the King, Isabella, and Mortimer. It was through this passage that Montagu would gain access to the castle.

In order to carry out his plan, Montagu enlisted the support of at least two dozen other young courtiers whose loyalty to the King could be counted on. Among them were Edward's cousins, the ailing John de Bohun, Earl of Hereford, and his brothers Humphrey and William; Ralph de Stafford; Robert de Ufford; William de Clinton; John Neville of Hornby; William Latimer; Thomas Garton; and Robert Digby.[268]

Many historians have claimed that Lancaster was involved in this conspiracy, but this is unlikely, unless it was secretly to offer his moral support. Lancaster had no means of gaining access to the King, and his name is not recorded among the conpirators. Nevertheless, Edward must have known that, when the time came, he could count on him as an ally.

The council met at Nottingham on 15 October. The chief items on its agenda were Philip VI's refusal to ratify the recent peace treaty unless Edward III paid liege homage, and matters of national security, which needed to be addressed in the wake of the recent invasion scare. At this council, according to Baker, Mortimer "shone with all too transient honour as Isabella's chief adviser, whose word was law to those assembled."

On 16 October, Lancaster appeared in Nottingham and took up lodgings near the castle. He was virtually blind now and, according to Baker, looked like an old man, even though he was not yet fifty, but Mortimer did not believe him harmless and angrily objected to his presence, demanding, "Who made him so bold to take up his lodgings close to the Queen?" As a result, Lancaster was moved to new accommodation a mile out of the town, with John de Bohun.[269]

Some members of the King's household, realizing that something was afoot, warned Mortimer and Isabella that Edward was plotting to overthrow them and that Montagu had openly asserted that Mortimer had had Edward II murdered.[270] On 18 or 19 October, the King, Montagu, and eight of their friends were summoned before Isabella, Mortimer, Chancellor Burghersh, and the council and interrogated.[271] Mortimer, "wrathful as a devil,"[272] dramatically accused the King and his companions of plotting against him. Edward denied it, as did Montagu, who sprang to his feet and defied any man to call the King a traitor, then sharply declared that he himself had done nothing against his allegiance. Mortimer snapped back that, when the King's wishes were in conflict with his own, they were not to be obeyed.[273] Afterward, realizing that it was only a matter of time before Mortimer moved against them, Montagu warned Edward "that it was better that they should eat the dog than let the dog eat them"; the King, despite some misgivings, agreed that they should strike now before it was too late and commanded Eland to leave the postern gate open, on pain of death. Montagu and the rest of the conspirators then left Nottingham, intending that Mortimer should think that they had fled for their lives.[274]

At midnight on 19 October, Montagu and his men returned and, carrying torches, made their way up the secret passage to the keep. The King, who knew he was watched by Mortimer's spies,[275] had had to remain inside the castle; since his physician was later rewarded for assisting in the plot, it is possible that he had connived to help Edward feign illness. This would have given the King an excuse to withdraw to his chamber, where his mother and Mortimer would have expected him to remain.[276] But after everyone had retired for the night, Edward emerged and made his way downstairs, probably in disguise (it is tempting to speculate that he had changed clothes with his physician). When Montagu and the rest appeared, he was waiting for them in the kitchen or hall, ready to lead them upstairs to the royal apartments.

They advanced with drawn swords, but outside the door of the Queen's chamber, they were challenged by Hugh de Turpington, the Steward of the Household, and Richard Monmouth, Mortimer's squire, who had escaped from the Tower with him in 1323. Turpington shouted, "Traitors! You shall die an evil death here!" But in the short but fierce fight that followed, it was he who perished under the violent impact of Sir John Neville's mace, while Monmouth was fatally stabbed.

The King did not want his mother to see him, so he stayed just outside the door to keep watch, "his weapon at the ready," while Montagu and his companions burst into the Queen's chamber,[277] where they found Isabella, Mortimer, Chancellor Burghersh, Simon de Bereford, and Oliver Ingham, who had just concluded a meeting at which they had resolved to arrest Montagu and his friends and were all about to retire for the night. Mortimer drew his sword and sprang to defend himself, killing one of his assailants, but he was quickly overpowered by Sir John de Moleyns, who arrested him in the King's name. Bereford and Ingham were seized and bound, and Bishop Burghersh was apprehended while trying to escape down the privy shaft.

Isabella watched in horror as her lover was pinioned. It had all happened so quickly, but she was fast realizing that her world was falling in ruins about her. She could not see her son, but she suspected that he was nearby, and in her anguish, she screamed, "Bel fitz! Bel fitz! Eiez pitie du gentil Mortimer!" ("Fair son! Fair son! Have pity on the good Mortimer!"). But Edward ignored her and would not show his face. Passionately, she begged Montagu and the others "to do no harm to the person of Mortimer because he was a worthy knight, her dear friend and well-beloved cousin," but they heeded her not. Mortimer and the other captives were marched out of the chamber and down to the great hall to meet their fate, and the door slammed shut on the Queen, locking her in with her fears and her misery.[278]

PART THREE

Isabella

Our Lady Queen Isabella

CHAPTER ELEVEN

❧

Our Dearest Mother

After Mortimer and the others had been taken away, Isabella's door was locked and the room placed under guard.

When the worst happened, Isabella's first thoughts had been for Mortimer's safety. Maybe she had feared that he would be summarily executed. That was in Edward III's mind, too, but having summoned and conferred with Lancaster during the night, he was persuaded that that would be just another act of tyranny and agreed to send Mortimer to London to be tried by his peers in Parliament.[1] Early the next morning, the once-mighty Earl of March was taken south to Leicester in chains.[2] The lords and the people gathered to watch as he and the other prisoners were escorted through Nottingham, and at his approach, they shouted loudly. A jubilant Lancaster was among them, wildly gesticulating for joy and throwing his cap in the air.[3]

On 20 October, the day after his successful coup, Edward III proclaimed that he had arrested Mortimer and wished all men to know that he had assumed personal control of the government of his realm and would "henceforth govern his people according to right and reason, as befits his royal dignity."[4] Edward's liberation from the tutelage of Mortimer and Isabella was greeted by his subjects as if it were the release of the Israelites from bondage,[5] for it was recognized that he had freed the realm from tyranny, civil war, and anarchy.

A day or so later, Edward left Nottingham, but before his departure, he sent his mother, who was in a very distressed state, to Berkhamsted Castle.[6] This eleventh-century fortress, which consisted of a strong keep on a very high hill, surrounded by a unique double moat, had once been owned by Thomas à Becket, and later by Piers Gaveston, so it had mixed associations for Isabella, although she may not have been in any state to care where she was at this time.[7] Here, she was to live under house arrest until the King had made up his mind what to do with her.

Once news of the overthrow of Mortimer became known, Maltravers, Gurney, Ockle, Deveril, and several more of Mortimer's followers panicked and fled abroad.[8] Lord Berkeley, who had helped them to flee, made no move to escape and was taken into custody.[9]

The King, accompanied by Lancaster, arrived in Leicester on 22 October, on his way south to London.[10] Mortimer was taken from Leicester four days later, with an escort of a hundred guards.[11] He was at Lutterworth on the twenty-seventh, but then nothing more is heard of his whereabouts until 26 November, when he is recorded as being a prisoner in the Tower of London,[12] possibly in the Beauchamp Tower. He was probably sent there as soon as he reached the capital.[13] This time, there was to be no chance of escape, for he was guarded by six men-at-arms.[14]

By 3 November, Edward had joined Queen Philippa at Woodstock. On that day, Parliament was summoned to meet at Westminster on 26 November,[15] which would allow time for Mortimer and his associates to be questioned. The King also invited his subjects to lay any charges against Mortimer before him in Parliament; as it turned out, not one petition would mention Isabella.[16] On 13 November, Edward celebrated his eighteenth birthday.

Parliament met at Westminster from 26 November to 9 December. Edward now had his chance to exact retribution from those who had perpetrated the crimes that had so discredited the previous regime. On the opening day, Berkeley was tried for the murder of Edward II.[17]

He was asked how he wished to acquit himself of responsibility for that murder. His reply was astonishing: "He said that he had never consented to the King's death, procured it or helped the murderers. Indeed, he never even knew that Edward was dead until this present Parliament." He asked, therefore, to be acquitted. Of course, if Edward had escaped from Berkeley Castle, as Fieschi claims, Berkeley would have been telling the truth, even though he had publicly escorted what was assumed to be the King's body to

Gloucester for burial. Not surprisingly, Berkeley's inquisitors did not accept this defense. It was hugely in Edward III's interests that it be rejected.

Furthermore, there was no way that Berkeley was going to be allowed to plead innocence on the grounds that Edward II was not dead, because Mortimer had probably confessed to his murder under interrogation in the Tower, and Edward III did not want the Crown's case against him undermined. So Berkeley changed tack and asked to be acquitted of the charge of murder on the grounds that he was not at his castle at the time it had been committed but had been recovering from an illness at his manor of Bradley near Wootton-under-Edge, a plea that was accepted. But he was then charged with having appointed the two other alleged murderers, Gurney and Ockle, to help guard Edward. He admitted that he had done so, but without any evil intent, and his guarantors—who had doubtless been well primed beforehand—declared that those two were the guilty ones. Parliament released Berkeley on a surety, leaving this charge to hang over his head for the next seven years.[18]

On 28 November, in the King's presence, Mortimer was arraigned for high treason by his peers in Parliament. He was allowed to be present but was bound and gagged, and dressed in a tunic on which were emblazoned the words "quid glorians" ("Where is your glory?").[19] He was indicted on several counts of treason, the most serious being that he had "traitorously, feloniously and falsely murdered and killed" Edward II; he had also arrogated to himself the royal power and ignored the regency council; he had lured Kent to his illegal execution; he had attacked Lancaster; he had dared to question the King's word; he had set spies upon the King; he had stirred up dissension in the kingdom; he had extended his territories to the disinheritance of the Crown; he had planned the destruction of the King's friends; and he had embezzled public funds.[20]

Later sources allege that Mortimer was accused of being "over-homely" with the Queen,[21] but their relationship is not referred to in the indictment in the Rolls of Parliament. In fact, Isabella is only once referred to in the charges, which reflects the King's determination to preserve what was left of her reputation. The charge that mentions her claims that "the said Roger falsely and maliciously sowed discord between the father of our Lord the King and the Queen his companion, making her believe that if she came near her husband, he would poinard her, or murder her in some other manner. Wherefore, by this cause, and by other subtleties, the said Queen remained absent from her said lord, to the great dishonour of the King and of his mother, and great damage, perhaps, to the whole nation hereafter, which God avert." This placed the responsibility for the rift between Edward and Isabella firmly on Mortimer's shoulders.

Mortimer was quite clearly guilty on all counts, and because he had sent Kent to his death without giving him a chance to speak in his own defense, and perhaps because there were fears that he might incriminate Isabella, his judges forbade him to plead. Thus, he was condemned unheard and sentenced "as a traitor and enemy of the King and of the realm to be drawn and hanged" and to the forfeiture of all his titles and property.[22] It has been credibly suggested that it was at the request of Isabella that Edward refrained from exacting the full penalty of the law for traitors or that he did so in order to exacerbate Isabella's terrible distress.[23]

That day, Burghersh, who had been imprisoned in the Tower, was deprived of the office of Chancellor and Bishop Stratford elected in his place. Burghersh, however, was a man of some ability, and it was not long before he was released and able to regain his political influence. In 1334, he was back in high office, as Treasurer, and he would serve Edward well as a diplomat. John Stratford became Edward's chief minister, held the office of Chancellor three times, and in 1333, was elected Archbishop of Canterbury. He died in 1348.

Now that Mortimer had been condemned, Parliament made an official vote of thanks to William de Montagu, who had been largely responsible for bringing him to justice and freeing the King and the realm from tyranny;[24] in reward, he received many of Mortimer's confiscated estates. William d'Eland was rewarded for admitting Montagu and his fellows to Nottingham Castle.[25] Archbishop Melton was appointed Treasurer. Later on, several of those who had helped to overthrow Mortimer were advanced by Edward III: in 1333, Richard de Bury was appointed Bishop of Durham and was made Chancellor the next year; in 1337, Montagu was created Earl of Salisbury, Robert de Ufford Earl of Suffolk, and William de Clinton Earl of Huntingdon; and in 1351, Ralph de Stafford was created Earl of Stafford.[26] All who had taken part in the coup were indemnified by Parliament against charges of murder, so that they could not be prosecuted for killing Mortimer's defenders on the night of the coup.[27]

On 29 November, Mortimer, attired in the black tunic that he had worn for Edward II's funeral, was brought from the Tower and drawn on an oxhide tied to two horses along the three miles to the Elms at Tyburn. The hordes of spectators jeered and chanted the words of Psalm 52, which began, "Why boastest thou in mischief, O mighty man? Thou lovest evil more than good."[28]

The Elms was London's common gallows from 1196 until 1783 and consisted of two uprights and a crossbeam long enough to accommodate ten felons. Here, Mortimer was allowed, or made, to say a few words to the watching crowds: he made no reference to Edward II's murder but confessed that Kent had been the innocent victim of a cruel conspiracy.[29] Then he was stripped naked, and "the same measure that he had meted out to others was measured to him." In those days, it could have taken him up to twenty minutes to die of slow strangulation. His body was left hanging from the gallows for two days and nights.[30]

That same day, in Parliament, Simon de Bereford, John Deveril, Bogo de Bayouse, John Maltravers, Thomas Gurney, and William Ockle were all condemned to death—Gurney and Ockle for Edward II's murder; Maltravers, Deveril, and Bayouse for assisting in Kent's destruction; and Bereford, "by common repute," for aiding and abetting Mortimer "in all his treasons, felonies and plots."[31] Bereford was the only one of the five in captivity, the rest having fled into exile. It is surprising that Maltravers was not indicted for Edward II's murder, especially since Berkeley had admitted to being away at the time and Maltravers had been left in charge of the former King, but Berkeley may have told his interrogators that Maltravers knew no more of the murder than he did, which would explain why Edward III was to concentrate his efforts on finding Gurney and Ockle. According to Baker, Deveril had confessed to murdering Edward II, but there is no evidence that he was involved. Since efforts to find the condemned had so far proved fruitless, warrants for their arrest were issued on 3 December, and rewards were offered to anyone apprehending them, alive or dead.[32] At the end of November, the lands and property of all Mortimer's principal adherents were seized by the Crown.[33]

On 1 December, Mortimer's body was cut down from the gallows and delivered to the Franciscans, who initially took it to their church at Newgate. Murimuth says he was buried there, but it was a grand resting place for so great a traitor, and other sources state that he was actually interred in the convent of the Grey Friars at Coventry.[34]

Knighton voiced what was probably the opinion of many when he asserted that Isabella deserved to be executed. She herself feared that she would be punished severely.[35] Yet it would be left to Henry VIII to order the first execution of an English queen consort, two centuries in the future. The Pope, as soon as he had learned of the toppling of Isabella and Mortimer, had written to Edward III, urging him in his righteous wrath not "to expose his mother's shame" but to treat her with honor.[36] It is unlikely that Edward had had any intention of doing anything else, not only because of his filial love for Isabella but also because his claim to the throne of France derived from her, and any scandal attaching to her name would certainly prejudice that claim. It would, furthermore, cause untold damage to the English monarchy, whose prestige, after more than two decades of misrule and factional fighting, was lower than it had been for two centuries. Public censure might also damage his mother's health at this time and would have meant the scandalous exposure of any illicit pregnancy.

Edward decided, therefore, that he would spare Isabella any public disgrace and instituted the official line that all the evils of the regency were to be blamed upon Mortimer, while his "dearest mother" was to be portrayed as just another of that tyrant's victims—which, in a sense, of course, she was. Her adulterous relationship with Mortimer would be airbrushed from history. Had Edward been convinced of Isabella's involvement in Edward II's murder—and she would surely have been questioned about this—he would hardly have been as lenient. Yet his treatment of her suggests that he held her responsible in part for the misrule of the past three years. Clearly, he was determined that she should never again wield any political power but should live out the rest of her life in honorable and comfortable retirement. She was to be treated with respect and courtesy and would henceforth be referred to as "Madame the Queen Mother" or "our Lady Queen Isabella."[37]

For the present, considering her pregnancy and the grief she must have been experiencing as a result of Mortimer's execution, it was decided that she be kept out of the public eye and that Philippa at last assume her rightful place as Queen of England.

On 1 December, Isabella "simply and spontaneously" surrendered all her lands to the King.[38] In January 1331, she would be assigned a fixed income of £3,000 per annum to live on and "maintain her noble estate all the days of her life,"[39] while Philippa would receive the lands that Isabella had held in dower.[40]

In December 1330, the King issued a general pardon to all opponents of the previous regime; invited exiles such as Wake, Beaumont, Hugh de Audley, and Rhys ap Gruffydd to come home; and restored their property.[41] On 7 December, Kent's son, Edmund, was restored to his father's earldom and lands, on the grounds that the late Earl had "been at all times good and loyal, though deceived by wicked men." Kent's daughter Joan was taken into the royal household to be brought up by Queen Philippa.[42] In 1361, after a checkered marital career, she married the King's heir, Edward, Prince of Wales, and, by him, became the mother of Richard II.

Oliver Ingham was pardoned on 8 December[43] and soon afterward restored as Seneschal of Gascony. On the fifteenth, Edward ordered that the bones of Hugh le Despenser, which had been on public display for more than four years, be taken down and given decent burial. Despenser's widow, Eleanor de Clare, had them interred in Tewkesbury Abbey and built a fine tomb in his memory. Their son, another Hugh, was restored to the Despenser barony.

Simon de Bereford was executed on 24 December, the only one of Mortimer's associates to share his fate.[44]

At Christmas, Isabella was with the court at Windsor.[45] After Mortimer's execution, Lord Wake, John Lestraunge, and the Bohun brothers had been ordered to escort her from Berkhamsted to the King.[46] She apparently remained at Windsor for the next two years, in the "safe-keeping" of the constable. Effectively, she was under house arrest; in a grant of 1331, Edward refers to the year 1330–31 having been "the first year of her imprisonment."[47] But it was a gilded cage. The King, "by the advice of his council," had "ordered his mother to be confined in a goodly castle, and gave her plenty of ladies and damsels to wait upon her, as well as knights and squires of honour. He made her a handsome allowance to keep and maintain the state to which she had been accustomed, but forbade her ever to go out or show herself abroad, except at certain times and when any shows were exhibited in the court of the castle,"[48] such as those put on by mummers and traveling players.

We do not know whether Isabella mingled with the King and his courtiers that first Christmas after her fall or whether she was simply in residence in the castle at that time and unable to participate in the festivities. If she had conceived around May, she would have been seven months pregnant at Christmas. But there is no further mention of her pregnancy in any source. The likelihood is, therefore, that, in the wake of the disaster that had overtaken her, she had lost her baby while she was at Berkhamsted.

Strickland and other writers have claimed that Isabella was shut up at Windsor because she suffered a period of mental derangement after Mortimer's execution. Strickland mentions a persistent contemporary rumor that she actually died on the day that Mortimer's corpse was cut down, which reveals that very few people could say with any certainty what had happened to Isabella. A nervous breakdown is a possibility. The shock of learning of her lover's death perhaps coincided with the depression that follows a stillbirth and caused such a breakdown. We do know that the King paid large sums for a physician to attend his mother during this period.[49] It has also been claimed that, for the rest of her life, Isabella suffered from periodic attacks of insanity or neurosis, but there is no evidence for this. If she did suffer initially from a mental illness, it is more likely to have been depression or anxiety than a personality disorder such as schizophrenia.

Isabella passed her time at Windsor "meekly."[50] She was certainly receiving spiritual comfort, for the King gave his chaplain, Edmund de Rammersby, "on behalf of our mother, the first year of her imprisonment, two crystal vases containing minute bones, relics of the Holy Innocents; one silver flask, containing relics of St. Sylvester; part of the side of St. Lawrence, enclosed in silver; and a joint of John the Baptist's little finger."[51]

Queen Philippa was extremely kind to Isabella at this time, and in the summer of 1331, the Pope wrote to thank and commend her for the sympathy and consolation that she had shown to her mother-in-law in her tribulation. He urged her "to aim at restoring the good fame of the Queen Mother, which has been undeservedly injured." It may be that the shrewd John XXII was following the official line that Isabella was sinned against rather than sinning, in the interests of fostering harmonious relations in the English royal family and boosting the prestige of the monarchy. Or he could have been told of Isabella's mental state. He was not supposed to know about her liaison with Mortimer, and would surely not have referred to it in a letter, so in speaking of "her tribulation" he was perhaps alluding to her nervous collapse.

Edward III was to enjoy a long and largely successful reign. To his subjects, he came to epitomize what a king should be: powerful, magnificent, warlike, merciful, wise, and "familiar and gentle to all men." According to Murimuth, "he was glorious among all the great ones of the world." Physically, he seems to have taken after his Plantagenet ancestors, being more than six feet tall with good bone structure and an aquiline nose, and he had the good looks of their race—"his face was like the face of a god."[52]

His marriage to Philippa of Hainault was enduringly happy, and the couple produced thirteen children. Edward was fortunate in that Philippa turned a blind eye to his many infidelities, for he was unable to control "the dissolute lusts of the flesh."[53] It is unfair to speculate that he inherited his sensual bent from Isabella, since many of his royal forebears were as promiscuous as he.

Edward put an end to the factional fighting that had so long dominated English politics, and unified his realm. By creating his sons dukes and marrying them into the great aristocratic families, he identified the interests of the nobility with those of the monarchy. He also ensured that the martial instincts of the baronage were channeled into a popular war. The military victories he won during that war restored the prestige of the monarchy and assured Edward of great popularity and renown. He established a famously brilliant court and raised the cult of chivalry to an art form. When he died in 1377, the epitaph on his tomb in Westminster Abbey described him as "the glory of the English, the flower of kings past, the pattern for kings to come." Isabella had given England a ruler to be proud of.

After the removal of Mortimer, Edward could afford to be tolerant and conciliatory. There was no purge of those who had supported Isabella and Mortimer. Bishops were left in their sees. Airmyn was appointed Treasurer in February 1331 and would hold the post for a year. He died in 1336. Bartholemew, Lord Burghersh, became one of the King's chief advisers and helped administer Isabella's dower lands in Ponthieu. Richard FitzAlan was restored to the earldom of Arundel. Hugh de Audley was created Earl of Gloucester.

Although Lancaster largely retired from public life in the 1330s, he remained in favor with the King until his death in 1345. In 1359, his granddaughter and heiress, Blanche of Lancaster, would marry Edward's fourth son, John of Gaunt, who thereby became Duke of Lancaster. In 1399, their son, Henry IV, became the first sovereign of the House of Lancaster.

Edward took measures to reverse the injustices of the previous regime. He promised his people that, in future, he would rule his realm with the advice of the council of magnates. He removed corrupt sheriffs and officials and dealt with complaints against them. In January 1332, in order to prevent an avalanche of disputes over land and titles, the King declared that the validity of a grant could not be questioned on the grounds that it had been made in the time of evil counselors.[54]

Before long, Edward had reestablished the authority and standing of the Crown, enlisted the support of the barons, and made foreign alliances that would lead to greater prosperity.

Edward was still anxious to get his hands on the men he believed to be his father's murderers and had paid a secret agent, Giles of Spain, to search for them. Ockle proved impossible to track down, having disappeared without trace, but before 20 May 1331, Giles had reported that Thomas Gurney was in Castile. Edward immediately requested King Alfonso XI to have Gurney arrested and sent warrants and letters of protection to ensure his safe passage. Alfonso complied, and when he received news of Gurney's arrest in Burgos, Edward rewarded both the captor and the messenger handsomely. Giles of Spain took Gurney in custody to Bayonne in Gascony, where, on the specific orders of the King, they were to board a ship bound for England. But Gurney gave his custodian the slip and disappeared.[55] On 17 June, Giles turned up at Dover without his prisoner and presented his bill for 372 days spent in pursuing him. Clearly, he was attempting to cheat the King, for Gurney had been out of England for only six or seven months.[56]

Edward III's treatment of the Mortimer family was just. In October 1331, Wigmore and other lordships were restored to Roger's eldest surviving son, Edmund. The following month, Roger's widow was given license to move his body to Wigmore Abbey, to lie with those of his ancestors; although there have been claims that it was moved to Wigmore or Shrewsbury,[57] recent research suggests that it remained undisturbed at Coventry.[58] Edmund Mortimer died of a fever on 16 December, leaving a three-year-old son, Roger, as his heir.

During the remaining years of her life, we only have occasional glimpses of Isabella in contemporary sources. She was not present, nor was Edward III, when, on 24 November 1331, King David II of Scotland and Queen Joan were crowned at Scone Abbey.

In January 1332, Isabella wrote "to her very dear sovereign lord the King" to inquire about two of the grants that he had made to her in December 1330. The manor of Bristlesham in Berkshire had turned out to belong to Alice de Lacy, Countess of Lincoln, and the rents of the town of Derby were swallowed up in an annuity to one Edward Chandos. Naturally, Isabella wanted compensation; clearly, she was in full possession of all her faculties. "As his dearest mother had surrendered her dower into his hands," the King assigned her other lands to the value of the Derby rents and persuaded Alice de Lacy to surrender Bristlesham in return for another manor. Edward also assigned to Isabella "divers other castles and lands, to the amount of £2,000."[59] With an income of £5,000 a year, more than her original dower as Queen Consort, Isabella could live very comfortably.

In March 1332, Queen Philippa bore a daughter, who was named Isabella in honor of the Queen Mother. This suggests that a conscious effort was being made to rehabilitate Isabella and also that Edward was anxious for harmonious relations with his mother.

Certainly, by March 1332, Isabella had been permitted to leave Windsor and had regained a degree of freedom, for that month, the constable of Windsor Castle secured the payment of "expenses incurred by him in safe-keeping Queen Isabella in that castle for some time, by the King's order."[60] At Easter, she was with the court when it stayed for ten days at Peterborough Abbey.

She may also have been involved in preparations for the wedding of her elder daughter, Eleanor, now nearly fourteen, who married Reginald II, Duke of Gueldres, at Nijmegen in May 1332. The marriage had been arranged by Isabella's cousin, the Countess of Hainault, but the auguries for the future were not good. Reginald, a widower, was dark of coloring and character. He had seized power from his feebleminded father and imprisoned him for six years.

Isabella's hand may perhaps be detected in the trousseau that was prepared for Eleanor. The Princess's wedding gown was of Spanish cloth of gold embroidered with brilliant silks and was worn with a crimson velvet mantle and a white lawn veil. When she sailed from Sandwich, she took with her caps, gloves, shoes of Cordoba leather, a bed hung with green velvet and silk curtains, rare spices, and loaves of sugar and traveled in a painted chariot upholstered in purple velvet and decorated with gold stars.

The new Duchess was well received by her husband's subjects. She bore him two sons, Reginald and Edward, who succeeded him in turn. But the catastrophic events of her unhappy childhood had left her nervous and overeager to please, and Reginald soon tired of her. In 1338, he sent her from court, pretended she had leprosy, and attempted to have the marriage annulled so that he could take another wife. Eleanor now proved that she had something of her mother's spirit: she turned up at Reginald's palace in Nijmegen and, before the whole court, removed her cloak; beneath it, she was either completely naked, according to some chroniclers, or was wearing only a diaphanous shift that left little to the imagination. Either way, everyone could see that there were no signs of leprosy on her body. Reginald had to take her back, and they remained together until he died after a fall from his horse in 1343.

After Eleanor's departure, Isabella probably took up residence at Castle Rising in Norfolk, a place indelibly associated with her, and the setting for most of her legends. The fact that Sir John de Moleyns was appointed her steward there indicates that she was still under the King's supervision, as does the fact that, in 1332, she was given permission to dwell at Eltham Palace, which was restored to her in November of that year, "whenever her health required a change of air."[61] Isabella cannot have relished Moleyns's presence, since it was he who had arrested Mortimer. However, he must have been absent for much of the time, since he was often in attendance on the King or serving abroad, and in 1340, he was dismissed from all his offices and imprisoned for acts of oppression and for failing to supply money he had promised to lend the King.[62]

Castle Rising was Isabella's own property, purchased in 1327. Built by William d'Albini, Earl of Arundel, the husband of Henry I's widow, Adeliza of Louvain, around 1150, it was a fine example of a Norman fortress, with a massive square keep that stood fifty feet high and boasted walls three yards thick decorated with Romanesque arcading, and doors with chevron decoration. The keep was surrounded by a deep ditch and massive ramparts, on which stood a stout curtain wall with three towers. It was not only a secure residence but also afforded complete privacy.

The castle was approached through a gateway protected by a portcullis, then entered by a processional stair enclosed by a richly sculpted wall. A passage led from the vaulted vestibule to the chapel. Inside the keep was a great hall; a great chamber, probably for the Queen's private use; the chapel; a kitchen; and a dungeon. In the basement were storerooms. Passages had been cut into the thickness of the walls, while garderobes were set into mural recesses. The castle kitchen was too small to cater for a household as large as Isabella's, so another was built outside in the bailey. The chapel, already described, was magnificently furnished.

Isabella's private lodgings were not in the castle itself but in a range of half-timbered buildings that were squeezed into the southern area of the narrow bailey. Their foundations were discovered in the late twentieth century. Isabella's private chambers were laid with black carpets and hung with painted cloths. She maintained a small library, and her *Household Book* records the constant preparation of parchment and vellum for it.[63]

At Castle Rising, Isabella maintained a considerable degree of state and lived a life of affluent leisure, passing her time "quite comfortably."[64] She had her own steward, treasurer, seneschal, falcon-bearer (William of Lakenham), surgeon (Master Lawrence), knights, huntsmen, grooms of the stable, thirty-three clerks and squires, eight ladies of her chamber, several damsels, and many menial servants.[65]

Isabella entertained regularly. Edward III visited her two or three times a year,[66] sometimes accompanied by Queen Philippa and Prince Edward. When the King came to stay, his household lodged nearby at a place called Thorndenes, which cannot now be identified, and he or his nobles brought with them troupes of minstrels to entertain the company. At other times,

Edward kept in touch with Isabella by letter and sent her choice delicacies, such as fresh game, wild boar, a falcon, a pair of lovebirds, pipe after pipe of Gascon wine, and barrels of sturgeon.

The burghers of nearby Bishop's (now King's) Lynn were often called upon to supply the Queen Mother with delicacies, at their own cost, which suggests that Isabella's rapacious instincts were still lively. These gifts included wine, meat, swans, barrels of sturgeon, turbot, herrings, lampreys, bread, barley, and candle wax, some of which were transported by her servant, Pierrot. In 1334, the Queen sent to Lynn for eight carpenters to make preparations for the coming visit of the King and Prince Edward. She also received a quarter of the customs dues at the port of Lynn. Relations between Castle Rising and Lynn were not always cordial, and quarrels frequently broke out between the townsfolk and the Queen's numerous retainers.[67] One can sense that the good burghers were sometimes relieved to learn that the Queen Mother had gone to stay elsewhere.

In retirement, Isabella spent much of her time hunting; hawking; reading the romances of which she was so fond; listening to the music of her minstrels; collecting religious relics, such as a ring made by Saint Dunstan; and looking to the salvation of her soul.[68] She owned casket-loads of jewels, singing birds, and many precious falcons.[69] After a time, her movements were not restricted, and starting in 1332, she made several pilgrimages to the shrine of Our Lady of Walsingham in Norfolk.[70] She also went to stay at other houses, such as Eltham Palace and Havering-atte-Bower, although she was rarely seen in London. Never again did she give any cause for scandal. Her rehabilitation was complete when orders were given that she was to be regularly prayed for after the King and Queen in church services throughout the kingdom.

To begin with, at Castle Rising, Isabella still had a physician in regular attendance. Master Pontio de Courtrone had formerly been on Edward II's medical staff, and the King had assigned him to look after Isabella. But in 1333, he was pensioned off with £100 a year, which the bailiffs of Norwich were ordered to deliver at Easter and Michaelmas, "for as long as he lives, for his great services to the Queen Mother."[71] We may perhaps conclude that Isabella had now recovered from whatever ailment had troubled her.

Clearly, she was more than able to look after her affairs. When the lieges of her forest of Macclesfield notified the King that the local bailiffs were killing her venison and destroying her wood, Edward replied, "Let this petition be shown to the Queen, that her advice may be learned thereon."[72] And when it came to recovering money owed to her administration, he referred his council to her for advice. Her name appears frequently as a witness to state documents, and in 1337, the King gave her permission to dispose of her goods by will and leave them to whomever she chose. In 1348, she was quick to defend her interests by urging that her stewards should sit on judicial commissions "to save and maintain our right and that which pertains to us."[73] None of these are the actions of a woman who was in the relentless throes of a mental illness.

Edward had not ceased to hunt for his father's assassins. In December 1332, Gurney was again tracked down and arrested by a royal agent, this time in Naples, and a Yorkshire baron, William, Lord Thweng, was sent to escort him back to England. On 13 February, Edward III sent Bernard de Pynsole with a ship to Bayonne to bring Thweng and Gurney back to England.[74] But Gurney fell ill on the long trek north through Italy. Thweng did everything he could for him, purchased clothes, shoes, and a comfortable bed, and paid two physicians to save him, but he died in prison in Bayonne, taking his secrets with him.[75] Murimuth, Baker, and Walsingham all claim, incorrectly, that he was beheaded at sea to prevent him from incriminating "the magnates, priests and other nobles."

The King had offered a reward for Gurney alive or dead, so Thweng had the body embalmed and sailed back to Tynemouth with it, landing early in July. Its place of burial is unknown, but Thweng rode north to report to Edward at Berwick, taking with him his escort of thirty men and some of the sailors who had manned the ship, presumably so that they could corroborate his story. He met with the King on 6 July and stayed for thirteen days.[76]

Why did Edward III go to such lengths to track down his father's reputed assassin? It was probably because Edward believed that Gurney was one of the men who had actually carried out the murder and could reveal to him the names, and perhaps the whereabouts, of the others involved and the circumstances in which the murder had taken place. He could also corroborate or dispute Berkeley's story. For this reason, Edward wanted to question him before ensuring that he received his just punishment.

During 1333, the King paid Simon de Bury, Master of the King's Scholars at Cambridge, £10 in compensation for the books that Edward II had given them, which had been confiscated by Isabella.[77]

In October that year, Edward led an English army to victory over the Scots at the Battle of Halidon Hill. Isabella's younger son, John of Eltham, now seventeen, commanded the first division. After the battle, David II and Queen Joan were sent by the anxious Scottish lords to France, where Philip VI gave them a safe refuge at Château Gaillard in Normandy. It was here, in 1315, that Marguerite of Burgundy had been murdered. David and Joan were to remain there for the next seven years, while Scotland was governed by regents.[78]

On 1 December, after bringing pressure to bear on the Pope, Adam Orleton was translated from Worcester to Winchester, the wealthiest see in England. Edward III was furious and had Orleton charged with complicity in the murder of Edward II. The Bishop protested his innocence, and as there was no evidence to convict him, he was acquitted[79] and later received back into favor. After distinguishing himself as a diplomat, he went blind and died in 1345.

In March 1334, Sir John Maltravers wrote to Edward III from exile in Flanders, informing him that he was in possession of sensitive information about the "honour, estate and well-being of the realm." Edward sent William de Montagu to see Maltravers and hear what he had to say, and it is likely that Maltravers confessed to him what had really happened at Berkeley in 1327.[80] This tied in with what Berkeley had told Parliament, but there was no proof of its being true, and if Edward II had escaped, where was he now? No one knew, so the matter was left well alone.

In June 1334, Isabella traveled north with King Edward, Queen Philippa, and the rest of the court to Durham Castle to attend a feast to celebrate Richard de Bury's enthronement as Bishop of Durham. Among the huge concourse of guests were Archbishops Stratford and Melton, five bishops, seven earls, numerous northern barons, and the commons of Durham. Among the mountains of food consumed were 2,300 herring, 1,100 eggs, fifteen piglets, and a porpoise.

In October, John of Eltham was granted a dispensation to marry the Infanta Maria, daughter of Ferdinand IV, King of Castile; the marriage never took place because Maria died soon afterward.

On 2 May 1336, Edward III granted a petition made by Mortimer's widow for restitution of her lands in Ireland. On 4 July, he paid compensation to the Genoese for the ship and goods seized by Despenser during his pirating days. This may have been prompted by his having received the first information about his father's survival from Nicolinus de Fieschi, who brought Edward letters in July 1336 and was rewarded with the hefty sum of 8,000 marks. This probably marks the beginning of Edward's dealings with the Fieschis that were to lead to Edward II's being confirmed the following spring. The theory supports the contention that the earliest date on which the Fieschi letter could have been written was early in 1336. It is more likely to have been the final letter connected with this matter and to have been written early in 1337.

Edward was campaigning in Scotland in the autumn of 1336 when, on 13 September, his brother, John of Eltham, died at Perth of wounds received in a skirmish, aged only twenty. Already, he had distinguished himself by his harshness toward the Scots, and in 1335, Edward had appointed him Warden of the Northern Marches. The loss of one of her children, the first she had had to bear, must have been deeply painful to Isabella. The King, whose accounts record that his brother's death gave him nightmares, came south in December, and, on the orders of their mother, Prince John was buried in January 1337 in Saint Thomas's Chapel in Westminster Abbey, Archbishop Stratford officiating. In 1339, in accordance with Isabella's wishes, Edward ordered his brother's body to be moved to Saint Edmund's Chapel, which was nearer the royal tombs. There, the Prince's bereft relations raised a beautiful tomb and effigy to his memory; it was probably made by the same sculptor and workshop responsible for Edward II's monument at Gloucester, which is thought to have been completed around this time. One of the female weepers on John of Eltham's tomb is likely to be Isabella. This figure stands to the left of the one that represents Edward II and wears a figure-skimming gown, a widow's chin-barbe and wimple, and a crown; in her hand, she holds a scepter.

John's death evidently left Isabella preoccupied with her own mortality, for it was at this time that Edward gave her permission to make her will.

On 16 March 1337, Thomas de Berkeley was finally acquitted in Parliament of all the charges against him and absolved of all responsibility for the death of Edward II.[81]

Two days later, William de Shalford, who had disclosed Rhys ap Gruffydd's plot to Mortimer in 1327 and urged him to find a remedy, was, at the instance of the Earl of Arundel and William de Montagu, rewarded by Parliament for his long service to the Crown.[82]

The sudden pardoning of Berkeley and the rewarding of Shalford were almost certainly prompted by Edward III's receipt of Manuele de Fieschi's letter. In the months since he had probably received the first intimation of his father's survival from Nicolinus de Fieschi, efforts had doubtless been made to question the hermit and establish proof of his identity. It now appears that Edward was satisfied that no murder had taken place and that Berkeley was innocent.

Thereafter, Berkeley went on to command Edward's armies in Scotland and France. In 1361, he was sent on an embassy to the Pope. He died later that year.

Isabella may also have been a beneficiary of Fieschi's revelations. In 1337, Edward restored to her the revenues of Ponthieu and Montreuil, which had been part of her original dower.[83]

On 24 May, Philip VI confiscated Gascony, an act that led to the outbreak of what would later become known as the Hundred Years' War. Later, in October, Edward III declared war on France. That year, Isabella's former ally Count William of Hainault was killed in Friesland, and his brother John went over to the French.

In 1338, Edward III formally laid claim to the French Crown, which he asserted was rightfully his in view of his descent through his mother from Philip IV. English propagandists had a field day comparing Edward's claim with Jesus Christ's descent from the House of David through His mother, the Virgin Mary.

During these years, the evidence about Isabella's life is fragmentary at best. There are various records of grants and gifts made to and by her.[84] She was with the King and his court at Pontefract in June 1338.[85] Otherwise, little is known of her activities.

At the beginning of September 1338, Edward III traveled to Germany to be made Vicar of the Holy Roman Empire. When he arrived at Koblenz, a man named William le Galeys (William the Welshman) was secretly brought to him from Cologne, escorted by an Italian called Francisco the Lombard and two men-at-arms, at a cost of 25s. 6d. According to the diplomatic documents of the Exchequer, this man had been "arrested" at Cologne for claiming that he was "the father of the present King."[86] Given his escort, it is more probable that he had not been arrested at all but had been summoned from Lombardy. Francisco certainly came from there, and while he is described as a royal sergeant at arms, there is no other mention of him in the household records. It is more likely that he was in the employ of the Fieschis.

Edward was crowned Vicar at Cologne on 5 September and had returned to Antwerp by the end of that month. William le Galeys is known to have been with him there on 18 October, and he stayed with the royal party, which included the young Prince Edward, at Antwerp until December, the King outlaying 13s. 4d. a week for his keep, a generous sum for one whose needs were probably modest. On 29 November, during this mysterious man's stay at Antwerp, Queen Philippa gave birth there to her third son, Lionel. After December, William le Galeys disappears from the records.

It may be significant that, until January 1339, Nicolinus de Fieschi was also in Antwerp. On 7 September, Edward III had given him a testimonial for his good service. It may have been Nicolinus who led the escort that brought "William le Galeys" to Edward or who arranged the meeting, which lends credence to the theory that William really was Edward II. Royal pretenders were usually dealt with harshly—Edward II himself had hanged one—but this one remained with the King for three or four months, and there was no public or private denunciation of his claim. Furthermore, he had come from Cologne, a place that Edward II had, according to Fieschi, visited in circa 1332. Then there is the pseudonym "William the Welshman": Edward II had been known as "Edward of Caernarvon," after the place of his birth, and Caernarvon is in Wales; moreover, Edward had been the first English Prince of Wales. We know that William le Galeys was kept under guard, but this may have been because Edward III did not want him to be recognized. There is a strong probability, therefore, that he was no imposter and that this was a private reunion between father and son, and a chance for the former King to give his blessing to his successor before retiring to Lombardy to end his days as a hermit. Either Edward III had requested the meeting or his father had suggested it. We may even speculate that he knew he did not have long to live and wanted to see his son one last time.

Edward III had every reason to keep his father's continuing existence a secret: he did not want him to be the focus of any plots for his restoration, although that was unlikely; he did not want to lose face after having Mortimer publicly convicted of Edward's murder in Parliament; nor would he have wanted to rake up old scandals that could harm his mother. It was for these reasons that the anniversary of Edward's death continued to be observed with religious services throughout the kingdom on 21 September every year, right up until the end of Edward III's reign.[87]

Edward now set about the rehabilitation of Maltravers. It is probably significant that, by 1339, Edward was employing Maltravers on official business in Flanders. In 1342, he permitted his wife, Agnes de Bereford, to visit him there for as long as she wished, "notwithstanding that he is banished from the realm of England."[88] Maltravers was still under sentence of death for his enticement of Kent, which is why the King could not openly favor or forgive him, but his use of him as an agent proves that he recognized his abilities and was working toward his eventual rehabilitation. At length, in 1345, Maltravers formally submitted to Edward at Sluys, pleading that he had been condemned unheard for procuring the execution of Kent, and asking for leave to go home. That August, in consideration of the excellent service he had rendered to Edward in Flanders, he was granted the King's safe-conduct to return to England to face trial.[89] Not surprisingly, he remained in Flanders, yet Edward continued to employ him on official business. In 1351, he was received back into favor when he was summoned to sit in Parliament as a baron and made Governor of the Channel Islands. When Parliament met at Westminster in January 1352, it acquitted Maltravers of all the charges against him, and his honors and estates were finally restored to him the following month.[90] Thereafter, he served Edward III faithfully until his death in 1365.

In 1352, after Maltravers's rehabilitation, Edward summoned Ranulph Higden to come to Westminster with all his manuscripts and papers "to have certain things explained to him." The King had evidently read Higden's gory description of Edward II's being murdered with a red-hot spit and was determined to set the record straight. Whatever was said at this audience, Higden kept quiet about it. Nor did he add any more to his chronicle, although he lived another thirteen years.[91]

How would the knowledge that her husband was still alive have affected Isabella? She may well have felt an overwhelming sense of relief that she bore no responsibility, even indirectly, for his brutal murder. She would naturally have wanted to know whether he had forgiven her and what he now thought of her. There is no evidence that they ever met again, although, equally, there is no evidence that they did not. After all, Edward had traveled around Europe in the guise of a humble friar. It would have been easy for him to slip unnoticed across to England to see his wife, especially if the King himself was easing his passage. Yet Edward had now turned to God and was living a celibate and solitary life. He had never been interested in women anyway, and there had been a lot of issues between him and Isabella. He may not have wished to see her or had resolved to put his worldly life firmly behind him. In the absence of any evidence to the contrary, it is probably safe to say that Isabella never set eyes on him again.

In December 1340, Isabella made a rare visit to London to be present in the great chamber of Winchester Palace in Southwark when the King delivered the Great Seal to the new Chancellor, Robert Bourchier.[92]

In defiance of public opinion, on 28 April 1342, Edward ratified Manuele de Fieschi's retention of his English benefices.[93] It is easy to see now why he should have done so.

Diplomatic negotiations with France had reached an impasse, and the clouds of war were gathering. On 26 January 1340, at a ceremony in the marketplace at Ghent, Edward III assumed the title and the royal arms of the King of France. In the summer, his forces won a great naval battle off Sluys in Holland, destroying a French fleet.

In November of that year, Isabella was among those who welcomed the King at the Tower of London, on his return from the Continent. She stayed on there to celebrate his birthday with him.[94] It must have been around this time that Edward returned Leeds Castle to Isabella. She would now hold it until her death, and both she and the King would pay for repairs to the walls, which had begun to collapse.[95] In 1341, Edward made provision for daily Mass to be sung in the chapel of Leeds Castle for the good estate of his mother.

That year, David II and Queen Joan were at last able to return to Scotland. Joan was now twenty, "seemly and very beautiful," like her mother, but David neglected her for his mistresses, and the marriage remained childless.[96]

On 27 February 1343, Parliament granted Edward III an aid of thirty thousand sacks of wool toward the war effort, but it was agreed that the Queen Mother's lands should be exempted, since, unlike most noble landowners, she did not sit in Parliament, and "it was unreasonable that a person exempt and not summoned to Parliament should be burdened with aids granted by Parliament."[97]

In March 1343, Edward and Philippa made a pilgrimage to Edward II's tomb at Gloucester.[98] There is no record of any earlier visit by the King, although work on the tomb had probably been going on apace throughout the early 1330s. The likelihood is that the real Edward II had recently died at Cecima, and perhaps been temporarily buried there, and that his body had been secretly brought home to England and buried in the tomb at Gloucester, from which the porter's body had now been removed.[99] Edward's heart would also have been substituted for the porter's, which had doubtless been removed from the casket held by Isabella.

Edward had perhaps died in 1341, when Edward III paid Nicolinus de Fieschi one mark a day plus generous expenses to travel to "divers parts beyond the sea" on what were evasively described as "certain affairs."[100]

There can be little doubt that Isabella's enthusiasm for the legends of King Arthur had been absorbed early on in life by her son. Edward was passionately interested in the ideal of chivalry, and by 1344, he had decided to found a new order of knights of the Round Table at Windsor. On 1 January that year, it was proclaimed that a great feast and tournament would shortly be held there, and invitations were sent out.

Isabella was present for at least some of these festivities, which lasted from around 15 to 23 January. She certainly graced the Round Table feast, at which there was "an indescribable host of people to delight in so great a solemnity." Minstrels played in the gallery and "the most alluring of drinks and dances were not lacking, [nor] embracings and kissings." Edward spent much of the evening organizing the seating arrangements and personally showing the ladies to their places in the great hall. Isabella was also present at the feast held in honor of Saint George on Sunday, 18 January, which was followed by three days of jousts.[101]

It is unlikely that she stayed for these, for she had business to attend to at Westminster, where, on 20 January, she granted certain liberties to the men of her manor of Cheylesmore, which lay to the south of Coventry, "out of consideration" for her eldest grandson, who had been created Prince of Wales the previous year, and to whom she intended the manor to come on her death.[102]

She was back at Windsor on 23 January when the King and Queen, "nobly adorned," led "the Lady Queen Mother" and the rest of the royal family to hear Mass in state in Henry III's chapel. Afterward, Edward III, wearing his crown and a suit of "very precious velvet," took an oath on the Gospels before the assembled throng, swearing "that he would begin a Round Table in the manner of King Arthur," for three hundred knights. Then the trumpets sounded, summoning the guests to yet another feast.[103]

In the event, the order of knighthood that Edward founded four years later would be the Order of the Garter. Legend has it that, while dancing with Montagu's wife, Katherine de Grandison, Countess of Salisbury, the King saw some male courtiers sniggering because her garter had fallen off. Edward picked it up, handed it back to her with a bow, and sternly announced, "Honi soit qui mal y pense" ("Be he disgraced who thinks evil of it"). His words were adopted as the Order's motto. Recent research has tended to corroborate this picturesque story.

When, in 1349, Edward admitted Queen Philippa and other ladies to the Order of the Garter as "Dames of the Fraternity," Isabella was not among them.

In November 1344, Isabella celebrated Edward's birthday with him at Norwich,[104] probably in the castle. The next year, the King, "of our special favour, and at the request of Isabella, Queen of England, our most dear mother," granted special privileges to that city.[105]

On 16 June 1345, perhaps to mark her fiftieth birthday, Edward bestowed on Isabella further rights in the manor of Cheylesmore, and that year, too, he granted a royal charter to her town of Coventry.[106] In 1345 also, Edward stayed for some time with his mother at Castle Rising, as several letters that he wrote to the Pope were sent from there.[107]

In September that year, Lancaster died, and Isabella was among the mourners at his state funeral in the collegiate church in The Newarke at Leicester.

England won a great victory over the French on 27 August 1346, at the Battle of Crécy, during which the Prince of Wales, now sixteen, won his spurs of knighthood. Then, on 4 September, the King laid siege to Calais, which would fall to him after a year.

The English scored another victory in October, this time against the Scots, who were France's allies, at the Battle of Neville's Cross, at which David II was taken prisoner. His shocked wife, Joan, now twenty-five, followed him to England, and Isabella had a chance to catch up with the daughter she had not seen for nineteen years. There is a lot of evidence to suggest that they became very close. David was held in honorable captivity in the Tower of London, where Joan was permitted to visit him,[108] while she spent much of her time at Hertford Castle, which was owned by Isabella. The King provided her with a suitable household, and both Isabella and Queen Philippa visited her frequently.[109] Isabella herself is known to have stayed there in 1347.

Hertford Castle was a royal residence that had been built by William the Conqueror on a stretch of low-lying ground partly encircled by the River Lea. King John improved the fortifications and living quarters, and Henry III provided further embellishments, repairing the hall, commissioning paintings for his chapel and chamber, and building another chapel for his queen. The castle was accessed through a great outer gateway and bridge.

The castle had been part of the dower of Marguerite of France, but she had transferred it to the late Earl of Pembroke. His widow had surrendered it to Isabella in 1327, and it was among the properties granted to the Queen Mother by Edward III. By now, the castle was falling into disrepair; the curtain wall was crumbling, some of the outer defenses had collapsed, and the roofs needed replacing. Yet there is no record of any repairs being carried out during Isabella's time.[110]

Sometime in 1347, Isabella gave the convent of the Poor Clares, or Minoresses without Aldgate, the advowsons, or right to present a benefice, of three churches. The Poor Clares were the female branch of the Franciscan Order, and this convent had been founded by Edmund Crouchback, Earl of Lancaster, the father of Earls Thomas and Henry, in 1293; his heart was buried beneath the high altar. Crouchback had been the second husband of Isabella's maternal grandmother, Blanche of Artois, and it was she who had introduced the Order of Poor Clares into England. It is therefore understandable that Isabella should have wished to patronize this foundation.

After the fall of Calais, England and France had agreed to a truce, but in September 1348, this had to be extended because of the devastation caused in both countries by the plague known as the Black Death. There had been hopes anyway of reaching a peace settlement, and Philip VI had proposed that Queen Isabella and Jeanne of Evreux, Queen Dowager of France, act as mediators. He suggested that they meet between Calais and Boulogne to discuss terms, but Edward III was having none of it. He was aware of his mother's poor reputation in France and knew that her involvement in the peace process would do his cause no good. Instead, he sent the new Duke of Lancaster, Henry of Grosmont, while Philip abandoned the idea of sending Queen Jeanne and substituted the Count of Eu.[111]

Isabella lived through the plague, which lasted until 1349. We have no record of her whereabouts, but she was probably living quietly in the country, perhaps at Castle Rising, or moving from house to house to escape the pestilence. She was a witness, therefore, to one of the most cataclysmic episodes in English history, for the Black Death decimated the population and changed the social order in England forever. Nor was the royal family spared, for the plague carried off her thirteen-year-old granddaughter Joan, the King's second daughter, while she was traveling through Gascony to her wedding.

Around 1350, Isabella perhaps suffered bouts of ill health, for in January 1351, a London physician or apothecary, Bartholemew Thomasyn, was rewarded for his services to King Edward, Queen Isabella, and Queen Philippa by being granted the full liberties of the City of London.

That Isabella was still seen to hold considerable influence over the King was clear in January 1354, when Charles, King of Navarre, the grandson of Louis X and Marguerite of Burgundy, was seeking protection from Philip VI's successor, John II, after having murdered the Constable of France. He appealed in writing to Edward III, the Prince of Wales, and Henry, Duke of

Lancaster. The Duke wrote back diplomatically that he was too busy to be of assistance just now but that he had forwarded copies of Charles's letter to the King, the Prince of Wales, the Queen, and the Queen Mother and was waiting for news from them. Whether Isabella was instrumental in persuading Edward to back Charles is not known, but he did so and thereby violated the terms of a recent peace he had negotiated with King John, which would lead to the reopening of the war.[112] Isabella made another of her few ventures into politics in May 1354, when, at the request of the Pope, she pleaded with Edward III to release the Duke of Brittany, whom he was holding hostage.

That year, Edward had the sentence on Mortimer reversed, on the grounds that the latter had been prevented from speaking in his own defense, and restored his grandson, another Roger Mortimer, to the earldom of March. In 1368, this Roger, who had been one of the luminaries of the court since 1350, would marry the King's granddaughter, Philippa of Clarence. In 1398, their grandson, Roger, the third Earl, would be Richard II's acknowledged heir. His descendants founded the royal House of York, which would occupy the throne of England itself from 1461 to 1485. The present Queen, Elizabeth II, is a descendant of both Roger Mortimer and Isabella of France.

Isabella spent the Christmas of 1354 being entertained by her grandson, the Prince of Wales, at Berkhamsted Castle.

The following spring, she received the sad news that her daughter Eleanor, Duchess of Gueldres, had died in poverty at the age of thirty-seven. Eleanor had helped to rule the duchy during the minority of her quarrelsome eldest son, but on reaching his majority, he had resented her efforts to make peace between him and his brother and had confiscated all her property, something that Isabella had experienced herself. But for Eleanor, there had been no restitution: she had lived out her remaining years in a Cistercian abbey, too proud to beg for assistance from her brother, Edward III. Now only two of Isabella's children remained. It is to be hoped she found some comfort in her eight surviving grandchildren; the last of Philippa's brood, Thomas of Woodstock, had been born the previous January. That year, Isabella again visited her grandson, the Prince of Wales, at Berkhamsted. In many ways, he was like her—good-looking, dynamic, intelligent, and ruthless—and evidently, they were close.

On 19 September 1356, the Prince of Wales again distinguished himself at the Battle of Poitiers, in which the King of France was taken prisoner. King John was to remain in England, treated as an honored guest, for the next four years, while the terms of his release were negotiated. During that time, John often visited his cousin Isabella at Hertford Castle; it is unlikely that he remembered her or had even met her, for he had been only seven years old when she had left France for the last time in 1326. Evidently, they struck up a rapport; he sent her messages by his servant John of Paris, and she, knowing that he loved reading, sent him in return two books about Lancelot and the Holy Grail.[113] Isabella's growing political influence may have encouraged her to intercede with Edward on John's behalf.

During 1356, Isabella was occupied with renovating her palace at Sheen in Surrey. Carpenters, tilers, and roofers were employed "at the Queen Mother's wages for her works at Sheen."[114] This suggests that, at sixty-one, she was still as fit and active as ever.

Mortimer's widow, Joan de Genville, died at the age of sixty in October 1356. She was probably buried with her husband at Coventry, Wigmore, or Shrewsbury.

In 1357, after eleven years of captivity, David II was finally freed and allowed to return to Scotland. A joyful Queen Joan accompanied him, but when she found out that he was making up for lost time with another woman, she returned to England for good in December on the pretext of discussing peace terms with her brother.[115] Edward III again permitted her to use Hertford Castle as a residence, and Isabella paid for her clothes and food. As before, she and Queen Philippa were frequent visitors.[116] Squabbles over the payment of his ransom money continued well after King David had returned to Scotland, and in 1358, he sent an envoy called William of Leith to Isabella, to request her "to act as mediatrix with King Edward" in the matter.[117] It appears that, despite her enforced retirement, kings still had respect for Isabella's undoubted political skills and that, as old memories faded, she was beginning to be regarded as a kind of elder stateswoman. It was, after all, more than twenty-seven years since Mortimer had faced the hangman's noose and Isabella had been placed under house arrest.

In 1357, the burghers of Lynn sent their last recorded gift to the Queen Mother, a pipe of wine.[118] Her *Household Book* for the year 1357–58, the last of three to survive, contains evidence that she was continuing to enjoy a pleasant existence with many diversions. She was still taking an interest in both domestic and public affairs and corresponded frequently with the King, Queen Philippa, Queen Joan, King John of France, the Duke of Lancaster, the Chancellor, and the Earl Marshal. At New Year 1358, they all brought her gifts and at other times sent her presents of Bordeaux wine, boars' heads, barrels of bream, and copper quadrants. These last were instruments for measuring circles and were sometimes used in navigation. They seem strange gifts to send an aging lady, but perhaps Isabella had discovered a latent interest in astronomy or geometry.

She was still following fashion and decking herself out as befitted a queen. During this year, she spent the princely sum of £1,400 on jewelry.

Isabella was clearly popular and well-thought-of, for visitors came to see her at an average rate of two or three a day; among them were the King, Queen Joan, the Prince of Wales, any French lords who were in England to see King John, and William, Earl of Douglas, one of the hostages for King David's ransom, who was making frequent visits to England at this time to negotiate a peace treaty. The Earl was the grandson of Sir James Douglas, that same Black Douglas who had twice attempted to abduct the young Queen Isabella. Other frequent visitors were Elizabeth de Clare, Edward II's niece and the foundress of Clare Hall in Cambridge; Isabella's long-standing cousin and friend Marie de Saint Pol, Dowager Countess of Pembroke, and foundress of Pembroke College in Cambridge, to whom Isabella gave a breviary in 1357; Mortimer's daughter Agnes, the widow of Lawrence Hastings, Earl of Pembroke; and his grandson and namesake, the Earl of March, now a successful courtier in his early thirties, who was married to Montagu's daughter Philippa and had one son, Edmund. March was Isabella's dinner guest three times in the space of one month. Did she, one wonders, tell him and his aunt tales of their notorious forebear?[119]

Yet there was a more pious dimension to her life, for now that she was in her sixties, her mind was becoming increasingly preoccupied with thoughts of her own mortality and the inevitability of divine judgment. During this last year, she prepared herself for death. She had always been a great patron of the Franciscans, and it was at this time that she took the habit of the Third (or Tertiary) Order of Saint Francis, which she wore under her outer robes.[120] This lay branch of the Franciscans had been founded twenty years earlier chiefly for penitents who wished to remain in the world; its members were not bound by conventual vows but by a requirement to maintain Franciscan observances and principles in their daily lives. In joining this Order, Isabella clearly wished to make reparation for her past transgressions, as her deeds plainly show.

During this last year of her life, she undertook many charitable works. She maintained poor scholars at Oxford, distributed alms to 150 selected paupers on Holy Days and the principal feasts of the Church, and paid for thirteen other needy persons to be fed every day and three more each Monday, Friday, and Saturday.[121]

It was natural that, as a tertiary of their Order, Isabella should wish to be buried in the Grey Friars' church at Newgate, of which she had been so generous a benefactress. We should not believe the jealous accusation of the Westminster monk John of Reading that the Queen had been "seduced" by the Grey Friars to change her will and leave her bones among them, after allegedly expressing a wish to be laid to rest at Westminster. The fact that the community of Westminster wanted her at all, and considered her worthy of interment in their royal mausoleum, is proof of how thoroughly she had redeemed her reputation. Whether Isabella herself considered that she was worthy of such a sepulchre is a matter for speculation.

Yet her burial at Grey Friars was to prove controversial in another respect. In the sixteenth century, the antiquarian John Stow listed the ruined royal tombs in that church and perpetrated the myth that Roger Mortimer's was among them. More recently, several historians, misreading contemporary sources, have asserted that he was buried there before being removed elsewhere. Thus, another myth about Isabella has arisen, that she deliberately chose to be buried near her lover, or at least near the place where his remains had briefly lain. That myth can be disposed of, for it is almost certain that Mortimer was buried at Coventry.

In February 1358, Isabella was slightly unwell. She had evidently recovered enough to accompany Queen Philippa, King John, and his son Philip, the future Duke of Burgundy, to the Saint George's Day celebrations at Windsor in April, which included a magnificent tournament in which many foreign knights took part. The occasion was to mark the completion of Edward's new college in the great court at Windsor, which was to be the focus of the Order of the Garter, and doubtless the King took great pleasure in showing Isabella around. This was to prove her last public appearance.

The Queen Mother may have had a hand in the shaping of the peace treaty that was concluded between King Edward and King John the following month, whereby John agreed to pay 4 million gold crowns in ransom and recognize Edward as sovereign ruler of Gascony, Calais, Guisnes, Ponthieu, and Montreuil. These last counties formed part of Isabella's dower, and she had a vested interest in any settlement, so it is unthinkable that this agreement would have been reached without her being consulted.

In June of that year, Isabella, who was now approaching sixty-three, made a final pilgrimage to the shrine of Becket at Canterbury, taking with her her daughter Joan. She had been here many times before, either alone or with Joan's father: Saint Thomas had not only been Edward II's favorite saint but Isabella's, too, so it was natural that she should seek his intercession in her present need to redeem her sins. Shortly beforehand, she had donated £2 to the the Abbess of the Minoresses' convent outside Aldgate so that that good lady could buy food for the community on the anniversaries of the deaths of "Edward, late King of England" and John of Eltham.[122] The dead were apparently very much in Isabella's thoughts at this time.

The fact that mother and daughter stayed at Leeds Castle from 13 June to 2 July suggests that it was at this time that Isabella was again taken ill. According to her *Household Book,* she became unwell immediately after overdosing on a potent medicine, which she presumably had been taking for some preexisting condition, possibly that which had struck her down in February, which was probably the first manifestation of the disease that killed her.[123] On 1 August, a London apothecary, Nicholas Thomason, received payment for spices and ointments for the Queen Mother, which were perhaps purchased as the two Queens journeyed east of the capital to Hertford Castle. Doherty points out that these were not necessarily medicines but may have been required for making perfumes or flavoring food.

But on 12 August, messengers were dispatched from Hertford to London for medicines, and on the twentieth, Isabella's condition was causing sufficient concern for two doctors to be summoned "with the greatest haste": one was an eminent London physician and the other, Master Lawrence, was the Queen's surgeon, who had accompanied her to Canterbury and was still there. His presence on this pilgrimage is further evidence that Isabella was already ailing when she embarked upon it.

It is unlikely that Master Lawrence got to Hertford in time, for Isabella died there on 22 August 1358, with her daughter Joan nearby.

The Prince of Wales was at Vale Royal when he received news of his grandmother's death. On 28 August, the King gave orders for the taking over of the late Queen Mother's estates, and by 19 September, the Prince was at Cheylesmore and Coventry, having taken possession of them as Isabella had intended.[124] She also left him Castle Rising and all her other castles, and most of her personal possessions, as well as a quarter share of the customs dues of Lynn.[125] Hertford Castle was granted by Edward III to his fourth son, John of Gaunt, while the rest of Isabella's lands went mainly to Queen Philippa.[126]

Some of her books—among them, a Bible, an Apocalypse, and a psalter—she had willed to her daughter Joan, while the rest, including a genealogy, went to the monks at Easton Royal in Wiltshire.[127]

Planning a magnificent funeral such as Edward III arranged for his mother took time. As she had directed, Isabella's embalmed body was wrapped in her wedding cloak, which she had preserved for half a century[128]—another indication that her late husband was very much in the forefront of her mind during her final months—and in her Franciscan habit, "as a protection against the attacks of the Devil." It lay in the chapel at Hertford Castle for three months, until 23 November, watched over constantly by fourteen poor persons, who were paid 2d. a day by the King. John Gynwell, Bishop of Lincoln, the Abbot of Waltham, and the Prior of Coventry all came to celebrate Requiem Masses in the chapel.[129]

On 21 November, Edward commanded the sheriffs of London to clean the streets of dirt and all impurities and to strew gravel along Bishopsgate and Aldgate "against the coming of the body of his dearest mother, Queen Isabella," to the City for her burial and gave them £9 to defray their expenses. Meanwhile, the Queen's body was being brought south with great solemnity from Hertford.[130] Prior to the funeral, it lay at Mile End, in the house of John Galeys, where members of the royal family watched over it. Galeys was later paid £10 as recompense for "the loss he suffered by the relinquishment of his house."[131] He may have been the same John Galeys who had been rewarded by Roger Mortimer in 1330 for his good service to him.[132]

Edward had arranged "a sumptuous funeral."[133] On 27 November, with great ceremony, Isabella's body was carried in procession through London, followed by the Prince of Wales, as chief mourner, "all the prelates and barons of England, as well as those French lords who were at that time detained in England as hostages," and a host of dignitaries.[134] There is no record of the King's being present, but in medieval times, protocol generally precluded English monarchs' attending funerals. Among the watching crowds was a youth called Geoffrey Chaucer, a page in the household of the King's third son, Lionel of Antwerp; this same Chaucer would later achieve renown as the first great writer in the English language and the author of *The Canterbury Tales*.

After a funeral service conducted by Simon Islip, Archbishop of Canterbury, the Queen's corpse was laid to rest in the center of the choir of the Grey Friars' church at Newgate; the tomb of her aunt, Marguerite of France, was nearby to the east, before the altar.[135] On 12 February 1359, five poor men were given money and a robe each by the King to pray for Isabella's soul.[136] In various places throughout the kingdom, chantries were founded so that intercessions could be made for her safe passage to Heaven.

Since the twelfth century, separate heart burial had been practiced within the royal families of Europe. Those who could afford it wished to profit from being prayed for at more than one sepulchre and so speed their passage through Purgatory. Richard I's body had been buried at Fontevrault in 1199, but a full-size tomb and effigy had been built to contain his heart at Rouen; while, more recently, three more or less identical tombs had been raised to the memory of Eleanor of Castile: one, for her viscera, in Lincoln Cathedral; another, for her heart, in the conventual church of the Black Friars in London; and the third, for the rest of her body, in Westminster Abbey. In 1299, Pope Boniface VIII had banned the division of royal bodies, but by 1304, this ruling had been relaxed for members of the French royal family, and other dynasties took their cue from that, although the practice died out in England in the fourteenth century. In 1323 and 1345, Isabella had obtained papal permission for her remains to be buried in three separate places,[137] but this does not seem to have happened. It is likely that her heart is buried beneath the simple gray stone inscribed ISABELLA REGINA in the Norman parish church dedicated to Saint Lawrence at Castle Rising; but there is no record of, or evidence for, any visceral burial.

It is on record that, at her own request, Edward II's heart in its silver casket was placed in Isabella's coffin on her breast.[138] Since she would hardly have wished to be buried with the heart of the porter, this is more or less conclusive evidence that the body in Gloucester Cathedral is Edward II's.[139]

Many writers[140] have condemned Isabella for what they see as this final act of hypocrisy, yet it was probably another act of reparation, like being buried in her wedding cloak. Entering a religious order as a penitent suggests that she was more preoccupied with remorse, absolution, and redemption than with memories of the wrongs that Edward had done her or of sharing the pleasures of the flesh with Mortimer. And, who knows, the hermit at Cecima might well have extended his forgiveness to her before his death.

Edward III saw that Isabella's servants were rewarded after her death.[141] Later, when the great middle window of the church in which she lay blew in, he paid for it to be replaced "for the repose of the soul of the most illustrious Queen Isabella."[142] Every year until his own passing in 1377, the King solemnly observed the anniversary of her death with prayers and intercessions.[143] In accordance with her instructions, for she had planned her own memorial, he also raised a beautiful marble tomb and alabaster effigy over her remains. The tomb was, unusually, the work of a female sculptor, Agnes de Ramsey, who had taken over her father's workshop. A craftsman, Nicholas of Louth, also worked on it, along with masons, smiths, and painters. The monument was evidently finished within a year, for in 1359, Andrew the Ironsmith was paid £110 for making decorative iron railings to surround it. Five years later, a painted canopy was erected over the tomb.[144]

In 1362, Isabella's daughter Joan died and, at her own request, was buried near her mother in the Grey Friars.[145] Twenty years later, the body of Isabella's granddaughter and namesake was also laid to rest there. Two of Isabella's confessors and one of her damsels were buried in the church.

Alas, Isabella's monument, along with all the rest, is irrevocably lost to us. It was damaged and defaced when the convent of the Grey Friars was dissolved during the Reformation of the 1530s. Then, before 1566, when the friars' former place of worship was made the local parish church in the reign of Elizabeth I, Sir Martin Bowes, Lord Mayor of London, sold it off with nine other tombs of royal personages and several gravestones for £50.[146] Nothing is known of what became of them.

The church in which they had stood was destroyed in the Great Fire of 1666 and afterward rebuilt by Sir Christopher Wren as Christ Church. It was Wren's church that was devastated during the Blitz and whose few ruins we see today. The site of the convent is now occupied by a small park, a building owned by the Post Office, and a busy main road. Somewhere, below the ground, lies the dust of a long-dead queen.

History has been unkind to Isabella. For centuries, she has been condemned, mostly by male historians, for her adultery, her violation of marital conventions, her cruelty, her misgovernment, and her connivance in a murder that probably never took place. She is the femme fatale of the English monarchy.

Yet Isabella is deserving of great pity for the impossible situation in which she found herself and also of admiration for the way in which she dealt with it. The deposition of Edward II had become a political imperative, and she successfully led a revolution to achieve it. In so doing, she brought about the first constitutional deposition by Parliament of an English king, setting a precedent for the depositions of Richard II in 1399, Henry VI in 1461 and 1471, Edward IV in 1470, Edward V in 1483, and Charles I in 1648. Thus, Isabella's importance in the history of Britain cannot be overestimated, for the process instigated by her in France and Hainault in 1326–27 set in motion a political trend that would lead directly to the decline of monarchical power itself and the emergence of democracy, a development that she herself, the daughter of Philip IV, would doubtless have been horrified to contemplate.

Isabella's dynastic importance cannot be overstated either, for she not only transmitted her claim to France to her son but also actively encouraged him to pursue it, thus instituting a war that was famously to last for more than a hundred years. Again, though, the long-term effects were disastrous, for England ended up losing nearly all its continental territories, and the political unrest generated by defeat was one of the causes of the Wars of the Roses, another dynastic catastrophe.

For these reasons, Isabella was one of the most important figures of the early fourteenth century, despite being in the political spotlight for only five years.

Isabella's downfall lay in her involvement with the rapacious Mortimer, for while she was undoubtedly an able and competent stateswoman, and was capable of launching the sole successful invasion of England since the Norman Conquest, her talents were ultimately wasted on policies that were calculated only to ensure the survival of an unpopular and tyrannical regime. Had Mortimer never come into her life, and had she ruled alone, with the help of Lancaster, after Edward's abdication, the outcome would have been very different, not only in historical terms but in terms of her reputation, which has suffered largely because of her perceived immorality with Mortimer. Nowadays, society is inclined to view a relationship such as theirs with far greater tolerance and understanding, so it is at last possible to take a kinder view of Isabella than in the past, when she was condemned largely because she was a woman who dared to violate the mores of the world in which she lived.

If there are ghosts in Newgate and at Castle Rising, they are surely not those of a mad and demented queen lamenting the brutal murder of her husband. Nor could it be claimed with any truth that Isabella of France deserves to be remembered by the epithet "She-Wolf."

Genealogical Tables

Clementina = King John   1. m. Isabella of   m. 2.   Hugh de Lusignan,
Pinel   1166–1216   Angoulême   Count of La Marche
    c. 1187–1249   d. 1249

Joan   m.   Llywellyn   William de Valence,   m.   Joan de
c. 1200–1237   of Jorwerth,   Earl of Pembroke   Munchensi
    Prince of Wales   c. 1230–1296   d. 1307
    1173–1240

Gwladus   m.   Ralph   Aymer de Valence,   m. 1. Beatrice de
Du   Mortimer,   Earl of Pembroke   Clermont
d. 1251   Baron of   1270?–1326   d. 1320
    Wigmore
    d. 1247   2.   Marie de
    Châtillon
Roger   m.   Matilda   Henry III,   m. Eleanor of   d. 1377
Mortimer,   de Braose   King of England   Provence
Baron of   d. 1301   1207–1272   c. 1233–1291
Wigmore
1231?–1282

Edmund   m.   Margaret   Edward I,   m. 1.   Eleanor   Edmund
Mortimer,   de Fiennes   King of England   of Castile   "Crouchback,"
Baron of   d. 1334   1239–1307   c. 1244–1290   Earl of Lancaster
Wigmore   1245–1296
d. 1304
    2. Marguerite
    of France
Roger   m.   Joan de   c. 1282–1318
Mortimer,   Genville
1st Earl of   Thomas,   Edmund,   m.   Margaret
March   Earl of Norfolk   Earl of Kent   Wake
1287?–1330   1300–1338   1301–1330   c. 1300–1349

Edmund   m. Elizabeth de   Eleanor   Joan of Acre   Alfonso   Elizabeth
Mortimer,   Badlesmere   1264–1298   1272–1307   1273–1284   1282–1316
knight   c. 1313–1355   m.   m. Gilbert   m.
d. 1332   Henry III,   de Clare,
    Count of Bar   Earl of   Humphrey
    d. 1302   Gloucester   de Bohun,
Roger   m.   Philippa   Edward I,   1243–1295   Earl of Hereford
Mortimer,   ↓   de Montagu   Count of Bar   1276?–1322
2nd Earl of   d. 1382   1294–1337   John,   Humphrey,   William,
March   Earl of   Earl of   Earl of
1328–1360   Hereford   Hereford   Northampton
    1306–1336   1309–1361   c.1310–1360

Gilbert,   Eleanor   m. 1.   Hugh le   Margaret   m. 1.   Piers Gaveston,
Earl of   1292–1337   ↓   Despenser   1293–1342   ↓   Earl of Cornwall
Gloucester   d. 1326   d. 1312
1291–1314
    2.   Sir William   2.   Hugh de Audley,
    la Zouch   Earl of Gloucester
    d. 1337   d. 1347

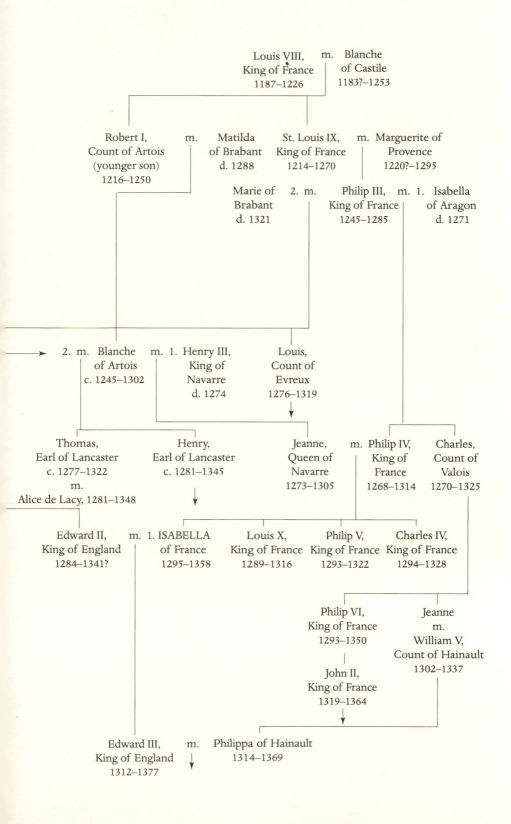

Louis VIII,   m.   Blanche
King of France   of Castile
1187–1226   1183?–1253

Robert I,   m.   Matilda   St. Louis IX,   m.   Marguerite of
Count of Artois   of Brabant   King of France   Provence
(younger son)   d. 1288   1214–1270   1220?–1295
1216–1250

Marie of   2. m.   Philip III,   m. 1.   Isabella
Brabant   King of France   of Aragon
d. 1321   1245–1285   d. 1271

2. m.   Blanche   m. 1.   Henry III,   Louis,
        of Artois   King of   Count of
        c. 1245–1302   Navarre   Evreux
                           d. 1274   1276–1319

Thomas,   Henry,   Jeanne,   m.   Philip IV,   Charles,
Earl of Lancaster   Earl of Lancaster   Queen of   King of   Count of
c. 1277–1322   c. 1281–1345   Navarre   France   Valois
m.   1273–1305   1268–1314   1270–1325
Alice de Lacy, 1281–1348

Edward II,   m. 1.   ISABELLA   Louis X,   Philip V,   Charles IV,
King of England   of France   King of France   King of France   King of France
1284–1341?   1295–1358   1289–1316   1293–1322   1294–1328

Philip VI,   Jeanne
King of France   m.
1293–1350   William V,
                  Count of Hainault
John II,   1302–1337
King of France
1319–1364

Edward III,   m.   Philippa of Hainault
King of England   1314–1369
1312–1377

Philip IV,　m.　Jeanne,
King of France　│　Queen of Navarre
1268–1314　　　1273–1305

Marguerite　Louis X,　m. 1.　Marguerite　　Blanche　Philip V,　m.　Jea[
d. young　King of France　　of Burgundy　d. young　King of France　　of Bur
　　1289–1316　　　d. 1315　　　　1293–1322　　1294-

　　　　　　　2.　Clémence
　　　　　　　　of Hungary
　　　　　　　　d. 1328

Jeanne,　　　　John I,
Queen of　　King of France
Navarre　　　b. & d. 1316
1312–1349
m.
Philip,
Count of
Evreux,
King of Navarre

Jeanne　Marguerite　　Isabella　Philip　Blanche　Louis　Daughter
1308–1347　1310–1382　　1312–1348　1313–1321　(a nun)　1315–1316　(unnamed)
m.　　m.　m. 1. Guiges VIII,　　1313–1358　　b. & d. 1322
Gudes IV,　Louis II,　　Dauphin of
Duke of　Count of　　Viennois
Burgundy　Flanders　　d. 1333
d. 1350　d. 1345
　　　　　2.　Jean,
　　　　　　Sieur de
　　　　　　Faucogney

Edward,　Isabella　Joan　William　Lionel　m.　Elizabeth
Prince of　b. 1332　1335–1348　c. 1336–1337?　b. 1338　│　de Burgh,
Wales　　　　　　　　　　　↓　Countess
b. 1330　　　　　　　　　　　　of Ulster
　　　　　　　　　　　　　　b. 1332

Charles IV,　　m. 1.　Blanche of　ISABELLA　m.　Edward II,　Robert
King of France　　　Burgundy　of France　　King of　1297–1308
1296–1328　　　　(annulled 1322)　1295–1358　　England
　　　　　　　　　　　　　　　　　　　　　　1284–1341?

　　　　　　　　2.　Morie of
　　　　　　　　　　Luxembourg
　　　　　　　　　　d. 1324

　　　　　　　　3.　Jeanne
　　　　　　　　　　of Evreux
　　　　　　　　　　d. 1371

Philip　　　Jeanne
d. young　d. young
1313　　　　1321

Daughter　Louis (?)
(unnamed)　d. young
b. & d. 1323　1324

Jeanne　　　Marie　　　Blanche
1326–1327　d. young　1328–1392
　　　　　　　　　　　　　m.
　　　　　　　　　　　　Philip,
　　　　　　　　　Duke of Orléans
　　　　　　　　　　　d. 1375

Edward III,　m.　Philippa　John of　Eleanor　m.　Reginald II,　Joan
King of England　of Hainault　Eltham,　1318–1355　　Count of　1321–1362
1312–1377　　　　1314–1369　Earl of　　　　　　　Gueldres　　m.
　　　　　　　　　　　　　　Cornwall　　　　　　d. 1343　David II,
　　　　　　　　　　　　　　1316–1336　　　　　　　　　King of Scots
　　　　　　　　　　　　　　　　　　　　　　　　　　　1324–1371

John　　　Edmund　　Blanche　　Mary　　Margaret　Thomas　　William　　Thomas
f Gaunt,　b. 1341　b. & d. 1342　b. 1344　b. 1346　1347–1348?　b. & d. 1348　b. 1355
Earl of
ichmond
b. 1340

Abbreviations Used in the Notes and References

PRINTED CALENDARS OF DOCUMENTS

CCR   *Calendar of the Close Rolls*
CFR   *Calendar of the Fine Rolls*
CPR   *Calendar of the Patent Rolls*

COLLECTIONS OF DOCUMENTS IN THE PUBLIC RECORD OFFICE

Chancery

C.47   Miscellanea
C.49   Parliament and Council Proceedings
C.53   Carter Rolls
C.61   Gascon Rolls
C.62   Liberate Rolls
C.81   Chancery Warrants

Duchy of Lancaster

D.L.10   Royal Charters
D.L.28   Accounts Various
D.L.41   Miscellanea
D.L.42   Miscellaneous Books

Exchequer

E.30   Diplomatic Documents
E.41   Ancient Deeds
E.101   King's Remembrancer, Wardrobe Accounts: Accounts Various
E.159   King's Remembrancer: Memoranda Rolls
E.163   Miscellanea
E.199   Sheriffs' Accounts
E.370   Miscellaneous Rolls, Including Pipe Rolls
E.403   Issue Rolls
E.404   Writs and Warrants for Issue

Special Collections

S.C.1   Ancient Correspondence
S.C.6   Ministers' Accounts
S.C.8   Ancient Petitions

Miscellaneous

CP   *Complete Peerage*
DNB   *Dictionary of National Biography*

All of the other sources listed can be identified by the author's name or an abbreviated title. All titles are given in full in the bibliography.

Notes and References

CHAPTER ONE   *The Fair Maiden*

1. For the betrothal, see Rishanger.
2. *Foedera;* Archives Nationales.
3. *Foedera;* Cotton MSS, Julius.
4. *Foedera.*
5. Ibid.
6. Cotton MSS, Julius.
7. Archives Nationales.
8. *Acta Imperii.*
9. *Foedera;* E.30.
10. Fawtier; Doherty, thesis.
11. *Annales Monastici.*
12. *Foedera;* Doherty, "Date of the Birth of Isabella."
13. *Foedera.*
14. *Letters of Edward, Prince of Wales.*
15. *Foedera.*
16. Knighton; Doherty, *Isabella.*
17. Bernard Sasset, Bishop of Pamiers, cited in *The Plantagenet Encyclopaedia.*
18. Froissart.
19. The title "Dauphin" was not used for the French King's eldest son until the middle of the fourteenth century.
20. The surname *Capet,* originally borne by Hugh Capet, founder of the dynasty, was not in fact used by any of the Capetian kings. It was revived by French revolutionaries in the late eighteenth century as a derisory surname for the deposed Louis XVI and his family

(whose true surname was Bourbon) and was thereafter used by historians to describe the dynasty that ruled France from 987 to 1328.

21. A few grants to her are recorded in *Les Journaux de Trésor de Philippe le Bel* and in *Receuil des Historiens de France.*

22. The earliest surviving signature of an English queen is that of Joan of Navarre, wife of Henry IV (reigned 1399–1413).

23. *Receuil des Historiens des Gaules.*

24. *Letters of Edward, Prince of Wales.*

25. S.C.1.

26. Archives Nationales.

27. Ibid.; *Foedera.*

28. Bibliothèque Nationale, Collection Brienne, 7007.

29. Piers of Langtoft; Walter of Guisborough.

30. *Vitae Paparum.*

31. *Chronicle of Lanercost.*

32. Additional MSS; E.101.

33. E.101; *CCR.*

34. Doherty, thesis.

35. *Annales Monastici;* Walsingham; Rapin-Thoyras.

36. E.101; Additional MSS.

37. *Foedera.*

38. *CCR; Foedera;* Additional MSS.

39. *CPR.*

40. "Chronicle of the Civil Wars."

41. Chaplais, *Gaveston; Foedera.*

42. Lizerand.

43. *Receuil des Historiens de France.*

44. For the wedding preparations, see *CCR* and *Les Journaux de Trésor de Philippe le Bel.*

45. *Foedera.*

46. Johnstone, *Edward of Caernarvon.*

47. Trevet.

48. E.101; Harleian MSS.

49. *Vita Edwardi Secundi.*

50. Trokelowe.

51. Baker.

52. *Annales Paulini;* Walter of Guisborough.

53. "Chronicle of the Civil Wars."

54. *Chronicle of Lanercost.*

55. See, for example, *Vita Edwardi Secundi* and Higden.

56. *Vita Edwardi Secundi.*

57. *Annales Paulini.*

58. Trokelowe.

59. *The Brut.*

60. Patroclus was the dearest friend of Achilles, and when he was killed by King Hector of Troy, Achilles was stricken by grief. Seeking revenge, he slew Hector, then staged a magnificent funeral for Patroclus. The author of the *Vita Edwardi Secundi* was of course writing with the benefit of hindsight.

61. Stowe MSS.

62. *Vita Edwardi Secundi; Chronicle of Meaux.*

63. Additional MSS; *CPR.*

64. *CFR.*

65. *Annales Londonienses.*
66. Walter of Guisborough; "Chronicle of the Civil Wars."
67. Some chroniclers refer to "divers accusations" (*Eulogium Historiarum;* Trevet; Walsingham); Murimuth says Gaveston was exiled because he gave "evil counsel" to Edward.
68. *Foedera; CCR.*
69. *Foedera.*
70. Additional MSS; E.101.
71. *CCR.*
72. Walter of Guisborough.
73. Robert of Reading.
74. *Vita Edwardi Secundi.*
75. Ibid.
76. E.101.
77. *Foedera;* C.53; *CCR; CPR.* It was commonly believed that Edward I had intended to bestow this earldom on one of his sons by Marguerite of France, Thomas of Brotherton or Edmund of Woodstock.
78. *Vita Edwardi Secundi;* Walter of Guisborough; Trokelowe.
79. *Vita Edwardi Secundi;* cf. Walter of Guisborough, Trokelowe, and Walsingham.
80. *Vita Edwardi Secundi.*
81. *Annales Paulini;* Walter of Guisborough. The *Chronicle of Lanercost* attests to the enmity between Gaveston and Langton.
82. Murimuth; *Vita Edwardi Secundi.*
83. Walter of Guisborough; *Annales Paulini; Foedera.*
84. *Literae Cantuarienses.*
85. Froissart.
86. E.101.
87. *Vita Edwardi Secundi.*
88. Ibid.; *Annales Paulini;* Trokelowe; Walsingham.
89. *Vita Edwardi Secundi.*
90. *Foedera; Parliamentary Writs; CPR.*
91. Trokelowe; *Vita Edwardi Secundi;* Walsingham.
92. Silk woven with gold.
93. That means that they were made of a rich silk ("marbrinus") woven to look like veins of marble.
94. At that time, "scarlet" was a richer-quality silk than normal.
95. For Isabella's trousseau, see E.101.
96. E.101; *Foedera.*
97. Murimuth.
98. Studer.
99. *Geoffrey de Paris.*
100. Latin MSS.
101. Now in the British Library.
102. In support of this theory, it should be noted that the head of Edward II on the Oxenbridge tomb bears a very close resemblance to that on his tomb effigy in Gloucester Cathedral.
103. Bayerische Staatsbibliothek, Munich.
104. *Vita Edwardi Secundi.*
105. Grey, *Scalacronica.*
106. *Vita Edwardi Secundi.*
107. *Roll of Arms.*
108. Archives Nationales; *Registre du Trésor des Chartres.*
109. Additional MSS.

110. This church was destroyed during the French Revolution, and only the crypt remains. The present cathedral was built between 1827 and 1866. For Isabella's wedding, see *Annales Londonienses* and *Annales Paulini*. A manuscript illumination of the wedding, dating from circa 1470–71, appears in Jean de Waurin's *Chronique d'Angleterre* in the British Library.
111. "Sindon" was either satin or very fine linen.
112. Blackley, "Isabella . . . and the . . . Cult of the Dead"; Costain.
113. Costain.
114. *CCR.*
115. Now in the British Museum.
116. l'Arsenal de Paris MSS, 3346; *Receuil des Historiens de France; Annales Paulini.*
117. E.101.
118. Ibid.
119. Cotton MSS, Nero; C.47; Additional MSS.
120. Phillips, *Aymer;* Maddicott; Mortimer. Among the ten were the Earls of Lincoln, Surrey, Pembroke, and Hereford and the Bishop of Durham; the other five were barons.
121. E.101.
122. *Vita Edwardi Secundi.*

CHAPTER TWO   *The King Is Lovesick for His Minion*

1. *Foedera; Parliamentary Writs.*
2. Trokelowe; *Foedera.*
3. *Foedera;* E.101.
4. *CCR.*
5. *Foedera.*
6. Trokelowe.
7. Archives Nationales, MS J655; Doherty, thesis.
8. *Annales Paulini;* Rhodes; Maddicott. The jewelry that Isabella brought from France is included in a list of her effects in the French Archives Nationales.
9. Trokelowe; Walsingham; *Foedera.*
10. *Annales Paulini; Gesta Edwardi;* Maddicott; E.403; *Foedera; Parliamentary Writs; CCR.*
11. E.101.
12. Henry III's palace was demolished in the seventeenth century by Charles II. The medieval royal apartments in Saint Thomas's Tower and the Wakefield Tower were partially restored in 1993. The Chapel of Saint Peter ad Vincula was rebuilt by Henry VIII. Only the foundations of the Coldharbour Gate remain today. In 1828, the royal menagerie became the basis of the new London Zoo.
13. Under Henry VIII, York Place became Whitehall Palace and replaced Westminster Palace as the seat of government.
14. *History of the King's Works;* Gee. Nothing survives of Edward the Confessor's palace. Richard II heightened Westminster Hall and built the magnificent hammerbeam roof that survives today. Of Saint Stephen's Chapel, only the fourteenth-century crypt now remains; it was heavily restored after 1834. Much of the medieval Palace of Westminster was destroyed by a fire in 1512, which ended its use as a royal residence. What remained, including the Painted Chamber, was nearly all destroyed in another fire in 1834. The Houses of Parliament, completed by 1860, now occupy the site.
15. For the coronation, see the eyewitness account in the *Annales Paulini; Vita Edwardi Secundi; Gesta Edwardi.*
16. *Annales Paulini;* Walsingham; *Parliamentary Writs.*
17. *Foedera.*
18. *Annales Paulini;* Robert of Reading; Walsingham.

19. Robert of Reading.
20. *Annales Paulini.*
21. Ibid.
22. Ibid.
23. Ibid.
24. *Select Documents of English Constitutional History; Foedera.*
25. This crown has long since disappeared. The only English medieval crown to survive is the tin burial crown of Edward I, which was found in his tomb in 1774 (Steane).
26. *Annales Paulini;* Walsingham; *Annales Londonienses.*
27. *Annales Paulini.*
28. *Annales Paulini;* Walsingham.
29. *Foedera.*
30. E.101.
31. *Annales Paulini.*
32. *Vita Edwardi Secundi.*
33. *Chronicle of Lanercost;* Cotton MSS, Nero.
34. *Vita Edwardi Secundi.*
35. Higden.
36. Higden; Robert of Reading; Knighton; *Vita Edwardi Secundi.*
37. Fabyan; Studer.
38. *Annales Paulini; Calendar of Entries in the Papal Registers.*
39. *Letters of Edward, Prince of Wales.*
40. Johnstone, *Edward of Caernarvon.*
41. Higden.
42. *Vita Edwardi Secundi.*
43. Johnstone, *Edward of Caernarvon.*
44. *Antiquarian Repertory.*
45. Strickland.
46. *Antiquarian Repertory; Chronicle of Meaux; Gesta Edwardi; CCR.*
47. *Vita Edwardi Secundi.*
48. Higden.
49. See, for example, Rishanger, and below in the text.
50. *Register of Thomas Cobham, Bishop of Worcester.*
51. Higden.
52. Mortimer.
53. Murimuth.
54. Robert of Reading.
55. *Annales Paulini; Gesta Edwardi; Annales Londonienses;* Trokelowe; Walsingham; *Vita Edwardi Secundi.*
56. *Vita Edwardi Secundi.*
57. Ibid.
58. *Annales Paulini.*
59. Robert of Reading.
60. Trokelowe.
61. Murimuth; *Chronicle of Lanercost.*
62. *Foedera.*
63. *CCR; Foedera.*
64. *Vita Edwardi Secundi.*
65. She was the daughter of Eleanor, daughter of Edward I, who had married Henry III, Count of Bar. Surrey, however, was living in open adultery with his mistress, Matilda de Nerford, who bore him children. In 1316, he was excommunicated by Pope John XXII for his adultery.

66. William de Valence was the son of Henry III's mother, Isabella of Angoulême, by her second husband, Hugh X de Lusignan, Count of La Marche.
67. He was the son of Henry III's daughter Beatrice by her marriage to John II, Duke of Brittany.
68. *Vita Edwardi Secundi.*
69. Burney MSS, 277; *Vita Edwardi Secundi.*
70. *Vita Edwardi Secundi.*
71. *Gesta Edwardi.*
72. *Vita Edwardi Secundi.*
73. E.101.
74. *CPR;* E.101; Harleian MSS.
75. *Wigmore Abbey Annals.* She was descended from King John's queen, Isabella of Angoulême. Mortimer's own mother had been a third cousin, and he himself was a descendant of King John.
76. Mortimer.
77. E.159.
78. *The Brut;* Tout, "Captivity and Death."
79. "Inventory of the Effects of Roger Mortimer."
80. *Annales Paulini; Vita Edwardi Secundi.*
81. *Annales Londonienses; Gesta Edwardi;* Maddicott.
82. *Les Journaux de Trésor de Philippe le Bel.*
83. Maddicott; Doherty, thesis; Robert of Reading.
84. By Anna Taylor in "The Career of Peter Gaveston."
85. Maddicott.
86. Maddicott; Doherty, thesis.
87. *CPR;* Doherty, thesis; E.101.
88. Archives Nationales, MS J356.
89. Higden; Robert of Reading; *Chronicle of Meaux.*
90. *Foedera; CPR.*
91. MS in the Wren Library of the Dean and Chapter of Lincoln Cathedral; Maddicott; Doherty, thesis; Robert of Reading.
92. *Foedera; CPR; Annales Londonienses.*
93. *Annales Londonienses;* Rawlinson MSS.
94. *History of the King's Works.*
95. *CPR; Foedera;* E.159.
96. *Vita Edwardi Secundi; Parliamentary Writs; CPR.*
97. *Foedera.*
98. E.101.
99. E.159.
100. Murimuth; *Annales Londonienses; Chronicle of Lanercost;* Davies, *Baronial Opposition.*
101. *Chronicle of Lanercost.*
102. *Annales Paulini; Vita Edwardi Secundi.*
103. *Vita Edwardi Secundi.*
104. *Foedera; CPR; CCR; Annales Paulini;* C.53.
105. Latin History MS C.5 (R).
106. *Chronicle of Lanercost.*
107. Latin History MS C.5 (R).
108. *Foedera; Les Journaux de Trésor de Philippe le Bel.*
109. Latin History MS C.5 (R); *Foedera.*
110. C.53; Maddicott.
111. C.53.
112. E.403; *CPR.*

113. Latin History MS C.5 (R).

114. A commote was a self-contained administrative area within Wales.

115. *CPR.*

116. *Foedera.*

117. *CPR.*

118. *Foedera.*

119. S.C.1; *Foedera.*

120. *Foedera.*

121. Ibid.

122. Latin History MS C.5 (R); *Rotuli Parliamentorum.*

123. Latin History MS C.5 (R); Maddicott.

124. *Foedera.*

125. *Annales Londonienses;* Latin History MS C.5 (R); *Vita Edwardi Secundi.*

126. *Vita Edwardi Secundi.*

127. Ibid.

128. *Foedera.*

129. *CPR.*

130. *Gesta Edwardi; Foedera.*

131. *Vita Edwardi Secundi.*

132. Ibid.

133. Robert of Reading; Walsingham; *Vita Edwardi Secundi; Chronicle of Lanercost; The Brut.*

134. *Chronicle of Lanercost.*

135. Walsingham.

136. Walsingham; *Chronicle of Lanercost; Annales Londonienses.*

137. *Vita Edwardi Secundi;* Robert of Reading.

138. *Annales Londonienses; Vita Edwardi Secundi; Gesta Edwardi;* Trokelowe; Walsingham; Knighton; Murimuth.

139. All that remains of the friary today is its boundary wall along the riverside.

140. Walter of Guisborough.

141. *Calendar of Documents Relating to Scotland.*

142. Walter of Guisborough.

143. *Vita Edwardi Secundi.*

144. *Vita Edwardi Secundi; Annales Londonienses.*

145. *Calendar of Letterbooks.*

146. Burney MS 277.

147. *Vita Edwardi Secundi.*

148. *Annales Londonienses; Foedera;* Robert of Reading; *Vita Edwardi Secundi;* Trokelowe.

149. *Annales Londonienses; Foedera;* Robert of Reading; *Vita Edwardi Secundi;* Trokelowe; *Parliamentary Writs.*

150. *CCR.*

151. *CFR;* C.53; *Foedera.*

152. *Foedera.*

153. C.81; *Annales Paulini; CCR.*

154. *Rotuli Scotiae;* C.81.

155. C.53; *CFR.*

156. E.101.

157. *Foedera.*

158. E.101.

159. *Annales Paulini; Vita Edwardi Secundi.*

160. *Vita Edwardi Secundi.*

161. E.101.

162. Ibid.

163. *CPR; CFR.*

164. *Annales Londonienses.*

165. *Chronicle of Lanercost.*

166. Simon de Montfort had led the barons against Henry III in the 1260s and had been instrumental in founding Parliament.

167. *Foedera.*

168. *Parliamentary Writs.*

169. Walter of Guisborough.

170. *Parliamentary Writs.*

171. *CCR.*

172. They are printed in *Rotuli Parliamentorum* and *Statutes of the Realm.*

173. *Vita Edwardi Secundi.*

174. *Foedera.*

175. *Vita Edwardi Secundi.*

176. *Household Book.*

177. Ibid.

178. Ibid.

179. Ibid.

180. *Household Book; Foedera.*

181. *Household Book.*

182. Trokelowe; Robert of Reading; *Annales Paulini.*

183. Robert of Reading; Walter of Guisborough; *Annales Paulini.*

184. *Household Book.*

185. *Foedera; CPR.*

186. *Foedera.*

187. *Foedera; CCR.*

188. E.403.

189. *Household Book.*

190. Ibid.

191. Ibid.

192. *Foedera;* Cotton MSS, Nero.

193. *Foedera.*

194. *CPR.*

195. Ibid.

196. *History of the King's Works;* Exchequer Plea Rolls, PRO.

197. Steane.

198. Very little from Isabella's time survives at Eltham. There are traces of Bek's hall and cellar. The hunting park was destroyed by the Commonwealth.

199. *Household Book.*

200. Cotton MSS, Nero.

201. *Household Book.*

202. *Annales Londonienses; Annales Paulini.*

203. Trokelowe says he went to France but was forced to flee after King Philip ordered his arrest, but this cannot be correct since Philip had issued a safe-conduct. The *Annales Paulini* state, probably correctly, that Gaveston went to Bruges.

204. *Le Livere de Reis; Annales Londonienses; Household Book; Rotuli Parliamentorum.*

205. *Vita Edwardi Secundi.*

206. "Chronicle of the Civil Wars."

207. *Foedera; Vita Edwardi Secundi.*

208. *Vita Edwardi Secundi.*

209. *Household Book.*

210. Ibid.

211. Ibid.

212. *Gesta Edwardi; Annales Londonienses; Vita Edwardi Secundi;* Walsingham.

213. Capgrave.

214. *Household Book.*

215. Ibid.

216. Ibid.

217. *Vita Edwardi Secundi.*

218. *Foedera.*

219. *Foedera; CCR.*

220. Ibid.

221. *Annales Paulini; Annales Londonienses;* Trokelowe; Cotton MSS, Nero.

222. *Foedera.*

223. E.403.

224. *Household Book.*

225. *Gesta Edwardi.* Joan Gaveston died in 1325 at Amesbury Priory, where Edward had arranged for her to be brought up with his niece, Eleanor de Bohun. Her elder sister, Amy, had been born early in the previous year. She, too, apparently died young (*CP*).

226. *Household Book.*

227. Cotton MSS, Nero.

228. *Household Book.*

229. *Foedera.*

230. *Household Book.*

231. *Foedera; Vita Edwardi Secundi;* Robert of Reading.

232. *Household Book.* In March and April, she also wrote to the Abbot of Saint Mary's, York, the Prior of Durham (twice), William de Boudon, William Melton, and the Abbot of Newburgh.

233. *CFR.*

234. Cotton MSS, Nero.

235. Tanner MS 197; Cotton MSS, Nero; Doherty, thesis.

236. *CPR.*

237. *Household Book; Calendar of Chancery Rolls.*

238. *Foedera.*

239. Cotton MSS, Nero.

240. *Household Book.*

241. Ibid.

242. Cotton MSS, Nero; Doherty, thesis.

243. The priory and castle are now in ruins.

244. *Vita Edwardi Secundi.*

245. *Foedera.*

246. *Foedera; CPR; CCR.*

247. *Parliamentary Writs; CPR; CCR; Foedera.*

248. Cotton MSS, Nero; *CCR; CFR.*

249. *Foedera;* Trokelowe; Walsingham.

250. *Household Book.* On 29 June, four of the Queen's men were paid 8s. 8d. for guarding her equipment at South Shields and taking it back to York.

251. *Household Book; CPR;* E.101; Cotton MSS, Nero.

252. *Annales Londonienses;* Robert of Reading; Trokelowe; *Vita Edwardi Secundi;* Cotton MSS, Nero; *Foedera; CCR.*

253. Robert of Reading; *Gesta Edwardi; Chronicle of Lanercost; Annales Paulini; Vita Edwardi Secundi; Annales Londonienses;* Harleian MS 636; *Literae Cantuarienses.*

254. C.53; Trokelowe.

255. Robert of Reading; *Vita Edwardi Secundi;* Trokelowe.

256. *Annales Londonienses;* Robert of Reading; Trokelowe.
257. *Vita Edwardi Secundi;* Robert of Reading.
258. Robert of Reading; *Annales Londonienses.*
259. *Vita Edwardi Secundi.*
260. Ibid.
261. *Household Book.*
262. *Annales Londonienses;* Robert of Reading; Trokelowe; *Vita Edwardi Secundi.*
263. *Vita Edwardi Secundi.*
264. Trokelowe; *Vita Edwardi Secundi.*
265. *Gesta Edwardi;* Cotton MSS, Cleopatra.
266. *Household Book.*
267. *Vita Edwardi Secundi.*
268. *Gesta Edwardi.*
269. *Vita Edwardi Secundi.*
270. Ibid.
271. Ibid.
272. *Vita Edwardi Secundi; Annales Londonienses; Annales Paulini;* Robert of Reading; Trokelowe; Walsingham; Baker; Murimuth; *Gesta Edwardi.*
273. For the fate of Gaveston's body, see *Annales Londonienses; Vita Edwardi Secundi;* Robert of Reading; *Annales Paulini;* Baker; *Gesta Edwardi;* Trokelowe; Walsingham.
274. "Chronicle of the Civil Wars."
275. *Vita Edwardi Secundi.*

CHAPTER THREE   *All That Is Prudent, Amiable, and Feminine*

1. *Vita Edwardi Secundi;* Robert of Reading; *The Brut;* Trokelowe.
2. *Chronicles . . . of Edward I and Edward II.*
3. Cotton MSS, Nero; *Vita Edwardi Secundi;* Trokelowe.
4. Cotton MSS, Nero.
5. E.101; E.403.
6. *Annales Londonienses; Chronicle of Lanercost.*
7. *Vita Edwardi Secundi; Annales Londonienses.*
8. *Chronicles . . . of Edward I and Edward II; Political Poems and Songs.*
9. *Vita Edwardi Secundi.*
10. Ibid.
11. *Household Book.*
12. Ibid.
13. Doherty, thesis.
14. E.101.
15. *Annales Londonienses; Chronicle of Lanercost; Vita Edwardi Secundi;* Robert of Reading.
16. *Calendar of Letter Books; Parliamentary Writs; Foedera; CCR.*
17. *Foedera; CPR; CCR; Vita Edwardi Secundi.*
18. *Foedera; Parliamentary Writs; CCR; Vita Edwardi Secundi;* Robert of Reading; Trokelowe.
19. *Vita Edwardi Secundi.*
20. Ibid.
21. *Vita Edwardi Secundi; Annales Londonienses; Annales Paulini;* Robert of Reading; Trokelowe; Walsingham.
22. *Household Book.*
23. *Annales Paulini.*
24. E.101.
25. Trokelowe.
26. *Annales Londonienses; Vita Edwardi Secundi;* Phillips, *Aymer.*

27. *Vita Edwardi Secundi.*
28. E.101.
29. Strickland.
30. Matthew Paris.
31. *History of the King's Works;* Gee; Robinson, *Royal Palaces;* Brindle and Kerr. Henry III's royal apartments at Windsor were either destroyed or completely transformed by the extensive alterations carried out by Edward III between 1350 and 1370. These royal apartments were again remodeled or rebuilt for Charles II in the seventeenth century and George IV in the nineteenth. Only a few traces of the buildings in which Isabella lived survive today, several having been revealed during restoration after the fire of 1992.
32. *CCR.*
33. Walsingham; E.101.
34. *Foedera.* This was the first occasion on which the time of the birth of an English king was recorded.
35. *Vita Edwardi Secundi.*
36. *CCR;* E.159; *CPR.*
37. Additional MSS; E.159. This is the Queen's first extant letter.
38. Fawtier.
39. Walsingham.
40. Ibid.
41. *Annales Londonienses.*
42. *Foedera;* Cotton MSS, Julius; *CCR.*
43. C.53.
44. Ibid.
45. E.101.
46. *Vita Edwardi Secundi.*
47. *CFR; Annales Londonienses; Foedera;* Lambeth MS 1213; *Annales Paulini.*
48. *Vita Edwardi Secundi.*
49. E.101.
50. *Annales Londonienses.*
51. *CPR; Foedera.*
52. Mortimer; Menache; Geoffrey de Paris.
53. E.101; *Household Book.*
54. For the Queen's household, see her *Household Book* and Johnstone, "The Queen's Household." Johnstone drew on the first and second surviving *Household Books* for her study.
55. *CPR; Household Book.*
56. Tout, *Chapters; Household Book.*
57. *Household Book;* Tout, *Chapters;* E.101.
58. Tout, *Chapters; Household Book.*
59. E.101.
60. *Household Book;* Davies, *Baronial Opposition.*
61. *Household Book; CPR.*
62. *Household Book; Letters of the Queens of England;* Johnstone, "The Queen's Household."
63. *Household Book; CPR.*
64. *Household Book.*
65. Ibid.
66. Ibid.
67. Ibid.
68. *CPR.*
69. Tout, *Chapters.*
70. Now in the British Museum.
71. Strickland.

72. Vale.
73. *Household Book.*
74. An inventory of the books owned by Isabella at her death is in Vale. See also Tout, *Chapters,* and Johnstone, "Isabella."
75. Cited by Rose.
76. An antiphon, usually from the Psalms, is sung or recited immediately after the Epistle at Mass.
77. The Isabella Psalter is now in the Staatsbibliothek, Munich.
78. Sandler, *Gothic Manuscripts; Age of Chivalry* catalog.
79. Evans, *English Art;* Martin; Royal MS 2.B.VII.
80. Lewis. The Isabella of France Apocalypse is MS Fr. 13096 in the Bibliothèque Nationale, Paris.
81. Strickland.
82. *Vita Edwardi Secundi.*
83. It was badly damaged in 1643 and completely destroyed in 1692.
84. Palmer, "The King's Confessors."
85. Vale.
86. Martin.
87. *CCR.*
88. Prestwich.
89. *Household Book; Age of Chivalry* catalog.
90. Matthew Paris; Parsons.
91. *Antient Kalendars; Household Book.*
92. *Household Book;* E.101.
93. The site of the hospital building is now under Saint Katharine's Dock.
94. *Household Book.* For full details of Isabella's financial resources, see Johnstone, "The Queen's Household."

CHAPTER FOUR   *His Dearest Companion*

1. E.101.
2. *Annales Londonienses.*
3. *CCR;* C.53.
4. E.101.
5. Ibid.
6. *CPR.*
7. *Vita Edwardi Secundi.*
8. *CCR; Foedera; Parliamentary Writs.*
9. *Vita Edwardi Secundi.*
10. Ibid.
11. Ibid.
12. *Gascon Rolls,* ed. Renouard.
13. Brown, "Diplomacy."
14. *Recueil des historiens de France; Recueil des historiens des Gaules; Vita Edwardi Secundi.*
15. *Gascon Rolls,* ed. Renouard; S.C.1; Archives Municipales; Cotton MSS, Julius.
16. Favier.
17. Doherty, thesis; Cotton MSS, Julius.
18. E.101.
19. *Receuil des historiens des Gaules.*
20. E.30.
21. *Receuil des historiens des Gaules;* Geoffrey de Paris; Strickland; *Comptes royaux.*
22. *Gascon Rolls,* ed. Renouard.

23. *Chronique de Pays-Bas;* Grey, *Scalacronica; Chronicum comitum Flandriae;* Jean des Preis.

24. For what became known as the affair of the Tour de Nesle, see *Chronique de Pays-Bas;* Grey, *Scalacronica;* Doherty, thesis; Brown, "Diplomacy"; Cordier; Castries; Bouyer; Kirchhoff; Leblanc-Ginet; Guinle; Jean des Preis; Molinier; Lescot; *Normanniae nova chronica;* Pirenne; *Chronicum Comitum Flandriae; Chronicon Comitum Flandrensium.*

25. *CCR; Parliamentary Writs.*

26. *Chronicle of Lanercost.*

27. Ibid.

28. *Vita Edwardi Secundi.*

29. I.e., the Parliament that met on 23 September 1313.

30. S.C.1; *Letters of the Queens of England.*

31. E.101.

32. *Foedera.*

33. *Vita Edwardi Secundi.*

34. *Gesta Edwardi; Chronicle of Meaux; Vita Edwardi Secundi;* Robert of Reading; *Foedera.*

35. *Foedera;* Walsingham; Strickland; Trokelowe.

36. *Vita Edwardi Secundi.*

37. For the reconciliation, see *Foedera;* Walsingham; *Vita Edwardi Secundi;* Trokelowe; *CPR;* Strickland.

38. In 1959, G. E. Trease noted that the Queen was being attended by her doctors at this time but erroneously concluded that she had suffered a miscarriage or stillbirth.

39. E.101; Trease.

40. Cotton MSS, Julius.

41. E.101; E.404.

42. E.101.

43. *CCR; Gascon Calendar;* E.101.

44. *Foedera.*

45. E.101.

46. E.101. For details of Isabella's trip to France, I am indebted to Brown, "Diplomacy."

47. E.101; E.404; C.47.

48. E.101.

49. Kentish Chronicle.

50. Leland; *Annales Paulini.*

51. E.101.

52. *Foedera; CPR.*

53. E.101.

54. Ibid.

55. Ibid.

56. E.101; *Foedera; CPR.*

57. E.101.

58. Ibid.

59. Ibid.

60. Seward, *Monks of War;* Doherty, thesis.

61. Doherty, thesis; *Foedera;* C.47; E.101; E.30; Langlois, "Rouleaux"; Cotton MSS, Julius. Isabella's petitions are in E.30. For a full account, see Brown, "Diplomacy."

62. E.101.

63. E.101. The castle in which Isabella stayed was destroyed by her grandson, the Black Prince, during the Hundred Years' War, but the Sainte Chapelle founded by Saint Louis in circa 1235 survives, although without its original stained glass. The present-day château dates mainly from the sixteenth century.

64. E.101.

65. *CPR.*

66. E.101.
67. E.101; *Foedera.*
68. E.101.
69. Brown, "Prince Is Father."
70. E.101.
71. Lambeth MS 242; E.101.
72. E.101.
73. Geoffrey de Paris.
74. Grey, *Scalacronica.*
75. Grey, writing some years after these events, states incorrectly that two of the Princesses were put to a shameful death and that the third was imprisoned without food or drink and starved to death.
76. Archives Tallandier.
77. *Chronique de Pays-Bas;* Grey, *Scalacronica.*
78. Hallam, *Capetian France;* Langlois; Fawtier.
79. Langlois, "Rouleaux"; Cotton MSS, Julius.
80. Doherty, thesis.
81. *Vita Edwardi Secundi; Chronicle of Meaux.*
82. E.101.
83. Ibid.
84. He was later exchanged for Bruce's wife, Elizabeth de Burgh, who had been held prisoner in England since 1306.
85. Trevet; Gransden.
86. E.101; Tout, *Chapters.*
87. Johnstone, "Eccentricities"; *Vita Edwardi Secundi;* Madox.
88. E.101.
89. *Vita Edwardi Secundi.*
90. *Rotuli Parliamentorum;* Doherty, thesis.
91. Doherty, thesis; *Household Book.*
92. E.101.
93. E.101; Christie; E.403.
94. *Vita Edwardi Secundi.*
95. Trokelowe; Phillips; *Aymer;* E.101.
96. *Annales Londonienses; Vita Edwardi Secundi; Annales Paulini;* Trokelowe; E.403; *CPR;* C.81; Additional MSS; Stowe MSS; E.101.
97. *Vita Edwardi Secundi.*
98. *Vita Edwardi Secundi;* E.101.
99. Doherty, thesis.
100. *CPR.*
101. Saaler; Cotton MSS, Nero; Cooper.
102. E.101; Lambeth MS 242.
103. *Vita Edwardi Secundi.*
104. Walsingham; *Vita Edwardi Secundi.*
105. *Gesta Edwardi.*
106. *Vita Edwardi Secundi.*
107. McKisack.
108. E.101.
109. Robert of Reading.
110. *Irish Exchequer Payments;* Barrow; *Chartularies of St. Mary's Abbey, Dublin.*
111. *Parliamentary Writs.*
112. *Rotuli Parliamentorum; Foedera; Vita Edwardi Secundi; Parliamentary Writs.*
113. *Foedera.*

114. *CPR.*
115. Household book of Thomas of Lancaster, in Stow, *London.*
116. *Foedera.*
117. E.101.
118. *CPR.*
119. Ibid.
120. Phillips, *Aymer;* Maddicott.
121. Society of Antiquaries MS 120.
122. *Brief Summary of the Wardobe Accounts of Edward II;* Society of Antiquaries MS 120.
123. *Household Book; Foedera; Brief Summary of the Wardrobe Accounts of Edward II.*
124. *CPR.*
125. E.404.
126. Society of Antiquaries MS 120.
127. E.404.
128. Description from tomb epitaph in Durham Cathedral.
129. Doherty, thesis; Maddicott.
130. *Historia Dunelmensis;* Doherty, thesis; Packe.
131. *CCR;* Mortimer; *CPR; Foedera.*
132. *CCR;* E.404.
133. *CPR.*
134. Packe. In 1589, Jeanne's direct descendant would ascend the French throne as Henry IV, first king of the House of Bourbon.
135. Clarendon was last used as a royal residence in 1453, by Henry VI. The palace has now largely disappeared, and only ruined fragments remain. The site was excavated in 1936 and in the 1960s. The tiled pavement from the Queen's chamber is now in the British Museum.
136. E.404.
137. *Vita Edwardi Secundi.*
138. *Historia Dunelmensis;* Doherty, thesis; Packe.
139. *Rotuli Parliamentorum; Foedera; Vita Edwardi Secundi; Parliamentary Writs.*
140. Dene; Additional MSS; Phillips, *Aymer.*
141. *Chronicon Abbatiae Ramesiensis.*
142. *Vita Edwardi Secundi.*
143. It was said to have been named in honor of Prince Edward and his younger brother, John of Eltham.
144. E.403.
145. *Vita Edwardi Secundi; CP;* Robert of Reading; *Chronicle of Meaux; Annales Paulini; Gesta Edwardi;* Walsingham. After Lancaster's death, Alice married Sir Eubulo Lestraunge second and Hugh, Baron Freyne, third. She died in 1348.
146. *Foedera.*
147. *Vita Edwardi Secundi.*
148. Walsingham.
149. *Brief Summary of the Wardrobe Accounts of Edward II.*
150. *CPR.*
151. Society of Antiquaries MS 121.
152. C.53.
153. *Brief Summary of the Wardrobe Accounts of Edward II.*
154. Baker.
155. *Rotuli Parliamentorum.*
156. E.404; Tanner MS 197.
157. *Vita Edwardi Secundi.*
158. Doherty, thesis; *CPR; CCR;* Lists and Indexes; E.404.

159. Davies, *Baronial Opposition;* Tout, *Chapters;* Tout, *Place.*

160. *Rotuli Parliamentorum.*

161. E.101.

162. Knighton; Gee.

163. E.159.

164. *CPR.*

165. Ibid.

166. *CPR; CCR.*

167. Phillips, *Aymer;* Maddicott.

168. *Rotuli Parliamentorum;* Doherty, thesis; Maddicott; *Documents Illustrative of English History.*

169. *CPR.*

170. Much of Woodstock was destroyed during the Civil War, and the remaining buildings were swept away in the early eighteenth century when Blenheim Palace was built in the palace grounds. A pillar now marks the site.

171. Society of Antiquaries MS 121; E.101; Lambeth MS 242.

172. E.101.

173. E.101; *Vita Edwardi Secundi.*

174. *Vita Edwardi Secundi;* Robert of Reading.

175. For the imposter, see *Vita Edwardi Secundi; Chronicle of Lanercost;* Walsingham; Johnstone, "Isabella."

176. *Vita Edwardi Secundi.*

177. D.L.28.

178. *Vita Edwardi Secundi.* Leake is in Nottinghamshire.

179. *Beverley Chapter Act Book.*

180. *Rotuli Parliamentorum.*

181. Robert of Reading.

182. *Rotuli Parliamentorum; Documents Illustrative of English History;* Tout, *Place;* Maddicott.

183. E.403; S.C.1.

184. *Annales Paulini.*

185. "War of Saint Sardos."

186. *Vita Edwardi Secundi.*

187. *Vita Edwardi Secundi;* Trokelowe.

188. This was Sir James Douglas (1286?–1330), one of Scotland's most famous heroes.

189. *Vita Edwardi Secundi;* Robert of Reading.

190. Barbour.

191. *Gesta Edwardi.*

192. *Vita Edwardi Secundi.*

193. "Chronicle of the Civil Wars"; *Vita Edwardi Secundi.*

194. *Vita Edwardi Secundi.*

195. See also Doherty, thesis, and Society of Antiquaries MS 120.

196. Maddicott; *CCR;* E.101.

197. *Vita Edwardi Secundi;* Trokelowe.

198. Additional MSS; *CFR.*

199. Additional MSS.

200. Ibid.

201. *Vita Edwardi Secundi.*

202. *Annales Paulini.*

203. Doherty, thesis.

204. *Register of Thomas Cobham.*

205. Robert of Reading.

206. *History of the King's Works;* Robert of Reading.

207. Lambeth MS 242.

208. E.159.
209. E.101.
210. Additional MSS.
211. *CPR;* Phillips, *Aymer.*
212. *Annales Paulini; Foedera;* Baker.
213. Trevet; Cotton MSS, Nero; *Lettres Secrètes.*
214. S.C.1.
215. Walsingham.
216. *Vita Edwardi Secundi.*
217. *Foedera.*
218. Ibid.; *Chronicles . . . of Edward I and Edward II.*
219. S.C.1.
220. *Chronicle of Lanercost;* Davies, "Despenser War."
221. Froissart.
222. *Chronicles . . . of Edward I and Edward II.*
223. Robert of Reading.
224. Ibid.
225. *Vita Edwardi Secundi.*
226. Ibid.
227. Robert of Reading.
228. *Vita Edwardi Secundi.*

CHAPTER FIVE   *The Displeasure of the Queen*

1. *Vita Edwardi Secundi.*
2. Ibid.
3. *CCR.*
4. Smith, "Revolt of William Somerton"; Walsingham.
5. C.81; *CPR;* Doherty, thesis; Lists and Indexes.
6. *CCR.*
7. *CCR;* Robert of Reading; Murimuth; Dugdale, *Monasticon; Annales Paulini.*
8. *Vita Edwardi Secundi.*
9. *Vita Edwardi Secundi;* Robert of Reading.
10. *Annales Paulini.*
11. Strickland.
12. Additional MSS; C.53; *CCR.*
13. *Wigmore Abbey Annals; Annales Paulini.*
14. *Vita Edwardi Secundi.*
15. *CCR.*
16. Murimuth; *Vita Edwardi Secundi;* Baker; *Chronicles . . . of Edward I and Edward II;* Maddicott.
17. *Chroniques de London.*
18. *Annales Paulini.*
19. *Vita Edwardi Secundi.*
20. *CCR; Statutes of the Realm; Parliamentary Writs; CPR;* Harleian MSS; *Vita Edwardi Secundi.*
21. *Vita Edwardi Secundi;* Robert of Reading; *Chronicles . . . of Edward I and Edward II.*
22. *Foedera.*
23. *Vita Edwardi Secundi.*
24. Kentish Chronicle.
25. E.101.
26. *History of the King's Works; CPR; CCR; CFR.*
27. Kentish Chronicle.

28. Walsingham; Higden.

29. Kentish Chronicle. Murimuth and Baker assert that Isabella reached Leeds on 29 September; the *Annales Paulini* place her arrival as late as 13 October. See Doherty, thesis, for a fuller discussion of this. It seems that the likeliest date for her arrival was 2 October, since her request for soldiers was sent to the King (then at Witley) on 3 October (E.101).

30. Doherty, thesis; E.101.

31. CCR. This was probably Leeds Priory in the village of Leeds, which had been founded by the builder of the castle, Robert de Crevecouer. The priory site has recently been excavated. For the episode at Leeds Castle, see *Foedera; Le Livere de Reis;* Walsingham; *Annales Paulini;* Trokelowe; Kentish Chronicle; Baker; *Vita Edwardi Secundi;* Robert of Reading.

32. Walsingham; E.101.

33. E.101; *Foedera.*

34. *Foedera.*

35. CCR; *Foedera.*

36. CCR.

37. *Annales Paulini.*

38. *Anominalle Chronicle.*

39. Grey, *Scalacronica;* Murimuth.

40. *Vita Edwardi Secundi;* Robert of Reading.

41. She was released on 12 November 1322.

42. *Vita Edwardi Secundi.*

43. CCR; S.C.6.

44. CFR; S.C.6; *History of the King's Works.*

45. CCR; E.101.

46. Kentish Chronicle; *Vita Edwardi Secundi.*

47. *Anominalle Chronicle.*

48. Strickland; Denholm-Young, introduction to *Vita Edwardi Secundi.*

49. *Foedera; Chronicles . . . of Edward I and Edward II;* Murimuth; *Annales Paulini.*

50. Haskins, "Doncaster Petition."

51. Cotton MSS, Nero.

52. *Vita Edwardi Secundi.*

53. Ibid.

54. CPR; *Foedera.*

55. *Foedera;* CCR.

56. *Chronicle of Meaux; Vita Edwardi Secundi.*

57. CPR.

58. *Parliamentary Writs;* Murimuth.

59. CPR.

60. Walsingham; *Parliamentary Writs;* Murimuth; *Anominalle Chronicle.*

61. CCR; CPR.

62. *Vita Edwardi Secundi;* Robert of Reading.

63. *Foedera.*

64. *Foedera; Annales Paulini.*

65. Walsingham.

66. For the Battle of Boroughbridge, see Grey, *Scalacronica; Vita Edwardi Secundi;* Mason, "Sir Andrew de Harcla"; Tout, "Tactics"; *The Brut; Chronicle of Lanercost.*

67. *Vita Edwardi Secundi.*

68. *Rotuli Parliamentorum.*

69. For Lancaster's trial and condemnation, see *Gesta Edwardi;* Keen, *Treason Trials;* Robert of Reading; Fryde, *Tyranny.*

70. *Vita Edwardi Secundi; The Brut;* Trokelowe; Robert of Reading; *Annales Paulini; Foedera.*

71. CCR; Sayles; Murimuth.

72. Kentish Chronicle; E.101; *CPR;* Murimuth.

73. D.L.42; *CPR.*

74. *Calendar of Entries in the Papal Registers.*

75. Murimuth; *CP; Anominalle Chronicle;* Fryde, *Tyranny.*

76. Cotton MSS, Vitellius.

77. S.C.8; *CP.*

78. Froissart.

79. *Parliamentary Writs; Statutes of the Realm.*

80. Cotton MSS, Vitellius.

81. *Vita Edwardi Secundi; Annales Paulini;* Robert of Reading; Baker; *Chronicle of Lanercost;* Froissart.

82. Froissart.

83. *CCR.*

84. Froissart.

85. *CCR;* Tout, *Place.*

86. Dene; *CP.*

87. Taylor, "Judgement."

88. Shepherd.

89. D.L.42.

90. *Vita Edwardi Secundi.*

91. Ibid.

92. Grey, *Scalacronica.*

93. Tout, *Place;* Tout, *Chapters.*

94. E.101.

95. *Vita Edwardi Secundi.*

96. Ibid.

97. *CPR;* Plucknett.

98. *Parliamentary Writs.*

99. "War of Saint Sardos."

100. Trokelowe.

101. Stowe MSS; Blackley, "Adam."

102. E.163.

103. Stowe MSS.

104. *Chronicle of Lanercost;* Barrow; *Calendar of Documents Relating to Scotland.*

105. *Chronicle of Lanercost.*

106. *Calendar of Documents Relating to Scotland.*

107. Stowe MSS.

108. Ibid.

109. *Chronicle of Lanercost.*

110. E.163.

111. Stowe MSS.

112. The continuator of William de Nangis, in *Receuil des historiens des Gaules.*

113. Stowe MSS.

114. *The Brut;* Stowe MSS; Robert of Reading; Grey, *Scalacronica;* Barbour; Trokelowe.

CHAPTER SIX   *Then Let Her Live Abandoned and Forlorn*

1. *CCR; CPR.*

2. Stowe MSS; E.101; Additional MSS.

3. *Chronographia Regum Francorum.*

4. *Vita Edwardi Secundi.*

5. *Historiae Anglicana Decem Scriptores.*

6. *The Brut.*
7. See Doherty, *Isabella,* and Susan Howatch in her fictionalized version of these events in the novel *Cashelmara.*
8. *CCR; Foedera.*
9. Cappellani.
10. Ibid.
11. *Foedera.*
12. *CPR.*
13. E.101; *Calendar of Plea and Memoranda Rolls.*
14. *Foedera.*
15. *Stonor Letters.*
16. E.101; S.C.1.
17. Doherty, thesis.
18. Mortimer.
19. Knighton; Robert of Reading.
20. C.81; *CPR; Political Poems and Songs;* Higden; Riches; *Anominalle Chronicle.*
21. Robert of Reading; *Chroniques de London.*
22. Knighton.
23. *Chronicle of Lanercost;* Mason, "Sir Andrew de Harcla"; *Foedera;* Trokelowe; *Gesta Edwardi;* Murimuth; Robert of Reading; *The Brut;* Walsingham; *Annales Paulini; Letters and Papers from Northern Registers.*
24. *Calendar of Documents Relating to Scotland; Foedera;* Robert of Reading; *Vita Edwardi Secundi.*
25. *Foedera.*
26. E.159; *Beverley Chapter Act Book.*
27. *Le Livere de Reis.*
28. The original Lanthorn Tower was gutted by fire in 1774; the present building is a Victorian reconstruction.
29. For Mortimer's escape, see *Foedera;* Bayley; Knighton; Strickland; Murimuth; Mortimer; Stones, "Date"; *Anominalle Chronicle;* Robert of Reading; *Chroniques de London;* Trokelowe. Murimuth incorrectly dates the escape to 1322.
30. *Chronicle of Meaux;* "War of Saint Sardos."
31. Kentish Chronicle; Doherty, thesis.
32. "War of Saint Sardos."
33. *Mortimeriados* (1596), revised as *The Barons' Wars* (1619); and *England's Heroical Epistles* (1619).
34. Hopkinson and Speight.
35. Mortimer; Hicks.
36. Trokelowe.
37. Haines, *Church and Politics;* Williams, *Mediaeval London; Registrum Ade de Orleton.*
38. Edwards, "Political Importance"; "War of Saint Sardos."
39. Froissart.
40. Trokelowe; Mortimer.
41. Mortimer.
42. *CCR; Foedera.*
43. *CCR.*
44. E.159.
45. Mortimer; Fryde, *Tyranny; Chronicle of Meaux.*
46. "War of Saint Sardos."
47. Ashmole MS 794; E.101.
48. Additional MSS; E.159; *CPR.*
49. *Chronicles of London,* ed. Kingsford; Trokelowe; Baker; "War of Saint Sardos."

50. E.403; *Foedera;* Tout, *Place; Chronicle of Lanercost.*
51. "War of Saint Sardos."
52. *CPR;* Walsingham.
53. *The Brut.* Pembroke was buried near the high altar in Westminster Abbey. His tomb and effigy still survive. His widow, Marie, survived him for fifty-three years.
54. *Vita Edwardi Secundi.*
55. *Foedera.*
56. *Le Livere de Reis.*
57. *CFR;* Walsingham; *Foedera;* Baker.
58. *Vita Edwardi Secundi.*
59. Walsingham; *Foedera.*
60. *Rotuli Parliamentorum.*
61. *CCR.*
62. *The Brut.*
63. C.61; "War of Saint Sardos"; *Vita Edwardi Secundi.*
64. *Foedera;* E.403.
65. Doherty, thesis.
66. E.403; Green, *Lives of the Princesses; CCR.* His first wife had been Edward's sister, Joan of Acre, who had died in 1307. Isabella le Despenser had previously been the wife of John, Baron Hastings (d. 1313).
67. *Rotuli Parliamentorum.*
68. *Foedera;* Strickland; Walsingham.
69. Baker; *Chronicle of Lanercost.*
70. "War of Saint Sardos."
71. E.403; *Foedera;* Tout, *Place; Chronicle of Lanercost.*
72. C.61; Doherty, thesis; E.404.
73. E.403; Doherty, thesis; E.404.
74. Blackley, "Isabella and the Bishop."
75. "War of Saint Sardos."
76. Froissart.
77. *Calendar of Entries in the Papal Registers.*
78. *Select Cases in the Court of King's Bench; CP.*
79. *Calendar of Entries in the Papal Registers.*
80. Tanquerery; Clarke, "Some Secular Activities."
81. "War of Saint Sardos."
82. *Foedera.*
83. "War of Saint Sardos."
84. Doherty, thesis.
85. *CCR.*
86. Doherty, thesis.
87. "War of Saint Sardos."
88. Ibid.
89. Walsingham.
90. Parliamentary Writs; "War of Saint Sardos."
91. *Chronicle of Lanercost.*
92. *Register of Thomas Cobham.*
93. *Literae Cantuarienses.*
94. *DNB.*
95. Dene; Baker; Hicks.
96. *Chronicles . . . of Edward I and Edward II;* Murimuth; *Foedera.*
97. "War of Saint Sardos"; Blackley, "Isabella and the Bishop."
98. *Literae Cantuarienses.*

99. "War of Saint Sardos"; Doherty, thesis.
100. *Foedera; CPR.*
101. "War of Saint Sardos."
102. Strickland.
103. E.101; *CPR.*
104. *Literae Cantuarienses.*
105. E.403; E.101. Isabella's expenses rolls, drawn up by William de Boudon, are in E.101.
106. "War of Saint Sardos."
107. *Literae Cantuarienses.*
108. *Lettres Secrètes.*
109. *Foedera.*
110. *Vita Edwardi Secundi.*
111. *Literae Cantuarienses.*

CHAPTER SEVEN   *Mortimer and Isabel Do Kiss When They Conspire*

1. For Isabella's stay in France, and her itinerary, see Thomas of London's accounts in E.101; Hunter, "Journal"; "War of Saint Sardos."
2. *CPR.*
3. "War of Saint Sardos."
4. Baker.
5. "War of Saint Sardos."
6. Ibid.
7. Ibid.
8. A late fifteenth-century manuscript illumination of Isabella's arrival in Paris is in the Bibliothèque Nationale, Paris, and shows Charles IV riding out to meet her. There are miniatures of Isabella being received at Boulogne and laying her complaints before Charles IV in an inferior copy of Froissart's *Chronicles* in the British Library.
9. Costain; Norris.
10. Froissart.
11. Ibid.
12. *Foedera.*
13. E.101.
14. *Foedera.*
15. "War of Saint Sardos."
16. *Foedera.*
17. Ibid.
18. Doherty, thesis; "War of Saint Sardos."
19. "War of Saint Sardos."
20. *Foedera.*
21. *Vita Edwardi Secundi.*
22. *CCR; Foedera;* Baker; Murimuth; *Vita Edwardi Secundi.*
23. E.101.
24. E.403.
25. "War of Saint Sardos."
26. Ibid.
27. *Foedera.*
28. *Vita Edwardi Secundi;* Baker.
29. Bodleian MS 751; *CPR.*
30. *Vita Edwardi Secundi; Literae Cantuarienses.*
31. *Foedera.*
32. "War of Saint Sardos."

33. Harleian MSS; "War of Saint Sardos"; Murimuth; *Vita Edwardi Secundi.*
34. Baker.
35. Murimuth.
36. Baker.
37. *Foedera;* Baker; Additional MSS; Walsingham; *CPR.*
38. *CCR; Foedera.*
39. Ibid.
40. Ibid.
41. *Vita Edwardi Secundi.*
42. *Le Livere de Reis; Vita Edwardi Secundi.*
43. *Vita Edwardi Secundi.*
44. Harleian MSS; "War of Saint Sardos"; Murimuth; *Vita Edwardi Secundi.* The date of the homage is sometimes incorrectly given as 21 September.
45. Froissart.
46. Baker.
47. *Parliamentary Writs; Annales Paulini.*
48. Walsingham.
49. *Foedera.*
50. *Vita Edwardi Secundi.*
51. Rose.
52. Knighton; Bury, *Philobiblon.*
53. Froissart.
54. Baker.
55. Ibid.; Walsingham.
56. *CCR; Foedera.*
57. *Foedera;* Grassi, "William Airmyn."
58. Baker.
59. *CCR; Foedera.*
60. *CCR; Foedera;* Baker; Murimuth; *Vita Edwardi Secundi.*
61. *Foedera.*
62. Froissart.
63. *Vita Edwardi Secundi.*
64. Ibid.
65. S.C.1.
66. Ibid.
67. *Vita Edwardi Secundi.*
68. Baker.
69. E.101. There is no record in Isabella's expenses roll of her entertaining Stapledon.
70. S.C.1.
71. E.101.
72. S.C.1; Baker.
73. E.101.
74. *Vita Edwardi Secundi; Rotuli Parliamentorum; Foedera.*
75. E.101.
76. Baker; *CCR;* S.C.1; Walsingham.
77. S.C.1; Baker.
78. Hunter, "Journal."
79. *Vita Edwardi Secundi.*
80. *Chroniques de London.*
81. *Vita Edwardi Secundi.*
82. *CCR;* Baker; Walsingham.
83. *Vita Edwardi Secundi.*

84. Ibid.
85. Ibid.
86. Ibid.
87. *Grandes Chroniques de France;* Walsingham.
88. S.C.1; Society of Antiquaries MS 122.
89. Cotton MSS, Faustina; Buck.
90. S.C.1.
91. *Le Journal de Trésor de Charles IV; Grandes Chroniques de France.*
92. *CCR;* Baker; Walsingham.
93. *CCR; Foedera.*
94. Ibid.
95. Ibid.
96. Ibid.
97. Ibid.
98. S.C.1; Baker.
99. *Chronique Parisienne Anonyme.*
100. Doherty, thesis.
101. *Vita Edwardi Secundi;* Murimuth.
102. Mortimer.
103. Baker.
104. Johnstone, "Isabella."
105. Mosley.
106. *Receuil des historiens des Gaules;* Murimuth; Knighton; Baker.
107. *Literae Cantuarienses.*
108. Lyubimenko.
109. E.101.
110. S.C.1.
111. *CPR.*
112. *CPR; CCR.*
113. S.C.1.
114. *Literae Cantuarienses; Receuil des historiens des Gaules;* Doherty, thesis.
115. *Foedera; CCR.*
116. Society of Antiquaries MS 122; *CCR; Foedera; CPR.*
117. Society of Antiquaries MS 122.
118. Kentish Chronicle.
119. Society of Antiquaries MS 122.
120. "Rekeningen van . . . Joanna Van Valois."
121. *CFR.*
122. *Historiae Anglican Decem Scriptores.*
123. *CCR.*
124. *Foedera.*
125. *Calendar of Entries in the Papal Registers.*
126. Ibid.
127. Ibid.; Knighton.
128. Baker.
129. *CCR;* E.101; *History of the King's Works;* E.159.
130. *Foedera.*
131. *CCR.*
132. *Literae Cantuarienses.*
133. Dene.
134. Ibid.; *Rotuli Parliamentorum.*
135. Additional MSS.

136. *Literae Cantuarienses.*
137. *Foedera.*
138. Ibid.; *Annales Paulini.*
139. Register of Walter Reynolds.
140. *CCR; Foedera.*
141. *Foedera; CPR.*
142. *CCR; Foedera.*
143. Ibid.
144. Ibid.
145. *CCR.*
146. Ibid.
147. *Foedera.*
148. *Calendar of Entries in the Papal Registers.*
149. Ibid.
150. Ibid.
151. *Foedera.*
152. Register of Walter Reynolds.
153. *CCR; Foedera.*
154. *Foedera.*
155. Kentish Chronicle; Historical Manuscripts Commission, Various Collections, I.
156. *Calendar of Entries in the Papal Registers.*
157. *CPR.*
158. *Foedera.*
159. Ibid.; *Annales Paulini.*
160. Archives Nationales MS J.237.
161. Society of Antiquaries MS 122.
162. Dene.
163. Ibid.; Book of Esther, Old Testament.
164. Cf. Grey, *Scalacronica.*
165. *CCR; Foedera.*
166. *Vita Edwardi Secundi;* Cappellani.
167. *Foedera.*
168. Ibid.
169. *CCR; Foedera.*
170. *CCR.*
171. *Literae Cantuarienses.*
172. E.101.
173. *CCR.*
174. *Foedera.*
175. *CFR.*
176. *Foedera.*
177. *Parliamentary Writs; Foedera;* C.49.
178. *CPR.*
179. Ibid.
180. Froissart.
181. Society of Antiquaries MS 122.
182. Baker.
183. Froissart.
184. *Foedera; CPR.*
185. Walsingham; Froissart.
186. Froissart.
187. Ibid.

188. Walsingham; Dene.
189. Walsingham.
190. Holmes, "Judgement"; Walsingham; Grey, *Scalacronica; The Brut.*
191. *The Brut; CCR.*
192. Walsingham; Grey, *Scalacronica; Receuil des historiens des Gaules; Chronographia Regum Francorum; Recits d'un Bourgeois;* Froissart.
193. Fryde, *Tyranny.*
194. Froissart.
195. Ibid.
196. The continuator of William de Nangis, in *Receuil des Historiens des Gaules.*
197. Society of Antiquaries MS 122.
198. See Doherty, thesis.
199. Hicks; Knighton.
200. *Table Chronologique.*
201. Froissart. The d'Ambreticourt family later settled in England with much honor. In 1360, at Wingham Church in Kent, Sir Eustace's son married Elizabeth of Juliers, granddaughter of Count William of Hainault, and widow of John, Earl of Kent, second son of Earl Edmund.
202. Epitaph on Philippa of Hainault's tomb in Westminster Abbey, by John Skelton.
203. Froissart.
204. *Groot Charterboek.*
205. *Wigmore Abbey Annals.*
206. "Rekeningen van . . . Joanna Van Valois."
207. Froissart.
208. Baker.
209. Ibid.
210. Froissart.
211. *Foedera.*
212. *CCR; Foedera.*
213. Bibliothèque Nationale, Paris, Collection Moreau, vol. 225.
214. C.62; *Chronicle of Lanercost.*
215. *Regesta Hanonensia.*
216. *Cronijke van Nederlandt.*
217. *Table Chronologique.*
218. Froissart.
219. "War of Saint Sardos"; C.61; C.81.
220. *CCR; CPR;* Fryde, *Tyranny.*
221. "Rekeningen van . . . Joanna Van Valois."
222. *Foedera.*
223. *CPR; CCR.*
224. Waller-Zeper.
225. "Rekeningen . . . van Joanna Van Valois."
226. Knighton.
227. Froissart.
228. *Groot Charterboek;* Smit.
229. Waller-Zeper; Knighton; Baker.
230. Froissart.

CHAPTER EIGHT   *Welcome, in God's Name, Madam and Your Son*

1. Froissart; *Chroniques de London;* Kentish Chronicle; *CCR;* Doherty, thesis; Fryde, *Tyranny; CPR;* Ronciere.

2. Froissart; Jean le Bel; *Chronique de Pays-Bas.*
3. *Annales Paulini;* Round; Baker.
4. *Annales Paulini; Foedera;* Baker; *Chronicle of Lanercost; Chronicles . . . of Edward I and Edward II.*
5. *Chronique de Pays-Bas.*
6. Froissart.
7. *Chronographia Regum Francorum; Annales Paulini.*
8. *Chroniques de London.*
9. Ibid.
10. Walsingham; Baker; Murimuth; *Chronicle of Lanercost.* All these chroniclers incorrectly claim that Lancaster and several bishops joined Isabella immediately, but, as will be seen, they did not come until later. Doherty suggests that her landing surprised many of her allies.
11. Froissart; Murimuth.
12. *Calendar of Plea and Memoranda Rolls;* E.101.
13. *Chronique de Pays-Bas;* Froissart.
14. *Annales Paulini.* An entry in the *CCR* shows that Isabella later repaid this money.
15. Froissart; *Chronographia Regum Francorum; Annales Paulini; Receuil des historiens des Gaules.*
16. *Chronicle of Lanercost;* Baker.
17. Knighton.
18. Froissart.
19. Barnwell Abbey House was built on the site in 1678.
20. Baker; Knighton; Murimuth.
21. Murimuth.
22. Baker.
23. *Foedera.*
24. *The Brut.*
25. *CPR.*
26. Kentish Chronicle.
27. *Chroniques de London; Chronicle of Meaux.*
28. *Foedera.*
29. *CPR.*
30. *Foedera; CCR;* Walsingham.
31. *Foedera; Receuil des historiens des Gaules; CCR.*
32. *Foedera.*
33. *Annales Paulini.*
34. *CPR; CCR.*
35. A beautiful miniature of Isabella and Mortimer entering Oxford is to be found in the late fifteenth-century manuscript of the "Chronicle of the Counts of Flanders" (Holkham MS 569, in the Collection of the Earl of Leicester).
36. Wood, *Oxford.*
37. *Historiae Anglicana Decem Scriptores.*
38. Wood, *Oxford.* Nothing remains of the great abbey of Oseney; the site is now occupied by Oxford Station.
39. *Chronicle of Meaux;* E.403; Society of Antiquaries MS 122; C.62.
40. *The Brut.*
41. *Chroniques de London.*
42. Walsingham; Kentish Chronicle.
43. See C.62 and *Parliamentary Writs* for Edward's itinerary during his flight.
44. Knighton; Baker; Walsingham.
45. *Chroniques de London; Annales Paulini.*
46. Walsingham.

47. *Annales Paulini.*
48. *CFR.*
49. Ibid.; *CCR.*
50. *Chronicle of Meaux.*
51. Froissart.
52. *CCR;* Society of Antiquaries MS 122.
53. Dene.
54. Robert of Reading; Murimuth.
55. *Literae Cantuarienses.*
56. Dene.
57. Robert of Reading; *The Brut;* Society of Antiquaries MS 122.
58. Wallingford Castle, which dates from 1071, was razed by Cromwell's forces in the seventeenth century. Only fragmentary ruins and remains of the ramparts can be seen today.
59. *Foedera.*
60. *Historiae Anglicana Decem Scriptores;* Baker.
61. Baker.
62. *Chartulary of Winchester Cathedral.*
63. Stow, *London.*
64. Dene; *Chroniques de London; Annales Paulini.*
65. Dene.
66. *Foedera.*
67. *Annales Paulini;* Walsingham; Williams, *Mediaeval London;* Murimuth.
68. Dene.
69. *Annales Paulini; Chroniques de London; Calendar of Plea and Memoranda Rolls.*
70. *CPR.*
71. *Chroniques de London; Chronicles . . . of Edward I and Edward II.*
72. Froissart.
73. Gloucester Castle was in ruins by the sixteenth century. A prison has stood on the site since the reign of Charles II.
74. Murimuth; *CPR;* Robert of Reading; Baker.
75. Higden; Froissart.
76. Baker.
77. Thynne. This diligent historian and antiquarian probably had access to sources lost to us.
78. Murimuth; *Chronicles . . . of Edward I and Edward II;* Walsingham; *Annales Paulini;* Robert of Reading.
79. Murimuth.
80. Baker.
81. Society of Antiquaries MS 122.
82. Froissart. Bristol Castle has long since been demolished.
83. Froissart is incorrect in stating that the King and the Younger Despenser were also in the castle.
84. Society of Antiquaries MS 122; *Gesta Edwardi.*
85. Froissart; *Calendar of Plea and Memoranda Rolls;* Society of Antiquaries MS 122.
86. Baker.
87. Walsingham; *Chronicle of Lanercost.*
88. Society of Antiquaries MS 122.
89. *Calendar of Plea and Memoranda Rolls.*
90. Historical Manuscripts Commission, Various Collections, I.
91. *Calendar of Plea and Memoranda Rolls.*
92. *Register of Robert Mortival.*
93. *Receuil des historiens des Gaules;* Baker.

94. Isabella's entry into Bristol is shown in manuscript illustrations in fifteenth-century chronicles in the British Library and the Bibliothèque Nationale, Paris.
95. Froissart.
96. Ibid.
97. *Foedera; CPR.*
98. *CCR.*
99. Dene.
100. Ibid.; Historical Manuscripts Commission, Various Collections, I.
101. Froissart.
102. Ibid.
103. For the trial of the Elder Despenser, see *Annales Paulini; Gesta Edwardi;* Kentish Chronicle. The arms of the Elder Despenser are borne today by the Earl Spencer (Fryde, *Tyranny*).
104. Doherty, thesis; *Memorials of St. Edmund's Abbey.*
105. Kentish Chronicle; *Berkeley Manuscripts; Annales Paulini;* Baker; Murimuth.
106. *CPR.*
107. Society of Antiquaries MS 122.
108. Froissart.
109. *Parliamentary Writs; Foedera.*
110. *Parliamentary Writs.*
111. Society of Antiquaries MS 102; Doherty, thesis.
112. E.101; *Calendar of Plea and Memoranda Rolls.*
113. Froissart.
114. Today, the palace, which was restored in 1954, boasts a fine Georgian facade.
115. E.101.
116. *Calendar of Plea and Memoranda Rolls.*
117. Ibid.
118. *CPR; Parliamentary Writs.*
119. *CFR; CPR.*
120. *Foedera.*
121. Baker.
122. *Foedera.*
123. Murimuth; *Annales Paulini;* Robert of Reading; Walsingham; Baker.
124. *Annales Paulini; The Brut;* Kentish Chronicle; *CPR;* Foedera; Ormrod, "Edward II at Neath"; Knighton. A ruined tower is all that remains of Llantrissant Castle.
125. *Chartulary of Winchester Cathedral.*
126. *CPR.*
127. *Annales Paulini;* Murimuth.
128. *Annales Paulini.* Knighton says he was hanged and his body divided.
129. Murimuth; *Chroniques de London.*
130. Froissart.
131. Doherty, thesis; Knighton; Kentish Chronicle.
132. *Foedera.*
133. *The Brut.*
134. Ibid.
135. For the Younger Despenser's trial, see *Gesta Edwardi;* Holmes, "Judgement"; Taylor, "Judgement"; Robert of Reading.
136. Froissart.
137. For the charges against Despenser, see *Annales Paulini;* Robert of Reading.
138. *The Brut;* Leland; Fryde, *Tyranny;* Holmes, "Judgement." A manuscript illustration of Isabella (wearing armor) and Mortimer with their army at Hereford shows Despenser's execution taking place in the background (BL Royal MS 15 EIV f31bv).

139. Michelet.
140. For Despenser's execution, see Froissart; *Annales Paulini;* Kentish Chronicle; Walsingham; Knighton. A graphic manuscript illustration of the execution is in a version of Froissart's *Chronicles* in the Bibliothèque Nationale, Paris.
141. *The Brut.*
142. *CCR.*
143. *CCR; CP.*
144. Froissart.
145. Knighton.
146. Froissart.
147. *CCR; Annales Paulini.*
148. *CPR.*
149. Ibid.; *Foedera; CCR.*
150. Baker.
151. See, for example, Johnstone, "Isabella."
152. *Annales Paulini.*
153. Cf. Mortimer.
154. Doherty, thesis.
155. Froissart.
156. Ibid.
157. *CCR.*
158. Ibid.
159. *CPR.*
160. *CCR.*
161. *CPR.*
162. Ibid.; C.62.
163. For their itinerary between 26 November and 21 December, see E.101.
164. *CFR.*
165. *Parliamentary Writs.*
166. *Annales Paulini.*
167. Thynne. He was finally interred on 28 March 1327, and a beautiful tomb was later raised to his memory by the high altar, which can still be seen today.
168. *Foedera.*
169. Baker.
170. *Foedera.*
171. *CCR; CFR.*
172. *CCR.*
173. Froissart.
174. Dene.
175. *Literae Cantuarienses.*
176. *Chroniques de London;* Historical Manuscripts Commission, Various Collections, I.
177. *Chartulary of Winchester Cathedral.*
178. Froissart; *Chartulary of Winchester Cathedral.*
179. *The Brut.*
180. *Chartulary of Winchester Cathedral.*
181. E.101; Froissart; Kentish Chronicle.
182. Society of Antiquaries MS 122.
183. E.101; *CFR.*
184. *Calendar of Plea and Memoranda Rolls.*
185. E.101; Froissart; Kentish Chronicle; Cotton MSS, Nero; Baker; *Annales Paulini; Rotuli Parliamentorum.*
186. Froissart; *Rotuli Parliamentorum.*

187. *Chronicle of Lanercost.*
188. *Literae Cantuarienses; The Brut.*
189. Pipewell Chronicle; Clarke, "Committees of Estates"; *Literae Cantuarienses; Rotuli Parliamentorum; Chronicle of Lanercost.*
190. Dene.
191. Higden; Lichfield Chronicle; Pipewell Chronicle; *Chronicle of Lanercost.* The sources for this Parliament are contradictory and confusing. See Doherty, thesis; Fryde, *Tyranny;* Clarke, "Committees of Estates"; Valente.
192. *Rotuli Parliamentorum.*
193. *CCR.*
194. *CPR.*
195. *Chronicle of Lanercost.*
196. Bodleian MS 956; Kentish Chronicle.
197. Dene.
198. *Calendar of Plea and Memoranda Rolls; Annales Paulini.*
199. *Calendar of Plea and Memoranda Rolls; Annales Paulini;* Dene.
200. *Literae Cantuarienses.*
201. Walsingham.
202. Bodleian MS 956; Kentish Chronicle.
203. Kentish Chronicle.
204. Dene; *Chronicle of Lanercost;* Kentish Chronicle.
205. *Chronicle of Lanercost.*
206. Dene.
207. Dene; *Chronicle of Lanercost;* Kentish Chronicle.
208. Dene.
209. *Chronicle of Lanercost.*
210. Kentish Chronicle.
211. Dene.
212. Dene; *Chronicle of Lanercost;* Kentish Chronicle.
213. Kentish Chronicle.
214. *Chronicle of Lanercost.*
215. *Chartulary of Winchester Cathedral.*
216. The Articles of Deposition are in *Select Documents of English Constitutional History.* See also *Foedera; Chartulary of Winchester Cathedral; Annales Paulini; The Brut; Historiae Anglicana Decem Scriptores.*
217. Dene.
218. Ibid.
219. Walsingham.
220. Harding, "Isabella and Mortimer"; E.101.
221. Walsingham.
222. Knighton; Baker. Baker's account of the deputation's mission was based on information given him by his patron, Sir Thomas de la More, who was one of its members and an eyewitness to these events.
223. *Chronicle of Lanercost.*
224. Clarke, "Committees of Estates"; Baker.
225. Walsingham.
226. Ibid.
227. For Edward's abdication, see Baker; Clarke, "Committees of Estates"; Higden; Lichfield Chronicle; Pipewell Chronicle; Kentish Chronicle; *Chronicle of Lanercost;* Doherty, thesis; Fryde, *Tyranny.*
228. *CCR.*
229. Baker.

CHAPTER NINE   *Plots and Stratagems*

1. C.62.
2. Baker.
3. Cuttino and Lyman.
4. For Edward III's coronation, see *Annales Paulini;* Dene; E.101; Walsingham; Murimuth; Baker.
5. Edward III's seal of 1327 is now the property of Durham Cathedral.
6. *CPR.*
7. *Political Poems and Songs.*
8. *Calendar of Entries in the Papal Registers;* Doherty, thesis.
9. Pipewell Chronicle.
10. In 1359–66, Edward III converted Sheen Manor into a sumptuous palace. It was demolished by a grieving Richard II in 1395, after his queen, Anne of Bohemia, had died of plague there. Henry V rebuilt it, but it was again burned down in 1497. A few years later, Henry VII raised it anew as Richmond Palace.
11. *CPR.*
12. *History of the King's Works.* Since Isabella's time, Leeds has been extensively renovated, but her apartments largely survive, much altered. Two of these rooms have been furnished in the manner they would have been in the time of Henry V's queen, Katherine of Valois (d. 1437).
13. *History of the King's Works; CPR; CCR; CFR.*
14. Doherty, thesis.
15. *Victoria County History: Hertfordshire; History of the King's Works.*
16. E.101.
17. *Calendar of Plea and Memoranda Rolls.*
18. *Rotuli Parliamentorum; Chroniques de London.*
19. For the regency council, see *The Brut; Chronicle of Meaux; Rotuli Parliamentorum;* Knighton.
20. Doherty, thesis.
21. Robert of Avesbury.
22. Doherty, thesis.
23. Froissart; Walsingham; Baker.
24. This treatise is in Christ Church College, Oxford (MS 92, f.4v).
25. Dene.
26. *CPR.*
27. *Chronicle of Meaux.*
28. *Calendar of Plea and Memoranda Rolls; Foedera;* Somerville; *CP.*
29. *Rotuli Parliamentorum.*
30. *Rotuli Parliamentorum;* Strickland; Rapin-Thoyras; *Foedera; The Brut.*
31. *Statutes of the Realm.*
32. E.101.
33. C.53; *Syllabus of Documents Relating to England;* Nicholson.
34. *CPR.*
35. Ibid.
36. Ibid.
37. *Calendar of Plea and Memoranda Rolls; CFR.*
38. C.53; *CPR.*
39. *Foedera.*
40. *CCR; CPR; CFR; Foedera;* C.62.
41. *CFR.*
42. *CPR.*

43. Murimuth; Walsingham; *Annales Paulini; Historiae Anglicana Decem Scriptores; Gesta Edwardi;* Froissart.

44. *Historiae Anglicana Decem Scriptores; Chartulary of Winchester Cathedral.*

45. *Foedera; Chronicle of Lanercost.*

46. *Foedera.*

47. Ibid.

48. Ibid.

49. Murimuth; Walsingham; Baker; Rapin-Thoyras.

50. *The Brut.*

51. Gransden.

52. The Latin poem is printed in Fabyan's *New Chronicles.* There are various different versions of these poems. Fabyan gives the verses in Latin, but the Norman-French original is in a manuscript at Longleat (Historical Manuscripts Commission). Studer accepts these poems as authentic, while Galbraith is skeptical.

53. *CPR;* Tout, "Captivity and Death"; Doherty, thesis.

54. *CFR.*

55. E.101; Dene.

56. E.101.

57. Knighton.

58. E.101; Knighton; *Rotuli Parliamentorum.*

59. Clarke, "Committees of Estates"; *Foedera.*

60. Ibid.

61. E.101; *Foedera.*

62. E.101.

63. *CFR.*

64. *Foedera.*

65. Ibid.

66. Fryde, *Tyranny.*

67. Baker; *CPR;* Mortimer; *Berkeley Manuscripts.*

68. "Documents Relating to Death and Burial"; Harleian MSS; *Foedera.*

69. *Annales Paulini;* Tout, "Captivity and Death"; Baker; *Berkeley Manuscripts.*

70. *Berkeley Manuscripts.*

71. Tout, "Captivity and Death"; Murimuth; *Berkeley Manuscripts.*

72. *Annales Paulini; Foedera.*

73. Baker.

74. Ibid.

75. *Chartulary of Winchester Cathedral; Rotuli Parliamentorum;* Baker; *Historiae Anglicana Decem Scriptores.*

76. *CPR;* Doherty, thesis.

77. S.C.1; *CPR;* Doherty, thesis.

78. *Foedera.*

79. E.101; Froissart.

80. Froissart.

81. *Literae Cantuarienses.*

82. S.C.1; *CPR;* Doherty, thesis.

83. C.53; *CPR.*

84. *Calendar of Entries in the Papal Registers.*

85. Doherty, thesis.

86. E.101.

87. Froissart; *The Brut.*

88. It became a market garden in the eighteenth century and, in 1839, the site of York's first railway station, which is now occupied by railway offices and a hotel.

89. Froissart; Walsingham; Baker.
90. Froissart; Walsingham; Baker; Murimuth; *The Brut;* Jean le Bel.
91. *Foedera; The Brut.*
92. *CPR.*
93. *Foedera; The Brut.*
94. *Rotuli Scotiae.*
95. E.101.
96. *Foedera;* E.370; *History of the King's Works.*
97. E.101; *Foedera.*
98. E.101.
99. *The Brut;* Grey, *Scalacronica.*
100. Murimuth.
101. *Berkeley Manuscripts;* Doherty, *Isabella.*
102. Murimuth.
103. Tanquerery; *Foedera.*
104. *CPR;* Harding, "Isabella and Mortimer."
105. Doherty, thesis.
106. Tanquerery; S.C.1.
107. *CPR.*
108. Tanquerery.
109. Ibid.
110. *Annales Paulini;* Tanquerery; Tout, "Captivity and Death"; *The Brut.*
111. *Foedera.*
112. *CCR;* King's Bench Records; *CPR;* Doherty, *Isabella.*
113. *Foedera.*
114. *CCR;* Froissart.
115. Ibid.
116. *Calendar of Entries in the Papal Registers; Foedera.*
117. Froissart.
118. Ibid.
119. C.53.
120. E.101.
121. Froissart; E.101; E.159.
122. E.101; *Foedera; CPR;* E.159.
123. *Foedera; CPR;* E.404; *Calendar of Plea and Memoranda Rolls; Rotuli Scotiae; Rotuli Parliamen-torum; Letters and Papers from Northern Registers;* Knighton. For further details, see Doherty, thesis.
124. Tout, "Captivity and Death"; Edwards, "Sir Gruffydd Lloyd."
125. *CCR; Chronicle of Lanercost.*
126. *CPR.*
127. E.101.
128. *CCR; CPR.*
129. Ibid.
130. *CPR.*
131. Tout, "Captivity and Death"; Doherty, *Isabella.*
132. For the full text of Hywel ap Gruffydd's statement, which comes from the Coram Rege Rolls, 5, EdIII, see Tout, "Captivity and Death."
133. *CCR.*
134. Tout, "Captivity and Death"; Murimuth; *Berkeley Manuscripts;* Doherty, thesis; Mortimer; Gransden.
135. *Chartulary of Winchester Cathedral.*
136. Gransden.

137. Tout, "Captivity and Death."
138. *The Brut;* Taylor, "French Brut"; *Anominalle Chronicle;* Taylor, *English Historical Literature.*
139. Fryde, *Tyranny.*
140. *Rotuli Parliamentorum.*
141. Johnson, *Edward III.*
142. *Rotuli Parliamentorum.*
143. Taylor, "French Brut"; Mortimer.
144. A copy of this letter was discovered by a French archivist in the nineteenth century in the binding of an official register dated 1368, which had been the property of Gaucelm de Deaux, Bishop of Maguelonne and was preserved in the Archives Departementales d'Herault at Montpellier in southern France, where it still rests today (GM23, Carte de Maguelonne, Reg. A, fol. 86r [r]).
145. Cuttino and Lyman.
146. Haines, "Edwardus Redivivus"; Mortimer.
147. Now in the possession of the Society of Antiquaries.
148. *Rotuli Parliamentorum.*
149. See Mortimer.
150. Haines, "Edwardus Redivivus."
151. Ibid.; Mortimer.
152. Cuttino and Lyman.
153. Doherty, *Isabella;* Cuttino and Lyman.
154. Ibid.
155. Haines, "Edwardus Redivivus." A contemporary description of the opening of the tomb is in MS 55 in Gloucester Cathedral Library.
156. *Calendar of Entries in the Papal Registers.*
157. For Manuele Fieschi, see Cuttino and Lyman; Mortimer; Doherty, *Isabella;* Doherty, thesis.
158. "Documents Relating to Death and Burial."
159. *Berkeley Manuscripts.*
160. Doherty, *Isabella; Berkeley Manuscripts.*
161. Mortimer.
162. *Rotuli Parliamentorum.*
163. *The Brut.*
164. Hope.
165. D.L.10; Harding, "Isabella and Mortimer"; *Berkeley Manuscripts;* Haines, "Edwardus Redivivus"; *Letters and Papers from Northern Registers.* The Berkeley accounts show that Gurney arrived on 28 September with news of Edward's death, and Doherty is of the opinion that an earlier messenger arrived on the twenty-third, but I think that there must be an error in the accounts and that we should read twenty-third for twenty-eighth.
166. D.L.10; Harding, "Isabella and Mortimer."
167. *Rotuli Parliamentorum.*
168. *Berkeley Manuscripts; Letters and Papers from Northern Registers.*
169. *Letters and Papers from Northern Registers.*
170. "Documents Relating to Death and Burial."
171. *Letters and Papers from Northern Registers.*
172. C.53.
173. *Foedera;* E.403.
174. *Foedera.*
175. Baker; *Anglo-Scottish Relations.*
176. *Historia Sancti Petri Gloucestriae.*
177. Knighton.
178. Tout, "Captivity and Death."

179. *Chronicle of Lanercost.*
180. *Rotuli Parliamentorum.*
181. Hunter, "Gurney."
182. *Berkeley Manuscripts.*
183. Tout, "Captivity and Death"; "Documents Relating to Death and Burial"; E.101.
184. E.101; E.41.
185. E.101.
186. *CPR.*
187. *CCR.*
188. E.101.
189. S.C.1.
190. *CPR.*
191. Historical Manuscripts Commission, 5th Report.
192. *Annales Paulini.*
193. *CPR.*
194. *Foedera;* E.403.
195. *CPR.*
196. E.101; *Foedera.*
197. E.101.
198. Hallam, "Royal Burial."
199. Murimuth.
200. For Edward II's funeral, see Additional MSS; Doherty, thesis; Harding, "Isabella and Mortimer"; "Documents Relating to Death and Burial"; Haines, "Edwardus Redivivus"; E.101; *Berkeley Manuscripts.*
201. Walker.
202. *Historia Sancti Petri Gloucestriae.*
203. Murimuth.

CHAPTER TEN   *Now, Mortimer, Begins Our Tragedy*

1. "Documents Relating to Death and Burial."
2. Ely Place was demolished in 1772.
3. Hardyng; Froissart.
4. *Annales Paulini.*
5. C.53; *CPR.*
6. *CPR.*
7. Froissart.
8. *The Brut;* Froissart; *Annales Paulini.*
9. *The Brut.*
10. C.53; *CPR.*
11. *Calendar of Plea and Memoranda Rolls.*
12. *Foedera.*
13. Ibid.
14. C.53.
15. Doherty, thesis.
16. C.61.
17. E.101.
18. C.53; *CPR; CFR.*
19. C.53.
20. *Annales Paulini; Foedera.*
21. *Foedera.*
22. Nicholson; Robert of Avesbury; Walsingham.

23. Grey, *Scalacronica.*
24. Knighton.
25. Grey, *Scalacronica;* Baker; *The Brut.* Cf. *Chronicle of Lanercost:* "The peace was made through them and no others."
26. *The Brut.*
27. Baker.
28. *Rotuli Parliamentorum.*
29. *CPR; Rotuli Parliamentorum.*
30. Doherty, thesis.
31. *The Brut.*
32. Doherty, thesis.
33. *Rotuli Parliamentorum.*
34. See, for example, S.C.8.
35. *CPR.*
36. *Statutes of the Realm.*
37. Doherty, thesis; *CPR; Foedera; Calendar of Plea and Memoranda Rolls.*
38. *Foedera.*
39. Ibid.
40. Froissart.
41. C.47; *Foedera;* C.61. The marriage negotiations were soon abandoned.
42. E.101; *Calendar of Plea and Memoranda Rolls;* Doherty, thesis.
43. Murimuth; Mortimer.
44. Mortimer.
45. *CPR;* Dugdale, *Monasticon.*
46. *Foedera;* Nicholson.
47. *Calendar of Plea and Memoranda Rolls; Dignity of a Peer;* Doherty, thesis.
48. *Foedera; Chronicle of Lanercost.*
49. *Calendar of Plea and Memoranda Rolls.*
50. *Chronicle of Lanercost; Calendar of Plea and Memoranda Rolls;* Nicholson; Doherty, thesis.
51. *Rotuli Parliamentorum;* C.53; Tout, *Chapters; CFR; CPR.*
52. Knighton.
53. *Foedera;* Barbour; *Chronicle of Lanercost;* Knighton; *Chroniques de London; Annales Paulini;* Walsingham.
54. *CCR.*
55. *Chronicle of Lanercost.*
56. Yates Thompson MS 13, 1325–35.
57. Sandler, *Gothic Manuscripts.*
58. Vale.
59. Little.
60. Barbour.
61. *Chronicle of Lanercost.*
62. *The Brut.*
63. *Chronicle of London,* ed. Nicholas.
64. *Anglo-Scottish Relations; Syllabus of the Documents Relating to England.*
65. E.403; *CFR.*
66. *CFR.*
67. *CCR.*
68. C.53.
69. Ibid.
70. *Dignity of a Peer.*
71. *Foedera; CPR; CCR.*
72. Baker; Walsingham; Strickland.

73. *Rotuli Parliamentorum.*
74. Walsingham; Baker; Knighton.
75. Doherty, thesis.
76. Ibid.
77. *Calendar of Plea and Memoranda Rolls.*
78. E.101.
79. *CPR;* Harding, "Isabella and Mortimer."
80. *CPR; Wigmore Abbey Annals.*
81. E.101; *Calendar of Plea and Memoranda Rolls.*
82. *Foedera; CFR;* C.53.
83. C.53; E.101.
84. *Calendar of Plea and Memoranda Rolls; The Brut.*
85. E.101.
86. *Calendar of Plea and Memoranda Rolls.*
87. E.101; *Calendar of Plea and Memoranda Rolls;* Doherty, thesis.
88. *Calendar of Plea and Memoranda Rolls; The Brut.*
89. *CPR; CCR; CFR; Foedera;* C.53.
90. Packe.
91. *Annales Paulini.*
92. *Foedera.*
93. E.101.
94. *The Brut; Annales Paulini;* Knighton.
95. *The Brut.* In 1346, he would obtain a pardon for one of Holland's murderers (*CPR;* Harding, "Isabella and Mortimer").
96. C.53.
97. *Rotuli Parliamentorum; Foedera.*
98. *Calendar of Plea and Memoranda Rolls; The Brut;* Knighton; *Rotuli Parliamentorum. The Brut's* claim is repeated by the pro-Lancastrian Knighton.
99. *Calendar of Plea and Memoranda Rolls.*
100. *Calendar of Plea and Memoranda Rolls; Rotuli Parliamentorum;* Dene; Harding, "Isabella and Mortimer"; *Foedera.*
101. *Calendar of Plea and Memoranda Rolls.*
102. C.53; Dugdale, *Monasticon;* E.101; Murimuth.
103. *Annales Paulini; CP.*
104. Harding, "Isabella and Mortimer"; E.101; *The Brut.*
105. *Dignity of a Peer.*
106. *Calendar of Plea and Memoranda Rolls.*
107. Ibid.
108. *Foedera; The Brut;* Murimuth.
109. *Calendar of Plea and Memoranda Rolls.*
110. Ibid.
111. C.53.
112. *Calendar of Plea and Memoranda Rolls.*
113. *Foedera.*
114. *Calendar of Plea and Memoranda Rolls.*
115. C.53; Harleian MSS.
116. *Annales Paulini.*
117. Déprez; *Grandes Chroniques de France.*
118. Dene.
119. *Annales Paulini.*
120. Holmes, "Rebellion"; C.53.

121. *CPR;* Eyton.
122. *Calendar of Plea and Memoranda Rolls.* This is the letter on which much of the account in this chapter is based. It is the chief source for the early stages of Lancaster's rebellion.
123. *Annales Paulini.*
124. *Calendar of Plea and Memoranda Rolls; Annales Paulini.*
125. *Annales Paulini;* Holmes, "Rebellion."
126. *Calendar of Plea and Memoranda Rolls.*
127. *The Brut.*
128. Knighton; Holmes, "Rebellion"; Baker.
129. Knighton; Holmes, "Rebellion"; *CP; C.53;* Dene.
130. Knighton.
131. Holmes, "Rebellion"; McKisack; Knighton.
132. *CCR.*
133. *C.53; Annales Londonienses.*
134. *Annales Londonienses; Calendar of Plea and Memoranda Rolls;* E.101; *CPR.*
135. E.101; *C.53.*
136. E.101; *Annales Londonienses.* Chigwell claimed benefit of clergy and was given into the custody of the Bishop of London.
137. *CCR.*
138. Haines, *Church and Politics.*
139. *Annales Londonienses.*
140. *Grandes Chroniques de France;* Froissart.
141. *Foedera.*
142. *CCR.*
143. *CPR.*
144. E.101.
145. S.C.1; *CPR; C.53.*
146. *Foedera.*
147. *CPR.*
148. *CFR.*
149. *CPR;* E.101; *CCR; CFR.*
150. *CFR; C.53.*
151. *C.53;* E.101.
152. *Foedera; CCR.*
153. *Foedera; CCR; CPR.*
154. *Foedera; Annales Paulini; CCR; Rotuli Parliamentorum.*
155. Strickland.
156. Knighton.
157. E.101.
158. Ibid.; *CCR; C.53.*
159. Murimuth; Baker.
160. *CPR; CCR; CFR; Foedera;* Doherty, thesis; Mortimer.
161. *CPR;* S.C.1.
162. *The Brut;* Mortimer; E.101; Robert of Avesbury; Murimuth; Baker; Knighton; Griffin (both). This tournament is sometimes incorrectly said to have taken place in the summer of 1328 at Bedford, but the court did not visit Bedford at that time. Some chroniclers were obviously confused by two Mortimer double weddings.
163. *CPR.*
164. Ibid.
165. Crump. A letter bearing this sign and Edward's signature is now in the Vatican Archives.
166. *CPR.*

167. For Kent's conspiracy, see *Foedera; The Brut;* Murimuth; Baker; Walsingham; *Chronicle of Meaux;* Knighton. Kent's confession is in Murimuth. Baker has apparently embroidered the facts with several details not recorded in contemporary accounts.

168. *The Brut;* Baker.

169. Murimuth; *Calendar of Entries in the Papal Registers.*

170. For the sources for Kent's conspiracy, see note 167.

171. E.101; S.C.1.

172. *CFR.*

173. C.53.

174. *CPR;* C.53; *CFR.*

175. Kenilworth is now a ruin. In 1649, it was wrecked by Cromwell's troops and dismantled soon afterward, at which time the lake was drained. John of Gaunt, Duke of Lancaster, and Robert Dudley, Earl of Leicester, added palatial ranges in the fourteenth and sixteenth centuries, respectively, the remains of which survive.

176. For a full discussion of his theory, see Mortimer.

177. Harleian MSS; Eyton.

178. "Two Effigies in Montgomery Church"; Mortimer.

179. Harleian MSS; Eyton.

180. *CPR;* C.53.

181. Ibid.

182. *Foedera; Dignity of a Peer.*

183. *Foedera.*

184. *CPR.*

185. *Foedera.*

186. C.53; *CPR.*

187. *Annales Paulini; Gesta Edwardi.*

188. *CPR; Rotuli Parliamentorum;* C.53.

189. The great hall was partially rebuilt in 1394 and still stands. The Round Table also survives and is displayed on the wall of the great hall. The rest of the castle was dismantled in 1651 by Cromwell's troops.

190. For the sources for Kent's conspiracy, see note 167.

191. *CCR; CPR.*

192. Tout, "Captivity and Death"; Doherty, thesis.

193. *CFR.*

194. *CCR.*

195. *The Brut; Chronicle of Lanercost; Rotuli Parliamentorum.*

196. *Foedera.*

197. Doherty, *Isabella.*

198. CPR.

199. Ibid.

200. *Rotuli Parliamentorum.*

201. Doherty, thesis; Doherty, *Isabella.*

202. See note 167.

203. *The Brut.*

204. *CFR.*

205. *The Brut.*

206. *Rotuli Parliamentorum; The Brut;* Walsingham.

207. *The Brut;* Knighton.

208. In *Foedera,* he is referred to as "the late Earl of Kent" on 15 March.

209. *Chronicle of Meaux;* Knighton; *The Brut.* His remains were later removed to Westminster Abbey.

210. Murimuth.

211. *CPR; CFR.*
212. *Foedera.*
213. Doherty, *Isabella; Foedera.*
214. Murimuth; Baker.
215. Robert of Avesbury.
216. *The Brut; Chronicle of Meaux.*
217. Doherty, thesis; Schama; Ormrod, *Edward III.*
218. *The Brut;* Baker.
219. *The Brut.*
220. *The Brut;* Stow, *Annals.*
221. *CPR;* S.C.1; C.53; Harleian MSS.
222. *CFR.*
223. Murimuth; *DNB.*
224. *Rotuli Parliamentorum; Select Cases in the Court of King's Bench.*
225. *CPR.*
226. *Foedera.*
227. Ibid.
228. S.C.8; *CPR.*
229. Society of Antiquaries MS 121.
230. *CPR.*
231. *Foedera; CCR.*
232. *The Brut; Annales Paulini.*
233. Galbraith.
234. Murimuth.
235. *CCR; CPR.*
236. *Foedera; Annales Paulini; CCR; Rotuli Parliamentorum.*
237. *Foedera; CCR; CPR; CFR.*
238. *CPR.*
239. C.53; *CPR.*
240. C.53.
241. *Annales Londonienses.*
242. *CPR;* C.53; *CFR.*
243. Harding, "Isabella and Mortimer."
244. C.53.
245. *Calendar of Entries in the Papal Registers.*
246. S.C.1.
247. *Annales Paulini;* C.53.
248. C.53; *CPR.*
249. *Foedera.*
250. C.53; Harleian MSS.
251. Murimuth; *Annales Paulini.*
252. *CCR; CPR.*
253. C.53.
254. *Annales Londonienses; CPR.*
255. *CPR; CCR; Calendar of Entries in the Papal Registers.*
256. *CCR; CPR; CFR.*
257. C.53.
258. *Dignity of a Peer;* C.81; S.C.1; C.53; *CPR;* Harleian MSS; *Calendar of Entries in the Papal Registers.*
259. *Calendar of Entries in the Papal Registers;* Doherty, *Isabella.*
260. *History of the King's Works;* Steane. By 1651, the castle was ruinous, and most of it had to be demolished. In 1674–79, the Duke of Newcastle converted what was left into a fine

mansion known as "The Castle," but it was gutted after an arson attack by a mob during the Reform Bill riots of 1831. It was restored in 1878 and is now the property of Nottingham City Council and houses the City Museum and Art Gallery.

261. *The Brut;* Walsingham; Knighton; E.101; *Rotuli Parliamentorum; CPR.*
262. Baker; *Anominalle Chronicle.*
263. *Rotuli Parliamentorum.*
264. Knighton.
265. Crump.
266. *The Brut;* Grey, *Scalacronica.*
267. Its location remained unknown for centuries before it was rediscovered in 1864. Today, it is lit by electric lights.
268. E.101; *The Brut; CFR.*
269. Baker; Stow, *Annals.*
270. *The Brut.*
271. For this meeting, see *The Brut;* Grey, *Scalacronica; Rotuli Parliamentorum;* Shenton.
272. *The Brut.*
273. Ibid.; *Rotuli Parliamentorum;* Grey, *Scalacronica.*
274. *The Brut;* Grey, *Scalacronica.*
275. *Rotuli Parliamentorum.*
276. Mortimer.
277. Murimuth and Baker both state that Mortimer was taken "in the room of the Queen Mother."
278. For the events of the night of 19 October 1330, see *Chroniques de London; Annales Paulini; Chronicle of Meaux;* Murimuth; Baker; Stow, *Annals; The Brut;* Grey, *Scalacronica; Rotuli Parliamentorum;* Knighton; *Gesta Edwardi.*

CHAPTER ELEVEN   *Our Dearest Mother*

1. Grey, *Scalacronica.*
2. Stow, *Annals;* Baker.
3. Stow, *Annals.*
4. *CCR; Foedera.*
5. *De Speculo Regis Edwardi III.*
6. S.C.8; Baker; E.403; *CPR.*
7. Berkhamsted Castle was in ruins by the sixteenth century. Today, little remains except the castle mound.
8. *The Brut;* Knighton; *Berkeley Manuscripts;* Murimuth.
9. *Berkeley Manuscripts.*
10. Baker.
11. S.C.8; Baker; E.403.
12. Baker; *Annales Paulini.*
13. Stow, *Annals;* Baker.
14. Harding, "Isabella and Mortimer."
15. *CCR.*
16. *Chartulary of Winchester Cathedral.*
17. For Berkeley's trial, see *Rotuli Parliamentorum.*
18. *Rotuli Parliamentorum;* Tout, "Captivity and Death"; *Berkeley Manuscripts;* Mortimer.
19. *Chronicle of Meaux.*
20. The charges against Mortimer are in *Rotuli Parliamentorum.*
21. See, for example, Capgrave.
22. *Rotuli Parliamentorum;* Knighton; Baker; Walsingham; Stow, *Annals.*
23. Doherty, *Isabella.*

24. *Rotuli Parliamentorum.*
25. *CPR.*
26. *CP; Handbook of British Chronology; CCR;* C.53; D.L.10.
27. *Rotuli Parliamentorum.*
28. *Chronicle of Meaux.*
29. S.C.1.
30. For Mortimer's execution, see Murimuth; Baker; Knighton; Stow, *Annals;* Walsingham; Abbott. The site of the gallows is now called Tyburn Way and lies just to the west of Marble Arch.
31. *Rotuli Parliamentorum;* Murimuth.
32. *Foedera.*
33. *Rotuli Parliamentorum.*
34. Murimuth; *Foedera; CCR;* Baker; S.C.8.
35. *Chronicle of Lanercost.*
36. *Calendar of Entries in the Papal Registers.*
37. Doherty, *Isabella.*
38. C.53; *CFR;* E.403; S.C.6; E.199.
39. *Foedera;* S.C.1; Froissart.
40. *CPR.*
41. *Rotuli Parliamentorum;* S.C.8; *Chronicle of Lanercost; CCR; CPR.*
42. Froissart.
43. *CCR; CPR.*
44. *Rotuli Parliamentorum.* Baker claims incorrectly that Deveril was executed on Christmas Eve, but he had fled abroad.
45. *CPR.*
46. Ibid.
47. *CPR; CCR;* E.159; *Foedera.*
48. Froissart; cf. the continuator of William de Nangis, in *Receuil des historiens des Gaules.*
49. Doherty, *Isabella.*
50. Froissart.
51. *Foedera.*
52. Murimuth.
53. Ibid.
54. *Rotuli Parliamentorum; CFR;* S.C.8; *CPR.*
55. *Foedera.*
56. Doherty, *Isabella.*
57. Dugdale, *Monasticon.*
58. *Foedera; CCR.* The *Wigmore Abbey Annals,* however, claim that Mortimer was buried at Shrewsbury. Wigmore Abbey was dissolved in the sixteenth century and the graves destroyed. The site is now a garden.
59. *Foedera; CPR.*
60. *CPR; CCR;* E.159.
61. *CPR; CFR.*
62. *CP.*
63. Cotton MSS, Galba; Bond, "Notices"; Doherty, *Isabella.*
64. Froissart.
65. Cotton MSS, Galba; Bond, "Notices"; Doherty, *Isabella.*
66. Froissart.
67. Johnson, *Edward III.*
68. *Foedera.*
69. Cotton MSS, Galba; Bond, "Notices"; Doherty, *Isabella.*
70. Latin records of King's Lynn, in Historical Manuscripts Commission, 11th Report.

71. *Foedera;* Strickland.
72. *Rotuli Parliamentorum.*
73. S.C.1.
74. *Foedera.*
75. Hunter, "Gurney"; Doherty, *Isabella; CP; CPR; CCR; Foedera; Chronicle of Meaux;* Additional MSS.
76. Ibid.
77. E.403.
78. Nicholson; Marshall.
79. *Chartulary of Winchester Cathedral.*
80. Harding, "Isabella and Mortimer"; Mortimer.
81. *Foedera.*
82. *Rotuli Parliamentorum.*
83. CPR.
84. C.53.
85. Murimuth.
86. E.30. For William le Galeys, see also "War of Saint Sardos"; Doherty, thesis; Doherty, *Isabella;* Mortimer.
87. *Foedera.*
88. CPR.
89. *CPR; Foedera.*
90. *Rotuli Parliamentorum.*
91. Gransden; Mortimer.
92. *CP; Handbook of British Chronology.* Strickland says that this event took place in 1339 and names the Chancellor as Robert Burghersh, but as there was never a chancellor of that name, she must be referring to Robert Bourchier, who was appointed in 1340.
93. *CPR;* Cuttino and Lyman; Neve.
94. *Foedera.*
95. CPR.
96. Marshall.
97. *Foedera.*
98. Murimuth.
99. Cuttino and Lyman.
100. *CCR;* Mortimer.
101. Murimuth; Jean le Bel.
102. C.53.
103. Murimuth; Jean le Bel.
104. Murimuth.
105. C.53.
106. Ibid.
107. *Calendar of Entries in the Papal Registers.*
108. *Foedera.*
109. Leland; Green, *Lives of the Princesses of England.*
110. E.370; *Victoria County History: Hertfordshire;* C.62; *History of the King's Works;* E.101. The castle was much decayed by 1609. It later became a private residence but was restored in 1967 and now houses the council offices. The gatehouse dates from the fifteenth century. Very little has survived from Isabella's time.
111. *Foedera;* Murimuth.
112. Fowler, *King's Lieutenant;* Ormrod, *Edward III.*
113. Cotton MSS, Galba; Bond, "Notices"; Doherty, *Isabella.*
114. CPR.
115. *Foedera.*

116. Cotton MSS, Galba; Bond, "Notices"; Doherty, *Isabella.*

117. *Foedera.*

118. Latin records of King's Lynn, in Historical Manuscripts Commission, 11th Report.

119. Isabella's last surviving *Household Book* is in Cotton MSS, Galba, but this was partially burned during the Cottonian Library fire of 1731. For extracts, see Bond, "Notices" and Doherty, *Isabella.*

120. *Monumenta Franciscana; Chronicle of Lanercost.*

121. Cotton MSS, Galba; Bond, "Notices"; Doherty, *Isabella.*

122. Ibid.

123. Doherty, *Isabella;* Knighton.

124. The royal manor house at Cheylesmore was, according to Leland, "somewhat in ruin" by 1549. The last remains of it were demolished in 1956, and the site is now a registrar's office. In Coventry stands the collegiate church of Saint John the Baptist, which was built by Isabella.

125. Dupuy.

126. *History of the King's Works; CCR.*

127. Stow, *London.*

128. Blackley, "Isabella . . . and the . . . Cult of the Dead"; E.101.

129. Doherty, *Isabella;* Knighton.

130. Knighton; E.403; *Foedera.*

131. E.403.

132. *CPR.*

133. Froissart.

134. Ibid.

135. Kingsford.

136. *CCR.*

137. Brown, "Death and the Human Body"; Duffy; *Calendar of Entries in the Papal Registers.*

138. Kingsford; Johnstone, "Isabella."

139. Haines, "Edwardus Redivivus."

140. See, for example, Strickland.

141. E.403.

142. Shepherd.

143. Parsons.

144. Gee; Blackley, "Isabella . . . and the . . . Cult of the Dead"; Blackley, "Tomb"; E.101; Cotton MSS, Galba; Stow, *London;* Duffy.

145. Grey, *Scalacronica.*

146. Stow, *London.*

Notes on the Chief Sources

What follows is a brief description and evaluation of each of the main contemporary sources to which I have referred in the text and notes. They are arranged in alphabetical order. Full details of these works are given in the bibliography.

ADAM OF USK, an able lawyer from Monmouth, was educated at Oxford and later enjoyed the patronage of the powerful Mortimer family. His chronicle mainly covers the period 1377 to 1421 and is based on firsthand evidence, but it lacks a critical eye.

The *ANNALES LONDONIENSES* cover the period 1194 to 1330 and were written by a citizen of London who enjoyed access to the archives of the Corporation of London. These annals are particularly important for the first half of the reign of Edward II, containing as they do a number of transcribed documents.

The *ANNALES PAULINI,* a valuable contemporary source that covers the years 1307 to 1341 and deals primarily with events in London, was probably written by a canon of Saint Paul's Cathedral, London, who was a close associate of another canon, Adam Murimuth (see below), on whose chronicle these annals were probably partly based.

GEOFFREY LE BAKER (flourished circa 1350), the parish priest of Swynbroke (Swinbrook) in Oxfordshire, wrote a chronicle covering the years 1303 to 1356, at the behest of his patron, Sir Thomas de la More (or Moore) of Northmoor (d. after 1347), an Oxfordshire knight and MP who was a loyal servant and follower of Edward II and was present at his abdication. Besides receiving eyewitness information in a memoir from his patron, Baker also drew heavily on the earlier chronicle of Adam Murimuth (see below). Baker's style is lively, descriptive, and frequently melodramatic, but he is not often reliable as a historian, being inclined to embroider the facts; his vivid imagination sometimes even led him to invent material. His work has a strong royalist and patriotic bias. His chronicle was begun in circa 1350 and completed in 1358. Until the late nineteenth century, when E. Maunde Thompson correctly identified its author, Baker's chronicle was erroneously ascribed to Sir Thomas de la More.

THE BRUT CHRONICLE exists in several versions that cover the period to 1333. Most of these are translations from a French original. The most important for this work are the London *Brut* and the northern *Brut,* both written in the 1330s.

The CHRONICLE OF LANERCOST, which covers the period 1297 to 1346, was probably compiled in circa 1346 at Lanercost Priory, a Franciscan house near Hadrian's Wall; it is partly based on a lost work that was probably written by a Franciscan monk of Carlisle. It deals mainly with northern affairs and includes an eyewitness account of the Battle of Bannockburn.

The CHRONICLE OF MEAUX was written in a Yorkshire abbey and covers the period to 1406.

The CHRONIQUES DE LONDON cover the period 1260 to 1344; written purely as annals, they are nevertheless useful as a source for events in the capital.

WILLIAM DENE, a notary public, wrote the *Historia Roffensis,* an important source for the deposition of Edward II. He was an eyewitness to some of the events about which he wrote.

JEAN FROISSART (circa 1335–37 to circa 1407–10), the celebrated Flemish chronicler, was born at Valenciennes in Hainault and later became a priest. He was in England from 1360 to 1366, as a page in the service of Queen Philippa of Hainault, wife of Edward III. During this period, he began his famous *Chronicles.* Thereafter, he traveled all over western Europe, collecting information for his great work. He was close to the English royal family and accompanied the Black Prince to Bordeaux in 1366 and the Duke of Clarence to Italy in 1368. He visited the court of Richard II in 1394–95. His *Chronicles* are written in French. They cover the years 1325 to 1400; the earlier period, up to 1361, is based on what he calls "the true chronicle" of another Hainaulter, Jean le Bel (see below). Froissart's *Chronicles* are lively, detailed, and eminently readable, but they are romanticized, unreliable, and inconsistent in parts and often based too indiscriminately on court gossip, and should therefore be treated with caution.

The GESTA EDWARDI DE CARNARVON, written by an anonymous Canon of Bridlington between 1327 and 1340, is an important source for Edward II's reign. It chiefly deals with events in the North.

SIR THOMAS GREY OF HETON (d. 1369) was a Northumbrian knight of some standing who, while being held in an Edinburgh prison in 1355, wrote the *Scalacronica,* a dramatic yet competent account of mainly northern history during the reigns of Edward I, Edward II, and Edward III. His father had served at Bannockburn in 1314. Grey based much of his chronicle on works by Geoffrey of Monmouth, the Venerable Bede, and Ranulph Higden, as well as the *Historia Aurea* of John, Vicar of Tynemouth (see under Walter of Guisborough, below). His manuscript, now in Corpus Christi College, Cambridge, is dedicated to Edward III. Of all contemporary chroniclers, Grey is perhaps the most sympathetic toward Edward II.

RANULPH HIGDEN (d. 1364), a Benedictine monk at Saint Werburgh's Abbey, Chester, from 1299, wrote his celebrated *Polychronicon* in circa 1347. This work, intended as an exhaustive universal history up to the year 1342, is vividly written but disjointed and repetitive. It nevertheless gained great popularity and was translated into English in 1387 by John Trevisa (see below). A later continuation, to 1381, was added by John of Malvern, a monk of Worcester.

JEAN LE BEL was a native of Hainault, a canon at Saint Lambert of Liège, and the favored confessor and adviser of his patron, Sir John of Hainault, Queen Isabella's champion. He was present during Edward III's Scottish campaign of 1327. His chronicle is a blend of history, chivalry, and romance, but while it is less colorful than Froissart's, it is more reliable.

HENRY KNIGHTON (or Cnitthon) (d. 1396) was an Augustinian canon at the abbey of Saint Mary of the Meadows, Leicester. His chronicle, which covers the period from the tenth century to 1395, is more valuable for the reign of Richard II than for the earlier part of the fourteenth century. It has a strong Lancastrian bias and deals in some detail with the life of Thomas of Lancaster. Knighton drew heavily on Higden and Walter of Guisborough for source material.

ADAM MURIMUTH (1275?–1347), whose family came from Fifield, Oxfordshire, was educated at Oxford and became a canon of Saint Paul's Cathedral, London, and held several other church offices. He was employed on several diplomatic missions to the papal Curia (1312–17, 1319, and 1323) and was also a royal councillor and a friend of Archbishop Reynolds and Henry Eastry, Prior of Canterbury, as well as being on good terms with Bishops Burghersh and Orleton. His kinsman Richard Murimuth was a royal clerk in 1328–29. In 1327, Adam Murimuth was one of a deputation sent by the Chapter of Exeter Cathedral to Edward III. Murimuth's chronicle, which covers the period 1303 to 1347, and must have been written after 1325, is of immense value, as it is based on what he himself had witnessed during his career. It deals not only with the general history of the period but also with the fate of Edward II, events in London, and ecclesiastical affairs.

WILLIAM RISHANGER (circa 1250–1312?), a Benedictine monk of Saint Albans, wrote a continuation of the Saint Albans chronicles, covering the period 1259 to 1307. He may also have been the author of the chronicle ascribed to John Trokelowe and Henry Blaneford (see below). Rishanger's work is useful, if mediocre in quality.

ROBERT OF READING (d. 1325), a monk at Westminster Abbey, wrote his *Flores Historiarum*, one of the most important sources for Edward II's reign, in circa 1327. Intended as a continuation of the *Great Chronicle* of Matthew Paris, it covers the years 1307 to 1325. (The earlier portion, from 1265 to 1306, was probably the work of John Bever of London [d. 1311], a monk of Westminster, who was commissioned by Margaret of France to write a eulogy on the death of Edward I.) Robert's is a thorough and detailed account, and of great value to the historian, despite his bombastic style, his strong Lancastrian bias, and his determination to demonstrate that Edward II was unfit to rule and that his deposition was justified.

JOHN TREVISA (circa 1340–42 to 1402), a Fellow of Exeter and Queen's Colleges, Oxford, became Vicar of Berkeley, Gloucestershire, and chaplain to the Berkeley family. His vigorous translation of Ranulph Higden's *Polychronicon*, to which he added a short continuation, was completed in 1387.

The chronicle ascribed to JOHN TROKELOWE and HENRY BLANEFORD, both monks of Saint Albans, which covers the years 1307 to 1323, may have been written by William Rishanger (see above); this is a continuation of the Saint Albans chronicles and, despite its poor chronology, is one of the chief authorities for Edward II's reign. It must have been written after 1330, since it refers to the execution of Roger Mortimer.

The *VITA EDWARDI SECUNDI*, an anonymous life of Edward II, formerly incorrectly ascribed to a monk of Malmesbury, is one of the chief independent sources for the reign and for the life and character of the King. Its author was well informed, shrewd, keenly observant, and not overcritical of his subject, even though it is clear that he was a supporter of the baronial opposition. His work stops abruptly in November 1325. Since he refers to Bishop Stapledon as being still alive, it must have been written before September 1326 and therefore does not anticipate the invasion of Isabella and Mortimer. The author, who was almost certainly not a monk, was highly educated, well versed in civil law, and of mature years. He has been tentatively identified by Denholm-Young with John Walwayn, a Herefordshire lawyer and clerk to the Earl of Hereford. Walwayn retired in January 1324 and was dead by July 1326.

THOMAS WALSINGHAM (d. 1422?), an Oxford scholar who became a Benedictine monk at Saint Albans, was a prolific writer who revived the tradition of chronicle writing at that abbey. He began the first of his six chronicles before 1388; these included a continuation of Matthew Paris's *Chronica Majora* from 1259 to 1422 and a chronicle of England and Normandy from 911 to 1419. Walsingham was a competent and authoritative writer, but he was more competent at collating material than he was at historical analysis and also overfond of occupying the high moral ground. For the early fourteenth century, he drew heavily on Murimuth, Trokelowe, and others.

WALTER OF GUISBOROUGH (or de Gisburn), or WALTER OF HEMINGBURGH (sometimes incorrectly given as Hemingford) (d. after 1313 or possibly after 1338), was an Austin canon at Guisborough (Gisburn) Priory, Yorkshire, who wrote an excellent, largely reliable, and perceptive chronicle of events from 1066 to 1312, drawing extensively on contemporary sources for the period commencing in 1290 and transcribing important documents. It has been suggested that a continuation covering the years 1327 to 1346 (which cannot all have been written by Walter) is loosely based on a work known as the *Historia Aurea*, which was written by John, Vicar of Tynemouth, around 1346.

Select Bibliography

PRIMARY SOURCES

Acta Imperii Angliaze et Franciae (ed. F. Kern, Tubingen, 1911).

Additional MSS, British Library.

Anglo-Scottish Relations, 1174–1328: Some Selected Documents (ed. E. L. G. Stones, London, 1965).

Annales Londonienses (ed. W. Stubbs, in *Chronicles of the Reigns of Edward I and Edward II*, 2 vols., Rolls Series, HMSO, London, 1882–83).

Annales Monastici (5 vols., ed. H. R. Luard, Rolls Series, HMSO, London, 1864–69).

Annales Paulini (ed. W. Stubbs, in *Chronicles of the Reigns of Edward I and Edward II*, 2 vols., Rolls Series, HMSO, London, 1882–83).

The Anominalle Chronicle, 1307–1344, from Brotherton Collection MS 29 (ed. W. R. Childs and J. Taylor, Yorkshire Archaeological Society Record Series 147, Leeds, 1991).

The Anominalle Chronicle, 1331–1388 (ed. V. H. Galbraith, Manchester, 1927).

Antient Kalendars and Inventories of the Treasury of His Majesty's Exchequer (3 vols., ed. F. Palgrave, London, 1836).

The Antiquarian Repertory (1779; 4 vols., ed. F. Grose, 1807–9).

The Apocalypse of Queen Isabella (c. 1280–1300; MS Fr. 13096, Bibliothèque Nationale, Paris).

Archaeologia (102 vols., ed. H. Nicholas et al., Society of Antiquaries of London, 1773–1969).

Archives Municipales d'Agen (Chartres) (ed. G. Tholin and A. Magen, Villaneuve-sur-Long, 1876).

Archives Nationales, MSS, Paris.

Archives Tallandier, Bibliothèque Nationale, Paris.

l'Arsenal de Paris MSS.

Ashmole MSS, Bodleian Library, Oxford.

Baker, Geoffrey le. *Chronicon Galfridi le Baker de Swynebroke* (ed. E. Maunde Thompson, Oxford, 1889).

Barbour, John. *The Bruce* (3 vols., ed. Walter Skeat, Early English Text Society, 1870–77; ed. W. M. Mackenzie, London, 1909).

The Berkeley Manuscripts: The Lives of the Berkeleys (3 vols., compiled by their steward, Sir John Smyth of Nibley, in the 17th century; ed. J. MacLean, Gloucester, 1883–85).

The Beverley Chapter Act Book, 1286–1347 (ed. A. Leach, Surtees Society, 1898).

Bibliothèque Nationale, Paris, Collections Brienne and Moreau.

Bodleian MSS, Bodleian Library, Oxford.

The Brut Chronicle, or The Chronicles of England (ed. F. W. D. Brie, Early English Text Society, Original Series, CXXXI, London, 1906, 1908).

Burney MSS, British Library.

Bury, Richard de. *Philobiblon* (ed. E. C. Thomas, London, 1960).

Calendar of Chancery Rolls (Various), 1277–1326 (HMSO, London, 1912).

Calendar of Chancery Warrants, 1244–1326 (HMSO, London, 1927).

Calendar of the Charter Rolls Preserved in the Public Record Office, 1222–1516 (6 vols., HMSO, London, 1903–27).

Calendar of the Close Rolls Preserved in the Public Record Office: Edward I, Edward II, and Edward III (24 vols., HMSO, London, 1892–1927).

Calendar of Documents Relating to Scotland Preserved in Her Majesty's Public Record Office, London (4 vols., ed. J. Bain, Edinburgh, 1881–88).

Calendar of Entries in the Papal Registers Relating to Great Britain and Ireland (8 vols., ed. W. H. Bliss and W. W. Blom, HMSO, London, 1893–1904).

Calendar of the Fine Rolls Preserved in the Public Record Office: Edward I, Edward II and Edward III, 1327–1347 (5 vols., HMSO, London, 1912–29).

Calendar of Inquisitions Post Mortem and Other Analogous Documents Preserved in the Public Record Office: Edward I, Edward II and Edward III (13 vols., HMSO, London, 1906–52).

Calendar of Letterbooks Preserved among the Archives of the Corporation of the City of London, 1275–1498 (11 vols., ed. R. R. Sharpe, London, 1899–1912).

Calendar of Memoranda Rolls, Michaelmas 1326–Michaelmas 1327 (HMSO, London, 1968).

Calendar of the Patent Rolls Preserved in the Public Record Office: Edward I, Edward II and Edward III (27 vols., HMSO, London, 1894–1916).

Calendar of Plea and Memoranda Rolls of the City of London, 1323–1412, Preserved among the Archives of the Corporation of London at the Guildhall (6 vols., ed. A. H. Thomas and P. E. Jones, Cambridge, 1926–61).

Calendar of Various Chancery Rolls: Supplementary Close Rolls, Welsh Rolls, Scutage Rolls, Preserved in the Public Record Office, 1277–1326 (HMSO, London, 1912).

Capgrave, John. *The Chronicle of England* (ed. F. C. Hingeston, Rolls Series, HMSO, London, 1858).

Cappellani, William. *Willelmi Cappellani in Brederode postea Monachi et Procuratoris Egmundensis Chronicon* (ed. C. Pijnacker Hondyk, *Historisch Genootschap*, 3rd Series, XX, Amsterdam, 1904).

Cartulaire de Notre Dame de Boulogne (ed. D. Hagnière, Paris, 1844).

Chancery Miscellanea (C.47), Public Record Office.

Chancery: Parliament and Council Proceedings (C.49), Public Record Office.

Chancery Records: Warrants for the Great Seal (C.81), Public Record Office.

Charter Rolls (C.53), Public Record Office.

Chartularies of St. Mary's Abbey, Dublin: With the Register of Its House at Dunbrody and Annals of Ireland (2 vols., ed. John T. Gilbert, Rolls Series, HMSO, London, 1884).

Chartulary of Winchester Cathedral (ed. A. W. Goodman, Winchester, 1927).

"Chronicarum Comitum Flandria" (ed. Joseph-Jean De Smet, in *Corpus Chronicorum Flandriae*, 4 vols., Brussels, 1837–65).

The Chronicle of Bury St. Edmunds, 1212–1301 (ed. and trans. Antonia Gransden, Nelson's Mediaeval Texts, London, 1964).

"A Chronicle of the Civil Wars of Edward II," also known as the Cleopatra Chronicle (ed. G. L. Haskins, *Speculum*, XIV, 1939).

Chronicle of the Grey Friars of London (ed. J. Nichols, Camden Society, 1852).

The Chronicle of Lanercost, 1272–1346 (2 vols., ed. J. Stevenson, Bannatyne Club, Edinburgh, 1839; ed. and trans. Sir Herbert R. Maxwell, Maitland Club, Glasgow, 1913).

Chronicle of London, 1089–1483 (ed. H. Nicholas, Society of Antiquaries of London, 1827).

Chronicle of Meaux: Chronica Monasterii de Melsa, a Fundatione usque ad Annum 1396, Auctore Thoma de Burton, Abbate. Accedit Continuato as Annum 1406 a Monacho Quodam ipsius Domus (3 vols., ed. E. A. Bond, Rolls Series, HMSO, London, 1866–68).

Chronicles Illustrative of the Reigns of Edward I and Edward II (2 vols. [Vol. I: *Annales Londonienses; Annales Paulini;* Vol. II: *Commendiato lamentablis in transita magni regis Edwardi; Gesta Edwardi de Carnarvon auctore canonico Bridlingtoniensi; Monachi cujusdam Malmesberiensis; Vita et mors Edwardi II conscripta a Thoma de la Moore*], ed. W. Stubbs, Rolls Series, HMSO, London, 1882–83).

The Chronicles of London (ed. and trans. E. Goldsmid, Edinburgh, 1885).

Chronicles of London (ed. C. L. Kingsford, 1905).

Chronicon Abbatiae Ramesiensis (ed. W. Mackay, Rolls Series, HMSO, London, 1886).

Chronique de Pays-Bas (ed. J. Smet, Receuil des Chroniques de Flandre, Brussels, 1856).

Chroniques de London depuis l'an 44 Hen III jusqu'à l'an 17 Edw III (ed. G. J. Aungier, Camden Society, Old Series, XXVIII, London, 1844).

Chronographia Regum Francorum (ed. H. Moranville, Société de l'Histoire de France, Paris, 1891–97).

A Collection of the Wills of the Kings and Queens of England from William the Conqueror to Henry VII (ed. J. Nichols, 1780).

Comptes royaux, 1285–1314 (3 vols., ed. Robert Fawtier and François Maillard, Paris, 1953–56).

"The Continuator of William de Nangis" (ed. P. C. F. Daunou and J. Naudet, in *Receuil des Historiens de France,* Paris, 1840).

Cotton MSS, Cleopatra, Faustina, Galba, Julius, Nero, and Vitellius, British Library.

Cronijke Van Nederlandt (ed. Charles Piot, Brussels, 1867).

Dene, William. "Historia Roffensis" (in *Anglia Sacra,* 2 vols., ed. H. Wharton, London, 1691).

De Speculo Regis Edwardi III (ed. Joseph Moisant, Paris, 1891).

The Dignity of a Peer: Report from the Lords' Committees for All Matters Touching the Dignity of a Peer (4 vols., London, 1820–29).

Documents concerning the rebellion of Roger Mortimer in 1321–22 (Hereford Cathedral Library).

Documents Illustrative of English History in the Thirteenth and Fourteenth Centuries (ed. H. Cole, London, 1844).

"Documents Relating to the Death and Burial of King Edward II" (ed. S. A. Moore, *Archaeologia,* L, 1887).

Douce MS (the French *Brut*), Bodleian Library, Oxford.

Duchy of Lancaster: Accounts Various (D.L.28), Public Record Office.

Duchy of Lancaster Miscellanea (D.L.41), Public Record Office.

Duchy of Lancaster: Miscellaneous Books (D.L.42), Public Record Office.

Duchy of Lancaster: Royal Charters (D.L.10), Public Record Office.

Egerton MSS, British Library.

English Coronation Records (ed. L. G. W. Legg, London, 1901).

English Historical Documents, Vol. III, 1189–1327 (ed. H. Rothwell, London, 1975–77).

English Historical Documents, Vol. IV, 1327–1485 (ed. D. C. Douglas and A. R. Myers, London, 1969).

Eulogium Historiarum (3 vols., ed. F. S. Haydon, Rolls Series, HMSO, London, 1858–63).

Excerpta Historica (ed. H. Nicholas, 1831).

Exchequer Records: Ancient Deeds (E.41), Public Record Office.

Exchequer Records: Diplomatic Documents (E.30), Public Record Office.

Exchequer Records: Issue Rolls (E.403), Public Record Office.

Exchequer Records: King's Remembrancer, Memoranda Rolls (E.159), Public Record Office.

Exchequer Records: King's Remembrancer, Wardrobe Accounts, Accounts Various (E.101), Public Record Office.

Exchequer Records: Miscellanea (E.163), Public Record Office.

Exchequer Records: Miscellaneous Rolls, including Pipe Rolls (E.370), Public Record Office.

Exchequer Records: Sheriffs' Accounts (E.199), Public Record Office.

Exchequer Records: Writs and Warrants for Issue (E.404).

Extracts from the Issue Rolls of the Exchequer (ed. F. Devon, London, 1837).

Fabyan, Robert. *The New Chronicles of England and France: The Concordance of Histories* (ed. H. Ellis, London, 1811).

Foedera, Conventiones, Literae et cujuscumque generis Acta Publica, or Rymer's Foedera, 1066–1383 (20 vols., ed. Thomas Rymer, 1704–35; 4 vols., ed. Adam Clarke, J. Caley, F. Holbrooke, J. W. Clarke, and T. Hardy, Records Commission, London, 1816–69).

Froissart, John. *Chronicles of England, France and Spain and the Adjoining Countries* (2 vols., ed. T. Johnes, London, 1839; 25 vols., ed. Kervyn de Lettenhove as *Oeuvres de Froissart,* Brussels, 1867–77; 15 vols., ed. S. Luce, G. Raynaud, and L. and A. Mirot as *Chroniques de Jean Froissart,* Société de l'histoire de France, Paris, 1869–1975; trans. John, Lord Berners, 1523–25, and ed. G. C. Macaulay, London, 1899, and, in 6 vols., by W. P. Ker, 1901–3; ed. and trans. Geoffrey Brereton, London, 1968, revised 1978; abridged and ed. J. Jolliffe, 1967–68).

The Gascon Calendar of 1322 (ed. G. P. Cuttino, Camden Society, 3rd Series, LXX, 1949).

Gascon Rolls Preserved in the Public Record Office, 1307–1317 (ed. Yves Renouard, HMSO, London, 1962).

Geoffrey de Paris: La chronique metrique attribué à Geoffrey de Paris (ed. Armel Diverrès, Paris, 1956).

Gesta Edwardi de Carnarvon auctore Canonico Bridlingtoniensi (ed. W. Stubbs in *Chronicles of the Reigns of Edward I and Edward II,* 2 vols., Rolls Series, HMSO, London, 1882–83).

Les Grandes Chroniques de France (Sloane MSS, British Library; ed. M. Paulin, Paris, 1837; 8 vols., ed. Jules Viard, Paris, 1934–37).

The Great Chronicle of London (ed. A. H. Thomas and I. D. Thornley, 1938; reprinted Gloucester, 1983).

Grey of Heton, Sir Thomas. *Scalacronica: A Chronicle of England and Scotland from A.D. MLXVI to A.D. MCCCLXII* (ed. J. Stevenson, Maitland Club, XL, Edinburgh, 1836); *Scalacronica: The Reigns of Edward I and Edward II, as Recorded by Sir Thomas Grey of Heton, Knight* (ed. and trans. Sir Herbert R. Maxwell, Glasgow and London, 1907).

Groot Charterboek de Graaven Van Holland (ed. F. Mieris, Leyden, 1754).

Guildhall MSS, Guildhall Library, London.

Hardyng, John. *The Chronicle of John Hardyng, from the First Beginning of England unto the Reign of King Edward the Fourth* (London, 1543; ed. H. Ellis, 1812; reprinted New York, 1974).

Harleian MSS, British Library.

Higden, Ranulph. *Polychronicon Ranulphi Higden Monachi Cestrensis, with the English Translations of John Trevisa* (9 vols., ed. C. Babington and J. R. Lumby, Rolls Series, HMSO, London, 1864–86; ed. John Taylor, as *The Universal Chronicle of Ranulph Higden,* Oxford, 1966—includes John Trevisa's English translation completed 1387).

Historia Dunelmensis Scriptores Tres (ed. J. Raine, Surtees Society, Edinburgh, 1839).

Historia Sancti Petri Gloucestriae (3 vols., ed. W. H. Hart, Rolls Series, HMSO, London, 1863–67).

Historiae Anglicana Decem Scriptores (ed. Roger Twysden, London, 1652; ed. A. H. Davis, 1934).

Historiae et Cartularium Monasterii Gloucestriae (2 vols., ed. William Henry Hart, Rolls Series, HMSO, London, 1863).

Historical Manuscripts Commission, 5th Report.

Historical Manuscripts Commission, 11th Report.

Historical Manuscripts Commission, Various Collections, I.

The History of the King's Works, Vols. I and II: The Middle Ages (ed. R. A. Brown, H. M. Colvin, and A. J. Taylor, London, 1963).

The Household Book of Queen Isabella of England for the Fifth Regnal Year of Edward II, 8th July 1311–7th July 1312 (ed. F. D. Blackley and G. Hermansen, University of Alberta, Edmonton, Classical and Historical Studies, I, 1971).

Inventaires des Manuscrits concernant les Relations de Flandre et l'Angleterre (ed. J. de St. Genois, Messager des Sciences Historiques, 1842).

"Inventory of the Effects of Roger Mortimer at Wigmore Castle and Abbey, Herefordshire" (ed. Lambert P. Larking, *The Archaeological Journal*, XV, 1858).

Irish Exchequer Payments (ed. Philomena Connolly, Irish MSS Commission, Dublin, 1998).

The Isabella Psalter (1303–1308). Bayerische Staatsbibliothek.

Issues of the Exchequer . . . from King Henry III to King Henry VI (ed. F. Devon, London, 1834–47).

Istoire et Croniques de Flandres (ed. Kervyn de Lettenhove, Brussels, 1879–80).

Jean le Bel. *Vray Chroniques de Jean le Bel* (ed. M. L. Polain, Brussels, 1863; 2 vols., ed. J. Viard and E. Déprez as *Chronique de Jean le Bel*, Sociéte de l'Histoire de France, Paris, 1904–5).

Jean des Preis dit d'Outremeuse: Lej Myreur des Histors (7 vols., ed. Ad. Borgnet and Stanislas Bormans, Brussels, 1864–68).

Jeanne d'Evreux Hours (1325–1328). The Cloisters, Metropolitan Museum of Art, New York.

John of Reading. *Chronica Johannis de Reading and Anonymi Cantuarensis* (ed. J. Tait, Manchester, 1914).

Les Journaux du Trésor de Charles IV (ed. Jules Viard, Paris, 1840).

Les Journaux de Trésor de Philippe le Bel (ed. Jules Viard, Paris, 1840).

The Kentish Chronicle (Trinity College Cambridge, MS R.5.41).

King's Bench Records, Public Record Office.

Knighton, Henry. *Chronicon Henrici Knighton, vel Cnitthon, monachi Leycestrensis* (2 vols., ed. J. R. Lumby, Rolls Series, HMSO, London, 1889–95; ed. and trans. G. H. Martin as *Knighton's Chronicle, 1337–1396*, Oxford, 1995).

Lambeth MSS. Lambeth Palace.

Lansdowne MSS. British Library.

Larking, Lambert B. "Inventory of the Effects of Roger Mortimer at Wigmore Castle and Abbey, Herefordshire" (*Archaeological Journal*, XV, 1858).

Latin History MS C.5 (R). Bodleian Library.

Latin MSS. Bibliothèque Nationale, Paris.

La Tour Landry, Geoffrey. *The Book of the Knight of La Tour Landry* (ed. T. Wright, London, 1868; trans. William Caxton, ed. M. Yofford, Early English Text Society, 1971).

Leland, John. *Collectanea* (6 vols., ed. T. Hearne, Chetham Society, 1770–74).

Lescot, Richard. *Chronique de Richard Lescot, religieux de Saint-Denis (1328–1344), suivie de la continuation de cette chronique (1344–1364)* (ed. Jean Lemoine, Paris, 1896).

Letters of Edward, Prince of Wales, 1304–5 (ed. Hilda Johnstone, Roxburghe Club, Cambridge, 1931).

Letters of the Kings of England (ed. J. O. Halliwell, 1846).

Letters and Papers from Northern Registers (ed. J. Raine, Rolls Series, HMSO, London, 1873).

Letters and Papers Illustrative of the Wars of the English in France (2 vols., ed. J. Stevenson, 1861–64).

Letters of the Queens of England, 1100–1547 (ed. Anne Crawford, Stroud, 1994).

Letters of Royal and Illustrious Ladies of Great Britain (3 vols., ed. Mary Anne Everett Wood, 1846).

"Lettre de Manuel de Fiesque concernant les dernières années du roi d'Angleterre Edouard II" (ed. Alexandre Germain, *Mémoires de la Société Archéologique de Montpellier,* VII, 1881).

Lettres de Jean XXII (1316–34) (ed. A. Fayen, Paris, 1808–12).

Lettres des Rois, Reines et Autres Personnages des Cours de France et d'Angleterre (2 vols., ed. J. J. Champollion-Figeac, 1839–47).

Lettres Secrètes et Curiales du Pape Jean XXII (1316–1334) relatives à la France (ed. Auguste Coulon and S. Clemençet, Paris, 1901–2, reprinted 1965).

Liberate Rolls (C.62), Public Record Office.

The Lichfield Chronicle (Bodleian Library, MS 956).

The Life of Edward II by the So-Called Monk of Malmesbury (see *Vita Edwardi Secundi*).

Lincoln, Dean, and Chapter Muniments, D.II/56/1.

Li Livres de Justice et de Plet (ed. F. A. B. Chabaille, Paris, 1850).

Lists and Indexes, Public Record Office.

Literae Cantuarienses (3 vols., ed. J. B. Sheppard, Rolls Series, HMSO, London, 1887–89).

Le Livere de Reis de Brittaniae (ed. J. Glover, Rolls Series, HMSO, London, 1865).

Memorials of St. Edmund's Abbey (3 vols., ed. T. Arnold, Rolls Series, HMSO, London, 1890–96).

Le Ménagier de Paris (ed. Jerome Pichon, Paris, 1846).

Monumenta Franciscana (ed. J. S. Brewer, Rolls Series, HMSO, London, 1858).

Moore, Thomas de la. *Vita et mors Edward II conscripta a Thoma de la Moore* (in *Chronicles Illustrative of the Reigns of Edward I and Edward II,* 2 vols., ed. William Stubbs, Rolls Series, HMSO, London, 1882–83) (see Baker, Geoffrey le).

Munimenta Gildhallae Londoniensis (ed. H. T. Riley, Rolls Series, HMSO, London, 1859–62).

Murimuth, Adam. *Adae Murimuth, Continuatio Chronicarum* (ed. E. Maunde Thompson, Rolls Series, HMSO, London, 1889).

"Normanniae nova chronica ab anno Christi CCCCLXXIII ad annum MCCCLXXVIII e tribus chronicis mss. Sancti Laudi, Sanctae Catherinae et Majoris Ecclesiae Rotomagensium collecta" (ed. A. Chérciel, *Mémoires de la Société des Antiquaires de Normandie,* XVIII, Series 2, 8, 1851).

Original Letters Illustrative of English History (ed. H. Ellis, 1827).

The Parliamentary Writs and Writs of Military Summons (4 vols., ed. Francis Palgrave, Records Commission, London, 1827–34).

Philippe of Navarre. *Les Quatre Ages de l'Homme* (ed. M. Freville, 1846).

Piers of Langtoft. *The Chronicle of Pierre de Langtoft, in French Verse, from the earliest period to the death of King Edward I* (2 vols., ed. Thomas Wright, Rolls Series, HMSO, London, 1866–68).

The Pipewell Chronicle (in M. V. Clarke, "Committees of Estates and the Deposition of Edward II," in *Historical Essays in Honour of James Tait,* ed. J. G. Edwards, V. Galbraith, and E. F. Jacob, Manchester, 1933).

Political Poems and Songs Relating to English History, from the Reign of John to That of Edward II (2 vols., ed. Thomas Wright, Rolls Series, HMSO, London, 1859–61).

Rawlinson MS A.273, Bodleian Library.

Receuil des Historiens de France: Documents Financiers (Comptes Royaux, 1285–1314) (ed. R. Fawtier, Paris, 1956).

Receuil des Historiens des Gaules et de la France (ed. M. de Wailly, Paris, 1855–76).

Receuil des Lettres Anglo-Françaises (1265–1399) (ed. J. F. Tanquerey, Paris, 1916).

Récits d'un Bourgeois de Valenciennes (ed. Kervyn de Lettenhove, Louvain, 1877).

Records of the Trial of Walter Langton, 1307–1312 (ed. A Beardwood, Camden Society, 4th Series, VI, London, 1969).

Regesta Hanonensia (ed. P. C. Muller, Gravenhage, 1882).

Register of Robert Mortival, Bishop of Salisbury, 1315–1330 (ed. S. Reynolds, Canterbury and York Society, 1965).

Register of Thomas Cobham, Bishop of Worcester, 1317–1327 (ed. E. H. Pearce, Worcester Historical Society, XL, Worcester, 1930).

Register of Walter Reynolds, MS in Lambeth Palace Library.

Register of Walter Stapledon, Bishop of Exeter, 1307–1326 (ed. F. C. Hingeston, London and Exeter, 1892).

Registre du Trésor des Chartres (ed. R. Fawtier, Paris, 1958).

Registrum Ade de Orleton, Episcopi Herefordensis (ed. A. T. Bannister, Canterbury and York Society, 1908).

"Rekeningen Van de Herberge Van Joanna Van Valois, 1319–1326" (ed. H. Smit, *Historisch Genootschap,* 3rd Series, XLVI, 1924).

Rishanger, William. *Willelmi Rishanger quondam monachi S. Albani et quorundam anonymorum Chronica et Annales regnantibus Henrico Tertio et Edwardo Primo, 1259–1307* (ed. H. T. Riley, Rolls Series, HMSO, London, 1865).

Robert of Avesbury. *Robertus de Avesbury: De Gestis Mirabilibus Regis Edwardi Tertii* (ed. E. M. Thompson, Rolls Series, HMSO, London, 1889).

Robert of Reading. *Flores Historiarum* (3 vols., ed. H. R. Luard, Rolls Series, HMSO, London, 1890).

The Roll of Arms of Caerlaverock (ed. T. Wright, Rolls Series, HMSO, London, 1864).

Rotuli Parliamentorum: ut et petitiones, et placita in Parliamento, 1272–1503; together with an Index to the Rolls of Parliament, comprising the Petitions, Pleas and Proceedings of Parliament (8 vols., ed. J. Strachey, John Pridden, and Edward Upham, Records Commission, 1767–1832).

Rotuli Parliamentorum Anglie hactenus inediti (ed. H. G. Richardson and G. O. Sayles, Camden Society, 3rd Series, LI, 1935).

Rotuli Scotiae in Turri Londinensi et in Domo Capitulari Westmonasteriensi Asservati, vol. I (ed. D. Macpherson, J. Caley, W. Illingworth, and T. H. Horne, London, 1814).

Royal MSS, British Library.

Select Cases in the Court of King's Bench (7 vols., ed. G. O. Sayles, Selden Society, London, 1936–71).

Select Documents of English Constitutional History, 1307–1485 (ed. Sloane MSS, British Library.

Society of Antiquaries MSS 120, 121, 122.

Special Collections. Ancient Correspondence (S.C.1), Public Record Office.

Special Collections. Ancient Petitions (S.C.8), Public Record Office.

Special Collections. Ministers' Accounts (S.C.6), Public Record Office.

Statutes of the Realm (11 vols., Records Commission, London, 1810–28).

The Stonor Letters (ed. C. L. Kingsford, Camden Society, 3rd Series, XXIX, London, 1919).

Stow, John. *The Chronicles of England* (London, 1580; republished as *The Annales of England,* London, 1592; ed. E. Howe, London, 1631).

Stow, John. *The Survey of London* (London, 1598).

Stowe MSS, British Library.

Syllabus of the Documents Relating to England and Other Kingdoms Contained in the Collection Known as "Rymer's Foedera" (3 vols., ed. T. Hardy, HMSO, London, 1869–85).

Table Chronologique des Chartres et Diplomes (ed. A. Wautier, Brussels, 1896).

Tanner MSS (including *Wardrobe Book,* 1311–12), Bodleian Library.

The Taymouth Hours (1325–1335); Yates Thompson MS 13, British Library.
Treaty Rolls Preserved in the Public Record Office (ed. Pierre Chaplais, HMSO, London, 1955).
Trevet, Nicholas. *Nicolai Triveti Annalium Continuato: Annals of Six Kings of England* (ed. A. E. Hall, Oxford, 1722; ed. Thomas Hog, English Historical Society, London, 1845).
Trokelowe, John, and Henry Blaneford. *Johannis de Trokelowe et Henrici de Blaneford Chronica et Annales* (ed. H. T. Riley, Rolls Series, HMSO, London, 1866).

Vita Edwardi Secundi Monachi Cuiusdam Malmsberiensis: The Life of Edward II by the so-called Monk of Malmesbury (perhaps written by John Walwayn; trans. and ed. N. Denholm-Young, Nelson's Mediaeval Texts, ed. V. H. Galbraith and R. A. B. Mynors, Oxford, 1957).
Vita et Mors Edwardi Secundi (ed. W. Stubbs, in *Chronicles of the Reigns of Edward I and Edward II*, 2 vols., Rolls Series, HMSO, London, 1882–83).
Vitae Paparum Avenionensium (ed. E. Baluze, Paris, 1921).

Walsingham, Thomas. *Chronicon Angliae, ab anno Domini 1322–8 usque ad annum 1388. Auctore Monacho Quodam Sancti Albani* (ed. E. M. Thompson, Rolls Series, HMSO, London, 1874).
Walsingham, Thomas. *Gesta Abbatum S. Albani* (3 vols., ed. H. T. Riley, Rolls Series, HMSO, London, 1867–69).
Walsingham, Thomas. *Historia Anglicana, 1272–1422* (2 vols., ed. H. T. Riley, Rolls Series, HMSO, London, 1863–64).
Walsingham, Thomas. *Ypodigma Neustriae* (ed. H. T. Riley, Rolls Series, HMSO, London, 1876).
Walter of Guisborough, or Walter of Hemingburgh. *Chronicon Domini Walteri de Hemingburgh* (2 vols., ed. H. C. Hamilton, English Historical Society, 1848–49; ed. Harry Rothwell, Camden Society, 3rd Series, LXXXIX, London, 1957).
"The War of Saint Sardos, 1322–1325" (ed. Pierre Chaplais, Camden Society, 3rd Series, LXXXVII, 1954).
Westminster Abbey Muniments.
Wigmore Abbey Annals (Latin MS 215, John Rylands Library, University of Manchester); in Sir William Dugdale, *Monasticon Anglicanum*, 3 vols., ed. J. Caley, H. Ellis, and B. Bandinel, 1830; published as "The Anglo-Norman Chronicle of Wigmore Abbey" (ed. J. C. Dickinson and P. T. Ricketts, *Transactions of the Woolhope Naturalists Field Club*, XXXIX, 1969).
Yates Thompson MSS, British Library.
Year Books of Edward II: 6 Edward II (ed. W. C. Bollard, Selden Society, Vol. 14, II, London, 1927).

SECONDARY SOURCES

Abbott, Geoffrey. *Tortures of the Tower of London* (Newton Abbot, 1986).
The Age of Chivalry (exhibition catalog, ed. J. Alexander and P. Binski, Royal Academy, London, 1987).
Age of Chivalry: Art and Society in Late Mediaeval England (ed. Nigel Saul, London, 1992).
The Age of Edward III (ed. J. S. Bothwell, York, 2001).
Alexander, J. J. G. "Painting and Manuscript Illuminations for Royal Patrons in the Later Middle Ages" (in *English Court Culture in the Later Middle Ages*, ed. V. J. Scattergood and J. W. Sherborne, London, 1983).
Altschul, M. *A Baronial Family in Mediaeval England: The Clares, 1217–1314* (London and Baltimore, 1965).
Ashley, Mike. *British Monarchs* (London, 1998).

Backhouse, Janet. *The Illuminated Page: Ten Centuries of Manuscript Painting* (British Library, London, 1997).

Baldwin, J. F. "The Household Administrations of Henry Lacy and Thomas of Lancaster" (*English Historical Review,* LXIII, 1927).

Banstead History Research Group. *Banstead: A History. How a Village Grew and Changed* (Southampton, 1993).

Barber, M. "The World Picture of Philip the Fair" (*Journal of Mediaeval History,* VIII, 1982).

Barber, Richard. *Edward, Prince of Wales and Aquitaine: A Biography of the Black Prince* (London, 1978).

Barker, J. R. V. *The Tournament in England, 1100–1400* (Woodbridge, 1986).

Barnes, Joshua. *The History of That Most Victorious Monarch, Edward III* (Cambridge, 1688).

Barrow, G. W. S. *Robert Bruce and the Community of the Realm of Scotland* (London, 1965; rev. ed., Edinburgh, 1988).

Barton, John, and Joy Law. *The Hollow Crown* (London, 1971).

Bayley, J. *History and Antiquities of the Tower of London* (London, 1830).

Bayliss, D. G. "The Lordship of Wigmore in the Fourteenth Century" (*Transactions of the Woolhope Naturalists Field Club,* XXXVI, I, 1959).

Beaumont-Maillet, L. *Le Grand Couvent de Cordeliers de Paris* (Paris, 1975).

Bell, S. Groag. "Mediaeval Women Book Owners: Arbiters of Lay Piety and Ambassadors of Culture" (*Signs: The Journal of Women in Culture and Society,* VII, IV, 1982).

Benedetti, Anna. *Edoardo II d'Inghilterra all' Abbazia di S. Alberto di Butrio* (Palermo, 1924).

Bertière, Simone. *Les Reines de France* (Paris, 1994).

Bevan, Bryan. *Edward III: Monarch of Chivalry* (London, 1992).

Beverley Smith, J. "Edward II and the Allegiance of Wales" (*Welsh History Review,* VIII, December 1976).

Bingham, Caroline. *The Life and Times of Edward II* (London, 1973).

Binski, Paul. *Mediaeval Death: Ritual and Representation* (London, 1996).

Binski, Paul. *The Painted Chamber at Westminster* (London, 1986).

Blackley, F. D. "Adam, the Bastard Son of Edward II" (*Bulletin of the Institute of Historical Research,* XXXVII, 1964).

Blackley, F. D. "Isabella and the Bishop of Exeter" (in *Essays in Mediaeval History Presented to Bertie Wilkinson,* ed. T. Sandquist and F. M. Powicke, Toronto, 1969).

Blackley, F. D. "Isabella of France, Queen of England (1308–1358) and the Late Mediaeval Cult of the Dead" (*Canadian Journal of History,* XV, I, 1980).

Blackley, F. D. "The Tomb of Isabella of France, Wife of Edward II of England" (*International Society for the Study of Church Monuments Bulletin,* VIII, 1983).

Bond, Arthur. *The Walsingham Story through 900 Years* (Walsingham, 1988).

Bond, E. A. "Notices on the Last Days of Isabella, Queen of Edward II, Drawn from the Account of the Expenses of Her Household" (*Archaeologia,* XXXV, 1853–54).

Bordonove, G. *Philippe le Bel* (Paris, 1994).

Borenius, T. "The Cycle of Images in the Palaces and Castles of Henry III" (*Journal of the Warburg and Courtauld Institutes,* VI, 1943).

Boswell, J. *Christianity, Social Tolerance and Homosexuality* (Chicago, 1980).

Bouyer, Christian. *Les Reines de France: Dictionnaire Chronologique* (Saint-Amand-Montrand, Cher, 1992; rev. ed., 2000).

Brewer, Clifford. *The Death of Kings: A Medical History of the Kings and Queens of England* (London, 2000).

Brewer, H. W. "The Greyfriars at Newgate" (*The Builder,* 21 April 1894).

Brindle, Steven, and Brian Kerr. *Windsor Revealed: New Light on the History of the Castle* (English Heritage, London, 1997).

Broglie, Emmanuel de, Bruno Centorame, Emmanuel Ducamp, Stéphane Guegan, Guillaume Picon, and Luc Thomasin. *l'ABCdaire des Rois de France* (Paris, 2000).

Brook, R. *The Story of Eltham Palace* (London, 1960).

Brooke-Little, J. R. *Boutell's Heraldry* (London, 1973).

Brown, Elizabeth A. R. "Customary Aid and Royal Finance in Capetian France: The Marriage Aid of Philip the Fair" (MA thesis, University of Cambridge, 1989).

Brown, Elizabeth A. R. "Death and the Human Body in the Later Middle Ages: The Legislation of Boniface VIII on the Division of the Corpse" (*Viator*, XII, 1981).

Brown, Elizabeth A. R. "Diplomacy, Adultery and Domestic Politics at the Court of Philip the Fair: Queen Isabelle's Mission to France in 1314" (in *Documenting the Past: Essays in Mediaeval History Presented to George Peddy Cuttino*, ed. J. S. Hamilton and Patricia J. Bradley, Woodbridge, 1989).

Brown, Elizabeth A. R. "The Marriage of Edward II of England and Isabelle of France: A Postscript" (*Speculum*, LXIV, 1989).

Brown, Elizabeth A. R. "The Political Repercussions of Family Ties in the Early Fourteenth Century: The Marriage of Edward II of England and Isabella of France" (*Speculum*, LXIII, 1988).

Brown, Elizabeth A. R. "The Prince Is Father of the King: The Character and Childhood of Philip the Fair of France" (*Mediaeval Studies*, XLIX, 1987).

Brownrigg, L. "The Taymouth Hours and the Romance of Beves of Hampton" (*English Manuscript Studies*, I, 1989).

Brundage, J. A. *Law, Sex and Christian Society in Mediaeval Europe* (Chicago, 1987).

Bryant, Arthur. *The Age of Chivalry* (London, 1963).

Buck, Mark C. *Politics, Finance and the Church in the Age of Edward II: Walter Stapledon, Treasurer of England* (Cambridge, 1983).

Burke's Guide to the British Monarchy (ed. H. Montgomery-Massingberd, Burke's Peerage, 1977).

Butler, L. H. "Archbishop Melton, His Neighbours and His Kinsmen, 1317–1340" (*Journal of Ecclesiastical History*, II, 1951).

Butler, R. M. *The Bars and Walls of York* (York, 1974).

Caley, J., H. Ellis, and B. Bandinel. *Monasticon Anglicanum: A History of the Abbeys and Other Monasteries, Hospitals, Friaries and Cathedral and Collegiate Churches, with their Dependencies in England and Wales* (6 vols., London, 1817).

Cam, H. M. "The General Eyres of 1329–1330" (*English Historical Review*, XXXIX, 1924).

Cannon, John, and Ralph Griffiths. *The Oxford Illustrated History of the British Monarchy* (Oxford, 1988).

Cannon, John, and Anne Hargreaves. *The Kings and Queens of Britain* (Oxford, 2001).

Carey, Henry, Viscount Falkland(?). *The History of the Life, Reign and Death of Edward II, King of England and Lord of Ireland, with the Rise and Fall of His Great Favourites, Gaveston and the Spencers* (written by "E.F.," 1627; London, 1680).

Castries, Duc de. *The Lives of the Kings and Queens of France* (London, 1979).

Cave, C. J. P. *Mediaeval Carvings in Exeter Cathedral* (London, 1953).

Cawthorne, Nigel. *Sex Lives of the Kings and Queens of England* (London, 1994).

Chambers Biographical Dictionary (ed. Magnus Magnusson, Edinburgh, 1990).

Chapelot, Jean. *Château de Vincennes* (NRS, 1994).

Chaplais, Pierre. "Le Duché-Pairie de Guyenne" (*Annales du Midi*, LXIX, 1957).

Chaplais, Pierre. *Piers Gaveston: Edward II's Adopted Brother* (Oxford, 1994).

Christie, A. G. I. *English Mediaeval Embroidery* (Oxford, 1938).

Chronicles of the Age of Chivalry (ed. Elizabeth Hallam, London, 1987).

Clapham, A. W., and W. H. Godfrey. *Some Famous Buildings and Their Story* (London, 1913).

Clarke, Maude V. "Committees of Estates and the Deposition of Edward II" (in *Historical Essays in Honour of James Tait*, ed. J. G. Edwards, V. H. Galbriath, and E. F. Jacob, Manchester, 1933).

Clarke, R. "Some Secular Activities of the English Dominicans" (MA thesis, University of London, 1930).

Clayton, H. *Royal Faces: 900 Years of British Monarchy* (1977).

Coad, Jonathan. *Dover Castle* (English Heritage, London, 1997).

Cole, Hubert. *The Black Prince* (London, 1976).

The Complete Peerage of England, Scotland, Ireland, Great Britain and the United Kingdom, extant, extinct or dormant, or a History of the House of Lords and all its Members from Earliest Times (13 vols., ed. G. E. Cokayne, V. Gibbs, H. A. Doubleday, G. H. White, D. Warrand, and Lord Howard de Walden, London, 1910–59).

Cook, Petronelle. *Queen Consorts of England: The Power behind the Throne* (New York, 1993).

Cooper, W. D. *The History of Winchelsea* (London, 1850).

Cordier, H. "Annales de l'Hôtel de Nesle" (*Mémoires de l'Institut National de France*, XLI, 1920).

Costain, Thomas B. *The Pageant of England, 1272–1377: The Three Edwards* (New York, 1958; London, 1973).

Coulton, George C. *Chaucer and His England* (London, 1908).

Crump, Charles George. "The Arrest of Roger Mortimer and Queen Isabel" (*English Historical Review*, XXVI, 1911).

Cunnington, P., and C. Lucas. *Costume for Births, Marriages and Deaths* (London, 1972).

Cussans, Thomas. *The Times' Kings and Queens of the British Isles* (London, 2002).

Cuttino, George Peddy, and Thomas W. Lyman. "Where Is Edward II?" (*Speculum*, LIII, no. 3, July 1978).

Dalzell, W. R. *The Shell Guide to the History of London* (London, 1981).

Daniell, C. *Death and Burial in Mediaeval England, 1066–1550* (London, 1997).

Dart, J. *The History and Antiquities of the Abbey Church of St. Peter's, Westminster* (2 vols., London, 1723).

Davies, James. *Wigmore Castle and the Mortimers* (Woolhope Club, 1881–82).

Davies, J. Conway. *The Baronial Opposition to Edward II* (Cambridge, 1918).

Davies, J. Conway. "The Despenser War in Glamorgan" (*Transactions of the Royal Historical Society*, 3rd Series, IX, 1915).

Davies, R. R. *Lordship and Society in the Marches of Wales, 1282–1400* (Oxford, 1978).

De La Noy, Michael. *Windsor Castle, Past and Present* (London, 1990).

Delderfield, Eric R. *Kings and Queens of England and Great Britain* (Newton Abbot, 1966).

Denton, J. H. *Robert Winchelsey and the Crown, 1294–1313* (Cambridge, 1980).

Déprez, E. *Les Préliminaires de la Guerre de Cent Ans* (Paris, 1902).

Dictionary of National Biography (63 vols., ed. L. Stephen and S. Lee, Oxford, 1885–1900).

Dimitresco, M. Marin. *Pierre de Gavaston, comte de Cornouailles: son biographie et son rôle pendant la commencement du régne d'Édouard II, 1307–1314* (Paris, 1898).

Dodge, Walter Phelps. *Piers Gaveston: A Chapter in Early Constitutional History* (London, 1899).

Doherty, Paul C. "The Date of the Birth of Isabella, Queen of England" (*Bulletin of the Institute of Historical Research*, XLVIII, November 1975).

Doherty, Paul C. "Isabella, Queen of England, 1296–1330" (D.Phil. thesis, Exeter College, Oxford, 1977).

Doherty, Paul C. *Isabella and the Strange Death of Edward II* (London, 2003).

Douch, R. "The Career, Lands and Family of William Montagu, Earl of Salisbury, 1301–44" (MA thesis, University of London, 1950).

Duffy, Mark. *Royal Tombs of Mediaeval England* (Stroud, 2003).

Dugdale, William. *The Baronage of England* (2 vols., London, 1675–76).

Dugdale, William. *Monasticon Anglicanum* (6 vols., ed. J. Caley et al., London, 1846).

Dupuy, M. *Le Prince Noir* (Paris, 1971).

Eames, E. S. "A Tile Pavement from the Queen's Chamber, Clarendon Palace, Dated 1250–2" (*British Archaeological Society Journal*, 3rd Series, XX, 1957).

Earle, Peter. "Edward II" (in *The Lives of the Kings and Queens of England*, ed. Antonia Fraser, London, 1975; rev. ed., 1998).

Edwards, J. G. "The Negotiations of the Treaty of Leake, 1318" (in *Essays Presented to R. Lane Poole,* London, 1927).

Edwards, J. G. "Sir Gruffydd Lloyd" (*English Historical Review,* XXX, 1915).

Edwards, Kathleen. "The Personal and Political Activities of the English Episcopate during the Reign of Edward II" (*Bulletin of the Institute of Historical Research,* XVI, 1938).

Edwards, Kathleen. "The Political Importance of the English Bishops during the Reign of Edward II" (*English Historical Review,* LIX, 1944).

Edwards, Kathleen. "The Social Origins and Provenance of the English Bishops during the Reign of Edward II" (*Transactions of the Royal Historical Society,* 5th series, IX, 1959).

Edward the Second (ed. C. R. Forker, Manchester, 1994).

Egbert, D. D. "A Sister to the Tickhill Psalter: The Psalter of Queen Isabella of England" (*Bulletin of the New York Public Library,* XXXIX, 1935).

Emerson, Barbara. *The Black Prince* (London, 1976).

England in the Fourteenth Century (ed. W. Mark Ormrod, London, 1985).

England in the Later Middle Ages: Portraits and Documents (ed. D. Baker, London, 1968).

English Court Culture in the Later Middle Ages (ed. V. J. Scattergood and J. W. Sherborne, London, 1983).

Erlande-Brandenburg, Alain. *Saint-Denis' Basilica* (Rennes, 1984).

Evans, B. Penry. "The Family of Mortimer" (Ph.D. thesis, University of Wales, 1937).

Evans, J. *English Art, 1307–1461* (Oxford, 1949).

Evans, Michael. *The Death of Kings: Royal Deaths in Mediaeval England* (London and New York, 2003).

Exchequer Plea Rolls (Public Record Office).

Eyton, R. W. *Antiquities of Shropshire* (12 vols., 1854–60).

Fairbank, F. R. "The Last Earl of Warenne and Surrey" (*Yorkshire Archaeological Journal,* XIX, 1907).

Favier, Jean. *Philippe le Bel* (Paris, 1978).

Fawtier, Robert. *Les Capétiens de France: leur rôle dans sa construction* (Paris, 1942). Published in Britain as *The Capetian Kings of France: Monarchy and Nation, 987–1328* (trans. Lionel Butler and R. J. Adam, London and Glasgow, 1960).

Fletcher, Benton. *Royal Homes near London* (London, 1930).

Fowler, Kenneth. *The Age of Plantagenet and Valois* (London, 1967).

Fowler, Kenneth. "Edward II" (in *The History of the English Speaking Peoples,* vol. II, 1970).

Fowler, Kenneth. *The King's Lieutenant: Henry of Grosmont, First Duke of Lancaster, 1310–1361* (London, 1969).

Frame, Robin. "The Bruces in Ireland, 1315–18" (*Irish Historical Studies,* XIX, LXXIII, 1974).

Fryde, E. B. "The Deposits of Hugh Despenser the Younger with Italian Bankers" (*Economic History Review,* 2nd series, III, 1951).

Fryde, Natalie. "John Stratford, Bishop of Winchester, and the Crown, 1323–1330" (*Bulletin of the Institute of Historical Research,* XLIV, 1971).

Fryde, Natalie. *The Tyranny and Fall of Edward II, 1321–1326* (Cambridge, 1979).

Galbraith, V. H. "The Literacy of the Mediaeval English Kings" (*Proceedings of the British Academy,* XXI, 1935).

Gardner, John. *The Life and Times of Chaucer* (London, 1977).

Gardner, Rena. *The Story of Tewkesbury Abbey* (Blandford, 1971).

Gee, Loveday Lewes. *Women, Art and Patronage from Henry III to Edward III* (Woodbridge, 2002).

Gilbert, J. T. *History of the Viceroys of Ireland* (Dublin, 1865).

Given-Wilson, C., and A. Curteis. *The Royal Bastards of Mediaeval England* (London, 1984).

Gordon, Dillon. *Making and Meaning: The Wilton Diptych* (London, 1993).

Gransden, Antonia. *Historical Writing in England.* Vol. II, *1307 to the Early Sixteenth Century* (London, 1982).

Grassi, J. L. "William Airmyn and the Bishopric of Norwich" (*English Historical Review,* LXX, 1955).

Green, David. *The Black Prince* (Stroud, 2001).

Green, Mary Anne Everett. *The Lives of the Princesses of England* (6 vols., London, 1849–55).

Green, V. H. H. *The Later Plantagenets: A Survey of English History between 1307 and 1485* (London, 1955; rev. ed., 1966).

Griffe, Maurice. *Les Souverains de France: Tableau genealogique et dynastique* (Le Cannet, 1997).

Griffin, Mary E. "Cadwalader, Arthur and Brutus in the Wigmore Manuscript" (*Speculum,* XVI, 1941).

Griffin, Mary E. "A Wigmore Manuscript at the University of Chicago" (*National Library of Wales Journal,* VII, 1952).

Griffiths, John. *Edward II in Glamorgan* (London, 1904).

Griffiths, Ralph. *Conquerors and Conquered in Mediaeval Wales* (Stroud, 1994).

Griffiths, Ralph. *The Principality of Wales in the Later Middle Ages: The Structure and Personnel of Government.* Vol. I, *South Wales, 1277–1536* (Cardiff, 1972).

Guinle, Jean-Philippe. *Le Livre des Rois de France* (Mohndruck, 1997).

Haines, R. M. "Adam Orleton and the Diocese of Winchester" (*Journal of Ecclesiastical History,* XXIII, 1972).

Haines, R. M. *Archbishop John Stratford* (Toronto, 1986).

Haines, R. M. *The Church and Politics in Fourteenth Century England: The Career of Adam Orleton, c. 1275–1345* (Cambridge, 1978).

Haines, R. M. "Edwardus Redivivus: The Afterlife of Edward of Caernarvon" (*Transactions of the Bristol and Gloucester Archaeological Society,* CXIV, 1996).

Hallam, Elizabeth M. *Capetian France, 987–1328* (London and New York, 1980).

Hallam, Elizabeth M. "The Eleanor Crosses and Royal Burial Customs" (in *Eleanor of Castile: Essays to Commemorate the 700th Anniversary of Her Death,* ed. David Parsons, Stamford, 1991).

Hallam, Elizabeth M. *The Itinerary of Edward II and His Household, 1307–1328* (List and Index Society, CCXI, London, 1984).

Hallam, Elizabeth M. "Royal Burial and the Cult of Kingship in France and England, 1060–1330" (*Journal of Mediaeval History,* IV/VIII, 1982).

Hamilton, Jeffrey S. *Piers Gaveston, Earl of Cornwall, 1307–12: Politics and Patronage in the Reign of Edward II* (London, 1988).

Hammond, Peter. *Her Majesty's Royal Palace and Fortress of the Tower of London* (Historic Royal Palaces, London, 1987).

Handbook of British Chronology (ed. F. Maurice Powicke and E. B. Fryde, Royal Historical Society, London, 1961).

Harding, D. A. "The Regime of Isabella and Mortimer, 1326–1330" (M.Phil. thesis, University of Durham, 1985).

Hardy, B. C. *Philippa of Hainault and Her Times* (London, 1910).

Harper, Charles G. *Abbeys of Old Romance* (London, 1930).

Harris, Alma. *In Days of Yore: Queen Isabella and Sir Roger Mortimer: A Royal Romance* (Nottingham, 1995).

Harrod, H. *Report of the Deeds and Records of the Borough of King's Lynn* (King's Lynn, 1874).

Hartshorne, C. H. "The Itinerary of Edward II" (*Collectanea Archaeologica,* I, 1861).

Harvey, J. *English Mediaeval Architects* (Stroud, 1984).

Harvey, John. *The Black Prince and His Age* (London, 1976).

Harvey, John. *The Plantagenets* (London, 1948).

Haskins, G. L. "The Doncaster Petition of 1321" (*English Historical Review,* LIII, 1938).

Hassall, W. O. *Who's Who in History.* Vol. I, *British Isles, 55 B.C. to 1485* (Oxford, 1960).

Hearsey, J. E. *Bridge, Church and Palace in Old London* (London, 1961).

Hedley, Olwen. *Royal Palaces* (London, 1972).

Hedley, Olwen. *Windsor Castle* (London, 1967).

Herbert, P. "Excavations at Christ Church, Greyfriars, 1976" (*London Archaeologist,* III, no. XII, 1979).

Hibbert, Christopher. *The Court at Windsor* (London, 1964).

Hibbert, Christopher. *The Tower of London* (London, 1971).

Hicks, Michael. *Who's Who in Late Mediaeval England* (London, 1991).

Hill, B. J. W. *The History and Treasures of Windsor Castle* (London, 1967).

Hill, J. W. F. *Mediaeval Lincoln* (Cambridge, 1948).

Hippisley-Cox, Anthony D. *Haunted Britain* (London, 1973).

The History of the City and County of Norwich (ed. R. Browne, 1768).

The History of the King's Works. Vols. I–III, *The Middle Ages* (ed. H. M. Colvin and A. J. Taylor, HMSO, London, 1963).

The History Today Companion to British History (ed. Juliet Gardiner and Neil Wenborn, London, 1995).

Holmes, G. A. *The Estates of the Higher Nobility in Fourteenth Century England* (Cambridge, 1957).

Holmes, G. A. "The Judgement on the Younger Despenser, 1326" (*English Historical Review,* LXX, 1955).

Holmes, G. A. "A Protest against the Despensers, 1326" (*Speculum,* XXX, 1955).

Holmes, G. A. "The Rebellion of the Earl of Lancaster, 1328–1329" (*Bulletin of the Institute of Historical Research,* XXVIII, 1955).

Hope, W. H. St. John. "On the Funeral Effigies of the Kings and Queens of England" (*Archae-ologia,* LX, 1907).

Hopkinson, Charles, and Martin Speight. *The Mortimers: Lords of the March* (Logaston, 2002).

Howard, P. *The Royal Palaces* (London, 1970).

Hoyt, R. S. "The Coronation Oath of 1308" (*English Historical Review,* LXXI, 1956).

Huguer, P. le. *Histoire de Philippe le Long* (Paris, 1975).

Hunter, Joseph. "Journal of the Mission of Queen Isabella to the Court of France; and of Her Residence in That Country" (*Archaeologia,* XXXVI, 1855).

Hunter, Joseph. "On the Measures Taken for the Apprehension of Sir Thomas de Gurney, One of the Murderers of Edward II" (*Archaeologia,* XXVII, 1838).

Hutchison, Harold F. "Edward II and His Minions" (*History Today,* XXI, VIII, 1971).

Hutchison, Harold F. *Edward II: The Pliant King* (London, 1971).

Impey, Edward, and Geoffrey Parnell. *The Tower of London: The Official Illustrated History* (Historic Royal Palaces, London, 2000).

Jamison, Catherine. *History of the Royal Hospital of St. Katharine by the Tower of London* (Oxford, 1952).

Jenkinson, H. "Mary de Sancto Paulo, Foundress of Pembroke College, Cambridge" (*Archae-ologia,* LXVI, 1914–15).

Jenner, Heather. *Royal Wives* (London, 1967).

Joannis, J. D. de: *Les Seizes Quartiers Généalogiques des Cápetiens* (Lyons, 1958).

Joelson, Annette. *Heirs to the Throne* (London, 1966).

Johnson, Paul. *The Life and Times of Edward III* (London, 1973).

Johnson, T. "Excavations at Christchurch, Newgate St." (*Transactions of the London and Middle-sex Archaeological Society,* XXV, 1974).

Johnstone, Hilda. "The County of Ponthieu, 1279–1307" (*English Historical Review,* XXIX, 1914).

Johnstone, Hilda. "The Eccentricities of Edward II" (*English Historical Review,* XLVIII, 1933).

Johnstone, Hilda. *Edward of Caernarvon, 1284–1307* (Manchester, 1946).

Johnstone, Hilda. "Isabella, the She-Wolf of France" (*History,* New Series, XXI, 1936–37).

Johnstone, Hilda. "The Queen's Exchequer under the Three Edwards" (in *Historical Essays in Honour of James Tait,* ed. J. G. Edwards, V. H. Galbraith, and E. F. Jacob, 1933).

Johnstone, Hilda. "The Queen's Household" (in *The English Government at Work, 1327–1336,* 3 vols., ed. J. F. Willard and W. A. Morris, The Mediaeval Academy of America, Cambridge, Mass., 1940).

Jones, Christopher. *The Great Palace: The Story of Parliament* (London, 1983).

Jones, Richard. *Walking Haunted London* (London, 1999).

Kay, F. George. *Lady of the Sun: The Life and Times of Alice Perrers* (London, 1966).

Keen, Maurice H. *England in the Later Middle Ages: A Political History* (London, 1973).

Keen, Maurice H. "Treason Trials under the Law of Arms" (*Transactions of the Royal Historical Society,* 5th series, XII, 1962).

Keevill, Graham D. *Mediaeval Palaces: An Archaeology* (Stroud, 2000).

Kerling, N. *Commercial Relations of Holland and Zeeland with England* (Leyden, 1954).

Kershaw, I. "The Great Famine and Agrarian Crisis in England, 1315–1322" (*Past and Present,* LIX, 1973).

Key Poets (ed. Jenny Green, London, 1995).

King, Edmund. *Mediaeval England, 1066–1485* (Oxford, 1988; rev. ed. Stroud, 2001).

The Kings and Queens of England (ed. W. Mark Ormrod, Stroud, 2001).

Kingsford, C. L. *The Grey Friars of London* (Aberdeen, 1915).

Kirchhoff, Elisabeth. *Rois et Reines de France* (Paris, 1996).

Labarge, Margaret Wade. *Gascony, England's First Colony, 1204–1453* (London, 1980).

Lane, Henry Murray. *The Royal Daughters of England* (2 vols., London, 1910).

Langlois, Charles Victor. "Rouleaux d'arrêts de la cour au roi au XIIIe siècle" (*Bibliothèque de l'École des Chartes,* L, 1889).

Langlois, Charles Victor. "Saint Louis–Philippe le Bel: Les dernières Capétiens directs" (in *Histoire de France illustrée,* vol. III, 2, ed. Ernest Lavisse, Paris, 1911).

Leadman, A. D. H. "The Battle of Myton" (*Yorkshire Archaeological and Topographical Journal,* VIII, 1883–84).

Leblanc-Ginet, Henri. *Les Rois de France* (Éditions Morena et Actualité de l'Histoire, 1997).

Lee, Christopher. *This Sceptred Isle, 55 B.C. to 1901* (London, 1997).

Leeds Castle Guidebook (London, 1994).

Leese, T. Anna. *Blood Royal* (Maryland, 1996).

Levis-Mirepoix, Duc de. *Le Siècle de Philippe le Bel* (Paris, 1961).

Lewis, S. "The Apocalypse of Isabella of France: Paris, Bibliothèque Nationale, Ms. Fr. 13096" (*Art Bulletin,* LXXII, 1990).

Lindley, P. *Gothic to Renaissance: Essays on Sculpture in England* (Stamford, 1995).

Lingard, John. *History of England* (London, 1819–30).

Little, A. G. *Franciscan History and Legend in English Mediaeval Art* (Manchester, 1937).

The Lives of the Kings and Queens of England (ed. Antonia Fraser, London, 1975, with relevant text by John Gillingham and Peter Earl; rev. eds., London, 1998 and 2000).

Lizerand, G. *Clement V et Philippe le Bel* (Paris, 1906).

Llywelyn, Alun. *The Shell Guide to Wales* (London, 1969).

Lofts, Norah. *Queens of Britain* (London, 1977).

The London Encyclopaedia (ed. Ben Weinreib and Christopher Hibbert, London, 1983).

Longman, William. *The Life and Times of Edward the Third* (2 vols., London, 1869).

Longmate, Norman. *Defending the Island: From Caesar to the Armada* (London, 1989).

Lucas, H. S. "The Great European Famine of 1315, 1316 and 1317" (*Speculum,* V, 1930).
Lucas, H. S. *The Low Countries in the Hundred Years War* (Michigan, 1926).
Lyubimenko, I. *Jean de Bretagne, Comte de Richmond* (Lille, 1908).

MacCann, Nick. *Leeds Castle* (Derby, 2000).
Mackinnon, James. *The History of Edward III* (London, 1900).
Mackworth-Young, Robin. *The History and Treasures of Windsor Castle* (Andover, n.d.).
Maddicott, J. R. *Thomas of Lancaster, 1307–1322: A Study in the Reign of Edward II* (Oxford, 1970).
Madox, Thomas. *The History and Antiquities of the Exchequer* (2 vols., London, 1711, 1749).
Mansel, Philip, and Robin W. Winks. *The Lily and the Lion: Royal France, Great Britain* (London, 1980).
Marsden, Simon. *The Journal of a Ghosthunter* (London, 1994).
Marshall, Rosalind K. *Scottish Queens, 1034–1714* (East Linton, 2003).
Martin, A. R. *Franciscan Architecture in England* (Manchester, 1937).
Mason, J. J. "Sir Andrew de Harcla, Earl of Carlisle" (*Transactions of the Cumberland and Westmorland Antiquarian and Archaeological Society,* n.s., XXIX, 1929).
Mason, John. *Haunted Heritage* (English Heritage, London, 1999).
McDonnell, Kevin. *Mediaeval London Suburbs* (London, 1978).
McFarlane, K. B. *The Nobility of Later Mediaeval England* (Oxford, 1973).
McKisack, May. *The Fourteenth Century, 1307–1399* (Oxford, 1959).
McNair, Scott. *Robert: Robert the Bruce, King of Scots* (New York, 1989).
Mediaeval Monarchs (ed. Elizabeth Hallam, London, 1990).
Mediaeval Queenship (ed. John Carmi Parsons, Stroud, 1993).
Menache, Sophia. "Isabella of France, Queen of England: A Reconsideration" (*Journal of Mediaeval History,* X, 1984).
Mertes, Kate. *The English Noble Household, 1250–1600* (Oxford, 1988).
Mexandeau, L. *Les Capétiens* (Lausanne, 1969).
Michelet, Jules. *L'Histoire de France* (24 vols., Paris, 1833–67).
Moir, L. *Historic Ludlow Castle and Those Associated with It* (Ludlow, 1950).
Morris, David S. *The Honour of Richmond: A History of the Lords, Earls and Dukes of Richmond* (York, 2000).
Morris, R. "Tewkesbury Abbey: The Despenser Mausoleum" (*Bristol and Gloucestershire Archaeological Transactions,* XCIII, 1993).
Mortimer, Ian. *The Greatest Traitor: The Life of Sir Roger Mortimer, 1st Earl of March, Ruler of England, 1327–1330* (London, 2003).
Mosley, Charles. *Blood Royal* (London, 2002).

Neve, John le. *Fasti Ecclesiae Anglicanae, 1300–1541* (Oxford, 1854; reprinted London, 1962–67).
Newton, Stella Mary. *Fashion in the Age of the Black Prince* (Woodbridge, 1980).
Nicholson, Ranald G. *Edward III and the Scots: The Formative Years of a Military Career, 1327–1335* (Oxford, 1965).
Nigra, Costantino. "Uno dogli Edoardi in Italia: Favola o Storia?" (*Nuova Antologia: revista di lettere, scienze ed arti,* series 4, XCII, 1901).
Norris, H. *Costume and Fashion.* Vol. II, 1066–1485 (London, 1927).
Norwich, John Julius. *Shakespeare's Kings* (London, 1999).

Ormrod, W. Mark. "Edward II at Neath Abbey, 1326" (*Neath Antiquarian Society Transactions,* 1988–89).
Ormrod, W. Mark. "The Lovers Who Ruled England" (*BBC History Magazine,* May 2003).
Ormrod, W. Mark. *The Reign of Edward III: Crown and Political Society in England, 1327–1377* (Stroud, 1990; reprinted, 2000).

Packe, Michael Seaman. *King Edward III* (London, 1983).

Palmer, Alan. *Kings and Queens of England* (London, 1976).

Palmer, Alan. *Princes of Wales* (London, 1979).

Palmer, Alan, and Veronica Palmer. *Royal England: A Historical Gazetteer* (London, 1983).

Palmer, C. F. R. "The King's Confessors" (*The Antiquary*, XXII, 1890).

Parker, T. H. *The Knights Templar in England* (University of Arizona, 1963).

Parsons, John Carmi. " 'Never Was a Body Buried in England with Such Solemnity and Honour': The Burials and Posthumous Memorials of English Queens to 1500" (in *Queens and Queenship in Mediaeval Europe*, ed. A. J. Duggan, Woodbridge, 1997).

Peers, C. *Berkhamsted Castle* (HMSO, 1948).

Phillips, J. R. S. *Aymer de Valence, Earl of Pembroke, 1307–1324: Baronial Politics in the Reign of Edward II* (Oxford, 1972).

Phillips, J. R. S. "The "Middle Party" and the Negotiating of the Treaty of Leake, August 1318: A Reinterpretation" (*Bulletin of the Institute of Historical Research*, XLVI, 1973).

Pine, L. G. *Princes of Wales* (London, 1959).

The Plantagenet Encyclopaedia (ed. Elizabeth Hallam, Godalming, 1996).

Poirel, D. *Philippe le Bel* (Paris, 1991).

Poole, Austin Lane. *Mediaeval England* (2 vols., 1958).

Porter, Arnold. *Tewkesbury Abbey* (Andover, 1992).

Pratt, Derek. "The Marcher Lordship of Chirk, 1329–1330" (*Transactions of the Denbighshire Historical Society*, XXXIX, 1990).

Prestwich, Michael C. "The Charges against the Despensers, 1321" (*Bulletin of the Institute of Historical Research*, LVIII, 1985).

Prestwich, Michael C. *Edward I* (London, 1988; rev. ed., 1997).

Prestwich, Michael C. "Isabella de Vescy and the Custody of Bamburgh Castle" (*Bulletin of the Institute of Historical Research*, XLIV, 1971).

Prestwich, Michael C. *The Three Edwards: War and State in England, 1272–1377* (London, 1980).

Price, J. E. "On Recent Discoveries in Newgate Street" (*Transactions of the London and Middlesex Archaeological Society*, V, 1881).

Raban, Sandra. *England under Edward I and Edward II, 1259–1327* (Oxford, 2000).

Ramsay, Sir James H. *The Genesis of Lancaster, or the Reigns of Edward II, Edward III and Richard II, 1307–1399* (2 vols., Oxford, 1913).

Rapin-Thoyras, Paul de. *Histoire d'Angleterre* (10 vols., The Hague, 1724–36).

Rawnsley, Hardwicke D. "Did Edward II Escape to Italy?" (*The British Review*, 12, 1915).

Rhodes, W. E. "The Inventory of the Jewels and Wardrobe of Queen Isabella (1307–08)" (*English Historical Review*, XII, 1897).

Riches, Samantha. *St. George: Hero, Martyr and Myth* (Stroud, 2000).

Roberts, R. A. "Edward II, the Lords Ordainers and Piers Gaveston's Jewels and Horses, 1312–13" (*Camden Miscellany*, 3rd series, XLI, 1929).

Robinson, C. "Was King Edward the Second a Degenerate?" (*American Journal of Insanity*, LXVI, 1910).

Robinson, John Martin. *Royal Palaces: Windsor Castle* (London, 1996).

Roncière, Charles de la. *Histoire de la Marine Française* (Paris, 1899).

Rose, Alexander. *Kings in the North: The House of Percy in British History* (London, 2002).

Rose, Tessa. *The Coronation Ceremony of the Kings and Queens of England, and the Crown Jewels* (HMSO, London, 1992).

Round, J. H. "The Landing of Queen Isabella" (*English Historical Review*, XIV, 1899).

Rowse, A. L. *The Tower of London in the History of the Nation* (London, 1972).

Rowse, A. L. *Windsor Castle in the History of the Nation* (London, 1974).

Saaler, Mary. *Edward II: 1307–1327* (London, 1997).

St. Aubyn, Giles. *Edward II* (London, 1979).

Sandford, Francis. *A Genealogical History of the Kings and Queens of England and Monarchs of Great Britain, 1066–1677* (1677).

Sandler, L. F. "A Follower of Jean Pucelle in England" (*Art Bulletin*, LII, 1970).

Sandler, L. F. *Gothic Manuscripts, 1285–1385* (2 vols., London, 1986).

Saul, Nigel. *A Companion to Mediaeval England, 1066–1485* (London, 1983; rev. ed. Stroud, 2000).

Saul, Nigel. "The Despensers and the Downfall of Edward II" (*English Historical Review*, XCIX, 1984).

Saul, Nigel. *Richard II* (London, 1997).

Saunders, Hilary St. George. *Westminster Hall* (London, 1951).

Sayles, G. O. "The Formal Judgements on the Traitors of 1322" (*Speculum*, XVI, 1941).

Scammel, Jean. "Robert I and the North of England" (*English Historical Review*, LXXIV, 1958).

Schama, Simon. *A History of Britain.* Vol. I, *At the Edge of the World, 3000 B.C.–A.D. 1603* (London, 2000).

Schramm, P. E. *A History of the English Coronation* (trans. L. G. Wickham Legg, 1937).

Seward, Desmond. *The Monks of War* (London, 1974).

The Shell Guide to England (ed. John Hadfield, London, 1975).

Shenton, Caroline. "Edward III and the Coup of 1330" (in *The Age of Edward III*, ed. J. S. Bothwell, York, 2001).

Shepherd, E. B. S. "The Church of the Friars Minor in London" (*Archaeological Journal*, LIX, 1902).

Sheppard, Francis. *London: A History* (Oxford, 1998).

Smalley, B. *English Friars and Antiquity in the Early Fourteenth Century* (Oxford, 1960).

Smit, H. T. *Bronnen Tot de Geschiedenis Van den Handel met England, Schotland, en Ierland, 1140–1450* (Gravenhage, 1928).

Smith, J. B. "Edward II and the Allegiance of Wales" (*Welsh History Review*, VIII, 1976).

Smith, W. E. L. *Episcopal Appointments and Patronage in the Reign of Edward II* (Chicago, 1938).

Smith, W. J. "The Revolt of William Somerton" (*English Historical Review*, LXIX, 1954).

Softly, Barbara. *The Queens of England* (Newton Abbot, 1976).

Somerville, R. *The History of the Duchy of Lancaster* (London, 1953).

Stanley, A. P. *Historical Memoirs of Westminster Abbey* (London, 1882).

Steane, John. *The Archaeology of the Mediaeval English Monarchy* (London, 1993; rev. ed., 1999).

Stone, Lawrence. *Sculpture in Britain: The Middle Ages* (Baltimore, 1972).

Stones, E. L. G. "The Anglo-Scottish Negotiations of 1327" (*Scottish Historical Review*, XXX, 1951).

Stones, E. L. G. "The Date of Roger Mortimer's Escape from the Tower of London" (*English Historical Review*, LXVI, 1951).

Stones, E. L. G. "The English Mission to Edinburgh" (*Scottish Historical Review*, XXVIII, 1949).

Stones, E. L. G. "The Treaty of Northampton, 1328" (*History*, n.s., XXXVIII, 1953).

Strickland, Agnes. *Lives of the Queens of England* (8 vols., London, 1850–59; reprinted, Bath, 1973).

Studer, P. "An Anglo-Norman Poem by Edward II" (*Modern Language Review*, XVI, 1921).

Swynnerton, C. "Certain Chattels of Roger Mortimer of Wigmore" (*Notes and Queries*, 11th series, X).

Tanner, L. "Westminster Abbey and the Coronation Service" (*History*, XXI, 1936–37).

Tanquerery, F. J. "The Conspiracy of Thomas Dunheved, 1327" (*English Historical Review*, XXXI, 1916).

Taylor, Anna A. "The Career of Peter Gaveston" (M.A. thesis, University of London, 1939).

Taylor, John. *English Historical Literature in the Fourteenth Century* (Oxford, 1987).

Taylor, John. "The French Brut and the Reign of Edward II" (*English Historical Review*, LXXII, 1957).

Taylor, John. "The Judgement on Hugh Despenser the Younger" (*Medievalia et Humanistica*, XII, 1958).

Thornton-Cook, Elsie. *Her Majesty: The Romance of the Queens of England, 1066–1910* (London, 1926; reprinted, New York, 1970).

Thornton-Cook, Elsie. *Kings in the Making: The Princes of Wales* (London, 1931).

Thynne, Francis, Lancaster herald. Lives of the Lord Treasurers (MSS, c. 1580, in the collection of Sir Thomas Phillipps, Bart, at Middle Hill).

Tomkinson, A. "Retinues at the Tournament of Dunstable, 1309" (*English Historical Review*, LXXIV, 1959).

Tout, Thomas Frederick. "The Captivity and Death of Edward of Caernarvon" (in *Collected Papers of Thomas Frederick Tout,* Manchester, 1920–34, and *Bulletin of the John Rylands Library,* VI, 1921).

Tout, Thomas Frederick. *Chapters in the Administrative History of Mediaeval England* (6 vols., Manchester, 1920–33).

Tout, Thomas Frederick. "Isabella of France" (*Dictionary of National Biography;* see above for full details).

Tout, Thomas Frederick. *The Place of the Reign of Edward II in English History* (Manchester, 1914; revised by Hilda Johnstone, Manchester, 1936).

Tout, Thomas Frederick. "The Tactics of the Battles of Boroughbridge and Morlaix" (*English Historical Review*, XIX, 1904).

Trease, G. E. "The Spicers and Apothecaries of the Royal Household in the Reigns of Henry III, Edward I and Edward II" (*Nottingham Mediaeval Studies,* III, 1959).

Trease, Geoffrey. *Nottingham: A Biography* (Otley, 1984).

Tristram, E. W. *English Mediaeval Wall Painting* (3 vols., Oxford, 1944–50).

Tristram, E. W. *English Wall Painting of the Fourteenth Century* (London, 1955).

Trueman, J. H. "The Personnel of Mediaeval Reform: The English Lords Ordainers of 1310" (*Mediaeval Studies,* XXI, 1959).

Tuchman, Barbara W. *A Distant Mirror: The Calamitous Fourteenth Century* (New York, 1978).

Tuck, A. J. *Crown and Nobility, 1272–1461: Political Conflict in Later Mediaeval England* (London, 1985).

Turner, Michael. *Eltham Palace* (English Heritage, London, 1999).

"Two Effigies in Montgomery Church" (*Archaeologia Cambrensis,* LXXX, 1925).

Underwood, Peter. *Haunted London* (London, 1973).

Usher, G. A. "The Career of a Political Bishop: Adam de Orleton (c. 1279–1345)" (*Transactions of the Royal Historical Society,* 5th series, XXII, 1972).

Vale, Juliet. *Edward III and Chivalry* (Woodbridge, 1982).

Valente, C. "The Deposition and Abdication of Edward II" (*English Historical Review*, CXIII, 1998).

Vansittart, Peter. *Happy and Glorious: A Collins Anthology of Royalty* (London, 1988).

Victoria County History: Surrey and Hertfordshire (London, 1914; reprinted, 1967).

Volkman, Jean-Charles. *Bien Connaître les Généalogies des Rois de France* (Luçon, 1996).

Walker, Simon. "Political Saints in Later Mediaeval England" (in *The McFarlane Legacy: Studies in Late Mediaeval Politics and Society,* ed. R. H. Britnell, and A. J. Pollard, Stroud, 1995).

Waller-Zeper, S. A. *Jan Van Henegowwen, Heer Van Beaumont* (Gravenhage, 1914).

Watson, G. W. "Geoffrey de Mortimer and His Descendants" (*Genealogist,* n.s., XXII, 1906).

Waugh, Scott L. *England in the Reign of Edward III* (Cambridge, 1991).

Waugh, Scott L. "For King, Country and Patron: The Despensers and Local Administration, 1321–22" (*Journal of British Studies, XXII, 1983*).

Waugh, Scott L. "The Profits of Violence: The Minor Gentry in the Rebellion of 1321–22 in Gloucestershire and Herefordshire" (*Speculum, LII, 1977*).

Weir, Alison. *Britain's Royal Families: The Complete Genealogy* (London, 1989; rev. ed., London, 2002).

Wenzler, Claude. *The Kings of France* (Rennes, 1995).

Who's Who in British History (ed. Juliet Gardiner, London, 2000).

Wilkinson, Bertie. "The Coronation Oath of Edward II and the Statute of York" (*Speculum, XIX, 1944*).

Wilkinson, Bertie. "The Negotiations Preceding the Treaty of Leake, August 1318" (in *Studies in Mediaeval History Presented to Frederick Maurice Powicke,* ed. R. W. Hunt, W. A. Pantin, and R. W. Southern, Oxford, 1948).

Wilkinson, Bertie. "The Sherburn Indenture and the Attack on the Despensers, 1321" (*English Historical Review, LXIII, 1948*).

Williams, G. A. *Mediaeval London: From Commune to Capital* (London, 1963).

Williams, Neville. *The Royal Residences of Great Britain* (London, 1960).

Williamson, David. *The National Portrait Gallery History of the Kings and Queens of England* (National Portrait Gallery, London, 1998).

Wilson, C. "The Origins of the Perpendicular Style and Its Development to c. 1360" (D.Phil. thesis, University of London, 1980).

Wilson, Derek. *The Tower of London: A Thousand Years* (London, 1978).

Wismes, Armel de. *Genealogy of the Kings of France* (Nantes, n.d.).

Wood, Anthony à. *History and Antiquities of the University of Oxford* (ed. J. Gutch, Oxford, 1729).

Wood, Charles T. "Personality, Politics and Constitutional Progress: The Lessons of Edward II" (*Studia Gratiana, XV, 1972*).

Wood, Charles T. "Queens, Queans and Kingship: An Inquiry into the Theories of Royal Legitimacy in Late Mediaeval England and France" (in *Order and Innovation in the Middle Ages: Essays in Honour of Joseph R. Strayer,* ed. William C. Jordan, Bruce McNab, and Teofilo F. Ruiz, Princeton, 1976).

Woods, A. "Excavations at Eltham Palace" (*Transactions of the London and Middlesex Archaeological Society, XXXIII, 1982*).

Woolgar, C. M. *The Great Household in Late Mediaeval England* (New Haven and London, 1999).

FICTION

Barnes, Margaret Campbell. *Isabel the Fair* (London, 1957).

Druon, Maurice. *The She-Wolf of France* (London, 1960).

Graham, Alice Walworth. *The Vows of the Peacock* (London, 1956).

Holt, Emily Sarah. *The Lord of the Marches, or the Story of Roger Mortimer: A Tale of the Fourteenth Century* (London, 1884).

Howatch, Susan. *Cashelmara* (London, 1974).

Lewis, Hilda. *Harlot Queen* (London, 1970).

Illustration Credits

Isabella and Roger Mortimer ride toward Oxford (Collection of the Earl of Leicester, Holkham Hall, Norfolk/Bridgeman Art Library)

Isabella takes possession of Bristol, from Jean Froissart, *Chroniques* (Bibliothèque nationale de France [MS FR 2643, f.9])

SECOND SECTION

Isabella and her army before Hereford, from Jean de Waurin, *Chroniques d'Angleterre* (British Library, London/Bridgeman Art Library)

The execution of Hugh le Despenser, from Jean Froissart, *Chroniques* (Bibliothèque nationale de France [MS FR 2643, f.ii])

Edward II abdicates in favor of his son, Edward III, from Piers of Langtoft, *Chronicle of England* (The British Library [MS Royal 20 A B, f.10])

Fortune turning a wheel, from the *Holkham Bible Picture Book* (The British Library [MS Add. 47682, f.iv])

Coronation of Edward III, from Jean Froissart, *Chroniques* (Bibliothèque nationale de France [MS FR 2643, f.12])

Berkeley Castle, Gloucestershire (Collections/Quintin Wright)

Edward's cell, Berkeley Castle, Gloucestershire (Collections/Michael Jenner)

Isabella with her son, Edward III, from an illuminated treatise by Walter de Milemete (The Governing Body of Christ Church, Oxford [MS 92, f.4v])

A Queen at Mass, from the *Taymouth Hours* (The British Library [MS Yates Thompson 13, f.7])

The Virgin presents a kneeling Queen to Christ, from the *Taymouth Hours* (The British Library [MS Yates Thompson 13, f.139])

A King and Queen kneeling, from the *Taymouth Hours* (The British Library [MS Yates Thompson 13, f.118v])

Castle Rising, Norfolk (Collections/John D. Beldom)

John of Eltham, tomb effigy in Westminster Abbey (Conway Library, Courtauld Institute of Art)

Isabella of France, weeper from the tomb of John of Eltham (Copyright Dean and Chapter of Westminster)

Philippa of Hainault, drawing by Smirko of an original wall painting (now destroyed) in St. Stephen's Chapel in the Palace of Westminster (© Society of Antiquaries, London)

Isabella, roof boss from Exeter Cathedral, c.1350 (Conway Library, Courtauld Institute of Art)

The Fieschi letter (Archives Départmentale Hérault, Montpellier [MS G1123, f.86])

Index

ABOUT THE AUTHOR

ALISON WEIR is the *New York Times* bestselling author of *Eleanor of Aquitaine; Mary, Queen of Scots, and the Murder of Lord Darnley;* and several other historical biographies. She lives in Surrey with her husband and two children.

ABOUT THE TYPE

This book was set in Monotype Dante, a typeface designed by Giovanni Mardersteig (1892–1977). Conceived as a private type for the Officina Bodoni in Verona, Italy, Dante was originally cut only for hand composition by Charles Malin, the famous Parisian punch cutter, between 1946 and 1952. Its first use was in an edition of Boccaccio's *Trattatello in laude di Dante* that appeared in 1954. The Monotype Corporation's version of Dante followed in 1957. Though modeled on the Aldine type used for Pietro Cardinal Bembo's treatise *De Aetna* in 1495, Dante is a thoroughly modern interpretation of that venerable face.